THE TALMUD

NORMAN SOLOMON is a Senior Associate of the Oxford Centre for Hebrew and Jewish Studies and a member of Wolfson College, Oxford. He was born in Cardiff, South Wales, and educated at Cardiff High School and St John's College, Cambridge. He was ordained in 1961 and served as rabbi to Orthodox congregations in Manchester, Liverpool, Hampstead (London) and Birmingham. He is actively involved in international interfaith dialogue, and 1983–94 directed the Centre for the Study of Judaism and Jewish/Christian Relations in Birmingham, of which he was a founder.

He is a past president of the British Association for Jewish Studies, and has published more than seventy papers on ethical and environmental topics as well as on various aspects of Jewish studies. His previous books include *Judaism and World Religion*, *The Analytic Movement: Hayyim Soloveitchik and his School*, *A Very Short Introduction to Judaism* and *Historical Dictionary of Judaism*.

The Talmud

A Selection

Selected, Translated and Edited by
NORMAN SOLOMON

PENGUIN BOOKS

PENGUIN CLASSICS

Published by the Penguin Group
Penguin Books Ltd, 80 Strand, London WC2R ORL, England
Penguin Group (USA) Inc., 375 Hudson Street, New York, New York 10014, USA
Penguin Group (Canada), 90 Eglinton Avenue East, Suite 700, Toronto, Ontario, Canada M4P 2Y3
(a division of Pearson Penguin Canada Inc.)
Penguin Ireland, 25 St Stephen's Green, Dublin 2, Ireland
(a division of Penguin Books Ltd)
Penguin Group (Australia), 250 Camberwell Road, Camberwell, Victoria 3124, Australia
(a division of Pearson Australia Group Pty Ltd)
Penguin Books India Pvt Ltd, 11 Community Centre, Panchsheel Park, New Delhi – 110 017, India
Penguin Group (NZ), 67 Apollo Drive, Rosedale, North Shore 0632, New Zealand
(a division of Pearson New Zealand Ltd)
Penguin Books (South Africa) (Pty) Ltd, 24 Sturdee Avenue, Rosebank, Johannesburg 2196, South Africa

Penguin Books Ltd, Registered Offices: 80 Strand, London WC2R ORL, England

www.penguin.com

This edition first published in Penguin Classics 2009

009

Selection, translation and editorial material copyright © Norman Solomon, 2009
All rights reserved

The moral right of the translator and editor has been asserted

Set in 11.25/12.25 pt PostScript Adobe Garamond
Typeset by Rowland Phototypesetting Ltd, Bury St Edmunds, Suffolk
Printed in England by Clays Ltd, St Ives plc

ISBN: 978-0-141-44178-8

www.greenpenguin.co.uk

Penguin Books is committed to a sustainable
future for our business, our readers and our planet.
This book is made from Forest Stewardship
Council™ certified paper.

ALWAYS LEARNING

PEARSON

Contents

List of Illustrations

Preface

The Talmud, frequently censored and occasionally banned and burned by the Catholic Church, is one of the most influential, though seldom acknowledged or properly understood, writings of Late Antiquity. It touches and illumines every facet of human life; ostensibly a code of law, it is a refreshingly human document.

Making this entirely new translation and abridgement has given me a great deal of pleasure, but also posed some difficult problems. In particular, how was I to condense about 5,500 large pages (in modern editions) of concise and often obscure Hebrew and Aramaic with commentary, into less than a tenth of that quantity of intelligible English? The selection inevitably reflects personal bias, and I apologize to those whose favourite pages I have omitted; my aim was to include at least something on each significant topic, as well as illustrating the rich variety of styles. A special feature of this volume is that it contains a selection from each of the Talmud's 63 tractates, set out in the traditional order; this should help the reader to appreciate the range and structure of the work as a whole.

People read Talmud for diverse reasons. To the pious Jew, it is an act of piety – it is virtuous to 'meditate on the law of the Lord' (Psalm 1:2) even if you can't always make sense of it; no doubt many *Daf Yomi* readers – members of the international circle set up by Rabbi Meir Shapira in 1923 with the aim of getting Jewish men to read a page a day – fall into this category. The less religious may read it as an exploration of personal identity, as a source for history or anthropology or law, or perhaps find its way of argument a congenial training for the mind.

And there are different ways to study it. A theologian may mine it for material to support his/her own interpretation of religion, a traditional Jew will look for practical guidance in religious observance, while an academic scholar will harness historical, philological, literary and sociological skills to elucidate the stages of its development and to place it in the broader context of human history.

All these approaches are reflected in this volume, though the volume of available scholarship, both traditional and academic, is so vast that no more than a sample of each can be offered. The emphasis here is on the historical; we must start by asking who the rabbis of the Talmud were, what they were trying to achieve, what sort of world they lived in and how they perceived it. That is why maps, illustrations and a timeline are included – the Talmud did not descend in perfect form from the sky, but came into being in this world among real people, with all the worries, confusions and imperfections that implies.

Nor can the text be properly understood without serious consideration of its literary formation – who actually compiled the documents of which it consists, what were their motives, how were the documents transmitted and how do they relate to historical reality?

Most readers will not previously have read any Talmud; some will have dipped into it and struggled to make sense of it; others will have lived with it and already feel familiar with its world. I hope there is something for all of them here. As the rabbis wisely observed (Ḥagiga 3a), there is no school in which novelty is not to be found, so perhaps even the learned will find some new perspectives in which to set their knowledge. Or they may find errors, in which case let them correct me.

But if you are a newcomer in this strange world, where do you start? How do you take your first steps in 'the sea of the Talmud', as it is often called?

Apart from your native wit and an inquisitive and open mind, you will need only one piece of equipment for your voyage, and that is a Bible ('Old Testament'). Use any translation you have to hand, but don't be surprised if it does not correspond exactly with the translation here; the Sages (as the rabbis of the Talmud are more properly called) read the Bible in Hebrew and picked up nuances in its words and idioms which elude a reader unfamiliar with the original language, and I have frequently translated Scripture unconventionally to accord with their interpretation.

There is no need to start at the first page, since the Talmud is not written in a stepwise fashion. Browse, and you will quite soon find something that attracts you, perhaps some amusing anecdote about an incident in the Schools (there is far more humour in the Talmud than it is generally credited for),[1] or perhaps some unexpected gem of wisdom. Make that your starting point. Turn over the pages at random to pick up something of the range and rhythm of the Talmud. Wade in, splash about; you may soon discover that you can swim a few strokes.

If you want to go further than this book can take you, you will need an instructor; by the time you have read it, you should be able to discriminate between who will lead you forward and who is likely to lead you astray.

Above all, enjoy it! The rabbis say that there is no greater joy than that of the day on which the Torah was revealed; wherever the Torah is studied something of that joy is present.

I acknowledge an incalculable debt to the many rabbis and scholars who have devoted their energy over the centuries to elucidating the Talmud, and most of all to those teachers, friends and students with whom I have personally enjoyed the privilege and stimulation of textual study.

The editorial team at Penguin have been extremely helpful and pleasant to work with. I should like to thank Adam Freudenheim, Elisabeth Merriman and Lindeth Vasey for guiding me into producing what I hope is a readable and not too daunting 'Talmud in miniature'; Lin, in particular, has been a model of patience in ironing out inconsistencies of style and content and in eliminating obscurities.

I may well not have completed the work at all if not for the constant support and encouragement of my wife, Dr Hilary Nissenbaum.

Thanks are due also to the Jewish Publication Society for

permission to use their translation of the Hebrew Scriptures, 2nd edn (Philadelphia: Jewish Publication Society, 1999).

NOTE

1. Kovelman, *Alexandria and Jerusalem*, Chapter 3 (see Bibliography for full citation), draws attention to the humour to be found in rabbinic *aggada*; but there is a lightness of touch in the *halakha* too.

Introduction

The Babylonian Talmud, with its kernel the Mishna, is the classic text of Judaism, second only to the Bible. If Scripture is the sun, the Talmud is the moon that reflects its light; its authority derives from its claim to interpret Scripture rightly.

Judaism is firmly rooted in the Bible, that is, in the Hebrew Scriptures that make up the work called by Christians the 'Old Testament'. But to describe Judaism as 'The Religion of the Old Testament' is inadequate; it is as if someone who had read, say, the works of Shakespeare (perhaps in a Japanese translation), imagined that he had grasped the essence of modern British or American culture. No one would deny that Shakespeare's dramas contribute significant, even essential, features to the modern cultures of the English-speaking world, but to mistake this input for the whole of contemporary reality is to ignore centuries of development before and after Shakespeare as well as all that derives from other sources.

Likewise, Judaism did not remain static after the period covered by its Sacred Scriptures, or even after the emergence of Christianity; to the present day it continues to evolve in response to changing historical circumstances and in interaction with surrounding cultures. The language of the Hebrew Scriptures still lives, and makes for both tradition and continuity, while the vocabulary has matured, extended and acquired fresh layers of meaning with each generation. Old Testament theology, that is, the attempt by Christians to understand the religious thought of ancient Israel, is a perfectly legitimate area of study, but it is *not* the study of Judaism.

Rabbinic texts, including the Talmud, rarely use the Hebrew

equivalents for the terms 'religion' or 'Judaism'; instead, they say, 'Torah'. The Hebrew word *Torah* is often translated as 'law', but this is misleading. 'Teaching' or 'the way' would be better; however, the word may also refer to a particular topic of law or moral instruction, to the text of the first five books of the Bible (the 'Five Books of Moses', the Written Torah) or to the whole of received tradition. I leave it untranslated.

Differences between the Judaism of the Talmud and the *apparent* meaning of the Bible are legion. For instance, the Hebrew Bible has nothing clear to say of life after death, and rarely so much as hints at such a possibility in contexts where one might expect it to; yet the rabbis who compiled the Talmud regarded belief in life after death as fundamental to Torah, implicit in Scripture, and they routinely invoked the future life as the place of ultimate bliss for the faithful and torment for the wicked. Another illustration may be drawn from the criminal code. Scripture lays down the rule of 'an eye for an eye' (Exodus 21:24) and demands capital punishment for a range of offences; the Talmud refuses to countenance the literal interpretation of the phrase, and though retaining capital punishment in theory, limits its application to such an extent that it would be virtually impossible in practice (*Bava Qama* 83b; see pp. 447–8[1]).

The Oral Torah

The relationship of rabbinic teaching to Scripture is complex, and obviously worried the Sages themselves. In the third century CE, in an attempt to address the issue, they formulated the concept of the Dual Torah.[2] According to this, side by side with the Written Torah (Genesis to Deuteronomy) that was dictated by God to Moses, there is an Oral Torah, also received from God at Sinai; this oral tradition, complementing the written Word, was preserved through the centuries by successive generations of faithful teachers, and is articulated in the teachings of the Sages; as they expressed it, 'Moses received the Torah at Sinai. He handed it to Joshua, Joshua to the elders, the elders to the prophets, and the prophets transmitted it to the men of the Great Synod' (*Avot* 1:1; see p. 553).

Roman law distinguished between *jus scriptum* ('written law') and *jus non scriptum* ('unwritten law'). To the Romans 'un-written law' was custom (*consuetudo*), while 'written law' meant laws based on any written source. The first-century Jewish historian Flavius Josephus made a similar distinction, which may well have been shared by the Pharisees.[3] However, the distinction between Written Torah and Oral Torah is different. By 'Oral Torah' the rabbis meant not only – nor even principally – unwritten laws, but the correct interpretation of those that *were* written; they recognized local custom (*minhag*) and communal enactments (*taqqanot*) as lesser categories of law, binding indeed, but only as sanctioned by the Written or Oral Torah.

How to Read the Talmud

The Talmud was not designed as literature for reading nor as oratory for inspiration, but for oral transmission with expla-nation by an authorized teacher;[4] brief texts were preferred, and an arrangement of material that commended itself to memory rather than logic. Like the works of Aristotle, the Talmud consists mainly of lecture notes, often compiled by zealous disciples rather than the master, and never polished as a whole for publication; the occasional 'purple patch', whose narrative or analytical skill seizes the imagination, comes as a welcome reward to the reader.

The editors did not of course have the modern English reader in mind, nor were they thinking of the non-Jewish world or even the general Jewish public. Rather, their notes were a resource for dedicated disciples within a culture dominated by biblical texts; they aimed to facilitate a discourse in progress. This discourse is set, moreover, in unfamiliar landscapes; the Mishna (the core of Talmud, as explained below) is a product of first- to third-century Roman Palestine, and the 'Babylonian' Talmud which comments on it arose in third- to seventh-century Meso-potamia, essentially under Iranian rule, though frequently a battleground between Rome and Iran.

Once these factors are appreciated, Talmud can be addressed at a universal human level. We all have to deal with other people, with the opposite sex, with law and government, with food production, commerce and crime, celebration and commemoration, life and death, and with God (or at least, the possibility of some form of ultimate reality). Part of the art of reading Talmud is to see that these are the things *it* is concerned with, too; much of it is down to earth, mundane, practical, not at all what might be expected of a work that sets out to guide people in the service of God.

The Talmud's length – one of the complete English translations runs to 69 volumes – is due neither to long-windedness nor to repetitiveness, but to the desire to be thorough and comprehensive. Indeed, its style is frequently terse to the point where the reader must turn to later commentators for elucidation.

Talmud is essentially an activity, not a book; you engage in it, rather than read it as you would a piece of literature. The word *talmud* means 'study', and stands for the creative study of Torah, that is, of the Bible and tradition; the student is not so much reading, as participating joyfully in the elucidation and implementation of God's Word. Talmud is how God's Word is made to relate to real-life situations.

The Sages expressed reluctance to commit Oral Torah to writing; they did not want to set it on a par with sacred Scripture, the 'Written Torah', nor did they want its dynamic character to be dampened down by fixing it in writing.[5] In the course of time the material became so voluminous, and the difficulties of accurate oral transmission so great, that notes were made and edited into the corpus we now call *the* Talmud. No doctrine of verbal inspiration attaches to the text, as it does to holy Scripture, and scribal errors are readily acknowledged.

Structure – The Framework of the Talmud

The framework of the Talmud is provided by the Mishna (often spelled 'Mishnah'). Tradition maintains that this was edited by Rabbi Judah ha-Nasi[6] in Galilee, Palestine, at the beginning of the third century CE; modern scholarship accepts this time and location of redaction, while acknowledging that there has been much subsequent editorial activity.

A glance at the contents of this volume will show that Mishna comprises six major divisions, or Orders (Hebrew, *seder*; plural, *sedarim*). Each Order is subdivided into tractates, and since the Middle Ages the tractates have been subdivided into chapters and the chapters into paragraphs, each of which is referred to as *a* Mishna.

It may seem paradoxical that the same term, Mishna, is used for the whole and also for the smallest part. Strictly speaking, *mishna* is the correct term for a brief rule or teaching of the kind that forms the characteristic building block of the work, and it would be more accurate to refer to the whole by the plural *mishnayot*, as some people do. Hebrew *mishna* derives from a root that means 'to repeat'; it is the succinct formulation that the master passes to the disciple to repeat and so memorize as a summary of the lesson. The Christian Jerome, writing *c.* 410, refers to the traditions of the Pharisees, 'which nowadays they call *deuterōseis*'[7] – a literal Greek equivalent of Hebrew *mishnayot*. Clearly, Mishna was conceived as oral teaching, and its detailed articulation as well as the ordering of its content are best appreciated within a context of orality.

The Mishna is set out as a systematic code of law, but its contents cover numerous aspects of life which would not be contained in a secular law code, such as ethics, religious ritual and sexual morality. It was produced at about the same time as Papinian (probably from Emesa, Syria) and Ulpian (a native of Tyre) were setting the course of Roman law; a major school of law, perhaps founded by the emperor Septimius Severus, functioned in the adjoining province of Berytus (Beirut).[8]

Mishna was never, in its entirety, the law that governed an actual society. For one thing, it contains detailed regulations for Temple ritual, even though by the time it was compiled there had been no Temple for well over a century; for another, it is unlikely that its leading exponents, prior to the time of Judah ha-Nasi, had much impact on any significant sector of Jewish society.

Scholars debate the extent to which Mishna incorporates: (a) actual Israelite or Temple law of an earlier time, (b) law as implemented by rabbis where possible in third-century Galilee and (c) formulations of what *ought* to be the law in an ideal Israelite polity reconstituted under messianic rule; certainly, all these elements are present. Mishna projects Torah as a seamless, eternal whole, the blueprint for an ideal 'Israel' which can be realized only partially and imperfectly in the here and now; through Torah, Israel (the Jewish nation), though politically helpless, can shape its own world in partnership with God.[9]

The Reception of the Mishna – Bavli and Yerushalmi

Mishna was quickly accepted as authoritative in significant circles of Palestinian and Babylonian Jewry even though there, as well as throughout the Jewish Diaspora, many different forms of Judaism persisted. Mishna articulated the distinctive Judaism of the Sages (Rabbinic Judaism), functioned as a guide to legal practice and served as the focus for instruction and debate in schools and courts. The discussion it generated as the rabbis sought to harmonize its contradictions, to relate its provisions to reports of teachings that had not been included in it and to clarify its intimate relationship with Scripture, comprises the essence of Talmud or, as it later became known, *Gemara* ('learning', 'completion', 'decision').[10]

Throughout the third century, exposition and implementation of Mishna proceeded in parallel in Palestine and Babylonia, with frequent contact and scholarly exchange between them. In the fourth century Abbaye and Rava, in Babylonia, introduced new approaches to the reading of texts and the interpretation of law; these differences of approach, as well as cultural disparities between the Hellenistic (subsequently Byzantine) environment of Palestine and the Iranian culture of Babylonia, were accentuated as time went on, though they did not result in a sectarian division.

The divergence between Palestine and Babylonia is reflected in two Talmudim (plural of Talmud). The Palestinian Talmud, or Yerushalmi (Jerusalem Talmud), also known as the Talmud of the Land of Israel, was completed by about 450 CE and the Babylonian Talmud, or Bavli, was completed about 600 CE; both were subject to later editing. Strictly speaking, neither was ever 'completed'; as we now have them they mark arbitrary stages, brought to a 'temporary' halt by outside events, in a continuous process.

The two Talmudim differ in their Aramaic dialects, and not infrequently in the decisions they endorse. Zacharias Frankel (1801–75) noted that the Yerushalmi was less verbose than the Bavli, that the Yerushalmi often raises questions without responding to them and that argumentation in the Yerushalmi rarely proceeds beyond a few steps, whereas in the Bavli it may continue for several pages.[11] Twentieth-century scholarship has elaborated considerably on this basic foundation. Saul Lieberman demonstrated that the Yerushalmi contains not merely occasional Greek and Latin words (as does the Bavli to a lesser extent), but frequently whole Greek phrases and proverbs. Jacob Neusner points to the insistence on alternatives, on justifying different positions in the light of reasoned argumentation, as the distinctive feature of the Bavli. David Kraemer claims that in the Bavli, at least in its anonymous redactional sections: 'Many options frequently are offered apparently for their own sake, and . . . [final] decisions are frequently avoided, preference being given instead to the support of contradictory opinions. In the Bavli speculation is paramount and . . . sagacity (called "talmud torah") is a central value. This contrast in overall compositional preferences may be the most important difference between the Bavli and the Yerushalmi.'[12]

The Bavli eventually came to be regarded by Jews as possessing greater authority. This is due not only to the fact that it continues discussions that the Yerushalmi does not pursue, but because its decisions were favoured by the Babylonian Geonim (heads of the academies) in the early Islamic period from the seventh century onward, and it is they who effectively transmitted the rabbinic tradition to mediaeval Jewry: Talmud reached Western Europe, from about 1000 CE, via North Africa from Babylonia rather than from Palestine.

The structure of both Yerushalmi and Bavli is determined by

the Mishna. Both follow the order of the Mishna's tractates and comment on them, at the same time reviewing other texts of the Mishna period,[13] and introducing anecdotes and additional material ranging from biblical exposition to popular medicine and superstition.

The Talmud translated in this volume is the Bavli (Babylonian).

How the Talmud Started
The Mishna under Roman Rule

The Romans invaded Judaea in 63 BCE, renaming it Palestine after 135 CE; the country remained under Roman and then Byzantine government for several centuries.

The earliest Mishna-type teachings were formulated in the late Second Temple period, many of them in the context of Temple worship; this is the period of the 'Schools'[14] of Hillel and Shammai. Teachings that can be assigned to this period tend to be either (a) straightforward clarifications of biblical law, (b) 'fences around the Torah', i.e. measures to protect the integrity of the law, or (c) laws regarded as ancient though they are not explicit in the Torah.[15]

In 66 CE Judaea revolted against Rome; the revolt was quashed and the Jerusalem Temple destroyed by Titus in 70. Yoḥanan ben Zakkai, a disciple of Hillel, escaped from the siege of Jerusalem and set up a court for the interpretation and application of Torah law in Yavné (Jamnia), a village not far from Jerusalem, where he modified the teaching of the Schools to adapt it to the new circumstances. He was displaced, probably in the 80s, by Gamaliel II, a strong leader who coordinated the existing teachings and introduced major changes in the liturgy.

Under the leadership of Simeon bar Koziba ('Bar Kokhba') Judaea tried again, in 131, to put an end to the Roman occupation, but was defeated by Hadrian in 135 with huge loss of life;[16] this, rather than the destruction of the Temple, marks the effective end of Jewish independence; Jews were excluded from Jerusalem and much of the country was rapidly paganized.[17] The Yavné court transferred to Usha in Galilee, and there the foundations of the Mishna in the form that we know it were laid, particularly by Meir. The law was articulated in greater detail than it had been at Yavné, and serious consideration was given to the intention and perception of 'Israelites' – a term the Sages preferred to 'Jews' – in fulfilling it.

By the third century CE, when Judah ha-Nasi, a grandson of Gamaliel II, set about collecting and refining the teachings of the Sages of the Land of Israel and compiling the Mishna, Jewish relations with Rome had somewhat eased, to the extent that Jewish legend dwells on the friendship between 'Rabbi' (Judah) and 'Antoninus'; whether 'Antoninus' was an Antonine emperor, the regional prefect or some more lowly Roman official, is unclear. The Talmud attributes several conversations to them on theological rather than political or administrative issues.

Judah and his descendants assumed the Hebrew title *nasi* ('prince', or 'president'; plural, *nesi'im*), perhaps with Leviticus 4:22 in mind.[18] In adopting this title Judah was presumably laying claim to leadership of the Jewish people, and when later allied to claims of Davidic descent, there may have been a covert message that he and his family – not Jesus, let alone any Roman – were the rightful rulers of Israel; at the same time, it established the pedigree of the Palestinian *nesi'im* vis-à-vis the Babylonian exilarchs, who claimed Davidic ancestry in the male line.

There is no independent evidence that Judah held any office formally recognized by Rome, nor does the Talmud make such a claim.[19] Perhaps the Roman administration recognized him as the spokesman of the Jews, since there are reports that he journeyed to the governor in Syria to receive 'authority' and also to Rome to intercede for his people.[20] Martin Goodman has suggested that the administration would have regarded him as a religious rather than an ethnic leader, a pattern that through the third century was increasingly being adopted with respect to Christian bishops, who were settling disputes among members of their flocks, by mediation rather than adjudication.[21] In time, Judah's successors were recognized as 'patriarchs', or occasionally 'ethnarchs', of the Jewish community, whatever those terms implied, but no term applied to them in

Latin or Greek literary sources or inscriptions corresponds to the Hebrew *nasi*.[22]

Whether or not Judah enjoyed official status, he certainly established the Sages as the effective religious leadership of Jews in Galilee and Judaea in the third century, and by default as a quasi-political leadership. Shaye Cohen writes:

The social standing of the rabbinic movement changed dramatically under the leadership of Judah the Patriarch. In his time the rabbinic movement expanded its base socially, economically and politically. The rabbis moved into the cities of the Galilee, Judea, and the coast; they began to find ways to include the poor among their number, and achieved unambiguous recognition from the Romans. This period marks a major transition in the development of the rabbinate in the land of Israel.[23]

Martin Jacobs argues that the summit of de facto power was reached by the *nesi'im* only under the Christian emperors, towards the end of the fourth century; an entry in the *Codex Theodosianus* for the year 392 addresses the Jewish leadership, presumably including the *nasi*, with the formula *viri clarissimi et inlustres* ('distinguished and illustrious sirs'), a formal indication of rank.[24] However, the entry for 415 explicitly downgrades the patriarch Gamaliel VI and another entry, dated 429, confiscates taxes raised by the Jewish *primates* and patriarchs.[25] Jacobs doubts whether this last reference in the *Codex* to the patriarchate indicates the disappearance of the institution; Theodoret, Bishop of Cyrrhus (Syria), refers to the Jewish patriarchs as late as 447/8,[26] but as this is only to scoff at their claim to Davidic ancestry it does not provide firm evidence that the institution still functioned. The archaeological record indicates that there was a vigorous resurgence of synagogue building in the fifth century, perhaps in response to the growing number of Christian churches in the Holy Land;[27] however, this does not imply that there was a functioning patriarchate.

Judah's assumption of authority and his relationship with the governing power both facilitated Roman control and placed power and authority in the hands of the Jewish religious authorities who followed his teachings. Roman patronage of, or at least benevolence toward, the patriarchate, even if not formal, would have strengthened the hand of the Sages in imposing Mishna in Galilee and its neighbourhood as the authoritative Jewish code of law. Judah is said to have been accompanied by some sort of armed guard,[28] a statement that is confirmed by the Church Father Origen's dubious claim to have observed that the 'ethn-arch' in his time differed little from a true king, and inflicted capital punishment with the knowledge if not the sanction of the Roman government.[29] Jews nevertheless remained subject to Roman jurisdiction in their external relations, and many Palestinian Jews, not to speak of those elsewhere in the Empire, were beyond reach of the *nasi* and his interpretation of Judaism.

Iran (Parthians, Sasanians) and the Bavli

If the de facto authority of Judah and his associates explains Mishna's acceptance among Jewish communities in Galilee and the surrounding areas, what accounts for its acceptance in Baby-lonia? In Judah's time Mesopotamia was temporarily under Roman rule, though contested by the Parthians (also known as Arsacids from the name of their founder Arsaces), who ruled much of what is now Iran and Iraq from roughly 247 BCE until 224 CE, and whose successors regained control of Mesopotamia in 226. The Parthian aristocracy had taken over much of the administrative apparatus established by the Seleucids, the ethnic-ally Greek rulers who succeeded Alexander, and adopted a fairly relaxed attitude to the internal affairs, including the religion, of the ethnic groups over whom they ruled; Jews were able to flourish as an independent ethnic group with a distinctive religion. In 117 CE, when the Revolt of the Diaspora was quelled under Trajan, as well as after the Bar Kokhba Revolt, refugees swelled the numbers of the Babylonian Jewish community, which had existed since the deportation of Israelites in biblical times.

Even so, for the time being Palestine remained the main centre of Jewish learning and attracted students from Babylonia, including Judah's outstanding disciple, Ḥiyya. Ḥiyya's nephew Abba ben Aivu, also called Abba Arika ('Abba the Tall'), returned in 219 to Sura in southern Babylonia (close to Ḥilla in modern Iraq), where he taught Torah and pioneered the application of Mishna as the Jewish legal system. The Talmud implies that Abba ben Aivu had studied prior to completing his education in Palestine – teachings are reported in his name from before that time;[30] he probably received ordination from Judah, and is generally referred to throughout the Talmud simply as 'Rav' (the master, or rabbi).

Rav's younger counterpart in Babylonia was Shmuel (Samuel) of Nehardea, on the east bank of the Euphrates a little below the level of Baghdad. The two were personally acquainted; a Talmudic anecdote records a meal they shared and at which Shmuel addressed Rav as 'Abba', a term denoting affection as well as respect.[31] Though the Talmud relates how he effected a cure for Judah's eye problem and Judah wished to ordain him (Bava Metzi'a 85b/86a), some scholars doubt that Shmuel ever visited Palestine. However, he certainly acquired a thorough knowledge of Mishna; his father was a scholar, and he also had contact with Levi ben Sisi, a disciple of Judah, who travelled frequently between Palestine and Babylonia and eventually settled in Nehardea.

Rav and Shmuel brought Mishna to Babylonia, but how did they gain power to implement its provisions as the Jewish legal system? From at least the middle of the second century Babylonian Jewry was governed by an officially recognized Resh Galuta ('Head of the Exile', or Exilarch). Rabbinic tradition attributes the origin of this institution to the exile of King Jehoiachin of Judah in the sixth century BCE (2 Kings 25:27; 1 Chronicles 3:17); Jacob Neusner has more plausibly speculated that the Parthian government under Vologases I (d. 79 CE) established the office as part of its reorganization of the administration, and with its aid enlisted Jewish support for Parthia against the Romans.[32] Whatever the origins, the earliest Exilarch named as such in rabbinic literature is Huna I, who flourished in the latter part of the second century.[33]

The Exilarch, if he was to maintain an independent Jewish 'nation in exile', needed judges and administrators and, moreover, judges who would administer distinctively Jewish justice;

affairs could not be left in the hands of Jewish 'strong-men',[34] nor could Jews submit to the jurisdiction of the Sasanian justices, for they were Magian priests, so accepting their authority would have been tantamount to conversion to the Zoroastrian religion. Rav, Shmuel and their disciples were uniquely equipped to establish Jewish law, for the Mishna, far more than the unmediated Bible, constituted a ready-made legal corpus that, with minimum adjustment, could be tailored to the needs of Babylonian Jewry.[35]

Both Rav and Shmuel remained subordinate to the exilarchs of their time. For about a century the followers of each tended to recognize their own master as the significant authority, but by the fourth generation the two came to be regarded as equals and were represented as debating with each other on terms of equality. Perhaps there were rival schools, though David Goodblatt has urged that any notion of Babylonian 'schools' at this time, in the sense of organized academic institutions, is an unsupported retrojection.[36]

The major political event in third-century Babylonia was the overthrow, in 224, of the Parthians by another Iranian dynasty, the Sasanians. Rabbi Yoḥanan, Rav's contemporary in Palestine, recoiled with horror when he received news that 'the Magi are coming to Babylon',[37] that is, that the Sasanians were prevailing over the Parthians; he feared their missionary zeal for Zoroastrianism as much as the inevitable ravages of war. Rav himself is said to have mourned when the last Arsacid ruler, Artabanus IV, was slain in battle by the victorious Sasanians under Ardashir in 224: 'When Antoninus died, Rabbi [Judah the Patriarch] lamented, "The bond is snapped"; when Ardavan died, Rav lamented, "The bond is snapped"'; other comments attributed to Rav are 'under a Roman, but not under a Magus', and 'Whoever learns anything from a Magus is deserving of death.'[38]

Ardashir (reigned 226–41) was the son of Papak, a Magian High Priest of Anahita at Stakhr, close to Persepolis; Ardashir's elder brother, Shapur, ruled over the sacred fire of Ormuzd, and the Byzantine poet and historian Agathias reports that Ardashir 'was initiated to the ceremonies of the magi and performed the mysteries himself'.[39] With such a background, and on the heels of his victories over the 'foreign' and heretical Arsacids and the Romans, Ardashir was motivated to impose his religion on the people now within his power; missionary fervour combined with a more invasive system of administration to oppress Jews and other dissident minorities, though not until the reforms of the priest Kartir towards the end of the third century can one speak of a 'state religion'.

Ardashir's son Shapur I (reigned *c.* 241–72) adopted a more tolerant policy, perhaps with a view to placating the peoples in the west of his empire and so securing his borders against Rome; in 260 he defeated and took captive the Roman emperor Valerian, an event commemorated in a series of rock reliefs in the cliffs at Bishapur. His protection of the prophet Mani, eponymous founder of the Manichaean religion, may indicate a cooler commitment towards the dominant form of Zoroastrian orthodoxy and an openness towards other forms of religion. Jews benefited from his tolerant policy though Rav, who died *c.* 247, seems not to have become reconciled to the new regime. Shmuel on the other hand is said to have visited Shapur frequently at Ctesiphon, the Sasanian winter-capital on the Tigris about 20 miles south-east of Baghdad, and to have established a cordial working relationship, possibly together with the Exilarch Mar Uqba I; there is even an anecdote (*Sukka* 53a) about Shmuel juggling eight wine glasses for Shapur's amusement.[40] The stories of their relationship, if embroidered, rest on a more solid foundation than those of Rabbi and 'Antoninus'.

A ruling attributed to Shmuel that 'The law of the realm is law' (*Bava Qama* 113a; see p. 451) was to have momentous consequences for the relationships of Jews with governing authorities in later ages. Superficially akin to the statement attributed to Jesus, 'Render into Caesar the things which are Caesar's, and unto God the things that are God's' (Matthew 22:23), it was never interpreted as signifying a difference between the material and spiritual realms; rather, it recognized the right of a legitimate government to control land tenure and raise reasonable taxes, and it recognized the legitimacy of the Sasanian government.[41] Whether it was devised by Shmuel, imposed by Shapur or simply emerged out of common practice, matters little; the ingenious compromise, while acknowledging Sasanian over-lordship, left the Jewish authorities free to administer all religious matters including family law, as well as internal com-mercial dealings and criminal behaviour. Jewish courts certainly administered punishments including flogging on miscreants, though they did not impose fines or capital punishment.[42]

The Sasanian regime ultimately proved propitious for Rav, Shmuel and their successors to develop a distinctive Jewish legal system on the basis of Judah's Mishna; their legal enactments, discussions, elaborations, commentaries, preaching and specu-lations comprise a significant part of the Babylonian Talmud.

In the fourth century a marked disparity emerged between Jewish law and learning in Palestine and that in Babylonia, reflecting changing political circumstances. The long reign (309–73) of Shapur II ensured stability for Babylonian Jewry; Jews did their best to evade the onerous taxes he demanded to finance his military operations, and individuals were punished for this,[43] but Jews were not subjected to systematic persecution. Abbaye and Rava, followed by Rav Papa, together with their associates, developed legal practice and theory in ways that were neither precedented nor emulated in Palestine, and were able to implement the law without state hindrance.

During Shapur's reign some seventeen Roman Emperors ruled; in 395 Rome formally split into an Eastern Empire ruled from Constantinople and a Western Empire ruled from Rome, and the Jews of Palestine suffered both from the general political instability and from the growing dominance of Christianity in the wake of Edict of Milan in 313;[44] matters were aggravated by the brutal crushing by Gallus of a revolt in 352[45] and by the earthquake of 363, which Christians gleefully interpreted as punishment on the Jews for daring, with the encouragement of the Emperor Julian (361–3), to commence rebuilding the Temple.[46] Despite this, material remains of synagogues in Pales-tine in the pre-Islamic period suggest that Jewish life enjoyed some respite under the Byzantines;[47] but Palestinian Jews focused on Bible, midrash, poetry and liturgy rather than on Talmudic dialectics.

Babylonia of the Talmud – Social and Religious Background

Sasanian society, as reformed in the fourth century under Shapur II, comprised four hereditary social estates: Magian priests and judges; warriors; scribes (administrators); cultivators, craftsmen and merchants. Each estate had its own head and empire-wide bureaucracy.[48]

Jews were not stratified in this way, though they too placed the law in the hands of the religious authorities; however, the Sages were not priests nor did they constitute a hereditary class, and the hereditary Jewish priestly families retained only vestigial privileges and functions. The only significant hereditary office was that of the Resh Galuta, the political head, who claimed descent in the direct male line from David; other positions of authority, such as those of the Sages who functioned as judges, were in principle open to all Jewish males.

There were three main levels of Sasanian administration below the Shah,[49] the supreme ruler, but Jewish 'Babylonia' coincides more or less with the *Šahrab* of Asōrestān (Assyria), under his direct rule. Thus the Jews, through the mediation of the Resh Galuta, had direct access to him, and could rely on the backing of the authorities for the implementation of their laws as interpreted by the rabbis. In regions under Iranian priestly administration it would have been far more difficult for the rabbis to impose their will; this is perhaps why rabbinic Judaism developed in Babylonia rather than elsewhere in the Iranian Empire.

In the course of the third century Mazdean Zoroastrianism was consolidated as the Iranian state religion and Mishnaic Judaism as the law code of the Jews of Babylonia. Christianity penetrated Mesopotamia via Edessa, while at the Indian end of the Empire were substantial Buddhist enclaves; the prophet Mani spent several years in a Christian–Jewish Elkasite monastery before proclaiming his brand of Gnostic syncretism, the highly successful Manichean religion, in Babylonia *c.* 250. There was also a general expansion of cults derived from Zoroastrianism, including the Mithraic popular in the Roman Empire.

Religious leaders poured scorn on one another's faith and did their best to 'protect' their own followers from being 'contaminated' by those of rival religions. Jews didn't lag behind. Christianity and dissident forms of Judaism were rejected by the Sages as *minut* (heresy), particularly for what the rabbis regarded as their misappropriation and perversion of Scripture; other faiths were rejected as idolatrous. But whatever was preached from the pulpit, economic interests brought people of different religious and ethnic communities together. Material culture, science, medicine and superstition crossed boundaries in the marketplace, though this is not always apparent in the literary sources, since these were compiled by the religious.

Early in the seventh century[50] the Sasanian Empire, under its last ruler Yazdegerd III, fell before the Muslim Arabs. The new era, welcomed by many Jews, marks the closure of the Talmud and the beginning of the so-called Geonic period with its symbiosis of Jewish and Arabic culture.

The Men Who Made Mishna and Talmud

In the 980s Jacob ben Nissim ibn Shahin sent an enquiry on behalf of the Jewish community of Kairouan, Tunisia, to the leading rabbi of the time, Sherira, the Gaon of Pumbedita, in far-off Babylonia. Who wrote the Mishna? he wanted to know. Had it been started by the Men of the Great Assembly (a partly legendary body of Sages in the period of the Second Temple), and had more been added by the Sages in each generation until it was completed by Rabbi Judah ha-Nasi? And who composed Tosefta, baraita and Talmud?

The epistle sent in reply by Sherira in 987, known as *Iggeret Rav Sherira Gaon*, is a classic of Jewish historiography, and still provides the basic chronology of rabbinic Judaism in the Talmudic and Geonic periods.[51] It is from Sherira that we inherit our chronology of Tannaim and Amoraim, who were followed by Sevoraim, who contributed to the Talmud, and who in turn were followed by the Geonim at Sura and Pumbedita.

Sherira insists that neither the Mishna nor the Talmud was a written document; orality was of their essence, and they were taught by repetition and memorization.[52] Despite this, there is evidence that some written records were kept for reference, though no one is sure what form they took prior to the Geonim.[53]

Tannaim; singular, Tanna

The Sages whose teachings are recorded in the Mishna are known collectively as the Tannaim. They were active in the Land of Israel from the late first century BCE until about 220 CE.

Other works, not all of which survive, contain teachings attributed to them, though none was as carefully preserved as the Mishna. A parallel collection, attributed to Judah's disciple Ḥiyya, shares the Mishna's structure and is known as Tosefta ('supplement'). As well as supplementary teachings, Tosefta contains elaborations of and commentary on the Mishna; it is frequently cited in the Talmud, though its status is secondary to that of the Mishna. Other teachings in similar style, not found in any extant collection though cited in the Talmud, are known collectively as baraitot (singular, baraita), or 'external' collections.

Many of the teachings were also arranged in the form of running commentary on the books of the Bible, the most important collections being (with no precise dates for any):

Mekhilta, on parts of Exodus. The Mekhilta of Rabbi Ishmael and The Mekhilta of Rabbi Simeon ben Yoḥai represent different exegetical traditions.
Sifra (or *Sifra d'bei Rav*), on Leviticus.
Sifré on Numbers and Deuteronomy.

The teaching of the Tannaim consists for the most part of succinct statements of law, in Hebrew, designed to be memorized; the meaning is not always clear, since it is assumed that a teacher will explain both meaning and context.

Tannaim present their teachings as authoritative; in the eyes of their successors, these teachings constitute Oral Torah.

Amoraim; singular, Amora

Amora (Aramaic, 'speaker') is the collective term for the rabbis who followed the Tannaim; they were active in the Land of

Israel until the late fourth century and in Babylonia until the
late fifth century.

   In a narrower sense, an Amora is the man who relays the
master's teaching to the students, translating from Hebrew to
Aramaic where necessary. It was thought undignified for the
master to teach directly, as the following amusing exchange
illustrates. (The point at issue is whether a Hebrew expression
used in the Mishna with reference to early morning means 'the
cock crowed' or 'the crier called'.)

Rav arrived [incognito] at Rabbi Shila's place. Rabbi Shila had no
Amora available, so Rav volunteered. [Rav] relayed [the Mishna] to
the students: 'The crier called.' Rabbi Shila intervened, 'Why don't
you say, "The cock crowed"?' Rav responded, 'The flute that sounds
sweet to freemen is rejected by [mere] weavers! When I said this in
the presence of Rabbi Ḥiyya he made no criticism, yet you tell me to
say, "The cock crowed"!' 'Ah,' said Rabbi Shila, 'You must be Rav!'
(*Yoma* 20b)

   Amoraim saw themselves as subordinate to the Tannaim;
they did not exercise independent judgement in matters decided
by Tannaim, but clarified and developed their rulings. This is
similar to the difference between the *mujtahids*, the early Islamic
jurists, and the *muqallids* who followed them, using *taqlid*
(rational arguments) to analyse and develop the decisions of
their predecessors.

   The sense of being inferior to their predecessors is articulated
in this comment attributed to a fourth-century Amora:

Rabbi Zeira said in the name of Rava bar Zimuna: 'If the former ones
were sons of angels, we are sons of men; if they were sons of men, we
are like donkeys, and not like the donkey of Rabbi Ḥanina ben Dosa
or Rabbi Pinḥas ben Yair, but like ordinary donkeys.' (*Shabbat* 112b)

   The boundary between Tannaim and Amoraim is not sharp.
First-generation Amoraim such as Rav and Shmuel in Babylonia
and Rabbi Yoḥanan in Palestine often formulated their teachings
in similar language and form to the Tannaim; later generations

recognized that Rav issued rulings just as a Tanna might and was not bound by the decisions of previous Tannaim.[54]

A fundamental distinction emerged between the mode of formulation of Tannaitic texts and that of Amoraic texts, and was fully established by the fourth Amoraic generation, that of Abbaye and Rava. Though Hebrew is used by early Amoraim to formulate teachings supplementing or clarifying those of the Mishna, most Amoraic teachings are recorded in Aramaic; they frequently *refer to* Tannaitic statements, and use an Aramaic technical vocabulary developed for second-level discussion.

Substance even more than language separates Amoraic discourse from Tannaitic. Where Tannaim disagree their views are set down side by side; only in a minority of instances are detailed arguments preserved. Moreover, they do not attempt to explain or justify each other's view. Amoraim, on the other hand, do spend a lot of time explaining or justifying the views of Tannaim – and arguing with each other. Of course, Tannaim might have argued in similar fashion, but it has not been preserved.

Through at least four generations there were frequent contacts and interchanges between Palestine and Babylonia; for instance, from the third generation of Amoraim onwards the influence of the Palestinian Rabbi Yoḥanan in Babylonia is very strong.[55] However, from the time of the fourth generation, Babylonian Torah diverged from that of Palestine, and became increasingly occupied with the analysis of legal concepts; much of Amoraic discourse is devoted to reviewing ranges of cases that help them to establish boundaries of the law.

The role of *hora'a* (decision-making) diminishes in proportion to that of analysis and argumentation. This is partly because most of the major decisions had been taken, but also because Torah study as such, irrespective of decision-making, is increasingly seen as a sacred duty. An anecdote about Shmuel includes the statement, attributed to a legendary 'Book of Adam', that 'Rav Ashi and Ravina are the end of *hora'a*' (*Bava Metzi'a* 85b–86a); Sherira likewise writes that Amoraic activity came to an end with Rav Ashi and Ravina early in the fifth century, few decisions being made subsequently.[56]

Sevoraim; singular, Savora[57]

Sherira wrote: 'And after [the Amoraim], even though there was certainly no *hora'a*, there were interpreters who explained things and were close to *hora'a*; they are called our Masters the Sevoraim.'[58] He cited a lengthy and complex passage at the beginning of tractate *Qiddushin* as an example of the work of Ina and Simuna, two of the latest Sevoraim,[59] but as their names do not appear there he evidently relied on information received from other sources. Scholarly controversy still surrounds the nature of the Sevoraic contribution to Talmud; conservative scholars maintain that the Sevoraim 'completed the ordering of the Talmud, clarified certain unsettled halakhic decisions, introduced additional discussions and explanations of existing texts, and inserted brief technical guide phrases to facilitate study of the texts'.[60]

It is perhaps no accident that the collecting and editing of rabbinic traditions that started with Amoraim in the time of Shapur II coincides roughly with the period in which Zoroastrian scholars were collecting and editing their own traditions in the Avesta.

Stammaim

The conventional view, derived from Sherira, is that the Sevoraim, who completed the Talmud were followed by the Geonim, possibly after an interval caused by political instability in the declining years of the Sasanians. Scholars' eyebrows were therefore raised in 1968 when David Weiss Halivni, in a monumental study in Hebrew of the literary formation of part of the Talmud, noted that despite the numerous citations of authorities on almost every page, most of the text of the Talmud consists of anonymous discussions; the inference was that these anonymous scholars were the real authors – they had 'changed the sources into traditions'.[61] He named them Stammaim (from Hebrew *stam*, 'anonymous'), and dated their activity from 427 to *c.* 520 (though he later extended this).

Since the Sevoraic contributions to Talmud are also for the most part anonymous, how does Halivni distinguish their contributions from those of the Stammaim? Indeed, why does he think that Stammaim more or less completed the Talmud, and were followed by Sevoraim who didn't do much? He offers two reasons:

1. [The Geonim and the Rishonim[62]] speak of the Saboraim as having added texts to the Talmud, which creates the impression that the Talmud was more or less complete during the time of the Saboraim.
2. Amoraic quotations in the materials generally attributed to the Saboraim can be traced to other places in the Talmud and were undoubtedly taken from there, whereas Amoraic quotations in the anonymous parts of the Talmud often have no parallel anywhere else in the Talmud.[63]

If 'Stammaim' really existed, as distinct from the Sevoraim, why did Sherira not notice them? Perhaps the answer to this lies in the evaluation of the kind of work they accomplished; essentially, they would have gathered and worked upon reports of the argumentation of the immediately preceding generations. A modern scholar like Halivni realizes how important such work is; it lays the foundation for the way in which all future generations will read the tradition. Sherira might well have dismissed such activity as unimportant, because to him the real tradition was the oral, of which he still felt himself a part, and the important activity was that of living and interpreting Torah in each generation. The Sevoraim had attained this level through their limited decision-making and the clarifications they had introduced, but the disciples who had jotted down or memorized anecdotes and debates in the academies would not, in his view, have qualified to be set on a par with Tannaim and Amoraim as a distinct stage in the chain of tradition.

Style of the Talmud
Halakha *and* Aggada

The content of the Talmud falls into two genres, *halakha* ('law') and *aggada* ('narrative'); both may occur in one *sugya* (unit) and they may even merge into one another, as in *Bava Qama* 60a–b (see p. 440).

Halakha is more precisely defined than *aggada*; law cannot function if it is vague. The complexity of *halakhic* argumentation was problematic, for a chain of reasoning might lead to conclusions that appear to challenge tradition. Some Sages were known for their facility in reasoning, and others for their reliable transmission of tradition:

When Rav Ḥisda and Rav Sheshet met, Rav Ḥisda's lips trembled before Rav Sheshet's knowledge of Mishna; Rav Sheshet's whole body shook at Rav Ḥisda's fine reasoning. (*Eruvin* 67a)

The choice of Rav Yosef rather than Rabba to head the academy of Pumbedita *c.* 320 CE indicates that the Sages valued soundness of tradition more than forensic skill.[64]

The Talmud's *halakhic* decisions were received in later Jewish tradition as binding, but the eleventh-century Spanish poet and scholar Shmuel Ha-Nagid characterized *aggada* as inspirational rather than definitive. Rashi, commenting on an *aggadic* remark about the saving life on the Sabbath, candidly stated: 'This is not the reason that the saving of life is permitted on the Sabbath . . . but [the compiler wanted] to make it appeal to [the general public] through an *aggada*, since women and ignorant people attended the sermon and the preachers had to attract their attention [with stories].'[65]

Style and Exegesis

A wide range of literary forms and styles is needed to articulate legal argumentation, biblical exegesis, homiletics, parables, folk tales, historical narrative, poetry, science, superstition and popular proverbs.

Legal and exegetical discussions have distinctive structures and vocabularies; narratives are often worked into set patterns with threefold examples. Vitality is ensured by the inclusion of anecdotes about the Sages and their disciples and often, as Louis Jacobs pointed out, by dramatic presentation of an argument.[66]

Bible exegesis builds on techniques evolved before the rabbinic period, for instance in the *pesher* commentaries of the Dead Sea Scrolls.[67] Rules of rhetoric such those attributed to Rabbi Ishmael and to Rabbi Yosé the Galilean were devised to govern the process and to save it from arbitrariness; these are explained below.

Language

Judah ha-Nasi, hoping for a national revival in Galilee, objected to Jews speaking Aramaic: 'In the Land of Israel, why should anyone speak Aramaic? Either the holy tongue, or Greek!' Rav Yosef, in early fourth-century Pumbedita, similarly declared, 'Why should anyone speak Aramaic? Either the holy tongue, or Persian!'[68] Aramaic nevertheless persisted as the vernacular among Jews and other minorities in the Near East for some centuries, and is still spoken by Mandaeans.

A baraita, probably of the third century, refers to Scriptures written in 'Coptic, Median, [paleo-]Hebrew [script], Elamite or Greek' (*Shabbat* 115a). Mishna, aside from documentary citations, is in Hebrew. Early Amoraim, in Babylonia as well as Palestine, continued to formulate their 'official' teaching in Hebrew, if slightly modified from the Hebrew of the Mishna. Later Amoraic statements, other than some formal rulings of Mishna-like character, tend to be made in Aramaic, while the language in which discussion takes place is mostly Aramaic. Some Persian ('Middle Iranian', or Pahlavi) loan-words occur, especially for administrative and military terms, but they are fewer than those of Latin or Greek origin.

Units of Discourse – Sh'ma'ta *and* Sugya

The *sh'ma'ta* (Aramaic: 'that which is heard', a discourse) is a brief summary of a *halakhic* lesson; when several are woven together into discussion of a specific topic, the whole is referred to as a *sugya* (unit, or pericope), a term derived from the Aramaic for 'step';[69] several *sugyot* may be strung together to form a collection.

The composition of *sugyot* was probably commenced in the

fourth century,[70] though it was not completed until the sixth or seventh. Many *sugyot* have survived in parallel versions in tractates of the two Talmudim, reflecting different stages in their development. Frequently, competing versions of a *sh'ma'ta* are set side by side in a single *sugya*; examples in this volume are *Megilla* 2a (see p. 262), *Nedarim* 22a (p. 356), *Nazir* 16b–17a (p. 363), *Bava Batra* 17b (p. 488) and *Horayot* 2a (p. 557). The evolution and literary construction of the *sugya* are among the topics most hotly debated by Talmudic scholars today.

Attributions

To report a teaching in the name of the master who formulated it 'brings redemption to the world';[71] as well as being intrinsically virtuous, it serves the practical purpose of establishing what authority attaches to the teaching.

Attributions, however, are open to question. The Gemara itself often carries conflicting reports of what a Sage said, identifications are frequently uncertain[72] and copyists sometimes confuse names. In this striking instance an attribution is *deliberately* modified to enhance the authority of a ruling:

Rabbi Simeon ben Pazi said in the name of Rabbi Joshua ben Levi in the name of Rabbi Yosé ben Shaul in the name of Rabbi [Judah ha-Nasi] on behalf of the holy congregation of Jerusalem, Rabbi Simeon [ben Yoḥai] and his colleagues said that the law is in accordance with the view of Rabbi Meir. (*Betza* 27a)

The Gemara immediately points out that this is anachronistic; Simeon ben Yoḥai preceded Meir. The laconic reply, that Simeon's ruling was the same as that given by Meir, acknowledges that the attribution is a fiction designed to lend authority to Meir's view.

Also, the Gemara frequently uses the formula 'X said . . .' in the course of an argument, when what it means is, 'Had X been confronted with this objection, he could have countered by saying . . .' Asher ben Yeḥiel ('the Rosh', *c.* 1250–1327) drew attention to this form of expression;[73] it is a form of shorthand rather than 'pseudepigraphy', as some scholars call it, since there was no intention of misleading anyone into the belief that X *actually* said what was hypothesized.

Interpretation of Scripture

A sacred text cannot guide on its own. It has to be read, and all reading is interpretation.

The Torah has privileged status as God's Word revealed to Moses at Sinai. A law is regarded as biblical only if derived from a verse in one of these five books. The festival of Purim, since it is based solely on the Book of Esther, is classified as a rabbinic, not a biblical, institution (it is *mid'rabbanan*, not *mid'Oraita*).

Three assumptions govern rabbinic interpretation of the Torah text:

The text is free from error and inconsistency. God does not make mistakes! Apparent contradictions can be resolved by correct interpretation, though we do not always know what this is.

The text is free from redundancy. Some laws are repeated – e.g. Deuteronomy reviews topics covered in the earlier books – but the precise formulation always reveals some new aspect.

The text is comprehensive, containing whatever we need to know (not necessarily 'all knowledge', though there have been rabbis in more recent times who claimed this[74]).

These three assumptions apply only to the Torah. The rest of the Hebrew Bible – Prophets and Writings – is held to be free from error, but not from redundancy; it cannot create *halakha*, only throw light on it.

The Bavli does not treat the text of the Mishna and other tannaitic works as sacrosanct like the Bible, but as a repository of law which can be 'corrected' if need be; it proposes emendations for clarification, to avoid inconsistencies, or to establish the 'correct' version of a law.[75] Amoraim sometimes say of a Mishna text, *m'shabeshta hi* ('it is incorrect');[76] Shmuel deliberately reverses attributions in a Mishna to ensure that the rabbis infer the correct *halakha* from it (*Pesaḥim* 27a); an anonymous comment adjusts the text of a Mishna to fit a ruling of Rava

(*Yevamot* 12b (see p. 304)), and so on. Although later Amoraim generally work on the assumption that Tannaim did not preserve superfluous statements, they are prepared to admit, as Rav Yosef did, that on occasion 'Rabbi included a superfluous Mishna.'[77]

Halivni notes that common technical terms such as *hakhi qa'amar* ('this is what he means to say') or *eima* ('I might say') 'hover between emendation and explanation', and he describes a process of 'interpreting out', which Amoraim use to restrict the application of a Mishna statement to a limited context or a special instance.[78]

Rules of Interpretation

In the third century scholars listed rules they believed to have been used by the Tannaim in their interpretation of Scripture. Seven hermeneutic rules (*middot*) were attributed to Hillel, thirteen to Rabbi Ishmael and thirty-two to Rabbi Yosé the Galilean;[79] they cover reasonableness, rhetoric and grammar, and have points of resemblance with ways in which Stoics interpreted Homer and Romans interpreted legal texts.[80] They can be reduced to four basic types:

Qal va-ḥomer: 'Minor and major', the argument a fortiori. It is reasonable to infer that if so-and-so is true in such-and-such a case, it will certainly be true in a case where the relevant factor is stronger. Examples (in this volume): *Pesaḥim* 66a (p. 161), *Yevamot* 87b (p. 324), *Sanhedrin* 73b (p. 521).

G'zera shava: 'Similar formulation', also known as *heqesh* ('analogy'). If a word or phrase occurs in two separate passages, an analogy may be drawn for the application of the law in both cases. Examples: *Berakhot* 31b (see p. 25), *Sota* 37b (p. 370).

The use of general (*k'lal*) and specific (*p'rat*), or inclusive (*ribbui*) and exclusive (*mi'ut*), terms. Examples: *Pesaḥim* 95a (see p. 175), *Sukka* 50b (pp. 218–19).

Meaning determined by context. Examples: *Rosh Hashana* 2b (p. 239), *Bava Metzi'a* 61a (p. 474).

In addition to these four types of reasoned interpretation, two artificial devices are sometimes used which seem to treat

Scripture as a code to be deciphered rather than a text to be read:

Gematria, the numerical value of the letters of a word. Examples: *Sanhedrin* 97b (see p. 516), *Makkot* 23b (p. 524).[81] A variety of anagrams, abbreviations and letter substitutions belong in this category.

Im eino 'inyan. If a word is superfluous in its own context, it is transposed elsewhere. Even a letter may be transposed from one word to another. Example: *Yoma* 48a.

Titles and Names

Hannah Cotton has observed that none of the sixty known documents reflecting Jewish life in Judaea in the period from 66 to 135 CE refers to anyone as 'Rabbi'.[82] The word was a courteous form of address to a master, whether of Torah or some secular discipline, but there is no evidence that it designated a category of religious scholar and leader prior to the third century. While Mishna uses the title, it consistently refers to men in this category as *ḥakhamim* Sages, not rabbis, a usage noted by Jerome.[83] The Mishna also uses the title Rabban; Bavli adds 'Rav' and 'Mar' ('master').

Sherira claimed that the Talmud applies the title 'Rabbi' to scholars in the Land of Israel and 'Rav' to Babylonians,[84] and in a letter to the community of Kairouan he wrote, 'Rabbi is greater than Rav, Rabban is greater than Rabbi, the untitled name is greater than Rabban.' Yochanan Breuer has disputed this traditional analysis, arguing that Rav was originally a dialectical variant of Rabbi, consistent with the Eastern Aramaic habit of dropping possessive endings; Rabban (as is generally agreed) was a title reserved for the Nasi,[85] and the 'untitled name' by which Hillel and Shammai, for instance, are known is because they predated the use of titles.[86]

The title Mar is occasionally used, as it was by Syriac Christians. It is likely that it was used for those lacking ordination; this may be why it was commonly applied to the Resh Galuta, though Sherira says it is either a proper name or a title of importance.[87]

Titles are sometimes conflated with names; Rava, for instance, is a conflation of Rav Abba, and Ravina of Rav Avina.

Theology

Many scholars have attempted to formulate the Talmud's 'theology', one of the most notable being Solomon Schechter, who drew attention to the non-systematic nature of the sources.[88] Rabbinic theology has to be based on material like this:

Said Rabbi Ḥama bar Ḥanina: If not for these three verses, sinners in Israel[89] would not have a leg to stand upon. It is written, [I WILL GATHER THE OUTCAST,] AND THOSE I HAVE CAUSED TO DO EVIL[90] (Micah 4:6); it is written, AS CLAY IN THE HAND OF THE POTTER[, SO ARE YOU IN MY HAND, SAYS THE LORD] (Jeremiah 18:6); it is written, AND I WILL PUT MY SPIRIT INTO YOU. THUS I WILL CAUSE YOU TO FOLLOW MY LAWS, AND FAITHFULLY TO OBSERVE MY RULES. (Ezekiel 36:27 JPS)

In the School of Rabbi Yannai they said, This may be derived from [the name] DI ZAHAV (Deuteronomy 1:1). What is DI ZAHAV? In the school of Rabbi Yannai they said, This is what Moses said to the Holy One, blessed be He: Lord of the Universe! Because of the silver and gold [zahav] you lavished on Israel until they said, enough! [dai] – that is what led them to sin ... Rabbi Ḥiyya bar Abba said in the name of Rabbi Yoḥanan, It is like a man who had a son; he bathed him, anointed him, gave him food and drink, hung a purse of money around his neck and set him by the door of a brothel. How could the son not sin? (Berakhot 32a)

Clearly, the rabbis were speculating about the relationship between free will and determinism, or between 'nature' and 'nurture': can a person be held responsible for his actions if they are strongly influenced or determined by God or by the environment? But they do not formulate systematic philosophical answers. If 'theology' is taken to mean 'the study of God's word', they were theologians; if it is taken to mean 'the construction of rational systems of thought to explicate God's word', they were not. In this latter sense, known Jewish theology ceased with the Hellenistic Jewish philosopher Philo of Alexandria early in the first century and was not revived until Saadia Gaon and others in the tenth century were confronted with Greek philosophy, mediated to the Islamic world by Syriac Christian scholars. The Talmud may provide building blocks that theologians can use to construct their systems, but it does not itself engage in systematic speculation.

The Bavli's values and its attitudes to society are reasonably consistent, though it is stretching the evidence somewhat to say that it gives 'a cogent account of the social order'. God and His providence, the authenticity and veracity of Torah and the rabbinic tradition, and the centrality of Israel in God's 'economy' are never doubted, and to this extent 'the authorship of the Talmud speaks in a single way'.[91] But if certain forms of argumentation are common, none is universal; sections composed at different times and places reflect different concerns and attitudes. Richard Kalmin rightly stresses that the Bavli is the work of different editors from the fourth-generation Amoraim onwards.[92] Moreover, no one knows to what extent the Bavli represents the full range of Jewish life and thought in Sasanian Babylonia rather than the limited perceptions of the religious scholars who compiled the Talmud.

The Talmud and Christianity

Christians were present in growing numbers in both Palestine and Babylonia during the formative period of rabbinic Judaism; their writings contain intemperate and vitriolic attacks on Jews and Judaism, among the most notorious of which are the *Homilies* of John Chrysostom (c. 347–407).[93]

Modern printed editions of the Talmud have been subjected to Christian censorship, and lack obvious references to Christianity. Uncensored manuscripts preserve a number of statements that appear to refer to Jesus, though not always by name; an example in this volume is *Sanhedrin* 42–3 (see pp. 504–5). He is said, for instance, to have been conceived illegitimately, to have defied his rabbinic teacher and to have practised sorcery. Peter Schäfer argues that 'These (mainly) Babylonian stories about Jesus and his family are deliberate and highly sophisticated counternarratives to the stories about Jesus' life and death in the Gospels – narratives that presuppose a detailed knowledge of the New Testament, in particular of the Gospel of John.'[94]

There is no explicit discussion of Christian theology and its claims for Jesus, though such matters must have been debated in Palestine in towns such as Caesarea[95] and Sepphoris where Jews and Christians lived in close proximity, and in Nisibis and other Mesopotamian towns with Christian populations. There are occasional references to Christian practice; it is said, for instance, that Rabbi Yoḥanan held that the men of the *ma'amad* refrained from fasting on Sundays 'because of the Nazarenes'.[96]

However, much *aggada* may be read as *implicit* responses to Christian teaching. For example, the frequent emphasis on the constancy of God's love for Israel, even though they have sinned, counters Christian claims that God had rejected Israel on account of their sinfulness and that Christians constituted the New Israel. Reaction to Christian teaching on the abrogation of the law is evident in the strong rabbinic emphasis on its enduring valdity, and in the claim (contrary to Galatians 3) that the patriarchs observed the law, and even rabbinic safeguards, before it was revealed at Sinai.[97] The rabbinic zeal for adducing proof-texts is, at least in part, a response to Christocentric appropriation of those texts.[98]

In Palestine from the fourth century, when Christian rulers conceived a new interest in the 'earthly' Jerusalem and the Holy Land, the Jewish response became evident in synagogue iconography; the early-fifth-century synagogue of Sepphoris has mosaics depicting such themes as the daily sacrifice and the Aaronic priesthood, presumably in rebuttal of Christian appropriation of such symbols.[99]

Transmission of the Text
Textual Criticism

The lack of final editing of the Bavli left the way open for minor adjustments and interpolations in its text in succeeding centuries; moreover, copyists often did not understand what they were copying and frequently 'corrected' the text to something they found more intelligible.

Some manuscript variants arose when comments written on the margin of a handwritten text were then copied into the main text, as is known to have occurred with Geonic comments and rulings; Rashi, for instance, deletes a phrase from the text because he considers it was 'from the *Halakhot Gedolot*', a work of the ninth-century *halakhic* authority Simeon Kayyara.[100] Mediaeval scholars often 'corrected' texts for the sake of intellectual consistency. The twelfth-century Tosafist Jacob Tam praised his grandfather, Rashi, for including proposed changes in his commentary rather than tampering with the text itself, and took his brother, Samuel (Rashbam), to task for eliminating older versions to suit his own interpretation.[101]

The earliest known fragment of rabbinic writing is an inscription in the Rehov Synagogue (near Bet Shean, Israel) probably from the sixth century; manuscript fragments of Talmud recovered from the Cairo Geniza and elsewhere have been dated by scholars to as early as the eighth century. The oldest dated manuscript of any part of the Talmud is in the Bodleian Library, Oxford; it is part of tractate *Keritot*, and carries a date equivalent to 1123. The earliest datable manuscript containing whole tractates is the Florence Codex of 1177, and the earliest nearly complete Talmud manuscript is the 1343 Munich Codex.[102]

Rashi and the Recovery of the Talmudic Text

The reputation of Rabbi Shlomo Yitzḥaqi (Solomon ben Isaac) of Troyes, Champagne (France) (1040–1105), more commonly known by his acronym Rashi, rests on several outstanding achievements. His Bible commentaries are justly admired for their philological advances, his *halakhic* rulings were influential, and he contributed to the development of the Jewish liturgy. His running commentary on the Babylonian Talmud remains, after 900 years, the first port of call for almost everyone who wishes to read Talmud in the original language, justifying the adage that 'without Rashi, the Talmud would have been forgotten in Israel'.[103]

The eleventh and twelfth centuries in Christian Europe were

a period of personal and collective religious revival. Associated with this was a renewed interest in ancient texts, often mediated through Muslims and Jews, and a desire to recover the *prisca philosophia*, the original and true wisdom that we, in our sins, had lost sight of even though it was implicit in God's word in Scripture. Ancient texts, that is, were to be translated and read carefully, and to be reconciled with Scripture.[104]

The Jews of north-west Europe shared this ideal, though their focus was what they perceived as their own special heritage, the Hebrew Scriptures and the writings of the rabbis. The Scriptures had never been forgotten, even if they were not well understood; the rabbinic tradition had been received in somewhat garbled form through Midrash, liturgical practice and poetry, and ancestral custom, but the more disciplined rabbinic Judaism enshrined in the Babylonian Talmud and cultivated by the Geonim did not reach Western Europe (except for Italy) until the tenth century. The routes by which it arrived were similar, and in some cases identical, to those that brought learning in general from the Islamic to the Christian world.

Abraham ibn Daud (1100–1180), a Spanish Jewish Aristotelian philosopher, relates how four Babylonian scholars captured by pirates in the Mediterranean were ransomed by Jewish communities in the West; one was Ḥushiel, who settled in Kairouan, Tunisia, where his son Ḥananel (c. 990–1055) was born.[105] While Ibn Daud's account has not survived modern historical scrutiny, it does illustrate the transfer of learning from the Islamic heartlands to the Maghreb, including Andalusia, and ultimately to the Christian West. Some of Ḥananel ben Ḥushiel's correspondence with the Babylonian Hai Gaon of Pumbedita has been preserved, showing how he channelled the scholarship of the Babylonian academies through the Maghreb to Spain. His commentaries on the Talmud draw heavily on Hai's work, which he often cites verbatim. By Ḥananel's time, however, it is clear that Talmud was already cultivated as far north as the Rhineland ('Lotharingia'), where Rabbenu Gershom of Mainz (c. 960–1028) had established an academy and was writing the first running commentary. When Rashi, as a young man, left his native Troyes to study in Worms, and later

Mainz, he was taught by Gershom's disciples, and read the commentaries and absorbed the teachings of both Gershom and Ḥananel. Rashi probably first studied Talmud under the guidance of his father, but his main teacher in Worms was Ya'aqov ben Yakar, whom he frequently cites (e.g. *Pesaḥim* 111a).

Jonah Fraenkel maintains that although Rashi uses his own words, he normally adopts the interpretation of his teachers;[106] however, there are numerous instances in which Rashi explicitly departs from them. In at least 767 places Rashi states *hakhi garsinan*, 'This is the correct reading.' This demonstrates a deep concern with the unreliability of available manuscripts, and Rashi's understanding that a reliable text must be established before progress could be made in the comprehension and application of Talmudic law. This is fully consistent with the emerging European attitude to the production of accurate texts of the ancient sources of knowledge; even the recovery of ancient texts as a basis for lawmaking is paralleled by the rediscovery of Justinian's *Digest* (*c.* 1070), and by the influential *Decretum* and *Panormia* of Saint Ivo of Chartres (*c.* 1040–1116), an almost exact contemporary of Rashi.[107] Rashi's creation of a rabbinic school may be seen in the context of the growth of scholasticism and the emergence of cathedral schools such as those of Paris and Chartres.[108]

Rashi did not rely on manuscript evidence alone, but sometimes adjusted texts to accord with his speculation as to what the rabbis intended to say. For instance, he wrote:

This is the reading in the manuscripts, but it is wrong, and [came about] through mistaken interpreters who did not understand the topic and explained it incorrectly on the basis of that reading.[109]

Though he was prepared, if necessary, to emend a text without manuscript support, he preferred to find such support if possible:

Since my youth I laboured to reconcile my understanding of Talmud with this reading but could not do so. I then came across a manuscript

with [my reading] written in the hand of Rabbenu Gershom ben
Judah, may he rest in peace, and [found the same] in an uncorrected
manuscript of Rabbi Isaac bar Menaḥem, and it seems right to me.[110]

Rashi distinguished statements from questions (the question
mark had not yet been invented); explained the context of
unattached statements; clarified whether a particular statement
was a hypothesis to be rejected or the conclusion of an argument;
and defined the reference of unattached pronouns. Above all,
he solved innumerable syntactical and lexical problems, skilfully
utilizing the Geonic traditions he had received as well as those
lexicographic and grammatical works with which he was
familiar; often, he supplied a translation into Old French, which
certainly would have been helpful to his original readers.
Occasionally, he clarified a practical *halakhic* point. His attitude to *aggada* was flexible and he sometimes interpreted it
metaphorically or homiletically.

A NOTE ON THIS TRANSLATION

Words and phrases in square brackets [   ] have been inserted
to assist the reader; they are not part of the text, and may be
conjectural.

Constant repetitions of 'he said' are irritating, so I have
amended freely to 'he replied', 'he observed', 'he commented'
and the like, without indicating the change.

No distinction has been made between 'Rabbi X said Rabbi
Y said . . .' and 'Rabbi X said in the name of Rabbi Y', even
though some scholars think this is significant.

Manuscripts and most printed copies use copious abbreviations, and these often create ambiguity. 'R'I', for instance,
might mean Rabbi Yehuda (there were many of the same name),
Rabbi Ishmael or Rabbi Isaac. Also, the names Rava and Rabba
are often confused.[111]

Modern English lacks a ready vocabulary for such concepts
as tithes, purity laws or sacrifices. These are explained in the
introductory notes to the relevant sections.

Rabbinic Aramaic and Hebrew have specially tailored formulae to handle *halakhic* argument and biblical exegesis; English needs to employ circumlocutions.

English has evolved in a Christian context and therefore English theological words, e.g. 'salvation' or 'Messiah', have acquired connotations which are not present in the Hebrew. Care must be taken not to read Christian theology into the texts.

Bible Translation

The richness of the Bible's Hebrew cannot be fully captured in translation. This was well recognized in ancient times; as the Greek translator of the apocryphal book Ecclesiasticus wrote in his Prologue: 'For the same things uttered in Hebrew, and translated into another tongue, have not the same force in them.'[112]

Where appropriate, I have used the Jewish Publication Society's translation of the Hebrew Scriptures, 2nd edition (Philadelphia, 1999, slightly modified to British spelling and punctuation), and occasionally the King James Version – respectively, 'JPS' and 'KJV'. Other translations are my own, tailored to fit the Talmud's reading of Scripture; some may unwittingly coincide with existing translations. Chapter and verse numbers are those used in printed Hebrew Bibles (there are none in the manuscripts). Protestant versions follow this with minor deviations; Catholic versions differ more often.

The Sages were thoroughly familiar with the Hebrew text, but later Jewish Bible commentators and modern English translators may read it differently. The Sages picked up different resonances, and often indulged in imaginative word play. For instance:

THESE ARE THE WORDS (Deuteronomy 1:1). The Holy One, blessed be He, said, My children play a role in the world like bees, through their pious ones and their prophets. Alternatively, just as the bee's honey is sweet and its sting is bitter, so are the words of Torah [to those who obey or disobey]. (Midrash *Deuteronomy Rabba* 1:6).

This is incoherent in English, but in Hebrew it is striking: *devarim* ('words') and *devorim* ('bees') are written with the same consonants.

One of the most extreme instances in this volume involves Isaiah 22:5. JPS translates the latter half of this verse: **KIR RAGED [IN THE VALLEY OF VISION], AND SHOA ON THE HILL**; KJV has: **[A DAY OF] BREAKING DOWN THE WALLS, AND OF CRYING IN THE MOUNTAINS**. I have translated (in *Ta'anit* 29a; see p. 259) in the way I believe the rabbis understood the verse: **HE WAILED AND MOANED FOR THE MOUNTAIN**.

The Bible texts the rabbis used differed in only minor detail from the now standard Hebrew text,[113] known as the 'masoretic' text since it has come to us as mediated by the Masoretes, Jewish scholars in the Land of Israel who in the fifth to ninth centuries devoted their attention to its accurate determination and preservation.

'Israel', 'Jew', 'Palestine'

The English word 'Jew' derives from Latin *Judaeus*, itself derived from Hebrew *yehudi*, from the proper name Yehuda (Judah); 'Judaea', the name originally assigned by the Roman administration to the province centred on Jerusalem, derives from this. Jewish coins and documents produced during the Revolt of 66–70, however, use the name 'Israel', in conscious rejection of Roman authority. Likewise the Mishna, with rabbinic literature generally, rarely uses the term *yehudim* as a collective for Jews, but *Israel*, the name given by God to Jacob, ancestor of the Twelve Tribes of Israel.[114] There are several possible reasons for this:

Since, strictly speaking, *yehudi* denoted a descendant of Judah, ancestor of only one of the twelve tribes of Israel, it could not be used for members of other tribes; Israel was therefore a more accurate, inclusive term.

Yehudi might have been understood too narrowly as denoting inhabitants of Judaea.

There may have been an element of polemic against Christian claims to be *verus Israel*, the 'true' Israel.

The term *yehudi* may have acquired pejorative overtones, as 'Jew' eventually did in English. It may have been to counter such a trend that Rabbi Yoḥanan declared, apropos of 'a Jew (*yehudi*) . . . called Mordecai' (Esther 2:5): Whoever rejects idolatry is called *yehudi* (*Megilla* 13a).

The geographical area promised by God to the patriarchs is called by the rabbis *Eretz Israel*, the Land of Israel, or simply The Land, never just *Israel*. In the Mishna period and for some time afterwards, three regions within this area contained substantial Jewish populations: *Yehuda* (Judaea), *Ever ha-Yarden* (Transjordan) and *Galil* (Galilee).

The name Syria Palaestina (later simply Palaestina) from which 'Palestine' derives was imposed by the Romans on the province of Judaea after Julius Severus quelled the Bar Kokhba Revolt. The nearest Hebrew equivalent would be *Eretz P'lishtim*, 'The Land of the Philistines', which occurs in the Bible (e.g. Exodus 13:17), but never in rabbinic literature. 'Palestine' is used in this volume as the conventional name for the area in late antiquity; it bears no modern political connotation.

Page Layout

Readers are often confused because the Talmud operates at different levels of discourse and it is not always easy to identify the level or the speaker. One Sage might, for instance, make a comment on a Mishna that interprets a verse in the Bible, and another challenges that comment. The manuscripts do not make this clear; they have no punctuation or paragraphing, no quotation marks, no references to chapter and verse, and often use pronouns without clear antecedent.

To assist the reader I have used different typefaces and spacing:

Italic type is used for all editorial material.
BOLD CAPITALS AND SMALL CAPITALS are used for biblical quotations.
Bold upper and lower case is used for Mishna and other Tannaitic texts.

The rest of the text of the Talmud is set in ordinary upper and lower case type.

There are often digressions or comments in the Talmud itself. As these might distract from the main line of argument they have been indented; if you ignore the indented material you will have a continuous text. Where there are digressions from the digression, or comments on the digression, inserted by later editors or copyists, they are indicated by a second level of indentation.

References

References to Mishna and Tosefta are by tractate name, chapter and paragraph, e.g. *Berakhot* 4:2. References to the Babylonian Talmud are by tractate name and folio number, for instance *Berakhot* 31a, while references to this volume add the page number (*Berakhot* 31a (see p. 25)). References to the Talmud of the Land of Israel are indicated by the word Yerushalmi, followed by tractate name, chapter, and section and/or folio number.

Marginal numbers indicate the folio number in the standard (Vilna 1886) edition of the Babylonian Talmud, based on the first complete printed edition (Venice: Daniel Bomberg, 1520–23).[115]

Footnote references to secondary works are abbreviated to author's name, short title and page with full citations in the Bibliography.

NOTES

1. See 'References', above.
2. Kraemer, *Mind*, pp. 117–18. Some well-known stories anachronistically put this terminology into the mouths of the schools of Hillel and Shammai at the beginning of the first century; see, for instance, *Shabbat* 31a (see pp. 105–6).
3. Julianus, in *Digest* 1.3.32; Josephus, *Antiquities* 13:297. See Sanders, *Jewish Law*, p. 99.

4. Even those scholars who maintain that elements were committed to writing early concede that most students relied on memorization, not on written copies, until the later Middle Ages.

5. Resh Laqish (third century) said, 'That which is oral should not be written; that which is written should not be oral' (*Gittin* 60b; *Temura* 14b). The precise motives are a matter for speculation.

6. The title *nasi* is explained in 'How the Talmud Started', p. xxiii.

7. Jerome, *Letter* 121:10, no. 884, in Vol. 22, p. 1054, of Migne's *Patrologia Latina* (1864 edn). Jerome refers to the rabbis as 'Pharisees'; that is how he saw them and how they saw themselves, but historians now emphasize the differences between Pharisees and rabbis while acknowledging some continuity.

8. Kovelman, *Alexandria and Jerusalem*, argues on the basis of petition texts that law was the 'flavour of the times' in second-century Egypt and Palestine.

9. This thought is well focused in Neusner, *Vanquished Nation*.

10. The change in terminology derives from the demand of the Christian censor of the Basel edition of the Talmud (1578–81) that *talmud* be changed to *gemara* throughout. See Albeck, *Talmud*, p. 3, for references.

11. Frankel, *Mavo*, pp. 28b–36b.

12. Lieberman, *Greek* and *Hellenism*; Neusner, *Judaism in Society*, pp. 110–11; Kraemer, *Mind*, p. 95.

13. These texts are described in the section 'The Men Who Made Mishna and Talmud', pp. xxxiff.

14. Literally, 'houses'.

15. Examples are the laws of *eruv* and *muqtzé* – see Glossary.

16. Cassius Dio, *Roman History* 69.14.1, claims that 50 fortresses and 985 villages were destroyed, and 580,000 soldiers killed. For an up-to-date assessment, see Schäfer, *Bar Kochba War*.

17. Millar, 'Transformations', pp. 144ff.

18. Gamaliel II's grandfather, Gamaliel I, at whose feet Paul claimed to have sat (Acts 22:3), may have had some connection with the Herodian dynasty (*Pesaḥim* 88b); this would hardly have been a matter of pride in rabbinic circles, but would explain the family's closeness to Rome. Simeon bar Koziba signed with the title and had it impressed on his coins. See Yadin, *Cave of Letters*, pp. 369–72.

19. Rashi *Shabbat* 122a, under *I mishum*, makes the suggestion. However, as Roman administration was organized on the basis of territory, not religion or ethnic identity, it is difficult to see what office Judah might have held.

20. Mishna *Eduyot* 7:7; Bavli *Sanhedrin* 11a; Yerushalmi *Sanhedrin* 7:19.

21. Goodman, 'Roman State', pp. 127–37; Harries, 'Resolving Disputes', p. 73, based on *Didascalia apostolorum*.

22. M. Jacobs, *Institution*, p. 232.

23. S. Cohen, 'Place of the Rabbi', p. 172.

24. *Codex Theodosianus* 16,8,13, No. 81, in M. Jacobs, *Institution*, pp. 284–7. The use of the plural means that whatever rank was implied was not restricted to the *nasi* (if he was indeed included), but applied to the Jewish leaders collectively. The *Codex*, compiled under Theodotion and published in 438, sets out the laws of the Roman Empire under the Christian emperors from 312.

25. Ibid., 16,8,22, No. 83, in M. Jacobs, *Institution*, pp. 287–91; ibid., 16,8,29, No. 88, in M. Jacobs, *Institution*, pp. 284–7. Note use of the plural.

26. M. Jacobs, *Institution*, p. 307; ibid., p. 327, from Theodoret, *Eranistes* 36, ed. Ettlinger, pp. 82–3.

27. See S. Schwartz, *Imperialism*, chapters 8–10.

28. *Berakhot* 16b (see p. 9). No one is sure of the meaning of *q'tzutzé*; perhaps these were lictors akin to those who preceded Roman magistrates.

29. The claim is put forward to make a theological point in Origen's *Epistola ad Africanum* 20; M. Jacobs, *Institution*, p. 251, rightly argues that it does not imply formal recognition by Rome of the ethnarch's status. *Midrash Rabba* on Ecclesiastes 10:2 implies that Judah ordered physical punishment, but does not specify that this was capital punishment.

30. For instance, in *Berakhot* 45b.

31. *Berakhot* 47a. The report is not necessarily accurate and, as suggested by Nathan ben Yeḥiel of Rome, it may simply be that Shmuel was addressing Rav by his personal name (Tosafot *Yevamot* 57b, under *Amar Shmuel*). *Shabbat* 53a seems less respectful, and 108a records a decidedly frosty reception by Shmuel when Rav returned from Palestine. Kalmin, *Sages, Stories*, p. 157, records examples of mutual hostility between the two Sages, but on pp. 187–9 Kalmin is more judicious.

32. Neusner, *Jews in Babylonia*, Vol. I, pp. 56–8. Ben Zeev (*Diaspora Judaism*, p. 266), in connection with the events of 116–17, writes: 'The Jewish revolt may therefore be regarded as one of the developments that prevented Rome from making Babylonia a Roman province.'

33. Yerushalmi *Ketubot* 12:3 (35a) and *Kil'ayim* 9:3 (32b); *Genesis Rabba* 33:3. Sherira (Lewin, *Iggeret*, p. 76) states that Huna I was Exilarch in the days of Rabbi.

34. The rise and fall of two such men, Anileus and Asineus, is narrated by Josephus, *Antiquities* 18:9.

35. An analogous situation arose for Christians under Sasanian rule. The *Synodicon Orientale*, edited by Jean-Baptiste Chabot in 1902, gives some indication of how the Christian Church, at least by the sixth century, began to issue legislation not only in ecclesiastical matters but in areas of civil jurisdiction, creating a quasi-Talmud of their own. For examples, see Erhart, 'Canon Law', pp. 123–9.

36. Goodblatt, *Rabbinic Instruction*, especially pp. 63–92. Brody, 'Chronology', p. 104, suggests that Rav Huna and Rav Ḥisda founded the academies.

37. *Yevamot* 63b.

38. *Avoda Zara* 10b–11a; *Shabbat* 11a and 75a.

39. J. Duschene-Guillemin, in Yarshater, *History of Iran*, Vol. 3, Part 2, p. 875.

40. The traditional date for Shmuel's death, based on Sherira's *Epistle* (Lewin, *Iggeret*, p. 82; Schlüter, *Auf welche Weise*, p. 213) is 253, six years before the sack of Nehardea by the Palmyrenes under Septimius Odenathus; *Berakhot* (see pp. 15–16), also indicates that Shmuel died relatively young. Neusner (*Jews in Babylonia*, Vol. II, p. 48–51) and Goodblatt (*Rabbinic Instruction*, p. 39) have argued that the sack of Nehardea must have taken place later, possibly in 263, in which case a later date may be assigned to Shmuel's death, too; this would accommodate the attribution to Shmuel in *Mo'ed Qatan* 26a of a comment on Shapur I's slaughter of inhabitants of Caesarea Mazaca, an event not earlier than 260.

41. It would have been far more problematic to recognize the legitimacy of Roman rule in Palestine.

42. Rava's own life was in danger when an offender died as a result of lashes he had imposed (*Ta'anit* 24b).

43. *Ḥagiga* 5b, *Bava Metzi'a* 86a; see also *Bava Qama* 116b–117b (see pp. 454–60).

44. Perhaps the statement that 'The son of David [i.e. the Messiah] will not come until the entire state reverts to heresy' (*Sanhedrin* 97a) refers to this.

45. Geiger, 'Gallus Revolt'.

46. According to a letter attributed to Cyril, Bishop of Jerusalem, when the Jews were ready to commence work on the Temple it was miraculously prevented by a terrible disaster which shook the country killing many people on '19 Iyyar of the year 674 of the kingdom of Alexander the Greek', that is, 19 May 363; the letter interprets the death of Julian as punishment for his rejection of

Christ. Brock, *Syriac Perspectives* X:267–86, translates the letter, which he believes is an early fifth-century pseudepigraph rather than the authentic work of Cyril (p. 283).

47. This is documented in Milson, *Art and Architecture*. Remains of the fifth-century synagogue of Sepphoris were discovered in 1993; see Weiss, *Sepphoris Synagogue*.

48. Parikhanian, in Yarshater, *History of Iran*, Vol. 3, Part 2, pp. 632–46. Three of the estates are brilliantly described in Tafazzuli's *Sasanian Society* (the author did not live to complete the work with an account of the priests and judges). The most valuable source of information about Sasanian law and society is Parikhanian, *The Book of a Thousand Judgements*, compiled *c.* 500 in the reign of Khosrow II Parviz. It is a catalogue of decisions, lacking the kind of argumentation that characterizes Talmud or commentaries on the *Avesta*, and it is not known how far it reflects third-century practice.

49. More properly, Shahinshah ('king of kings'). Sasanian administration is described in Gyselen, *Géographie*, pp. 27–40.

50. The precise date of the Battle of al-Qādishīyah, often given as 635 or 636, is disputed; in any case, the defeat was a lengthy process.

51. Abraham ibn Daud (G. Cohen, *Ibn Daud*), in twelfth-century Andalusia, drew on a range of Geonic sources; he is responsible for the arrangement of Tannaim and Amoraim into 'generations'. Brody, *Chronology*, argues that Sherira and the *Seder Tannaim v'Amoraim* drew independently on a source compiled for the Exilarchs commencing before the Amoraic academies were formed.

52. Lewin, *Iggeret*, p. 71; Schlüter, *Auf welche Weise*, p. 193, no. 144.

53. See 'Transmission of the Text'.

54. *Rav Tanna hu u-falig* (*Eruvin* 50b and parallels).

55. Kalmin, *Sages, Stories*, p. 59.

56. Presumably Ravina I, as Ravina II died only in 499.

57. Alternative spellings include S'vora, Sevora, Sebora, etc.

58. Lewin, *Iggeret*, p. 69; Schlüter, *Auf welche Weise*, p. 192, no. 143. The term *savora* carries several nuances: one who holds an opinion, offers a reason, makes a decision.

59. Simuna died *c.* 540. Other authorities, such as (Cohen,) Ibn Daud in his *Sefer ha-Qabbala*, extend the period of the Sevoraim as far as Rav Sheshna, died *c.* 689.

60. Sperber, in *Encylopaedia Judaica*, entry on Savora.

61. Halivni, *M'qorot*, p. 15 (my translation).

62. Rishonim ('early ones') are rabbinic authorities from the tenth to the early sixteenth centuries.

63. Halivni, *Midrash*, reprinted in Chernick, *Essential Papers*, pp. 141–2.

64. *Horayot* 14a (see p. 564) and *Berakhot* 64a.

65. Shmuel Ha-Nagid, *Introduction to the Talmud*, based on a work of that name by Shmuel ben Ḥofni, the Gaon of Sura (d. 1013); Rashi *Shabbat* 30b.

66. L. Jacobs, *Structure and Form*. See *Bekhorot* 5b (see p. 621).

67. The word *pesher* ('interpretation') is applied in some of the Dead Sea Scrolls, for instance the Habakkuk Commentary, to indicate a form of exegesis by which a prophecy is read in terms of its fulfilment in persons and events belonging to the age of the interpreter.

68. *Sota* 49b, and paralleled in *Bava Qama* 83a (see p. 444). The attributions are not necessarily correct. The word used by Rabbi for 'Aramaic' is *sursi* (Syrian, or Syriac), probably a contemptuous term.

69. In *Shabbat* 66b, *l'terutzé sugya* means 'to straighten [his] step'.

70. See Kalmin, *Sages, Stories*, pp. 169–73.

71. *Megilla* 15a, based on Esther 2:22.

72. E.g. which of seven Gamaliels or innumerable Judahs is meant? Or confusion like that resolved in *Pesaḥim* 113b–114a: 'Yosef of Hutzal is Yosef the Babylonian; Isi ben Gur Aryeh is Isi ben Yehuda, Isi ben Gamaliel or Isi ben Mahalal, but his real name is Isi ben Aqavia; Rabbi Isaac ben Tavla is Rabbi Isaac ben Ḥaqla.'

73. Rosh, comment on *Nazir* 17a in the margin of the Vilna 1886 edition.

74. For instance Elijah of Vilna (1720–99): 'Everything that was, is and will be throughout time is included in the Torah . . . And not only the general principles, but even the details of each species and of each human individual, whatever happens to him from the day of his birth until his end, and all his transmigrations, all in full detail' (Commentary on *Sifra di-Tsni'uta*, Chapter 5).

75. For instance, *Shabbat* 66a, where it is proposed to emend 'the lame may go out on his supports, but Rabbi Yosé forbids it' to 'the lame may not go out on his supports, but Rabbi Yosé permits it'.

76. Examples: *Shabbat* 121a, *Pesaḥim* 100a, *Gittin* 73a, *Qiddushin* 47b, *Ḥullin* 141b.

77. *Yevamot* 50a.

78. Halivni, *Peshat & Derash*, pp. 36, 37–9. He claims that although Amoraim did not make the assumption that the tannaitic texts were free of redundancy, Stammaim did.

79. Hillel's rules are listed in Tosefta *Sanhedrin* 7:11 (Zuckermandel edn); Ishmael's and Yosé's are independent baraitot attached as

introductions to Sifra and Mishnat Rabbi Eliezer (ed. Enelow) respectively.

80. On Homeric interpretation, see Lamberton and Keaney, *Homer's Ancient Readers*. Lieberman, *Hellenism*, pp. 47–82, reviews Talmudic parallels.

81. This is equivalent to the Greek *isopsēpha*; cf. Artemidorus, *Interpretation* 3:28.

82. Cotton and Yardeni, *DJD*, Vol. XXVII, pp. 153f.

83. Jerome, *Letter* 121:10.

84. Lewin, *Iggeret*, p. 125. Rashi (*Ketubot* 43b) explained that this was because the rabbis of the Land of Israel were ordained while those of Babylonia were not.

85. It is also used for Yoḥanan ben Zakkai, perhaps because later generations thought of him as a *nasi*.

86. Breuer, 'Rabbi is greater'. Breuer also disputes the Talmudic assertion (*Sanhedrin* 14a and Yerushalmi *Bikkurim* 65d) that the rabbis of Babylonia were not ordained (pp. 47, 48).

87. Lewin, *Iggeret*, p. 126.

88. Schechter, *Aspects*.

89. Literally, 'enemies of Israel'; sinners are regarded as enemies of the people.

90. The last phrase is a possible literal rendering of the Hebrew, though the context demands a translation such as JPS's 'those I have treated harshly'.

91. Neusner, *Judaism in Society*, Preface to the Second Printing, pp. xxvii, xxxiii.

92. Kalmin, *Sages, Stories*, p. 215.

93. On Chrysostom's *Homilies on the Jews*, see Wilken, *Chrysostom*. For early Christian anti-Semitism in general, see Ruether, *Faith and Fratricide*; Limor and Stroumsa, *Contra Iudaeos*; Simon, *Verus Israel*; and Dunn, *Parting of the Ways*.

94. Schäfer, *Jesus*, p. 8. See also Krauss, *Handbook*.

95. See de Lange, *Origen*.

96. *Ta'anit* 27b. 'Nazarenes' are most likely Christians; *ma'amad* is the group of townsmen whose turn it is to represent the people at the Temple service.

97. *Yoma* 28b.

98. On the relationship between Christian and Jewish Bible exegesis, see Horbury, *Jews and Christians*, especially chapter 8 (pp. 200–225).

99. Weiss, *Sepphoris Synagogue*, pp. 250–52. The mosaic band is reproduced and interpreted on pp. 79–81.

100. *Shita Mequbbetzet* to *Bava Metzi'a* 13b. Rashi's correction is on *Berakhot* 38a.
101. *Sefer ha-Yashar* (ed. Schlesinger), Introduction, p. 9.
102. Maimonides (*Mishné Torah: Malvé v'lové* 15:2) refers to a manuscript he found in Egypt 'written on parchment as they did some five hundred years ago', i.e. about 650, but it is presumed lost. David Rozental (Rosenthal) edited a facsimile of the *Babylonian Talmud, Codex Florence* (3 vols. Jerusalem: Maqor, 1972); he lists earlier manuscripts, pp. 1–2. Raphael N. Rabbinovicz, in the late nineteenth century, based his monumental but incomplete *Diqduqei Soferim* on the Munich manuscript.
103. Shereshevsky, *Rashi*, p. 149, attributed the statement to Menaḥem ben Zeraḥ, in his introduction to *Tzedah La-Derekh*.
104. Haskin, *Renaissance*. For more recent evaluations, see Benson and Constable, *Renaissance and Renewal* and Swanson, *Renaissance*.
105. G. Cohen, *Ibn Daud*, pp. 46–9 and 63–7. Some early authorities refer to Ḥananel as 'of Rome'; his father had travelled to Italy where he became acquainted with the Yerushalmi, which figures prominently in Ḥananel's commentary.
106. Fraenkel, *Rashi's Methodology*, p. 2.
107. See Stephen Kuttner, 'The Revival of Jurisprudence', in Dahan, *Rashi*, pp. 299–323.
108. R. W. Southern, 'The School of Paris and the School of Chartres', in Dahan, *Rashi*, pp. 113–33.
109. *Keritot* 4a, under *v'hakha*. Other instances include *Betza* 12a, under *v'af Rabbi Yoḥanan*; *Shavuot*, 3b, under *qashya* ('some confused student who had a problem wrote this in the margin'); and *Zevaḥim* 115a, under *v'h'g l'olam bizmano*; nor does he spare the errors he attributes to his own teachers (*Shabbat* 85a and 101a).
110. *Sukka* 40a, under *h'g etzim d'hasaqa*.
111. Kalmin, *Sages, Stories*, p. 179, n. 19, refers to Shamma Friedman who proposed in an article in *Sinai* 55 (1992), pp. 140–64, that the orthographic distinction was the invention of mediaeval copyists. I have been unable to check this.
112. See Brock, *Syriac Perspectives*, III:69–87, for an account of translation techniques in antiquity; he stresses that the biblical translators and others who chose the method of *verbum e verbo* (word for word) did so not in ignorance of literary propriety but for quite specific motives.
113. Some twenty instances of rabbinic interpretations based on a different text are listed by Aqiva Eger (1761–1837) in his marginal note on *Shabbat* 55b, but this is certainly an underestimate.

114. Genesis 32:29 and 35:10. On the use of 'Israel' in coins and docu-
    ments, see Goodman, *Rome*, p. 19.
115. The format is that of the twenty-five individual tractates printed by
    Joshua and Gershom Soncino between 1484 and 1519. See Haber-
    mann, *Ha-Madpisim* and *Ha-Madpiss*, and Yardeni, *Hebrew Script*.

Further Reading

See Bibliography. For general background, the following should be helpful.

The Cambridge Companion to the Talmud and Rabbinic Literature, ed. C. E. Fonrobert and Martin S. Jaffee (Cambridge: Cambridge University Press, 2007).

Chajes, Z. H., *The Student's Guide Through the Talmud*, tr. Jacob Shachter (London: East and West Library, 1952).

Chernick, Michael (ed.), *Essential Papers on the Talmud* (New York and London: New York University Press, 1994).

Halivni, David Weiss, *Peshat & Derash: Plain and Applied Meaning in Rabbinic Exegesis* (New York and Oxford: Oxford University Press, 1991).

Harris, Jay, *How Do We Know This?* (New York: SUNY Press, 1994).

Jacobs, Louis, *Structure and Form in the Babylonian Talmud* (Cambridge: Cambridge University Press, 1991).

Jastrow, Marcus, *Dictionary of Talmud Babli, Yerushalmi, Midrashic Literature and Targumim*, 2 vols. (reprinted, New York: Pardes, 1950).

Katz, Steven T. (ed.), *The Cambridge History of Judaism, Vol. 4: The Late Roman and Rabbinic Period* (Cambridge: Cambridge University Press, 2006).

Kraemer, David, *Reading the Rabbis: The Talmud as Literature* (New York: Oxford University Press, 1996).

Neusner, J., *Vanquished Nation, Broken Spirit: The Virtues of the Heart in Formative Judaism* (New York: Cambridge University Press, 1987).

Schwartz, Seth, *Imperialism and Jewish Society, 200 B.C.E. to 640 C.E.* (Princeton: Princeton University Press, 2001).

Strack, H. L. and G. Stemberger, *Introduction to the Talmud and Midrash* (Edinburgh: T. & T. Clarke, 1991).

The Talmud:
Selections

FIRST ORDER

ZERAIM (SEEDS)

INTRODUCTION

The Mishna opens with a tractate on prayer. This establishes the continuity of Oral with Written Torah and suggests that relationship with God is the key to the Sages' understanding of the world.

The rest of the Order, as the title Zeraim (Seeds) suggests, has to do with land. Land – that is, the sacredness of the Land of Israel and its indissoluble link with the people – was particularly emphasized since Mishna was compiled at a time when the Land was under Roman occupation.

The second tractate, Pe'ah (Corner of the field), covers aspects of provision for the poor, such as leaving the gleanings of the field for them to collect. Most of the remaining tractates cover different kinds of tithing, while Shevi'it *deals with the sabbatical year and the remission of debt; these matters are summed up in Appendix II.*

Both Shevi'it *and* Kil'ayim *(Mixtures) contain material that has been cited in discussion of environmental issues. The prohibition of agricultural work in the sabbatical and Jubilee years teaches responsibility for the conservation of soil resources, while the prohibition of mixed species can be read as a warning against unwarranted manipulation of the natural order.*

FIRST TRACTATE
BERAKHOT (BLESSINGS)

The Bible makes no provision for regular private prayer but 'conversation with God' is a major feature. Abraham prayed for an heir, Jacob for protection from Esau, Moses for forgiveness for the people, Solomon at the inauguration of the Temple, and Daniel three times a day in Babylon; much of the Book of Psalms would have been recited in the Second Temple in Jerusalem, and additional daily prayers were recited there, too.[1]

Dead Sea Scrolls texts reaching back to the second century BCE comprise the earliest evidence of regular Jewish confessional and communal prayer outside the Temple; they include the Apocryphal Psalms, Shema, benedictions, the Ten Commandments and grace over meals, and use phrases and themes similar to those formulated by the rabbis.

The Jewish prayer liturgy was consolidated under Gamaliel II at Yavné (Jamnia), near Jerusalem, about 100 CE, and his institutions underlie this tractate. There are two major constituents: the Shema, recited morning and evening, and the Tefilla, or Prayer, originally recited morning and afternoon, but already in the second century at all three daily services (morning, afternoon and evening). The rabbis also formulated blessings for various occasions and prescribed public Torah readings.

Shema consists of three scriptural readings: Deuteronomy 6:4–9, 11:13–21 and Numbers 15:37–41. The opening verse, HEAR, O ISRAEL! THE LORD IS OUR GOD, THE LORD IS ONE, is the fundamental Jewish declaration of faith, akin to the Islamic Shahada (testimony of faith). Reciting the verse with

1.   See Mishna *Tamid* Chapter Five.

commitment is called 'accepting the yoke of the kingdom of heaven'; the remainder of the first paragraph is 'accepting the yoke of the commandments'. The second paragraph is a declaration of faith in reward and punishment; the third concludes with a reminder of God's redemptive power as manifested at the Exodus from Egypt.

The Tefilla ('Prayer' par excellence) is also known as amida ('standing') since it is normally said while standing, or as shemoné esré ('eighteen'), since it originally consisted of eighteen blessings (later increased to nineteen) or paragraphs, organized as praise, petitions and thanksgiving. It is said quietly, maintaining a reverent attitude, feet together, right hand over left on breast, facing Jerusalem. Unless otherwise indicated 'Prayer' below refers specifically to this prayer.

Ten men of the age of thirteen or over constitute a minyan, or quorum, for public prayer. However, Mishna regards the three daily services as individual rather than communal obligations; though it is virtuous to join others for communal prayer, individuals recite the daily prayers irrespective of whether they are in the synagogue or together with others.[2]

This tractate defines, regulates and explores the significance of prayers with which it assumes the student is already familiar.

CHAPTER ONE

MISHNA:

2a   **From what time should one recite *Shema* in the evenings? According to Rabbi Eliezer, from the time that *Kohanim* enter to partake of *teruma*,[3] until the end of the first [night-]watch;[4]**

---

2.   Daniel 6:11. This was the view of the early Church, too: 'Pray thus three times a day' (*Didache* 8:3).

3.   *Kohanim* receive *teruma* (a gift of food) from the people, and may eat it only in a state of purity. A *Kohen* who has been polluted, e.g. by contact with the carcass of an unclean beast, bathes for purification during the day but does not regain purity until nightfall. See *T'vul Yom*.

4.   The night, from dusk to dawn, is divided into watches; there is a difference of opinion as to whether there are three or four.

the [majority of] Sages say, Until midnight; Rabban Gamaliel says, Until dawn. On one ocasion [Gamaliel's] sons returned [late] from a feast and told him that they had not [yet] recited *Shema* ; he said to them, If it is not yet dawn you should recite it. Moreover, whenever the Sages said [that something should be done] before midnight, the *mitzva* extends until dawn: the *mitzva* of burning of the fats and limbs [of sacrifices] extends until dawn, and the *mitzva* of eating [sacrifices] within the day extends until dawn. If so, why did the Sages say 'until midnight'? [It was] to safeguard people from [the possibility of] sin.

GEMARA:

What is the Tanna[5] referring to when he says, **From what time?** And why does he mention evening first, rather than teaching us [what happens in] the morning?

The Tanna refers to Scripture, for it is written, **WHEN YOU LIE DOWN AND WHEN YOU RISE UP** (Deuteronomy 6:7). He explains to us that the recital of *Shema* **WHEN YOU LIE DOWN** is **from the time that** *Kohanim* **enter to partake of** *teruma*.

Alternatively, he infers [that evening comes first] from the [story of] creation of the world, for it is written, **AND IT WAS EVENING AND IT WAS MORNING, THE FIRST DAY** (Genesis 1:5).

If [evening should be mentioned first], why does the Mishna state later, **In the morning he says two blessings before it and one after; in the evening two before and two after?**[6] Surely he should deal with the evening first? The Tanna opens with the evening [*Shema*] and continues with the morning; as he is dealing with the morning [*Shema*] he completes what he has to say about it then reverts to matters concerning the evening.

Not everyone was pleased with Gamaliel's institution of fixed prayers and regular prayer times, for it could undermine the spontaneity of prayer; as Rabbi Eliezer puts it later in this tractate, **He whose prayer is a fixed thing, his prayer is not supplication** *(Mishna 4:4). But Gamaliel had certainly not*

5.   The one who formulated the Mishna. See p. xxxii.
6.   *Berakhot* 1:4 (11a).

intended to discourage spontaneous, individual prayer. Chapter Two contains a collection of personal prayers of some of the leading rabbis of the Mishna and the early Talmudic period, introduced by the third-century Palestinian sage Eleazar ben Pedat's affirmation of the value of reciting Shema *and* Tefilla *regularly with full devotion. The careful stylization of the reports, each commencing 'When he had completed his prayer, X used to say . . .', indicates a lengthy process of literary formation; parallel versions vary in detail. Over the centuries, several of these prayers have been incorporated in the liturgy; Rav's, for instance, is widely used as a public prayer for the new month, and Mar the son of Ravina's is the basis for private prayer following the* Tefilla.

CHAPTER TWO

GEMARA:

16b   Rabbi Eleazar said: What is the meaning of the verse: I BLESS YOU ALL MY LIFE, I LIFT UP MY HANDS, INVOKING YOUR NAME (Psalm 63:5 JPS)? I BLESS YOU ALL MY LIFE refers to *Shema*; I LIFT UP MY HANDS, INVOKING YOUR NAME refers to the Prayer. Of one who does this [the Psalmist] says: I AM SATED AS WITH A RICH FEAST; even more, he inherits two worlds, this world and the next, for it continues: I SING PRAISES WITH JOYFUL LIPS (Psalm 63:6 JPS).[7]

When he had completed his Prayer, Rabbi Eleazar used to say this: May it be Your will, Lord our God, to make present among us love, brotherhood, peace and friendship. Increase the number of our disciples, make us successful, give us purpose and hope, and grant us our portion in the Garden of Eden. [While] in Your world, may we enjoy virtuous company and inclinations. May we arise early to accomplish our hearts' aspiration to fear Your Name, and may our happiness appear before You as worthy.[8]

7. 'Praises' is plural: one who does this praises God here, and will praise him again in the World to Come.
8. The last phrase is obscure. Rashi reads it as a prayer for our material needs to be satisfied.

When he had completed his Prayer, Rabbi Yoḥanan used to say this: May it be Your will, Lord our God, when You see our shame and our evil, to clothe Yourself in mercy, to wrap Yourself with strength, envelop Yourself in kindness and gird Yourself with grace; and may Your attributes of goodness and patience be manifest through You.

When he had completed his Prayer, Rabbi Zeira used to say this: May it be Your will, Lord our God, that we do not sin, or act shamefully, or more disgracefully than our fathers.

When he had completed his Prayer, Rabbi Ḥiyya used to say this: May it be Your will, Lord our God, that Your Torah should be our occupation; let us not despair nor our eyes dim.

When he had completed his Prayer, Rav used to say this: May it be Your will, Lord our God, to grant us long life, a life of goodness, of blessing, of sustenance, of good health, a sin-fearing life, a life free from shame and embarrassment, a life of wealth and honour, a life of love of Torah and fear of heaven, a life in which You fulfil our desires for good.

When he had completed his Prayer, Rabbi [Judah the Patriarch] used to say this: May it be Your will, Lord our God, to protect us from insolence and insolent people, from malicious people and accidents, from the evil inclination, from bad company and neighbours, from Satan the destroyer and from harsh litigation and litigants, whether or not of the covenant.

And this despite the fact that Rabbi was accompanied by lictors![9]

When he had completed his Prayer, Rav Safra used to say this: May it be Your will, Lord our God, to set peace in the family above and in the family below, and among the disciples who engage in [the study of] Your Torah, whether [they do so] out of pure or improper motives; as to those who study out of improper motives, may their motives become pure!

When he had completed his Prayer, Rabbi Alexandri used to say this: May it be Your will, Lord our God, that the place

17a

---

9. The lictor (Latin) was an officer in attendance on a Roman magistrate, equipped to execute summary justice. The point is that though Rabbi was accompanied by human bodyguards he realized that ultimately his safety lay in the hands of God.

where we stand be a place of light, not darkness; let us not despair nor our eyes become dim.

> Some say that was what Rav Hamnuna said, but Rabbi Alexandri, when he had completed his Prayer, used to say this: Lord of the universe! It is clear to You that we desire to fulfil Your will. What stops us? The yeast in the dough,[10] and oppression by the nations. May it be Your will to save us from both, that we may return [to You] and, with a perfect heart, obey the laws that are Your will.

When he had completed his Prayer, Rava used to say this: O my God, before I was created I was of no worth, and now that I have been created it is as if I were not created; I am [but] dust in my lifetime, how much more so when I die. I [stand] before You as a vessel full of shame and contempt. May it be Your will, Lord my God, that I sin no more; purge my sin, in Your abundant mercy, but not by means of chastisements and severe sickness.

> That was [also] the prayer of Rav Hamnuna the Younger on the Day of Atonement.

When he had completed his Prayer, Mar the son of Ravina used to say this: O my God, guard my tongue from evil and my lips from uttering guile. To such as curse me may I be silent; may I be as dust to all. Open my mind to Your Torah, so that I may pursue Your commandments. Save me from evil inclination, evil women and all the troubles that occur in the world; frustrate the plans and intentions of those who plot evil against me. **MAY THE WORDS OF MY MOUTH AND THE PRAYER OF MY HEART BE ACCEPTABLE TO YOU** (Psalm 19:15 JPS).

If someone is preoccupied with another mitzva, *he may be exempt from reciting* Shema, *either because he would not have time to do both, or because he would be unable to focus his mind properly. Chapter Three cites as an example someone who has lost a close relative and is responsible for arranging the*

10. The evil inclination.

*burial. In the course of the discussion the Gemara considers
how to show respect in the presence of a corpse, and enquires
whether the dead are aware of what the living do. While the
doctrine of life after death is accepted without question, there
is no agreement as to whether communication between the living
and the dead is possible.*

CHAPTER THREE

GEMARA:

Let us consider that point. **He who keeps vigil for the dead,**   18a
**even though not his own [relative, for whom he is responsible],
is exempt from reciting the *Shema*, from the *tefilla*, from
tefillin and from all *mitzvot* of the Torah. If two [were keeping
vigil together], one keeps vigil and the other recites *Shema*.
Ben Azzai says, If they are on a boat, they may leave [the
corpse] in one corner and pray together in another corner.**

On what do [Ben Azzai and the anonymous
Mishna] differ? Ravina said, They differ as to whether
[we need] to allow for the possibility that rats [might
attack the corpse if the watchers move away]; [the
anonymous Mishna] is concerned [about this], [Ben
Azzai] is not.

The rabbis taught: **Someone who is taking bones from one
place to another should not put them in a bag,**[11] **place it on
his donkey and ride [sitting] on them, for that would be
treating them disrespectfully. However, if he was afraid that
non-Jews or robbers [might otherwise take them], it is permitted. The same applies to a Torah scroll as to bones.**

What does [this last sentence] refer to? If to the first
part [of the baraita, that one should not put the bag
of bones on a donkey and sit on it], it is obvious –
surely a Torah scroll is no less [demanding of respect]
than bones! So it must refer to the latter part[, namely
that it is permitted to place the scroll in a bag on a

11.   Probably Greek *dissakion*, a double bag.

donkey and sit on the bag in order to protect the scroll
from non-Jews or robbers].

Reḥava said in the name of Rav Yehuda: Anyone who sees
the corpse[12] and does not accompany it transgresses [the verse]:
HE WHO MOCKS THE POOR AFFRONTS HIS MAKER (Proverbs
17:5 JPS). If he does accompany it, what is his reward? Rav Assi
said, of such a man Scripture says, **HE WHO IS GENEROUS TO
THE POOR MAKES A LOAN**[13] **TO THE LORD** (Proverbs 19:17
JPS), and **HE WHO SHOWS PITY FOR THE NEEDY HONOURS
HIM** (Proverbs 14:31 JPS).

Rabbi Ḥiyya and Rabbi Jonathan were conversing as they
walked through a cemetery, and Rabbi Jonathan's fringes were
brushing on the ground. Rabbi Ḥiyya said to him, Raise them,
so that [the dead] don't say, 'Tomorrow they come to us, and
now they mock us!'[14] He said to him, Do they really know that
much? Is it not written, **BUT THE DEAD KNOW NOTHING**
(Ecclesiastes 9:5 JPS)? [Rabbi Ḥiyya] responded to him, If you
learned [Scripture] you did not review it, and if you reviewed it
you did not [go over it] a third time, and if you [went over it]
a third time they never explained it to you! **THE LIVING KNOW
THAT THEY WILL DIE** (Ecclesiastes 9:5 JPS) refers to the righteous, who even in their death are called 'living'; **BUT THE DEAD
KNOW NOTHING** refers to the wicked, who even in their lifetime
are called 'dead'.

18b

*The proof-texts in the next two paragraphs have been embedded
in Rabbi Ḥiyya's statement, though they are most probably later
additions to the report of the conversation between Ḥiyya and
Jonathan. For clarity, they are set out as an independent unit.*

[The righteous are called 'living' even in their
death], as it is written, **AND BENAIAH THE SON OF
JEHOIADA, SON OF A LIVING**[15] **MAN OF KABZEEL**

12. i.e. the funeral cortège.
13. Hebrew *m'lavé* ('accompany') and *malvé* ('lend') are written the same way.
14. We mock them by demonstrating that we observe the commandments, such as
    tzitzit (fringes on the corners of a garment, as in Numbers 15:37–41), whereas they
    are unable to do so.
15. Most translations have 'valiant' or 'hero', though the literal meaning of the Hebrew
    ḥai is 'living'; JPS refers the phrase to Benaiah, translating 'a brave soldier who
    performed great deeds'.

WHO HAD DONE GREAT DEEDS, SMOTE THE TWO
ALTAR HEARTHS OF MOAB; HE ALSO WENT DOWN
AND SLEW A LION IN ITS DEN ON A SNOWY DAY
(2 Samuel 23:20 and 1 Chronicles 11:22). SON OF A
LIVING MAN – surely everyone is the child of a living
man! But 'son of a living man' [here means] 'son of a
man who even in death would be called living'. A . . .
MAN OF KABZEEL WHO HAD DONE GREAT DEEDS –
he went out and gathered large numbers of workers
for Torah;[16] HE SMOTE THE TWO ALTAR HEARTHS
OF MOAB – he left no peer in the First or the Second
Temple; HE ALSO WENT DOWN AND SLEW A LION IN
ITS DEN ON A SNOWY DAY – some say, [This means]
he broke the ice, descended and immersed himself [for
purification];[17] some say, [It means] he taught *Sifra
d'bei Rav*[18] on a winter's day.

BUT THE DEAD KNOW NOTHING refers to the
wicked, who even in their lifetime are called 'dead' –
as it is written, AND THOU, O WICKED CORPSE,[19]
PRINCE OF ISRAEL (Ezekiel 21:30). Alternatively, [you
may infer it] from here – ON THE EVIDENCE OF
TWO WITNESSES OR THREE WITNESSES THE DEAD[20]
SHALL BE PUT TO DEATH (Deuteronomy 17:6) – he
is still alive[, but Scripture regards him] as already dead
[on account of his sin].[21]

Rabbi Ḥiyya's sons went out to the villages [to attend to their
father's estate after his death]; it was hard for them to study,
and they struggled to remember [what they had learnt]. One
said to the other, Is our father aware of our distress? The other

16. From this point on the interpretation is highly dependent on Hebrew wordplay,
and it would be futile to try to capture this in English. The military exploits of
David's heroes are interpreted as metaphors for Torah achievements.
17. In order to be able to study Torah – Rashi.
18. The *halakhic* Midrash on Leviticus – Rashi.
19. Hebrew *ḥalal*, which most translators treat in context as an adjective; 'dishonoured
wicked prince' (JPS), 'profane wicked prince' (KJV, verse 25).
20. This is literal. Translators expand; for instance, 'the one who is condemned to
die'.
21. The idea of the faithful as living and the sinful as dead is common in the New
Testament, e.g. John 11:25–6; Romans 8:13.

replied, How can he know? It is written, **HIS SONS ATTAIN HONOUR AND HE DOES NOT KNOW IT; THEY ARE HUMBLED AND HE IS NOT AWARE OF IT** (Job 14:21 JPS). The other said to him, But doesn't he know? [It continues] **HE FEELS ONLY THE PAIN OF HIS FLESH, AND HIS SPIRIT MOURNS IN HIM** (Job 14:22 JPS), and Rabbi Isaac said, Worms are as painful to the dead as a needle in the flesh of the living.

They say, [The dead] know their own suffering, but they don't know the suffering of others.

Don't [the dead know what happens among the living]? Surely it was taught: A Ḥasid[22] once gave a denarius to a poor man on the eve of the New Year festival in a period of famine. His wife was annoyed with him so he went and spent the night in the cemetery. He heard two spirits conversing. One said to the other, 'Come! Let's hear from behind the curtain[23] what disasters are to befall the world!' The other replied, 'I can't [come], as I was buried in a reed mat. You go, and tell me what you hear.' She went about the world, and returned. 'What did you find out from behind the curtain?' asked her friend. She replied, 'I heard that if anyone sows at the first rains, hail will destroy [his crops].' [The Ḥasid] went and sowed at the second rains; everybody else's crops were ruined, but his were not.

The next[24] year he again spent the night in the cemetery, and heard the same two spirits conversing. One said to the other, 'Come! Let's hear from behind the curtain what disasters are to befall the world!' The other said to her, 'Didn't I tell you that I can't [come], as I was buried in a reed mat? You go, and tell me what you hear.' She went about the world, and returned. 'What did you find out from behind the curtain?' asked her friend. She replied, 'I heard that if anyone sows at the second rains, drought will destroy [his crops].' [The Ḥasid]

22. Various groups have been known as *ḥasidim* ('pious ones', or 'lovers of God'). There is no connection with the contemporary Hasidic movement, which originated in the eighteenth century; here the term simply denotes a holy man.
23. The partition separating them from the *Shekhina* (divine presence) – Rashi.
24. Literally, 'another', but the context indicates 'next'.

went and sowed at the first rains; everybody else's crops were struck [by hail], but his were not.

His wife said to him, 'Why is it that last year everybody's crops were struck [by hail] and yours weren't, and now everybody's crops are affected by drought and yours aren't?' He told her the whole story.

Before very long a quarrel broke out between the Ḥasid's wife and the mother of the [second] girl. The Ḥasid's wife said, 'Look! I will show you that your daughter was buried in a reed mat!'

The next year he went and spent a night in the cemetery, and heard the same two spirits conversing. One said to the other, 'Come! Let's hear from behind the curtain what disasters are to befall the world!' The other said to her, 'Leave off! Our conversation has been heard among the living!'

[From this] you can see that the dead do know [what transpires among the living]. Not necessarily. Perhaps someone died and then went and informed them.

A proof [that the dead know what transpires among the living]: Zeiri used to entrust money to his landlady. While he was away studying she died. He went to her graveside to enquire from her where the money was. She said to him, 'Go and take it from beneath the door hinge in such-and-such a place, and ask my mother to send my comb and my tube of kohl with so-and-so who is coming tomorrow.' So you see that they do know![25] Not necessarily. Perhaps Duma[26] had already announced [the imminent death of her friend].

A proof [that the dead know what transpires among the living]: Shmuel's father was in charge of the orphans' money. Shmuel was not present when he died, but people called him 'the son who consumed the orphans' money'.[27] [Shmuel] looked for [his father] in the cemetery. He said [to the spirits], 'I want Abba!'[28] They said, 'There are plenty of Abbas here.' He said 'I

25. Since she was aware that the other woman was dying and would be buried the next day – Rashi.
26. The angel in charge of the dead.
27. That is, they were unable to locate the money.
28. Daddy.

want Abba son of Abba!' They said, 'There are plenty of Abba
son of Abbas here.' He said 'I want Abba son of Abba, the father
of Shmuel! Where is he?' They said, 'He has ascended to the
heavenly yeshiva.' While this was happening he spied Levi[29]
sitting outside. He said to him, Why are you sitting outside?
Why have you not ascended [to the heavenly yeshiva]? [Levi]
replied, I was told that [because of] all the years I upset Rabbi
Appas by failing to attend his yeshiva they would not take me
up [to the heavenly yeshiva]. Meanwhile, [Shmuel's] father
arrived, and [Shmuel] saw that he was crying and smiling. He
said, Why are you crying? He replied, Because soon you will be
coming here. And why are you smiling? Because you are highly
thought of in this world. [Shmuel] said, If I am highly thought
of, let them take Levi up [to the heavenly yeshiva]; and they
took him up. [Shmuel] said [to his father], Where is the orphans'
money? He replied, Go and take it out of the mill – what is
above and below is ours, what is in between belongs to the
orphans. Why have you done it that way? He replied, If thieves
come, they will take ours [money, not that of the orphans],
and if the ground erodes it, it will erode ours. So you see [from
the fact that his father knew Shmuel was coming] that [the
dead] do know [what happens to the living! Not necessarily].
Perhaps Shmuel was different – since he was so highly esteemed
they announced his arrival in advance and prepared the way
for him.

Rabbi Jonathan, too, changed his mind about this, as Shmuel
bar Naḥmani said in Rabbi Jonathan's name, How do we know
that the dead talk to each other? Since it says, **AND THE LORD
SAID TO HIM, 'THIS IS THE LAND OF WHICH I SWORE TO
ABRAHAM, ISAAC AND JACOB, TO SAY, "I WILL ASSIGN IT TO
YOUR OFFSPRING"'** (Deuteronomy 34:4). What does it mean
by 'to say'? Go, tell Abraham, Isaac and Jacob that I have now
fulfilled for their children the oath that I swore to them. Now,
if you think [the dead] don't know what happens in the world,
what was the point of saying anything to them? What, after all,

19a

29. Levi ben Sisi was Shmuel's teacher and colleague.

do they know? But if they do know, what was the point of telling them[, seeing that they already knew]? [The point could be] that they might express their thanks to Moses.

Chapter Four covers the times of prayer and aspects of its performance; it focuses on the tefilla. *Ever since the liturgy was consolidated during the Geonic period (c. 500–1100), there have been three daily prayers,* shaḥarit, minḥa *and* aravit *(morning, afternoon, evening); on festival days* musaf *('additional') is added, and on Yom Kippur and rain fasts there is a fifth service,* ne'ila *('closing of the gates').*

Gamaliel II arrived c. 90 CE in Yavné, where Yoḥanan ben Zakkai had established a court following the destruction of the Temple in 70. Gamaliel's family was wealthy and influential, and evidently in favour with Rome. He established himself as nasi *(president) of the court in place of Yoḥanan, who left Yavné and taught at Beror Ḥayil. The following story suggests an authoritarian tendency on Gamaliel's part; perhaps he perceived a need to show a united front to the Romans. Also evident is the social distance between the 'ruling class' that he represented, and the other Sages.*

The narrative is a composite, redacted some centuries after the events, and there are parallel accounts differing in detail from this one. Certainly, the 'takeover' of rabbinic Judaism by the family of the Nasi was memorable, and Gamaliel's strong personality and halakhic initiatives left a lasting impact. Beyond that, the stories tell us more about rabbinic attitudes and institutions in Sasanian Babylonia than about the events themselves; the description of Gamaliel's court as a bet ha-midrash *('House of Study') at which he presided over lectures given by an assistant seems anachronistic.*

CHAPTER FOUR

MISHNA:

26a [Time for] the morning prayer [extends] to midday; Rabbi Judah says, to [the end of] the fourth hour.[30] [Time for] the afternoon prayer [extends] to midday; Rabbi Judah says, to *plag ha-minḥa*.[31] The evening prayer is not fixed. The additional prayer [on Sabbath and festivals, may be recited] at any time of the day.

GEMARA:

27b **The evening prayer is not fixed.**

What does **is not fixed** mean?

If you say it means that if you haven't recited it earlier you may recite it at any time throughout the night, it should have said, **[Time for] the evening prayer [extends] throughout the night.**

So does it mean, it is not obligatory at all? This would accord with [the opinion] that the evening prayer is optional, for Rav Yehuda said in Shmuel's name, Rabban Gamaliel holds that the evening prayer is obligatory, and Rabbi Joshua that it is optional.

Abbaye said, The law is according to the one who says it is obligatory; Rava said, the law is according to the one who says it is optional.

The rabbis taught: **A disciple came before Rabbi Joshua and asked, Is the evening prayer obligatory or optional? He replied, Optional.**

[The disciple] then came before Rabban Gamaliel and asked, Is the evening prayer obligatory or optional? He replied, Obligatory. [The disciple] said, But Rabbi Joshua told me it was optional! [Gamaliel] replied, Wait until the shield-bearers[32] enter the House of Study!

When the shield-bearers entered the House of Study, the questioner arose and enquired, Is the evening prayer obligatory or optional?

---

30. The day from sunrise to sunset is divided into twelve hours.
31. An hour and a quarter before sunset.
32. The Sages – warriors for Torah.

Rabban Gamaliel replied, Obligatory. Then he turned to the Sages and said, Does anyone disagree?

Rabbi Joshua said, No!

[Gamaliel said,] Have I not heard in your name that it is optional? Stand up, Joshua, and let them testify against you!

Joshua got to his feet and said, If I were alive and he were dead, the living could contradict the dead, but seeing that he lives and I live, how can the living contradict the living?

Rabban Gamaliel resumed his seat and [continued to] expound, while Rabbi Joshua remained standing, until the people became restive and told Ḥutzpit the lecturer[33] to stop; so [Ḥutzpit] stopped.

They said, How long will [Gamaliel] continue to vex [Rabbi Joshua]? Some time ago he vexed him over [the calculation] of the New Year [and then] he vexed him in the matter of Rabbi Zadok's first-born lamb.[34] Now he is at it again! Let us depose him!

Who can we put in his place? Can we appoint Rabbi Joshua? [Hardly,] since he is involved in the matter. Can we appoint Rabbi Aqiva? [Not really,] since he lacks 'merit of the fathers'[35] and [Gamaliel] may victimize him. [So] let's appoint Rabbi Eleazar ben Azaria, since he is learned, wealthy and a tenth-generation descendant of Ezra.

He is learned –[36] if anyone poses a question he can answer it.

He is wealthy – if he has to bribe Caesar he can do so.

He is a tenth-generation descendant of Ezra – he has 'merit of the fathers', so [Gamaliel] cannot victimize him.

---

33. Literally, 'translator'. The storyteller assumes that Gamaliel would have had an assistant to deliver the lecture, a procedure later adopted as the norm in the Babylonian academies.
34. Respectively Mishna *Rosh Hashana* 2:9 and *Bekhorot* 36a, where similar phraseology is used to that here.
35. Aqiva's parents were converts to Judaism.
36. At this point the narrative moves from Hebrew to Aramaic; clearly a later section has been grafted on.

They went and said to [Eleazar], Would Sir agree to become head of the *metivta*?[37]

He replied, I must consult my household.

28a   He consulted his wife. She said, Perhaps they will depose you[, too]?

He replied, A person can enjoy[38] the cup of honour for a day, and the next day let it be smashed.

She said, You don't have a hoary head![39]

That day was his eighteenth birthday. Miraculously, eighteen rows of his hair turned white.

That's why [Mishna] says, **Rabbi Eleazar ben Azaria says, I am like a seventy-year old man . . .**[40]

They taught: **On that day they removed the doorkeeper, and disciples were allowed to enter, for Rabban Gamaliel had pronounced, No disciple who lacks complete integrity shall enter the House of Learning! On that day many benches were added [for the disciples Gamaliel had excluded].**

Rabbi Yoḥanan said, Abba Joseph ben Dostai and the [other] rabbis argued about this; one said 400 benches were added, and the other said 700 benches.

Rabban Gamaliel was upset [when he saw so many disciples enter]. He thought, Perhaps, God forbid, I have withheld Torah from Israel! In a dream, he was shown white jars full of smoke; but it wasn't so[41] – he was only shown that to put his mind at rest.

They taught: **On that day [the tractate] *Eduyot* was taught, and wherever [Mishna] says 'on that day', it is [the day Gamaliel was deposed]; no point of law**

37. The Babylonian term for a rabbinic session, or perhaps academy (see Goodblatt, *Rabbinic Instruction*, pp. 76–92); another anachronism.
38. Literally, 'use'.
39. You don't look old enough to exercise authority.
40. Mishna *Berakhot* 1:5. The plain meaning of Eleazar's words is 'I am about seventy years old.'
41. The extra disciples were not in fact insincere 'jars of smoke'.

that called for decision[42] in the House of Study remained undecided.

Nor did Rabban Gamaliel absent himself from the House of Study for a moment, for Mishna says: **On that day Judah, the Ammonite proselyte, presented himself before the House of Study and enquired, May I enter the congregation?[43] Rabban Gamaliel said to him, You are forbidden to enter the congregation; Rabbi Joshua said to him, You are permitted to enter the congregation. Rabban Gamaliel [then] said to [Rabbi Joshua], Is it not said, No Ammonite or Moabite shall be admitted into the congregation of the Lord** (Deuteronomy 23:4 JPS)? **Rabbi Joshua replied to him, But are Ammon and Moab still in their places? Sennacherib came and mixed up all the nations, as it is said, I have erased the borders of peoples; I have plundered their treasures, And exiled their populations** (Isaiah 10:13 JPS) – and whoever is separated is regarded as from the majority.[44] **Rabban Gamaliel responded, Does it not also say, But afterwards I will restore the fortunes of the Ammonites – declares the Lord** (Jeremiah 49:6 JPS)? **Rabbi Joshua rejoined, And does it not say, I will restore my people Israel** (Amos 9:14 JPS), **though they have not [yet] been restored? They immediately permitted [Judah] to enter the congregation.**

Rabban Gamaliel said, Since that is how things are, I shall go and seek reconciliation with Rabbi Joshua.

When he arrived at [Joshua's] house, he saw the walls were black [with soot]. He [exclaimed,] From the walls of your house it seems you are a smith!

---

42. Literally, 'that depended on'.
43. *Yadayim* 4:4 (see p. 715). That is, May I marry a native-born Jewish woman?
44. That is, Judah the proselyte belongs to the general, non-Ammonite, population. This phrase is a gloss on the words attributed to Joshua.

[Joshua] said, Woe to the generation whose leader you are! Little do you comprehend the sufferings of the learned, how they support themselves and how they are provided for!

[Gamaliel] said, I humble myself before you! Forgive me!

[Joshua] ignored him.

[Gamaliel: Forgive me] for the sake of my father's house!

He forgave.

They said, Who will inform the rabbis [that we have made up the quarrel]? A fuller [was present, and] said to them, I'll go.

Rabbi Joshua sent [this message] to the House of Study: Let him who wears the robe don the robe! Should he who does not wear the robe say to the one who wears the robe, doff your robe that I may wear it?[45]

Rabbi Aqiva said to the rabbis,[46] Lock the door, so that Rabban Gamaliel's servants cannot come and punish us!

Rabbi Joshua said, It is better that I should go in person [to inform the rabbis].

He came and knocked on the door, and said, Let the sprinkler, the son of a sprinkler, sprinkle! Should the one who is neither a sprinkler nor the son of a sprinkler say to the sprinkler, Your water is cave water and your ashes are ashes of the roast?[47]

The rabbis said, What can we do now [with Eleazar, seeing Gamaliel has resumed office]? [We can't] dismiss him, for it has been decided that one should increase holiness, not decrease.[48] Should one of them preside[49] one week and the other in alternate weeks? That would be invidious. So let Rabban Gamaliel preside for two weeks, and Rabbi Eleazar ben Azaria in the third week.

That is why the teacher says, Whose week was it? It was Rabbi Eleazar ben Azaria's.

---

45. The coded messages tell the rabbis that Gamaliel, of the house of the Nasi, should be restored to his hereditary position.

46. Presumably in response to the message conveyed by the fuller.

47. It was the High Priest's prerogative to sprinkle the blood of the red heifer to prepare the ashes for purification of those who had come into contact with a corpse (Numbers 19:4). Ironically, Eleazar was of priestly descent, but Gamaliel was not. 'Cave water' and 'ashes of the roast' are unfit for performance of the ceremony.

48. Cf. *Shabbat* 21b (see p. 99).

49. Literally, 'expound'.

The disciple [who posed the question about the evening prayer] was Rabbi Simeon ben Yoḥai.

The externals and 'mechanics' of prayer must never be allowed to interfere with its essence, the relationship between the worshipper and God. In the next passage we see this exemplified in the prayer of Hannah.

Kavvana, *the 'direction of the heart', is essential to the performance of* mitzvot; *however, there are many levels of* kavvana. *An important distinction was articulated by the Lithuanian Rabbi Hayyim Soloveitchik (1853–1917): '*Halakha *has much to say about focusing on the meaning of the words as you pray, and about being aware that you are fulfilling a* mitzva, *But transcending such matters is the need to banish all stray thoughts from your mind and to feel that you are standing in the Holy Presence; this is not a mere "halakhic requirement", but part of the very* definition *of prayer – without it, you are not praying at all, and the* halakhic *modalities do not even begin.'*[50]

CHAPTER FIVE

GEMARA:
The rabbis taught: **He who prays must direct his heart**[51] **to heaven. Abba Saul says, This is what is meant by, YOU MAKE THEIR HEARTS FIRM; YOU INCLINE YOUR EAR** (Psalm 10:17). ₃₁a

It was taught: Rabbi Judah says, When Rabbi Aqiva prayed with the congregation he made it brief so as not to inconvenience them, but when he prayed on his own you could leave him in one corner and find him in another, so much did he bend the knee and prostrate himself.

Rabbi Ḥiyya bar Abba said, One should always pray in a house with windows, as it is said: HE HAD WINDOWS MADE, ETC. Do you think you should spend the whole day in prayer?

50. Soloveitchik, *Ḥiddushei R'Ḥ*, on *Tefilla* 4:1.
51. The heart was understood as the seat of intellect as well as emotions; 'direct his mind' would be an equally satisfactory translation.

[No,] Daniel made this clear: THREE TIMES A DAY, ETC. Do you think this began when he arrived in Babylon? [No,] for it is written: AS HE DID BEFORE THIS TIME. Do you think it is all right to pray in any direction you like? [No,] that is why it says: FACING JERUSALEM (Daniel 6:11).[52] Do you think that [all three daily Prayers] might be said at one time? [No,] this was made clear by David, as it is written: Evening, morning and afternoon (Psalm 55:18). Should one pray aloud? [No,] this was made plain through Hannah, as it is said, HER LIPS MOVED, BUT HER VOICE WAS NOT HEARD (1 Samuel 1:13). Should you first petition for your [personal] needs, and then praise? [No,] this was made plain by Solomon, as it is said, HEAR THE PRAYER AND SUPPLICATION OF YOUR SERVANT (1 Kings 8:28) – first praise, then supplication.

One should not make a private petition after *emet v'yatziv*,[53] but after the Prayer it is all right [to make petitions, and they may be] even as long as the Day of Atonement confession.

Rav Hamnuna said: [See] how many important laws may be derived from [what] Scripture [says] about Hannah! NOW HANNAH WAS PRAYING IN HER HEART – from this [you learn] that when you pray you must direct your heart; ONLY HER LIPS MOVED – from this [you see that] you should articulate the words; BUT HER VOICE COULD NOT BE HEARD – from this [you see that] you should not raise your voice in prayer; SO ELI THOUGHT SHE WAS DRUNK – from this [you learn] that it is forbidden to pray when drunk (1 Samuel 1:13 JPS).

ELI SAID TO HER, HOW LONG WILL YOU MAKE A DRUNKEN SPECTACLE OF YOURSELF? (1 Samuel 1:14 JPS). Said Rabbi
31b Eleazar, From this [you learn] that if you see some impropriety in another person you should rebuke him.

AND HANNAH REPLIED, 'OH NO, MY LORD . . .' (1 Samuel 1:15 JPS). Ulla said in the name of Rabbi Yosé, She [meant to] say, 'You are no lord in this matter, nor does the holy spirit rest

52. Weiss, *Sepphoris Synagogue*, p. 45, remarks that the position of the Tannaim on this was 'fluid'; the orientation of the fifth-century Sepphoris synagogue was determined on architectural grounds rather than by the direction of Jerusalem.
53. A blessing preceding the main morning prayer.

on you, since you suspect me of such a thing!' Some say that this is what she [meant to] tell him: 'You are no lord, and the *Shekhina* and the holy spirit are not with you, since you have judged me guilty and not innocent. Can't you see that I AM A VERY UNHAPPY WOMAN [AND] I HAVE DRUNK NO WINE OR OTHER STRONG DRINK BUT I HAVE BEEN POURING OUT MY HEART TO THE LORD (1 Samuel 1:15 JPS)? Said Rabbi Eleazar, from this [you learn] that if someone wrongly suspects you of an impropriety you should inform him [of the facts].

DO NOT TAKE YOUR MAIDSERVANT FOR A DAUGHTER OF BELIAL[54] (1 Samuel 1:16). Said Rabbi Eleazar, from this [you learn] that if a person prays in a state of inebriation it is as if he was worshipping idols; here we have the term 'daughter of Belial' and there we have 'sons of Belial' – SONS OF BELIAL[55] FROM AMONG YOU HAVE GONE AND SUBVERTED THE INHABITANTS OF THEIR TOWN (Deuteronomy 13:14); just as there the context is idolatry, so here idolatry [is meant].

'THEN GO IN PEACE,' SAID ELI (1 Samuel 1:17 JPS). Said Rabbi Eleazar, from this [you learn] that if you have suspected anyone of something of which he is innocent you should conciliate him. Not only that, but you should bless him, as it is said, 'AND MAY THE GOD OF ISRAEL GRANT YOU WHAT YOU HAVE ASKED OF HIM' (1 Samuel 1:17 JPS).

AND SHE MADE THIS VOW: 'O LORD OF HOSTS . . .' (1 Samuel 1:11 JPS). Said Rabbi Eleazar: From the day that the Holy One, blessed be He, created the world, no one addressed the Holy One, blessed be He, as Lord of Hosts until Hannah called [on] Him as [Lord of] Hosts.[56] Hannah was saying to the Holy One, blessed be He, 'Lord of the universe! Of all the immense multitude that You have created in Your world, is it too much for You to grant me one son?'

What is this like? A king of flesh and blood made a feast for his servants. A poor man was standing at the

---

54. In place of 'daughter of Belial' JPS translates 'worthless woman', but the literal translation is required to make sense of the comment.
55. JPS: 'scoundrels'.
56. Hebrew *tz'vaot* (Hosts) means 'multitudes' or 'crowds'; 1 Samuel 1 is the first time that Scripture applies the term to God.

gate; he asked for a piece of bread, but no one took any notice. He pushed his way [into the presence of] the king, and said, 'Your majesty! From this great feast you have made, is it too much for you to grant me a morsel of bread?'

... IF YOU WILL LOOK UPON THE SUFFERING OF YOUR MAIDSERVANT (1 Samuel 1:11 JPS). Said Rabbi Eleazar: Hannah said to the Holy One, blessed be He, 'Lord of the universe! If You see [my suffering], fine! But if not, just see [what I will do]![57] I will seclude myself [with another man] before my husband, Elkanah. When I seclude myself they will have to give me the [bitter] waters to drink as a wife suspected of adultery. You will not allow Your Torah to be falsified, and it says, IF SHE IS INNOCENT, SHE WILL BE CLEARED [OF GUILT] AND CONCEIVE SEED (Numbers 5:28).'

This is all very well according to those who interpret CONCEIVE SEED as 'if she was barren, she will give birth'. But how can you explain it according to those who say it means, 'If she would have given birth in pain, she will give birth with ease; if she would have borne females, she will bear males; dark, she will bear fair; short, she will bear tall'?

For it was taught: SHE WILL BE CLEARED [OF GUILT] AND CONCEIVE SEED. This teaches that if she was barren, she will give birth. This is the view of Rabbi Ishmael, but Rabbi Aqiva objected, If this was so, all barren women will go and seclude themselves [with other men], and whoever had not committed adultery would conceive! So it must mean, 'If she would have given birth in pain, she will give birth with ease; short, she will bear tall; dark, she will bear fair; one child, she will bear two.'

On this latter view, how do you explain, IF YOU

57. The Hebrew for 'look upon' is literally 'if to see you will see'. Biblical Hebrew achieves emphasis by duplication of the verb; this idiom was no longer current in Eleazar's day, and he interprets it as a peculiarity.

WILL LOOK UPON? [Answer: No explanation is called for, since] the Torah speaks in human language.[58]

THE SUFFERING OF YOUR MAIDSERVANT . . . NOT FORGET YOUR MAIDSERVANT . . . GRANT YOUR MAIDSERVANT . . . Rabbi Yosé the son of Rabbi Ḥanina said, Why three times **MAIDSERVANT?** Hannah said to the Holy One, blessed be He, 'Lord of the universe! You made three mortal tests for women (some say, three approaches to death): [the laws of] menstruation, the setting aside of dough [for the priest] and [the kindling of] the Sabbath light. Have I transgressed any of them?'

AND GRANT YOUR MAIDSERVANT SEED OF MEN.[59] What is [meant by] 'seed of men'? Rav said, A man among men! Shmuel said, Seed that will anoint two men, namely Saul and David.[60] Rabbi Yoḥanan said, Seed that would be on a par with two men, namely Moses and Aaron, as it is said, **MOSES AND AARON AMONG HIS PRIESTS, SAMUEL, AMONG THOSE WHO CALL ON HIS NAME** (Psalm 99:6 JPS). But the disciples say, **SEED OF MEN** [means] seed that is 'mixed' [i.e. average] among men. When Rav Dimi came he said, Not a giant nor a dwarf, not too weak nor too strong,[61] not too ruddy nor too pale, not too clever nor too stupid.

I AM THE WOMAN WHO STOOD HERE BESIDE YOU (1 Samuel 1:26 JPS). Rabbi Joshua ben Levi said, From here [you can infer] that it is forbidden to sit within four cubits of someone who is praying.

The whole world belongs to God, its creator; we humans are not owners, but trustees. The rabbis instituted a simple form of prayer to thank God for any pleasure we derive from His creation; it consists of six Hebrew words – Blessed are You, God, our God and ruler of the world – followed by an appropriate description of the benefit enjoyed, for instance smelling a rose, viewing a wonder of nature, or consuming food or drink.

58. i.e. it is normal linguistic usage and does not call for special interpretation.
59. JPS translates 'a male child'.
60. Hannah's son, the prophet Samuel, anointed both of them.
61. 'Too thin or too fat' – Rashi.

Mishna sets out appropriate generic formulae for food of various kinds, and the Gemara enquires as to whether there is a scriptural basis for the prayer; the Amoraim conclude that there is no scriptural basis, but that it is simply common sense to thank the Creator for what He has provided.

CHAPTER SIX

MISHNA:

35a   What blessing should you recite [before eating or drinking] produce? For produce of the tree you say, [Blessed are You, God, our God and ruler of the world,][62] Who creates the produce of the tree; but for wine you say, Who creates the produce of the vine. For produce of the earth you say, Who creates the produce of the earth; but for bread you say, Who produces bread from the earth. For vegetables you say, Who creates the produce of the earth; but Rabbi Judah says, You say, Who creates different kinds of vegetation.

GEMARA:

What is the [scriptural] basis for this? It is as the rabbis taught: HOLY – PRAISES TO THE LORD (Leviticus 19:24)[63] – this teaches that [the fruit] requires blessing both before and after [eating]. On this basis Rabbi Aqiva said that a person should not taste anything before blessing [God].

Is that what [the expression] HOLY – PRAISES is for? Surely it is needed either because the Torah is telling us, 'redeem it before eating it', or because it is telling us, 'That which requires songs [of praise] must be redeemed; that which does not require songs [of praise] need not be redeemed' – as Rabbi Shmuel bar Naḥmani said in Rabbi Jonathan's name, How do we know that songs [of praise] should be [sung] only over wine? Since it says, BUT THE VINE REPLIED, 'HAVE I STOPPED YIELDING MY NEW WINE, WHICH

62. This formula is assumed in all instances; Mishna discusses only the generic ending of the blessing.
63. A literal translation. KJV reads, 'shall be holy to praise the Lord withal'.

GLADDENS GOD AND MEN . . . ?' (Judges 9:13 JPS) –
Granted it gladdens men, how does it gladden God?
From this you see that songs of praise [that 'gladden
God'] are sung only over wine.

This argument is fine for those who [apply the verse in
Leviticus to] 'fourth-year planting'[, since they would reject
these alternative interpretations of the verse], but what can those
who [restrict it to] 'fourth-year vine' say[, seeing that they need
the verse for the alternative interpretations]?

Moreover, even if you [apply the verse in Leviticus to] 'fourth-
year planting', it will work if you make inferences from the
verbal parallel –

> For it was taught: **Rabbi says, In one place it is
> said, THAT YOU MAY INCREASE ITS YIELD FOR YOUR-
> SELVES** (Leviticus 19:25), **and in another it says, AND
> THE YIELD OF THE VINEYARD** (Deuteronomy 22:9);
> **just as in [Deuteronomy] 'yield' is specifically that of
> the vineyard, so in the [Leviticus] 'yield' is specifically
> that of the vineyard[, and not that of 'planting' in
> general].**

– You would still have one 'praise'[64] left over as a basis for
blessing. But if you do not make that inference, on what can
you base [the duty to say] a blessing [when eating]?

Also, even if you make the inference, you would have a
[scriptural] basis for blessing only after eating, not before.

> That's no question, since we could argue from
> minor to major: If you have to bless [God] when you
> are satisfied, how much more so when you are hungry!

That settles the need for saying a blessing over wine[, since the
verse in Leviticus, as we now interpret it, refers to the vineyard and no other planting]. What about other kinds [of food]?

We can make the inference from [the need to bless God for
the produce of] the vineyard. Just as the vineyard is something
you enjoy, and you must bless [God for it], so must you bless
[God] for anything you enjoy.

You could object to this line of argument that stricter laws

64. The term for 'praise' in Leviticus 19:24 is plural.

apply to the vineyard, [for instance that] you must leave the young grapes [for the poor].[65]

You can counter [the objection by citing] flour. Flour is also strict, since it is liable to the laws of *ḥalla*.[66]

The argument goes to and fro, This is not like that, and that is not like this; the common factor is that they are things that are enjoyed, and they[67] require a blessing. We infer that whatever is enjoyed requires a blessing.

But [wine and flour] have in common that they [are offered] on the altar[, so how can we argue on that basis that a blessing is required, too, for foods other than] the olive, [the oil of] which is [poured as a libation] on the altar?

> Do we need the [association with] the altar to include the olive? Is it not written, And flame spread from stacks and standing grain to the olive-*kerem*[68] (Judges 15:5) — Rav Papa said, *Kerem* never means 'olive plantation' unless it is joined with the word *zayit*.

The question remains: The common factor [among those items for which we find a scriptural basis for blessing] is their connection with the altar.

Then perhaps we should derive [the principle of blessing] from the Seven Species.[69] Just as the Seven Species are something you enjoy, and you must bless [God for them], so must you bless [God] for anything you enjoy.

You could object to this line of argument that [stricter laws apply to the Seven Species, since] first-fruits must be offered from them. Also, [Deuteronomy 8:10] says that you should bless after [eating]; how do you know that you should bless before?

> That's no question, since we could argue from minor to major: If you have to bless [God] when you are satisfied, how much more so when you are hungry!

Anyway, even if you say [Leviticus 19:24] applies to all plants[,

---

65. See introductory note to *Pe'ah*.
66. These are explained in *Ḥalla*.
67. Wine, as we have demonstrated; flour, on the basis of Deuteronomy 8:10 – Rashi.
68. *Kerem* on its own means 'vineyard'.
69. Wheat, barley, grapes, figs, pomegranates, olives and dates (Deuteronomy 8:8).

not just the vine], how do you know that you should bless for food other than plants, for instance eggs or fish?

So[, abandon the search for a scriptural basis! We conclude that] it is common sense – a person should not enjoy anything in this world without blessing [his Creator].

Chapter Nine opens with formulae of thanksgiving to God for His gracious saving acts. The Gemara's discussion generates a series of sayings about groups of three, including this attributed to Rav Yehuda in the name of Rav: 'Three need mercy: a good king, a good year and a good dream.' On this slender peg the editors hung the material available to them on dreams.

Manuals of dream interpretation are an ancient genre, from the Chester Beatty Papyrus record of the Egyptian twelfth dynasty (1991–1786 BCE) through the Babylonian dream guide found in Ashurbanipal's (668–627 BCE) library at Nineveh. Artemidorus, in second-century CE Rome, summed up dream interpretation to his time and responded to criticisms by Sceptics and others. He makes the important distinction between enhypnion, *a dream reflecting the present, and* oneiros, *a dream pointing to the future.*[70] *The Gemara takes a similar position: not all dreams are predictive. A passage not translated here lists the significance of various dream symbols, and like Artemidorus (and more recently Freud) frequently interprets the 'dream work' through wordplay; however, the material has all been thoroughly Judaized, most of the symbols being linked to biblical texts.*

The collection opens in sceptical mode. Joseph's dream (Genesis 37) is cited by way of illustration that even the truest of dreams contains some nonsense; he dreamed that sun, moon and eleven stars, that is, his father, mother and brothers, would bow down to him, yet his mother was already dead. Shmuel, if he had a bad dream, cited Zechariah 10:2: **DREAMS SPEAK FALSEHOOD;** *if he had a good dream, he cited it as a question:* **DO DREAMS SPEAK FALSEHOOD?** *An ambivalent statement is*

70. Artemidorus, *Oneirocriticon*, pp. 14–15.

attributed to Rabbi Bana'a: 'There were 24 interpreters of
dreams in Jerusalem. I once had a dream and visited all of them.
Each gave a different interpretation, and each came true, which
proves what is said, that "interpretation follows the mouth".'
Shmuel bar Naḥmani, moreover, said in the name of Rabbi
Jonathan, A person is shown only the thoughts of his own mind,
as it is said, AND YOU, O KING, YOUR THOUGHTS AROSE ON
YOUR BED (Daniel 2:29).

Two anecdotes, one set in a Roman context, the other in the
Sasanian court, reflect the constant warfare between Rome and
Iran. Again, there is scepticism; play on the ruler's secret fear
and he will dream about it.

The tale of Bar Hedya, with its touches of humour and its
providential ending, is an ingenious literary sketch of the lives
of Abbaye and Rava, based on the implausible plot that the two
men simultaneously had identical dreams over a long period
and sought the ministrations of the same interpreter. In a deep
sense, of course, Abbaye and Rava did share the same dreams,
and these were dreams filled with biblical texts. But there is
scepticism here, too; if indeed the interpreter caused the fulfilment of his own interpretations, those interpretations were arbitrary, tailored to suit his own needs, not possessing objective
validity. And anyway, doesn't God exercise providence over the
affairs of humankind (see Shabbat 156a)?

CHAPTER NINE

GEMARA:

56a   Caesar[71] said to Rabbi Joshua ben Ḥanania, You [people] think
you are very clever, so tell me what I will see in my dream! He
replied, You will see the Persians impress you to the royal levy,
seize you and make you tend pigs with a golden staff. [Caesar]
mulled this over all day, and at night he saw it [in his dream].

King Shapur said to Shmuel, You [people] think you are very
clever, so tell me what I will see in my dream! He replied, You

---

71. 'Caesar' would be some local Roman official; but most likely, this is a literary
    fiction devised to convey a tradition of Joshua's understanding of Roman fears.

will see the Romans come and take you captive and make you crush datestones in a golden mill. [Shapur] mulled this over all day, and at night he saw it [in his dream].

Bar Hedya was an interpreter of dreams: if you paid him, he gave you a favourable interpretation; if you didn't pay him, the interpretation was unfavourable.

Abbaye and Rava had [similar] dreams; Abbaye paid [Bar Hedya to interpret] but Rava didn't.

They said, In our dream they recited to us,[72] YOUR OX IS SLAUGHTERED BEFORE YOUR EYES ... (Deuteronomy 28:31). To Rava he said, Your business will fail and you will have no pleasure from what you eat. To Abbaye he said, Your business will prosper, and you will be too happy to eat.

They said, They recited to us, YOU WILL BEGET SONS AND DAUGHTERS, BUT THEY WILL NOT BE YOURS, FOR THEY WILL GO INTO CAPTIVITY ... (Deuteronomy 28:41). To Rava he interpreted in the [plain,] bad sense. To Abbaye he said, You will have many sons and daughters; your daughters will marry into other families, and it will seem as if they are in captivity.

They said, They recited to us, YOUR SONS AND DAUGHTERS WILL BE GIVEN TO ANOTHER PEOPLE ... (Deuteronomy 28:32). To Abbaye he said, You will have many sons and daughters; you will want [to marry them] to your relatives, [your wife] will want [to marry them] to hers; she will prevail upon you to give them to her relatives, who are like 'another people'. To Rava he said, Your wife will die, and her sons and daughters will fall into the hands of another woman.

[This corresponds with what] Rava [himself] observed that Rabbi Jeremiah had said in the name of Rav: What does YOUR SONS AND DAUGHTERS WILL BE GIVEN TO ANOTHER PEOPLE mean? [It refers to] the father's wife [who is not the children's mother].

In our dream, they recited to us, GO, EAT YOUR BREAD IN JOY! (Ecclesiastes 9:7). To Abbaye he said, Your business will prosper; you will eat and drink and recite this verse out of

---

72. Alternatively, 'they got us to recite', or 'they showed us the text'; though the mind fabricates, the essence of the dream is 'sent'.

[sheer] joy. To Rava he said, Your business will fail; you will slaughter [your animals] but not eat; you will drink, and recite [the verse] to allay your fears.

In our dream, they recited to us, THE FIELD WILL BRING FORTH MUCH SEED; YOU WILL GATHER LITTLE, FOR THE LOCUST WILL DESTROY IT (Deuteronomy 28:38). To Abbaye, he applied the first half of the verse; to Rava, the end.

They recited to us, YOU WILL HAVE OLIVE TREES THROUGH-OUT YOUR BORDERS; YOU WILL NOT ANOINT WITH THEIR OIL, FOR YOUR OLIVES WILL DROP (Deuteronomy 28:40). To Abbaye, he applied the first half of the verse; to Rava, the end.

They recited to us, ALL THE NATIONS OF THE EARTH WILL SEE THAT THE NAME OF THE LORD IS UPON YOU, AND THEY WILL FEAR YOU (Deuteronomy 28:10). To Abbaye he said, Your reputation as head of the academy will flourish; people will hold you in awe. To Rava he said, The king's treasury will be broken into and you will be charged with theft; everyone will learn a lesson from you.[73] The next day the king's treasury was broken into and Rava was arrested.

They said, [In our dream] we saw lettuce on the wine keg. To Abbaye he said, Your merchandise will thrive like lettuce. To Rava he said, Your merchandise is bitter as lettuce.[74]

They said, We saw meat on the wine keg. To Abbaye he said, Your wine is tasty, and everyone will come to buy meat and wine from you. To Rava he said, Your wine is strong; everyone will have to buy meat to eat with it.

They said, We saw a jug suspended in a palm tree. To Abbaye he said, Your merchandise spreads like a palm. To Rava he said, Your merchandise is sweet[75] like dates.

They said to him, We saw a pomegranate on a keg of wine. To Abbaye he said, Your merchandise is expensive like a pom-egranate. To Rava he said, Your merchandise is tart like a pomegranate.

They said, We saw a jug fall into the well. To Abbaye he

73. Literally, 'will reason a fortiori from you'.
74. Ancient varieties of lettuce were bitter (see Pliny, *Historia Naturalis* 19:38); that is why it is the 'bitter herb' of choice for Passover (Mishna *Pesaḥim* 2:6 (39a)).
75. You will have to sell it cheap – Rashi.

said, Your merchandise is in demand, as the saying goes, 'The bread fell in the well and there's nothing left.' To Rava he said, Your merchandise has failed; you could throw it down the well.

They said, We saw a young donkey standing on our pillow braying. To Abbaye he said, You will be king and have an *amora* [to speak for you].[76] To Rava he said, The words *peter ḥamor*[77] are erased from your *tefillin*. [Rava] retorted, But I have seen them and they are there! He said, The letter *vav* in *peter ḥamor* has certainly been erased.[78]

Rava then went to him alone, and said, [In my dream] I saw the outer door of the house collapse. [Bar Hedya] said, Your wife will die.

He said, I saw molars and front teeth fall out. [Bar Hedya] said, Your son and daughter will die.

He said, I saw two doves flying. [Bar Hedya] said, You will divorce two wives.

He said, I saw two turnip heads. [Bar Hedya] said, You will suffer two blows. Rava went and sat in the House of Study all that day.[79] Then he found two blind men fighting and went to separate them, and they hit him twice; they would have hit him again, but he said, Enough! I saw only two!

After that, Rava went and paid him. He said, I saw a wall fall down. [Bar Hedya] said, You will acquire property without limit.

He said, I saw Abbaye's mansion collapse and cover us with dust. [Bar Hedya] said, Abbaye will die and you will take over the academy.

He said, I saw my own mansion collapse, and everyone came and helped themselves to bricks. [Bar Hedya] said, Your teachings will spread through the world.

76. That is, Abbaye would be head of the academy; as a matter of prestige he would not personally deliver the lectures, but an *amora* would deliver them in his presence.
77. 'First-born donkey' (Exodus 13:13).
78. This is puzzling; *ḥamor* could be spelled with a *vav* and is in fact spelled without one in the Masoretic Hebrew text. Rashi therefore suggests that in Rava's *tefillin* the scribe had incorrectly written it with a *vav* and then erased it. Other manuscripts preserve readings that are not open to this objection.
79. To avoid the predicted blows.

He said, I saw my head split and my brains fall out! [Bar Hedya] said, It was the feathers falling out of your pillow.

He said, In my dream the Hallel of Egypt [Psalms 113-18] was recited. [Bar Hedya] said, A miracle will happen to you.

[Bar Hedya] was about to accompany him on a boat, but thought to himself, Why should I go with a man to whom a miracle is about to happen?[80] As he disembarked he dropped his scroll. Rava found it and read: 'All dreams go by the mouth [of the interpreter].' Scoundrel! he exclaimed. You had the power and you caused all this distress! I can forgive you all, but not [the death of] the daughter of Rav Ḥisda. May you fall into the hands of a government that will show you no mercy!

[Bar Hedya] thought, What can I do? The curse of a Sage, even if undeserved, takes effect. I will go into exile, for the teacher says that exile expiates sin. He went into exile among the Romans, and sat at the chief treasurer's gate. The chief treasurer had a dream and said to [Bar Hedya], I dreamed that a needle stuck in my finger. [Bar Hedya] said, Pay me a *zuz* [to interpret]. He didn't pay, so [Bar Hedya] remained silent. [The chief treasurer] said, [I dreamed that] I saw two of my fingers rot. [Bar Hedya] said, Pay me a *zuz* [to interpret]. He didn't pay, so [Bar Hedya] remained silent. [The chief treasurer] said, [I dreamed that] I saw my whole hand rot. [Bar Hedya] said, All the silk garments [under your care] have rotted away.

News got to the palace and the chief treasurer was summoned and sentenced to death. He protested, Why me? Fetch that man who knew but said nothing! They fetched Bar Hedya and said to him, Because of your *zuz* the king's 566 silk garments have rotted away! They attached ropes to two cedar trees and bound one of his thighs to each; when they released the ropes his head split,[81] then each [tree sprung back] to its place, and he split and fell into two parts.

Berakhot *ends on a more elevated note:*

64a   Said Rabbi Eleazar in the name of Rabbi Ḥanina: The disciples of the Sages augment peace in the world, as it is said, **AND**

---

80. The boat might founder; he will be saved but I won't.
81. Obscure.

ALL YOUR CHILDREN SHALL BE DISCIPLES OF THE LORD, AND GREAT SHALL BE THE PEACE OF YOUR CHILDREN (Isaiah 54:13) – read not *banayikh* [your children] but *bonayikh* [your builders].

GREAT PEACE TO THOSE WHO LOVE YOUR TORAH, AND NO ADVERSITY TO THEM (Psalm 119:165); **MAY THERE BE PEACE WITHIN YOUR RAMPARTS, PEACE WITHIN YOUR PALACES; FOR THE SAKE OF MY BROTHERS AND FRIENDS, I PRAY THAT YOU HAVE PEACE; FOR THE SAKE OF THE HOUSE OF THE LORD OUR GOD, I SEEK PEACE FOR YOU** (122:7–9); **MAY THE LORD GRANT STRENGTH TO HIS PEOPLE, MAY HE BLESS HIS PEOPLE WITH PEACE** (29:11)!

SECOND TRACTATE
PE'AH (CORNER OF THE FIELD)

This tractate deals with rights of the poor to agricultural produce. The main entitlements are:

1. Pe'ah – *the 'corner' or 'edge' of the field – from which the tractate takes its name. This is derived from Leviticus 19:9:* **WHEN YOU REAP THE HARVEST OF YOUR LAND, YOU SHALL NOT COMPLETELY REAP THE CORNERS OF YOUR FIELD.**

2. Leqet – *'gatherings' –* . . . **NOR SHALL YOU GATHER THE GLEANINGS OF YOUR HARVEST** *(Leviticus 19:9). Defined below 4:10.*

3. Shikh'ḥa – *'that which has been forgotten' –* **WHEN YOU REAP THE HARVEST OF YOUR FIELD, AND FORGET A SHEAF IN THE FIELD, DO NOT GO BACK TO FETCH IT, BUT LEAVE IT FOR THE STRANGER, THE ORPHAN AND THE WIDOW** *(Deuteronomy 24:19). Discussed below 5:7.*

4. Peret – *'berries' –* **YOU SHALL NOT GLEAN YOUR VINEYARD OR GATHER THE FALLEN BERRIES; YOU SHALL LEAVE THEM FOR THE POOR AND THE STRANGER. I AM THE LORD YOUR GOD** *(Leviticus 19:10; cf. Deuteronomy 24: 20, 21). Defined below 7:3.*

5. 'Ol'lot – *'orphan grapes' –* **WHEN YOU GATHER THE GRAPES FROM YOUR VINEYARD, DO NOT TAKE THE YOUNG**[1] **[GRAPES]; THEY ARE FOR THE STRANGER, THE ORPHAN AND THE WIDOW** *(Deuteronomy 24:21). Defined below 7:4.*

6. Maaser 'Ani – *'tithe for the poor' (Deuteronomy 14:28, 29 and 26:12 – see Appendix II).*

   Ruth, in the Bible, illustrates some of these laws in practice.

---

1. The Hebrew term is obscure, but probably related to a word meaning 'suckling'.

*Mishna's opening paragraph, now included in the Ortho-
dox daily liturgy, places* pe'ah *with benevolence in general in
the category of* mitzvot *for which there is in principle no
upper limit.*

*Mishna is concerned with definition and boundaries. What
crops are liable to* pe'ah *or* peret? *How do we balance the
claims of poor and landowner? Who qualifies as 'poor'? How
do these laws interact with those of tithing? Some of the laws
were implemented in the time of the Mishna; studying them,
even when they could not be put into practice in their original
form, would have inculcated in Jews a sense of responsibility
for the welfare of the needy.*

CHAPTER ONE

1. These are the [*mitzvot*] for which there is no fixed measure:
   Pe'ah, first-fruits, the offering on 'being seen [before the
   Lord at the Temple in Jerusalem]', the practice of benevolence and the study of Torah. These are the things of which
   one enjoys the fruit in this world, while the stock remains
   for the World to Come: Honouring father and mother; the
   practice of benevolence; bringing peace among men. But
   study of Torah is equal to them all.[2]
2. You should leave no less than a sixtieth [of the crop] as
   pe'ah. Though they said there is no fixed measure, it all
   depends on the size of the field, the number of the poor and
   the size of the crop.[3]
3. *Pe'ah* is left at the beginning and the middle of the field.
   Rabbi Simeon says, It is essential to leave some at the end
   of the field [too].[4] Rabbi Judah says, It is sufficient to leave

2. Textual variants in this Mishna include the addition of 'effecting reconciliation
   between man and wife'.
3. The phrase translated 'size of the crop' is obscure; some have understood it to
   mean the humility, or piety, of the landowner.
4. 'Beginning', 'middle' and 'end' here refer to the process of harvesting, not to
   location in the field (Rashi, *Shabbat* 23a, on the phrase *l'sof sadehu*).

a single stalk of *pe'ah* at the end, but if [the owner] does not do that, what he gave [at the beginning and the middle] is [regarded merely as] *hefqer*.[5]

4. [The Sages] formulated a general principle for *pe'ah*: Whatever is edible, keeps, grows from the land, is harvested all at one time and stored, is liable to *pe'ah*; this includes grains and pulses.

5. Among trees, the sumach, the carob, the walnut, the almond, the grape vine, the pomegranate, the olive and the date are liable to *pe'ah*.

CHAPTER FOUR

10. What is *leqet*? Whatever falls off as you reap. If he reaped an armful, or plucked a handful, and a thorn stung him so that he dropped [the produce] on the ground, it belongs to the landowner;[6] but if something fell into his hand or on to the scythe, it belongs to the poor. What falls off his hand or the scythe belongs to the poor; Rabbi Aqiva says, It belongs to the landowner.

CHAPTER FIVE

7. If the workers forgot a sheaf, but the landowner had not forgotten it, or if the landowner forgot it, but the workers had not forgotten it, or if the poor stood in the way [of the reapers] or concealed [the sheaf] under straw, this is not *shikh'ha*.[7]

---

5. *Hefqer* means 'ownerless'. The poor (or anyone else) may indeed take it, but the landowner has not fulfilled his obligation.
6. Because the produce dropped as a result of an accident, not in the course of reaping.
7. It remains property of the landowner.

CHAPTER SIX

1. The School of Shammai say, [If someone declares something] *hefqer* for the poor [only], it is *hefqer*; but the School of Hillel say it is only *hefqer* if it is declared *hefqer* for rich [and poor alike],[8] as is the case in the sabbatical year.

   If the sheaves in a field were all one *kab* [in volume] and one was four *kabs*, and [the owner] forgot [the four-*kab* sheaf], the School of Shammai say it is not *shikh'ḥa*, but the School of Hillel say it is.

CHAPTER SEVEN

3. What is *peret*? Whatever falls off as the grapes are harvested. If someone was harvesting grapes, cut a bunch and got tangled in foliage so that [the bunch] fell to the ground and [grapes] fell off, these belong to the landowner. If he placed a basket beneath the vine as he was harvesting [to catch falling grapes], he robs the poor; of such a person it is said, DO NOT REMOVE ANCIENT BOUNDARY STONES; DO NOT ENCROACH UPON THE FIELD OF ORPHANS (Proverbs 23:10 JPS).[9]

4. What are *'ol'lot*? [Grapes that hang where there is] neither shoulder nor bough.[10] If there are shoulder and bough, [the grapes] belong to the landowner, but if there is any doubt they go to the poor. If there are solitary grapes in the fork [where the cluster joins the main vine], if they break off together with the cluster they belong to the landowner, otherwise to the poor. Rabbi Judah says, Solitary grapes may

---

8. You cannot relinquish your ownership and then specify who has a right to the object.
9. Only the first half of this verse is cited in the standard Mishna text, but presumably the second half is intended.
10. 'Orphaned' grapes that are not part of the main bunches. A shoulder is a main branch from which hang boughs each with their individual clusters.

rank as a cluster, but the Sages say, They are *'ol'lot* [to which the poor are entitled].

After rounding off some details of pe'ah *and the associated gifts, the Mishna moves on to rules governing the tithe for the poor; it concludes with general considerations on entitlement to social assistance.*

CHAPTER EIGHT

5. The poor at the barn should each be given not less than half a *kab* of wheat; a *kab* of barley – Rabbi Meir says, Half a *kab*; a *kab* and a half of spelt; and a *kab* of figs or a *maneh* of dates – Rabbi Aqiva says, Half a *maneh*; a half *log* of wine – Rabbi Aqiva says, A quarter; a quarter of [olive] oil – Rabbi Aqiva says, An eighth; and of any other fruits, Abba Saul says, Sufficient for him to sell and to buy food for two meals [with the proceeds].

6. This measure [applies equally] to *Kohanim*, Levites and Israelites. If [the landowner] was retaining some [of the crop for his poor relatives], he may withhold half and distribute half. If he had only a little,[11] he may place it before [the poor] and let them share it among themselves.

7. An itinerant poor person should be given not less than a loaf worth a *dupondium* when [flour] is four *seahs* for a *sela*.[12] If he [wishes to] remain overnight he should be given what he needs for an overnight stay; if over Shabbat he should be given food for three meals.

   If anyone has food [enough] for two meals, he should not take from the soup kitchen. If he has food for fourteen meals, he should not take from the [weekly charity] fund; the fund is collected by two and distributed by three.[13]

8. If anyone has 200 *zuz*[14] [in cash], he should not take *leqet*,

---

11. i.e. not enough to distribute the recommended quantities to each of the poor.
12. A quarter-*kab* loaf.
13. To ensure that it is seen to be honest and fair.
14. The amount of money deemed sufficient for a year's maintenance.

shikh'ḥa, pe'ah or the poor tithe. If he is one denarius short [of the 200 *zuz*], then even if a thousand people simultaneously give him [a denarius], he may accept.

He is not obliged to sell his home or the tools of his trade.[15]

9. If anyone has 50 *zuz* with which to trade he should not take [poor benefits].

Whoever has no need but takes will not depart this world until he becomes dependent on others. Whoever is in need but does not take will not depart this world until he is in a position to support others, and of such a one Scripture says, BLESSED IS HE WHO TRUSTS IN THE LORD, WHOSE TRUST IS IN THE LORD ALONE (Jeremiah 17:7 JPS). The same [applies to] a judge who issues correct verdicts in truth and integrity.

Whoever is not blind or lame but pretends to be [in order to get charity] will not die of old age until he has become so, as it is said, JUSTICE, JUSTICE SHALL YOU PURSUE (Deuteronomy 16:20). [Likewise,] any judge who accepts bribes and perverts judgement will not die of old age until his eyes dim, as it is said, DO NOT TAKE BRIBES, FOR BRIBES BLIND THE CLEAR-SIGHTED AND UPSET THE PLEAS OF THOSE WHO ARE IN THE RIGHT (Exodus 23:8 JPS).

15. Even if he owns a house and tools worth more, he may claim benefits provided his liquid assets are less than 200 *zuz*.

THIRD TRACTATE
DEMAI (DOUBTFULLY TITHED PRODUCE)

Ancient Israelite society depended on a priesthood supported by tithes. Although by late Second Temple times the economic structure of Palestine had changed radically from that envisaged in the Torah, some forms of tithing remained widespread. A form of fellowship developed among Pharisees to strengthen the observance of the laws of tithing and of ritual purity; this played a significant role in the formation of Rabbinic Judaism.[1] There were two levels: a person might establish himself as trustworthy (ne'eman) in respect of tithing only, or in respect of both tithing and ritual purity. Members of the fellowship were known as ḥaverim (friends, associates), in distinction from 'amé ha-aretz (people of the land, i.e. 'ordinary' people).

A procedure for induction is hinted at in Chapter Two and more fully developed in Tosefta;[2] perhaps it was something like the procedures described in the 'Rule of the Community' in the Dead Sea Scrolls.

When a man took on the responsibilities of a ḥaver, his family and servants were expected to commit themselves as well, in his presence; should he subsequently marry a woman from a family of 'amé ha-aretz, he would be responsible for her acceptance.[3]

While initiation rites for the privileged few were common in the 'mystery cults' popular in the Roman Empire at the time,

1. See Neusner, *Fellowship* and Oppenheimer, *'Am ha-aretz*. For definitions of *'am ha-aretz*, see Tosefta *Avoda Zara* 3:10; *Berakhot* 47b; *Sota* 21b–22a; *Gittin* 61a.
2. Tosefta *Demai* 2:14 (Lieberman edition) is explicit: 'One who accepts [the obligations of the *ḥaver*] in the presence of the fellowship . . .'
3. Ibid. 2:16. Sarason, *History*, p. 91, translates as if the woman or servant formally accepts the new status; if this is correct, it would be in the presence of the husband or master, not before the assembled fellowship.

*fellowship of tithing- and purity-groups was open to all Jews who were prepared to accept their terms; members (*ḥaverim*) were expected to follow a normal lifestyle, differing from others only in their stricter adherence to the laws of tithing and ritual purity, their higher ethical standards and their devotion to Torah.*

This tractate gives the impression that some degree of social conflict arose between ḥaverim *and* 'amé ha-aretz; *the former looked down on the latter as neglectful of the divine commands, and the latter resented their 'holier-than-thou' attitude. The conflict finds an echo in the New Testament, where Jesus says: 'Woe to you scribes and Pharisees, hypocrites, for you tithe mint, dill and cumin and have neglected the weightier provisions of the law: justice, mercy and faithfulness. But these are the things you should have done without neglecting the others' (Matthew 23:23) – an assessment in agreement with that of the rabbis themselves (see 3:1 below). Here we are concerned with the practical arrangements instituted by* ḥaverim *to safeguard their own compliance with tithing law.*

Demai – *the word may derive from the Aramaic for 'perhaps' – is defined as produce of an* 'am ha-aretz. *Essentially, the problem of* demai *is social: how does a* ḥaver *interact with an* 'am ha-aretz? *He cannot be certain that food he receives from the* 'am ha-aretz, *whether in a social or a commercial context, has been tithed. Must he tithe it again? The* ḥaverim *decided that it was safe to assume that an* 'am ha-aretz *had set aside the* teruma *(priests'-due), since that was a matter for which the Torah imposed severe penalties and which in any case was a small amount, but not that he had tithed; therefore, the* ḥaver *has to tithe. However, since most* 'amé ha-aretz *did in fact tithe, the requirement to tithe again might be relaxed where either (a) the law on tithing was not stringent, or (b) there was special need, such as hospitality for guests.*

CHAPTER ONE

1. The [foods treated most] leniently in [respect of] *demai* are wild figs, the fruit of the Christ's-thorn jujube,[4] sorbus fruits, white figs, sycamore fruits, dates unripened on the tree, late grapes and caperberries; in Judaea also the sumach[-fruit], Judaean vinegar and coriander.[5] Rabbi Judah says, Wild figs are exempt except for those that bear twice a year; jujube fruits are exempt except for those that come from Shiqmona; sycamore fruits are exempt except for those that ripen fully on the tree.
3. If someone buys [produce] for seed or for cattle-fodder, flour for [tanning] hides, oil for lighting or for polishing utensils, he is exempt from [tithing as] *demai.*

    Beyond K'ziv[6] one is exempt from *demai.*

    The *ḥalla* of an *'am ha-aretz*, any mixture containing *teruma*, food paid for with second-tithe money, and the remains of grain-offerings, are [all] exempt from *demai.*[7]

CHAPTER TWO

1. The following have to be tithed as *demai* everywhere: figs, dates, locust beans, rice and cumin. If anyone uses rice from outside the land [of Israel], it is exempt.
2. When someone undertakes to be trustworthy [in respect of tithes], he must tithe what he eats, what he sells and what he buys, and must not accept hospitality from an *'am ha-aretz.* Rabbi Judah says, One who accepts the hospitality of an

---

4. *Ziziphus spina-christi*, still a common plant in Israel. The Latin name with its reference to Jesus was given by mediaeval Christians to the plant known in Hebrew as *rim*.
5. These fruits listed are not normally cultivated, being of little value.
6. Ecdippa, on the northern border of the Land of Israel.
7. Details of these commodities can be found in the relevant tractates; there is no reason to suspect that an *'am ha-aretz* has somehow contaminated them.

'*am ha-aretz* [may be regarded as trustworthy; the other Sages] retorted, If he is not trustworthy for himself, how can others trust him?

3. When someone undertakes to be a *ḥaver*, he may not sell either liquid or dry [products] to an '*am ha-aretz*, nor may he purchase liquid [products] from him; he may not accept hospitality from an '*am ha-aretz*, nor offer him hospitality if clothed.[8] Rabbi Judah says, He should also not raise sheep and goats,[9] nor be given to vows or frivolity, nor defile himself for the dead, and he should attend to the needs of scholars in the House of Study; [the other Sages] replied, These matters are not relevant.

Charity and hospitality should not be allowed to suffer through zeal for tithing.

CHAPTER THREE

1. [A *ḥaver*] may give *demai* to the poor to eat or to [his] guests; Rabban Gamaliel used to give his workers *demai*. The School of Shammai say that the charity commissioners give what has been tithed to those [they know] will not tithe, and that which has not been tithed to those [they know] will tithe, so that everyone gets what is suitable; but the Sages say, They should distribute without discrimination, and whoever wishes to tithe may do so.

CHAPTER FOUR

1. If you buy fruit from someone who cannot be relied upon to tithe, and you forgot to tithe [and it is now the Sabbath], you may ask him on the Sabbath [whether he has tithed],

8. Clothes convey impurity.
9. Because it is difficult to prevent them from grazing on other people's crops.

and eat on the strength of his word;[10] [however,] once darkness has fallen at the end of the Sabbath you must tithe before eating. If you can't find him, but another person who is not trustworthy for tithes said that it had been tithed, you may eat on the strength of his word, but once darkness has fallen at the end of the Sabbath you must tithe before eating. Rabbi Simeon Shezuri says that even on a weekday you may question him about [a quantity of] levitical tithe which has fallen back into *demai* and eat on the strength of his word.

2. If someone places his friend under oath to eat with him,[11] but [the friend] does not trust him to tithe, [the friend] may eat with him on the first Sabbath [following his wedding][12] despite not trusting him to tithe, provided that he assures him that he has tithed. On the second Sabbath, however, he should not eat without tithing even if the host vows not to benefit from him[13] [in any way unless he partakes in the feast].

Chapters Six and Seven resolve awkward situations between tithers and non-tithers.

CHAPTER SIX

7. If two men, one who tithes and one who does not, harvested their grapes in the same vat, the tither should set aside tithe for his own, and also for the share of the non-tither wherever it may be.

8. If two men[, one who tithes and one who does not,] rented a field or inherited it or [owned it as] partners, [the tither] can say [to the non-tither], You take the wheat in such-and-such a location, and I [will take] the wheat in such-and-such a location, or You [take] the wine in such-and-such a

---

10. Tithing is not permitted on the Sabbath. An *'am ha-aretz* might tell a lie in the normal course of things, but would not do so on the Sabbath!

11. He swears to have nothing to do with him unless he attends the feast.

12. It would be extremely offensive to snub him on this occasion.

13. This form of vow was in effect a threat to break off relations.

location, and I [will take] the wine in such-and-such a
location; but he should not say, You take wheat and I [will
take] barley, or You take wine and I [will take] oil.

9. If a *ḥaver* and an *'am ha-aretz* inherited [land from] their
father, the *ḥaver* may say, You take the wheat in such-and-
such a location, and I [will take] the wheat in such-and-such
a location, or You [take] the wine in such-and-such a location, and I [will take] the wine in such-and-such a location;
but he should not say, You take wheat and I [will take]
barley, or You take the liquid and I [will take] the dry.

10. If a proselyte and an idolater inherited their father's [estate],
[the proselyte] may say [to the idolater], You take the idols
and I will take money, You [take] wine and I [will take]
fruit; but if [the estate] has already come into the possession
of the proselyte, this is forbidden.

FOURTH TRACTATE
KIL'AYIM (MIXTURES)

This tractate elaborates several biblical verses that forbid mixtures of one sort or another:

YOU SHALL NOT LET YOUR CATTLE MATE WITH A DIFFERENT KIND; YOU SHALL NOT SOW YOUR FIELD WITH TWO KINDS OF SEED; YOU SHALL NOT PUT ON CLOTH FROM A MIXTURE OF TWO KINDS OF MATERIAL. (Leviticus 19:19 JPS)

YOU SHALL NOT SOW YOUR VINEYARD WITH TWO KINDS OF SEED, ELSE THE CROP – FROM THE SEED YOU HAVE SOWN – AND THE YIELD OF THE VINEYARD ARE CONDEMNED.[1] (Deuteronomy 22:10)

YOU SHALL NOT PLOUGH WITH AN OX AND AN ASS TOGETHER. (Deuteronomy 22:10 JPS)

YOU SHALL NOT WEAR CLOTH COMBINING WOOL AND LINEN. (Deuteronomy 22:11 JPS)

The word kil'ayim *occurs in the Bible only in the context of these laws, three times in Leviticus 19:19 alone. It is a dual plural, perhaps cognate with Arabic* kilān, *'both'.*

Mishna does not speculate on the 'philosophy' of forbidden mixtures; its purpose is simply to translate the law into practical terms. Later authorities have made up for this. The Italian kabbalist Menaḥem Recanati (c. 1300) related these mitzvot *to the prohibition of witchcraft which mixes, that is, confuses, the*

---

1.   Literally, 'will be holy'; the expression may be a euphemism.

'spiritual powers' and thus controverts God's creation; the more ethically oriented German Rabbi Samson Raphael Hirsch (1808–88) thought that these mitzvot *taught respect for the purity of nature and care of the environment (he believed that God had created each species as we now find it).*

Mishna opens by establishing which pairs of plants or animals are considered to be of the same species, and hence may be 'mixed' because this is not cross-breeding. The system of classification does not coincide with that used in modern biology; 'species' (Hebrew: min*) should be understood in terms of gross appearance, function and names.*

It is not possible to identify all the plants and animals with certainty; where there is doubt I rely on Yehuda Feliks in his Ha-Tsomeaḥ *and* Mishnah Shevi'it; *where an item cannot be identified the Hebrew is left untranslated.*

CHAPTER ONE

1. Wheat and rye-grass are not *kil'ayim* one with the other;[2] barley and oats, spelt and rye, broad beans and French vetch, red crasspeas and grass-peas, hyacinth bean and Nile cowpea, are not *kil'ayim* one with the other.

2. Cucumber and melons are not *kil'ayim* one with the other; Rabbi Judah says they are *kil'ayim*. Lettuce and wild lettuce, chicory and wild chicory, leeks and wild leeks, coriander and wild coriander,[3] mustard and white mustard, calabash[4] and roasting calabash, cowpea and locust bean, are not *kil'ayim* one with the other.

3. Turnips and rape, kale and *trubtor*,[5] beet and sorrel, are not

2. i.e. they are not considered separate species; rye-grass is merely a degenerate form of wheat.

3. Feliks, *Ha-Tsomeaḥ*, observing that all coriander was wild, suggests that the second plant is *Bifora testiculata*, which lacks an English name.

4. Or 'gourd', but often translated as 'pumpkin', to which it is closely related. Pumpkins, however, were a post-Columbus American introduction to the Old World.

5. 'A slim (thin-leaved?) cabbage' – Talmud Yerushalmi.

kil'ayim one with the other. Rabbi Aqiva added, Garlic and rocambole ['Spanish garlic'], onions and shallots, lupins and yellow lupins, are not *kil'ayim* one with the other.

4. Among trees, pear and crustaminum pear, plum and hawthorn, are not *kil'ayim* one with the other. [However,] apple and Syrian pear, peach and almond, jujube and Christ's-thorn jujube are *kil'ayim* one with the other even though they resemble each other [and might be thought identical species].

5. Radishes and rape, mustard and field mustard, Greek with Egyptian or roasting calabash, are *kil'ayim* one with the other even though they resemble each other.

6. Wolf and dog, wild dog and fox, goat and deer, ibex and lamb, horse and mule, mule and donkey, donkey and onager, are *kil'ayim* one with the other even though they resemble each other.

7. One should not bring[6] tree on to tree, vegetable on to vegetable, tree on to vegetable or vegetable on to tree. Rabbi Judah permits vegetable on to tree.

8. One should not plant vegetables in the stump of a sycamore, nor rue on to trifoliate orange, since it is vegetable on to tree. One should not plant a shoot from a fig tree on to squill [even] in order to cool it.[7] A vine shoot should not be inserted in a melon for [the melon] to exude moisture into it, since this is tree into vegetable. Calabash seeds should not be placed in mallow to preserve it, since this is vegetable into vegetable.

9. If someone stores turnips and radishes under a vine, provided that some of the leaves [remain] exposed there is no need to worry that it might be *kil'ayim*, that it might be [growing in] the sabbatical year [or] that it might need tithing; and it may be lifted out on the Sabbath.

If someone sows wheat and barley together, that is *kil'ayim*. Rabbi Judah says, It is only *kil'ayim* if he sows [at least] two wheat [grains] and a [grain of] barley, or a [grain

6. The term is vague; it could cover grafting where that is applicable.
7. Alternatively, 'for shade'. The squill (*Urginea maritima*) is a bulb of the lily family used as an expectorant.

of] wheat and two barley [grains], or [a grain each of] wheat
and barley and spelt.

*What is meant by 'planting together'? It would be absurd to think
that a farmer should not, for instance, sow two different crops in
a field of several acres. Mishna focuses here on appearance; what
looks like a mixture of crops is forbidden, and what looks like
separate crops is permitted. The definition culminates in 3:1,
where consideration is given to the maximum number of different
plants that might be planted in a square plot six by six palms.*

*Chapter Three Mishna 5 states that 'whatever the Sages for-
bade was on account of appearance'. With this and associated
statements in mind Avery-Peck has argued that 'order, and with
it holiness, is not dependent on a pre-ordained, transcendent,
model. It is . . . a function of each Israelite's own desire to order,
and thereby sanctify, the world.'[8] This builds much on a weak
foundation. Mishna defines what is perceived as a vineyard or
a distinct area in a field, but this is to do with the psychology of
perception and does not imply any special Israelite mystique or
power of consecration; Israelites do not perceive field boundaries differently from other people.*

CHAPTER TWO

6. If somebody wants to plant plots of different species in his
   field, the School of Shammai say that he should leave a space
   three furrows wide[9] between [the plots], but the School of
   Hillel say he should leave [a space as wide as] the yoke [used
   to plough in] the Sharon; [these measures] are close to one
   another.
7. If the corner of a plot[10] of wheat penetrated [a plot of]
   barley, this is permissible, since it would be seen as the end
   of the [wheat] field[, rather than as a mixed sowing].

8. Avery-Peck, *Agriculture*, p. 141.
9. According to the Yerushalmi this would be a rectangle 6 cubits by 2.
10. Literally, 'the end of a row', or perhaps 'the end of a triangle'.

If his field was sown with wheat and his neighbour's with another kind [of crop], he may [sow] next to [his neighbour's field] the same kind [of crop his neighbour is growing, since that would look like the extension of his neighbour's field].

If he and his neighbour are both growing wheat, he may [nevertheless] sow a row of flax, though not any other kind [of crop], next to [his neighbour's field]. Rabbi Simeon says, There is no difference between flax and other crops. Rabbi Yosé says, He may test a row of flax even in the middle of his [own] field.

9. If someone wants to make his field a patchwork of different species, he may plant twenty-four patches in [a field of the area required to sow] a *seah* [of grain], each patch [being the area required to sow a] quarter-*kab* [of grain], and he may sow any crop he wishes in [the patches].

According to Rabbi Meir, if there were [just] one or two [bare] patches [in a field of grain], he may sow mustard in them, but not [if there were] three, since that would look like a field of mustard [and it would look as if he was growing a mixed field]; the [majority of] Sages say nine would be all right, but not ten. Rabbi Eliezer ben Jacob says, Even if the field was [as large as the area required to sow a quarter-*kur* [of grain], he should not grow more than one patch [of mustard] in it.

10. Whatever is in the quarter-*kab* area is counted in the measure. If a vine [has spread through it], or there is a grave or a rock, they count towards the quarter-*kab* area.

If he sows [one sort of] grain in [a field planted with another sort of] grain, he must leave a space [between them] of a quarter-*kab* area. If he sows [one sort of] vegetable in [a field planted with other] vegetables, six palms [suffices]. Grain among vegetables, or vegetables among grain, [require a space of] a quarter-*kab*; Rabbi Eliezer says, six palms [is sufficient] for vegetables in grain.

*Chapters Four to Seven deal with the special problems arising
in a vineyard (the crunch case is 5:5). Deuteronomy 22:10
states that if you sow your vineyard with two kinds of seed the
vineyard as well as the the crop is 'holy', that is, condemned,
put beyond use. How far does this ban extend? The Schools rule
that planting in the vicinity of a vineyard is permissible only if
(a) enough room is left to till the vine and (b) sufficient is planted
to constitute a 'field', that is, a distinct crop. This leaves their
successors at Yavné and Usha to define what constitutes a 'vineyard' as distinct from a random planting of vines – how close
must the individual vines be, and what is the minimum number
that constitutes a vineyard.*

*Chapter Six deals with a trellis, Seven with layering, grafting,
and accidental intrusion of a vine into a vegetable plot. In
Chapter Eight Mishna sets the limits of 'mixing' of plants and
of ploughing with various animals.*

CHAPTER FOUR

1. The School of Shammai say, [If there is] a bare patch sixteen
   cubits wide in a vineyard, [you may sow other crops there];
   the School of Hillel say, Twelve cubits. What is 'a bare patch
   in a vineyard'? If [the bare patch is] less than sixteen cubits
   wide, you should not bring other seed there; if there are
   sixteen cubits you must give the vine enough space for
   tillage,[11] and then you may sow the rest.
2. What is a 'bare surround'? If there are less than twelve
   cubits [between the vine and a fence], you should not bring
   other seed there; if there are twelve cubits, you must give
   the vine enough space for tillage, and then you may sow the
   rest.

---

11. That is, four cubits adjoining the vine on each side of the bare patch, to allow
     oxen to draw a plough or cart.

CHAPTER FIVE

5. If someone plants vegetables in a vineyard, or maintains
them there, he condemns forty-five vines. When does this
apply? If the vines are planted four or five cubits apart. If
[the vines] were planted six or seven cubits apart, [the vegetables put beyond use everything] within sixteen cubits,
measured in a circle rather than a square.[12]

CHAPTER SIX

1. It is forbidden to sow, to maintain and to derive any benefit
from [the product of] mixed seeds in the vineyard. Mixed
seeds [elsewhere] may not be sown or maintained, but it is
permitted to eat [the product], and certainly to derive benefit
from it. Mixed material[13] in garments is permitted in all
[these] ways; only wearing it is forbidden. Crossbred animals
may be nurtured and kept; only [actually] breeding them is
forbidden. Crossbred animals may not be crossed with one
another.

2. Farm animal with farm animal, wild with wild, farm with
wild, wild with farm, unclean[14] with unclean, clean with
clean, unclean with clean, clean with unclean – it is forbidden to plough, to draw [a wagon] or to lead [together].

*Mishna rules that the driver and anyone who rides in the wagon
are equally culpable (disputed by Rabbi Meir); it then reviews
methods of hitching animals to vehicles, and discusses which
species certain animals belong to.*

12. A circle of 16 cubits diameter would enclose 45 vines spaced 4 cubits apart. The
commentators offer ingenious explanations as to why 45 vines would be rendered
forbidden if they were planted 5 cubits apart, seeing that a circle of 16 cubits
diameter would not enclose that many.
13. Wool and linen, as in the next chapter.
14. 'Unclean' in the sense of 'forbidden to eat', as in Leviticus 11.

CHAPTER NINE

1. Wool and linen are the only materials [forbidden to wear together as] *kil'ayim*. Wool and linen are [likewise] the only materials susceptible to defilement by plague. *Kohanim* wear wool and linen [together] to serve in the Temple.

   If someone mixed camels' wool with lambs' wool, if the majority was camels' wool it may [be worn with linen], but if the majority was lambs' wool it is forbidden, and if there were [exactly] equal quantities of each it is forbidden.

8. Only [material] which has been combed, spun and woven is forbidden as *kil'ayim*, as it is said, YOU SHALL NOT WEAR SHA'ATNEZ (Deuteronomy 22:11) – [that is,] anything which is *shu'a* (smooth, i.e. combed out), *tavui* (spun) and *nuz* (woven).[15]

---

15. Mishna interprets the obscure word *sha'atnez* as an acrostic. There is considerable doubt as to the meaning of *nuz*.

FIFTH TRACTATE
SHEVI'IT
(THE SEVENTH YEAR)

Three biblical passages drive this tractate:

SIX YEARS YOU SHALL SOW YOUR LAND AND GATHER IN ITS YIELD; BUT IN THE SEVENTH YEAR YOU SHALL LET IT REST AND LIE FALLOW. LET THE NEEDY AMONG YOUR PEOPLE EAT OF IT, AND WHAT THEY LEAVE LET THE WILD BEASTS EAT. YOU SHALL DO THE SAME WITH YOUR VINEYARDS AND YOUR OLIVE GROVES. (Exodus 23:10–11 JPS)

THE LORD SPOKE TO MOSES ON MOUNT SINAI: SPEAK TO THE ISRAELITE PEOPLE AND SAY TO THEM: WHEN YOU ENTER THE LAND THAT I ASSIGN TO YOU, THE LAND SHALL OBSERVE A SABBATH OF THE LORD. SIX YEARS YOU MAY SOW YOUR FIELD AND SIX YEARS YOU MAY PRUNE YOUR VINEYARD AND GATHER IN THE YIELD. BUT IN THE SEVENTH YEAR THE LAND SHALL HAVE A SABBATH OF COMPLETE REST: YOU SHALL NOT SOW YOUR FIELD OR PRUNE YOUR VINEYARD. YOU SHALL NOT REAP THE AFTERGROWTH OF YOUR HARVEST OR GATHER THE GRAPES OF YOUR UNTRIMMED VINES; IT SHALL BE A YEAR OF COMPLETE REST FOR THE LAND. BUT YOU MAY EAT WHATEVER THE LAND DURING ITS SABBATH WILL PRODUCE – YOU, YOUR MALE AND FEMALE SLAVES, THE HIRED AND BOUND LABOURERS WHO LIVE WITH YOU, AND YOUR CATTLE AND THE BEAST IN YOUR LAND MAY EAT ALL ITS YIELD. (Leviticus 25:1–7 JPS)

EVERY SEVENTH YEAR YOU SHALL PRACTISE REMISSION OF DEBTS. THIS SHALL BE THE NATURE OF THE REMISSION: EVERY CREDITOR SHALL REMIT THE DUE THAT HE CLAIMS FROM HIS FELLOW; HE

SHALL NOT DUN HIS FELLOW OR KINSMAN, FOR THE REMISSION
PROCLAIMED IS OF THE LORD. YOU MAY DUN THE FOREIGNER; BUT
YOU MUST REMIT WHATEVER IS DUE YOU FROM YOUR KINSMEN.
(Deuteronomy 15:1–3 JPS)

Other biblical references to the sabbatical year include Leviticus 26:34–5, which decrees national exile as a punishment for
its neglect, and Jeremiah 34:8–22, which castigates the upper
classes of Judah for failure to free their slaves in accordance
with the 'covenant of [their] fathers'. The Jubilee Year (Leviticus
25:8–16), marking the end of seven sabbatical cycles, does not
figure in the Mishna of this tractate.

Nehemiah (10:32) records the post-Exilic community's commitment to suspend agricultural work during the seventh year
and to remit debts; 1 Maccabees (6:49, 53–4) and Josephus
(Antiquities 11:338; 13:228–35; 14:202 and 14:475) confirm
observance of the sabbatical year in the late Second Temple
period. Josephus claims that Alexander the Great and Julius
Caesar exempted Jews from taxes in the sabbatical year, a privilege abolished in the wake of the Bar Kokhba Revolt. He also
indicates (Antiquities 14:475) that the year 37 BCE was a
sabbatical year; on this basis the first sabbatical year of the
current millennium would have been 2000/2001, a result consistent with current Orthodox practice.

Tosefta, followed by both Talmudim,[1] states that the opening
Mishna is not applicable, since 'Rabban Gamaliel and his court',
i.e. Gamaliel III,[2] rejected the ruling of the Schools and permitted ploughing throughout the sixth year. Mishna nevertheless continues with detailed definitions of a 'field of trees' and
of a 'white field', i.e. a field of grain or pulses, and it cites

---

1. Yerushalmi *Shevi'it* 1:1 and Bavli *Mo'ed Qatan* 3b–4a. Rav Ashi's surmise (*Mo'ed
    Qatan* 4a) that the ruling of the Schools was applicable only in Temple times,
    and that Gamaliel was therefore able to relax it, is followed by later authorities
    such as Maimonides (*Mishneh Torah: Shemita v'Yovel* 3:1).
2. So Feliks, *Yerushalmi*, p. 22, citing some earlier authorities, and David Rothkopff
    (*Encyclopedia Judaica* article on Sabbatical Year and Jubilee). Most commentators
    assume that Gamaliel II, of Yavné, is meant, but this raises the question of why
    Yavneans continued to elaborate the ruling of the Schools.

elaborations of the ruling of the Schools by rabbis of Yavné and Usha.

CHAPTER ONE

1. How long may you continue to plough in a field of trees in the year preceding the seventh year? The School of Shammai say, For as long as it is beneficial for [that year's] fruit; the School of Hillel say, Until Pentecost; these [times] are close to one another.
2. What [constitutes] 'a field of trees'? Wherever there are three trees to a *bet seah*, each capable of producing [the equivalent of] a cake of dried figs [weighing] sixty Italian[3] *maneh*, you may plough the whole field for their benefit; if there is less than that [amount], you may plough around [each tree] the distance [required for] a fig harvester and his basket.
3. There is no difference whether the trees are fruit-bearing or non fruit-bearing – if[, were they figs,] they would each be capable of producing a cake of dried figs [weighing] sixty Italian *maneh*, you may plough the whole field for their benefit; if the quantity is less than that, you may plough around [each tree] only as much as it needs.[4]

CHAPTER TWO

1. How long may you continue to plough a white field[5] in the year preceding the seventh year? For as long as [the soil] remains moist enough [from the winter rains] for people to plough for planting cucumbers and gourds. Rabbi Simeon says, In that case it would be up to each individual to decide

3. 'Italy of Greece', i.e. Magna Graecia, or southern Italy.
4. i.e. the distance [required for] a fig harvester and his basket.
5. i.e. a field of grain or pulses.

the law; [rather, you may plough] a field of trees until Pentecost and a white field until Passover.

6. You may not plant, graft or layer within thirty days of the New Year [festival] of the seventh year.[6] If anyone did plant, graft or layer [in that period], he must uproot it. Rabbi Judah says, A graft that does not take within three days will not take; Rabbi Yosé and Rabbi Simeon say, Two weeks.

Several jobs a person might legitimately do in his field in the sabbatical year could appear to the onlooker as agricultural work. He might, for instance, want to clear parts of the field to pen his sheep, or to gather sticks for fuel or to quarry stones for building; all of these incidentally improve the field, though that is not his primary intention. Mishna draws a fine line between what would and would not mislead others, or what could be used as 'cover' for forbidden activities.

CHAPTER THREE

4. If someone wishes to convert his field into pens [for his animals], he should fence off an area of two *seahs*. [When that is full of dung,] he should move three of the partitions [to form a pen in the adjoining area], leaving the one in the middle, so that altogether he uses an area of four *seahs*; Rabban Simeon ben Gamaliel says, [He may use] an area of eight *seahs*. If his whole field is [only] four *seahs*, he should leave a little [unpenned] in order to avoid any appearance [of intending to manure his field]. [When this is finished, he must] remove [the dung] from the enclosure and heap it up in his field in the ways [permitted to] those who [store] manure.[7]

---

6. This is to ensure that the plant or layer rooted, or the graft took hold, before the sabbatical year started.

7. This was dealt with earlier in the chapter; manure has to be stored in such a way that it does not appear that the farmer is fertilizing his field in the sabbatical year.

CHAPTER FOUR

1. At first they said that a man might gather sticks, stones or grass from his field, just as he might from anyone else's, the larger ones first. When sinners increased in number, [the Sages] ordained that you might gather [only] from someone else's field, and only if this is done without consideration, and certainly without arranging food as payment.[8]

YOU MAY EAT WHATEVER THE LAND DURING ITS SABBATH WILL PRODUCE (Leviticus 25:6). *The emphasis is on 'eat' – you may not use the produce for a different purpose, nor pick it when it is unripe.*

7. When may you eat fruit [that has grown of its own accord] in the seventh year? As soon as the young figs turn red, you may eat them with your bread in the field; when they are fully ripe, you may take them into the house [to eat]. Likewise, in other years, this is the time at which they must be tithed.

8. When the young grapes [first develop] juice, you may eat them with your bread in the field; when they are fully ripe, you may take them into the house [to eat]. Likewise, in other years, this is the time at which they must be tithed.

The laws of the sabbatical year, other than the remission of debts, apply fully only in the Land of Israel, but were extended by the rabbis to some contiguous regions such as 'Syria';[9] this may have been to discourage people from migrating in order to evade the sabbatical obligations.

8. The Yerushalmi explains that though in principle there is no reason why a person should not gather sticks in the sabbatical year if he needs them, some people abused this as 'cover' for preparing the field for sowing; they would be unlikely to prepare a neighbour's field for sowing without reciprocation or payment.

9. 'Syria' includes parts of modern Lebanon and Syria.

CHAPTER SIX

1. There are three regions for the seventh year. In those parts of the Land of Israel resettled by the returnees from Babylon,[10] as far [north-east] as K'ziv [Ecdippa], [produce] is not eaten and [the land] not cultivated. In the areas taken by those who came up from Egypt[11] [but which were not resettled by the returnees from Babylon], from K'ziv to the River, and to Amana, [produce] may be eaten but [the land] may not be cultivated. From the River and Amana inland, [produce] may be eaten and [the land] may be cultivated.
2. In Syria they may work on harvested [crops],[12] but not on what is still in the ground. They may thresh, winnow, tread and make sheaves, but not reap, nor harvest grapes and figs.

CHAPTER SEVEN

1. [The Sages] laid down a general principle regarding the seventh year: [the sanctity of] the seventh year applies to anything that is food for people or animals, or is a dyestuff, and that does not keep [if left] in the ground, [as well as to] what has been received in exchange for them; [all these] must be removed.

   What is [included in this category]? Wild ginger leaves, skale-fern fronds, chicory, leeks, purslane and orchid; of animal fodder, thistles and thorns, and of dyestuffs the aftergrowth of woad, and safflower. [All] these and what is exchanged for them are subject to the law of the seventh year, and they and what is exchanged for them[13] must be removed [at the proper time].

10. In the time of Ezra and Nehemiah.
11. In the time of Moses.
12. That is, even with people who are suspected of cultivating their fields in the seventh year.
13. Money paid or goods bartered.

2. And they laid down another general principle: [The sanctity of] the seventh year applies to anything that is food[14] for people or animals, or is a dyestuff, and that does keep [if left] in the ground[, as well as to] what has been received in exchange for them; but [these] things need not be removed.

What is [included in this category]? Wild ginger root, and the root of skale-fern, heliotrope, orchid and *bokhriya*;[15] of dyestuffs, *Rubia tinctorum*, dyer's reseda. [All] these and what is exchanged for them are subject to the law of the seventh year, but neither they nor what is exchanged for them need be removed [since they keep in the ground, and therefore remain available in the wild]. Rabbi Meir said, What is exchanged for them must be removed by the New Year; they replied, They themselves need not be removed, how much less need what is exchanged for them be removed!

CHAPTER EIGHT

2. [Produce of] the seventh year is for eating, drinking and anointing; [that is,] for eating that which is normally eaten, drinking that which is normally drunk, and anointing with that which is normally used as ointment; you may not anoint with wine or vinegar, but [only] with oil. The same applies to *teruma* and second tithe, but the seventh year is more lenient in that its oil may be used also for lighting.[16]

YOU, AND YOUR CATTLE AND THE BEAST IN YOUR LAND MAY EAT ALL ITS YIELD (Leviticus 25:1–7). *Fruit which grows in the sabbatical year may be eaten only for as long as it is available to 'the beast in your land'; any that remains must be 'removed' by the time that species no longer grows wild. The date for* bi'ur *(removal) varies by species and region.*

14. Mishna reads 'that is not food', but this appears to be an error. I have followed Maimonides' reading.
15. Uncertain; possibly spikenard.
16. Whereas *teruma* and second tithe oil may not be used for lighting.

CHAPTER NINE

2. There are three regions for *bi'ur*, Judah, Transjordan and Galilee, and each of these [is divided into] three districts. [Galilee is divided into] Upper Galilee, Lower Galilee and the valley. From K'far Ḥanania upwards, where sycamores do not grow, is Upper Galilee; below K'far Ḥanania, where sycamores grow, is Lower Galilee; the valley is [the area] around Tiberias.

   In Judah, [the three regions are] the mountain, the lowland and the valley. The lowland of Lydda is like the southern lowland, and the adjoining hills are like the King's Hill. From Bet Ḥoron to the Mediterranean is one district.

3. Why did they say three regions [rather than nine districts]? So that people could eat in each [region] until there was no more [growing in any of its districts].

   Rabbi Simeon said, Only Judah was divided into three districts; all other regions were like the King's Hill.

   All regions are [counted] as one for olives and dates.[17]

Jewish society in first- and second-century Palestine was more dependent on commerce than that envisaged in Leviticus and Deuteronomy. To enable commercial credit, Hillel devised the prosbul, *under the terms of which a debt might be placed, before the seventh year, in the hands of the court for collection; then, like a fine owing to the court, it would not be remitted in the seventh year.* Prosbul *is the Greek* prosbolē *or* pros boulēn, *'before the council'.*

CHAPTER TEN

1. The seventh year brings about remission of debts, whether documented or not. It does not cancel credit extended by a

---

17. That is, you could continue eating olives and dates so long as any grew wild in any part of the country.

shopkeeper, but if [the shopkeeper] had [converted the debt to] a loan, [the seventh year] remits it. Rabbi Judah says, It cancels one by one.[18]

It does not cancel wages due. Rabbi Yosé says, It cancels wages stipulated for work forbidden in the seventh year.

3. It does not cancel debts [incurred under the terms of a] *prosbul*. This is something Hillel instituted; when he saw that people refrained from lending to one another and so transgressed the words of the Torah, BEWARE LEST YOU HARBOUR THE BASE THOUGHT, 'THE SEVENTH YEAR, THE YEAR OF REMISSION, IS COMING', SO THAT YOU ARE MEAN TO YOUR NEEDY KINSMAN AND GIVE HIM NOTHING ... (Deuteronomy 15:9 JPS), he instituted the *prosbul*.

4. The essence of the *prosbul* is: I transfer to you, so-and-so, judges in such-and-such a place, all debts owing to me, so that I can collect them whenever I please. The judges or witnesses sign below.

8. If someone wants to repay a debt [owing to you] in the seventh year, you should say, I release it! If he insists, you may accept, as it is said, THIS SHALL BE THE WORD[19] OF THE REMISSION (Deuteronomy 15:2). The same applies to a manslayer who has been exiled to a city of refuge; if the people of the town wish to honour him, he should say, I have slain a man; if they insist, he may accept, as it is said, THIS IS THE WORD CONCERNING THE MANSLAYER (Deuteronomy 19:4).

9. If someone repays a debt in the seventh year, the Sages[20] are pleased with him. If someone borrows from a proselyte whose children converted with him, he is not obliged to repay the children [after the death of their father], but if he

---

18. If someone bought on credit, and before paying bought more on credit from the same shopkeeper, the first debt has become a loan and is cancelled by the sabbatical year; these opinions of Rabbi Judah and Rabbi Yosé were rejected.

19. This is literal. The more idiomatic translation given in the introductory note is 'nature'.

20. Literally, 'the spirit of the Sages'.

does repay the Sages are pleased with him. Chattels are acquired [only] when [the buyer] moves them, but the Sages are pleased with anyone who abides by his word.[21]

21. That is, do not go back on your word once you have agreed a bargain, even though technically the sale has not been completed.

SIXTH TRACTATE
TERUMOT
(HEAVE OFFERINGS)

*THIS THEN SHALL BE THE PRIESTS'-DUE FROM THE PEOPLE:
EVERYONE WHO OFFERS A SACRIFICE, WHETHER AN OX OR A
SHEEP, MUST GIVE THE SHOULDER, THE CHEEKS AND THE
STOMACH TO THE PRIEST. YOU SHALL ALSO GIVE HIM THE FIRST-
FRUITS OF YOUR NEW GRAIN AND WINE AND OIL, AND THE FIRST
SHEARING OF YOUR SHEEP.* (Deuteronomy 18:3–4 JPS)

These 'first-fruits' are known as teruma.[1] *The word means
'that which is raised' – or, as in modern Hebrew, 'contribution'
(cf. the English idiom 'to raise money'); a common English
translation is 'heave-offering'. The receiving* Kohen *need not be
a functioning Temple priest – any male descendant of Aaron in
the male line qualifies, as do his wife and dependants.*

Teruma *possessed sacred status. People who were not*
Kohanim *or not in a state of purity were strictly forbidden to
consume it; if the food became unclean it was not to be eaten.*

Teruma *remained in practice after Temple times. The second-
century Rabbi Tarfon, reproached by Gamaliel II for his
absence from the House of Study, excused himself on the
grounds that he was 'performing [priestly] service', i.e. eating*
teruma.[2]

---

1.   First-fruits proper are dealt with in *Bikkurim*.
2.   *Pesaḥim* 72b–73a.

CHAPTER FOUR

3. The quantity of *teruma*: A generous [person gives] a fortieth[3] [of the crop]; the School of Shammai say, a thirtieth. The average is a fiftieth; a sixtieth is niggardly. If someone set aside *teruma* and found [he had separated only] a sixtieth, it is [valid] *teruma*, and he does not need to set aside [any more as] *teruma*. If he found it was [only] one part in sixty-one, it is [valid] *teruma*, but he must set aside [more] *teruma* [to make up] his usual quantity by measure, weight and number. Rabbi Judah says, [This additional *teruma*] may be taken even from produce which does not adjoin [the main crop].

What happens if teruma *falls into unconsecrated food? What happens if impure* teruma *falls into pure? In general, if the quantity that falls in is less than one part in a hundred, it may be ignored, but there are many complex situations where the law is less clear. The rules on handling mixtures are of wide application, since they affect also everyday matters such as kosher and non-kosher food.*

CHAPTER FIVE

5. If a *seah* of *teruma* fell into a hundred [*seahs* of unconsecrated food], and then he took some of the mixture and it fell into some other [food], Rabbi Eliezer says, [The mixture] contaminates as if it was [all] real *teruma*, but the Sages say, It contaminates only in proportion [to the quantity of actual *teruma* it contains].

6. If a *seah* of *teruma* fell into less than a hundred [*seahs* of unconsecrated food] so that [the mixture] was contaminated, and some of the mixture fell into some other [food], Rabbi Eliezer says, [The mixture] contaminates as if it was [all]

3. The Yerushalmi derives this figure from Ezekiel 45:13.

real *teruma*, but the Sages say, It contaminates only in proportion [to the quantity of actual *teruma* it contains].

Contaminated food contaminates only in proportion; leaven makes leaven only in proportion; drawn water invalidates a *miqvé* only in proportion.

SEVENTH TRACTATE
MA'ASEROT (TITHES)

The tithe primarily dealt with in this tractate is Ma'aser Rishon (first tithe), designated for Levites, but the rules regarding liability apply to tithes generally:

AND TO THE LEVITES I HEREBY GIVE ALL THE TITHES IN ISRAEL AS THEIR SHARE IN RETURN FOR THE SERVICES THAT THEY PERFORM, THE SERVICES OF THE TENT OF MEETING. HENCEFORTH, ISRAELITES SHALL NOT TRESPASS ON THE TENT OF MEETING, AND THUS INCUR GUILT AND DIE; ONLY LEVITES SHALL PERFORM THE SERVICES OF THE TENT OF MEETING; OTHERS WOULD INCUR GUILT. IT IS THE LAW FOR ALL TIME THROUGHOUT THE AGES. BUT THEY SHALL HAVE NO TERRITORIAL SHARE AMONG THE ISRAELITES; FOR IT IS THE TITHES SET ASIDE BY THE ISRAELITES AS A GIFT TO THE LORD THAT I GIVE TO THE LEVITES AS THEIR SHARE. THEREFORE I HAVE SAID CONCERNING THEM: THEY SHALL HAVE NO TERRITORIAL SHARE AMONG THE ISRAELITES. (Numbers 18:21–4 JPS)

CHAPTER ONE

1. [The Sages] formulated a general rule for tithes: Whatever is edible, belongs to someone and grows from the ground is liable for tithing.

   And they formulated another general rule: Whatever is

edible to start with and edible later on[1] is liable for tithing both small and large, even though it is kept in order to increase [the amount] for eating. However, if it is not edible to start with but becomes edible later on, it is not liable for tithing until it becomes edible.

2. At what stage does fruit become liable for tithing? Figs as soon as they begin to ripen; grapes and wild grapes when the pips become visible; the sumach, berries and all red [fruit] when they redden; pomegranates when they soften; dates when they show [cracks like rising] dough; peaches when 'veins' appear; walnuts when the nut separates [from the husk]. Rabbi Judah says, Both walnuts and almonds [become liable for tithing] when the shell hardens.

Mishna defines stages of ripening for other fruits and vegetables, then considers a second stage, the 'harvest'. Prior to harvest, even though the fruit has reached the point at which it may be tithed, it is permissible to eat it casually without actually tithing; after harvest, casual consumption is forbidden.

5. What is 'harvest' with regard to tithing? For cucumbers and gourds it is when they lose their hairiness; if they don't lose their hairiness, it is when they are [gathered into] a heap. For melons it is when they lose their hairiness; if they don't lose their hairiness, it is when they are spread out [to dry]. For those vegetables that are bundled, it is when they are bundled; if they are not bundled, it is when he fills a container [with them]; if he doesn't fill a container, it is when he has gathered all he needs; [if he gathers them into] a basket, it is when he covers it [with leaves]; if he doesn't cover it, it is when he has filled the basket; if he doesn't fill the basket, it is when he has gathered all he needs.

[In what circumstances] does this apply? If he is taking [the produce] to market. If he is taking it home, he may eat [of it] casually until he arrives home.

---

1.   Literally, 'eaten at the end'; Mishna has in mind vegetables such as spinach which may be eaten at all stages of their growth.

*Similar rules are laid down for other crops and circumstances.
Even if a crop has not been fully harvested there are actions
which may 'fix' it for tithing, so that the person who has performed those actions would have to tithe even before eating
casually; illustrations are given for the application of these rules.
Mishna 2:7 alludes to Deuteronomy 23:25–6, where the right
of workers to help themselves to the crop on which they are
working is established;[2] it shows how the rabbis handle a potential conflict of law between workers' rights and the religious
duty of tithing.*

CHAPTER TWO

5. If someone says to his friend, 'Here is an *issar*, give me five
   figs for it', he must tithe before eating them. This is Rabbi
   Meir's opinion, but Rabbi Judah says, If he eats them one
   by one he need not [tithe], but if he puts them together he
   must. Rabbi Judah said, There was a rose garden in Jerusalem where figs were sold at three or four to the *issar*, and
   neither *teruma* nor tithe was ever set aside from them.

7. If someone hired a worker to string[3] his figs, and [the worker
   stipulated,] 'On condition that I may eat figs', he may eat,
   and is exempt [from tithing]; if [he stipulated,] 'On condition that I and my household may eat', or 'On condition
   that my son may eat as my wages', he may eat, and is exempt
   [from tithing,] but his son must tithe what he eats. [If he
   says,] 'On condition that I may eat [both] during and after
   stringing', he may eat during stringing, and is exempt [from
   tithing], but after stringing he must tithe what he eats, for
   the Torah does not grant him a right to eat [except when
   he is working]. The rule is, when someone eats [on the basis
   of a right granted by] the Torah, he is exempt from tithing,
   but if he is not eating [on the basis granted by] the Torah
   he must tithe.

2. The biblical text itself does not restrict the right to workers.
3. Alternatively, to lay the figs out to dry.

CHAPTER FOUR

1. If someone preserves, pickles or salts [before harvesting], he must [tithe]. If he digs [produce] into the ground [to ripen], he is exempt [from tithing]. If he [merely] dips [the produce in salt to eat it] out in the field, he is exempt [from tithing]. If he crushes olives to get the bitterness out, he is exempt [from tithing]. If he presses olives on to his flesh, he is exempt [from tithing], but if he squeezes [the oil] into his hand, he must tithe. If someone scoops the scum [off fermenting wine] into a dish of food, he is exempt [from tithing], but if into an [empty] pot, he must tithe, since that is like a small vat.

CHAPTER FIVE

1. If someone pulls up plants in his [land] to replant them elsewhere in his own land, he is exempt [from tithing]. If he bought growing plants he is exempt. If he bought [plants] to send to his friend, he is exempt; [but] Rabbi Eleazar ben Azaria says, If similar things are sold in the market, they must be tithed.

EIGHTH TRACTATE
MA'ASER SHENI
(SECOND TITHE)

Ma'aser Sheni (second tithe) produce must be taken to Jerusalem and eaten there in purity. Alternatively, the tither may 'redeem' the tithe, that is, exchange it for money, which he then takes to Jerusalem and spends there on comestibles to be consumed as second tithe.

YOU SHALL SET ASIDE EVERY YEAR A TENTH PART OF ALL THE YIELD OF YOUR SOWING THAT IS BROUGHT FROM THE FIELD. YOU SHALL CONSUME THE TITHES OF YOUR NEW GRAIN AND WINE AND OIL, AND THE FIRSTLINGS OF YOUR HERDS AND FLOCKS, IN THE PRESENCE OF THE LORD YOUR GOD, IN THE PLACE WHERE HE WILL CHOOSE TO ESTABLISH HIS NAME, SO THAT YOU MAY LEARN TO REVERE THE LORD YOUR GOD FOREVER. SHOULD THE DISTANCE BE TOO GREAT FOR YOU, SHOULD YOU BE UNABLE TO TRANSPORT THEM, BECAUSE THE PLACE WHERE THE LORD YOUR GOD HAS CHOSEN TO ESTABLISH HIS NAME IS FAR FROM YOU AND BECAUSE THE LORD YOUR GOD HAS BLESSED YOU, YOU MAY CONVERT THEM INTO MONEY. WRAP UP THE MONEY AND TAKE IT WITH YOU TO THE PLACE THAT THE LORD YOUR GOD HAS CHOSEN, AND SPEND THE MONEY ON ANYTHING YOU WANT – CATTLE, SHEEP, WINE, OR OTHER INTOXICANT, OR ANYTHING YOU MAY DESIRE. AND YOU SHALL FEAST THERE, IN THE PRESENCE OF THE LORD YOUR GOD, AND REJOICE WITH YOUR HOUSEHOLD. (Deuteronomy 14:22–7 JPS)

CHAPTER ONE

1. You may not sell, pawn or exchange second tithe, nor weigh things against it, nor may you say to your friend [when you arrive] in Jerusalem, 'Here is [second-tithe] wine for you; give me oil', and the same applies with other kinds of produce. You may, however, make gifts to each other [of second-tithe produce].

2. You may not sell cattle [reserved as] tithe, whether unblemished and alive, or blemished and slaughtered, nor is [second tithe] valid to betroth a wife;[1] first-born cattle[, however,] may be sold unblemished and alive, or blemished and slaughtered, and are valid to betroth a wife.

   You may not redeem second tithe against blanks, or coins that are not in circulation, or coins not [currently] in your possession.

3. If you buy cattle for peace-offerings, or beasts[2] for eating[, with the proceeds of second tithe], the hide loses consecrated status,[3] even if there is more hide than meat.

   [Similarly,] in a place where wine is sold in sealed jars, the jars lose consecrated status.

   The shells of walnuts and almonds lose consecrated status.

   Wine that is fermenting may not be bought for second-tithe money, but when fermentation is complete it may be bought for second-tithe money.

5. If you [use second-tithe money to] buy water, salt, produce still attached to the ground, or produce that cannot reach Jerusalem, the tithe purchase is invalid. If you did this unwittingly,[4] the [goods and] money must be returned; if deliberately, the items must be taken and consumed in

1. An object used as a token of betrothal, in the way a ring is now used, must be the bridegroom's personal property, available for monetary transaction; since cattle tithe cannot be sold, it is disqualified for this purpose.
2. i.e. animals other than sheep, goats and oxen, and which therefore cannot be peace-offerings.
3. It loses the status of second tithe, and you need not redeem it to use the proceeds to buy food to consume in Jerusalem.
4. i.e. you did not realize that the money was second-tithe money.

[Jerusalem], and if there is no Temple, they must [be left to] rot.

7. You may not buy male and female slaves, land or 'unclean' animals with second-tithe money, but if you did, you must consume the corresponding value [of legitimate second-tithe produce in Jerusalem].

You may not bring the pairs of birds for male and female discharge or childbirth offerings,[5] nor sin-offerings or reparation-offerings, from second tithe,[6] but if you did, you must consume the corresponding value [of legitimate second-tithe produce in Jerusalem].

The rule is, if you purchased with second-tithe money anything that is not for personal consumption, you must consume the corresponding value [of legitimate second-tithe produce in Jerusalem].

CHAPTER TWO

1. Second tithe is for eating, drinking and anointing – eating what is normally eaten, drinking what is normally drunk, anointing what is normally used as ointment. You must not anoint with [second-tithe] wine or vinegar, only with oil. You must not add herbs and spices to the oil,[7] nor purchase spiced oil with second-tithe money, but you may add herbs and spices to wine.

If honey or spices fell into [the wine] and improved it, the increase in value is reckoned proportionately. [Likewise,] if fish was improved by being boiled with second-tithe peas, the increase in value is reckoned proportionately. [However,] if [second-tithe] dough was improved by baking, the increase in value is [credited] to the second [tithe only]. The rule is, if the [unconsecrated item that brought about]

---

5. See *Zavim* and *Qinnim*.
6. All these involve burnt offerings that are not consumed by the one who brings them.
7. Herbs soak up oil and so divert it from its 'normal' use.

the improvement [remains] detectable,[8] the increase in value is reckoned proportionately, but if not, it accrues to the second [tithe].

Any procedure that involves buying and selling must come up against the realities of the market. Much of the tractate is therefore devoted to preserving the interest of second tithe, i.e. ensuring that no loss is involved in its sale or purchase, or in the changing of money.

CHAPTER FOUR

1. If someone transports second-tithe produce from a place where it is expensive to a place where it is cheap, or from a place where it is cheap to a place where it is expensive, he must redeem it according to the local price [whether high or low]. If he brings produce from the barn into town, the profit accrues to the second [tithe], and [he must pay] the expenses out of his own pocket.

2. Second tithe is redeemed at the lower market price, [that is, at the price] the retailer pays rather than the price at which he sells; [likewise, second-tithe money] is exchanged at the rate the money-changer gives change for larger denominations rather than the rate at which he accepts small for large.

   Second tithe may not be redeemed by conjecture. If the price is definite, it may be redeemed [in the presence of] one witness. If the price is indefinite – if, for instance, a film has formed on the wine, the fruit is going off or the coins are rusty – it must be redeemed [in the presence of] three witnesses.

   If the owner himself redeems the produce he must pay an extra fifth (Leviticus 27:31). The next Mishna considers some consequences.

3. If the owner offers a *sela* [to redeem second tithe], and someone else offers a *sela*, the owner takes precedence, since

8.   Like spices in wine or peas in fish, but unlike firewood used in baking dough.

he must add a fifth. If the owner offers a *sela*, and someone else offers a *sela* plus one *issar*, the one who offers a *sela* plus an *issar* takes precedence, since he offers the higher principal[, even though the total amount is less].

When you redeem your second tithe, you must add a fifth [to the price], whether it was [originally] your own or whether you received it as a gift.

The final chapter takes up two new themes. Fruit of the vine may not be consumed for three years from the time of planting; in the fourth year it is 'hallowed' (Leviticus 19:24), and like maʿaser sheni *must be taken to Jerusalem and eaten in purity.*

CHAPTER FIVE

2. [Fruits of the] fourth-year vine are taken to Jerusalem from a day's journey [away] in any direction.[9] What are the limits? Eilat[10] to the south, Aqrabat to the north, Lydda to the west and the Jordan to the east. When there was an excess of fruit, they ruled that even fruit from near the wall [of Jerusalem] might be redeemed [rather than physically brought to the city]; this was on the understanding that they might revert to the original procedure whenever they wished. Rabbi Yosé says, [The ruling] was given after the destruction of the Temple, and the understanding was that the original procedure would be restored when the Temple was rebuilt. *Several paragraphs are devoted to the 'removal' of tithes in the third and sixth years of the sabbatical cycle, and the declaration that accompanies this (Deuteronomy 26:12–15). The tractate concludes with a wistful if obscure reflection on the suspension of part of the biblical procedure by John Hyrcanus (Yoḥanan the High Priest), c. 175–104 BCE. The tithe declaration was perhaps abolished since it was in the time of John Hyrcanus that*

9. Fruit from further afield would be redeemed, and the money brought to Jerusalem to be spent there appropriately.
10. A village some fifteen miles from Jerusalem, not Eilat on the shore of the Red Sea.

Kohanim *usurped the tithe that had previously been allotted to Levites; it would no longer be true to declare I HAVE GIVEN IT TO THE LEVITE.* Lieberman argued that the awakening call and the 'knocking' were both abolished because they appeared idolatrous. Egyptian priests commenced their daily worship with an invocation to the gods to awaken, so to address God with the words of Psalm 44:24 might have been misunderstood as implying that He slept; it was common practice among idolaters to stun the animal prior to slaughter, a practice which would cause a blemish and render it unfit for sacrifice according to Torah law, and to avoid confusion Yoḥanan stopped the earlier Jewish practice of 'knocking', that is, marking the head of the animal prior to slaughter.[11]

15. Yoḥanan the High Priest stopped the tithe declaration and abolished the awakening call and the knockers. Until his day hammers had been heard in Jerusalem and no one had to enquire about *demai*.

11.   Lieberman, *Hellenism*, pp. 139–43. On John Hyrcanus, see Neusner, *Rabbinic Traditions*, 1:160–76. Josephus writes of him in *Wars* 1:54f. and *Antiquities* 13. Abbaye (*Qiddushin* 66a) seems to confuse him with Alexander Yannai.

NINTH TRACTATE
ḤALLA
(DOUGH OFFERING)

The Hebrew word ḥalla is familiar now as 'challah', a plaited white bread loaf enriched with eggs, eaten by Jews at the Sabbath meal; this loaf originated in fifteenth-century Europe. Ḥalla in the Bible is a general word for loaf, or cake. In rabbinic terminology it denotes the gift set aside for the Kohanim from each batch of bread baked, in accordance with Numbers. The practice is still followed today by Orthodox Jews, though as there is no possibility of giving the ḥalla to ritually pure Kohanim only a symbolic portion is set aside, then burnt.

THE LORD SPOKE TO MOSES, SAYING: SPEAK TO THE ISRAELITE PEOPLE AND SAY TO THEM: WHEN YOU ENTER THE LAND TO WHICH I AM TAKING YOU AND YOU EAT OF THE BREAD OF THE LAND, YOU SHALL SET SOME ASIDE AS A GIFT TO THE LORD: AS THE FIRST YIELD OF YOUR BAKING, YOU SHALL SET ASIDE A LOAF AS A GIFT; YOU SHALL SET IT ASIDE AS A GIFT LIKE THE GIFT FROM THE THRESHING FLOOR. YOU SHALL MAKE A GIFT TO THE LORD FROM THE FIRST YIELD OF YOUR BAKING, THROUGHOUT THE AGES.
(Numbers 15:17–21 JPS)

CHAPTER ONE

1. Five [grain species] are subject to the law of *ḥalla*. [Bread baked from] wheat, barley, spelt, oats or rye is liable for *ḥalla*; [all five] count together, are forbidden as *ḥadash*

before Passover and may not be reaped before the Omer;[1] if they take root before the Omer, the Omer releases them [for consumption], but if not they [remain] forbidden until the following Omer.

9. [Failure to set aside] *teruma* or *ḥalla* renders [the owner] liable to death [at the hand of heaven].[2] [Should a non-*Kohen* accidentally eat some,] he must pay a fifth [over the value in compensation]; [both] are forbidden to non-*Kohanim*; they are property of the *Kohanim*; they lose their character in [mixtures where they make up less than 1 part in] 101; [*Kohanim*] must wash their hands before eating them, and must [wait until] evening [for purification to take effect].

Pure [dough] may not be given [as *ḥalla*] for impure [dough]; [*ḥalla*] must be set aside from dough with which it is in contact, and which has been [kneaded].

If someone declares, 'My whole harvest is *teruma*', or 'The whole of my dough is *ḥalla*', his words are without effect; some must be left [unconsecrated].

CHAPTER TWO

6. Five quarter-*kabs* of flour, inclusive of sourdough, fine and coarse bran, are liable for *ḥalla*. If the coarse bran had been removed but [fell] back in, it is not counted.

7. The quantity to be set aside as *ḥalla* is one twenty-fourth. If someone prepares dough for himself, or his son's feast, it is one twenty-fourth; [for] a baker who bakes for the market, or a woman who sells to the market, [the proportion] is one forty-eighth. Should her dough become unclean, whether through carelessness or constraint, [the proportion] is one forty-eighth; should it be made unclean deliberately, a twenty-fourth [must be separated], so that the sinner does not profit.

1. See p. 87.
2. No penalty is exacted by a human court, though Leviticus 22:9 states: 'And they shall die, having profaned it.'

The final two chapters are concerned with intricate questions about the combination of various types of dough, with ritual purity and with the status of ḥalla *beyond the boundaries of Judaea.*

TENTH TRACTATE
'ORLA (FRUIT OF FIRST THREE YEARS)

WHEN YOU ENTER THE LAND AND PLANT ANY TREE FOR FOOD, YOU SHALL REGARD ITS FRUIT AS FORBIDDEN. THREE YEARS IT SHALL BE FORBIDDEN FOR YOU, NOT TO BE EATEN. IN THE FOURTH YEAR ALL ITS FRUIT SHALL BE SET ASIDE FOR JUBILATION BEFORE THE LORD; AND ONLY IN THE FIFTH YEAR MAY YOU USE ITS FRUIT – THAT ITS YIELD TO YOU MAY BE INCREASED: I THE LORD AM YOUR GOD. (Leviticus 19:23–5 JPS)

Hebrew 'orla *is related to the word that commonly denotes 'uncircumcised'; KJV translates, 'ye shall count the fruit thereof as uncircumcised'.*

Fourth-year fruit (neta' r'vai) *is not discussed in this tractate; there were brief references above, in* Berakhot *35a (see Chapter Six) and in* Ma'aser Sheni *Chapter Five.*

CHAPTER ONE

1. If you plant [trees] as a fence, or for timber, [the fruit] is exempt [from the laws of *'orla*]. Rabbi Yosé says, Even if the inner [growth] is for food and the outer for a fence, the inner is subject [to the law] and the outer exempt.
2. When our fathers entered the Land [in the days of Joshua], whatever was [already] planted was exempt [from the laws of *'orla*, but what] they planted [themselves], even though they had not yet conquered the Land, was subject [to the law].

If you plant for public [benefit, the fruit] is subject [to the laws of ʿorla], but Rabbi Judah exempts [it].

If [anyone] plants on public land, or a non-Jew plants, or a robber plants, or someone plants on a ship or produce grows of its own accord, [the fruit] is subject to [the laws of] ʿorla.

3. If a tree was uprooted together with the soil [around its roots] or a river flooded it together with the soil, if it can survive [with the attached soil], it is exempt [from recounting the years of ʿorla], but if not, [the years of ʿorla] must be [recounted].[1]

If the soil to one side was separated, or disturbed by the plough or shaken to dust, then if [the tree] can survive [with the remaining soil], it is exempt [from recounting the years of ʿorla], but if not, [the years of ʿorla] must be [recounted].

Chapters Two and Three form part of the rabbinic system regulating mixtures. If a forbidden substance falls into a permitted one, the mixture is not automatically condemned; it is usually relevant to enquire about the relative quantities, whether the forbidden substance has imparted a taste to the mixture, and so on.

CHAPTER TWO

1. *Teruma, terumat maʿaser, ḥalla* and first-fruits lose their character in [mixtures where they make up less than 1 part in] 101;[2] they count together [towards the 1 part], and [an equivalent part] must be removed [from the mixture].

ʿOrla and vine mixtures lose their character in [mixtures where they make up less than 1 part in] 201; they count together [towards the 1 part], but [no equivalent part] need be removed [from the mixture]. Rabbi Simeon says, They do not count together; Rabbi Eliezer says, They count

1. Since it is as if the tree has been newly planted.
2. That is, their presence may be ignored; the mixture is permitted.

together [if they] contribute a taste [to the mixture], but not [just] to render the mixture forbidden.

4. Any [quantity, however small,] that leavens, seasons or desecrates *'orla*, vine mixtures or *teruma*, [renders the mixture] forbidden. The School of Shammai say, [It may render it] impure [too], but the School of Hillel say, It can only [render it] impure if it is [at least] an egg-size.

5. Dostai of K'far Yotma was a disciple of the School of Shammai. He said, I heard Shammai[3] himself say that anything less than egg-size does not convey impurity.

6. Why, then, did they say 'any [quantity] that leavens, seasons or desecrates'? It was to exercise stringency in cases where [polluter and polluted] are of the same kind [of food], and both stringency and leniency where they are of different kinds. What does this mean? If[, for instance,] wheat sourdough fell into wheat dough in sufficient quantity to leaven it, then whether or not the quantity of wheat was more than 100 times that of sourdough, [the mixture] is forbidden; and if the quantity of wheat was less than 100 times that of sourdough, then whether or not the sourdough was sufficient to leaven it, [the mixture] is forbidden.

7. And what is meant by 'both stringency and leniency where they are of different kinds'? If[, for instance,] groats and lentils were boiled together, and there is sufficient [of the forbidden sort] to impart a taste [to the mixture], then whether or not the quantity [of the forbidden sort] is less than 1 in 100 [of the permitted, the mixture] is forbidden; but if there is not sufficient [of the forbidden sort] to impart a taste [to the mixture], then whether or not the quantity [of the forbidden sort] is less than 1 in 100 [of the permitted, the mixture] is permitted.

3.   Literally, 'Shammai the Elder'.

CHAPTER THREE

9. If doubt [has arisen as to whether the fruit of a tree is still subject to *'orla*], if in the Land of Israel it is forbidden; if in Syria it is permitted; if [further] beyond the Land, you may go and help yourself [to the fruit] so long as people are not watching you.[4]

   [Likewise, if] vegetables had been planted in a vineyard, and someone is selling vegetables nearby, if in the Land of Israel [the vegetables] are forbidden;[5] if in Syria it is permitted; if [further] beyond the Land, you may go and help yourself [to the vegetables] so long as you do not harvest them yourself.

The final sentence introduces the topic of ḥadash ('new'), that is, the new season's grain harvest. Leviticus 23:14 says that the new harvest is not to be eaten until the Omer, a sheaf of the new harvest, is presented in the Temple; this would normally happen on the second night of Passover.

Ḥadash is forbidden everywhere[6] as by the Torah; *'orla* is forbidden [beyond the Land of Israel] as law [received by Moses at Sinai]; *kil'ayim* is forbidden [beyond the Land of Israel] as an enactment of the scribes.

---

4. It is permissible, but others might misapprehend.
5. They may have come from the forbidden mixed sowing in the vineyard.
6. i.e. even beyond the Land of Israel.

ELEVENTH TRACTATE
BIKKURIM (FIRST-FRUITS)

Many religions have a formal ceremony to express gratitude for the fresh season's produce. Deuteronomy transforms the ancient rite to an acknowledgement of God's fulfilment of His promise to the ancestors of a land for their descendants; they hold this land under the terms of a covenant with God, whom they worship at a single, chosen shrine.

WHEN YOU ENTER THE LAND THAT THE LORD YOUR GOD IS GIVING YOU AS A HERITAGE . . . YOU SHALL TAKE SOME OF EVERY FIRST FRUIT OF THE SOIL . . . PUT IT IN A BASKET AND GO TO THE PLACE WHERE THE LORD YOUR GOD WILL CHOOSE . . . YOU SHALL GO TO THE PRIEST IN CHARGE AT THAT TIME AND SAY TO HIM, 'I ACKNOWLEDGE THIS DAY BEFORE THE LORD YOUR GOD THAT I HAVE ENTERED THE LAND THAT THE LORD SWORE TO OUR FATHERS TO ASSIGN US.' (Deuteronomy 26:1–3 JPS)

CHAPTER ONE

1. Some bring first-fruits and recite [the declaration]; some bring but do not recite; and some neither bring nor recite.

These do not bring: one who plants in his own land but layers into private or public land, and similarly one who layers from private or public land into his own. If someone plants in his own land and layers across private or public property into [another area of] his own land, he does not bring; Rabbi Judah says, Such a one does bring.

2. Why do [the preceding] not bring? Because it is said, THE CHOICE FIRST-FRUITS OF *YOUR* SOIL YOU SHALL BRING (Exodus 23:19 JPS) – that is, all the growth should be from your [own] land.

   Tenants, crop-sharers, men who have taken land by force, and robbers do not bring, for the same reason, that it is said, THE CHOICE FIRST-FRUITS OF *YOUR* SOIL YOU SHALL BRING.

3. First-fruits are brought only from the seven species [for which the Land of Israel is celebrated], but not from mountain dates, valley fruit or inferior kinds of olive.

   First-fruits should not be brought before Shavuot. The men of Mount Tz'vuim[1] brought their first-fruits before Shavuot, but they were not accepted, since it is written in the Torah, THE FEAST OF THE HARVEST, OF THE FIRST-FRUITS OF YOUR WORK, OF WHAT YOU SOW IN THE FIELD (Exodus 23:16 JPS).

The Sages were uncomfortable with the notion that someone who was not of Israelite descent might say 'God of our fathers Abraham, Isaac and Jacob', seeing that he was not physically descended from the three. Later rabbis rejected the alternatives proposed in this Mishna on the grounds that Abraham is the father of all God-fearers; all Jews, irrespective of their descent, pray to 'the God of our fathers'.

4. These bring but do not recite: The proselyte brings but does not recite, since he cannot say, THAT THE LORD SWORE TO OUR FATHERS TO ASSIGN US; but if his mother was an Israelite, he brings and recites. When he prays on his own, he says, 'God of the fathers of Israel', and in the synagogue, he says, 'God of your fathers'; but if his mother was an Israelite, he says 'God of our fathers'.

Ownership of land is a basic qualification for making the declaration. But what constitutes 'land'? Is it enough to own just two or three trees? What happens if the fruit is lost or spoiled en route? Such questions are dealt with in the rest of the chapter.

   Chapter Two defines the status of first-fruits in terms identical

---

1.   Identification uncertain.

to those given in Ḥalla 1:9. After stating that this is unlike the
status of tithes, Mishna defines differences of status across a
range of topics. Chapter Three is a vivid, possibly idealized
portrayal of the pilgrims' procession with the first-fruits. Lieber-
man pointed out that several features of this procession, such
as the gilding of the ox, the olive wreath and the flute player,
have no biblical precedent and do not occur again in the Mishna;
they are heathen rites, attested in Homer and other classical
works, permitted by the authorities as 'a concession to the
people who considered it a hiddur mitzva, *"an adorning of a*
pious deed"'.[2]

CHAPTER THREE

1. How are first-fruits set aside? A man goes down to his field
   and sees the first fig, the first bunch of grapes or the first
   pomegranate. He ties a reed around it. Rabbi Simeon says,
   Although he has done that, when he harvests them he again
   declares them first-fruits.
2. How do they take first-fruits up [to Jerusalem]? [Representa-
   tives of] all the towns in that area gather in the main town
   and sleep in the town square — they do not enter the
   houses. Early next morning the officer says, ARISE! LET US
   ASCEND TO ZION, TO (THE HOUSE OF)[3] THE LORD OUR
   GOD! (Jeremiah 31:6).
3. Those who [live near] Jerusalem bring figs and grapes; those
   [who come] from a distance bring dried figs and raisins. An
   ox precedes them, its horns overlaid with gold and a crown
   of olives on its head, and the flute plays before them until
   they approach Jerusalem. As they near Jerusalem, they send
   [messengers] ahead and adorn their first-fruits. Officials and
   treasurers come out to greet them, matching them in dignity,
   and all the artisans of Jerusalem stand before them, welcom-

2. Lieberman, *Hellenism*, pp. 144–6.
3. Mishna cites these words, but they are lacking in the received text of Jeremiah.

ing them: Our brothers of such-and-such a place, come in peace!

4. The flute was played before them until they arrived at the Temple Mount. Once they reached the Temple Mount, even King Agrippa would take a basket on his shoulder and enter the Temple courtyard. When they arrived in the Temple courtyard, the Levites burst into song: I EXTOL YOU, O LORD, FOR YOU HAVE LIFTED ME UP, AND NOT LET MY ENEMIES REJOICE OVER ME (Psalm 30:2 JPS).

5. The doves on the baskets flew upwards, and [the people] handed [their baskets] to the priests.

6. While the basket was still on his shoulder, [the pilgrim] would recite from I ACKNOWLEDGE THIS DAY BEFORE THE LORD YOUR GOD to the end of the passage. Rabbi Judah says, [He would recite only] as far as MY FATHER WAS A FUGITIVE ARAMEAN; when he reached MY FATHER WAS A FUGITIVE ARAMEAN, he would remove the basket from his shoulder and hold it by its edges, and the priest would put his hands beneath [the presenter's hands] and wave [the basket]; then [the pilgrim] would recite from MY FATHER WAS A FUGITIVE ARAMEAN to the end of the passage, set the basket down beside the altar, bow and leave.

7. At first whoever knew how to recite did so, and those who did not how to recite were prompted. [When they saw that] people were discouraged from bringing [first-fruits],[4] it was decided to prompt those who knew how and those who did not know how.

8. Wealthy people brought their first-fruits in baskets of silver and gold, poor people in wicker baskets of willow strips. Both baskets and first-fruits were donated to the priests.

---

4.   They were embarrassed at being unable to recite Hebrew fluently.

SECOND ORDER

MO'ED
(APPOINTED TIMES)

INTRODUCTION

Two tractates (Shabbat, Eruvin) cover the Sabbath laws in meticulous detail; Betza deals with their application to festivals. Appendix I has an explanation of the Jewish Calendar with a complete list of festivals.

Two festivals lack a dedicated tractate in this Order. Shavuot (Feast of Weeks, or of First-fruits) is to some extent covered in Bikkurim, in the Order Zeraim. Ḥanuka, however, comes in only for incidental mention,[1] and this omission may have been politically motivated; perhaps Judah ha-Nasi, under Roman administration, deemed it imprudent to publish a tractate on a festival celebrating resistance to an occupying power.

---

1.   *Bikkurim* 1:6, *Rosh Hashana* 1:3; *Ta'anit* 2:10; *Megilla* 3:4, 6; *Mo'ed Qatan* 3:9; *Bava Qama* 6:6.

FIRST TRACTATE
SHABBAT (THE SABBATH)

The Sabbath extends from sunset on Friday to starlight on Saturday, roughly 25 hours. First mentioned in Genesis 2:1–3 as the culmination of Creation, references to it occur throughout the Bible.

The two versions of the Ten Commandments articulate its dual significance. Exodus focuses on the spiritual aspect – the Sabbath celebrates the perfection of Creation, in which freemen, slaves and animals share:

REMEMBER THE SABBATH DAY AND KEEP IT HOLY. SIX DAYS YOU SHALL LABOUR AND DO ALL YOUR WORK, BUT THE SEVENTH DAY IS A SABBATH OF THE LORD YOUR GOD: YOU SHALL NOT DO ANY WORK – YOU, YOUR SON OR DAUGHTER, YOUR MALE OR FEMALE SLAVE, OR YOUR CATTLE, OR THE STRANGER WHO IS WITHIN YOUR SETTLEMENTS. FOR IN SIX DAYS THE LORD MADE HEAVEN AND EARTH AND SEA, AND ALL THAT IS IN THEM, AND HE RESTED ON THE SEVENTH DAY; THEREFORE THE LORD BLESSED THE SABBATH DAY AND HALLOWED IT. (Exodus 20:8–11 JPS)

Deuteronomy emphasizes the social aspect – God freed you from slavery in Egypt, therefore all of you, slaves and animals equally with free men and women, must rest on the Sabbath:

OBSERVE THE SABBATH DAY AND KEEP IT HOLY, AS THE LORD YOUR GOD HAS COMMANDED YOU. SIX DAYS YOU SHALL LABOUR AND DO ALL YOUR WORK, BUT THE SEVENTH DAY IS A SABBATH OF THE LORD YOUR GOD; YOU SHALL NOT DO ANY WORK – YOU, YOUR SON OR DAUGHTER, YOUR MALE OR FEMALE SLAVE, YOUR

OX OR YOUR ASS, OR ANY OF YOUR CATTLE, OR THE STRANGER IN
YOUR SETTLEMENTS, SO THAT YOUR MALE AND FEMALE SLAVE MAY
REST AS YOU DO. REMEMBER THAT YOU WERE A SLAVE IN THE
LAND OF EGYPT AND THE LORD YOUR GOD FREED YOU FROM
THERE WITH A MIGHTY HAND AND AN OUTSTRETCHED ARM;
THEREFORE THE LORD YOUR GOD HAS COMMANDED YOU TO
OBSERVE THE SABBATH DAY. (Deuteronomy 5:12–15 JPS)

Much of this tractate is concerned with activities that are
prohibited on the Sabbath. The Bible explicitly forbids certain
kinds of work, for instance the lighting of fires, but the connec-
tion between its idea of the Sabbath and the Mishna's elaborate
system is not obvious. Study of pseudepigrapha, such as the
Book of Jubilees, and of the Dead Sea Scrolls, has revealed a
gradual evolution in Sabbath law; the Mishna itself is evidence
of the later stages, moving from the first-century debates of the
Schools of Hillel and Shammai on matters such as Sabbath
preparation and muqtzé, *to the listing of 39 categories of for-*
bidden activity in Chapter Seven, most likely a product of third-
century Galilee.

The tractate opens with a consideration of the prohibition of
'carrying' on the Sabbath, that is, of physically transferring
objects from public to private areas or vice versa, or of carrying
anything more than four cubits within a public area; this is
illustrated by the example of a householder welcoming a needy
person at the door. Mishna then discusses preparations for the
Sabbath, and in Chapter Two the kindling of lights, to this day
a significant Friday evening feature in the Jewish home.

'With what materials may the Sabbath light be kindled?' The
materials rejected, whether as wicks or as fuel, either splutter
or generate an unpleasant smell. Wax candles, introduced in
tenth-century Europe, were unknown in Roman times, but are
now commonly used to inaugurate the Sabbath, though some
use olive-oil lamps as recommended by the Mishna.

The Gemara asks what materials may be used for the lights
kindled in honour of the eight-day midwinter festival of
Ḥanuka; this passage, of which part is translated below, is the
most informative rabbinic source for the festival, which Mishna
alludes to only incidentally.

Nowadays the eight-branched ḥanukiya, or menora, is a familiar object in Jewish homes, and a subject for artistic creativity. Such valuable metal articles were beyond private means in pre-modern times; as we glean from the following passage only 'important persons' could be expected to afford light as well as fire!

CHAPTER TWO

GEMARA:

Rav Huna said, Those wicks and oils that the Sages said may not be used for lighting on the Sabbath may not be used on Ḥanuka, whether on Sabbath or weekdays.   21a

Rava said: What is Rav Huna's reason? He holds that if the [Ḥanuka] light goes out you are obliged to relight it[, so you should use only the best materials, to forestall your negligently failing to relight it if it does go out]; and [he holds] that you are permitted to use its light [e.g. for reading, so you have to use the best materials when lighting it, since otherwise it may splutter and you might inadvertently adjust it, so infringing the Sabbath].

Rav Ḥisda said, Those wicks and oils that the Sages said may not be used for lighting on the Sabbath may be used on Ḥanuka on weekdays, but not on the Sabbath.

He holds that if the [Ḥanuka] light goes out you   21b
do not have to relight it, [and also that] you are permitted to use its light.

Rabbi Zeira said in the name of Rav Matna – some say Rabbi Zeira said it in the name of Rav – Those wicks and oils that the Sages said may not be used for lighting on the Sabbath may be used on Ḥanuka, whether on weekdays or on the Sabbath.

Rav Yirmiya says, What is Rav's argument? [Rav] holds that if the [Ḥanuka] light goes out, you do not have to relight it, and you are forbidden to use its light.

The disciples reported this to Abbaye in the name of Rav Yirmiya and he did not

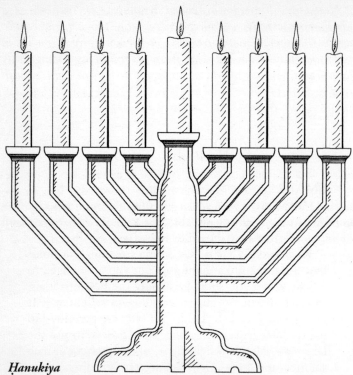

Ḥanukiya
Eight-branched *ḥanukiya (menora)*. The dedicated
ḥanuka lamp and the use of wax are medieval developments.

accept it, but when Ravin came and they
reported [the same statement] to Abbaye in
the name of Rabbi Yoḥanan, he accepted it.
He remarked, Had I been worthy I would
have learned this matter earlier! But he
learned it[, so why the regret]? It made a
difference with regard to ʻthe learning of
youthʼ.[1]

So if the [Ḥanuka] light goes out, donʼt you need to relight

1. What you learn in childhood is more firmly rooted in your mind. Kalmin (*Sages,
    Stories*, p. 162) suggests that Abbaye at first rejected the view because Rav Yirmiya
    was a lesser authority.

it? As against this, [we have learned,] **The *mitzva* [of the Ḥanuka light] extends from sunset until [the time that] people stop walking about in the streets.**[2] Doesn't this [imply] that if it goes out [during that period,] you must relight it? No, [the intention might be that] if you haven't lit it, you may still do so; alternatively, [it is an indication of] the quantity [of oil you should put in the lamp].

How long is that [period from sunset]? Rabba bar bar Ḥana says, until the Palmyrenes[3] stop walking around.

The rabbis taught: **The [basic] *mitzva* of Ḥanuka is to kindle one light per household [each night]; those who like to do better kindle a light for each person. As to those who like to do things in the best way possible, the School of Shammai say, Light eight on the first night, then decrease [by one each night]; the School of Hillel say, Light one on the first night, then increase [by one each night].**

Ulla said: Two Amoraim in the West,[4] Rabbi Yosé bar Avin and Rabbi Yosé bar Zevida, differed [as to the rationales of the Schools of Hillel and Shammai on this point]. One of them said, the School of Shammai [want the number of lights] to correspond to the days to come, and the School of Hillel to the days that have passed. The other said, the School of Shammai [want the number of lights] to correspond to the oxen sacrificed on the festival [of Tabernacles],[5] and the School of Hillel [follow that principle that] in holy matters one should increase rather than decrease.

2. In the days when there was no street lighting this would normally be half an hour or so after sunset.
3. The reference here is probably to itinerant sellers of kindling material; read *Tadmorai* instead of *Tarmodai*. Tadmor is Hebrew/Aramaic for Palmyra (cf. 1 Kings 9:18, though this is now thought to be a misreading of Tamar).
4. The Land of Israel.
5. Thirteen oxen were sacrificed on the first day of Tabernacles, the number decreasing by one each day for seven days (Numbers 29:12–34). 2 Maccabees 10:6 recounts how, when Judas Maccabeus regained the Temple on 25 Kislev, the Jews celebrated Tabernacles for eight days and ordained that there should be an eight-day celebration each year commencing on this date; this account of the origin of Ḥanuka links it explicitly to Tabernacles.

[Similarly,] Rabba bar bar Ḥana reported in the name
of Rabbi Yoḥanan that there were two elders in Sidon,
one of whom followed the School of Shammai and
the other the School of Hillel; one explained that
his reason was [that the number of lights should]
correspond to the oxen sacrificed on the festival [of
Tabernacles], the other that in holy matters one should
increase rather than decrease.

The rabbis taught: **It is a *mitzva* to place the Ḥanuka light
outside, next to the door. If you live in an upper storey, place
it in a window overlooking the street. In times of danger,**[6] **it
is sufficient to place it [indoors] on the table.**

Rava said, You need another light for personal use, but if you
have a fire this is not necessary. [However,] an important person
needs another light even if he has a fire.

What is Ḥanuka? The rabbis taught: **The eight days of
Ḥanuka commence on 25 Kislev; you may not deliver eulogies
or fast then. When the Greeks entered the Temple, they polluted all the oil there. When the Hasmoneans overcame them,
they searched and found just one jar of oil bearing the seal of
the High Priest, containing only enough oil to kindle [the
Temple candelabrum] for one day; a miracle happened, and
they kindled from it for eight days. In a later year they established [the eight days as an occasion] for celebration with
Hallel and thanksgiving.**[7]

*The canon of Scripture was fixed by a process of exclusion
rather than inclusion; books deemed contrary to Torah were
suppressed. Here, it is reported in Rav's name that some Sages
considered removing Ecclesiastes and Proverbs from the canon;
Mishna Yadayim 3:5 refers to attempts to exclude Song and
Ecclesiastes.*

30b   Rav Yehuda the son of Rav Shmuel said in Rav's name: The
Sages wanted to suppress[8] Ecclesiastes since its words contradict

---

6.   The rabbis had in mind persecution by Zoroastrians, to whom fire was sacred.
7.   This is a drastic revision of the history as given by Josephus and in Maccabees,
     neither of which mentions the miracle of the oil. The rabbis diverted attention
     from the military victories and focused on the spiritual aspect of the events.
8.   Literally, 'hide'; Apocrypha are 'hidden' books.

one another. So why didn't they? Because it begins and ends
with words of Torah. It begins with words of Torah, for it is
written, WHAT BENEFIT DOES A MAN GAIN FROM ALL HIS
LABOUR UNDER THE SUN? (Ecclesiastes 1:3); as they said in
Rabbi Yannai's School, From that which is UNDER THE SUN
there is no [benefit], but from that which preceded the sun
[namely the Torah – Rashi] there is [benefit]. And it concludes
with words of Torah, for it is written, AN END TO THE MATTER;
ALL HAS BEEN HEARD. FEAR GOD AND KEEP HIS COMMAND-
MENTS, FOR THIS IS ALL OF MAN[9] (Ecclesiastes 12:13).

What is [the meaning of] THIS IS ALL OF MAN?
Rabbi Eleazar said, The whole world was created just
for this purpose. Rabbi Abba bar Kahana said, This is
of equal value to the whole world. Simeon Ben Azzai
– some say Simeon Ben Zoma – said, The whole world
was created just as a means to this [purpose].

In what way do 'its words contradict one another'? It is
written, VEXATION IS BETTER THAN REVELRY (7:3 JPS), and
OF REVELRY I SAID, 'IT IS PRAISEWORTHY!' (2:2); it is written,
I THEREFORE PRAISED HAPPINESS (8:15), and OF MERRI-
MENT, 'WHAT GOOD IS THAT?' (2:2 JPS).

No problem. VEXATION[10] IS BETTER THAN REV-
ELRY [means], When the Holy one, blessed be He, is
angry with the righteous in this world, it is better than
when He is happy with the wicked in this world; OF
REVELRY I SAID, 'IT IS PRAISEWORTHY!' is when
He takes pleasure in the righteous in this world. I
THEREFORE PRAISED HAPPINESS refers to the joy
[experienced] in [the performance of] a *mitzva*; and
OF MERRIMENT, 'WHAT GOOD IS THAT?' is joy other
than that [experienced] in [the performance of] a
mitzva.

This teaches you that the *Shekhina* does not rest on
a man when he is miserable or slothful, or [engaged]
in revelry or frivolity or chatter or futile things, but

9.   Better, 'This is man's purpose'; but the literal translation supports the rabbis'
     interpretation.
10. The word generally means 'anger'.

only when he is in the joyful state attained through
[performing] a *mitzva*, as it is written, [**ELISHA
SAID . . .**] **'NOW THEN, GET ME A MUSICIAN.' AS
THE MUSICIAN PLAYED, THE HAND OF THE LORD
CAME UPON HIM** (2 Kings 3:15).

Rav Yehuda said, The same [i.e. approach-
ing it in a joyful mood – Rashi] applies to a
halakhic decision. Rava said, The same
applies to a favourable dream.

Can [Rav Yehuda be right when he says
that *halakha* should be approached in a joyful mood]? Didn't Rav Giddel say in the
name of Rav, If a disciple sits in the presence
of the master and his lips do not drip [with]
bitterness,[11] they will be burnt, as it is said,
**HIS LIPS ARE LIKE LILIES; THEY DRIP
FLOWING MYRRH** (Song 5:13 JPS) – do not
read *shoshanim* ('lilies') but *she-shonim*,
('That learn'), and do not read *mor* ('myrrh')
but *mar* ('bitterness'). No problem! The
master should approach the topic with joy,
the disciple with seriousness. Alternatively,
both statements may be applied to the
master, one before he commences, the other
through the discourse, as was Rabba's practice; before the discourse he would tell a
joke and the students would laugh, but then
he would sit reverently and begin the exposition.

They also considered suppressing *Proverbs*, since its words
contradict one another. Why didn't they? They said, Did we
not examine *Ecclesiastes* and resolve its contradictions?[12] We
will examine this [book] too [and resolve its contradictions].

In what way do 'its words contradict one another'? It is
written, **DO NOT ANSWER A FOOL IN ACCORD WITH HIS FOLLY**

11. He should attend seriously to the master's discourse.
12. Literally, 'Find reason [for them]'.

(Proverbs 26:4), and it is written, **ANSWER A FOOL IN ACCORD WITH HIS FOLLY** (26:5).

No problem! One [verse] refers to matters of Torah, the other to worldly things.

> This is like the man who came before Rabbi, saying, 'Your wife is mine and your children are mine!' [Rabbi] said to him, Would you like a cup of wine? He drank it and burst. [Likewise,] a man approached Rabbi Ḥiyya, saying, 'Your mother is my wife and you are my son.' [Rabbi Ḥiyya] said to him, Would you like a cup of wine? He drank it and burst. Rabbi Ḥiyya remarked, Rabbi's prayer helped that his children should not be [stigmatized as] bastards, for he used to pray: May it be Your will, Lord our God, to protect me this day from insolence and from insolent people.[13]

How does it apply in Torah matters? An example would be Rabban Gamaliel, who was expounding [the theme of the World to Come] and said, A woman will give birth every day, as it is said, **SHE WILL CONCEIVE AND GIVE BIRTH TOGETHER**[14] (Jeremiah 31:8). A disciple laughed at this, saying, **THERE IS NOTHING NEW UNDER THE SUN** (Ecclesiastes 1:9). [Rabban Gamaliel] said to him, Come! Let me show you something like it in this world! He showed him a hen.

Another time Rabban Gamaliel was expounding [the theme of the World to Come] and said, The trees will produce fruit every day, as it is said, **IT SHALL BRING FORTH BOUGHS AND PRODUCE FRUIT** (Ezekiel 17:23) – just as it always has branches, so will it bear fruit each day! A disciple laughed at this, saying **THERE IS NOTHING NEW UNDER THE SUN**. [Rabban Gamaliel] said to him, Come! Let me show you something like it in this world! He went out and showed him a caperberry bush.[15]

Another time Rabban Gamaliel was expounding [the theme of the World to Come], and said, The [trees of the] Land of

13. This prayer is found in an expanded form in the Orthodox Jewish morning liturgy.
14. This is a literal translation; JPS has 'Those with child and those in labour'.
15. The caperberry is always productive, bearing berries, flower buds and young shoots at different times of the year – Rashi, based on Mishna *Ma'aserot* 4:6. *Capparis spinosa* is a classic Mediterranean condiment still in common use.

Israel will one day produce loaves of bread and silken garments, as it is said, LET ABUNDANT[16] GRAIN BE IN THE LAND (Psalm 72:16 JPS). A disciple laughed at this, saying THERE IS NOTH-ING NEW UNDER THE SUN. [Rabban Gamaliel] said to him, Come! Let me show you something like it in this world! He went out and showed him mushrooms and toadstools [shaped like loaves – Rashi] and soft young palm fronds [with the appearance of silk – Rashi].

The Gemara moves abruptly on to a collection of stories about Hillel and Shammai, which contain many anachronisms and much evidence of literary development, so it is unlikely that they took their present form until centuries after the events described. David Kraemer, noting with other scholars that the section where Hillel sums up the Torah 'on one leg' is lacking in the earlier version of the conversion stories in Avot de Rabbi Nathan, *draws attention to the implied reduction of Written as well as Oral Torah to 'interpretation', a notion he believes to be peculiar to the Bavli, and to the emphasis on the equivalence and interdependence of both Torahs.[17] All three stories exhibit a markedly positive attitude towards converts.*

31a   The rabbis taught: You should always be patient like Hillel, not impetuous like Shammai. Two men laid a bet with one another; they said, Whoever of us gets Hillel into a rage wins 400 *zuz*. One said, I will provoke him! That day was the eve of the Sabbath, and Hillel was washing his hair. [The man] passed the door of [Hillel's] house shouting,[18] Is Hillel there? Is Hillel there?

[Hillel] robed himself, came out to greet him and said, My son, what is it you want?

He replied, I have a question to put to you!

Then ask, my son, ask!

Why do Babylonians have round heads?

[Hillel] replied, My son, you have asked an important ques-tion. It is because they lack skilful midwives.

16. The unusual Hebrew word used for 'abundant' suggests silk.
17. Kraemer, *Mind*, p. 157.
18. Literally, 'saying'.

[The man] went off, waited an hour, then came back and again shouted, Is Hillel there? Is Hillel there?

[Hillel] robed himself, came out to greet him and said, My son, what is it you want?

He replied, I have a question to put to you!

Then ask, my son, ask!

Why do Palmyrenes have tender eyes?

[Hillel] replied, My son, you have asked an important question. It is because they live in a sandy place.

[The man] went off, waited an hour, came back and again shouted, Is Hillel there? Is Hillel there?

[Hillel] robed himself, came out to greet him and said, My son, what is it you want?

He replied, I have a question to put to you!

Then ask, my son, ask!

Why do Africans have broad feet?

[Hillel] replied, My son, you have asked an important question. It is because they live among pools of water.

[The man said,] I have a lot of questions to ask, but I am afraid you will get angry.

[Hillel] robed himself, sat before him and said, Ask all the questions you want!

[The man said,] Are you Hillel, whom they call the Prince of Israel!

I am.

Then may there not be many like you in Israel!

Why [do you say that], my son?

Because through you I have lost 400 *zuz*!

[Hillel] replied, Restrain your emotions! Better you should lose 400 *zuz* and 400 *zuz* again than that Hillel should lose his temper!

[Another story]. The rabbis taught: A heathen came before Shammai and asked, How many Torahs do you have?

Two, he replied, the Written Torah and the Oral Torah.

[The man said,] I believe what you say about the Written Torah, but not what you say about the Oral Torah. Convert me on condition that you teach me [only] the Written Torah! Shammai rebuked him and angrily sent him away.

He came to Hillel [with the same request], and [Hillel] accepted him as a convert. The first day Hillel taught him *aleph, bet, gimmel, dalet*;[19] the next day he changed the order [of the letters]. But that's not what you taught me yesterday! the man protested. [Hillel] replied, Then you relied on me [for the order of the alphabet]! Rely on me also for the Oral Torah!

On another occasion a heathen presented himself to Shammai saying, Convert me on condition that you teach me the whole Torah while I stand on one leg! [Shammai] drove him away with the builder's measure he was holding.

He came to Hillel [with the same request], and [Hillel] accepted him as a convert. [Hillel] said to him, Do not do to others what you would not like them to do to you! That is the whole Torah; the rest is commentary, go and learn!

On another occasion a heathen was walking past the House of Study and overheard the scribe reading, THESE ARE THE VESTMENTS THEY ARE TO MAKE: A BREASTPIECE, AN EPHOD . . . (Exodus 28:4 JPS). For whom are these? he asked. They replied, For the High Priest. He thought to himself, I shall convert so that they will appoint me High Priest.

He presented himself to Shammai saying, Convert me on condition that you appoint me High Priest. [Shammai] drove him away with the builder's measure he was holding.

He came to Hillel [with the same request]; [Hillel] accepted him as a convert. [Hillel] said to him, No one can be appointed as a leader[20] unless he knows the strategies of leadership; go and learn the strategies of leadership! [The man] went and studied [Torah]. When he reached the verse, THE OUTSIDER THAT ENCROACHES SHALL BE PUT TO DEATH (Numbers 1:51 JPS), he enquired, To whom does this apply? [Hillel] told him, [It applies] even to David, King of Israel[, since he was not a descendant of Aaron]. The convert then reasoned, [Native-born] Israelites are called children of the All-present, and through His love for them he called them ISRAEL, MY FIRST-BORN SON (Exodus 4:22 JPS), yet of them it is written,

19. The first four letters of the Hebrew alphabet.
20. Literally, 'king'.

THE OUTSIDER THAT ENCROACHES SHALL BE PUT TO DEATH; how much more so does the verse apply to me, a humble stranger who comes with his stick and his bag! He went to Shammai and said, I am unfit to become High Priest! Is it not written, THE OUTSIDER THAT ENCROACHES SHALL BE PUT TO DEATH? Then he returned to Hillel and said, Patient Hillel, may blessings rest on your head, for you have brought me close beneath the wings of the *Shekhina*!

Later, the three [converts] met at an inn. They said, Shammai's impetuosity would have driven us from the world, but Hillel's patience brought us close beneath the wings of the *Shekhina*!

The Ten Commandments forbid people to work their animals on the Sabbath. Mishna interprets this to mean that an animal might wear ornaments or protective clothing on the Sabbath, but should not be used to carry any form of burden. Rabbi Eleazar ben Azaria allowed his cow to go out with a ribbon between her horns, contrary to the majority opinion that this constituted a burden; the Gemara concludes that it was his neighbour's cow, but that he was responsible since he ought to have informed her that she was doing wrong. This leads to a discussion of the extent to which we are responsible for our neighbours' actions, and to general reflections on the connection between sin and punishment. Can there can be suffering without sin; can anyone be entirely free of sin?

CHAPTER FIVE

Rabbi Ammi said: There is no death without sin, no suffering without guilt. There is no death without sin, as it is written, THE PERSON THAT SINS, HE SHALL DIE; THE SON SHALL NOT BEAR THE SIN OF THE FATHER, NOR SHALL THE FATHER BEAR THE SIN OF THE SON (Ezekiel 18:20); and no suffering without guilt, as it is written, I WILL VISIT THEIR SIN WITH THE ROD, AND THEIR GUILT WITH PLAGUES (Psalm 89:33).

55a

55b   An objection was raised [to Rabbi Ammi's view]: **The ministering angels said to the Holy One, blessed be He, Why did
you impose punishment on Adam? He said to them, I gave
him one simple commandment and he transgressed. They said
to Him, Did not Moses and Aaron observe the whole Torah,
yet still they died? He replied, ALL THINGS COME ALIKE TO
ALL; ONE [FATE] BEFALLS THE RIGHTEOUS AND THE WICKED,
THE GOOD, THE PURE AND THE IMPURE** (Ecclesiastes 9:2).

[Rabbi Ammi's opinion accords with that of] the Tanna who
taught: **Rabbi Simeon ben Eleazar says, Even Moses and Aaron
died through their [own] sin, as it is said, FOR YOU DID NOT
TRUST ME** (Numbers 20:12). [This implies,] If you had trusted
Me, your time would not yet have come to depart this world.

They objected: **Four died through the counsel of the serpent,**[21] **and these are they: Benjamin son of Jacob, Amram
father of Moses, Jesse father of David and Chileab son of
David.**

> All are *gemara*[22] except for Jesse father of David, to
> whom Scripture alludes: **AND ABSALOM HAD SET
> AMASA IN CHARGE OF THE ARMY IN PLACE OF JOAB.
> NOW AMASA WAS THE SON OF A MAN CALLED
> YITHRA THE ISRAELITE,**[23] **WHO HAD HAD INTER-
> COURSE WITH ABIGAIL, DAUGHTER OF NAHASH
> AND SISTER OF JOAB'S MOTHER ZERUIAH** (2 Samuel
> 17:25). But was [Abigail really] the daughter of Nahash?
> Surely she was the daughter of Jesse, as it is written [in
> a list of Jesse's children], **AND THEIR SISTERS WERE
> ZERUIAH AND ABIGAIL [. . . AND ABIGAIL BORE
> AMASA]** (1 Chronicles 2:16–17). [We must infer that
> Abigail was the daughter of] the man who died
> through the counsel of the *nahash* [serpent].

Who [raised this objection]? It cannot be the Tanna who
spoke about the ministering angels, for he would have included

---

21. i.e. through the counsel the serpent gave Eve, not through any other sin, for they
     did not sin themselves – Rashi. This view resembles the Christians' doctrine of
     'original sin' as later formulated by Augustine (354–430).
22. They have no biblical basis, but are traditional teaching.
23. In 1 Chronicles 2:17 the name is given as Jether the Ishmaelite.

Moses and Aaron [among those who] did not die on account of their sin. So must it not be Rabbi Simeon ben Eleazar, from which we may conclude that there is death without sin, and suffering without guilt.

Rabbi Ammi's [contrary] opinion is [therefore] refuted.

Pagan philosophers such as Celsus, and 'heretics' such as Marcion and Faustus the Manichee,[24] *attacked the Bible on the grounds that it attributes apparently evil deeds to God and to prominent figures whom we are encouraged to regard as virtuous. Plato had expressed similar criticism of the traditional Greek myths, but whereas he was ready to accuse Homer of error and to recommend that such stories not be taught to the young, the rabbis felt obligated to defend the Word of God as it stood. They achieved this, much as the Alexandrian scholars who had defended Homer, by radical reinterpretation of the text, filling gaps in the narrative so as to present their heroes in a more favourable light.*

Rabbi Jonathan ben Eleazar immigrated from Babylonia to Sepphoris, Galilee, early in the third century, and established a reputation for his polemics against heretics. His defences of biblical heroes have been worked into a literary unit in which each 'portrait' shares these features:

1. *Attribution to 'Rabbi Shmuel bar Naḥmani in the name of Rabbi Jonathan'.*
2. *The formula 'Whoever says X sinned is mistaken.'*
3. *A proof-text demonstrating that X was not a sinner.*
4. *The text indicating X's apparent misdeed.*
5. *Reinterpretation of the text, claiming though X's sin was comparatively minor, Scripture accounts it 'as if' he had sinned greatly.*

Rabbi Shmuel bar Naḥmani said in the name of Rabbi   56a
Jonathan: Whoever says David sinned is mistaken, for it is said,

---

24. Celsus' *Alēthēs Logos* ('The True Discourse') was written *c.* 178; it is known through its refutation (*Contra Celsum*) by the Christian Origen of Caesarea (185–254), who had extensive contacts with the Jewish Sages (see de Lange, *Origen*). Marcion and Faustus were attacked by Tertullian and Augustine respectively.

AND DAVID PROSPERED IN ALL HIS WAYS, AND THE LORD WAS WITH HIM (1 Samuel 18:14). Is it possible that if the *Shekhina* were with him he would be led to sin?

In that case, what is meant by [Nathan's condemnation]: **WHY HAVE YOU DESPISED THE WORD OF THE LORD TO DO**[25] **EVIL IN MY SIGHT? YOU SMOTE URIAH THE HITTITE BY THE SWORD AND TOOK HIS WIFE TO BE YOUR WIFE, AND SLEW HIM WITH THE SWORD OF THE AMMONITES!** (2 Samuel 12:9)?[26] He did [indeed] intend to sin, but did not [actually] do so.

> Rav said, Rabbi [Judah the Patriarch] who was descended from David reinterpreted in David's favour: **WHY HAVE YOU DESPISED THE WORD OF THE LORD TO DO EVIL?** This 'evil' is different from other 'evils' in the Torah, for elsewhere it is written, **AND HE DID**, but here it says [merely], **TO DO** – that is, he intended to sin, but did not [in fact] do so.

YOU SMOTE URIAH THE HITTITE BY THE SWORD. You ought to have had him tried [independently] by the Sanhedrin, but you failed to do so.

AND TOOK HIS WIFE TO BE YOUR WIFE. The 'taking' was valid since, as Rabbi Shmuel bar Naḥmani said in the name of Rabbi Jonathan, Whoever went [to fight] in a war of the House of David [first] wrote a [conditional] divorce for his wife, as it is said, **AND BRING THESE TEN CHEESES TO THE CAPTAIN OF A THOUSAND, AND TO YOUR BROTHERS BRING GREETINGS, AND TAKE THEIR *ARUBA*** (1 Samuel 17:18). What is 'their *aruba*'? Rav Yosef taught, Matters involving him and her [i.e. bills of divorce].[27]

AND SLEW HIM WITH THE SWORD OF THE AMMONITES! Just as you are not held responsible[28] for the sword of the

---

25. This is a literal translation of the infinitive, to fit the next paragraph. A more idiomatic translation would be 'and done' or 'by doing'.

26. The obvious answer, that the latter verse refers to the much later episode of Uriah and Bathsheba, has been ruled out by the notion that the *Shekhina* was resting on him, a notion comparable to that of those Muslim theologians who hold that a prophet cannot sin, a view not shared by Jewish theologians.

27. *Aruba* generally means 'pledge', but here it is obscure. The word is derived from a root meaning to mix, or involve, hence Rav Yosef's interpretation.

28. Literally, 'punished'.

Ammonites, so you will not be held responsible in the matter of Uriah the Hittite.

What is the reason for that? [Uriah was guilty of treason, hence liable to the death penalty, since] he had rebelled against the king, for he said MY LORD JOAB AND MY LORD'S SERVANTS ARE ENCAMPED ON THE OPEN FIELD (2 Samuel 11:11) [, thereby declaring his allegiance to Joab rather than to David].

Rav said, When you look into the affairs of David, you find nothing amiss except in the matter of Uriah, as it is written, [DAVID DID WHAT WAS RIGHT IN THE EYES OF THE LORD, AND DEPARTED FROM WHAT HE COMMANDED HIM] ONLY IN THE MATTER OF URIAH THE HITTITE (1 Kings 15:5).

Abbaye the Elder noted a contradiction [in the words of Rav]. Could Rav have said that? Did not Rav [himself] say that David [sinned, since he] accepted slander [against Mephibosheth]? [This is a good] question.

On that point. Rav said, David accepted slander, as it is written, AND THE KING SAID TO HIM, 'WHERE IS HE?' AND ZIBA SAID TO THE KING, HE IS IN THE HOUSE OF MACHIR THE SON OF AMMIEL IN LO-DEBAR (2 Samuel 9:4), and it is written, THEN KING DAVID SENT AND FETCHED HIM OUT OF THE HOUSE OF MACHIR THE SON OF AMMIEL FROM LO-DEBAR (2 Samuel 9:5). Now [David] had already seen that [Ziba] lied, so when [Ziba] again slandered [Mephibosheth] why did [David] listen, for it says, AND THE KING SAID, 'WHERE IS YOUR MASTER'S SON?' AND ZIBA SAID TO THE KING, HE IS IN JERU-SALEM, FOR HE SAYS, TODAY THE HOUSE OF ISRAEL WILL RESTORE MY FATHER'S KINGDOM TO ME (2 Samuel 16:3). And how do we know that the king listened [to this accusation]? For it says, AND THE KING SAID TO ZIBA: ALL THAT BELONGS TO MEPHIBOSHETH IS NOW YOURS! AND ZIBA SAID, I PROSTRATE MYSELF; MAY I FIND FAVOUR IN YOUR EYES, LORD KING! (16:4).

But Shmuel says David did not accept slander.

[David] perceived indications [of Mephibosheth's treachery], as it is written: AND MEPHIBOSHETH THE SON OF SAUL CAME DOWN TO MEET THE KING; HE HAD NOT DRESSED HIS FEET, NOR TRIMMED HIS BEARD, NOR WASHED HIS CLOTHES ... AND THE KING SAID TO HIM, 'WHY DID YOU NOT COME WITH ME, MEPHIBOSHETH?' AND HE SAID, 'MY LORD KING, MY SERVANT DECEIVED ME, FOR HE SAID, I WILL SADDLE AN ASS TO RIDE UPON AND GO TO THE KING, FOR YOUR SERVANT IS LAME. AND HE SLANDERED YOUR SERVANT TO MY LORD THE KING; BUT MY LORD THE KING IS LIKE AN ANGEL OF GOD, SO DO WHATEVER SEEMS GOOD TO YOU' ... AND THE KING SAID TO HIM, 'WHY SPEAK ANY MORE OF YOUR MATTERS? I SAY, YOU AND ZIBA SHOULD SHARE THE FIELD.' AND MEPHIBOSHETH SAID TO THE KING, 'LET HIM TAKE IT ALL, SEEING THAT MY LORD THE KING HAS COME IN PEACE TO HIS OWN HOUSE' (19:25–8, 30–31).

[What Mephibosheth meant was,] I said, 'When will you come in peace', and you are doing this to me? My quarrel is not with you, but with the One who brought you [back] in peace. That is the meaning of AND JONATHAN'S SON WAS MERIB-BAAL (1 Chronicles 8:34; 9:40). Was his name Merib-Baal? Surely it was Mephibosheth! But when he stirred up a quarrel with his master,[29] a heavenly voice declared of him, Strife, son of Strife – Strife, as we have said;[30] Son of Strife, [grandson of Saul, of whom] it is written, AND SAUL ARRIVED IN THE CITY OF AMALEK AND STROVE IN THE VALLEY[31] (1 Samuel 15:5) – Rabbi

29. 'Quarrel with his master' is a loose interpretation of the Hebrew words *merib* and *baal*.
30. He rebelled against the house of David.
31. The usual translation is 'lay in wait in the valley', but the Hebrew for 'lay in wait' is the normal word for 'strove' or 'quarrelled'. Rabbi Mani held that Saul objected to the command to exterminate the Amalekites (*Yoma* 22b).

Mani says, [Saul strove] concerning [that which was to take place] in the valley.

Rav Yehuda said in the name of Rav, When David said to Mephibosheth, **YOU AND ZIBA SHOULD SHARE THE FIELD**, a voice from heaven proclaimed, 'Rehaboam and Jeroboam will divide the kingdom.'

Rav Yehuda said in the name of Rav, If David had rejected [Ziba's] slander, the kingdom of the house of David would never have been divided, Israel would not have served idols and we would not have been exiled from our land.

Mishna lists the 39 melakhot *(activities) forbidden on the Sabbath. These are broad categories, extended in later Judaism to cover new inventions and technologies; for instance, the prohibition of lighting fire was extended to cover operating an internal combustion engine, hence driving a car.*

CHAPTER SEVEN

MISHNA:

Forty 'fathers'[32] of activity less one [are forbidden on the Sabbath]: sowing [seed], ploughing, harvesting, gathering into sheaves, threshing, winnowing, sorting, grinding and sifting, kneading, baking; shearing wool [from the sheep], bleaching it, snapping off the ends of the threads, dyeing it, spinning, stretching [threads] across the loom, making two loops [to fix them to the loom], weaving two threads, breaking off [the ends of the woven] threads, tying [knots], loosening [knots], stitching two threads, tearing [material] in order to stitch two threads; trapping a deer, slaughtering it, flaying it, salting [its hide], tanning it, scraping it, cutting it into strips; writing two characters, erasing in order to write two characters; building, demolishing, extinguishing [fire], lighting fire, the final

73a

32. Principal categories.

hammer blow,[33] [and] carrying from one domain to another –
these are the forty 'fathers' less one.

GEMARA:

73b   Why the number? Rabbi Yoḥanan said, [This is to indicate]
that if somebody did [all the activities] in one 'forgetting', he
would be liable under each and every heading.

Sowing and ploughing. Surely people plough first and then
sow, so shouldn't the Mishna first say 'plough' and then 'sow'?
[No.] The Tanna was in the land of Israel, where they sow and
then plough a second time.[34]

It was taught: **Sowing, pruning, planting, layering and grafting are all one category of activity.** What does this teach us? It
teaches us that if someone does many activities that are of a
similar type, he is liable only once.

Rabbi Aḥa said in the name of Rabbi Ḥiyya bar Ashi, Pruning
renders liable as planting; planting, layering and grafting render
liable as sowing. Sowing but not planting? Say, Also as sowing.

Rav Kahana said, If someone prunes and needs the wood, he
is liable twice, once for harvesting and once for planting.[35]

Rav Yosef said, If someone cuts alfalfa,[36] he is liable twice,
once for harvesting and once for planting.

Abbaye said, If someone chops beet leaves,[37] he is liable twice,
once for harvesting and once for planting.

And ploughing. It was taught: **Ploughing, digging and
trenching are all one category of activity.**

Rav Sheshet said, If someone removed a mound indoors, he
would be liable for building; if outdoors, he would be liable for
ploughing.

Rava said, If someone filled up a hole indoors, he would be
liable for building; if outdoors, he would be liable for ploughing.

Rabbi Aḥa said, If someone digs a hole on Shabbat just
because he needs the earth,[38] he is exempt; even according to

---

33. Completing of an artefact, e.g. the final blow of the cobbler on his last.
34. Since the ground is hard the seed has to be ploughed in – Rashi.
35. As he needs the wood, he is harvesting; since pruning stimulates growth, it is like
    planting.
36. Or clover (Sokoloff, *Babylonian*, entry on *aspasta*).
37. Or 'mangel-wurzel' (ibid., entry, *silqa*).
38. i.e. he is not aiming to improve the soil condition, as in ploughing.

Rabbi Judah, who holds that a person may be liable for an activity that is not done for its normal purpose, that would only be if it is constructive, but this is destructive.

And harvesting. It was taught, **Harvesting cereals, picking grapes, dates, olives or figs,**[39] **are all one category of activity.**

Rava Papa said, If someone throws a clod of earth at a palm and knocks off dates, he is liable twice, once for picking and once for shelling. Rav Ashi said, This is not the normal way of picking or shelling[, so he is exempt].

And gathering into sheaves. Rava said, Someone who gathers salt from a saltpan is liable as for gathering into sheaves. Abbaye said, **Gathering into sheaves** applies only to plants that grow in the soil.

And threshing. It was taught, **Beating out cereals, flax and cotton are all one category of activity.**

Winnowing, sorting, grinding and sifting. Aren't winnowing, sorting and sifting the same thing? Abbaye and Rava both said, Activities that took place in [the construction of the Sanctuary] are listed, even when similar to one another. Then why not list crushing?[40] Abbaye answered, Because a poor man eats his bread without crushing [the flour]. Rava answered, [The list is compiled] in accordance with Rabbi, who said the fathers of activity were forty less one, and if you add crushing there would be forty. 74a

In that case delete one of the others and insert crushing! Abbaye's explanation is more plausible.

Several Amoraim try to make sense of an enigmatic Tannaitic ruling on 'sorting'. As a literary unit it is highly stylized, and presents in dialogue form discussions ranging over a century or so.

The rabbis taught: **If there were many kinds of food before him, he may sort and eat, he may sort and set aside, he should not sort, and if he sorts he is liable to bring a sin-offering.**

What does this mean?

---

39. Hebrew has a different verb for harvesting each kind of fruit, as it does for 'beating out' later.

40. Grinding very finely; this was done in preparing dyestuffs for the sanctuary – Rashi.

Ulla said, This is what it means: **He may sort and eat** – for that day; **he may sort and set aside** – for that day; for the next day, **he should not sort, and if he has sorted, he is liable to bring a sin-offering**.

Rav Ḥisda objected, Is it permitted to bake 'for that day', or to cook 'for that day'? So, said Rav Ḥisda, [It means:] **He may sort and eat** – less than the measurement;[41] **he may sort and set aside** – less than the measurement; if over the measurement, **he should not sort, and if he has sorted, he is liable to bring a sin-offering**.

Rav Yosef objected, Is it permitted to bake 'less than the measurement'? So, said Rav Yosef, [It means:] **He may sort and eat** – by hand; **he may sort and set aside** – by hand; if with a funnel or on a plate, **he should not sort**, and if with a sieve or a sifting-basket, **if he sorts, he is liable to bring a sin-offering**.

Rav Hamnuna objected, Does it say anything about a funnel or a plate? So, said Rav Hamnuna, [It means:] **He may sort and eat** – food out of waste; **he may sort and set aside** – food out of waste; but [by removing] waste from food, **he should not sort, and if he sorts, he is liable to bring a sin-offering**.

Abbaye objected, Does it say anything about food out of waste? So, said Abbaye, [It means:] **He may sort and eat** – for immediate consumption; **he may sort and set aside** – for immediate consumption; but for [later in] the day, **he should not sort, and if he has sorted** he is like one who sorts for storage **and is liable to bring a sin-offering**.

The disciples reported this to Rava, and he said, Naḥmani[42] spoke well!

Over-preoccupation with law might divert attention from the beauty and spirituality that characterize the Sabbath; the following sugya *reminds us that the meticulous regulations constitute a structure to safeguard and focus its spiritual essence and*

41. There is a fixed measurement for each activity below which there is no liability for infringing the Sabbath law.
42. A sobriquet of Abbaye, the ward of Rav Naḥman.

beauty. The term 'oneg Shabbat – 'Sabbath delight' – perfectly
articulates what the Sabbath means to the observant Jew: the
spiritual is achieved not in opposition to the material, but
through the celebration of God's material creation.

CHAPTER SIXTEEN

GEMARA:

Rabbi Simeon ben Pazzi said that Rabbi Joshu ben Levi said 118a
in the name of Bar Kappara, Whoever celebrates the Sabbath
with three meals[43] will be saved from three calamities: the
birthpangs of the Messiah, the judgement of Gehinnom and
the war of God and Magog. From the birthpangs of the Messiah,
for [of the Sabbath] it says, [REMEMBER THE SABBATH] DAY
(Exodus 20:8), and [of the birthpangs of the Messiah] it says, I
WILL SEND ELIJAH THE PROPHET TO YOU BEFORE THE
COMING OF THE AWESOME, FEARFUL DAY (Malachi 3:23 JPS);
from the judgement of Gehinnom, for [of the Sabbath] it says,
[REMEMBER THE SABBATH] DAY, and [of the judgement of
Gehinnom] it says, THAT DAY SHALL BE A DAY OF WRATH
(Zephaniah 1:15 JPS); from the war of God and Magog, for [of
the Sabbath] it says [REMEMBER THE SABBATH] DAY, and [of
the war of God and Magog,] it says, ON THAT DAY, WHEN
GOG SETS FOOT ON THE SOIL OF ISRAEL (Ezekiel 38:18 JPS).

Rabbi Yoḥanan said in the name of Rabbi Yosé, Whoever
makes the Sabbath a delight will enjoy unbounded heritage, as
it is said, WHEN YOU DELIGHT IN THE LORD, I WILL SET YOU
ASTRIDE THE HEIGHTS OF THE EARTH AND WILL LET YOU
ENJOY THE HERITAGE OF YOUR FATHER JACOB (Isaiah 58:14); 118b
[this is] not like [the heritage of] Abraham, to whom it was
said, UP, WALK ABOUT THE LAND, THROUGH ITS LENGTH
AND ITS BREADTH (Genesis 13:17 JPS), nor like [the heritage
of] Isaac, to whom it was said, I WILL ASSIGN ALL THESE
LANDS TO YOU AND TO YOUR HEIRS (Genesis 26:3 JPS), but
like [the heritage of] Jacob, of whom it is written, YOU SHALL

---

43. People normally ate only two meals a day.

SPREAD OUT TO THE WEST AND TO THE EAST, TO THE NORTH AND TO THE SOUTH (Genesis 28:14 JPS).

Rav Naḥman bar Isaac said, [Whoever makes the Sabbath a delight] will be saved from the suffering of exile. Here it is written, **I WILL SET YOU ASTRIDE THE HEIGHTS OF THE EARTH**, and there it is written, **AND YOU WILL TREAD UPON THEIR HIGH PLACES** (Deuteronomy 33:29).

Rav Yehuda said in the name of Rav, Whoever makes the Sabbath a delight will be granted the desires of his heart, as it says, **TAKE DELIGHT IN THE LORD, AND HE WILL GRANT THE DESIRES OF YOUR HEART** (Psalm 37:4). I would not know what delight is meant here, but when it says, **YOU SHALL CALL THE SABBATH A DELIGHT** (Isaiah 58:13), you must say, This [refers] to the Sabbath delight.

How do you make it a delight?

Rav Yehuda the son of Rav Shmuel bar Shelat said in Rav's name, With a dish of beet, and big fish, and the finest garlic.

Rav Ḥiyya bar Ashi said in Rav's name, Even a small thing, if you make it to honour the Sabbath, is 'a delight'.

What, for instance? Rav Papa said, a cup of *harsana*.[44]

Rav Ḥiyya bar Abba said, When someone observes the Sabbath properly, he can be forgiven even if he serves idols as in the generation of Enosh, as it is said, **HAPPY IS *ENOSH*[45] WHO DOES THIS ... WHO KEEPS THE SABBATH AND DOES NOT PROFANE IT** (Isaiah 56:2) – do not read *m'ḥal'lo* ('does not profane it') but *maḥul lo* ('he is forgiven').

Rav Yehuda said in Rav's name, If Israel had kept their first Sabbath, no nation or tongue could have prevailed against them. It is said, **YET SOME OF THE PEOPLE WENT OUT ON THE SEVENTH DAY TO GATHER**[46] (Exodus 16:27 JPS), and following that it is written, **AMALEK CAME AND FOUGHT WITH ISRAEL** (17:8 JPS).

Rabbi Yoḥanan said in the name of Rabbi Simeon ben Yoḥai,

---

44. 'A small fish found around rocks' – Sokoloff, *Babylonian*, entry on *harsana*.
45. A Hebrew term for 'man', roughly equivalent to the English 'mortal'; also the personal name of an allegedly degenerate descendant of Adam (Genesis 5:6–11).
46. i.e. they disobeyed the instruction to stay at home on the Sabbath day.

If only Israel were to keep two Sabbaths properly they would
be redeemed forthwith, as it is said, **AS FOR THE EUNUCHS
WHO KEEP MY SABBATHS**, and then, **I WILL BRING THEM TO
MY SACRED MOUNT** (Isaiah 56:4, 7 JPS).

Rabbi Yosé said, May my portion fall among those who enjoy
three meals on the Sabbath!

*Rabbi Yosé's saying opens a collection which the redactors of
the Talmud inserted here even though few of the sayings have
any bearing on the Sabbath; eventually the Gemara returns to
the theme of Sabbath delight. Several of the anecdotes should
be read against the backdrop of a highly stratified society in
which men did not think it dignified to engage in menial tasks;
such things could normally be left to women or servants, but to
honour the Sabbath was a personal privilege to be pursued
eagerly.*

Rabbi Ḥanina would robe himself on the eve of the Sabbath
and stand and proclaim, Come! Let us go forth to welcome
Queen Sabbath!

Rabbi Yanai dressed in his [finest] clothes on the eve of the
Sabbath and proclaimed, Come, O bride! Come, O bride!

Rabba bar Rav Huna dropped in on Rabba bar Rav Naḥman.
They served him three *seahs* of greased wafers. How did you
know I was coming? he asked. They replied, Are you more
important to us than she is?[47]

Rabbi Abba bought meat from thirteen butchers for thirteen
silver coins. He handed it [to his servants][48] on the threshold,
and said to them, Hurry! Hurry!

Rabbi Abbahu sat on an ivory chair to blow the fire.

Rav Anan wore a *gudna*,[49] for it was taught in the school of
Rabbi Ishmael, **Do not wear the garments in which you boiled
the pot for your master when you serve him wine.**

Rav Safra singed a [sheep's] head.

Rava salted the fish.

Rav Huna kindled the lamps.

47. 'She' is the Sabbath, in honour of whom (rather than Rabba) the delicacy had
    been prepared.
48. Rashi inserts these words.
49. Obscure word, evidently denoting a garment worn only on special occasions.

Rav Papa prepared wicks.

Rav Ḥisda chopped beet.

Rabba and Rav Yosef gathered wood.

Rabbi Zeira set the kindling alight.

Rav Naḥman bar Isaac carried burdens in and out on his shoulder. He said, If Rabbi Ammi and Rabbi Assi were to visit me, would I not carry burdens for them?

> Some say, Rabbi Ammi and Rabbi Assi carried burdens in and out on their shoulders. They said, If Rabbi Yoḥanan were to visit us, would we not carry burdens for him?

Joseph the Sabbath-honourer had a heathen neighbour who owned much property. The Chaldean [astrologers] said to the neighbour, Joseph the Sabbath-honourer will enjoy it all! [The neighbour therefore] sold all his property, [bought a jewel with the proceeds] and put it in his turban. As he was crossing on a ferry the wind blew it off and deposited it in the water, where a fish swallowed it. They caught the fish, brought it [to market] on the eve of the Sabbath, and offered it for sale. Who will buy it now? they asked. [People] said, Take it to Joseph the Sabbath-honourer; he always buys. They brought him [the fish] and he purchased it. When he opened it he found the jewel inside, and he sold it for thirteen gold pieces.[50] An old man met him and commented, Who borrows for the Sabbath, the Sabbath repays him!

Rabbi asked Rabbi Ishmael the son of Rabbi Yosé, What [special] merit do the wealthy of the land of Israel possess?[51] He replied, It is because they tithe, as it is said, YOU SHALL SET ASIDE TITHES (Deuteronomy 14:22) – tithe, and you will become wealthy.[52]

What [special] merit do [the wealthy of] Babylonia possess[, seeing that they do not tithe]? He replied, They honour the Torah.

50. Some understand this as 'thirteen lofts full of gold', but that seems exaggerated. It is assumed that Joseph did not know the provenance of the jewel.
51. It is assumed that if someone possesses wealth it is because God has blessed him on account of his virtue.
52. There is a play here on the words 'aser (tithe) and 'ashir (wealthy).

And those of other lands? They honour the Sabbath, as Rabbi Ḥiyya bar Abba related: I was once invited to [the home of] a gentleman in Laodicea, and they set before him a golden table that needed ten men to carry it; sixteen silver chains were fixed on it, and dishes and cups and jugs and jars, and all kinds of choice foods and spices were set out. As they served they said, THE EARTH IS THE LORD'S, AND ALL THAT IT HOLDS, ETC. (Psalm 24:1 JPS) and as they cleared away they said, THE HEAVENS BELONG TO THE LORD, BUT THE EARTH HE GAVE OVER TO MAN (115:16 JPS). I asked him, My son, what did you do to deserve this? He replied, I was a butcher, and whenever I came across a beast of good quality I said, Let this be for Shabbat! I said, Happy are you, and blessed be the Omnipresent who has granted what you deserve!

Caesar[53] said to Rabbi Joshua ben Ḥanania, How is it that the Sabbath meal smells so appealing? He said, We have a certan spice called Shabbat[54] that we put in it. Let me have some, he requested. [Joshua replied,] For those who observe Shabbat, it works; for those who don't, it doesn't.

The Exilarch asked Rav Hamnuna, What is the meaning of [IF YOU CALL . . .] THE LORD'S HOLY DAY 'HONOURED' (Isaiah 58:13 JPS)? He said, This refers to the Day of Atonement, when there is no eating or drinking; the Torah says, honour it [by wearing] fresh clothes.

AND IF YOU HONOUR IT (Isaiah 58:14 JPS) – Rav says, By starting it early; Shmuel says, By extending it late.

Rav Papa bar Abba's sons asked him, What can people like us who have meat and wine every day do differently [to honour Shabbat]? He said, If you normally eat early, eat later; if you normally eat late, eat earlier.

In summer Rav Sheshet used to seat his disciples [on the Sabbath] in the sun, and in winter in the shade, so that they would leave early [and enjoy the Shabbat].

Rabbi Zeira used to look for pairs of disciples [engrossed in   119b

---

53. i.e. a high Roman official.
54. The Hebrew for dill is *shevet*, spelled exactly the same as Shabbat; Joshua, or perhaps the storyteller, is playing on the word.

Torah study – Rashi]; he would say to them, Please do not profane [the Sabbath]![55]

Rava – though some say Rabbi Joshua ben Levi – said, Even if you pray alone on the Sabbath eve you should recite *vay'khulu* (Genesis 2:1–3), for Rav Hamnuna said, When anyone prays on the Sabbath eve and recites *vay'khulu*, the Holy One, blessed be He, regards him as a partner in the creation; it says *vay'khulu* ('and they were completed'), but read instead *vay'khallu* ('and they completed').[56]

Rabbi Eleazar said, How do we know that speech is like deed? It is written, BY THE WORD OF THE LORD THE HEAVENS WERE MADE (Psalm 33:6 JPS).[57]

Rav Ḥisda said in the name of Mar Uqba, When anyone prays on the Sabbath eve and recites *vay'khulu*, the two ministering angels who accompany each person lay their hands on his head and say, YOUR GUILT SHALL DEPART AND YOUR SIN BE PURGED AWAY (Isaiah 6:7 JPS).

It was taught: **Rabbi Yosé ben Yehuda says, Two ministering angels, one good and one bad, accompany each person home when he returns from the synagogue on the Sabbath eve. If he arrives home to find the lamp shining, the table laid and the divan spread, the good angel says, May it be [God's] will that it should be so on the Sabbath to come, and the bad angel is forced to say, Amen! But if not, the bad angel says, May it be [God's] will that it should be so on the Sabbath to come, and the good angel is forced to say, Amen!**

Rabbi Eleazar said, A person should always set his table on the Sabbath eve, even if he needs no more than an olive[-size to eat].

And Rabbi Ḥanina said, A person should always set his table after the Sabbath, even if he needs no more than an olive[-size to eat]. Hot water[58] after Shabbat is therapeutic; hot bread after Shabbat is therapeutic.

---

55. He wanted to encourage them to enjoy 'Sabbath delight' – Rashi.
56. That is, active rather than passive, and plural to indicate participation by the one who prays.
57. Hebrew uses the same root for 'deed' and 'made'.
58. For drinks or washing – Rashi.

They used to prepare a three-year-old calf for Rabbi Abbahu after Shabbat, but he [just ate] the kidneys. When his son, Abimi, grew up, he asked, Why do you waste all that [food]? Keep some kidney from the Sabbath eve! They left some, but a lion came and ate [the calf].[59]

Reference to a point of law 'written in Zeiri's notebook' leads to citations from the 'notebooks' of other rabbis, including one from the notebook of the third-century Palestinian aggadist Joshua ben Levi that seems to imply that a person's character or fortune is determined by the day of the week on which he was born. But Rabbi Ḥanina declares that a person's life is guided by the mazzal *in the ascendant at the time he was born. Mazzal has been left untranslated since its meaning varies; it can mean constellation, sign of the Zodiac or, as here, 'heavenly body that moves', i.e. sun, moon or planet.*

Greek and Indian astrology arrived in Iran, including Babylonia, shortly after Ardashir I founded the Sasanian Empire in 226, when Rav and Shmuel were active. The astrologers' belief that people's lives were controlled by influences from the heavenly bodies, though widespread in the ancient world, conflicts with basic Jewish teaching on free will, reward and punishment. Yoḥanan, Rav, Shmuel and several of their successors distance themselves from Ḥanina's genethlialogy and demonstrate that Israel stands directly under divine providence, immune from astrological influence so long as she is faithful to God's commandments.

Belief in astrology persisted among Jews into modern times, with only rare voices, such as that of Maimonides, daring to challenge it. The Jewish congratulatory expression mazzal tov *('good constellation') derives from this belief.*

59. i.e. the calf that would have been eaten after Shabbat – Rashi.

CHAPTER TWENTY-FOUR

GEMARA:

156a   Rabbi Ḥanina said: Go tell the son of Levi that it is not the *mazzal* of the day of birth that determines, but the *mazzal* of the hour. One who was [born] under the sun will be radiant; he will eat of his own and drink of his own, [but] his secrets will be disclosed, and he will not succeed if he [attempts to] steal. One who is [born] under Venus will be rich, a provider of sustenance, for light is born within him. One [born] under Mercury will be radiant and wise, for [Mercury] is the sun's scribe. He who is [born] under the moon will suffer hardship; he will build and it will be destroyed, will destroy and it will be built; he will eat that which is not his and drink that which is not his; his secrets will stay concealed; if he steals he will succeed. He who is [born] under Saturn will be one whose plans are frustrated; some say, plans [made] against him will be frustrated. He who is [born] under Jupiter will be just; Rav Naḥman bar Isaac says, Just in [the performance of] the commandments. He who is [born] under Mars will be a shedder of blood; Rav Ashi says, [He could be] a blood letter, a butcher, a robber or a *mohel*. Rabbah said, I was [born] under Mars[, but I am none of those things]; Abbaye [responded], Master, you too punish and slay.[60]

It was taught: Rabbi Ḥanina said, *Mazzal* makes wise, *mazzal* makes rich and Israel is subject to *mazzal*. Rabbi Yoḥanan said, Israel is not subject to *mazzal*.

[This view of Rabbi Yoḥanan is consistent with his teaching, for] Rabbi Yoḥanan said, How do we know that Israel is not subject to *mazzal*? It is written, **Thus says the Lord: Do not learn from the ways of the nations, and do not fear the signs in the sky as the nations fear them** (Jeremiah 10:1–2) – [that is,] let the nations fear [signs in the sky], but let not Israel fear.

---

60. Abbaye refers to Rabbah's activities as a judge. It is unlikely that Babylonian Jewish courts exercised capital jurisdiction, but they certainly flogged offenders.

Rav, too, held that Israel is not subject to *mazzal*, for Rav Yehuda said in Rav's name, How do we know that Israel is not subject to *mazzal*? It is written, **AND HE TOOK HIM OUTSIDE** (Genesis 15:5). Abraham said before the Holy One, blessed be He, Lord of the Universe, **ONE OF MY HOUSEHOLD WILL BE MY HEIR** (Genesis 15:3). He said, No, **ONE WHO ISSUES FROM YOUR LOINS WILL BE YOUR HEIR** (15:4). [Abraham] said to Him, Lord of the Universe, I have looked at my horoscope and I am not destined to produce a son. [The Lord] replied to [Abraham], Abandon your horoscope! Israel is not subject to *mazzal*! What is the reason you [think you cannot produce a son]? [Is it] because Jupiter is in the west? Then I shall return it to the east, as it is written, **WHO HAS RAISED JUPITER FROM THE EAST, SUMMONED IT TO DO HIS BIDDING?** (Isaiah 41:2).[61]

156b

And [you can infer that] Shmuel, too, [held that] Israel is not subject to *mazzal*, for Shmuel and Ablat[62] were sitting [together,] and some men passed [on their way] to the fields. Ablat said to Shmuel, That man is going but he will not return; a snake will bite him and he will die. Shmuel said, If he is an Israelite he will return. While they were [still] sitting there, he returned. Ablat got up, set [the man's] load down and found a snake inside that had been cut in half. Shmuel asked [the man], What did you do? He replied, Every day we [all] put food [in the basket] together and eat it. Today [I saw that] one of us had no food and [he] was embarrassed. I said [to my companions], I will [collect the food and] put it in the bag. When I reached [the man who had none], I pretended to take [food] from him so he shouldn't be embarrassed. Shmuel said, You did a *mitzva*. Shmuel [then] went out and preached: **CHARITY SAVES FROM DEATH** (Proverbs 10:2) – not just from painful[63] death, but from any death.

And [you can infer that] Rabbi Aqiva, too, [held that] Israel is not subject to *mazzal*. Rabbi Aqiva had a daughter, and the Chaldean [astrologer]s told him that on the day she walked in

61. This not the common translation, since *tzedeq* is 'victory' or 'righteousness'; however, it is also the Hebrew name for Jupiter.
62. A Gentile sage and astrologer in Babylonia, not known outside the Talmud.
63. Literally, 'different'.

the garden a snake would bite her and she would die. He worried
a lot about the matter. One day she took off the ornamental
plate she was wearing on her forehead and stuck it in the soil;
it pierced the eye of the snake. When she picked it up in the
morning, the [dead] snake was dragged behind her. Her father
asked her what she had done. [She said,] Last evening a poor
man called at the door, but everyone was busy at the feast and
no one heard him, so I took the portion of food you had given
me and gave it to him. Rabbi Aqiva [then] went out and
preached: CHARITY SAVES FROM DEATH (Proverbs 10:2) – not
just from painful death, but from any death.

And [you can infer] from Rabbi Naḥman bar Isaac['s story],
too, [that] Israel is not subject to *mazzal*. The Chaldean
[astrologer]s told Rabbi Naḥman bar Isaac's mother that her
son [was destined to be] a robber. She wouldn't let him uncover
his head, but said, Cover your head so that the fear of Heaven
should be upon you, and pray. He didn't know why she said
that. One day he was sitting under a palm tree studying, when
his garment slipped from his head; he looked up at the palm,
temptation overcame him, and he climbed up and tore off a
bunch of dates with his teeth.[64]

---

64. Though the palm did not belong to him – Rashi.

SECOND TRACTATE
ERUVIN (BOUNDARIES)

After bringing the Israelites out of Egypt, God fed them in the desert with 'bread from the sky', which they called 'manna'. Six days it rained down for them, but not on the Sabbath; instead, they collected a double portion on Fridays. Moses' instructions for the seventh day were LET EVERYONE REMAIN WHERE HE IS; LET NO ONE LEAVE HIS PLACE ON THE SEVENTH DAY *(Exodus 16:29).*

Some rabbis understood this to mean that people should remain within allotted boundaries on the Sabbath.[1] These boundaries would depend on where you were when it commenced. If, for instance, you were in a village, you would be permitted to walk anywhere in it and 2,000 cubits beyond, in any direction; a town or village you encountered within the 2,000 cubits would count as only 4 cubits, so you could move anywhere within it, too. If you wanted to visit the next village, say at a distance of 3,000 cubits, you could do this by establishing 'residence' at a spot which was within 2,000 cubits of both villages, either by being there at the commencement of the Sabbath, or by placing a meal there in advance. This meal is known as eruv teḥumin, *the eruv of boundaries.*

Another sort of boundary derives from private property. If you and I live in houses that open on to a common courtyard

---

1. *Eruvin* 48a; 51a. Jerome, *Letter* 121:10, no. 884, in Vol. 22, p. 1054, of Migne's *Patrologia Latina* (1864 edn), ridiculing the rabbis for following the 'carnal sense' of Scripture (he reads this into Colossians 2:18–23), wrote: 'Since it is commanded that on Sabbaths each one should sit in his home and not leave the place in which he lives . . . They say, "Our teachers, Barachibas and Simeon and Hellel, gave us the tradition that we may go two thousand paces on the sabbath".' Presumably these teachers are Aqiva, Simeon and Hillel.

(or nowadays in separate apartments in a block), there is a boundary to my property, a boundary to yours and a common area through which we both have rights of passage. While there is no restriction on our movements within any of these areas, since they fall within the 2,000-cubit limit, there is a rabbinic restriction on transferring objects from one area to another. The device by which the restriction is lifted is called eruv ḥatzerot, *the* eruv *of courtyards: all residents of the courtyard contribute to a common meal, placed in the house of one of them, so that they regard themselves as residing together for the Sabbath meal. The word* eruv, *literally 'mixture', or 'sharing', denotes that meal. As Shmuel remarks (*Eruvin 49a*), if someone insists on having his own piece of bread, the* eruv *would be invalid for all, since* eruv *denotes sharing. Clearly, the* eruv *carries social as well as religious significance.*

Our courtyard may be one of many that open on to a street (Hebrew: mavui*). In that case, as well as erecting a token boundary at the end(s) of the street, all the residents of the courtyards will share in a third kind of* eruv, *known as* shittuf m'vuot. *This kind of* eruv *is commonly set up around a town, or an area within a town, enabling observant Jews to carry within the designated area.*

A fourth type of eruv, eruv tavshilin, *allows the preparation of food for the Sabbath on festival days; see* Betza, *Chapter Two.*

CHAPTER FOUR

MISHNA:

41b   **If foreigners or a malign spirit removed someone [beyond his Sabbath boundary], he has only four cubits [within which to move]. If they return him, it is as if he never left.**

If they took him to another town, or placed him in a paddock or a prison, Rabban Gamaliel and Rabbi Eleazar ben Azaria say, He may move throughout it, [but] Rabbi Joshua and Rabbi Aqiva say, He has only four cubits.

Once they were departing from Brindisi[2] and their ship put out to sea. Rabban Gamaliel and Rabbi Eleazar ben Azaria walked throughout it, [but] Rabbi Joshua and Rabbi Aqiva did not budge beyond four cubits, for they wished to be strict with themselves.

On one occasion they did not enter port until nightfall [on Friday, when the Sabbath had already commenced]. They said to Rabban Gamaliel, May we disembark? He said, You may; I was looking out, and [saw that] we entered the boundary before dark.

GEMARA:

Boundaries through the Sky   43a

Rav Ḥanania enquired: Do boundaries apply[3] above a height of 10 [palms], or do boundaries not apply above a height of 10 [palms]?

> You need not ask with reference to a pillar 10 [palms] high and four wide, for that is a swelling of the ground[, so like the ground itself is subject to boundary rules]. Pose the question rather with reference to a pillar 10 high but less than four wide, or with reference to someone who leaps [through the air above 10 palms]; alternatively, with reference to someone in a boat.[4]

What [is the answer]?

Rav Hoshaya said, Here is a proof: **Once they were departing from Brindisi and their ship put out to sea.** Now, if you say that boundaries apply above a height of 10 [palms], that is why **they wished to be strict with themselves**; but if boundaries do not apply above a height of 10 [palms], why did **they wish** [to be strict with themselves, seeing that the whole question of boundaries did not arise]?

> Perhaps it is as Rava said [in another context: The boat was] in the shallows[, so the deck was less than

---

2. The standard Hebrew text reads PLNDRSN, but there are several manuscript variations. The journey of the four rabbis to Rome is attested in several places; Brindisi (Brindisium) was a major port in Roman times.
3. Literally, 'Are there boundaries?'
4. The boat deck is assumed to be more than 10 palms above solid ground.

10 palms above solid ground]; here also, [perhaps] they were in shallows.[5]

Another proof. **On one occasion they did not enter port until dark.** Now, if you say that boundaries apply above a height of 10 [palms], that is all right; but if boundaries do not apply above a height of 10 [palms], what was the problem?

Rava says, it was moving in the shallows[, so the boundary laws applied].

A proof. **Seven lessons were recited on the Sabbath morning in the presence of Rav Ḥisda at Sura, and late on the Sabbath afternoon in Rava's presence at Pumbedita.** Who recited them? Was it not Elijah, from which you can infer that boundaries do not apply above a height of 10 [palms]? Not [necessarily]; perhaps the demon Joseph recited them.[6]

A proof. **If someone says, 'I [vow] to be a Nazirite on the day the son of David comes', he may drink wine on Sabbaths and Festivals, but he is forbidden to drink wine on weekdays.[7]** Now, if you say that boundaries apply above a height of 10 [palms], that is why he would be permitted [to drink wine, since the son of David would not arrive then as his journey would infringe the Sabbath]; but if boundaries do not apply above a height of 10 [palms], why should he be permitted[, seeing that the son of David might arrive]?

That is for a different reason. Scripture says, LO, I WILL SEND THE PROPHET ELIJAH TO YOU BEFORE THE COMING OF THE AWESOME, FEARFUL DAY OF THE LORD (Malachi 3:23 JPS), and [as] Elijah didn't arrive the previous day[, the son of David will not arrive today, the Sabbath, even if his journey is permissible].

But if so, he should be permitted [to drink wine] on any weekday, too, seeing that Elijah did not come

43b

5. Rava (below) was commenting on their arrival in port, when they would have been in shallow water; here, they were in the open Mediterranean.
6. Elijah would most likely have travelled in his fiery chariot (2 Kings 2:11), well above 10 spans high, and would certainly not have contravened the Sabbath laws; demons, on the other hand, are not Sabbath observers.
7. Nazirites abstain from produce of the grape and from contact with the dead and let their hair grow (Numbers 6); 'son of David' is the Messiah.

the previous day! So we assume [that Elijah came, but the would-be Nazirite did not know about it since Elijah] presented himself [only] at the Great Court. [Then why should the Sabbath be different?] Elijah might have presented himself at the Great Court [on Friday]! [Not so;] Israel has already been assured that Elijah will not come on the eve of a Sabbath or festival, since it would be troublesome.[8]

This assumes that if Elijah wouldn't come [on the eve of Sabbath or festival], the Messiah wouldn't come either. In that case, [the intending Nazirite] should be permitted [to drink wine] on Friday! Elijah wouldn't come [on Friday], but Messiah might, since when Messiah comes everyone will be Israel's servants [and will undertake the Sabbath preparations for them, so his arrival would not be troublesome].

He should be permitted [to drink wine] on Sunday. [As this is not stated,] we can infer that boundaries do not apply [above a height of 10 palms], for if boundaries did apply, he should be permitted [to drink wine] on Sunday, as Elijah could not arrive on the Sabbath!

The Tanna is in doubt as to whether boundaries apply, and goes to the stricter side.

When did this person take his vow [to be a Nazirite]? If it was a weekday, then once he had become a Nazirite, how could the Sabbath exempt him? So he must have vowed on the Sabbath itself, or on the Festival, so that day he is permitted [to drink wine], but from then on he is forbidden.

The Absent-minded Disciple

On one occasion they did not enter port until dark.

It was taught: Rabban Gamaliel had a tube through which he could determine 2,000 cubits on dry land, and 2,000 on sea.[9]

If you want to know how deep a valley is, fetch a

8. It would interfere with the Sabbath or festival preparations.
9. That is, engineered to enable him to estimate the Sabbath boundary. This may have been an instrument like the dioptra, a primitive theodolite, in use as early as 300 BCE and described by Hero of Alexandria (first century CE).

tube and look through it, and you will see how deep the valley is.[10]

If you want to know how high a palm tree is, measure its shadow and your own shadow, and you will know how high the palm is.

If you want to make sure that wild animals will not take up residence in the shade of a tomb [memorial],[11] put up a cane at the fourth hour of the day and see which way its shadow falls, then slope [the memorial] up and down from there [so that it does not offer shade at that time of the day].

Rav Ḥanilai's son, Nehemiah, was deeply engrossed in his studies and [absent-mindedly] walked beyond the [Sabbath] boundary. Rav Ḥisda said to Rav Naḥman, Your disciple Nehemiah is in distress! [Rav Naḥman] replied, [Then] make a barrier with people[12] so that he can come back in!

Rav Naḥman bar Isaac was sitting behind Rava, and Rava was in front of Rav Naḥman.[13] Rav Naḥman bar Isaac said to Rava, What is Rav Ḥisda's problem? Is it that there are enough men [to make the barrier], but he wants to know whether the *halakha* is according to Rabban Gamaliel, or were there not enough men [to make the barrier], and he wants to know whether or not the *halakha* is according to Rabban Eliezer?

Obviously, we must be dealing with a case where there were not enough men [to make the barrier], for if there were enough men, what was the question? Hadn't Rav [already] said that the *halakha* was according to Rabban Gamaliel in the cases of paddock, prison and boat? So we must be dealing with a case where there were not enough men, and the enquiry is as to

44a

10. Rashi explains that you would first need to establish how distances appeared through the tube on flat land.

11. The fear is that the animal may smell the corpse and drag it out – Rashi.

12. Some men had presumably established a further boundary for themselves by means of an *eruv*.

13. Gafni, *Yehudei Bavel*, pp. 274–9, explains that two disciples of Rav Naḥman, Rava in the front row and Naḥman bar Isaac in the second row, were taking part in the discussion, but Naḥman bar Isaac was still subordinate to, and a disciple of, Rava. See also Goodblatt, *Rabbinic Instruction*, pp. 221–38, and Kalmin, *Sages, Stories*, p. 199.

whether the *halakha* is according to Rabbi Eliezer[, who said that if somone had strayed two cubits beyond the boundary he could re-enter – Rashi].

> This is evident on close examination, since [Rav Naḥman] said to him, 'He can come in'; surely 'come in' implies without a barrier!

Rav Naḥman bar Isaac objected to Rava, **If the wall [of the *Sukka*] fell down, he may not stand people or objects there or prop up a bed to spread a sheet [over the gap], since it is forbidden to make a new, temporary 'tent' on the festival, and even more so on the Sabbath.**

The discussion is inconclusive. We do not know whether the absent-minded student was left standing until after the Sabbath!

How do you define a boundary around a town, seeing that there is no obvious way to do this unless the town is circular? Mishna states that, irrespective of the shape of the town, the boundary is to be squared off to a perfect rectangle based on the maximum extent of the town; Gemara clarifies that the rectangle is to be aligned north–south by east–west. This sparks off some technical discussion, leading to a consideration of the lapse of time between equinoxes and solstices. The editors inserted here a collection of sayings on the value of learning Torah and on the best way to study; these are remarkable for their down-to-earth quality, the warm humanity of several of the anecdotes and the sense they exhibit of joy and love in learning Torah.

This selection begins with Joshua ben Ḥanania's humorous reflections on being outwitted; these are all the more pointed as he was himself celebrated for outwitting heretics and unbelievers. Then come some anecdotes involving Beruria, the wife of Rabbi Meir, one of few women cited with evident admiration by the rabbis (though this proved rather too much for medieval commentators, who fabricated scurrilous stories about her).

CHAPTER FIVE

GEMARA:

53b   Rabbi Joshua ben Ḥanania said: **The only people who ever outwitted me were a woman, a boy and a girl.** What happened with the woman? Once I stayed at an inn, and the innkeeper made me a dish of beans. On the first day I ate them and left nothing, and again on the second day I ate them and left nothing. On the third day she put too much salt in them, and after tasting them I abstained. She said, Sir, why don't you eat? I replied, I ate earlier in the day. She said, Then you should not have broken bread! Perhaps you have set aside[14] [these beans for the servant] as *pe'ah* for the previous ones, for don't the Sages say *pe'ah* is set aside from the dish, not from the cooking pot?

What happened with the girl? I was walking along and my route passed through a field. A girl said to me, Sir, isn't this a [private] field? I said to her, It is a well-trodden path [and therefore a public right of way]. She replied, Robbers like you have trodden it!

And what happened with the boy? I was on my way when I saw a boy sitting at the crossroads. I asked, Which is the way into town? He said, This way is short but long, and that one is long but short. I followed the short but long [route], but when I arrived at the town I found that it was surrounded by gardens and orchards, and I had to retrace my steps. I said, My son, didn't you tell me that was the short [route]? He said to me, But didn't I tell you it was long! I kissed his head and said to him, Happy are you, Israel, for you are all astute, from the greatest to the smallest!

Rabbi Yosé the Galilean was on his way when he met Beruria. He said to her, Which way do we go to Lydda? She said to him, Stupid Galilean! Didn't the Sages say, Don't talk

---

14. 'Have set aside' follows the reading of the Vilna Gaon; the standard texts read 'you have not set aside'. This is the only place in the Talmud where the notion of *pe'ah* is extended to leaving food for servants; it was codified in the *Shulḥan Arukh* but ignored by Maimonides.

too much to women![15] You should have said, Which way to Lydda?

[On another occasion] **Beruria chanced on a student who was reviewing his lessons silently. She rebuked him sharply[16] and said, Isn't it written, [FOR HE HAS GRANTED ME AN ETERNAL PACT,] DRAWN UP IN FULL AND SECURED** (2 Samuel 23:5 JPS) – if [your learning] is drawn up in full to the 248 parts of your body,[17] it will be secure, and if not, it will not be secure. [And indeed] they taught: **Rabbi Eliezer had a disciple who used to review his lessons silently, and after three years he forgot what he had learned.**

54a

More anecdotes on the virtue of learning aloud lead to sayings on the benefits and joys of Torah study. Here is a selection.

Rabbi Joshua ben Levi said, If you are on a journey and have no companion, study Torah, as it is said, **FOR THEY ARE A GRACEFUL ACCOMPANIMENT;**[18] if your throat is sore, study Torah, as it is said, **AND A NECKLACE ABOUT YOUR THROAT** (Proverbs 1:9 JPS); if you feel unwell internally, study Torah, as it is said, **IT WILL BE A CURE FOR YOUR BODY**; if your bones ache, study Torah, as it is said, **A TONIC FOR YOUR BONES** (3:8 JPS); if your whole body feels unwell, study Torah, as it is said, **HEALING FOR HIS WHOLE BODY** (4:22 JPS).

Rav Yehuda the son of Rabbi Ḥiyya said, See! The ways of the Holy One, blessed be He, are not like the ways of flesh and blood! [It is] the way of flesh and blood that if someone gives his friend a drug, it is good for this but bad for that; but when the Holy One, blessed be He, gave the Torah to Israel, it was a cure for all his body, as it is said, **HEALING FOR HIS WHOLE BODY.**

Rava the son of Rav Yosef bar Ḥama had upset Rav Yosef.[19] When the eve of the Day of Atonement drew near, [Rava] said,

15. Mishna *Avot* 1:5 (see p. 554).
16. Literally, 'kicked him'.
17. That is, if you use your voice and limbs as well as your mind; 248 body parts are listed in Mishna *Ohalot* 1:8 (see p. 673).
18. JPS translates 'a graceful wreath about your head'; the Hebrew term *l'viya* translated as 'wreath' is literally 'accompaniment'.
19. That is, Yosef bar Ḥiyya (died *c.* 333 CE), head of the academy of Pumbedita, who by that time had lost his sight.

I will go and make it up with him. He went, and found [Rav Yosef's] servant pouring wine [for his master]. He said, Let me pour! [The servant] handed it over and [Rava] poured it. When [Rav Yosef] tasted it he said, This tastes as if it was poured by Yosef bar Ḥama! He said, It is I! [Rav Yosef said,] Don't sit down until you tell me the meaning of these verses: **AND FROM MIDBAR TO MATTANAH, AND FROM MATTANAH TO NAHALIEL, AND FROM NAHALIEL TO BAMOTH, AND FROM BAMOTH TO THE VALLEY** (Numbers 21:18–20 JPS). He replied: When someone makes himself like the desert (*midbar*) on which everyone tramples,[20] [the Torah] will be handed to him as a gift (*mattana*); when he accepts it as a gift, God will take him as a possession (*naḥaliel*); as God takes possession of him, he ascends to greatness, as it says, **FROM NAHALIEL TO BAMOTH** (*high places*). But if he becomes proud, the Holy One, blessed be He, casts him down, as it is said, **AND FROM BAMOTH TO THE VALLEY**. If he [then] repents, the Holy One, blessed be He, will raise him again, as it is said, **EVERY VALLEY WILL BE RAISED** (Isaiah 40:4).

Rabbi Ḥiyya bar Abba said, What is the meaning of **HE WHO TENDS A FIG TREE WILL ENJOY ITS FRUIT** (Proverbs 27:18 JPS)? Why are the words of Torah compared to a fig tree? Just
54b as whenever you search a fig tree,] you find figs, so whenever you mull over Torah, you discover meaning.

Rabbi Shmuel bar Naḥmani said, What is the meaning of **A LOVING DOE, A GRACEFUL MOUNTAIN GOAT, LET HER BREASTS SATISFY YOU AT ALL TIMES; BE INFATUATED WITH LOVE OF HER ALWAYS** (Proverbs 5:19 JPS)? Why are the words of Torah compared to a doe? This tells you that just as the doe's womb[21] is narrow, and she satisfies her lover every time as she did the first time, so too the words of Torah constantly satisfy those who learn them as they did the first time. **A GRACEFUL MOUNTAIN GOAT** – [Torah] brings grace to all who learn her! **LET HER BREASTS SATISFY YOU AT ALL TIMES** – why are the words of Torah compared to the breasts? This tells you that just

20. i.e. if you are humble, and do not respond to insults.
21. Presumably a euphemism for vagina.

as whenever a baby sucks he finds milk, so too whenever you mull over words of Torah, you discover meaning. **BE INFATU-ATED WITH LOVE OF HER ALWAYS** – like Rabbi Eleazar ben Pedat, of whom they said, Eleazar sat engrossed in Torah in the lower market of Sepphoris while his goods were on display in the upper market of Sepphoris.[22]

Rabbi Perida had a disciple to whom he repeated everything 400 times, and [only then did the disciple] absorb it. One day [Perida received a message that] he was required for some *mitzva*. He repeated [the lesson to the disciple as usual 400 times,] but [the disciple] did not absorb it. [Perida] said to him, What is the difference [today]? He replied, Sir, the moment they said to you that there was a *mitzva* to attend to, I lost my concentration, because I kept thinking, Now sir is getting up [to go], now sir is getting up [to go]. [Perida] said to him, Put your mind to it and I will teach you [again]. He repeated [the lesson] another 400 times. A heavenly voice issued forth and addressed [Perida]: What would you prefer [as your reward]: that 400 years should be added to your life, or that you and your generation should attain the life of the World to Come? He said, That I and my generation should attain the life of the World to Come. The Holy One, blessed be He, proclaimed, Grant him both!

The theme of 'squaring' boundaries is resumed, plunging the student into one of the major issues of calendar calculation.

The rabbis taught: **When you square [the town's boundaries], you square them according to the world's squaring, north to the world's north and south to the world's south.**[23] The mnemonic for this is Aries to the north and Scorpio to the south.   56a

Rabbi Yosé says, **If you don't know how to square according to the world's squaring, you should square according to the sun's path. How do you do that? [The side where] the sun rises and sets on a long day is towards north; where the sun rises and sets on a short day is towards south; at the Nisan and Tishrei**[24] **equinoxes the sun rises directly east and sets**

22. So greatly did he love Torah that he neglected his business.
23. i.e. the northern and southern boundaries follow an east–west axis.
24. i.e. spring and autumn.

directly west, as it is written, IT GOES SOUTHWARD, THEN
ROUND TO THE NORTH (Ecclesiastes 1:6)[25] – IT GOES SOUTH-
WARD in the day, and ROUND TO THE NORTH [towards] night.

    ROUND AND ROUND GOES THE WIND (Ecclesiastes
    1:6) – this refers to the eastern and western sectors;
    sometimes it goes along them, sometimes around
    them.

Rav Mesharshya said, These rules don't apply, for it was
taught: **The sun never rose in the north-eastern quarter and
set in the north-west, nor did it rise in the south-eastern
quarter and set in the south-west.**[26]

Shmuel said, The Nisan equinox falls precisely at one of the
four quarters of the day, [that is,] the beginning of the day, the
beginning of the night, midday or midnight; the Tishrei equinox
falls at $1\frac{1}{2}$ or $7\frac{1}{2}$ hours, whether in the daytime or at night. From
one *tequfa* to the next is 91 days, $7\frac{1}{2}$ hours, and no *tequfa* may
drag more than half an hour from another.[27]

Shmuel also said: If the spring equinox coincides with Jupiter,
trees will be shattered [by storms]; if the winter solstice coincides
with Jupiter, plants will wither.

    That is, if the birth of the moon occurred at the
    hour of the moon or of Jupiter.[28]

---

25. The Talmud takes the sun to be the subject of this verse; some translators take
the wind as subject.
26. This statement is clearly incorrect; the text is supported by manuscripts, but may
be corrupt.
27. In clock time, Shmuel is saying that the spring equinox must fall precisely at
6 a.m., midday, 6 p.m. or midnight, and the autumn equinox $1\frac{1}{2}$ hours later. See
next note. Shmuel accepts the Julian year of precisely $365\frac{1}{4}$ days. As this has
remained the basis for the Jewish calendar for at least 1,500 years, festivals now
occur on average about 13 days earlier than they did when the calculation was
introduced. A more accurate value for the tropical year, of 365 days, 7 hours and
28 minutes, is attributed by late medieval sources to Shmuel's contemporary Ada
bar Ahava. See W. M. Feldman, *Mathematics*, p. 75.
28. For the possible interpretations of *molad*, or birth of the moon, see Stern, *Calendar*, pp. 99–112. The concept of 'planetary hours', i.e. hours 'ruled' by sun, moon,
Mercury, Venus, Mars, Jupiter and Saturn, was known to the Babylonians and is
perpetuated by astrologers today.

THIRD TRACTATE
PESAḤIM (THE PASSOVER)

**SEVEN DAYS YOU SHALL EAT UNLEAVENED BREAD; ON THE
VERY FIRST DAY YOU SHALL REMOVE LEAVEN FROM YOUR
HOUSES** (Exodus 12:15 JPS). ***NO LEAVEN SHALL BE FOUND IN
YOUR HOUSES FOR SEVEN DAYS*** (12:19).

CHAPTER ONE

MISHNA:

On the night of the fourteenth [of Nisan] you must search
for *ḥametz* [leaven] by the light of a lamp. There is no need
to search places where you do not put *ḥametz*.

In what circumstances did they say, Two rows [of barrels]
in the cellar [must be searched]? [Only if] you might have put
ḥametz there.

The School of Shammai say, Two rows [means] two rows
across the whole area of the cellar, but the School of Hillel
say, Two rows [means] the two outer rows, that is, the upper-
most ones.

*On the night of the fourteenth is literally 'at light on the four-
teenth'. The Gemara concludes that the expression is a euphemism – 'light' here stands for dark, as in the Aramaic idiom sagi
nahor, 'one who has plenty of light', for a blind person – and it
offers advice on the general use of euphemism to avoid
unpleasantness.*

It was generally accepted that ḥametz *was prohibited on the
afternoon of 14th Nisan, i.e. the afternoon preceding Pesach,*

though this is not clearly stated in Scripture. The Sages seek proof-texts.

Days are regarded as commencing at dark on the previous evening; if, for instance, 15th Nisan falls on a Thursday, it commences at nightfall on Wednesday evening. Daylight hours are reckoned by dividing the period from sunrise to sunset into twelve equal parts.

GEMARA:

4b   A Mishna[1] states: Rabbi Meir says, **They eat [*ḥametz*] throughout the fifth hour and burn [what is left over] at the beginning of the sixth. Rabbi Judah says, They eat [*ḥametz*] throughout the fourth hour, wait through the fifth and burn [what is left over] at the beginning of the sixth.** [Evidently,] they both agree that it is forbidden [to eat] *ḥametz* after the sixth hour. On what is this based?

Abbaye said, [It is based on] two verses. One states, **No leaven shall be found in your houses for seven days** (Exodus 12:19), and the other states, **But on the first day you shall remove leaven from your houses** (12:15). What does this imply? The fourteenth [of Nisan] is added [before the seven as the day] to remove *ḥametz*.[2]

Why not say [instead] that [the second verse is needed] to include the night of the fifteenth [as the time by which] *ḥametz* must be removed? We might, after all, think that as [Scripture] writes **days**, it means days not nights[, so the second verse is needed] to tell us that nights are included [in the prohibition]!

5a   [No. The verse] is not needed for that, since removal of leaven is compared to [the prohibition of] eating *ḥametz*, and [the prohibition of] eating *ḥametz* to [the command to] eat *matza*. Removal of leaven is compared to [the prohibition of] eating *ḥametz*, for it is written, **No leaven shall be found in your houses for seven days, for whoever eats**

---

1. Later in this chapter.
2. Abbaye's point is that if *ḥametz* is forbidden on 15 Nisan (the first day of Passover), it makes no sense to say it must be removed *on* that day; we must therefore understand *ba-yom ha-rishon* as 'by the first day' rather than 'on the first day'.

ḤAMETZ WILL BE CUT OFF (Exodus 12:19); [the pro-
hibition of] eating *ḥametz* is compared to [the com-
mand to] eat *matza*, for it is written, YOU SHALL EAT
NO ḤAMETZ; IN ALL YOUR DWELLINGS YOU SHALL
EAT *MATZA* (12:20), and of *matza* it is written, IN THE
EVENING YOU SHALL EAT *MATZA* (12:18).

Then perhaps [the second verse is needed] to add
the night of the fourteenth [as the time by which]
ḥametz must be removed? [No. That cannot be so,
since] Scripture says, [BUT ON THE FIRST] DAY
(Exodus 12:15). Perhaps it means in the morning? [No,
since] BUT implies a division [of the day].

It was taught in the School of Rabbi Ishmael: We find that
the fourteenth is called 'first', as it is said, IN THE FIRST, ON
THE FOURTEENTH DAY OF THE MONTH (Exodus 12:18).[3]

Rav Naḥman bar Isaac said, 'First' may mean 'previous', as
[when] Scripture says, WERE YOU THE FIRST OF MEN TO BE
BORN? (Job 15:7).

Then what about, YOU SHALL TAKE FOR YOUR-
SELVES ON THE FIRST DAY? Can that [possibly] mean
the previous day? [Surely not!] That is different, for it
[continues], AND YOU SHALL REJOICE BEFORE THE
LORD YOUR GOD FOR SEVEN DAYS (Leviticus 23:40);
just as the seventh [day must be] the seventh [day] of
the festival, so the first [day] is the first [day] of the
festival.

But [in connection with Pesach, likewise,]
it is written, BUT ON THE FIRST DAY YOU
SHALL REMOVE . . . FOR SEVEN DAYS YOU
SHALL EAT *MATZA* (Exodus 12:15[4])[, so how
can you claim in this context that 'first'
means 'previous']? If it just meant 'first'
Scripture should have written FIRST DAY.

3. A puzzling statement, since 'first' in this verse clearly refers to the month, not the
    day, and the occurrence of 'first' that would be relevant to interpret as 'previous'
    is in verse 15. *Tosafot* draws attention to the problem.
4. The phrases are in the reverse order in the Bible, but are cited this way to carry
    the argument forward.

Why then has it written *THE* FIRST DAY
[with the definite article]? This must be as we
said[, namely, that here it means 'previous'].

But the identical expression is used in the
verse cited from Leviticus in connection with
the festival of Sukkot[, so why is] THE FIRST
DAY [written] there, too? Moreover, there
[the definite article is used twice, for] it is
written ON THE FIRST DAY SHALL BE A
SOLEMN REST, AND ON THE EIGHTH DAY
A SOLEMN REST (Leviticus 23:39). That is
different; when Scripture writes THE EIGHTH
DAY [SHALL BE A DAY OF] SOLEMN REST it
must be referring to the eighth day of the
festival; so [likewise] when it states THE
FIRST, it must mean the first day of the
festival. Then why does it [use the definite
article]? It must be to exclude the middle
days of the festival. But [surely] that follows
from [explicitly stating] the first and the
eighth? [Not necessarily, since you might
have thought] that as Scripture writes AND
ON THE EIGHTH DAY, the conjunction AND
implies an addition to what is specified, that
is, we are to understand that the middle days
are included; [it therefore uses the definite
article] to inform us [that that would be an
incorrect inference].

Then let the Torah use neither the conjunction nor the definite article! Moreover,
since it states there, ON THE FIRST DAY YOU
SHALL HAVE A HOLY CONVOCATION (Leviticus 23:35), surely 'first' there [could be
understood as] 'previous'? [So] we must
[abandon the idea that 'first' in this context
means 'previous', and instead] use the threefold repetition of THE FIRST [in Leviticus 23]
as it was interpreted in the school of Rabbi

Ishmael, for it was taught in the school of Rabbi Ishmael:

Through the merit of three 'firsts' they earned three 'firsts', namely the destruction of the seed of Esau, the building of the Temple and the name of the Messiah: destruction of the seed of Esau, as it is written, AND THE FIRST CAME OUT RUDDY ALL OVER, LIKE A HAIRY CLOAK (Genesis 25:25); the building of the Temple, as it is written, A GLORIOUS HIGH THRONE FROM THE FIRST IS THE PLACE OF OUR TEMPLE (Jeremiah 17:12); the name of the Messiah, as it is written, BEHOLD, THE FIRST IN ZION! (Isaiah 41:27).

Rava said, [The prohibition of *hametz* on the afternoon preceding Pesach] is derived from this verse: YOU SHALL NOT SLAUGHTER MY SACRIFICE WITH LEAVEN (Exodus 34:25); [this means,] you shall not slaughter the Passover [lamb] while you still have leaven in your possession.

Perhaps that means [for each person] the time at which he slaughters his lamb? No. [It means] the [whole] period specified by the Torah for slaughter.

A baraita teaches the same: BUT ON THE FIRST DAY YOU SHALL REMOVE LEAVEN FROM YOUR HOUSE (Exodus 12:15). This means on the eve of the festival. Or could it mean on the [first day of the] festival itself? [No. For it is written,] YOU SHALL NOT SLAUGHTER MY SACRIFICE WITH LEAVEN (34:25); [this means,] you shall not slaughter the Passover [lamb] while you still have leaven in your possession. This is the opinion of Rabbi Ishmael, but Rabbi Aqiva says, [This interpretation] is not necessary. It says, BUT ON THE FIRST DAY YOU SHALL REMOVE LEAVEN FROM YOUR HOUSE (12:15), and it is written, NO WORK SHALL BE DONE ON [THOSE DAYS] (12:16); [since] burning is a principal category of forbidden work, it is clear that the removal of *hametz* should not take place on the festival day itself.

Rabbi Yosé says, [Ishmael's interpretation] is not necessary.

It says, BUT ON THE FIRST DAY YOU SHALL REMOVE LEAVEN
FROM YOUR HOUSE; [this must mean] on the eve of the festival.
Or could it mean on the festival itself? [No, for] BUT indicates
a division [of time], and it could not be permissible on the
festival itself, for the removal of leaven is compared to the
prohibition of eating *ḥametz*, and the prohibition of eating
ḥametz to the eating of *matza*.

5b   Rava said, We can make three inferences from Rabbi Aqiva's
statement. We can infer that *ḥametz* must be removed by burning; we can infer that the prohibition of kindling fire on Shabbat
is specified by the Torah as a category of forbidden activity; and
we can infer that we do not accept the ruling that since kindling
fires is permitted [on festivals] for [personal] needs, it is also
permitted when there is no need.

*Enough of proof-texts! The next section illustrates a radically
different kind of reasoning. It is a highly stylized academic
exercise; the disciples are challenged to explore their understanding of the principles behind various Tannaitic statements,
and to apply them to questions about the need to search for*
ḥametz *in a variety of circumstances. Underlying the discussion
is the assumption that the Torah is a seamless whole, whose
principles extend across all areas of law; there is joy in discovery
as answers to new questions are revealed. Aside from a comment
by Rava, the passage is an anonymous discussion of Tannaitic
sources, sparked off by the Mishna's common-sense advice not
to get over-anxious about remote possibilities.*

MISHNA:

9a   There is no need to worry whether a mouse[5] has dragged
[*ḥametz*] from one house to another or from one place to
another, since [if we were to consider such a possibility,] we
would need to worry whether it had dragged something from
courtyard to courtyard or from town to town, and there would
be no end to the matter.

GEMARA:

9b   Nine bundles of *matza* and one of *ḥametz*, and a mouse

5.   The word *ḥulda*, feminine of the biblical *ḥoled* (Leviticus 11:29), is variously
     translated by Jastrow, *Dictionary*, as 'mole', 'weasel', 'porcupine' and 'back-gate';
     in modern Hebrew it means 'rat'.

comes and takes one and we don't know whether it took the *matza* or the *ḥametz* – this corresponds to [the baraita of] the Nine Shops; if one [of the bundles] had separated, and then the mouse came and took it, this corresponds to the latter part [of the baraita]. For a baraita states: **There were nine shops all selling [correctly] slaughtered meat and one selling carrion, and he bought [meat] from one, but did not know which; [in such a case of] doubt[, the meat] is forbidden. If[, on the other hand, the meat] was found [outside the shops, we] go by the majority[, and the meat is permitted].**

Two bundles, one of *matza* and one of *ḥametz*, and in front of them two houses, one searched and the other not searched, then two mice arrive; one takes the *matza* and one the *ḥametz*, and we do not know which entered which house – this corresponds to [the baraita of] the Two Boxes. For a baraita states: **Two boxes, one of priests'-due and one of ordinary food, and in front of them are two sacks,[6] one of priests'-due and one of ordinary food, and food fell from the boxes into the sacks. It is [all] permitted, since I may assume[7] that the ordinary fell into the ordinary, and the priests'-due into the priests'-due.[8]**

[It is all very well to] say **I may assume** with regard to priests'-due, which [nowadays] is of rabbinical status only, but can we say it of *ḥametz*, which is *d'Oraita*? [Yes. The prohibition of *ḥametz* is indeed *d'Oraita*, but] is the search for *ḥametz d'Oraita*? [Surely] it is rabbinic, for the Torah requires only that [*ḥametz*] be declared null and void.

10a

A bundle of *ḥametz*, and two houses that have [already] been searched, and a mouse comes and takes it, and we do not know which [house] it entered – this corresponds to [the Mishna of] the Two Paths. For a Mishna states, **Two paths, one pure and one impure; someone walked along one of them and [prepared] pure [food], then someone else walked along the other and [prepared] pure [food], Rabbi Judah says, If they both enquired**

---

6. The word is *seah*; the reference is to a container, possibly a sack, that holds that measurement.
7. Literally, 'I say'.
8. Tosefta *Terumot* 6:11 (Lieberman edn).

independently, [the food prepared by] both is pure, but if they enquired together it is impure. Rabbi Yosé says, Either way it is impure.[9]

 Rava, and some say Rabbi Yoḥanan, observed [apropos of the Mishna], Everyone agrees that [if they enquired] together [the food is impure], and if one after the other it is pure. They dispute only the case where one enquires on behalf of the other; Rabbi Yosé compares this to [both enquiring] together, and Rabbi Judah compares it to one enquiring after the other.

If there is doubt as to whether [the mouse] entered the house or not, this corresponds to [the Mishna of] the Valley, and to the dispute between Rabbi Eliezer and the rabbis. For a Mishna states, **If someone entered a valley in the rainy season, and there was [a source of] impurity in a field, and he says, I passed through that place, but I don't know whether I entered that field or not, Rabbi Eliezer declared him pure, and the rabbis declared him impure, for Rabbi Eliezer held that if there is doubt as to whether someone entered [an impure place, he remains] pure, whereas if there is doubt as to whether he touched [the source of] impurity, he is impure.**[10]

If [the mouse] entered [the house, and the man] searched and found nothing, this corresponds to the dispute between Rabbi Meir and the rabbis. For a Mishna states, **Rabbi Meir used to say that wherever there is a presumption of impurity, the state of impurity remains until there is definite information as to where the source of impurity has gone; but the rabbis say, Search until you reach rock or virgin soil.**[11]

If [the mouse] entered [the house, and the man] searched and found the *ḥametz*, this corresponds to the dispute between Rabbi and Rabban Simeon ben Gamaliel.[12] For a baraita states, **If a grave was lost within a field and someone enters the field, he is impure; if a grave is located [within the field, the person who entered the field] is pure, because I may assume that the**

9.　Mishna *Tohorot* 5:5.
10.　Ibid., 6:5.
11.　Mishna *Nidda* 9:5 (61a).
12.　Judah the Patriarch and his father, Simeon ben Gamaliel II.

grave that was lost is the one that has been found. This is the opinion of Rabbi, but Rabban Simeon ben Gamaliel says, The whole field must be searched [in case this was not the same grave, and there is more than one].

If he left nine [bundles of *hametz*] and [came back and] found ten, this corresponds to the dispute between Rabbi and the [other] rabbis. For a baraita states, **If he left 100 [*zuz* of second-tithe money] and [came back and] found 200, [he must assume] that unconsecrated [money] and second-tithe [money] are mixed together. This is the opinion of Rabbi, but the [other] rabbis say, [The first money has been taken, and the 200 are] all unconsecrated [money].**[13]

If he left ten [bundles of *hametz*] and [came back and] found nine, this corresponds to the end of the baraita, for it states, **If he left 200 [*zuz*] and [came back and] found 100, 100 remains and 100 has been taken. This is the opinion of Rabbi, but the [other] rabbis say, [The first money has been taken, and the 100 are] all unconsecrated [money].**

If he left [*hametz*] in one corner and [came back and] found 10b
it in another, this corresponds to the dispute between Rabban Simeon ben Gamaliel and the [other] rabbis. For a baraita states, **If someone lost a spade in a house, the house is impure, for I must assume that an impure person entered[, rendering the contents of the house impure,] and took it. Rabban Simeon ben Gamaliel says, The house is pure, for I may assume that [the owner] lent [the spade] to someone else and forgot about it, or that he [himself] took it from one corner, placed it in another and forgot.**

Who said anything about a corner? Words are lacking from the baraita, and it should read, **If someone lost a spade in a house, the house is impure, for I must assume that an impure person entered[, rendering the contents of the house impure,] and took it. If [the owner] left [the spade] in one corner and found it another, the house is impure, for I must assume that an impure person entered, took [the spade] from one**

13. Tosefta *Ma'aser Sheni* 5:7 (Lieberman edn).

corner and deposited it in another. Rabban Simeon ben Gamaliel says, The house is pure, for I may assume that [the owner] lent [the spade] to someone else and forgot about it, or that he [himself] took it from one corner, placed it in another and forgot.

The following is a 'running commentary' on the Mishna, the interesting digressions not being allowed to obscure the interpretation. The Gemara makes clear that substances in the list are not 'true' ḥametz, but fall into two categories: mixtures containing ḥametz, and degraded forms of ḥametz.

As the text contains both Hebrew and Greek terms unfamiliar in Babylonia, the Amoraim have to engage in a certain amount of philology. The comparison of Judaean and Edomite wine carries a subtext: Edom is the symbol of Rome, and the alternating fortunes of Judah and Edom point to the eventual triumph of the former.

CHAPTER THREE

MISHNA:

42a   You transgress[14] [the laws of] Passover by retaining in your possession any of the following: Babylonian dip, Median beer, Edomite vinegar, Egyptian *zythos*, dyers' soup, butchers' dough, scribes' glue.[15] Rabbi Eliezer says, Women's cosmetics, also. In sum, you transgress by keeping anything [made of] grain.[16] The items in this list are forbidden, but do not render you liable to 'being cut off'.[17]

GEMARA:

The rabbis taught: **Three things are said of Babylonian dip: it blocks the heart, it blinds the eyes and it weakens the body.**

14. So Rashi.
15. *Zythos* is a Greek adaptation of an Egyptian word for beer (Jastrow, *Dictionary*). Mishna also has Greek *zōmos* (soup) and *kolla* (glue).
16. Wheat, barley, oats, rye or spelt, as specified in a previous Mishna.
17. One who eats leaven on Passover 'shall be cut off from his people [*karet*]' (Exodus 12:15).

It blocks the heart because of the whey it contains; it blinds the eyes because of the salt; it weakens the body because of the mouldy bread in it.

The rabbis taught: Three things increase faeces, bend the stature and rob a man of one five-hundredth of the light of his eyes. These are they: black bread,[18] unmatured beer and raw vegetables.

The rabbis taught: Three things decrease faeces, straighten the stature and lighten the eyes. These are they: refined bread, fat meat and mature wine – refined bread made from fine flour; fat meat, from a goat that has not yet given birth; mature wine, three years old.

Whatever is good for one [part of the body] is bad for another, and what is good for that is bad for this, other than fresh ginger, long peppers, refined bread, fat meat and mature wine, which are good for the whole body.

Median beer [is forbidden because] they put barley water in it.

Edomite vinegar [is forbidden because] they put barley in it.

> Rav Naḥman said, At first, when they used to bring [wine for] libations from Judaea, the Judaean wine did not turn sour unless they put barley in it; they called [the soured wine] 'vinegar' without qualification. Nowadays, it is Edomite wine that does not turn sour unless they put barley in it, so they call it 'Edomite vinegar'.[19] This fulfils what is said, **I SHALL BE FILLED, NOW THAT IT IS LAID IN RUINS**[20] (Ezekiel 26:2 JPS) – if the one [Israel] is full, the other [Edom] will be laid in ruins, and if the other [Edom] is full, this [Israel] will be laid in ruins.

> Rav Naḥman bar Isaac said, [The alternating fortunes of Israel and Edom] are derived from this: **ONE PEOPLE SHALL BE MIGHTIER THAN THE OTHER** (Genesis 25:23 JPS).

18. Latin *cibaria*.
19. He is saying that originally Judaean wine was better than Edomite; now it is the reverse.
20. In Ezekiel, it is Tyre that makes this boast.

Rabbi Judah said, Originally, if you bought vinegar from an 'am ha-aretz there was no need to tithe it, since you could assume it was made from husks; but now, if you buy vinegar from an 'am ha-aretz you must tithe it, since you have to assume it is made from wine.

> Does Rabbi Judah hold that husks do not have to be tithed? Surely a Mishna says, **If someone soaks husks in a measure of water, and finds the full measure of water there, he is exempt [from tithes], but Rabbi Judah says he must [tithe].**[21] What he means is, [If you bought vinegar from an 'am ha-aretz there is no need to tithe it, since] the 'am ha-aretz is not under suspicion of [having failed to tithe] husks. Alternatively, one statement concerns vinegar made with a strainer,[22] and the other concerns vinegar made by soaking pips.

Egyptian *zythos*. What is Egyptian *zythos*? Rav Yosef taught, [It consists of] one third barley, one third safflower seed and one third salt. Rav Papa substituted wheat for barley [in the recipe]. (The mnemonic is SISNI.[23]) They steep them, roast them, and grind them, and drink [the mixture] between Passover and Pentecost. If you are constipated it loosens you; if you suffer diarrhoea it constricts you. It is dangerous for sick people and pregnant women.

Dyers' soup. Here they understand it to be bran water with which they moisten lac.[24]

Butchers' dough. Bread made from grain less than a third ripe; they place it over a pot and it absorbs the moisture.

And scribes' glue. Here they understand it to be leather-

21. Mishna Ma'aserot 5:6.
22. And possibly containing lees of the wine – Rashi.
23. This is an abbreviation to help remember that YoSef included barley (Hebrew: se'or) among the ingredients.
24. Sokoloff, *Babylonian*, entry on *lakha*. The reading *laba* in the Vilna text is incorrect.

workers' glue. Rav Shimi of Ḥozna'a said, It is a cosmetic that rich girls use, then give what is left over to poor girls.[25]

[Rav Shimi] can't be right. Didn't Rabbi Ḥiyya teach that the Mishna lists four general items and three trades? If you say that [scribe's glue] is a rich girls' cosmetic, what is the [third] trade? Then what – if you say leatherworkers' glue [is meant], why is it called scribes' glue? It should be called leatherworkers' glue! Rav Oshaya said, It is certainly leatherworkers' glue, but it is referred to as scribes' glue since they use it too, to stick their papers together.

Rabbi Eliezer says, Women's cosmetics, also. Women's cosmetics? Surely he means women's applications. As Rav Yehuda said in the name of Rav, When Jewish girls have matured physically but not reached [adult] years, poor girls apply lime [as a depilatory], rich girls apply fine flour, and princesses oil of myrrh, as it is written, Six months with oil of myrrh (Esther 2:12).

43a

What is oil of myrrh? Rav Huna bar Yirmiya said, *Stakte.*[26] Rav Yirmiya bar Abba said, Oil [extracted from] olives less than a third ripe. Rabbi Judah said, *Omphakias,*[27] [that is,] oil [extracted from] olives less than a third ripe.

Why do they apply it? Because it removes [unwanted] hair and softens the flesh.

In sum, you transgress by keeping anything [made of] grain. It was taught: **Rabbi Joshua said, Seeing that the Mishna gives the [general] rule that you transgress by keeping anything [made of] grain, why did the Sages list these [specific] items? It was so that people should be familiar with them and their names.**

This is like what happened to a westerner[28] who came to Babylon. He had some meat with him, and

25. Scribes' daughters – Rashi.
26. Greek, meaning something that oozes or drips.
27. Greek, denoting wine from unripe grapes, rather than oil; there is perhaps some scribal confusion here.
28. From the Land of Israel.

asked, Pass me the food[-bowl]! He heard them say, Pass him the *kutaḥ*; as soon as he heard the word *kutaḥ* he desisted[, since he knew that it was the Babylonian dip and contained milk, which he could not eat with his meat].

What determined the class structure among Jews in the societies where the Mishna and the Babylonian Talmud came into being? The aggada below, like the opening of the final chapter of Qiddushin, assigns value to the 'holiness' of good family, here descent from Aaron the High Priest, but the highest value to Torah learning, a point expressed more forcefully in the final Mishna of Horayot (see p. 561).

To what extent do the social structures assumed by the Talmud correspond to the reality of Jewish life at that time? The 'near death' vision of Yosef the son of Rabbi Joshua ben Levi, in which he sees a reversed social order among all but the learned, points to a discrepancy between ideal and reality.

At times, there was tension amounting to hatred between the learned (the talmid ḥakham*) and the ignorant (the* ʿam ha-aretz*). Such hostility may well have arisen in reaction to the exclusiveness of the* ḥaverim, *who set themselves apart from the 'ignorant masses' by their meticulous tithing and ritual purity; it declines among the Amoraim.*[29]

MISHNA:

49a   **If someone is on the way to slaughter his Passover [lamb], or to circumcise his son, or to the betrothal feast in the home of his [prospective] father-in-law, and remembers that he has *ḥametz* in his house, if he has time to return home, get rid of it and still perform his *mitzva*,**[30] **he should return home and get rid of it. If there isn't enough time to do both, he should [not return home, but] mentally annul [the *ḥametz* and proceed with his *mitzva*].**

[If he was on his way] to rescue [people] from idolaters, a river, robbers, a fire or a collapsing building, he should [not

29. The passage is analysed in detail by Oppenheimer, ʿAm ha-aretz, pp. 172–88. See introductory note to Demai, pp. 44–5.
30. Used here in the sense of 'obligation'.

return home, but should] mentally annul [the *ḥametz* and proceed with his *mitzva*].

[If he was on his way] to establish Sabbath residence for some optional [purpose], he should return at once [to get rid of the *ḥametz*].

The same [applies] if someone left Jerusalem and discovered he was [still] carrying sacred meat. If he has passed the Mount of Olives, he may burn [the meat] wherever he is, but if not he should return [to Jerusalem] and burn it within the city with wood from the altar fire.

For what quantity is one obliged to return? Rabbi Meir says, In both cases, an egg-size; Rabbi Judah says, In both cases, an olive-size; the [majority of] Sages say, Sacred meat, an olive-size; *ḥametz*, an egg-size.

GEMARA:

They objected: If someone is on his way to the betrothal feast in the home of his [prospective] father-in-law, or to establish Sabbath residence for some optional [purpose], he should return at once [to get rid of the *ḥametz*].

Rabbi Yoḥanan said, There is no contradiction; one is [the opinion of] Rabbi Judah, the other is [the opinion of] Rabbi Yosé, for a baraita teaches: The betrothal feast is optional according to Rabbi Judah, but Rabbi Yosé says it is a *mitzva*.

[However, since] Rav Ḥisda stated that the dispute [between the Mishna and the baraita] concerned [only] the second meal [that the prospective bridegroom takes with his in-laws], but all agree that the first meal is a *mitzva*, you may say that both Mishna and baraita are in accordance with Rabbi Judah's opinion; one concerns the first meal, the other the second. [The basis for this is] the baraita which teaches: Rabbi Judah says, I have heard that only the betrothal meal itself is a *mitzva*, not the *sivlonot*[31] meal [which follows]. Rabbi Yosé replied, I heard that both the betrothal meal and the *sivlonot* meal [are obligatory].

It was taught: Rabbi Simeon says, A disciple should not benefit in any way from a feast that is not a *mitzva* feast.

31. Gifts presented by the groom to the bride at a second, 'follow-up' meal.

What, for instance, is not a *mitzva* feast? Rabbi Yoḥanan said, For example, [the marriage of] the daughter of a *Kohen* to an [ordinary] Israelite, or of the daughter of a scholar to an ignoramus. For Rabbi Yoḥanan said, The match of a *Kohen*'s daughter to an [ordinary] Israelite does not augur well.

What did he mean by that? Rav Ḥisda says, [He meant that] she would be widowed [early] or divorced or childless. A baraita says, **Either he will bury her [prematurely – Rashi], or she will bury or impoverish him.**

How can this be? Did not Rabbi Yoḥanan [himself] say, If you wish to get rich, cleave to the seed of Aaron,[32] so that Torah and priesthood may combine to produce wealth? No problem. One statement was addressed to a learned person, the other to an ignoramus.

Rabbi Joshua married a *Kohen*'s daughter and became sick. He said, Aaron is not pleased that I should cleave to his seed, and that he should have a son-in-law like me.

Rav Idi bar Avin married a *Kohen*'s daughter and had two sons by her who were ordained, Rav Sheshet and Rabbi Joshua.

Rav Papa said, Had I not married a *Kohen*'s daughter I would not have become wealthy.

Rav Kahana said, Had I not married a *Kohen*'s daughter I would not have been exiled. They said, to him, But you have been exiled to a place of Torah! [He replied,] I did not leave my home voluntarily.[33]

Rabbi Isaac said, Whoever benefits from a feast that is not a *mitzva* feast[34] will someday be exiled, as it is said, [**THEY LIE ON IVORY BEDS, LOLLING ON THEIR COUCHES,**] **FEASTING**

32. Marry the daughter of a *Kohen*.
33. The story of Rav Kahana's flight from Babylonia to Palestine is told in *Bava Qama* 117a (see pp. 457–60). Early commentators disagreed as to whether, despite his name, he was a *Kohen* (*Tosafot* to *Pesaḥim* 49b).
34. Literally, 'an optional feast'.

ON LAMBS FROM THE FLOCK AND ON CALVES FROM THE STALLS . . . ASSUREDLY, RIGHT SOON THEY SHALL HEAD THE COLUMN OF EXILES (Amos 6:4, 7 JPS).

The rabbis taught: The disciple who eats to excess, wherever it may be, will destroy his home, turn his wife into a widow and his brood into orphans; he will forget his learning and be drawn into quarrels; he will disgrace the Name of Heaven, as well as his father and his teacher, and bring himself, his children and his grandchildren for all generations into disrepute.

> What did they mean by 'into disrepute'? Abbaye said, [People] will call his children Son of the oven-heater; Rava said, Son of the dancer among the drinking-bowls; Rav Papa said, Son of the pan-licker; Rav Shemaia said, Son of the one who collapsed on the ground.

The rabbis taught: Sell whatever you possess so that you can marry the daughter of a man of learning; then if you die or have to go into exile, you can be confident that your children will be [numbered among the] disciples. But don't marry the daughter of an ignoramus (*'am ha-aretz*), for if you die or have to go into exile your children will become ignoramuses.

The rabbis taught: Sell whatever you possess so that you can marry the daughter of a learned man, and marry your daughter to a learned man; this is like [mixing] the grapes of a vine with the grapes of a vine, beautiful and acceptable. But don't marry the daughter of an ignoramus, for that is like [mixing] the grapes of a vine with the berries of a thorn-bush, ugly and unacceptable.

49b

The rabbis taught: Sell whatever you possess so that you can marry the daughter of a learned man. If you cannot find the daughter of a learned man, marry the daughter of a man outstanding in his generation;[35] if you cannot find the daughter of a man outstanding in his generation, marry the daughter of a community leader; if you cannot find the daughter of a community leader, marry the daughter of a charity trustee; if you cannot find the daughter of a charity trustee, marry the

35.   i.e. one who excels in good deeds – Rashi.

daughter of a teacher of children. But never marry the daughter of an ignoramus, for they are an abomination, and their women are an abomination, and of their daughters it is said, CURSED BE HE WHO LIES WITH ANY BEAST (Deuteronomy 27:21).

It was taught: Rabbi says, It is forbidden for an ignoramus to eat meat, as it is said, THIS IS THE TORAH FOR ANIMALS AND BIRDS (Leviticus 11:46) – whoever learns Torah may eat the meat of animals and birds, but who does not learn Torah may not eat the meat of animals and birds.

The comments that follow are hyperbole, a common rabbinic form of expression; they are counterbalanced by numerous rabbinic statements that call for compassion and love to be extended to all. The rabbis were convinced that life uninformed by the word of God is on a par with that of animals.

Rabbi Eleazar said: It is permitted to stab an ignoramus [even] on the Day of Atonement that falls on a Sabbath! His disciples said, But Master, why don't you say 'slaughter'?[36] He said, One needs a blessing, the other doesn't!

Rabbi Eleazar said: It is forbidden to accompany an ignoramus on a journey, for it is said, FOR [TORAH] IS [THE SOURCE OF] YOUR LIFE AND THE LENGTH OF YOUR DAYS (Deuteronomy 30:20); [the ignoramus] cares nothing for his own life, so he will care even less for anyone else's.

Rabbi Shmuel bar Naḥmani said in the name of Rabbi Yoḥanan, It is permitted to tear apart an ignoramus as if he was a fish; Rabbi Shmuel bar Isaac said, Even from his spine.

Rabbi Aqiva said, When I was an ignoramus I used to say, Who will let me get hold of a disciple so that I can bite him like a donkey! His disciples asked, Why didn't you say 'like a dog'? He replied, [The donkey] bites and breaks bones; [the dog] bites but does not break bones.

A baraita taught: Rabbi Meir used to say, If anyone marries his daughter to an ignoramus, it is as if he threw her before a lion, [for] just as a lion tramples and eats and has no shame,

---

36. The verb that is used for *kasher* slaughtering. It is not permitted to slaughter or stab any animal on the Sabbath or the Day of Atonement.

so an ignoramus beats [his wife] and has sex and has no shame.

A baraita taught: **Rabbi Eliezer used to say, If they didn't need us for commerce they would kill us.**

Rabbi Ḥiyya taught: If anyone discusses[37] Torah in the presence of an ignoramus, it is as if he had sex with his fiancée in front of him,[38] as it is said, **Moses commanded us the Torah as an inheritance** (Deuteronomy 33:4) – do not read *morasha* ('inheritance'), but *m'orasa* ('betrothed').

The ignorant, especially their women, hate the learned even more than the nations hate Israel. The Tannaim taught, Worse than any of them is he who has learned but abandoned [his learning].

The rabbis taught: **Six things are said of an** *'am ha-aretz*: **Do not invite him to give evidence; do not accept evidence from him; do not pass on a secret to him; do not appoint him as a guardian for orphans; do not set him in charge of the distribution of charity; do not travel in his company.** Some say, one should not proclaim his lost property;[39] but the Tanna [who drew up the list thought one should, since] he may produce a worthwhile heir who will benefit from it, as it is said, **He prepares it, but the righteous will wear it** (Job 27:17). *The Gemara returns to a discussion of the Mishna.*

The same [applies] if someone left [Jerusalem and discovered he was [still] carrying sacred meat.] Does this imply that Rabbi Meir holds that an egg-size is a significant [quantity], but Rabbi Judah holds that even an olive-size is significant? As against that, [a Mishna states:] **What is the [minimum] quantity [of food] for which** *zimmun* **is required? An olive-size, but Rabbi Judah says, An egg-size.**[40]

---

37. Literally, 'engages in'.
38. The point is that an ignorant person is not yet ready to understand. Presenting him with Torah before he is prepared for it is forbidden, as is engaging in sex before marriage.
39. Anyone who finds a lost object is obliged to make a public announcement so that the loser has an opportunity to claim his property.
40. *Zimmun* is the formula introducing grace among a quorum of three or more men. The Mishna referred to is *Berakhot* 7:2 (45a).

Rabbi Yoḥanan said, Reverse the opinions![41]

Abbaye said, Don't reverse the opinions! There[42] they argue from proof-texts, but here they argue by reason. There they argue from proof-texts: Rabbi Meir holds, **AND YOU SHALL EAT, AND YOU SHALL BE SATISFIED, AND YOU SHALL BLESS** (Deuteronomy 8:10) – **AND YOU SHALL EAT** refers to eating; **AND YOU SHALL BE SATISFIED** refers to drinking; 'eating' implies [as a minimum] an olive-size[, so one should **BLESS**, including *zimmun*, even for an olive-size]. But Rabbi Judah holds, **AND YOU SHALL EAT, AND YOU SHALL BE SATISFIED** implies eating that gives satisfaction, and that is an egg-size[, hence the requirement to **BLESS** commences only when one has eaten an egg-size]. Here [in the *ḥametz* case] they argue by reason: Rabbi Meir holds that [the quantity for which you are obliged] to return is the same as [the quantity that is susceptible to] impurity; just as [the quantity susceptible to] impurity is an egg-size, so [the quantity for which you are obliged] to return is an egg-size. But Rabbi Judah holds that [the quantity for which you are obliged] to return is the same as [the quantity that is] forbidden; just as [*ḥametz*] of an olive-size is forbidden, so [the quantity for which you are obliged] to return is an olive-size.

50a

A baraita states: **Rabbi Nathan said, in both cases the measure is two eggs; but the Sages did not agree with him.**

The next collection connects with the previous aggada through its concern that social position should be determined by learning.[43]

ON THAT DAY THERE SHALL BE NEITHER *YEQAROT* NOR *KIPPA'ON*[44] (Zechariah 14:6).

41. i.e. the attributions.
42. In the *zimmun* case.
43. Rashi thinks the connection is the reference to Jerusalem, but this overlooks the deeper relationship.
44. Both words are obscure. The root of *yeqarot* can mean 'precious', 'honourable', 'rare' or 'heavy'; the root of *kippa'on* means 'congeal', and Rashi points to its use in Aramaic and rabbinic Hebrew for material that precipitates out of a liquid and floats to the top. JPS translates, 'neither sunlight nor cold moonlight'; Brown, Driver and Briggs *Lexicon*, p. 430, following Symmachus, translates 'there shall not be light but cold and congelation'. Each rabbinic interpretation picks up a particular nuance of the Hebrew.

Rabbi Eleazar said, This [refers to] the light that is rare in this world, but which will be abundant[45] in the World to Come.

Rabbi Yoḥanan said, This [refers to the tractates] *Nega'im* and *Ohalot* that are difficult in this world but will prove easy in the World to Come.

And Rabbi Joshua ben Levi said, This [refers to] people who highly regarded in this world, but will sink in the World to Come.

This is like [what happened to] Rabbi Joshua ben Levi's son, Rav Yosef, who became ill and fainted away. When he revived, his father asked him, What did you see? He said, I saw a world turned upside-down; those who are high here were low there, and those who are low here were high there. [Joshua ben Levi] said, My son, you saw the world clearly[, as it should be]; but how were we [men of learning placed] there? [He replied, In the same order] we are here, so were we there, and I heard them say, 'Happy is he who has arrived here in possession of his learning!' I also heard them say, 'No one stands on as high a level as the [martyrs] slain by the [Roman] regime!'

Who was he referring to? If to Rabbi Aqiva and his colleagues, surely they would not have been placed on such a high level merely on account of their martyrdom? He must have been referring to those slain at Lydda.[46]

SPEAK TO THE WHOLE COMMUNITY OF ISRAEL AND SAY THAT ON THE TENTH OF THIS MONTH EACH OF THEM SHALL TAKE A LAMB TO A FAMILY, A LAMB TO A HOUSEHOLD ... YOU SHALL KEEP WATCH OVER IT UNTIL THE FOURTEENTH DAY OF THIS MONTH;

45. Literally, 'precipitated'. This is the wonderful light of Creation, stored up for the righteous in the World to Come.

46. Rashi refers to *Ta'anit* 18b, which he says was about two non-Jewish brothers who sacrificed their lives to save Jews from persecution; in his comment on *Bava Batra* 10b, he names them as Pappos and Julianus who were slain by 'Turnus Rufus' in 'Laodicea'. The probable reference is to the savage repression by Lusius Quietus of the so-called 'Revolt of the Diaspora' which broke out in Cyrenaica in 115 CE when Trajan was fighting the Parthians; it is referred to in the 'Rabbinic Apocalypse' at the end of Mishna *Sota*. 'Lydda' is almost certainly a misreading for Lydia, or more probably Laodicea (in Phrygia, Asia Minor). On this revolt, see Ben Zeev, *Diaspora Judaism*, and Goodman, *Rome and Jerusalem*, pp. 475–82.

*AND ALL THE ASSEMBLED CONGREGATION OF THE ISRAELITES
SHALL SLAUGHTER IT AT TWILIGHT.* (Exodus 12:3, 6 JPS)

*Rabbinic Judaism has few absolutes; more often, it is a case of
balancing one obligation against another. The Passover lamb
must be slaughtered on 14 Nisan and eaten the same night, the
15th. Only the daily and Sabbath sacrifices in the Temple may
be slaughtered on the Sabbath. What happens, then, if 14 Nisan
falls on a Sabbath?*

*Form criticism and historical evidence suggest that the story
of Hillel is not earlier than the second century and may have
been subsequently revised; the Amoraim remould it to fit their
own understanding of the* halakhic *principles involved.*

CHAPTER SIX

MISHNA:

65b   These aspects of the Passover [sacrifice] override the Sabbath: It may be slaughtered, its blood may be sprinkled [on
the altar], its inner parts may be cleaned and its fats burnt,
but it may not be roasted, nor may its inner parts be rinsed
on the Sabbath.

Carrying it on your shoulder, or bringing it from beyond
the Sabbath boundary, or cutting off scabs, do not override
the Sabbath; Rabbi Eliezer says, They do override [the Sab-
bath].

GEMARA:

66a   The rabbis taught: This law eluded the Bnei Bathyra.[47] On
one occasion 14 Nisan fell on the Sabbath; they had forgotten
[the law], and did not know whether or not it overrode the
Sabbath. They said, Does anyone know whether or not [the
slaughter of] the Passover [lamb] overrides the Sabbath?

[Someone] said to them, A man called Hillel the Babylonian
has come up from Babylon; he attended the two great

47. A family of Sages possibly originating from Bathyra, location uncertain.

[scholars] of the generation, Shemaia and Avtalion, and he knows whether or not the Passover overrides the Sabbath.

They sent him an invitation, and asked, Do you know whether or not the Passover overrides the Sabbath?

He responded, Is there only one Passover in the year? Surely we have more than two hundred a year that override the Sabbath.[48]

They said, On what [scriptural text] do you base that?

He replied, [The expression] IN ITS APPOINTED SEASON is used in connection with the Passover (Numbers 9:2), and IN ITS APPOINTED SEASON is used [also] of the daily sacrifice (28:2); just as IN ITS APPOINTED SEASON [indicates that slaughter of] the daily sacrifice overrides the Sabbath [prohibitions], so IN ITS APPOINTED SEASON [when] used in connection with the Passover [indicates that] it overrides the Sabbath [prohibitions]. Moreover, there is an a fortiori argument: If the daily sacrifice, neglect of which does not incur the penalty of *karet*, overrides the Sabbath [prohibitions], how much more so should the Passover, neglect of which does incur the penalty of *karet*, override the Sabbath [prohibitions]!

They immediately asked him to take the chair and appointed him president, and all day long he expounded the laws of Passover. He [then] began to criticize them and said, Whose fault is it that I should [have] come from Babylon to preside over you? It is your laziness, for you did not serve the two great [scholars] of the generation, Shemaia and Avtalion.

They asked, Sir! If someone forgot to bring the knife [to slaughter the lamb] prior to the Sabbath, what should he do?[49]

He replied, I did hear the law on that [point], but I have forgotten it. But leave it to Israel – if they are not prophets, they are the children of prophets.[50]

The following day, those who brought lambs stuck the knife in the lamb's fleece, and those who brought goats put it between their horns. When he saw what they did he

48. He means more than two hundred sacrifices, such as the daily sacrifice, that are offered in the Temple on the Sabbath.
49. It would not be permitted to carry the knife in the public domain on the Sabbath.
50. An allusion to Amos 7:14.

remembered the law, and said, This is [just] what I was told by Shemaia and Avtalion.

A teacher commented: [The expression] IN ITS APPOINTED SEASON is used in connection with the Passover (Numbers 9:2), and IN ITS APPOINTED SEASON is used [also] of the daily sacrifice (28:2); just as IN ITS APPOINTED SEASON [indicates that slaughtering] the daily sacrifice overrides the Sabbath [prohibitions], so IN ITS APPOINTED SEASON [when] used in connection with the Passover [indicates that] it overrides the Sabbath [prohibitions].

But how do we know that the daily sacrifice itself was offered on the Sabbath? If you say it is based on the expression IN ITS APPOINTED SEASON, this is written of the Passover too[, so why cite the daily sacrifice]? In fact, it is not the expression IN ITS APPOINTED SEASON on which the inference is based, but the verse A BURNT OFFERING EVERY SABBATH, AS WELL AS THE DAILY BURNT OFFERING AND ITS LIBATION (Numbers 28:10), which implies that that daily sacrifice is offered on the Sabbath [too].

A teacher commented: Moreover, there is an a fortiori argument: if the daily sacrifice, neglect of which does not incur the penalty of *karet*, overrides the Sabbath [prohibitions], how much more so should the Passover, neglect of which does incur the penalty of *karet*, override the Sabbath [prohibitions]!

But this is open to an objection: The daily sacrifice is both [more] frequent [than the Passover], and entirely [consumed on the altar, so one cannot make an a fortiori argument for the Passover, since the Passover is more lenient in these respects. They answered: Hillel] first gave them the a fortiori argument, but they rejected it, so he then argued by analogy.

Then if he [could produce a valid text-based] analogy, why did he [first] offer the a fortiori argument? He was arguing *ad hominem*, [as if to say,] You may not have learned the analogy, and you may not devise a text-based analogy on your own [initiative], but you may argue from minor to major on your own initiative, therefore do so! However, they refuted his argument [and he was thrown back on the analogy].

A teacher commented: **The following day, those who brought lambs stuck the knife in the lamb's fleece, and those who brought goats put it between their horns.** But surely this is making use of consecrated animals? [No. They acted] in accordance with [the known view of] Hillel, for it was taught: **They say of Hillel that in his day no one committed sacrilege with a burnt offering, since they brought [the animals] to the Temple courtyard unconsecrated, and [only then] consecrated them, laid their hands upon them and slaughtered them.**

66b

How could they consecrate the Passover [lamb] on the Sabbath? Does not a Mishna rule, **You may not consecrate, assess, devote or separate *teruma* and tithes; this is on festivals, and a fortiori on the Sabbath?**[51] This applies only to obligatory offerings that have no fixed time, but obligatory offerings that do have a fixed time may be consecrated [on the Sabbath, if that is their fixed time], as Rabbi Yoḥanan said, A man may consecrate his Passover [lamb] on the Sabbath and his festival offering on the festival.

But isn't [getting the lamb to carry the knife in its fleece a form of] driving a laden animal[, which is forbidden on the Sabbath? Yes, but] it is an abnormal

51. A truncated version of Mishna *Betza* 5:2 (36b) (see pp. 234–5).

way of driving. [Even if] it is an abnormal way of driving, and so not forbidden under Torah law, surely it is forbidden by the rabbis? That is precisely the question [the Bnei Bathyra put to Hillel]: If the Torah does not [actually] forbid something, but the rabbis forbid it as a protective measure, may it nevertheless be done in an abnormal manner in order to fulfil a *mitzva*? [It is in answer to this question that he responded:] **Leave it to Israel – if they are not prophets, they are the children of prophets.**

Hillel, in criticizing the Bnei Bathyra for their 'laziness', gave way to uncharacteristic anger and pride; this is the theme now addressed.

Rav Yehuda said in the name of Rav: Whoever is proud, if he is a wise man, his wisdom departs from him, if he is a prophet, prophecy departs from him. If he is a wise man, his wisdom departs from him – [this we see] from Hillel, as the teacher said, **He [then] began to criticize them** and then, **He replied, I did hear the law . . . but I have forgotten it**; if he is a prophet, prophecy departs from him – [this we see] from Deborah, for it is written, **DELIVERANCE CEASED, CEASED IN ISRAEL, TILL I, DEBORAH, AROSE, TILL I AROSE, A MOTHER IN ISRAEL** (Judges 5:7), and after that is written, **AWAKE, AWAKE, DEBORAH, AWAKE, AWAKE, BEGIN THE SONG**[52] (5:12).

Resh Laqish said, When a man becomes angry, even if he is a wise man, his wisdom departs from him; if he is a prophet, prophecy departs from him. If he is a wise man, his wisdom departs from him – [this we see] from Moses, for it is written, **MOSES BECAME ANGRY WITH THE COMMANDERS OF THE ARMY, ETC.** (Numbers 31:14 JPS), and [then], **ELEAZAR THE PRIEST SAID TO THE TROOPS WHO HAD TAKEN PART IN THE FIGHTING, 'THIS IS THE RITUAL LAW THAT THE LORD HAS ENJOINED UPON MOSES'** (31:21 JPS) – from which it appears that the law eluded Moses;[53] if he is a prophet, prophecy departs from him – [this we see] from Elisha, for it is written, '**WERE**

52. Deborah is trying to recover her prophetic power.
53. Otherwise he would have announced it himself.

IT NOT THAT I RESPECT KING JEHOSHAPHAT OF JUDAH, I WOULDN'T LOOK AT YOU OR NOTICE YOU' (2 Kings 3:14 JPS), and then, 'NOW THEN, GET ME A MUSICIAN.' AS THE MUSICIAN PLAYED, THE HAND OF THE LORD CAME UPON HIM, ETC.' (3:15 JPS).[54]

Rav Mani bar Patish said, When a man loses his temper he is brought low, even if heaven has already allotted him greatness. We know this from Eliab, for it is written, ELIAB BECAME ANGRY WITH DAVID AND SAID, 'WHY DID YOU COME DOWN HERE, AND WITH WHOM DID YOU LEAVE THOSE FEW SHEEP IN THE WILDERNESS? I KNOW YOUR IMPUDENCE AND YOUR IMPERTINENCE: YOU CAME DOWN TO WATCH THE FIGHTING!' (1 Samuel 17:28 JPS); and of Eliab it is written, [BUT THE LORD SAID TO SAMUEL,] 'PAY NO ATTENTION TO HIS APPEARANCE OR HIS STATURE, FOR I HAVE REJECTED HIM' (1 Samuel 16:7 JPS) – which implies that until then he had loved him.

The Passover lamb was offered in the Temple, i.e. presented to God, prior to being eaten at home. The party who were to share it had to be designated in advance. It might happen, for instance with a married woman, that she had been 'counted in' to two parties, that of her new family and that into which she was born; since an individual cannot be a member of more than one party, with which does she celebrate? The Gemara describes the felicity of a bride who is equally happy in her in-laws' home and her father's house.

CHAPTER EIGHT

MISHNA:

When a woman is living in her husband's home, if both her husband and her father slaughtered [a lamb] on her behalf, she partakes of her husband's.

87a

---

54. That is, Elisha had lost his prophetic power, and only regained it when the musician played.

If she goes to her father's house on the first festival [following her marriage], and both her husband and her father slaughtered [a lamb] on her behalf, she may partake of whichever she wishes.

If guardians slaughtered [on behalf of] an orphan, he may eat where he wishes.

A slave of two partners may not eat [the Passover lamb] of either.

Someone who is half slave and half freedman[55] may not eat of his master's [Passover lamb].

GEMARA:

[She may partake of whichever she wishes.] This implies that *berera* operates [retrospectively making her choice the valid one]. [No, not necessarily. Perhaps] whichever she wishes means whichever she wished at the time [the lamb] was slaughtered[, so the choice is not retrospective].

[A baraita] contradicts [the Mishna's ruling]: On the first festival [following her marriage], the bride eats [the Passover lamb] with her father; after that, if she wishes, she eats with her father, or if she wishes, with her husband.

[Answer:] There is no contradiction. The baraita speaks of a case where she is keen to go; the Mishna of a case where she is not keen. [The former case is] as it is written, So I became in his eyes As one who finds favour (Song 8:10 JPS) – Rabbi Yoḥanan said, This is like a bride who is at ease in her in-laws' home, and keen to go to her father's house to tell [her family] how happy she is; as it is written, On that day, says the Lord, you will call Me 'My Spouse', and no longer call Me 'My Master' (Hosea 2:18), on which Rabbi Yoḥanan commented, This is like a bride in her father-in-law's house, not like a bride in her father's house.

More homilies:

'We have a little sister, Whose breasts are not yet formed' (Song 8:8 JPS) – Rabbi Yoḥanan said, This [refers to] Elam, whose people were successful in learning but not in teaching.[56]

---

55. The classical illustration of an untenable personal situation: Mishna *Gittin* 4:5 (41a).
56. The Jews of Elam, 'little sister' of Babylonia, learned Torah but did not produce their own teachers.

I AM A WALL, MY BREASTS ARE LIKE TOWERS (Song 8:10 JPS) – Rabbi Yoḥanan said, I AM A WALL – this refers to Torah; MY BREASTS ARE LIKE TOWERS – this refers to the Sages [who nurture Israel]. Rava interpreted, I AM A WALL – this refers to the congregation of Israel; MY BREASTS ARE LIKE TOWERS – this refers to synagogues and houses of study [that nourish Israel spiritually].

Rav Zutra bar Tovia said in the name of Rav: What is the meaning of the verse, FOR OUR SONS ARE LIKE SAPLINGS, WELL-TENDED IN THEIR YOUTH; OUR DAUGHTERS ARE LIKE CORNERSTONES TRIMMED TO GIVE SHAPE TO A PALACE (Psalm 144:12 JPS)? FOR OUR SONS ARE LIKE SAPLINGS, WELL-TENDED IN THEIR YOUTH – these are the young men of Israel, who have not tasted sin; OUR DAUGHTERS ARE LIKE CORNERSTONES TRIMMED TO GIVE SHAPE TO A PALACE – these are virgins of Israel who preserve their virginity for their husbands; as it says, THEY SHALL BE FILLED AS A BOWL, AS THE CORNERSTONES OF THE ALTAR (Zechariah 9:15);[57] alternatively, as it says, OUR STOREHOUSES ARE FULL, SUPPLYING PRODUCE OF ALL KINDS (Psalm 144:13 JPS). LIKE CORNERSTONES TRIMMED TO GIVE SHAPE TO A PALACE – Scripture accounts it to both [young men and virgins] as if the Temple[58] were to be rebuilt in their days.

The prophet Hosea portrays the relationship of God and Israel as that of husband and wife. The background to the following interpretation is most likely the Christian claim that God had rejected Israel on account of its sins; the response is not denial that Israel had sinned, but affirmation that God's love overcomes sin.

THE WORD OF THE LORD THAT CAME TO HOSEA SON OF BEERI, IN THE REIGNS OF KINGS UZZIAH, JOTHAM, AHAZ AND HEZEKIAH OF JUDAH (Hosea 1:1 JPS). Four prophets prophesied in one period, and Hosea was the greatest of them, as it is said, THE BEGINNING OF GOD'S WORD WAS WITH

---

57. The virgins are filled with desire for their husbands since they have kept away from other men – Rashi.
58. *Heikhal*, translated 'palace', can refer to the Temple.

HOSEA[59] (Hosea 1:2). Now, was Hosea the first one He spoke with? Surely there were many prophets between Moses and Hosea. Rabbi Yoḥanan said, He was first among the prophets who prophesied at that time, namely Hosea, Isaiah, Amos and Micah.

The Holy One, blessed be He, said to Hosea, Your children [Israel] have sinned! [Hosea] should have replied, They are *Your* children, Your favoured ones, the children of Abraham, Isaac and Jacob; have mercy upon them! Not only did he not say that, but he said to Him, Lord of the Universe! All the world is Yours! Change them for another nation!

The Holy One, blessed be He, said, What can I do with this man? I shall say, Go, get yourself a whore for a wife, and beget children of whoredom, and then I will tell him, Send her away! If he can send her away, then I can send Israel away! [This is] as it is written, **GO, GET YOURSELF A WHORE FOR A WIFE, AND BEGET CHILDREN OF WHOREDOM** (Hosea 1:2).

The text then says, **SO HE WENT AND MARRIED GOMER THE DAUGHTER OF DIBLAIM** (Hosea 1:3 JPS) –

87b
> Rav said, [she was called] 'Gomer', because everyone consummated with her; 'Diblaim' – she was bad news, the daughter of bad news. Shmuel said, 'Diblaim' – everyone trampled her like a date.[60]
>
> Another [line of] interpretation: 'Gomer' – Rabbi Judah said, Because in her time [the enemy] sought to destroy Israel's possessions; Rabbi Yoḥanan said, They completely despoiled them, as it is said, **FOR THE KING OF ARAM HAD DECIMATED THEM AND TRAMPLED THEM LIKE THE DUST UNDER HIS FEET** (2 Kings 13:7 JPS).[61]

SHE CONCEIVED AND BORE HIM A SON, AND THE LORD INSTRUCTED HIM, 'NAME HIM JEZREEL; FOR I WILL SOON PUNISH THE HOUSE OF JEHU FOR THE

59. This is a literal translation; JPS has 'When the Lord first spoke to Hosea'.
60. The root GMR is 'to finish or complete'; Diblaim is (incorrectly) related to *dibba*, 'bad news' or 'bad report' (cf. Genesis 37:2 and Numbers 13:32); 'trample' is a sexual euphemism; *diblaim* is a plural of *devela* 'date'.
61. Both interpretations draw on the meaning of the root GMR.

BLOODY DEEDS AT JEZREEL AND PUT AN END TO THE MONARCHY OF THE HOUSE OF ISRAEL.' . . . SHE CONCEIVED AGAIN AND BORE A DAUGHTER; AND HE SAID TO HIM, 'NAME HER LO-RUHAMAH; FOR I WILL NO LONGER ACCEPT THE HOUSE OF ISRAEL OR PARDON THEM.' . . . SHE CONCEIVED AND BORE A SON. THEN HE SAID, 'NAME HIM LO-AMMI; FOR YOU ARE NOT MY PEOPLE, AND I WILL NOT BE YOUR [GOD].' (Hosea 1:3–4, 6, 8–9 JPS)

When two sons and a daughter had been born to Hosea, the Holy One, blessed be He, said to him, Perhaps you should have learned from Moses your master; when I spoke with him, he parted from his wife. Now you part from yours!

Hosea replied, Lord of the Universe! I have children from her; I can't send her away or divorce her!

The Holy One, blessed be He, retorted, If you, who have a harlot for a wife and don't even know whether her children are yours or someone else's, [can't bring yourself to part from her, how can you tell Me] to part from Israel, who are My children, the children of those I put to the test, the children of Abraham, Isaac and Jacob, one of My four possessions in the world!

One [of God's possessions] is the Torah, as it is written, **THE LORD TOOK POSSESSION OF ME AS THE BEGINNING OF HIS WAY** (Proverbs 8:22); one is heaven and earth, as it is written, [**GOD MOST HIGH,**] **WHO POSSESSES HEAVEN AND EARTH** (Genesis 14:19); one is the Holy Temple, as it is written, **THE MOUNTAIN HIS RIGHT HAND HAD ACQUIRED** (Psalm 78:54 JPS); and one is Israel, as it is written, **YOUR PEOPLE, WHOM YOU POSSESS** (Exodus 15:16).

When [Hosea] realized that he had sinned, he started to pray for mercy for himself. The Holy One, blessed be He, said, Rather than implore for mercy for yourself, implore for mercy for Israel; because of you I have made three decrees against them.[62]

---

62. i.e. you could have averted the decrees had you tried.

[Hosea then] prayed for them and averted the [harsh] decrees. Not only that, but he began to bless them, saying,

THE NUMBER OF THE PEOPLE OF ISRAEL SHALL BE LIKE THAT OF THE SANDS OF THE SEA, WHICH CANNOT BE MEASURED OR COUNTED, AND INSTEAD OF BEING TOLD, 'YOU ARE NOT-MY-PEOPLE', THEY SHALL BE CALLED CHILDREN-OF-THE-LIVING-GOD. THE PEOPLE OF JUDAH AND THE PEOPLE OF ISRAEL SHALL ASSEMBLE TOGETHER . . . (Hosea 2:1–2 JPS) – I WILL SOW HER IN THE LAND AS MY OWN; AND TAKE LO-RUHAMA BACK IN FAVOUR; AND I WILL SAY TO LO-AMMI, 'YOU ARE MY PEOPLE', AND HE WILL RESPOND, '[YOU ARE] MY GOD.' (2:25 JPS)

Rabbi Yoḥanan said, Woe to leadership! It buries those who exercise it; there is not a single prophet whose activities did not span the reigns of four kings, as it is said, THE PROPHECIES OF ISAIAH THE SON OF AMOZ . . . IN THE REIGNS OF UZZIAH, JOTHAM, AHAZ AND HEZEKIAH, KINGS OF JUDAH (Isaiah 1:1 JPS).[63]

Rabbi Yoḥanan said, Why did Jeroboam the son of Joash deserve to be numbered with the kings of Judah? Because he refused to accept slander against [the prophet] Amos. We know he was included, for it is written, THE WORD OF THE LORD THAT CAME TO HOSEA SON OF BEERI, IN THE REIGNS OF KINGS UZZIAH, JOTHAM, AHAZ AND HEZEKIAH OF JUDAH, AND IN THE REIGN OF KING JEROBOAM SON OF JOASH OF ISRAEL (Hosea 1:1 JPS). We know, too, that he rejected slander, for it is written, AMAZIAH, THE PRIEST OF BETHEL, SENT THIS MESSAGE TO KING JEROBOAM OF ISRAEL: 'AMOS IS CONSPIRING AGAINST YOU' . . . FOR AMOS HAS SAID, 'JEROBOAM SHALL DIE BY THE SWORD' (Amos 7:10–11 JPS); he reflected, God forbid that he said that! But if he has indeed said it, what can I do, seeing that God has told him [to say so].

Rabbi Eleazar said, Even when He is angry the Holy One, blessed be He, is mindful of mercy, as it is said, I WILL NOT CONTINUE, I WILL SHOW MERCY TO THE HOUSE OF ISRAEL[64]

63. Kings exercise leadership; prophets do not.
64. This is a literal translation; the idiom, however, means, 'I will not continue to show mercy . . .'

(Hosea 1:6). Rabbi Yosé ben Ḥanina derived [the same] from the end of the verse: BUT I WILL SURELY FORGIVE THEM.[65]

Rabbi Eleazar said, moreover, The Holy One, blessed be He, exiled Israel among the nations only that proselytes might be added to their number, as it is said, I WILL SOW HER IN THE LAND – No one sows a *seah* unless he intends to harvest several *kurs*. Rabbi Yoḥanan inferred the same from [the end of the verse]: AND TAKE LO-RUHAMA BACK IN FAVOUR[; AND I WILL SAY TO LO-AMMI, 'YOU ARE MY PEOPLE]'[66] (Hosea 2:25 JPS).

Rabbi Yoḥanan said in the name of Rabbi Simeon ben Yoḥai, What is the meaning of the verses: DO NOT INFORM ON A SLAVE TO HIS MASTER, LEST HE CURSE YOU AND YOU INCUR GUILT. THERE IS A BREED OF MEN THAT BRINGS A CURSE ON ITS FATHERS, AND BRINGS NO BLESSING TO ITS MOTHERS (Proverbs 30:10–11 JPS). How does DO NOT INFORM follow from BRINGS A CURSE ON ITS FATHERS, AND BRINGS NO BLESSING TO ITS MOTHERS? It signifies that even a generation that brings curses on its fathers and no blessing on its mothers should refrain from slandering a slave to his master. This is what we learn from Hosea.[67]

Rabbi Oshaya said, What is the meaning of the expression: HIS GRACIOUS DELIVERANCE OF ISRAEL (Judges 5:11 JPS)? The Holy One, blessed be He, acted graciously towards Israel by scattering[68] them among the nations. As a Roman[69] said to Rabbi Ḥanina, We are better than you. It is written of you, [FOR JOAB AND ALL ISRAEL] STAYED THERE FOR SIX MONTHS [UNTIL HE HAD KILLED OFF EVERY MALE IN EDOM] (I Kings 11:16 JPS); but you have been within our power for many years, and we have done nothing to you. He replied, May I get one of

---

65. Likewise, a literal translation of an idiom meaning 'I will not continue to forgive.'
66. Rashi points out that it is the latter part of this quotation, lacking in the Talmud texts, that demonstrates that those presently not God's people will be numbered among them.
67. Hosea got into trouble for slandering Israel, even though they had indeed sinned – Rashi.
68. The word translated 'deliverance' derives from a root that could mean 'scatter'. Rabbi Oshaya's point was that Israel would be more vulnerable if they were under the control of just one nation.
69. Literally, 'a sectarian'; the context makes is clear that it is a Roman.

my disciples [to respond]? Rabbi Oshaya joined [conversation] with [the Roman] and said, That is because you don't know what to do. You cannot destroy us all, since we are not all [within your territory; and were you to destroy just] those who are within your territory [people] would call you a lame power. By the Roman eagle, replied the other, we go out and we come in with that [thought]![70]

Rabbi Ḥiyya taught: What is meant by, GOD UNDERSTANDS THE WAY TO IT; HE KNOWS ITS PLACE (Job 28:23)? The Holy One, blessed be He, knows that Israel could not withstand the [harsh] Roman decrees, so he exiled them to Babylon.

Rabbi Eleazar said, The Holy One, blessed be He, exiled Israel to Babylon because it is as low as Sheol, as it is said, FROM SHEOL ITSELF WILL I SAVE THEM, REDEEM THEM FROM VERY DEATH (Hosea 13:14 JPS).

Rabbi Ḥanina said, [He exiled them to Babylon] because the language [of Babylon] is close to that of Torah.

Rabbi Yoḥanan said, Because he [wanted to] send them back to their maternal home. This is like a man who is angry with his wife. Where will he send her? Back to her mother.

Rabbi Alexandri likewise said, Three return to their place of origin: Israel, the silver of Egypt and the writing on the tablets [of stone that Moses brought down from Mount Sinai]. Israel, as we have said; the Egyptian silver, as it is written, IN THE FIFTH YEAR OF KING REHOBOAM, KING SHISHAK OF EGYPT MARCHED AGAINST JERUSALEM [AND CARRIED OFF THE TREA- SURES OF THE HOUSE OF THE LORD] (1 Kings 14:25 JPS); and the writing on the tablets, as it is written, AND I SMASHED THEM BEFORE YOUR EYES (Deuteronomy 9:17) – and it was taught, The stones were smashed, but the letters flew [heavenwards].

The sugya *is rounded off with a humorous anecdote, followed by reassuring homilies.*

Ulla said, [They were exiled to Babylon] so they might eat
88a   dates and study Torah. When Ulla arrived in Pumbedita they offered him a tray of dates. He asked, How many [trays of dates] can you get for a *zuz*? Three, they replied. He exclaimed, A

70. Oshaya plays on the Roman rivalry with Persia.

basketful of honey for a *zuz*, and [you] Babylonians don't study Torah! During the night [the dates] troubled him. [The next morning he proclaimed:] A basket of deadly poison goes for a *zuz* in Babylon, and despite that they learn Torah!

Rabbi Eleazar also said, What is the meaning of the verse, AND MANY NATIONS SHALL GO AND SAY, 'LET US ASCEND THE LORD'S MOUNTAIN, TO THE HOUSE OF JACOB'S GOD' (Isaiah 2:3)? Why the God of Jacob, and not the God of Abraham or Isaac? Not like Abraham, to whom God was like a mountain, as it is said, 'On the mount of the Lord there is vision' (Genesis 22:14 JPS); nor like Isaac, to whom God was like a field, as it is said, AND ISAAC WENT OUT TO MEDITATE IN THE FIELD (24:63); but like Jacob, to whom God was home, as it is said, AND HE CALLED THE PLACE THE HOME OF GOD [BETHEL] (28:19).

Rabbi Yohanan said, The ingathering of the exiles is as great as the day that heaven and earth were created, as it is said, THE PEOPLE OF JUDAH AND THE PEOPLE OF ISRAEL SHALL ASSEMBLE TOGETHER AND APPOINT ONE HEAD OVER THEM; AND THEY SHALL RISE FROM THE GROUND — FOR MARVEL-LOUS SHALL BE THE DAY OF JEZREEL (Hosea 2:2 JPS), and it is written, AND IT WAS EVENING AND IT WAS MORNING — ONE DAY (Genesis 1:5).[71]

Chapter Nine treats of the Second Passover:

AND THE LORD SPOKE TO MOSES, SAYING: SPEAK TO THE ISRAELITE PEOPLE, SAYING: WHEN ANY OF YOU OR OF YOUR POS-TERITY WHO ARE DEFILED BY A CORPSE OR ARE ON A LONG JOUR-NEY WOULD OFFER A PASSOVER SACRIFICE TO THE LORD, THEY SHALL OFFER IT IN THE SECOND MONTH, ON THE FOURTEENTH DAY OF THE MONTH, AT TWILIGHT. THEY SHALL EAT IT WITH UNLEAVENED BREAD AND BITTER HERBS, AND THEY SHALL NOT LEAVE ANY OF IT OVER UNTIL MORNING. THEY SHALL NOT BREAK A BONE OF IT. THEY SHALL OFFER IT IN STRICT ACCORD WITH THE LAW OF THE PASSOVER SACRIFICE. (Numbers 9:9–12 JPS)

71. The inference is made from the use of 'day' in each citation.

Although the sacrifice is the same on the First Passover and Second Passover, the Feast of Unleavened Bread is not repeated; there are consequently several differences between the two celebrations.

CHAPTER NINE

MISHNA:

95a   What is the difference between the first Passover and the second?

On the first, *ḥametz* may not be seen or found[72] [in your possession]; on the second, you may have both leavened and unleavened bread with you in the house.

On the first, Hallel[73] must be recited as [the Passover sacrifice] is eaten; on the second, Hallel need not be recited as [the Passover] is eaten.

On both, Hallel must be recited as the sacrifice is made. On both, the Passover is eaten together with unleavened bread and bitter herbs, and both override the Sabbath.

GEMARA:

The rabbis taught: THEY SHALL OFFER IT IN STRICT ACCORD WITH THE LAW OF THE PASSOVER SACRIFICE — Scripture speaks of those *mitzvot* that apply to the body [of the Passover lamb or kid]. How do we know that it speaks of *mitzvot* that apply to the body? Because it is written, THEY SHALL EAT IT WITH UNLEAVENED BREAD AND BITTER HERBS. Does it speak also of *mitzvot* that do not apply to the body? [No, since] it states, THEY SHALL NOT BREAK A BONE OF IT — just as the [prohibition of] breaking bones is a *mitzva* that applies specifically to the body, so all *mitzvot* that apply to the body [are included]. Issi ben Yehuda says, [You can infer from the words] THEY SHALL OFFER IT that Scripture speaks [only] of *mitzvot* that apply to the body.

---

72. Cf. Exodus 12:19 and Deuteronomy 16:4. The prohibitions are understood by the rabbis to mean that you may not have leaven in your possession during Passover.
73. Psalms 113–18.

A teacher commented: **Does it speak also of *mitzvot* that do not apply to the body [of the Passover]?** – but surely you just said, **Scripture speaks of those *mitzvot* that apply to the body**, [so what is the question? The baraita] means, Seeing that [Scripture] says, **THEY SHALL EAT IT WITH UNLEAVENED BREAD AND BITTER HERBS**, you can see that **THEY SHALL OFFER IT** is not limited to the [lamb or kid] alone.[74] I might [therefore] think that this is like a *p'rat* followed by a *k'lal*,[75] in which case the *k'lal* would broaden the *p'rat*, and perhaps include all [aspects of Passover; the baraita] wants to tell you that this is not the case.

What use does Issi ben Yehuda make of [the phrase], **THEY SHALL NOT BREAK A BONE OF IT**? He requires it [to establish] that no difference is made between a bone that contains marrow and one that doesn't.

What use do [the other] rabbis make of [the phrase] **THEY SHALL OFFER IT**? [They require it to establish] that a [Second] Passover [sacrifice] may not be slaughtered for just one person,[76] but one should try as hard as possible [to get others to share it].

The rabbis taught: **THEY SHALL OFFER IT IN STRICT ACCORD WITH THE LAW OF THE PASSOVER SACRIFICE.** Do you think that just as on the First Passover, *ḥametz* may not be seen or found [in your possession], so on the Second, *ḥametz* may not be seen or found [in your possession]? [This is not so, since Scripture says,] **THEY SHALL EAT IT WITH UNLEAVENED BREAD AND BITTER HERBS.**[77] But this would exclude only positive commandments [other than the one specified]. How do I know that negative commandments, too, [other than the one specified,] are to be excluded? Because it is written, **THEY**

74. It applies also to unleavened bread and bitter herbs.
75. A specific term (the lamb/kid) followed by a more general one (unleavened bread, etc.). See Introduction, 'Rules of Interpretation', pp. xli–xlii.
76. 'Offer' is plural.
77. The arguments that follow are based on the notion that if the Torah made a general statement – **IN STRICT ACCORD WITH THE LAW OF THE PASSOVER** – but then specified details, such as eating it with unleavened bread, this limits the generality of the first statement, so that not *all* laws for the First Passover apply to the Second.

SHALL NOT LEAVE ANY OF IT OVER UNTIL MORNING. I would infer from this only that a negative commandment joined to a positive one is excluded. How do I know that even pure negative commandments, [other than the one specified,] are to be excluded? Because it is written, THEY SHALL NOT BREAK A BONE OF IT. [To sum up:] just as the inclusions are specified – one positive commandment, one negative joined to a positive, and one pure negative – so [every other] positive, negative joined to a positive, and pure negative commandment [is excluded].

What, then, is included [by way of comparison] with UNLEAVENED BREAD AND BITTER HERBS? That [the Second Passover, like the First,] must be roasted in fire. And what is excluded? That [it is not necessary] to get rid of leavening agents.

Perhaps we should argue the other way round?[78]

[No, since it is] preferable to include *mitzvot* that apply to the body [of the Passover].

And what is included [by way of comparison] with THEY SHALL NOT LEAVE ANY OF IT OVER UNTIL MORNING? That [the meat of Second Passover, like that of the First,] may not be removed [beyond its boundary] (Exodus 12:46). And what is excluded? That it is not forbidden for *ḥametz* to be seen or found in one's possession.

Perhaps we should argue the other way round? [No, since it is] preferable to include *mitzvot* that apply to the body [of the Passover].

And what is included [by way of comparison] with THEY 95b SHALL NOT BREAK A BONE OF IT? That [the meat of Second Passover, like that of the First,] may not be eaten raw (Exodus 12:9). And what is excluded? YOU SHALL NOT OFFER THE BLOOD OF MY SACRIFICE WHILE YOU HAVE LEAVEN [IN YOUR POSSESSION] (Exodus 34:25).

Perhaps we should argue the other way round? [No, since it is] preferable to include *mitzvot* that apply to the body [of the Passover].

78. i.e. exclude roasting and include getting rid of leavening agents.

The final chapter is devoted to the Passover Eve meal, known as the Seder ('order'). This is a family feast at which the exodus from Egypt is recalled and reflected upon. The book containing the Order of Service is called haggada *('telling the story'), a word derived from* v'higgadta *in the verse,* **AND YOU SHALL TELL** [**V'HIGADTA**] **YOUR SON ON THAT DAY** *(Exodus 13:8 JPS).*

The opening Mishna is concerned with provision for the poor, for there cannot be a truly joyful occasion unless rich and poor alike are able to participate.

How could the rabbis set a requirement for four cups of wine – a double of doubles – to accompany the Seder, at a time when there was a widespread superstition that doubles, and in particular twins, were unlucky or dangerous? The rabbis do not directly challenge the superstition, but limit its impact to unlikely circumstances, or to particularly susceptible people. Their overall attitude is somewhat sceptical, though a range of views is presented.

CHAPTER TEN

MISHNA:
No one should eat on the Eve of Passover from the time of the afternoon prayer until darkness falls. Even the poorest Israelite should not eat until he reclines; even if he is so poor that he [normally depends on] the soup-kitchen [for his meals], they should give him not less than [the] four [required] cups of wine [together with the full Passover feast]. 99b

GEMARA:
They should not give him less than [the] four [required] cups of wine. How could the rabbis institute something that might lead to danger? Does not a baraita teach, **A person should not eat twice, nor drink twice, nor have sex twice?** 109b

Rav Naḥman said, [The four Seder cups are all right, since] Scripture says, **IT IS A NIGHT WHEN THE LORD WATCHES** (Exodus 12:42) – a night when you are protected from demons.

Rava said, The cup of blessing combines [with others] for good, not for bad.

Ravina said, The rabbis instituted four cups as a sign of
freedom; each is a *mitzva* in its own right.[79]

Nor have sex twice. Why not? Surely [having sex a second
time] is a separate decision[80] [rather than setting out to 'do a
double']. Abbaye said, What [the baraita] means to say is, a
person should not eat twice, drink twice and have sex even once,
in case he is weakened and [rendered susceptible] to harm
[occasioned by eating or drinking a double].

The rabbis taught: **If anyone drinks double, his blood is on
his head!**[81]

Rav Yehuda said, When does this apply? If he didn't take
fresh air[82] in between. But if he has taken fresh air, it is all right
[to drink a second time].

Rav Ashi said, I saw Rav Ḥanania bar Bibi go outside after
each cup.

[The danger] only applies if he intends to set off on a journey,
but not if he is staying home.

> Rabbi Zeira said, Sleeping is like setting off on a
> journey.

> Rav Papa said, Going to relieve oneself is like setting
> off on a journey.

But is it really all right if he is staying home? Didn't Rava
count walls?[83] And when Abbaye drank one cup, his mother[84]
held two cups [ready] in her hands [to ensure that he would
drink three rather than two], and [likewise] when Rav Naḥman
bar Isaac drank two cups, his servant held one ready, and when
he drank one his servant held two ready[, even though they
were staying home].

It is different for an important person [like Rava or Naḥman

---

79. i.e. they do not combine to form doubles.
80. Literally, 'a change of mind'; this is contrary to Rava's prescription for producing
     male offspring (*Eruvin* 100b).
81. He is responsible for any harm that may accrue to himself.
82. Literally, 'see the street'.
83. In order to keep tally of the number of cups he drank and to avoid doubles –
     Rashi and Rashbam.
84. Abbaye's mother died in childbirth; he regarded the nurse who brought him up
     as his mother (*Qiddushin* 31b), and she passed on to him numerous remedies and
     superstitions (cf. *Shabbat* 134a).

bar Isaac, since the demons are more likely to be out to get him].

Ulla said, 'Doubles' doesn't apply to ten cups.

> [In saying this,] Ulla follows his [usual] line. For Ulla – though some say it was taught in a baraita – said that the Sages instituted [the custom of drinking] ten cups in the house of mourning. If 'doubles' applied to ten cups, how could the Sages have introduced [a custom] that might be dangerous?

But 'doubles' does apply to eight [cups].

Rav Ḥisda and Rabba bar bar Ḥana both said, 'Peace' [that is, seven] joins for good, not for bad, [so eight is not harmful,] but 'doubles' does apply to six [cups].

Rabba and Rav Yosef both said, 'Grace' [that is, five] joins for good, not for bad, [so six is not harmful,] but 'doubles' does apply to four [cups].

Abbaye and Rava both said, 'Protect' [that is, three] joins for good, not for bad[, so four is not harmful].[85]

[In saying this,] Rava followed his habit, for Rava bade farewell to his students with four cups; even though [one of them,] Rava bar Livai, was harmed, he took no account of this, saying, It was because he kept badgering me at my lectures.

Rav Yosef said, The demon Joseph told me that Ashmodai, king of the demons, is in charge of all doubles, and that [as] a king it cannot be said [of him] that he harms [anyone].

> Others report this in the opposite sense, that to the contrary, [as] a king he is irascible and does what he likes, since **A king may break down fences to make a road for himself and no one can stop him.**[86]

Rav Papa said, The demon Joseph said to me, We [demons] kill for two but we don't kill for four. We cause harm for two, whether [the double was] deliberate or accidental; for four[, we cause harm if the double was] accidental, but not if it was

---

85. 'Peace' is the seventh and last word in the final sentence of the priestly blessing in Numbers 6:24–6; 'grace' is the fifth and last word in the middle sentence; 'protect' is the third and last word in the first sentence – Rashi and Rashbam.
86. *Sanhedrin* 20b.

deliberate. If someone carelessly allowed [a double] to happen, what remedy does he have? He should hold his right thumb in his left hand and his left thumb in his right hand, and say, You and I make three! If he hears a voice say, You and I make four, he should say, You and I make five; if it says, You and I make six, he should say, You and I make seven. That happened once, and when they got to 101 a demon popped out.[87]

Ameimar said, The chief sorceress once told me that if you meet sorceresses you should say, Hot shit out of torn baskets into your mouths, O sorceresses! May the hair with which you conjure be torn out[88] and the crumbs you do magic with blow away! May your potions be scattered, and may the wind blow the fresh saffron out of your hands, O sorceresses! As long as [heaven] cared for me, and I cared for myself, and you cared for me, I didn't come among you; now that I have come among you I know that you have cooled towards me and I have not taken care of myself.[89]

In the West they are not particular about doubles.

Rav Dimi of Nehardea was particular even about the [number of marks for] measurement on the wine barrels; it once happened that [that they came out to an even number and] the barrel burst.

The principle of the matter is, that if anybody is attentive to [doubles, the demons] are attentive to him; if he is not attentive to [doubles, the demons] don't bother with him.

Even so, one ought to take care.

When Rav Dimi came, he said, Two eggs, two walnuts, two cucumbers and [two of] the other thing, are [forbidden as] a law of Moses from Sinai![90] However, the rabbis didn't know what he meant by 'the other thing', so they forbade all doubles on account of 'the other thing'.

Now when we said that ten, eight, six or four don't count as

87. Or possibly, 'escaped'.
88. On the role of hair in incantation formulae, see Lieberman, *Greek*, p. 111.
89. This translation follows Rashbam, who cites Ezekiel 13:20 on the false prophetesses. Text and translation are dubious.
90. A hyperbole to stress how dangerous these doubles are.

doubles, this was in connection with demons, but for sorcery we have to worry about larger numbers. There was an incident with a man who divorced his wife. She went and married an innkeeper. [The ex-husband] used to go [there] every day to drink wine, but though she tried sorcery on him it didn't succeed as he always took care [to avoid] doubles. One day he drank a lot and lost count. Up to sixteen he kept a clear head, but after that he was confused and no longer careful. [The innkeeper] turned him out [when he reached] a double. On his way he met an Arab, who said to him, 'I see a dead man walking here.' As he continued on his way, he caught hold of a palm tree; the tree cried out and the man expired.

Rav Avira said, Doubles don't apply to dishes or to loaves of bread.

The principle is doubles don't apply to things completed by people; among things that are naturally complete, you must take care with food.[91]

Doubles don't apply to inns.[92]

Doubles don't apply to someone who changes his mind.

Doubles don't apply to guests.[93]

Doubles don't apply to women, unless she is an important woman.

Rav Ḥinena the son of Rabbi Joshua said, Asparagus wine combines for good, not for bad.

Ravina said in the name of Rav, One should go to the stricter side [in case of doubt] about doubles.

    Some say, [he said] to the more lenient side.

Every effort is made to involve children in the family celebration of the Passover, and some customs were devised explicitly to arouse their curiosity. The universal Jewish practice is for the youngest capable child present at the Seder to chant the 'Four Questions'.

91. In case the food in question is the 'other thing' that Rav Dimi failed to specify – Rashbam.
92. i.e. drinking in two inns is not a 'double'.
93. A guest is dependent on the host, so cannot know how many cups he will drink; each one is like a 'change of mind'. This applies equally to non-important women.

MISHNA:

116a   The second cup [of wine] is poured for him, and now[94] the child questions his father; if the child is not [yet] intelligent enough to ask, the father teaches him:

How different this night is from all [other] nights! On all [other] nights we may eat either *hametz* or *matza*, but tonight only *matza*; on all [other] nights we eat any vegetables, but tonight bitter [herb]; on all [other] nights we may eat roasted, cooked or boiled meat, but tonight only roasted; on all [other] nights we dip once, but tonight we dip twice.[95]

The father teaches according to the capacity of the son. He begins with shame, and ends with praise, and expounds from AN ARAMEAN TRIED TO DESTROY MY FATHER[96] (Deuteronomy 26:5).

GEMARA:

The rabbis taught: If the son is clever, he asks [the four questions]; if [the son] is not clever, the wife asks; if not, [the father] asks himself. Even if two learned disciples who know the laws of Passover [share the Seder], they question one another.

On all [other] nights we dip once, but tonight we dip twice. Rava objected, Surely there is no obligation to dip at all on any other night? The Mishna should read, On all [other] nights we don't have to dip even once, but tonight we must dip twice.

Rav Safra objected, But do children have any obligation?[97] So, said Rav Safra, the Mishna should read, On all [other] nights we don't dip even once, but tonight we dip twice.

He begins with shame, and ends with praise. What [does the Mishna mean by] 'shame'? Rav said, 'Our fathers of old were idolaters'; Shmuel said, 'We were slaves [in Egypt].'[98]

Rav Nahman said to his slave Daru [at the Seder], If a master grants his slave freedom and gives him silver and gold, what

---

94. Since it is not usual to take a second cup before the meal – Rashi.
95. Variant readings are reflected in the ensuing discussion.
96. This is a rabbinic interpretation of the verse which is more correctly translated, 'My father was a wandering Aramean.'
97. They have not yet reached the age of *bar mitzva* (13), when personal responsibility commences.
98. Both phrases occur in the *haggada*.

should [the slave] say? [Daru] replied, He should thank him and praise him. Rav Naḥman said, You have exempted us from the four questions! He went on to say, 'We were slaves [in Egypt] . . .'

MISHNA:

Rabban Gamaliel used to say, Whoever has not mentioned these three things at the Passover [meal] has failed in his duty; namely, *Pesaḥ, matza, maror*:

116b

Pesaḥ [Passover]: because God passed over our houses in Egypt, as it is said, YOU SHALL SAY, 'IT IS THE PASSOVER SACRIFICE TO THE LORD, BECAUSE HE PASSED OVER THE HOUSES OF THE ISRAELITES IN EGYPT WHEN HE SMOTE THE EGYPTIANS, BUT SAVED OUR HOUSES' (Exodus 12:27 JPS).

Matza [unleavened bread]: because our fathers were redeemed from Egypt, as it is said, AND THEY BAKED UN- LEAVENED CAKES OF THE DOUGH THAT THEY HAD TAKEN OUT OF EGYPT (12:39 JPS).

Maror [bitter herb]: because the Egyptians embittered the lives of our fathers in Egypt, as it is said, RUTHLESSLY THEY MADE LIFE BITTER FOR THEM WITH HARSH LABOUR AT MOR- TAR AND BRICKS AND WITH ALL SORTS OF TASKS IN THE FIELD (1:14 JPS).

In every generation you should imagine that you, yourself had come out of Egypt, as it is said, AND YOU SHALL EXPLAIN TO YOUR SON ON THAT DAY, 'IT IS BECAUSE OF WHAT THE LORD DID FOR ME WHEN I WENT FREE FROM EGYPT' (13:8 JPS). That is why we must thank, praise, glorify, exalt, honour, bless, acclaim and laud the One who performed all these miracles for our fathers and ourselves; He brought us from slavery to freedom, from anxiety to joy, from mourning to celebration, from darkness to great light and from oppression to redemption. So let us say, Hallelujah![99]

How much [of Hallel] should one say [at this point in the Seder, prior to the meal]? The School of Shammai said, As far as A HAPPY MOTHER OF CHILDREN (Psalm 113:9); but the

---

99. 'Praise the Lord', but here with special reference to Hallel, hence the ensuing questions as to how much to recite at this point prior to the meal.

School of Hillel said, As far as THE FLINTY ROCK INTO A MOUNTAIN (Psalm 114:8).

You conclude [this part of the Seder] with [the blessing of] redemption. Rabbi Tarfon said, [You say,] 'He who redeemed us and redeemed our fathers from Egypt', but do not end [with the formula of blessing]. Rabbi Aqiva said, [You say,] 'So may the Lord our God and God of our fathers bring us to other seasons and festivals in the future in peace, with joy in Your rebuilt city, and gladness in Your service; and may we partake there of the Passover and [other] sacrifices . . . Blessed are You, O Lord, who has redeemed Israel.'

GEMARA:

Rava said, You need to say, 'And He brought us out from there.'

Rava said, [When you come to the three items specified by Rabban Gamaliel,] you should raise the *matza* [by way of demonstration] and raise the bitter herb, but you need not raise the meat; indeed[, if you raised the meat] it would look as if you were eating sacrifices outside [the Temple].

Rabbinic legislation on disability seeks to strike a balance between 'normalization', and reluctance to impose obligations that might prove too onerous. A special problem arises with the Seder, since it is in some measure a visual demonstration of the Exodus; how can a blind person be obligated to take part? Two third-generation Amoraim, Rav Yosef and Rav Sheshet, were blind; what did they do?

Rav Aḥa bar Jacob said, A blind person is exempt from [the obligation] of *haggada* ['telling the story'. In connection with *haggada*,] it is written, BECAUSE OF *THIS* (Exodus 13:8), and [in connection with the rebellious son,] it is written, *THIS* SON OF OURS (Deuteronomy 21:20); just as there the blind are excluded, so here the blind are excluded.

How can this be? Didn't Maremar say, I asked Rav Yosef's disciples who recited the *haggada* in his house, and they told me Rav Yosef [himself did so, and when I asked] who recited the *haggada* in Rav Sheshet's house, they told me Rav Sheshet [himself did so]?

The disciples held that [the obligation to eat] *matza* is

nowadays[100] of rabbinic status [only, and therefore Rav Yosef and Rav Sheshet ruled leniently].

Then does it follow that Rav Aḥa bar Jacob held that [the obligation to eat] *matza* is nowadays *d'Oraita*? Surely Rav Aḥa bar Jacob himself stated that *matza* is nowadays *d'rabbanan*! [No, he does not hold that it is *d'Oraita*. But] he held that whatever the rabbis instituted, they instituted in the way that the Torah had done.

But surely Rav Yosef and Rav Sheshet would agree that whatever the rabbis instituted, they instituted in the way that the Torah had done? [Yes. But] while [in the Deuteronomy case,] 'this' may [serve to] exclude the blind, in [the case of] *matza*, what could the Torah have written other than 'because of this'; [it does not exclude the blind, but specifies] that *matza* and bitter herb [must be present].

100. i.e. since the destruction of the Temple and the cessation of the sacrificial service.

FOURTH TRACTATE
SHEQALIM (THE ANNUAL TEMPLE TAX)

*By the late Second Temple period there was a substantial Jewish
presence throughout the Roman and Parthian Empires. The
Jerusalem Temple was a focal point for Jewish identity, and
the link was expressed through the annual remission of the
half-*sheqel *(Exodus 30:13) as a per capita tax for its support.
The Romans had their eyes on the money, and after the destruction of the Temple in 70, Vespasian substituted for it a* fiscus
judaicus *('Jewish purse') of two drachmas per head for the
temple of Jupiter Capitolinus at Rome, a tax Jews understand-
ably did their best to evade; Rome continued to collect it until
at least the third century.*[1]

The tractate deals with the collection of and liability to the
sheqel *and with the administration of the Temple treasury.
Mishna weaves authentic tradition as to Temple procedure with
nostalgic reconstruction in hope of restoration.*

CHAPTER ONE

1. **On 1 Adar the [collection of] the *sheqel* and [ban on] *kil'ayim*
   are announced. On 15 [Adar] the scroll [of Esther] is read in
   the cities,[2] and [attention is paid to] maintenance of the
   roads, town squares, immersion pools and public works and**

1. Josephus, *Wars*, 7:216–18; Suetonius, *Twelve Caesars*, Domitian 12. In *Antiquities*
    18:311–14 Josephus describes the collection of the two-drachma coins in Nehardea,
    Babylonia, prior to their transmission to Jerusalem.
2. *Megilla* 2a (see p. 262).

to the marking of graves; [agents] of the court set out [to inspect fields] for *kil'ayim*.

2. Rabbi Judah says, At first they [simply] uprooted the [forbidden] crops and threw them down where they were, but when sinners increased [who took advantage of this free hoeing of their fields, the court] declared the fields *hefqer*.[3]

3. On 15 [Adar] collection facilities [for the *sheqel*] were opened in the city [of Jerusalem], and on 23 [Adar] in the Temple precincts. Once they had opened in the Temple precincts, [the courts] commenced impounding the goods [of those who had not paid]. Whose goods did they impound? [Those of] Levites, Israelites, proselytes and freed slaves, but not women, slaves or children.

If a father once paid a *sheqel* on behalf of his son, he should continue.

The goods of *Kohanim* are not impounded, in order to maintain peace.[4]

CHAPTER TWO

3. If someone hands in money and says, This is for my *sheqel*, the School of Shammai say, Any excess must be used for free-will offerings; the School of Hillel say, The excess is not consecrated. If he said, [Take] my *sheqel* from this [money], both Houses agree that the excess is not consecrated.

If he said, This [money] is for a sin-offering, both Houses agree that any excess must be used for free-will offerings; but if he said, I'd like to make a sin-offering[, to be paid for] out of this money, both Houses agree that the excess is not consecrated.

4. Rabbi Simeon said, Why is there a difference between the *sheqel* and the sin-offering? [It is because] the *sheqel* is a fixed amount, but the sin-offering is not of fixed value.

3. So the courts allowed anyone to help themselves.
4. *Kohanim* disputed their liability to pay the *sheqel*, and could become violent if the attempt was made to coerce them.

5. Rabbi Judah said, The *sheqel* does not have a fixed value [either]. When Israel returned from exile, they brought [half-]*darkonot*; later, they brought [half-]*sela*s, then [half-] *teva'in*; [finally,] they wanted to bring [half-]denarii.[5] Rabbi Simeon replied, Even so, they all gave an equal amount at any one time, whereas one person brings a sin-offering that costs a *sela*, one may bring one worth two *selas* and another brings one worth three.

CHAPTER THREE

1. They draw funds from the treasury three times a year – fifteen days before Passover, fifteen days before Shavuot and fifteen days before Sukkot – since these are the times for cattle tithe.[6] This is Rabbi Aqiva's opinion, but Ben Azzai said, [The three times were] 29 Adar, 1 Sivan and 29 Av. Rabbi Eleazar and Rabbi Simeon say, 1 Nisan, 1 Sivan and 29 Elul. Why not 1 Tishri rather than 29 Elul? Since [1 Tishri] is [the New Year] festival, and it is not possible to tithe on the festival, they advanced it to 29 Elul.

2. The money was put into three boxes, each of three-*seah* capacity, marked with *aleph*, *bet*, *gimmel*. (Rabbi Ishmael says they were marked in Greek: *alpha*, *beta*, *gamma*.) The man who withdrew the money was not to enter [the treasury] wearing long folding garments, *tefillin* or amulets, for if he became poor, people would suspect [it was as a punishment for] robbing the treasury, while if he became rich, they would suspect he had become rich [by robbing] the treasury; for a person should show himself in the clear before people just as he should show himself in the clear before God, as it is said, YOU SHALL BE CLEAR BEFORE THE LORD AND BEFORE ISRAEL (Numbers 32:22 JPS), and YOU WILL FIND

---

5. These denominations are not all identifiable, but the point is that they are in order of declining value.
6. Animals would be readily available for purchase as offerings.

FAVOUR AND APPROBATION IN THE EYES OF GOD AND MAN (Proverbs 3:4 JPS).

3. Members of Rabban Gamaliel's family would enter holding their *sheqel* between their fingers; they would throw it down in front of the collector, who would push it into the box.

Before drawing funds [from the treasury], the man who drew the funds would say [to those present], Shall I draw? They would say to him three times, Draw, draw, draw!

4. When he drew the first [boxful], he would cover [that part of the coffers] with a leather spread, and likewise for the second, but he did not cover after the third withdrawal in case he forgot and inadvertently drew from what had already been drawn from.

The first boxful was withdrawn on behalf of [the people of] the Land of Israel, the second on behalf of its walled cities and the third on behalf of Babylonia, Media and distant lands.[7]

CHAPTER FIVE

1. These were the Temple officials: Yohanan ben Phineas [was in charge] of the tokens, Ahijah of the libations, Mattathias ben Samuel of casting lots, Petahiah of the birds – Petahiah was actually Mordecai, but he was called Petahiah because he opened (*patah*) the discourse with his words and was fluent in seventy languages – Ben Ahijah [was in charge] of those with stomach ailments, Nehunia of digging wells, Gevini was the crier, Ben Gever [was in charge] of closing the gates, Ben Babi of the strap, Ben Arza of the cymbals, Hogros ben Levi of the music, Garmu's family of the shewbread, Avtinos' family of preparing the incense, Eleazar of the curtain and Phineas of the vestments.

2. There were [never] less than three [assistant] treasurers and

---

7. The money was mainly spent on the purchase of sacrifices, and these were offered on behalf of all Israel.

seven [principal] treasurers. No public financial office should
be discharged by fewer than two [officials], but Ben Ahijah
[was entrusted with responsibility] for those with stomach
ailments and Eleazar [with responsibility] for the curtain, as
a majority of the public had consented.

6. There were two chambers in the Temple, one [called] the
Quiet Chamber and the other the Chamber of the Vessels.
God-fearing people would place money secretly in the Quiet
Chamber, and poor relatives of people of good class[8] would
discreetly support themselves from it. Anyone who had a
vessel would throw it into the Chamber of the Vessels, and
once every thirty days treasurers would open it up. If they
found anything of use for the Temple, they would retain it;
they would sell the rest and add the proceeds to the Temple
maintenance fund.

CHAPTER SIX

1. There were thirteen horn-shaped receptacles, thirteen
[money-changing] counters and thirteen places to bow in
the Sanctuary. [The families of] Rabban Gamaliel and Rabbi
Ḥanina the deputy High Priest used to bow in fourteen
[places], the extra one being near the wood store; they had
a tradition that that was where the Ark was concealed.[9]

2. A priest was once busy [in the area] and noticed that the
floor was different from the adjoining areas. He went to tell
his friend, but fell down dead before he managed to complete
his statement; then they were sure that that was where the
Ark was concealed.

8. Or possibly, 'of good deeds'.
9. This tradition is elaborated in *Yoma* 54a.

CHAPTER SEVEN

6. Rabbi Simeon said, The court instituted seven measures [regarding Temple expenditure]. One was that when a non-Jew sent [an animal] from abroad for a burnt offering, if he sent libations with it they would be offered, but if not, libations would be provided at the public expense.[10]

   Similarly, if a proselyte died and left [animals for] sacrifice, if he left libations for them they would be offered, but if not, libations would be provided at the public expense.[11]

   The Court also ruled that if a High Priest died, his grain offering should be provided at the public expense; Rabbi Judah says, It must be paid for by his heirs. [Both agree that] it must be a full [tenth of an *ephah*].

7. [They also decreed that] priests might benefit from the wood, that the ashes of the red heifer were not subject to the law of sacrilege and that bird-pairs that had been rejected would be replaced at public expense. Rabbi Yosé said, Whoever provided the birds must replace the rejected ones.

Chapter Eight covers the purity status of saliva or vessels found in Jerusalem, methods of cleansing appurtenances such as the sanctuary curtain and disposal of the remains of offerings. Here is the final Mishna:

CHAPTER EIGHT

8. The limbs of the daily offering are placed [for disposal] on the lower half of the [altar] ramp on its east side; the limbs of the additional offering are placed [for disposal] on the lower half of the [altar] ramp on its west side; those of the New Moon offering [are placed for disposal] below the altar surround.

10. That is, from the Temple treasury.
11. The proselyte would not have relatives to provide the libations.

Sheqel and first-fruits operate only when the Temple is standing, but the tithes of grain and cattle and the law of first-born animals apply irrespective of whether the Temple is standing.

If someone declares *sheqel* and first-fruits consecrated [despite there being no Temple], they attain consecrated status. Rabbi Simeon says, If someone [nowadays] declares first-fruits consecrated, they are not consecrated.

FIFTH TRACTATE
YOMA (THE DAY)

*'The Day' is Yom Kippur, the Day of Atonement, that is, of
reconciliation with God. The first seven chapters set out in
meticulous detail the Temple procedure for the day, based on
Leviticus 16. In the eighth, final chapter the Mishna moves from
the public ritual of atonement to the personal aspects of the
day.*

CHAPTER ONE

MISHNA:

**Seven days prior to Yom Kippur the High Priest is moved
from his home to the Parhedrin[1] Chamber, and a deputy
is appointed in case anything occurs that might disqualify
him.**

Rabbi Judah says, Another wife is prepared for him, in case
his wife dies, for it is said, AND HE SHALL ATONE FOR HIMSELF
AND FOR HIS HOUSE (Leviticus 16:6) – 'his house' is his wife.
[The other Sages] said [to Rabbi Judah], If so, there would be
no end to the matter.

GEMARA:

[Another] Mishna states: **Seven days before the burning of
the [red] heifer they moved the priest who was to burn it from**

---

1.   Derived from Greek *paredros*, assistant or assessor.

his home to the north-eastern chamber in front of the *bira*, known as the Stone Chamber.[2]

Why was it called the Stone Chamber? Because all utensils there were made of dung, stone or earth. Why was that? It was because the red heifer might be processed by someone who had immersed only that day, as Mishna states: **They rendered the priest who was to burn the heifer impure, then immersed him [in the cleansing *miqvé*], in order to undermine the view of the Sadducees, who held that [the heifer might be burnt only] by someone on whom the sun had set [following his immersion];[3]** [the rabbis accordingly] insisted on dung, stone and earthern utensils that are not receptive to impurity, in order that people should not take the matter lightly.

Why [was the priest who burnt the heifer secluded] in the north-east? Because [the heifer] was a sin-offering, of which is written, [**HE SHALL SPRINKLE**] **TOWARD THE FRONT OF THE TENT OF MEETING** (Numbers 19:4); the rabbis therefore ordained that he should occupy the north-eastern chamber, which would be distinctive.[4]

What is the *bira*? Rabba bar bar Ḥana said in the name of Rabbi Yoḥanan, A place on the Temple Mount. But Resh Laqish said, The whole Temple is called *bira*, as [David said], **THE *BIRA* THAT I HAVE PREPARED** (1 Chronicles 29:19). What is the [scriptural] basis [for isolating the High Priest for seven days]?

The Gemara enquires whether we are to derive it from the isolation of the priest who burnt the red heifer (but what scriptural basis does that have?), from Aaron's separation at the inauguration of the priesthood (Leviticus 8 – then why not apply

2. Mishna *Parah* 3:1 (see p. 681).
3. Ibid., 3:7 (see p. 683). The topic of *t'vul yom* – one who had immersed but on whom the sun had not set – is dealt with in the tractate of that name.
4. Rashi explains that the priest stood on the Mount of Olives to carry out the ceremony, and from there looked towards the eastern gate of the Temple.

other procedures of the inauguration too?), or from Moses'
isolation prior to the Sinai covenant (Exodus 24:16 – but that
was only for six days). Discussion of Aaron's separation as
precedent yields what historically is the most plausible interpret-
ation, namely that it reflects the efforts of the Pharisees to
control Temple procedure.

A baraita supports the view of Resh Laqish: IN THIS WAY   4a
SHALL AARON ENTER THE SANCTUARY (Leviticus 16:3) – IN
THIS WAY, i.e. in the way indicated in the context of the
inauguration. What [happened] at the inauguration? Aaron
was set apart for seven days and served for one day; Moses
transmitted [God's word] to him throughout the seven days
to instruct him [on the performance of] the service. Likewise,
throughout the generations, the High Priest is set apart for
seven days and serves for one day; two of Moses' disciples –
that is, not Sadducees – transmit [the authentic tradition]
to him throughout the seven days to instruct him [in the
performance of] the service. That is why they said, Seven days
prior to Yom Kippur the High Priest is moved from his home
to the Parhedrin Chamber. Just as they move the High Priest,
so they move the priest who burns the red heifer to the
north-eastern chamber in front of the *bira*. Each day, they
sprinkle each of them with [prescribed amounts of] all [avail-
able purification waters].

CHAPTER THREE

GEMARA:

The rabbis taught: A poor man, a rich man and a wicked   35b
man come to Judgement. They ask the poor man, Why did
you not engage in the study of Torah? If he says, Because I
had such a hard time trying to earn a living, they reply: Were
you worse off than Hillel? They say that Hillel went to work
each day and earned a *tropaikos*; he paid half of it to the
doorkeeper of the House of Study, and supported himself and
his family on the other half. One day he couldn't make enough

money, so the doorkeeper wouldn't let him in. He climbed up
and sat on the skylight[5] so that he might hear the words of the
living God from the mouths of Shemaia and Avtalion. That
day, they say, was a Friday, the winter solstice, and snow was
falling. When dawn came [the next morning], Shemaia said to
Avtalion, Avtalion, my brother, this house is always light but
today it is dark: are there clouds? They looked up and saw the
shape of a man in the skylight, and when they went up they
found he was buried under three cubits of snow. They freed
him, washed him, anointed him and sat him by a roaring fire,
saying, It is right that we should override the Sabbath [laws]
for this man.

They ask the rich man, Why did you not engage in the
study of Torah? If he says, Because I was so busy with my
affairs, they say, Surely you were no wealthier than Rabbi
Eleazar ben Ḥarsom, of whom they say that his father left him
1,000 towns on dry land and 1,000 ships in the sea, yet every
day he took a jar of flour on his shoulder and wandered from
town to town and country to country [seeking] to learn Torah.
His servants once met him [but did not recognize him], and
tried to press him into the public levy.[6] He protested, I beg
you, leave me to study Torah! They retorted, By the life of
Rabbi Eleazar ben Ḥarsom, we won't let you go! [They
failed to recognize him] because he had never supervised them,
since all his days and nights were devoted to the study of
Torah.

They ask the wicked man, Why did you not engage in the
study of Torah? If he says, Because I was so handsome, and
was driven to satisfy my lust, they say to him, Were you more
handsome than Joseph? They say of Joseph, the virtuous man,
that Potiphar's wife tried every day to seduce him (Genesis
37). What she wore [to attract him] in the morning she did
not wear in the evening. She said to him, Just listen to me!

5.   Kushelevsky, 'Skylight', p. 375, in a semiotic appraisal of this passage, sees the
      image of 'the man in the skylight' as a sign of revelation: 'The revealed face
      through the skylight – an imperative of non-indifference . . . and of responsibility
      toward the Other'.
6.   Angaria (Greek) – forced labour, in this case levied on behalf of the owner of the
      town, namely Eleazar himself.

He said, No! She said, Then I will see that you are bound in the prison house; he said, THE LORD SETS FREE THE PRISONERS. She said, I will cripple you; he said, THE LORD STRAIGHTENS THE BENT. She said, I will blind you; he said, THE LORD GIVES SIGHT TO THE BLIND (Psalm 146:7, 8). She gave him 1,000 pieces of silver to lie with her, to be with her, but he wouldn't listen to her – TO LIE WITH HER in this world, TO BE WITH HER in the next (Genesis 39:10).

Hillel, then, shows up the guilt of the poor, Eleazar ben Ḥarsom that of the rich and Joseph that of the lustful.

The public Temple procedures described lovingly and at length in the first seven chapters are helpful, but not essential, to the forgiveness of sin and restoration to God. Penitence – teshuva ('return' to God) – is essential, and is a major theme of the final chapter, which addresses the private 'observances' of the Day of Atonement, including fasting and other forms of self-discipline.

CHAPTER EIGHT

MISHNA:
On Yom Kippur it is forbidden to eat, drink, wash, anoint, wear [leather] shoes, or have sex.   73b

A king and a bride may wash their faces. In the opinion of Rabbi Eliezer a woman who has [recently] given birth may wear shoes, but the [other] Sages forbid this.

The penalty is incurred if you eat the equivalent of a large date including the stone, or if you drink enough to fill your cheeks. All foods combine to a date-size, and all drinks to a mouthful, but food and drink do not combine.

GEMARA:
Forbidden? Surely it is [not merely forbidden, but] punishable by *karet*!

Rabbi Ila – some say Rabbi Jeremiah – said, It had to be [expressed this way] to cover the case of the half-measure[, since the penalty applies only to someone who has eaten or drunk a full measure].[7]

That [argument] holds if you maintain that the Torah forbids half-measures, but what could you say on the view that the Torah[, though not the rabbis,] permits half-measures?

For it was taught: Rabbi Yoḥanan says,
Half-measures are forbidden by the Torah;
Resh Laqish says, Half-measures are permitted by the Torah.

[The answer given] is satisfactory on Rabbi Yoḥanan's view, but what could you say on Resh Laqish's view?

Resh Laqish agrees that [half-measures are] forbidden by the rabbis.

In that case[, if he swore not to eat a half-measure of some forbidden food, but then ate it], he should not be obliged to bring sacrifice [for having broken an oath, since an oath to do something forbidden is invalid]. So why does a Mishna state: **[If someone said,] 'I swear I will not eat', and he ate non-kosher meat, or swarming or crawling creatures, he is liable [to the penalty for breaking an oath], but Rabbi Simeon holds he is exempt?**[8] The question was put, Why [should he be liable]? Surely he was already placed under oath at Mount Sinai [not to eat such things, so another oath not to eat them has no further effect, and is invalid? To this question] Rav, Shmuel and Rabbi Yoḥanan replied, [This is where his oath] included permissible things with the forbidden ones; but Resh Laqish said, It would only apply if either (a) in the view of the rabbis, he explicitly [swore not to eat] half-measures, or (b) in the view of Rabbi Aqiva, who maintained that even if he does not say so explicitly,

74a

7. Anything short of the full measure is called half-measure.
8. Mishna *Shavuot* 3:4 (22b).

[someone who binds himself with an oath] means to forbid even the smallest amount.

If you argue that on the view that the Torah permits half-measures he would be obliged to bring sacrifice, doesn't the Mishna say, **The oath of testimony applies only to people who are eligible to testify?**[9] [In considering that,] we asked, Whom [does the Mishna] exclude? Rav Papa said, It excludes a king; Rav Aḥa bar Jacob said, It excludes a [professional] dice-player. Now, [the testimony of] a [professional] dice-player would be acceptable in [strict] Torah [law], though the rabbis disqualified it, and nevertheless you find that he is exempt from taking the oath. [Answer:] That case is different, since Scripture says, IF HE DOES NOT TELL, HE SHALL CARRY THE RESPONSIBILITY (Leviticus 5:1), and [a dice-player] is incompetent to tell.[10]

[Is it true that] Mishna never says 'forbidden' when it teaches that something is punishable by *karet*? [What about the] baraita that says, **Even though they said all of them were forbidden, *karet* applies only to those who eat, drink or perform labour?** What that baraita means is, **When they said 'forbidden', they referred only to half-measures, but for full measures the punishment is *karet*; but even though the punishment is *karet*, it applies only to eating, drinking and performing labour.** Alternatively, you might say [simply] that the word 'forbidden' applies to the rest, as Rabba and Rav Yosef read in the other books of the rabbis:[11] **How do we know that eating, drinking, anointing, wearing [leather] shoes and sex are forbidden on Yom Kippur? [The prohibition] is derived from the word *shabbaton*, meaning 'desist'.**

To take up the point about half-measures: Rabbi Yoḥanan

9. Ibid., 4:1 (30a).
10. A professional gambler is assumed to be dishonest, so any testimony he gives would be worthless; consequently, he cannot have a duty to 'tell'.
11. An obscure phrase, which according to Rashi refers to the *midrashim* on Numbers and Deuteronomy.

says, They are forbidden by the Torah; Resh Laqish says, They are permitted by the Torah. Rabbi Yoḥanan says, They are forbidden by the Torah – since any bit can count towards the full measure, you are eating forbidden food[, however small the quantity]. Resh Laqish says, They are permitted by the Torah – the Torah forbids 'eating', and so [small a quantity] is not ['eating'].

Rabbi Yoḥanan objected[12] to Resh Laqish: **I might assume that whatever has a specified penalty is included in the prohibition. The** *koi*[13] **and half-measure involve no specified penalty; how do I know that they are nevertheless forbidden? Because Scripture says,** ALL FATS **(Leviticus 7:23).** [Resh Laqish could reply:] They are forbidden only by the rabbis; the proof-text is merely a support.

The obligation to fast on Yom Kippur is not absolute; anyone whose life may be endangered is forbidden to fast, on the general principle that the preservation of life takes precedence over all other commandments save those of idolatry, murder and adultery.[14] *Mishna gives some illustrations – for instance, a pregnant woman who smells some food that she craves should be given a little until the craving passes.*

84b   **And every doubt involving [danger to] life overrides Sabbath [observance].**

Rav Yehuda said in the name of Rav, They meant not only a doubt affecting this Sabbath, but even a doubt affecting an additional Sabbath. In what way? They meant to tell us [that if doctors] assessed that [the patient needed to take the cure] for eight days, and the first day was a Sabbath, we do not say, Wait until after the Sabbath [to apply the cure], so that we are not obliged to desecrate two Sabbaths.

This is taught also in a baraita: **You may heat water for a sick person on the Sabbath, whether for drinking or application, and not only for this Sabbath but for the next. Do not**

12. This is not a direct report, but a surmise as to an objection he might have raised.
13. The rabbis could not decide whether this animal, possibly an antelope, should be classified as domestic or wild; in the former case certain fats were forbidden, in the latter not.
14. *Sanhedrin* 73–4 (see pp. 510–12).

say, Wait and see if his condition improves, but heat the water immediately, because any doubt about [danger to] life overrides the Sabbath, and not just this Sabbath, but additional Sabbaths. [What needs to be done] should not be done by non-Israelites or Samaritans, but by adult Israelites. Do not say that these things should not be done on the advice of women or Samaritans – their opinion may be combined with that of others.

The rabbis taught: **Do whatever is needed to save life on Shabbat; whoever is quick off the mark is to be praised; do not seek authorization from the court.**

How does this work? If you see a child fall in the sea, spread a net and fish him out, and **whoever is quick off the mark is to be praised; do not seek authorization from the court** – even though you may [incidentally] be catching fish.[15]

If you see a child fall down a pit, dig it out and bring him up, and **whoever is quick off the mark is to be praised; do not seek authorization from the court** – even though you are [incidentally] building steps.

If you see a door closing on a child, smash it down and get him out, and **whoever is quick off the mark is to be praised; do not seek authorization from the court** – even though you are [incidentally] breaking it into planks.

Extinguish fires and place obstacles in their way, and **whoever is quick off the mark is to be praised; do not seek authorization from the court** – even though you are [incidentally] levelling the ground.[16]

All these cases need mention. If it mentioned only the sea, you might think that this is because he might be carried away, but if he was in a pit, he could remain there [until after Shabbat; the baraita tells you that this is not correct]. If it mentioned only the pit, you might think that this is because [the child] is frightened, but if he was locked behind a door, someone could sit on the other side and amuse him [by rattling] nuts [until after Shabbat; it tells you that this is not correct]. And why

15. Catching fish is a forbidden labour on the Sabbath, as are the examples that follow.
16. 'Levelling (the ground)' follows Sokoloff, *Babylonian*, p. 676. Rashi understands it to indicate levelling off the embers to use them as a grill after Shabbat.

mention extinguishing and placing obstacles? [Because this should be done] even if [no people are there, but only] in an adjoining courtyard.

MISHNA:

85b   Sin-offering and definite reparation-offering atone; death and the Day of Atonement atone together with *teshuva* [penitence]. *Teshuva* atones [immediately, at any time of the year,] for minor sins, both positive and negative; for major sins it tides over until the Day of Atonement [effects final atonement].

If someone says, I will sin, then repent, [then] sin [again] and repent, he is not given the opportunity to repent;[17] [if he says] I will sin, and the Day of Atonement will atone, the Day of Atonement does not atone for him.

The Day of Atonement atones for sins between man and God, but sins between one person and another are not forgiven until [the offending party effects] reconciliation.

Rabbi Eleazar ben Azaria expounded: FROM ALL YOUR SINS BEFORE THE LORD YOU SHALL BE CLEANSED (Leviticus 16:30) – The Day of Atonement atones for sins against God, but sins between one person and another are not forgiven until [the offending party effects] reconciliation.

Said Rabbi Aqiva: Happy are you, O Israel! Before whom do you cleanse yourselves [from sin], and who cleanses you? Your Father in Heaven, as it is said, I WILL SPRINKLE CLEAN WATER UPON YOU, AND YOU SHALL BE CLEAN (Ezekiel 36:25 JPS), and it says, THE LORD IS THE *MIQVÉ* OF ISRAEL (Jeremiah 17:13) – just as the *miqvé* purifies the unclean, so does the Holy One, blessed be He, cleanse Israel.[18]

GEMARA:

86a   Rabbi Matya ben Ḥarash asked Rabbi Eleazar in Rome, Do you know about the four categories of penitence that Rabbi Ishmael expounded?

---

17. If he does repent, he would of course be forgiven, but by deliberately sinning with the intention of repenting he has made genuine penitence more difficult.

18. The usual – and contextually correct – translation of Jeremiah's words, is 'O Lord, Israel's hope!' The noun *miqvé* occurs in the Bible both in the sense of 'hope' and as a 'gathering' of waters; Aqiva's exegesis exploits this ambivalence.

[Rabbi Eleazar] replied, There are three, and *teshuva* [is required] with each of them. If someone failed to observe a positive command, then repented, he is forgiven before he moves from the spot, as it is said, TURN BACK, O REBELLIOUS CHILDREN, I WILL HEAL YOUR AFFLICTIONS! (Jeremiah 3:22 JPS). If he transgressed a negative command, then repented, *teshuva* tides him over [until] the Day of Atonement brings forgiveness, as it is said, FOR ON THIS DAY ATONEMENT SHALL BE MADE FOR YOU (Leviticus 16:30 JPS). If he transgressed [any of those commandments for which Scripture assigns] *karet* or capital punishment, both *teshuva* and the Day of Atonement tide him over and suffering wrings [the sin out of him], as it is said, I WILL PUNISH THEIR TRANSGRESSION WITH THE ROD, THEIR INIQUITY WITH PLAGUES (Psalm 89:33 JPS). But if anyone has profaned God's Name, *teshuva* cannot tide him over, the Day of Atonement cannot bring forgiveness, nor can suffering wring out [the sin], as it is said, 'THIS INIQUITY SHALL NEVER BE FORGIVEN FOR YOU UNTIL YOU DIE,' SAID MY LORD GOD OF HOSTS (Isaiah 22:14 JPS).

What does 'profaning God's Name' (*ḥillul Hashem*) mean?

Rav said, For somebody like me, if I were to take meat from the butcher without paying immediately[, that would be *ḥillul Hashem*].[19]

> Abbaye commented: This would only apply in a place where they do not invoice [for payment], but where they invoice for payment it does not matter.[20]
> Ravina remarked: Mata Meḥasya[21] is a place where they invoice for payment.
> When Abbaye bought meat from two partners, he would make payment to each of them [separately],[22] then bring them together for a reckoning.

Rabbi Yoḥanan said, For one like me, if I were to walk four

---

19. People would suspect him of theft and learn to do likewise (Rashi), or think that he was taking advantage of his status to gain favours.
20. There is no obligation to pay until the invoice (written or otherwise) is presented.
21. The town where he resided.
22. So that neither could suspect that he had not paid.

cubits without [learning] Torah or without [wearing] *tefillin*[, that would be *hillul Hashem*].

Isaac of the school of Rabbi Yannai said, Hillul Hashem is when somebody gets talked about in such a way that his friends feel ashamed of him.

Rav Nahman bar Isaac commented, For instance, if people say, May God forgive so-and-so!

Abbaye said, As it was taught: AND YOU SHALL LOVE THE LORD YOUR GOD (Deuteronomy 6:5) – [you shall act in such a manner that] God's Name is loved because of you. Study Scripture and Mishna, wait upon the learned, deal with everyone in a pleasant manner. People will then say of you, Happy is his father who taught him Torah, and his teacher who taught him Torah! Woe to those who have not studied Torah! See how pleasant and fair are the ways of this man who has studied Torah! Of such a person Scripture says, AND HE SAID TO ME, 'YOU ARE MY SERVANT, ISRAEL IN WHOM I GLORY' (Isaiah 49:3 JPS). But if anyone studies Scripture and Mishna, waits upon the learned, but does not conduct his affairs honestly and does not speak to people pleasantly, what do people say of him? Woe to so-and-so who studied Torah, woe to his father who taught him Torah and woe to his teacher who taught him Torah! See how crooked are his deeds and unpleasant his ways! Of such a person Scripture says, THEY CAUSED MY HOLY NAME TO BE PROFANED, IN THAT IT WAS SAID OF THEM, 'THESE ARE THE PEOPLE OF THE LORD, YET THEY HAD TO LEAVE HIS LAND' (Ezekiel 36:20 JPS).

Rabbi Hama bar Hanina said, Great is *teshuva*, for it brings healing to the world, as it is said, I WILL HEAL THEIR AFFLICTION,[23] GENEROUSLY I WILL TAKE THEM BACK IN LOVE (Hosea 14:5 JPS).

Rabbi Hama bar Hanina noted a contradiction. It is written, TURN BACK, O REBELLIOUS CHILDREN, implying that their sin is now regarded as mere childish wilfulness, and it continues, I WILL HEAL YOUR AFFLICTIONS! [implying that though now

---

23. The unusual word *meshuva*, here translated 'affliction', is closely related to the Hebrew for penitence.

forgiven, their sin is regarded as a deep sickness that has left its
mark – Rashi] (Jeremiah 3:22 JPS). [There is no contradiction;]
one [expression is used of those who have repented] out of love,
the other [of those who have repented merely] out of fear.[24]

Rav Yehuda noted a contradiction. It is written, TURN BACK,
O REBELLIOUS CHILDREN, I WILL HEAL YOUR AFFLICTIONS!
and it is written, TURN BACK, REBELLIOUS CHILDREN, FOR I
HAVE BEEN YOUR MASTER;[25] I WILL TAKE YOU ONE FROM A
TOWN AND TWO FROM A CLAN, AND BRING YOU TO ZION
(Jeremiah 3:14 JPS). [The first of these speaks of penitents as
God's 'children', the second as His slaves, since He is their
master. There is no contradiction:] one [verse speaks of those
who return to God] out of love or fear, the other [of those who
return to God] as a result of suffering.

Rabbi Levi said, Great is *teshuva*, for it reaches the Throne
of Glory, as it is written, RETURN, O ISRAEL, TO THE LORD
YOUR GOD (Hosea 14:2 JPS).

Rabbi Yoḥanan said, Great is *teshuva*; it overrides a prohib-   86b
ition in the Torah, for it is written, [THE WORD OF THE LORD
CAME TO ME AS FOLLOWS]: IF A MAN DIVORCES HIS WIFE,
AND SHE LEAVES HIM AND MARRIES ANOTHER MAN, CAN HE
EVER GO BACK TO HER?[26] WOULD NOT SUCH A LAND BE
DEFILED? NOW YOU HAVE WHORED WITH MANY LOVERS,
YET YOU CAN RETURN TO ME, SAYS THE LORD (Jeremiah
3:1–2).

Rabbi Jonathan said, Great is *teshuva*; it brings redemption,
for it is written, HE SHALL COME AS REDEEMER TO ZION, TO
THOSE IN JACOB WHO TURN BACK FROM SIN – DECLARES
THE LORD (Isaiah 59:20 JPS) – Why does He come as redeemer?
Because there are in Jacob those who turn back from sin.

Resh Laqish said, Great is *teshuva*; it transforms deliberate
transgressions to unintentional ones, as it is written, RETURN,

24. i.e. if you repent out of love of God, your sin is treated as a mere youthful
    aberration; if you are motivated only by fear of punishment, the 'disease' may not
    be completely eradicated.
25. 'I have espoused you' (JPS); but this translation does not fit the interpretation.
26. Deuteronomy 24:1–4, though permitting both divorce and remarriage, does not
    allow this.

O Israel, to the Lord your God, for you have
stumbled in your sin (Hosea 14:2) – 'sin' is deliberate, yet
[the verse] calls it [mere] 'stumbling'.

That can't be. Surely Resh Laqish said, Great is
teshuva, for it transforms deliberate transgressions to
merits, as it is written, And when a wicked man
turns back from his wickedness and does
what is just and right, it is he who shall
live (Ezekiel 33:19 JPS)! [No problem.] One [verse]
speaks of those who have repented] out of love, the
other [of those merely] out of fear.

Rabbi Shmuel bar Naḥmani said in the name of Rabbi Jonathan, Great is *teshuva*; it lengthens a man's days, as it is written,
And when a wicked man turns back from his wicked-
ness and does what is just and right, it is he who
shall live.

Rabbi Isaac reported, They say in the West in the
name of Rabba bar Mari, Come and see, the ways of
the Holy One, blessed be He, are not like the ways of
flesh and blood. If a man provokes another, then
among flesh and blood it is uncertain whether [the
offended party] will accept reconciliation, and even if
he will, whether this can be achieved by words. But as
for the Holy One, blessed be He, should a man offend
against Him in private, he can be reconciled with Him
through words [alone], as it is said, Take words
with you And return to the Lord (Hosea 14:3).
More than that, he will be grateful to Him, as it
[continues], And take good; even more, Scripture
accounts it as if he had offered oxen, as it continues,
Instead of bulls we will pay by our lips – and
lest you think that means reparation-offerings, it states,
Generously[27] will I take them back, in love
(14:5).

It was taught: Rabbi Meir used to say, Great is *teshuva*, since
for the sake of one individual who repents, the whole world

27. Indicates a free-will offering.

is forgiven, as it is said, I WILL HEAL THEIR AFFLICTION,
GENEROUSLY WILL I TAKE THEM BACK, IN LOVE, FOR MY
ANGER HAS TURNED AWAY FROM HIM[28] (Hosea 14:5) – it does
not say 'from them', but 'from him'.

How can you tell someone is a genuine penitent? Rav Yehuda
says, If, for instance, he has the opportunity to commit the
[same] sin again on two occasions, but refrains from it. Rav
Yehuda indicated that he meant, [With] the same woman, at
the same time [of day] and in the same place.

Rav Yehuda reported that Rav noted a contradiction. It is
written, HAPPY IS HE WHOSE TRANSGRESSION IS FORGIVEN,
WHOSE SIN IS CONCEALED (Psalm 32:1), and it is written, HE
WHO CONCEALS HIS SINS WILL NOT PROSPER (Proverbs 28:13).
No contradiction. One [verse speaks of] a publicly known sin,
one of a sin which is not publicly known.[29] Rav Zutra bar Tuvia
said [in the name of] Rav Naḥman, One [verse speaks of] a sin
between man and man, the other of a sin between man and
God.

---

28. JPS has 'them', noting that the Hebrew is 'him'.
29. If the sin is publicly known, it is appropriate to make public amends.

SIXTH TRACTATE
SUKKA (TABERNACLES)

Three times a year you shall hold a festival for Me . . . the Feast of Ingathering at the end of the year, when you gather in the results of your work from the field.
(Exodus 23:14, 16 JPS)

Mark, on the fifteenth day of the seventh month, when you have gathered in the yield of your land, you shall observe the festival of the Lord [to last] seven days: a complete rest on the first day, and a complete rest on the eighth day. On the first day you shall take the product of hadar trees, branches of palm trees, boughs of leafy trees and willows of the brook, and you shall rejoice before the Lord your God seven days. You shall observe it as a festival of the Lord for seven days in the year; you shall observe it in the seventh month as a law for all time, throughout the ages. You shall live in booths seven days, all citizens in Israel shall live in booths, in order that future generations may know that I made the Israelite people live in booths when I brought them out of the land of Egypt. I am the Lord your God.
(Leviticus 23:39–43 JPS)

Numbers 29:12–34 lists the Temple sacrifices for the festival, and verses 35–8 introduce an Eighth Day of Solemn Assembly.

After the ingathering from your threshing floor and your vat, you shall hold the Feast of Booths for seven

DAYS. YOU SHALL REJOICE IN YOUR FESTIVAL, WITH YOUR SON
AND DAUGHTER, YOUR MALE AND FEMALE SLAVE, THE LEVITE,
THE STRANGER, THE FATHERLESS AND THE WIDOW IN YOUR COM-
MUNITIES. YOU SHALL HOLD A FESTIVAL FOR THE LORD YOUR
GOD SEVEN DAYS, IN THE PLACE THAT THE LORD WILL CHOOSE;
FOR THE LORD YOUR GOD WILL BLESS ALL YOUR CROPS AND ALL
YOUR UNDERTAKINGS, AND YOU SHALL HAVE NOTHING BUT JOY.
(Deuteronomy 16:13–15 JPS)

This tractate deals with the construction and correct use of
the sukka *(hut, booth, tabernacle), built in Jewish homes for the
festival of Sukkot (Tabernacles); the* Arba'a Minim *(Four Plant
Species) that represent the harvest; and the joyful celebration of
the festival.*

The opening chapter defines the sukka. *The essential element
is* s'khakh *('covering'), which must be made of approved
materials and placed at an appropriate height. Walls are
required to support the* s'khakh *and form an enclosure, but their
role is functional rather than intrinsic; they do not need to be
purpose-made.*

This sugya *forms a well-developed, highly stylized literary
unit. Many of the arguments put into the mouths of the earlier
rabbis are not reports, but speculations as to how they might
have justified their rulings. No one, for instance, had historical
information about Queen Helena's* sukka; *rather, it is being
're-designed' to accord with later theory.*

CHAPTER ONE

MISHNA:

If a *sukka* is more than 20 cubits high, it is not valid; but
Rabbi Judah says, It is valid.

If it is less than 10 palms high, or has fewer than three walls,
or has more light than shade, it is not valid.

GEMARA:

Elsewhere Mishna says, If [the beam bounding] a cul-de-

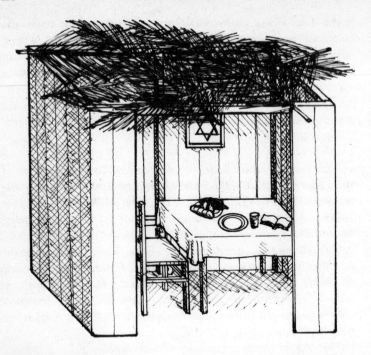

Sukka
Tabernacle.

sac is higher than 20 cubits, he should lower it.[1] Why does it
say 'not valid' here, whereas there it tells you how to put it
right?

Sukka is biblical, so it states 'not valid'; the [law of the]
cul-de-sac is rabbinic, so it tells you how to put it right.

Alternatively, [you may say that] even with a biblical command, it would tell you how to put it right; however, in the
case of *sukka*, where there is much to discuss, it simply says 'not
valid', whereas with the cul-de-sac, which is straightforward, it
tells you how to put it right.

1. The topic is the determination of boundaries by means of an *eruv*; see introductory
    note to *Eruvin*.

What is the [scriptural] basis for [the law about the height of a *sukka*]?

Rabba said, Scripture says, **IN ORDER THAT FUTURE GENERATIONS MAY KNOW THAT I MADE THE ISRAELITE PEOPLE LIVE IN BOOTHS WHEN I BROUGHT THEM OUT OF THE LAND OF EGYPT** (Leviticus 23:43 JPS). Up to a height of 20 cubits a person is aware that he is living in a *sukka*; above 20 cubits he is not aware that he is living in a *sukka*, since it does not catch the eye.

Rabbi Zeira[2] said, [It is derived] from here: **THERE SHALL BE A *SUKKA* FOR SHADE FROM THE HEAT BY DAY [AND AS A SHELTER FOR PROTECTION AGAINST FLOOD AND RAIN]** (Isaiah 4:6). Up to a height of 20 cubits a person is shaded by the *sukka*; if it is above 20 cubits he is shaded by the walls rather than by the *sukka*.

> Abbaye said to him, If that is so, suppose someone made a *sukka* in Ashtarot Qarnayim[3] – would it not be valid[, seeing that he is shaded by the sides of the gorge rather than by the covering of the *sukka*]? [Rabbi Zeira replied,] Take away Ashtarot Qarnayim and you still have a *sukka*; take away the walls, you do not have a *sukka*.

But Rava said, [It is derived] from here: **YOU SHALL LIVE IN BOOTHS SEVEN DAYS.** The Torah is saying, 'Leave your permanent abode for seven days and live in a temporary abode.' Up to a height of 20 cubits a person might make a temporary abode; higher than 20 cubits he would not make a temporary abode, but a permanent one.

> Abbaye asked him, If so, suppose someone erected iron walls and put a [*sukka*] covering over them, wouldn't that be a [valid] *sukka*? Rava replied, What I meant was, up to a height of 20 cubits, [a height at which] a man [might] make a temporary abode, even if he erects a permanent [construction] he has fulfilled the *mitzva*; over 20 cubits, [a height at which] a man

2. Zeira III, a disciple of Rav Yosef at Pumbedita.
3. 'Ashtarot of the twin peaks' (Genesis 14:5), understood by the rabbis to be a narrow gorge.

[would] make a permanent abode, even if he erects a temporary [construction] he has not fulfilled the *mitzva*.

2b   The others reject Rabba's proposal – his verse refers to future generations. They reject Rabbi Zeira's proposal – his verse refers to the messianic era. Rabbi Zeira himself would say, If that were so, Scripture would have said, 'The canopy[4] will be for shade by day'; as it says, THERE SHALL BE A *SUKKA* FOR SHADE . . . BY DAY, both inferences can be made.

[The other two] reject Rava's proposal because of Abbaye's objection.

With whom [of the foregoing] does the following observation made by Rabbi Josiah in Rav's name agree? The debate [between Rabbi Judah and the other Sages] concerns a case where the walls do not reach the *s'khakh*, but if the walls do reach the *s'khakh*, the *sukka* is valid even though it is higher than 20 cubits.

With whom? With Rabba, since he said it was because it does not catch the eye; if the walls extend to the *s'khakh*, it does catch the eye.

With whom does this observation made by Rav Huna in Rav's name agree? The debate [between Rabbi Judah and the other Sages] concerns a case where the [area of the] *sukka* is no more than 4 by 4 cubits, but if it is more than 4 by 4 cubits, the *sukka* is valid even though it is higher than 20 cubits.

With whom? With Rabbi Zeira, since he said it was because of shade; if the area is greater, the *sukka* casts a shade.

With whom does this observation made by Rav Ḥanan bar Rabba in Rav's name agree? The debate [between Rabbi Judah and the other Sages] concerns a case where the [area of the] *sukka* is just large enough to accommodate his head, most of his body and his table, but if it can accommodate more than his head, most of his body and his table, the *sukka* is valid even though it is higher than 20 cubits.

With whom? With none of them!

---

4.   This word is in the previous verse.

Clearly, Rabbi Josiah disagrees with [both] Rav Huna and Rav Ḥanan bar Rabba, since they give linear dimensions, and he does not. But do Rav Huna and Rav Ḥanan bar Rabba disagree about what is needed to make a *sukka* valid, one holding that the [minimum requirement] to make it valid is 4 by 4 cubits, and the other that the [minimum requirement] to make it valid is sufficient [volume] to accommodate his head, most of his body and his table?

No. All agree that the [minimum requirement] to make it valid is sufficient [volume] to accommodate his head, most of his body and his table. The dispute here is as to whether [Rabbi Judah and the Sages] differ about [a case] where the [area of the] *sukka* is just large enough to accommodate his head, most of his body and his table, but agree that if it can accommodate more than his head, most of his body and his table, the *sukka* is valid [even though it is higher than 20 cubits]; or whether [Rabbi Judah and the Sages] differ about [a case] where the [area of the] *sukka* is between what is large enough to accommodate his head, most of his body and his table, and is 4 [by 4] cubits, but if it is more than 4 [by 4] cubits, all agree that it is valid.

An objection was raised: **If a *sukka* is more than 20 cubits high, it is not valid; but Rabbi Judah says it is valid even if it is 40 or 50 cubits high. Rabbi Judah said, When Queen Helena**[5] **stayed at Lydda, her *sukka* was more than 20 cubits high; the elders went in and out and made no comment to her. [The Sages] replied to [Rabbi Judah]: What does that prove? She was a woman, and women are exempt from [the laws of] *sukka*. [Rabbi Judah] answered them, But didn't she have seven sons? Moreover, whatever she did, she did in accordance with [the rulings of] the Sages.**

Why does the baraita add, **Moreover, whatever she did, she did in accordance with [the rulings of] the Sages?** You might have thought that her children were young, and young children are exempt from *sukka*;

5. The conversion to Judaism of Queen Helena (d. 50 CE) of Adiabene (capital Arbela, now Irbil, Iraq) and her sons Monobazus II and Izates II is described by Josephus, *Antiquities* 20:34.

however, since there were seven, it is impossible that
none of them was old enough to be independent of
his mother. If you were to say, only the rabbis rule that
a child who is independent of his mother is obliged [to
live in the *sukka*], and [Queen Helena] did not follow
rabbinic law, they add, **Moreover, whatever she did,
she did in accordance with [the rulings of] the Sages**.

Now, if you say that the debate [between Rabbi Judah and
the other Sages] concerns a case where the walls do not reach
the *s'khakh*, a queen might dwell in such a *sukka* to enjoy the
air; but if you say the dispute is about a small *sukka*, a queen
would surely not dwell in a small *sukka*!

Rabba bar Rav Ada said, They must have been thinking of a
sukka divided into small cubicles.[6]

But would a queen dwell in a *sukka* divided into small
cubicles?

Rav Ashi said, They must have been thinking of a *sukka*
containing[, but not consisting exclusively of,] small cubicles.
The Sages thought that her sons were in the main *sukka*, but
she herself sat in a cubicle for privacy, which is why [the elders]
made no objection to her; Rabbi Judah thought her sons were
with her, and that despite that [the elders] made no objection.

3a

*The four plants listed in Leviticus 23:40 were identified by the
rabbis as citron (etrog), palm frond (lulav), myrtle and willow.
Three myrtle twigs and two willow twigs are bound to the palm
frond; worshippers hold them in the right hand, with the citron
next to them in the left, as they chant the Hallel psalms (113–
18). Chapters Three and Four set out the regulations as to
species, size, etc., for the plants; the extract below touches on
the concept of hiddur mitzva – items used in the performance
of a mitzva should be aesthetically pleasing as well as fulfilling
the letter of the law.*

6.   *Qitoniyot*; this may derive from Hebrew *qatan* 'small', or from Greek *koitē*, 'a
     place to lie down'.

CHAPTER THREE

It was taught: **A withered one is invalid, but Rabbi Judah**   31a
says it is valid. Rava said, this dispute was about the palm frond:
the Sages compare the palm frond to the citron, [reasoning that]
just as the citron must be beautiful, so must the palm frond,
but Rabbi Judah holds that we do not compare the palm frond
to the citron; all agree that the citron must be beautiful.

Doesn't Rabbi Judah hold that the palm frond must be
beautiful? Surely a Mishna says, **Rabbi Judah says, You must
bind [the palm frond] above.** Isn't this to make it look beautiful?
No, it's for the reason given: **Rabbi Judah says in the name of
Rabbi Tarfon, [Scripture says]** *kappot* **[fronds, and this can be
read as]** *kafut* **(bound) – if it spreads you should bind it
together.**

Doesn't he hold that it must be beautiful? Surely a Mishna
says, **Rabbi Judah says, You may only bind the palm frond
with its own species.** Isn't this so that it should look beautiful?
No, for Rava said, This could be even with the bast or the root
of the palm[, which are not beautiful]. So what is Rabbi Judah's
point? He holds that the palm frond must be bound, but if you
were to bind it with another species, you would have five species
[rather than the four that the Torah requires].

Does Rabbi Judah hold that the citron must be beautiful?
Surely a baraita says, **Just as you must not omit any of the four
species, so you must not add to them. If you can't obtain a
citron, you should not take a quince or a pomegranate or
anything else [in its place]. If [any of the four] is shrunken, it
is [still] valid, but if it is [completely] withered, it is not valid;
Rabbi Judah says, Even if it is [completely] withered[, it is
valid]. Moreover, said Rabbi Judah, there were towns where**   31b
**they passed their palm fronds as an heirloom to their grand-
children. The Sages retorted, How can you bring a proof from
that? Duress is different.**[7] At any rate, [it states clearly,] **Rabbi**

---

7.   i.e. since they were unable to obtain fresh palm fronds, they had no alternative.

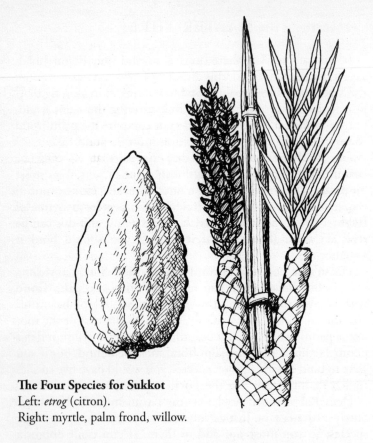

The Four Species for Sukkot
Left: *etrog* (citron).
Right: myrtle, palm frond, willow.

Judah says, Even if it is [completely] withered[, it is valid].
Isn't he referring to the citron? No, to the palm frond.

A teacher commented: **Just as you must not omit any of the four species, so you must not add to them.** Isn't this obvious? You might have thought that as Rabbi Judah says that the palm frond must be bound, even if you used another species each would be regarded as a distinct item[, and the extra species would not be seen as relating to the four]; [the baraita] tells you [that this would be a mistake].

A teacher commented: **If you can't obtain a citron,**

you should not take a quince or a pomegranate or anything else [in its place]. Isn't this obvious? You might have thought, Let him take [the substitute fruit], so that the idea of the citron should not be forgotten; [the baraita] tells you that could lead to error, for people would continue [to bring a substitute fruit even when citrons became available].

A proof [that Rabbi Judah does not require the citron to be beautiful]: **An old citron is not valid; Rabbi Judah holds it is valid.** This indeed refutes Rava's claim [that Rabbi Judah requires the citron to be beautiful].

[Still,] doesn't Rabbi Judah hold that the citron must be beautiful? Surely a Mishna states, **If it is pea-green, Rabbi Meir says it is valid, but Rabbi Judah rejects it?** [That is not because it isn't beautiful, but] because it is unripe.

Another proof: **Rabbi Meir says that the minimum size for a citron is a walnut-size; Rabbi Judah says, An egg-size.** Isn't that because he requires it to be beautiful? No, it is because it is unripe.

Another proof: **As to the maximum size, Rabbi Judah says, Whatever you can hold two of in one hand; Rabbi Yosé says, Even if [you can only hold] one in two hands.** Isn't that because [Rabbi Judah] requires it to be beautiful? No, it is as Rabba said, You must take the palm in your right and the citron in your left. Sometimes a person gets them mixed up and has to change hands, [and if the citron is too large,] he may [damage it and] invalidate it.

But Rabbi Judah [must surely acknowledge that] Scripture (Leviticus 23:40) calls it ['the fruit of the] *hadar* [tree', meaning 'beautiful'? No.] He takes *hadar* to mean *ha-dar* 'that dwells', i.e. that remains on the tree from year to year.[8]

Sukkot occurs before the rainy season in Israel, and from early times was associated with water-drawing ceremonies and prayers for rain. The first passage exemplifies the

8. Citrus fruits have no fixed season, but may be found on the tree throughout the year.

methods of textual interpretation by general and specific or by inclusive and exclusive terms, the latter leading to a broader interpretation.[9]

CHAPTER FIVE

MISHNA:

50a The flute is sounded on five or six days [of Sukkot]. This is the flute of the water-drawing, which does not override Sabbath or Festival.[10]

GEMARA:

50b The Rabbis taught: **The flute overrides the Sabbath; this is the opinion of Rabbi Yosé ben Yehuda. The [majority of] Sages say, It does not override even a festival.**[11]

Rav Yosef said, The argument is about the music accompanying the sacrifices: Rabbi Yosé holds that instrumental music is essential; it is therefore an act of service and overrides the Sabbath; the Sages hold that vocal music is essential, so [the playing of instruments] is not an act of service and does not override the Sabbath. However, all agree that the music at the water-drawing is simply for enjoyment and does not override the Sabbath.

Rav Yosef said, What leads me to say that this is what the argument is about? It is a baraita that states, **Rabbi rejects serving vessels that are made of wood; Rabbi Yosé ben Yehuda accepts them.** Surely the basis of their argument is that the one who rules that [wooden vessels] are acceptable holds that instrumental music is essential, so we can learn from the oboe of Moses;[12] the one who rejects [wooden vessels] holds that vocal music is essential, so we cannot learn from the oboe of Moses[, since it was not a vessel of divine service].

9. See Introduction, 'Interpretation of Scripture', pp. xli–xlii, and Solomon, *Interpretation*.
10. It is forbidden to play musical instruments on the Sabbath or major Festival days unless mandated as Temple service.
11. Festivals are less holy than the Sabbath.
12. This reed instrument (not strictly an oboe) was allegedly made of wood. As it was used for divine service, it demonstrates that wooden vessels are acceptable.

No. [Perhaps] both hold that instrumental music is essential, and the argument here is about inferring the possible from the impossible.[13] The one who accepts [wooden vessels] infers possible from impossible; the one who rejects them does not infer possible from impossible.

Alternatively, all agree that instrumental music is essential and that you cannot infer possible from impossible. The argument is about whether [the material for construction of] the candelabrum is derived from Scripture by 'general and specific' or by 'inclusive and exclusive' [interpretation]; Rabbi Yosé ben Yehuda interprets by 'inclusive and exclusive', but Rabbi interprets by 'general and specific'.

Rabbi interprets by 'general and specific': YOU SHALL MAKE A CANDELABRUM – general; OF PURE GOLD – specific; YOU SHALL MAKE THE CANDELABRUM OF BEATEN [WORK] (Exodus 25:31) – again general. A general term followed by a specific term and then another general one produces something similar to the specific; as the specific term here refers to a metal, [the candelabrum] must be metal.

Rabbi Yosé ben Yehuda interprets by 'inclusive and exclusive': YOU SHALL MAKE A CANDELABRUM – inclusive; OF PURE GOLD – exclusive; YOU SHALL MAKE THE CANDELABRUM OF BEATEN [WORK] – again inclusive. Inclusive, exclusive, inclusive includes all. What does it include here? Any material. What does it exclude? Pottery.

The next Mishna's nostalgic reminiscence of the joyful Temple ceremony is amplified in the Gemara, leading to a meditation on sin and temptation.

MISHNA:

Whoever has not witnessed the Joy of the Water-Drawing has never witnessed true joy. At the end of the first festival day, [priests and Levites] descended to the Women's Courtyard, where they had made a great improvement. Golden candelabra stood there; on top of each were four bowls, reached by four ladders. Four young priests, carrying 120-*log* pitchers, 51a

---

13. It is assumed that reed instruments cannot be made of material other than wood; Moses was too wise to invent the saxophone!

poured [oil] into each of the bowls. They used worn-out vestures and belts of the priests to light [torches], and every courtyard in Jerusalem shone from the lights of the Water-Drawing.

51b   Men of piety and good deeds danced before them with flaming torches, singing hymns and praises. Levites played harps, psalteries, cymbals, trumpets and countless musical instruments on the fifteen steps that descend from the Men's Courtyard to the Women's Courtyard – corresponding to the fifteen Songs of Ascent in the Book of Psalms[14] – where Levites stand with their instruments and sing.

Two priests stood at the upper gate of the steps from the Men's Courtyard to the Women's Courtyard, holding two trumpets. When the announcer called,[15] they sounded *teqi'a*, *teru'a*, *teqi'a*. When they reached the tenth step, they [again] sounded *teqi'a*, *teru'a*, *teqi'a*. They continued sounding [their trumpets] until they reached the eastern exit. When they reached the eastern exit, they turned from east to west[16] and said, Our fathers who were in this place turned their backs to the sanctuary and faced eastward, bowing east to the sun;[17] but as for us, our eyes are toward God. Rabbi Judah says, They doubled the phrase, saying, We are for God, and our eyes are toward God.

GEMARA:

The rabbis taught: Whoever did not witness the Joy of the Water-Drawing has never witnessed true joy; whoever did not gaze upon Jerusalem in its glory has never gazed upon a desirable city; whoever did not see the Temple in its glory[18] has never seen a beautiful building.

Which [Temple building did they mean]? Abbaye – but some say Rav Ḥisda – said, Herod's. Of what did he build it? Rabba said, Marble and alabaster. Some

14. Psalms 120–34.
15. Some understand this as 'when the cock crowed', but this is problematic, as pointed out by the Tosafot. The same ambiguity occurs in *Yoma* 20b.
16. To face the sanctuary.
17. An allusion to Ezekiel 8:16.
18. Literally, 'in its building'.

say[, he built it of] stibnite, marble and alabaster.[19] He made one row protrude and one recede, so that the plaster should grip. He wanted to overlay it with gold, but the rabbis said it was better as it was, for it looked like the waves of the sea.[20]

It was taught: **Rabbi Judah said, Whoever did not see the double colonnade in Alexandria has never seen the dignity of Israel.**

They say it was like a great basilica, one colonnade within another, and that sometimes it held 600,000 people, as many as left Egypt at the Exodus – some say it was double the number who left Egypt. Seventy-one golden thrones were there, corresponding to the number [of judges] in the great Sanhedrin, and each was made of not less than 21,000 talents of gold. In the centre was a wooden platform on which the overseer of the congregation stood with flags; when it was time to respond Amen!, he waved his flag, and all the people responded, Amen!

People did not sit at random, but goldsmiths in their [designated] place, silversmiths in their place, smiths in their place, brass workers[21] in their place and weavers in their place, so that when a needy person came in he could tell who were his fellow-artisans and approach them, so receive support for himself and his dependants.

Abbaye said, Alexander of Macedon killed them all.[22]

19. The names of the rocks are imprecise: it is unclear whether *kuhla* – literally, 'blue' – is the name of a separate one, such as stibnite (Sokoloff, *Babylonian*), or an adjective qualifying 'marble'.
20. Josephus, *Antiquities* 15:11, says when Herod, in 20/19 BCE, addressed the people of Judaea with his proposal for rebuilding the Temple, 'they were dismayed that he might tear down the whole edifice and not have sufficient means to bring his project to completion'; the rabbis, like Josephus, were wary of ambitious scemes that would inevitably be financed by heavy taxes.
21. Literally, 'Tarsians'. The translation follows Rashi. Jastrow (*Dictionary*) suggests they were artistic weavers of metallic thread (i.e. filigree workers), as opposed to common weavers.
22. This is impossible, and contradicts the Yerushalmi (*Sukka* 5:1), where the name is recognizably a form of Trajan. In 117 Lusius Quietus, on Trajan's orders, crushed

Why were they punished?[23] Because they transgressed these words of Scripture: [THE LORD HAS WARNED YOU,] 'YOU MUST NOT GO BACK THAT WAY AGAIN' (Deuteronomy 17:16 JPS).

When [the Roman leader] came, he found them reading in [their] book, THE LORD WILL BRING A NATION AGAINST YOU FROM AFAR, FROM THE END OF THE EARTH, [WHICH WILL SWOOP DOWN LIKE THE EAGLE] (Deuteronomy 28:49 JPS). He thought, Now, I come from ten days' distance by ship, but a wind carried me and the ship arrived in five days. So he attacked and killed them.

They had made a great improvement. What was the 'great improvement'? The [floor of the Women's Courtyard] was originally flat, so they surrounded it with a balcony and arranged that women should sit above and men below.[24]

[As] the rabbis taught: **At first, women sat inside and men outside, but this led to frivolity. They then directed that women should sit outside and men inside, but this still led to frivolity. So they directed that women should sit above and men below.**

How could they do that? Is it not written, ALL THIS THAT THE LORD MADE ME UNDERSTAND BY HIS HAND ON ME, I GIVE YOU IN WRITING[– THE PLAN OF ALL THE WORKS] (1 Chronicles 28:19 JPS)?[25] Rav said, They found a proof-text to interpret: THE LAND SHALL WAIL, EACH FAMILY BY ITSELF: THE FAMILY

52a

---

the Revolt of the Diaspora which had spread to Egypt. A diminished and impoverished Jewish community remained in Alexandria, despite a brief expulsion under the Christian patriarch Cyril in 414; it still has a fine Synagogue, though few Jews remain. Azaria dei Rossi (c. 1511–78) was the first Jew in modern times to question the text on the basis of external historical evidence; see Weinberg, *Light of the Eyes*, pp. 241–51.

23. Persecution is interpreted as punishment from God.

24. This is presumably the forerunner of the women's balcony in Orthodox synagogues.

25. David's words to Solomon. What right did anyone have to change the divinely revealed design of the Temple? Josephus' text of Herod's speech proposing the rebuilding, in *Antiquities* 15:11, likewise stresses that his intention was to restore the dimensions of Solomon's Temple, which had been beyond the means of Zerubbabel.

OF THE HOUSE OF DAVID BY THEMSELVES, AND
THEIR WOMENFOLK BY THEMSELVES (Zechariah
12:12 JPS). They [reasoned]: If, in days to come, when
[the people] are in mourning and they are not in the
thrall of the Evil Inclination, the Torah says that men
will be on their own and women on their own, how
much more so [should the sexes be segregated] here,
where people are busy enjoying themselves and the
Evil Inclination holds sway.

What will they be in mourning for? Rabbi
Dosa and the rabbis disputed this. One said,
[They will mourn] the Messiah son of Joseph
who has been slain; the other says, [They will
mourn] the Evil Inclination which has been
slain. Now, if you say, [They will mourn]
the Messiah son of Joseph who has been
slain, that is as it is written, THEY SHALL
LOOK TO ME [ON ACCOUNT OF] THE ONE
THEY HAVE PIERCED, AND MOURN FOR
HIM AS ONE WHO MOURNS FOR AN ONLY
SON (Zechariah 12:10); but if you say, [They
will mourn] the Evil Inclination which has
been slain, why mourn? Surely they should
[rather] rejoice! Why will they weep?

It is as Rabbi Judah expounded: In days
to come, the Holy One, blessed be He, will
take the Evil Inclination and slay him in the
presence of the righteous and the wicked.
To the righteous he will appear as a mighty
mountain, to the wicked as a thin thread.
Both [groups] will weep. The righteous will
weep, saying, How did we ever overcome
this mighty mountain! The wicked will weep,
saying, How could we have failed to overcome this thin thread! And the Holy One,
blessed be He, will share their astonishment,
as it is said, THUS SAYS THE LORD OF
HOSTS: IF, WHEN THOSE DAYS COME, IT

WILL BE ASTONISHING IN THE SIGHT OF THE REMNANT OF THIS PEOPLE, EVEN IN MY EYES IT WILL BE ASTONISHING (Zechariah 8:6).

[Likewise,] Rav Assi said, At first, the Evil Inclination is like a shuttle-thread;[26] eventually, it is like a cart rope, as it is said, **WOE TO THOSE WHO DRAW SIN WITH USELESS CORD[27] AND INIQUITY WITH CART ROPES** (Isaiah 5:18).

Both the Apocrypha and the Dead Sea Scrolls speak of two 'anointed ones', or messiahs – a priest descended from Aaron and a 'lay' messiah descended from David. The Talmud, however, identifies one messiah as a descendant of Joseph, who will fall in battle, and the other as a descendant of David, who will triumph. Though ignored by Maimonides and others, the concept of Messiah son of Joseph was adopted by Kabbalists and has come to signify the era just prior to the final Redemption.

The rabbis taught: The Holy One, blessed be He, says to Messiah son of David – may he be revealed speedily in our days! – Ask Me for anything and I shall grant it to you – as it is said, **LET ME TELL OF THE DECREE: [THE LORD SAID TO ME, 'YOU ARE MY SON,] I HAVE FATHERED YOU THIS DAY. ASK IT OF ME, AND I WILL MAKE THE NATIONS YOUR DOMAIN'** (Psalm 2:7–8 JPS). When he sees Messiah son of Joseph slain, he says to Him, Lord of the Universe! All I ask from You is life! [God] replies, Even before you asked, your father David prophesied, **HE ASKED YOU FOR LIFE; YOU GRANTED IT** (Psalm 21:5 JPS).

Rabbi Avira – some say Rabbi Joshua ben Levi – expounded: The Evil Inclination has seven names:

The Holy One, blessed be He, called it Bad, as it is said, **'FOR THE INCLINATION OF MAN'S HEART IS BAD FROM HIS YOUTH'** (Genesis 8:21).

Moses called it Uncircumcised, as it is said, **CIRCUMCISE THE FORESKIN OF YOUR HEARTS** (Deuteronomy 10:16).

26. Or possibly, a spider's web.
27. Other translations have 'cords of falsehood' or 'cords of vanity'; the point is that the weak cords that bring sin become strong ropes that bind the sinner.

David called it Impure, as it is said, **FASHION A PURE HEART FOR ME, O GOD** (Psalm 51:12 JPS) – which implies there is an impure one[, too].

Solomon called it Enemy, as it is said, **IF YOUR ENEMY IS HUNGRY, GIVE HIM BREAD TO EAT; IF HE IS THIRSTY, GIVE HIM WATER TO DRINK. YOU WILL BE HEAPING LIVE COALS ON HIS HEAD, AND THE LORD WILL REWARD YOU** (Proverbs 25:21–2 JPS) – do not read *y'shallem lakh* ('will reward you'), but *yashlimenu lakh* ('will deliver him into your hand').

Isaiah called it Obstacle, as it is said, **BUILD UP, BUILD UP A HIGHWAY! CLEAR A ROAD! REMOVE ALL OBSTACLES FROM THE ROAD OF MY PEOPLE** (Isaiah 57:14 JPS).

Ezekiel called it Stone, as it is said, **I WILL REMOVE THE HEART OF STONE FROM YOUR BODY AND GIVE YOU A HEART OF FLESH** (Ezekiel 36:26 JPS).

Joel called it Northern One,[28] as it is said, **AND I WILL DRIVE THE NORTHERNER FAR FROM YOU** (Joel 2:20 JPS).

The rabbis taught: **AND I WILL DRIVE THE NORTHERNER FAR FROM YOU** – this is the Evil Inclination. **I WILL THRUST IT INTO A PARCHED AND DESOLATE LAND** – to a place where there are no people to tempt; **ITS VAN ON THE EASTERN SEA** – for it set its eyes on the First Temple, destroyed it and slew its Sages; **AND ITS REAR TO THE WESTERN SEA** – for it set its eyes on the Second Temple, destroyed it, and slew its Sages; **AND THE STENCH OF IT SHALL GO UP, AND THE FOUL SMELL RISE** – for it ignores the nations of the world and devotes its attention to the enemies of Israel;[29] **FOR (THE LORD] SHALL WORK GREAT DEEDS** (Joel 2:20–21 JPS) – Abbaye said, [Its attention is focused] most strongly on the scholars.

This is like [what happened to] Abbaye. He overheard someone say to a woman, Let's travel together, [so] he thought, I will follow and prevent them from sin. He followed them three parasangs through open country, and when they parted he heard them say, It

28. Or, 'hidden'. Joel refers to a plague of locusts that had come from the north, the 'hidden' direction, since in the northern hemisphere the sun circles southward. Hebrew *tzafon* ('north') is cognate with *tzafun* ('hidden').
29. A euphemism for sinful Jews.

was a long journey, but the company was pleasant. [Abbaye] went and leaned miserably against the door hinge,[30] until an old man came and taught him, **Whoever is greater than another has a greater inclination [to evil].**

Rabbi Isaac said, A man's inclination rises against him each day, as it is said, **ONLY EVIL THE WHOLE TIME** (Genesis 6:5).

Rabbi Simeon ben Laqish said, A man's inclination rises against him each day and seeks to kill him, as it is said, **THE WICKED WATCHES FOR THE RIGHTEOUS, SEEKING TO PUT HIM TO DEATH** (Psalm 37:32 JPS), and if the Holy One, blessed be He, does not help him, he could not prevail against it, as it is said, **THE LORD WILL NOT ABANDON HIM TO HIS POWER; HE WILL NOT LET HIM BE CONDEMNED IN JUDGEMENT** (Psalm 37:33 JPS).

It was taught in the School of Rabbi Ishmael: **If that ugly one accosts you,[31] take him to the House of Study. If he is stone, he will melt; if he is iron, he will shatter. If he is stone, he will melt, for it is written, HO, ALL WHO ARE THIRSTY, COME FOR WATER** (Isaiah 55:1), **and it is written, WATER ERODES STONE** (Job 14:19). **If he is iron, he will shatter, as it is written, BEHOLD, MY WORD IS LIKE FIRE – DECLARES THE LORD – AND LIKE A HAMMER THAT SHATTERS ROCK** (Jeremiah 23:29 JPS).

30. Abbaye was confounded since the pair had not yielded to a temptation he would have found overwhelming.
31. i.e. if you are beset by temptation.

SEVENTH TRACTATE
BETZA (FESTIVAL LAWS)

The common name is its opening word, Betza *('Egg'); it is also known as* Yom Tov *('Festival'), since it defines the types of activity permitted or forbidden for festivals. The definition relates to the Sabbath laws; what is forbidden on Sabbaths is also forbidden on festivals, with the exception of carrying, lighting fires and the preparation of food. The circumstances in which these activities are permitted, and of what constitutes food preparation, are clarified.*

The tractate opens with an apparently trivial question. May one eat, on the festival, an egg laid by a hen that day? The School of Shammai, usually stricter, take the more lenient view in this instance. No one, however, seems to know quite what the original egg problem was about. Several Amoraic interpretations are investigated, and ultimately Rabba's prevails: Mishna is concerned that if a festival falls on a Sunday, the egg will have been 'prepared' (if only by 'heaven') on the Sabbath; since it is not permissible to prepare on the Sabbath for the festival, the egg may not be eaten.

The egg quickly becomes the test case for a much more significant issue: fixing the calendar. Why, in the diaspora, is each festival day observed twice, on succeeding days? Originally, diaspora Jews depended on receiving information from Jerusalem as to which day had been proclaimed the first of the month (a month might be 29 or 30 days). The festivals of Passover and Tabernacles begin on the fifteenth of the month; if messengers from Jerusalem did not arrive in time, there would be doubt as to which was the correct day to observe the festival. Was this doubling necessary if the correct date could be calculated? What

*would happen when the Temple was rebuilt and, as was antici-
pated, Jews reverted to fixing the calendar by observation and
dispatching messengers from Jerusalem with the information?*

*Underlying the discussion was a struggle to uphold the pri-
macy of the courts of the Land of Israel in calendar fixation.
The current system of calculation was finalized early in the tenth
century; that the doubled festival day was not then declared
obsolete is due to the conservative stance of Geonim including
Saadia and Hai.*[1]

CHAPTER ONE

MISHNA:

2a   If an egg was laid on the festival day, the School of Shammai
say, It may be eaten, but the School of Hillel say, It may not
be eaten.

The School of Shammai say, [The measure for getting rid
of] sourdough [before Passover is] a date-size, and [for getting
rid of] leaven an olive-size; the School of Hillel say, Both are
an olive-size.

If someone slaughters a wild animal or a fowl on the festival,
the School of Shammai say, He may dig with his spade to
cover [the blood],[2] but the School of Hillel say, He may not
slaughter unless he has earth ready before the festival. They
agree that if he [nevertheless] slaughtered, he should dig with
a spade and cover [the blood, and] that ashes in an oven [are
regarded as] prepared.

GEMARA:

4b   It was taught: Rav said, If an egg is laid on the [first] of the
double festival days in the diaspora, it is permitted [to eat it] on
the [second], but Rav Assi said, If it is laid on one day, it is
forbidden [to eat it] on the other.

   Could this be because Rav Assi regarded the two

1.   Stern, ʿSecond Dayʾ, and Stern, *Calendar*.
2.   Cf. Leviticus 17:13.

days as 'one holiness'[, i.e. as one long holy day? Surely
not, since] Rav Assi himself used to recite *havdala*
between one day and the other. Rav Assi was in doubt
[as to whether the double day should be regarded as
one long day or as two separate days, so] he went to
the stricter side on both counts.

Rabbi Zeira said, Rav Assi's ruling appears reasonable, since
nowadays we know the times of the moon, yet we still observe
double [festival] days. [But] Abbaye said, Rav's ruling appears
reasonable, since the Mishna states, **Originally, they used to
light beacons, but when the Samaritans interfered, they dispatched messengers [instead].**[3] If the Samaritans ceased [inter-
fering], we would [obtain the information quickly by beacon
signals and so] observe only one day; [even now,] in those places
that the messengers reach [in time for the festivals], we observe
[only] one day.

Now that we know when the new month is fixed,[4]
why do we keep two days? It is because they sent [a
directive] from there: Take heed [to uphold] your
ancestral custom; one day you may be persecuted and
error will ensue.

*The New Year festival falls on the first of the month, but the
day could not be determined until witnesses testified to the
appearance of the new moon on the day itself, by which time it
might be too late to inform anyone. Consequently, the New
Year festival was observed for two days even in the Land of
Israel.*

It was taught: Rav and Shmuel both said, An egg laid on the
[first] day of the New Year is forbidden on the [second], for

3.   Mishna *Rosh Hashana* 2:2 (22b). Each new month was proclaimed in Jerusalem
     on the basis of observation of the moon. Originally a system of hill beacons was
     used to convey the information as far as Babylonia, but opponents of the rabbis
     (the reading 'Samaritans' may not be correct) allegedly lit misleading signals.
     Messengers might not arrive in time for the festivals on the fifteenth of the month.
4.   Now that we in Babylon can calculate the appearance of the new moon. Following
     H. Y. Bornstein, some scholars have suggested that the reference is not to calcu-
     lation, but to annual notice of the dates of festivals received by the diaspora
     communities from the High Court of the Land of Israel (Yerushalmi *Eruvin* 3:9;
     Stern, 'Second Day', p. 51). This system might easily be disrupted should per-
     secution occur.

the Mishna teaches, **Originally, they would accept testimony [about appearance of the new] moon all day. On one occasion[,**
5a **however,] witnesses arrived late and the Levites were confused in [their choice of] hymns [to sing in the Temple], so [the Sages] decreed that witnesses should not be received after the afternoon sacrifice. If witnesses arrived later than the afternoon sacrifice, both that day and the next were treated as holy.**[5]

Rabba said, Since the time of Rabban Yoḥanan ben Zakkai's ordinance, the egg has been permitted, for the Mishna [goes on to] state, **After the Temple was destroyed, Rabban Yoḥanan ben Zakkai ordained that testimony [about appearance of the new] moon might be accepted throughout the [New Year's] day.**[6]

Abbaye said to him, But didn't Rav and Shmuel both say, An egg laid on the [first] day of the New Year is forbidden on the [second]?

[Rabba] retorted, I spoke to you about Rabban Yoḥanan ben Zakkai, and you cite Rav and Shmuel![7]

[Abbaye:] Then Rav and Shmuel have a problem with the Mishna?

[Rabba:] No problem. This is for us, that is for them.[8]

But Rav Yosef said, Even after Yoḥanan ben Zakkai's ordinance the egg remained forbidden. Why[, seeing there was no longer any substantive ground to forbid it]? Because [the prohibition] had been instituted by an authoritative court,[9] and any [legislation] instituted by an authoritative court can only be abrogated by an [equally] authoritative court.

A digression follows on the biblical foundation for Rav Yosef's principle. Abbaye returns to the argument:

5b Abbaye said to him, [Then] is the prohibition of the egg a matter instituted by an authoritative court? [Surely not.] It is [merely] a consequence of [the dispute concerning] testimony

5. Mishna *Rosh Hashana* 4:4 (30b).
6. Ibid.
7. Rav and Shmuel, as Amoraim, were of lesser authority than Yoḥanan ben Zakkai.
8. Rav and Shmuel's ruling applies to Babylonia, Yoḥanan ben Zakkai's to the Land of Israel.
9. Literally, 'by a number', i.e. of judges.

[about the new moon]; if testimony is accepted, the egg is permitted.

Rav Ada and Rav Salmon, both of Bei Kaluḥit, said that even after Yoḥanan ben Zakkai's ordinance the egg remained forbidden. Why[, seeing there was no longer any substantive ground to forbid it]? Because the Temple might be speedily rebuilt,[10] and people would than say, 'Last year we ate eggs [laid on the first day] on the second festival day, [so] we will do the same this year'; but they won't realize that last year there were two [separate] holinesses, this year only one.[11]

> Then how could we accept testimony? [The same argument might be used:] The Temple might be speedily rebuilt, and people would say, 'Last year we accepted testimony throughout the day, [so] we will accept it [also] this year.' [No.] [Acceptance of] testimony is a matter for the courts[, and they would not make a mistake]; eggs are everybody's business[, and mistakes would be made].

Rava said, Even after Yoḥanan ben Zakkai's ordinance the egg remained forbidden. Did not Yoḥanan ben Zakkai himself agree that if witnesses arrived [only] after [the time of] the afternoon sacrifice that both that day and the next would be holy?

Rava said, moreover, The *halakha* is according to Rav in these three matters, whether lenient or strict.

If a festival falls on a Friday, preparations must be made for the Sabbath before the festival begins. A simple Sabbath meal is prepared on Thursday, and on that basis it is permitted to continue the Sabbath preparations on the festival itself. The procedure is known as eruv tavshilin.

10. Jews would then revert to a system in which the Jerusalem court would decide the beginning of the month on the basis of observers' testimony, and distant places would rely on information relayed by messengers.

11. If the doubling of the day is due to doubt, one day is really the festival and the other not; there are two separate, distinct days ('two holinesses'). But if the doubling is due to the late arrival of witnesses, what happens is that the first day is extended into one day of double length ('one holiness'), and it no longer makes sense to speak of an egg laid on one day and eaten on the next.

CHAPTER TWO

MISHNA:

15b If a festival falls on a Friday, you may not cook on that day primarily for the Sabbath; you may, however, cook for the festival [itself], and whatever is left over [may be eaten] on the Sabbath. You may cook [for the Sabbath] on the eve of the festival, and on that basis [continue to] cook on the festival itself for the Sabbath.

The School of Shammai say, [For that procedure to be valid, you must] cook two dishes [for the Sabbath], but the School of Hillel say, One [is enough]; [both Schools] agree that fish with an egg dressing [counts as] two dishes.

If someone ate [the prepared food before the Sabbath] or lost it, so long as even a little remains he may rely on that [to cook on the festival] for the Sabbath.

GEMARA:

What is this [procedure] based on?

Shmuel said, Scripture says, REMEMBER THE SABBATH DAY TO MAKE IT HOLY (Exodus 20:8) – remember it in circumstances where you might forget it.

What did he mean?

Rava said, [He wanted to] ensure that people would choose a fine portion [of food] for the Sabbath, as well as a fine portion for the festival.

Rav Ashi said, It was so that people would reflect, If we mustn't cook on the festival for the Sabbath, how much worse would it be to cook on the festival for a weekday!

[Now,] the Mishna stated, **You may cook [for the Sabbath] on the eve of the festival, and on that basis [continue to] cook on the festival itself for the Sabbath.** That's all right according to Rav Ashi, since he says that it was so that people would reflect, If we mustn't cook on the festival for the Sabbath, how much worse would it be to cook on the festival for a weekday – that is why you may cook on the eve of the festival, but not on the festival itself. But on Rava's view, why does it say 'on the eve of the festival'? You should be permitted to cook on the festival itself. [Rava would agree that in principle] that would be permitted, if not for the danger that people might be negligent.

A Tanna bases [the procedure] on [the story of the manna]: BAKE WHAT YOU WOULD BAKE AND BOIL WHAT YOU WOULD BOIL (Exodus 16:23) – Rabbi Eleazar said, Bake on the basis of what has already been baked, and boil on the basis of what has already been boiled – from this verse the Sages derived the principle of *eruv tavshilin*.

The rabbis taught: Rabbi Eliezer once sat and expounded the festival laws throughout the day. A group of disciples left and he commented, These have large barrels![12] A second group left; he said, These have barrels! A third group left; he said, These have pitchers! A fourth group left; he said, These have jugs! A fifth group left; he said, These have jars! When the sixth group got up to leave, he said, A curse on these! He gazed at the [remaining] disciples and their faces paled. [The curse is] not on you, my children, he said, but on those who left, for they have abandoned the everlasting for the ephemeral. When he finally dismissed them, he said, 'GO, EAT CHOICE FOODS AND DRINK SWEET DRINKS AND SEND PORTIONS TO WHOEVER HAS NOTHING PREPARED, FOR THE DAY IS HOLY TO OUR LORD. DO NOT BE SAD, FOR YOUR REJOICING IN THE LORD IS THE SOURCE OF YOUR STRENGTH' (Nehemiah 8:10 JPS).

A teacher commented, They have abandoned the everlasting for the ephemeral? Surely it is a *mitzva* to rejoice on the festival!

Rabbi Eliezer is consistent with his own position, for he said that rejoicing on the festival was optional, as a baraita states: Rabbi Eliezer says, On a festival a person should either eat and drink [all day] or sit and learn [all day]; but Rabbi Joshua said, Divide it – half for God and half for you!

Rabbi Yoḥanan observed, They both interpreted the same verses. Scripture says, A GATHERING FOR THE LORD YOUR GOD (Deuteronomy 16:8), but it also

12. They are leaving early because they have so much to eat.

says, **A GATHERING FOR YOU** (Numbers 29:35). How can that be? Rabbi Eliezer thought, It must be entirely for God or entirely for you; Rabbi Joshua thought, Divide it – half for God and half for you!

CHAPTER FIVE

MISHNA:

36b   Whatever [form of activity] you would be held liable for as 'rest', 'option'[13] or *mitzva* [if you did it] on Shabbat, you are liable for on festivals too.

These activities are forbidden as 'rest': climbing trees, riding animals, swimming, clapping hands or thighs [in time with music], dancing.

These activities are forbidden as 'option': adjudicating, betrothal, *ḥalitza* and levirate marriage.

These activities are forbidden as *mitzva*: consecrating, valuing [for consecration], declaring *ḥerem*, separating *teruma* and tithes.

The only difference between [activity forbidden on] Sabbaths and [that forbidden on] festival days is with regard to food preparation.

GEMARA:

Climbing trees: [this is forbidden] in case he plucks a branch.

Riding animals: in case he passes the boundary. Are boundaries *d'Oraita* then? [Surely not. The reason for the prohibition must be] in case he cuts off a branch [to use as a spur].

Swimming: in case he makes a swimming aid.

Clapping hands or thighs, dancing: in case he mends a musical instrument.

These activities are forbidden as 'option': adjudicating. Isn't it a *mitzva* [to adjudicate]? [The baraita] covers a case where a

13. 'Rest' and 'option' are used here in the technical sense of activities forbidden by the rabbis, though not by the Written Torah. The distinction between them is not clear, and is not of significance in later *halakha*.

better [judge] is available[, so it would not be a *mitzva* for this one to judge].

Betrothal: but it is a *mitzva* [to marry]! [The baraita] covers a case where he already has a wife and children.[14]

Ḥalitza **and levirate marriage**: but [levirate marriage] is a *mitzva*! [The baraita] covers a case where there is an older brother; it would have been preferable for the older brother to undertake the levirate marriage.

What is the reason all these are forbidden? To prevent writing.

These activities are forbidden as *mitzva*: consecrating, valuing [for consecration], declaring *ḥerem*: because they are like doing business.

Separating *teruma* and tithes: isn't this obvious? Rav Yosef taught: It refers to [a situation] where he is delivering it to the *Kohen* on the same day. It is only [forbidden] if the produce became liable to tithing before [the festival]; if the liability arose [on the festival day] – for instance, if it was dough from which he needed to set aside *ḥalla* – he may set it aside and deliver it to the *Kohen*.

Are some [activities in the category of] 'option' but not 'rest', and some [in the category of] *mitzva* but not 'rest'? Rabbi Isaac said, It means 'not only . . .' – Not only is a mere 'rest' forbidden, but even a 'rest' linked with an 'option'; not only is a 'rest' linked with an 'option' forbidden, but even a 'rest' linked with a *mitzva*.

37a

14. Polygamy was permissible, but not a *mitzva*.

EIGHTH TRACTATE
ROSH HASHANA
(THE NEW YEAR)

This tractate is mainly concerned with calendar fixation (see Appendix I). The final chapter deals with the sounding of the shofar *at the New Year festival.*

When does the year begin? According to Exodus (12:2) the first month is 'the month of spring', i.e. Nisan. The festival celebrated by Jews as Rosh ha-Shana ('the beginning of the year') is, however, the 'sacred occasion commemorated with loud blasts' on the first day of the seventh month, i.e. Tishrei (Leviticus 23:24 JPS); this is how it was known to Philo and Josephus and in the Dead Sea scrolls. The Seleucid year, commonly used in documents, also began in autumn.

Today it is common for calendar years, tax years and school years to commence on different dates; the Sages of the Mishna likewise found it necessary to define the year separately for documents, tax, tithing and liturgy.

CHAPTER ONE

MISHNA:

There are four new years:

1 Nisan is the new year for kings and festivals.

1 Elul is the new year for tithing cattle; Rabbi Eleazar and Rabbi Simeon say, 1 Tishrei.

1 Tishrei is the new year for [numbering] years, for sabbatical and jubilee [years, and for] planting [fruit trees] and vegetables.

1 Shevat is the new year for trees according to the School of Shammai, but the School of Hillel say, 15 [Shevat].

GEMARA:

1 Nisan is the new year for kings. How does this affect the law?

Rav Ḥisda said, In respect of documents, for the Mishna teaches, **Antedated bills of debt are invalid, postdated ones are valid.**[1]

The rabbis taught: **If a king acceded to the throne on 29 Adar, [he is deemed to have] completed one year on 1 Nisan [even though he has reigned for only a day]; but if he acceded on 1 Nisan, his second year does not commence until 1 Nisan the following year.**

A scholar observed, **If he acceded on 1 Nisan, his second year does not commence until 1 Nisan the following year;** this teaches us that 1 Nisan is the new year for kings, and [also] that one day of the year counts as a [whole] year.   2b

If he acceded on 1 Nisan, his second year does not commence until 1 Nisan the following year. Isn't that obvious? No. It had to be [stated to cover a case where] he was appointed in Adar [but did not take over until Nisan]; you might have thought [that 1 Nisan should count as] his second year, but [the text] tells you [that this is not so].

The rabbis taught: **If [a king] died in Adar and another succeeded him in Adar, the year is counted for both; if he died in Nisan and another succeeded him in Nisan, the year is counted for both; if he died in Adar and another succeeded him in Nisan, the first year is counted for the first [king], and the second for the second.**

A scholar commented, **If [a king] died in Adar and another succeeded him in Adar, the year is counted for both.** Isn't this obvious? You might have thought that we would not count one year for two [kings], so it lets us know [that we do].

If he died in Nisan and another succeeded him in

---

1. An antedated claim may result in the creditor unjustly gaining priority over later creditors whose claims arose between the apparent and real dates of his bill.

Nisan, the year is counted for both. Isn't this obvious?
You might have thought that we only say one day
counts as a year if it is at the end of a year, but we
would not say so if it was at the beginning, so it lets
us know [that we do].

**If he died in Adar and another succeeded him in
Nisan, the first year is counted for the first [king],
and the second for the second.** Isn't this obvious? It
is needed [to cover the following case]: he was
appointed king in Adar and he was the son of the
previous king, so you might have thought both years
should count for him; it lets us know [that this is not
the case].

Rabbi Yoḥanan said, How do we know that regnal years are
counted from Nisan? It is said, IN THE FOUR HUNDRED AND
EIGHTIETH YEAR AFTER THE ISRAELITES LEFT THE LAND OF
EGYPT, IN THE MONTH OF ZIV – THAT IS, THE SECOND
MONTH – IN THE FOURTH YEAR OF HIS REIGN OVER ISRAEL,
SOLOMON, ETC. (1 Kings 6:1 JPS). Solomon's reign is compared
to the Exodus from Egypt; just as the Exodus from Egypt was
in Nisan, so Solomon's reign [was reckoned] from Nisan.

But how do we know that the Egyptian Exodus was itself
counted from Nisan? Perhaps it was counted from Tishrei? That
cannot be, since it is written, AARON THE PRIEST ASCENDED
MOUNT HOR AT THE COMMAND OF THE LORD AND DIED
THERE, IN THE FORTIETH YEAR AFTER THE ISRAELITES HAD
LEFT THE LAND OF EGYPT, ON THE FIRST DAY OF THE FIFTH
MONTH (Numbers 33:38 JPS), and it is also written, IT WAS IN
THE FORTIETH YEAR, ON THE FIRST DAY OF THE ELEVENTH
MONTH, THAT MOSES ADDRESSED THE ISRAELITES (Deuteronomy 1:3 JPS). Since he refers to Av as in the fortieth year
[from the Exodus] and to [the previous] Shevat as in the fortieth
year [too], it is impossible that the beginning of the year [for
counting from the Exodus] should be Tishrei.[2]

One of those verses explicitly [reckons] by the

2. This assumes that months are numbered from Nisan, a point demonstrated later
(but not translated here).

Exodus from Egypt, but how do we know that the other [reckons] by the Exodus from Egypt? It is as Rav Papa said, TWENTIETH YEAR (Nehemiah 2:1) is paralleled so that the two contexts should be compared; here, likewise, FORTIETH YEAR is paralleled so that the two contexts should be compared: just as one refers to the Exodus from Egypt, so does the other refer to the Exodus from Egypt.

How do we know that the event that took place in Av preceded the one in Shevat? Perhaps the Shevat one was first? This cannot be, for it is written, AFTER HE HAD DEFEATED SIHON KING OF THE AMORITES (Deuteronomy 1:4 JPS), and when Aaron died Sihon was [still] alive, as it is written, AND WHEN THE CANAANITE, KING OF ARAD, HEARD (Numbers 21:1) – what did he hear [that induced him] to come? He heard that Aaron had died and the clouds of glory had departed, so he concluded that an opportunity had come to wage war against Israel. That is why it is written, THE WHOLE ASSEMBLY SAW (*va-yir'u*) THAT AARON HAD EXPIRED (Numbers 20:29), which Rabbi Abbahu interpreted as *va-yiyr'u* ('they became afraid'), taking *ki* as 'because', for Resh Laqish taught that *ki* can mean 'if', 'in case', 'but' or 'because'.[3]

3a

How can you compare [the two]? In one case it is the Canaanite, in the other Sihon! They taught, Sihon, Arad and Canaan were the same [person]: [he was called] Sihon because he was like a desert colt (*sayah*); Canaan, because that was his realm; and what was his [personal] name? Arad. Others say, [He was called] Arad because he was like a wild ass (*arad*) of the desert; Canaan, because that was his realm; and what was his [personal] name? Sihon.

Perhaps the year begins with Iyar? No, this is impossible, for it is written, IN THE FIRST MONTH OF THE SECOND YEAR, ON THE FIRST OF THE MONTH, THE TABERNACLE WAS SET UP (Exodus 40:17 JPS), and it is written, IN THE SECOND YEAR, ON

3. Rabbi Abbahu translates, 'The whole assembly was afraid, because Aaron had expired.' On *ki*, see also *Gittin* 90a (see p. 397).

THE TWENTIETH DAY OF THE SECOND MONTH, THE CLOUD
LIFTED FROM THE TABERNACLE (Numbers 10:11 JPS). Since
it refers to Nisan as in the second year [from the Exodus] and
to [the following month,] Iyar as [also] in the second year, it
follows that Iyar cannot be the beginning of the year.

Then perhaps the year begins with Sivan? No, this is impossible, for it is written, IN THE THIRD MONTH AFTER THE
ISRAELITES LEFT EGYPT (Exodus 19:1). Now, if [Sivan, 'the
third month',] was the new year, it ought to have been written,
'in the second year'.

Then perhaps Tammuz, or Av, or Adar [is the new year]?

Rabbi Eleazar said, [We derive the months of the regnal new
year] from here: HE BEGAN TO BUILD ON THE SECOND,[4] IN
THE SECOND MONTH OF THE FOURTH YEAR OF HIS REIGN
(2 Chronicles 3:2). Surely, [the first] THE SECOND means the
second month of his reign?

> Ravina objected, Perhaps it means the second [day]
> of the month? If so, it would have said explicitly, 'the
> second day'. Then perhaps it means 'the second day
> of the week'? [No.] First, we do not find that Scripture
> anywhere specifies the second day of the week. Also,
> we must draw an analogy between the two uses of
> 'second': just as the first refers to the month, so the
> second refers to the month.

A baraita supports Rabbi Yoḥanan[, who derived the month
of the regnal new year from Kings]: How do we know that we
count the years of kings from Nisan? Because it is said, AND
IN THE FOUR HUNDRED AND EIGHTIETH YEAR AFTER THE
ISRAELITES LEFT EGYPT (1 Kings 6:1), and it is written, AARON
THE PRIEST ASCENDED MOUNT HOR (Numbers 33:38), and it
is written, AFTER HE HAD DEFEATED SIHON (Deuteronomy
1:4), and it is written, THE WHOLE ASSEMBLY SAW THAT
AARON HAD EXPIRED (Numbers 20:29 JPS), and it is written,
IN THE FIRST MONTH OF THE SECOND YEAR (Exodus 40:17),
and it is written, IN THE SECOND YEAR, ON THE TWENTIETH
DAY OF THE SECOND MONTH (Numbers 10:11), and it is
written, IN THE THIRD MONTH AFTER THE ISRAELITES LEFT

4.   English translations insert 'day' here, but it is lacking in the Hebrew.

EGYPT (Exodus 19:1), **and it is written, HE BEGAN TO BUILD** (2 Chronicles 3:2).

Rav Ḥisda said, This was taught only with reference to kings of Israel, but kings of [other] nations count from Tishrei, as it is said, THE NARRATIVE OF NEHEMIAH SON OF HACALIAH: IN THE MONTH OF KISLEV OF THE TWENTIETH YEAR (Nehemiah 1:1 JPS), and it is written, IN THE MONTH OF NISAN, IN THE TWENTIETH YEAR OF KING ARTAXERXES (Nehemiah 2:1 JPS). Since he refers to Kislev as in the twentieth year [of Artaxerxes' reign], and to [the following] Nisan as [also] in the twentieth year [of his reign], it is impossible that the beginning of the year [of Artaxerxes' reign] could have been Nisan.

Chapter Three introduces the topic of the shofar – *from which animal the horn may be taken, what sounds must be produced, what if the instrument is damaged, etc. Correct intention is all important; if one person blows and another listens, both must consciously intend to fulfil the* mitzva.

CHAPTER THREE

MISHNA:
If the *shofar* had split and was glued together, it is invalid. 27a
If someone glued parts of *shofarot* together, it is invalid. If it was pierced and the hole was stopped up, impeding the sound, this is invalid; otherwise, it is valid.

If someone sounds the *shofar* in a pit, a cistern or an earthenware jar, then if what he hears is the sound of the *shofar*, he has fulfilled his obligation, but if he heard only an echo, he has not.

Similarly, if someone was passing the synagogue, or his house was near the synagogue, and he heard the sound of the *shofar*, or of the scroll [of Esther] being read [on Purim], if he gave it his attention he has fulfilled his obligation, but if not, he has not. Even though two people heard [the same sound], one put his mind to it, but the other did not.

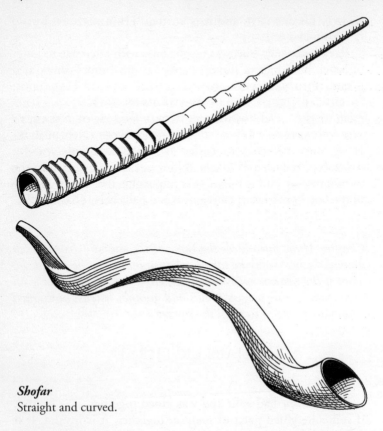

Shofar
Straight and curved.

GEMARA:
After clarifying some points about damaged shofarot, *the Gemara continues:*

If someone sounds the *shofar* in a pit, a cistern or an earthenware jar. Rav Huna said, This applies to people who are standing outside the pit [and therefore heard only an echo], but those who are in the pit have fulfilled their obligation[, since they heard the actual sound of the the *shofar*]. We find this also in a baraita: **If someone sounds the *shofar* in a pit or an earthenware jar, he has not fulfilled his obligation.** But doesn't the Mishna say he has? So it must certainly be as Rav Huna said.

Some formulate this as a contradiction: A baraita

says, **If someone sounds the *shofar* in a pit or an earthenware jar, he has not fulfilled his obligation.** But doesn't the Mishna say, **He *has* fulfilled his obligation?** Rav Huna said, There is no contradiction; one [ruling] applies to those who are standing by the edge of the pit, the other to those who are in the pit.

To fulfil one's obligation one must act intentionally. But there is a second level of intention (kavana) where the requirement is less obvious: granted you know what you are doing, is it also essential to be aware that you are fulfilling a mitzva?

They sent to Shmuel's father: **If someone was forced to eat** 28a **unleavened bread [on Passover], he has fulfilled [the *mitzva*].** Who forced him? If he was possessed by a demon, does not a baraita state, **If someone has periods of sanity and periods of madness, while he is sane [the law regards him as] sane in all respects, and while he is mad [the law regards him as] mad in all respects?**[5] Rav Ashi said, Forced by Persians.

Rava said, This implies that if someone sounded the *shofar* [merely] to make music, he has fulfilled his obligation. Isn't this obviously the same thing? [Not quite.] You might have thought that [in the case of the unleavened bread] the Torah said he should eat unleavened bread and he has, after all, eaten it. But in the present instance, the Torah says A REMEMBERING OF SOUNDING[6] (Leviticus 23:24), [which implies intention,] and this individual is preoccupied [with making music rather than with the performance of a *mitzva*], so [Rava] lets you know [that such is not the case].

The next Mishna is a more philosophical reflection on mental attitude and religious faith.

MISHNA:

WHENEVER MOSES HELD UP HIS HAND, ISRAEL PRE- 29a VAILED; BUT WHENEVER HE LET DOWN HIS HAND, AMALEK PREVAILED (Exodus 17:11 JPS). **Did Moses' hands, then, make or break the battle? [Surely not!] But this teaches you that so**

5. So the question could not arise; someone possessed by demons is mad, so not subject to any legal obligation.
6. A literal translation. For JPS, see introductory note to this tractate.

long as Israel looked upwards and submitted their minds to their Father in Heaven, they prevailed; otherwise, they foundered.

Similarly, MAKE YOURSELF A SERPENT AND MOUNT IT ON A STANDARD; WHOEVER HAS BEEN BITTEN SHOULD LOOK AT IT AND WILL BE HEALED (Numbers 21:8). Did the [brazen] serpent kill or cure? [Surely not!] But this teaches you that so long as Israel looked upwards and submitted their minds to their Father in Heaven, they were cured; otherwise, they perished.

A deaf-mute, an idiot and a minor cannot act on behalf of the public to fulfil their obligations. The rule is, Whoever is not himself obliged [to fulfil a *mitzva*] cannot carry it out on behalf of others.

The rabbis forbade the playing of musical instruments on the Sabbath. Does this mean that if Rosh Hashana falls on a Saturday the shofar *should not be sounded, or would the biblical command override the rabbis' precautionary measure?*

CHAPTER FOUR

MISHNA:

29b   If the festival of Rosh Hashana fell on the Sabbath, they would sound the *shofar* in the Temple but not in the city [of Jerusalem].

After the destruction of the Temple, Rabban Yoḥanan ben Zakkai ordained that [the *shofar*] should be sounded [on Rosh Hashana when it fell on the Sabbath] wherever there was a court. Rabbi Eleazar said, Rabban Yoḥanan ben Zakkai ordained this only for Yavné. They said [to Rabbi Eleazar], There is no difference [in this respect] between Yavné and any other location where a court sits.[7]

7.   Yoḥanan ben Zakkai set up court in Yavné following the fall of Jerusalem in 70. According to the fourteenth-century commentator Nissim ben Reuben of Gerona, Isaac Alfasi (c. 1013–1103) followed Yoḥanan ben Zakkai's ruling and sounded the *shofar* in his court (whether Fez or Lucena is unclear) when Rosh Hashana fell on the Sabbath; however, most authorities demurred.

In this respect, also, Jerusalem was superior to Yavné: they sounded [the *shofar*] on Rosh Hashana when it fell on the Sabbath] in any town from which you could see or hear [it], and which was near and accessible, but in Yavné it was sounded only in the court [itself].

GEMARA:

How do we know this? Rabbi Levi bar Laḥma said in the name of Rabbi Ḥama bar Ḥanina, One verse says, YOU SHALL HAVE A DAY OF SOLEMN REST, A REMEMBERING OF SOUND-ING (Leviticus 23:24), but another says, YOU SHALL HAVE A DAY OF SOUNDING (Numbers 29:1). There is no contradiction: one verse applies when the festival falls on Shabbat, the other when it falls on a weekday.

Rava [objected]: If [sounding the *shofar* on Shabbat] is for-bidden by the Torah, how could it be permitted in the Temple? Also, is [sounding the *shofar* forbidden] labour, that Scripture should need to exclude it? Surely it was taught in Shmuel's School that ['servile' in] YOU SHALL DO NO *SERVILE* LABOUR (Numbers 29:1) excludes [activities such as] sounding the *shofar* or ladling bread from the oven, since they are skills rather than labour? So, said Rava, the Torah permits [sounding the *shofar* on Shabbat], but the rabbis forbade it, as Rabba said: Everyone is obliged to sound the *shofar* [on Rosh Hashana,] but not everyone knows how to sound it; the rabbis therefore ordained that it should not be sounded on Shabbat, in case someone takes it in his hand to go to an expert [for instruction, and infringes Shabbat by] carrying it four cubits in the public domain. For the same reason [they forbade] taking the *lulav* or reading the scroll [of Esther on Shabbat].

NINTH TRACTATE
TA'ANIT (PUBLIC FASTS)

The tractate opens with rules as to when two short prayers should be inserted in the tefilla: *the 'declaration of God's might', i.e. 'He who makes the wind blow and the rain fall', is said throughout the winter; the 'request for rain' – 'Grant rain and dew' – was not said until pilgrims to Jerusalem had returned to their distant homes after the New Year festival cycle, and the time varied according to location. Both prayers remain in the liturgy.*

The rainy season in Israel begins in late autumn. If no rain had fallen by 17 Ḥeshvan (late October/early November), the court would initiate a series of progressively more severe fasts on which people would pray for rain. Much of the tractate is concerned with these and other fasts to forestall calamity.

The first three fasts were for scholars only; if there was no rain by the following month (Kislev), the court would declare three public fasts; these would be followed by another three, then seven, if required, on Mondays and Thursdays.[1] References to trumpeting priests and to courses of priests suggest Temple times, but other features relate to later periods.

1. Evidence that Mondays and Thursdays were especially propitious for prayer and fasting comes from the Christian *Didache*, written *c.*120: 'Let not your fasts be with the hypocrites, for they fast on Mondays and Thursdays, but do you fast on Wednesdays and Fridays' (*Didache* 8:1; Kirsopp Lake's translation, in Loeb *Apostolic Fathers*).

CHAPTER TWO

MISHNA:

What is the procedure for [rain] fasts?   15a

They take the [prayer-]lectern into the town square and spread ashes on it, and on the heads of the president and the chief justice, and everyone spreads ashes on his own head. The most senior present addresses them with words of reproof: Brethren! It is not said of the men of Nineveh that God saw their sackcloth and their fasting, but AND GOD SAW THEIR DEEDS, THAT THEY HAD REPENTED OF THEIR EVIL WAYS (Jonah 3:10); [likewise,] the prophet says, REND YOUR HEARTS, NOT YOUR GARMENTS (Joel 2:13). They stand in prayer, and the prayers are led by one who is venerable and fluent, who has children, but whose house is bare, so that his prayer will be heartfelt.

Mishna details twenty-four blessings and the accompanying blasts on horns and trumpets, then continues:

On the first three fasts the members of the course [of priests   15b serving that week] fast, but do not complete [the fast];[2] on the second three, the members of the course fast and complete, and the members of the serving family fast, but do not complete; on the final seven, both groups complete. This is the view of Rabbi Joshua, but the [other] Sages say, Neither of these groups observes the first three fasts; on the second three, the members of the course fast, but do not complete, and the members of the serving family do not fast at all; on the final seven, the members of the course [fast and] complete, and the members of the serving family fast but do not complete.

GEMARA:

What is the procedure for [rain-]fasts? They take the

2. i.e. they fast only in the daytime, not the previous evening (liturgical 'days' run from sunset one evening to starlight the next). There were 24 courses of *Kohanim*, as listed in 1 Chronicles 24:3–18, each in turn serving in the Temple for a week. The courses were each subdivided into seven 'father's houses', one to serve on each day of the week; for clarity, I have translated 'serving family' rather than 'father's house'.

[prayer-]lectern into the town square. Did this happen even
with the initial fasts? As against that: On the first three and the
second three fasts, they enter the synagogue and pray as they
do the rest of the year, but on the last seven they take the
[prayer-]lectern into the town square and spread ashes on it,
and on the heads of the president and the chief justice, and
everyone spreads ashes on his own head. Rabbi Nathan says,
They brought ashes from the roast. Rav Papa said, Our Mishna
too is speaking of the last seven fasts.

[The Mishna] states, On the head of the president and then
everyone spreads, etc. How can this be? Doesn't a baraita teach,
Rabbi says, With dignity start from the greater, with injury
from the lesser?

> With dignity start from the greater, as it is said,
> AND MOSES SPOKE TO AARON, AND TO HIS
> REMAINING SONS ELEAZAR AND ITAMAR (Leviticus
> 10:12); with injury from the lesser, for we find
> (Genesis 3) that the serpent was cursed first, then Eve,
> and then Adam.

Putting ashes on their heads is [according them] dignity, for
it signifies 'You are worthy enough to pray for all of us.'

Everyone spreads ashes on his own head. Rav Ada asked, If
everyone spreads ashes on his head, let the president and chief
justice do likewise! Why should other people put ashes on them?
Rabbi Abba of Caesarea said, One who humbles himself is not
like one who is humbled by others.

16a

On which part of the head are the ashes placed? Rabbi Isaac
said, In the position of the *tefillin*, as it is said, To PROVIDE
FOR THE MOURNERS IN ZION, TO GIVE THEM GLORY RATHER
THAN ASHES (Isaiah 61:3).[3]

Why do they go out into the town square? Rabbi Ḥiyya bar
Abba said, [It is as if] to say, We cried out in private but were
not answered; we will now abase ourselves openly. Resh Laqish
said, We have exiled ourselves [from our homes]; may our exile
atone for us! What [practical difference] is there between [the

---

3. *Tefillin* are understood as 'a glory'.

two opinions]? They would differ as to whether it would be sufficient to move from one synagogue to another.[4]

Why do they take the [prayer-]lectern into the town square? Rabbi Joshua ben Levi said, [It is as if] to say, We had a modest vessel [to carry our prayer], but through our sins it has been demeaned.

Why do they wear sackcloth? Rabbi Ḥiyya bar Abba said, [It is as if] to say, We are [but] animals.

Why do they spread ashes on the [prayer-]lectern? Rabbi Judah ben Pazi said, [It is as if] to say, I WILL BE WITH HIM IN DISTRESS[5] (Psalm 91:15 JPS); Resh Laqish said, IN ALL THEIR TROUBLES HE WAS TROUBLED (Isaiah 63:9 JPS).

Rabbi Zeira said, When I first saw the rabbis spread ashes on the [prayer-]lectern, my whole body trembled.

Why does each individual put ashes on his head? Rabbi Levi bar Ḥama and Rabbi Ḥanina differed on this. One said, [It is as if] to say, We are like ashes before You. The other said, It is a reminder of the ashes of Isaac. What is the difference? The difference would be if someone used plain earth.[6]

Ḥoni, Abba Ḥilkiah and Ḥanina ben Dosa (see Sota 49a) were charismatic miracle workers in Galilee from the first century BCE onward; the stories told about their healing activities and apparent 'familiarity' with God are similar to those told about Jesus.[7] Simeon ben Shetaḥ demonstrates the wariness with which they were regarded by the 'establishment'.

4. On Rabbi Ḥiyya bar Abba's theory, it would not do, for the synagogue is not 'open'; on Resh Laqish's it would be all right, since the move to another synagogue is an 'exile' of sorts.
5. The prayer-lectern is the symbol of God's presence.
6. It would symbolize abasement, but not correspond to the ashes of the sacrifice offered in place of Isaac.
7. Vermes, *Jesus*, chapter 3.

CHAPTER THREE

GEMARA:

Ḥoni the Circle-Maker

The rabbis taught: Once, most of Adar had passed and no rain had fallen. They sent to Ḥoni the Circle-Maker: Pray for rain! He said to them, Go and fetch in your Passover ovens so they do not disintegrate [in the rain]![8] He prayed but no rain fell. He drew a circle and stood in the middle of it, just as the prophet Habakkuk had done, as it is said, I WILL STAND UPON MY WATCH, AND SET ME UPON THE TOWER (Habakkuk 2:1). He addressed [God]: Lord of the Universe, Your children have turned to me as one of Your family. I swear by Your great name that I will not budge from here until You show mercy to Your children!

Rain began to fall, in drips. His disciples said to him: Master, with the greatest respect,[9] it seems to us that this [meagre] rain is falling just to absolve you from your oath.

Ḥoni [again] addressed [God]: This is not what I asked for, but rain [to fill] wells, ditches and caves! [At this, rain] poured down in torrents, in drops as large as the aperture of a barrel; the Sages estimated that none was less than a *log*.

His disciples said to him: Master, with the greatest respect, it looks to us that if the rain falls like this it will destroy the world!

Ḥoni [again] addressed [God]: This is not what I asked for, but rain of goodwill, blessing and generosity! [The rain then] fell in just measure, [but persisted until] the people [were forced to] ascend to the Temple Mount on account of it. They said to [Ḥoni]: Master! Just as you prayed for it to come, pray for it to cease!

He replied: My tradition is that one does not pray [to

---

8. This sentence, lacking in the baraita but preserved in the Mishna, is needed to demonstrate his boastfulness about his close relationship with God, and to explain his drawing of the circle and Simeon ben Shetah's reprimand.
9. Literally, 'We have looked upon you, may we not die!'

remove] an excess of good. Still, bring me an ox [to offer] by way of thanksgiving.

They brought him an ox [to make a] thanksgiving [offering]. He laid his hands on it and declared: Lord of the Universe! Your people Israel whom you brought out of Egypt cannot abide excess of either good or evil. When You were angry with them, they could not endure it; when You showered them with goodness, they could not endure it. May it be Your will that the rain stop and relief come to the world!

At once the wind blew, the clouds dispersed, the sun shone and the people went out to the countryside and gathered mushrooms.

Simeon ben Shetaḥ sent to [Ḥoni]: Were you anyone but Ḥoni I would excommunicate you! If these were the days of Elijah, to whom the keys of rain were entrusted, would not your actions have profaned the Name of heaven?[10] But what can I do, seeing that you play mischievously before the Holy One, blessed be He, and He gives in to whatever you want, like a mischievous child whose father gives in to him – if he says, Daddy, bathe me in hot water, give me a cold shower, give me walnuts, almonds, peaches, pomegranates, his father lets him have what he wants. Of you Scripture says, YOUR FATHER AND MOTHER ARE HAPPY; SHE THAT BORE YOU REJOICES (Proverbs 23:25)!

The rabbis taught: What message did the Men of the Chamber of Hewn Stone[11] send to Ḥoni? [THOU SHALT MAKE THY PRAYER UNTO HIM, AND HE WILL HEAR THEE . . .] THOU SHALT ALSO DECREE A THING, AND IT SHALL BE ESTABLISHED UNTO THEE, AND LIGHT SHALL SHINE UPON THY WAYS. WHEN THEY CAST THEE DOWN, THOU SHALT SAY: 'THERE IS LIFTING UP'; FOR THE LOWLY PERSON HE SAVETH. HE DELIVERETH HIM THAT IS NOT[12] INNOCENT. YEA, THOU SHALT BE DELIVERED THROUGH THE CLEANNESS OF THY

10. The reprimand is presumably directed at Ḥoni's confidence that God would send copious rain, even though drought had been decreed; Ḥoni appears to be thwarting God's will.
11. Seat of the High Court (Sanhedrin) in the Temple.
12. Several English translations omit 'not', but the Talmud's reading demands it.

HANDS (Job 22:27, 28–30). THOU SHALT ALSO DECREE A THING – You decree on earth below, and the Holy One blessed be He, fulfils your word in heaven! AND LIGHT SHALL SHINE UPON THY WAYS – Through your prayer you have brought light to a generation that was in darkness. WHEN THEY CAST THEE DOWN, THOU SHALT SAY: 'THERE IS LIFTING UP' – You have raised through your prayer the generation that was lowly; FOR THE LOWLY PERSON HE SAVETH – You have saved through your prayer the generation that was sunk in sin; HE DELIVERETH HIM THAT IS NOT INNOCENT – you have saved them through the purity of your deeds.

Honi Sleeps for Seventy Years

Rabbi Yoḥanan said: All his life long that good man [Honi] was troubled by the verse: WHEN THE LORD RETURNS THE CAPTIVES OF ZION, IT WAS AS IF WE HAD DREAMED (Psalm 126:1). He wondered, Is it possible to fall asleep and dream for seventy years?

One day he was out walking and saw a man plant a carob tree. He asked him, When will it bear fruit? In seventy years' time, [the other] replied. [Honi] said, Are you so sure you will live seventy years? [The man] replied, I entered a world in which carob trees had been planted; as my fathers planted for me, I plant for my sons.

[Honi] sat down, broke bread and dozed off. A grotto[13] formed around him, concealing him from sight, and he slept for seventy years.

[When he awoke] he saw a man pluck fruit from [the carob tree]. He said, Are you the one who planted it? [The man] replied, I am his grandson.

[Honi] thought to himself, I must have slept for seventy years! He saw that generations of foals had descended from his donkey. He went home and enquired, Is Honi the Circle-Maker's son alive? They replied, His son is no longer here, but his grandson is. He said to them, I am Honi the Circle-Maker, but they refused to believe him.

13. Probable meaning. Rashi understands the rare word *m'shunita* as a tooth, or projection, of rock.

He entered the House of Study and heard the students remark, The lectures are as clear as in the days of Ḥoni the Circle-Maker, who could answer every question the students put to him when he entered the House of Study.

He said, I am he! But no one would believe him, nor would they accord him the respect he deserved. He became depressed and prayed to die.

That's the meaning of the proverb, 'Companions or death'!

A Story of Ḥoni's Grandson

Abba Ḥilkiah was the son of Ḥoni's son. Whenever the world needed rain the rabbis would send to him; he would pray and rain would come.

Once the world was in need of rain. They dispatched two rabbis to ask him to pray for rain. When they arrived at his house he was not in, so they went out to the fields and found him hoeing. They greeted him, but he did not reply.   23b

Towards evening he gathered sticks. He put the spade and sticks on one shoulder, and [draped] his garment on the other. He did not wear shoes the whole way, but put them on only when he came to water. Where there were thorns and briars he raised his cloak[, exposing his flesh to them]. When he arrived back in town his wife adorned herself to come out and greet him. When they arrived at the house his wife entered first, he followed and the rabbis followed him. He sat down to break bread but did not invite the rabbis to partake. He broke bread for the children; to the elder he gave one portion, to the younger two. Then he said to his wife, I know the rabbis are here on account of rain; let's go up to the roof to pray, so if the Holy One, blessed be He, is willing to send rain we will not need to claim credit for ourselves.[14] They went up to the roof; he stood in one corner and she in the other, and clouds started to form on her side.

When they came back down, he said to the rabbis, What brings you here? They replied, The rabbis sent us to ask you to pray for rain.

14. That is, the rabbis will not see that we have had anything to do with it.

He said, Then blessed be the Omnipresent who has not put you in need of the services of Abba Ḥilkiah!

They replied, We know that the rain came on your account, but will you please explain those strange things you have been doing. Why did you not respond to our greetings?

He replied, I was hired by the day, and thought I should not neglect my work.

Why did you put the spade and sticks on one shoulder and drape your garment over the other?

He said to them, It was a borrowed garment; I had borrowed it for one purpose, not for the other.

Why did you not wear shoes all the way, but put them on only when you came to water?

He replied, All the way I could see [what was underfoot]; in the water I couldn't.

Why, when you came to thorns and briars, did you raise your cloak[, exposing your flesh to the thorns and briars]?

The one heals, the other does not.

Why, when you arrived back in town, did your wife adorn herself to come out and greet you?

So that I should not set my eyes on another woman.

Why did she enter the house first, then you, and we followed?

I did not know what sort of people you were[, and whether I could trust you with my wife].

Why, when you broke bread, did you not invite us to partake?

Because there was not much bread in the house, and I did not want to incur your gratitude for nothing.

Why did you give one portion of bread to the older [child] and two to the younger?

Because the one remains at home, but the other attends the synagogue [for study, and is away all day – Rashi].

Why did clouds form first from the direction that your wife was praying rather than in your direction?

Because a woman remains at home and gives bread to the poor, which is of immediate benefit, whereas I give only money, which is not of immediate benefit. Alternatively, because when the neighbourhood [was troubled by] criminals I prayed that they should die, but she prayed that they should repent, and they did so.

CHAPTER FOUR

MISHNA:
Five calamities befell our fathers on 17 Tammuz and five on   26a
Tisha b'Av (9 Av).

On 17 Tammuz the tablets of stone were smashed [by   26b
Moses], the daily sacrifice ceased, [the walls of] the city [of
Jerusalem] were breached, Apostomos burnt the Torah and an
image was set up in the sanctuary.[15]

On Tisha b'Av it was decreed that our fathers should not
enter the Land, both the First and Second Temples were
destroyed, Beitar was captured and the city [of Jerusalem] was
ploughed over.

Once [the month of] Av begins we reduce pleasure.

Haircutting and the washing of clothes are forbidden in the
week of Tisha b'Av, but are permitted on the Thursday in
honour of the Sabbath.

You should not eat two courses on the eve of Tisha b'Av,
nor eat meat or drink wine. Rabban Simeon ben Gamaliel
says, You should [merely] do something different [from the
usual]. Rabbi Judah [held that] overturning the couch[16] was
obligatory, but the Sages disagreed.

Rabban Simeon ben Gamaliel said, 15 Av and the Day of
Atonement were Israel's most joyful days. The girls of Jerusalem went out then in borrowed white dresses – that was so
that none should be embarrassed [by not having one of her
own], and all [the dresses] were immersed [for purification] –
the girls of Jerusalem went out and danced among the vineyards. What did they [sing]? Young man! Raise your eyes and

15.   On the last of these, see Daniel 12:11.
16.   *Mo'ed Qatan* 20b (see p. 282).

consider whom you choose! Look for breeding, not for beauty – GRACE IS DECEPTIVE, BEAUTY IS ILLUSORY; IT IS FOR HER FEAR OF THE LORD THAT A WOMAN IS TO BE PRAISED. EXTOL HER FOR THE FRUIT OF HER HAND, AND LET HER WORKS PRAISE HER IN THE GATES (Proverbs 31:30–31 JPS).

Likewise it is said, O MAIDENS OF ZION, GO FORTH AND GAZE UPON KING SOLOMON WEARING THE CROWN THAT HIS MOTHER GAVE HIM ON HIS WEDDING DAY, ON HIS DAY OF BLISS (Song 3:11 JPS): ON HIS WEDDING DAY – That is the day the Torah was revealed; ON HIS DAY OF BLISS – That is the day the Temple was built. May it be rebuilt speedily in our days![17]

GEMARA:

29a   On Tisha b'Av it was decreed that our fathers should not enter the Land. How do we know this? It is written, IN THE FIRST MONTH OF THE SECOND YEAR, ON THE FIRST OF THE MONTH, THE TABERNACLE WAS SET UP (Exodus 40:17 JPS). Now, a scholar said, In the first year Moses constructed the Tabernacle, and in the second he erected it and dispatched the spies. We then read, IN THE SECOND YEAR, ON THE TWENTIETH DAY OF THE SECOND MONTH, THE CLOUD LIFTED FROM THE TABERNACLE OF THE PACT . . . THEY MARCHED FROM THE MOUNTAIN OF THE LORD A DISTANCE OF THREE DAYS (Numbers 10:11, 33 JPS) – Rabbi Ḥama bar Ḥanina observed, That is when they turned aside from the Lord. We continue: THE RIFFRAFF IN THEIR MIDST FELT A GLUTTONOUS CRAVING; AND THEN THE ISRAELITES WEPT . . . A WHOLE MONTH (11:4, 20 JPS) – which brings us to 22 Sivan. [After that,] SO MIRIAM WAS SHUT OUT OF CAMP SEVEN DAYS (12:15 JPS) – which brings us to 29 Sivan, then, SEND MEN (13:2 JPS), and a baraita confirms that it was on 29 Sivan that Moses dispatched the spies; and then, AT THE END OF FORTY DAYS THEY RETURNED FROM SCOUTING THE LAND (13:25 JPS).

But surely there are only 39 days [from 29 Sivan to 9 Av]! Abbaye said, Tammuz that year was a full

17.   This paragraph interprets the lovers in Song as God and the people of Israel.

month,[18] as it is written, HE HAS PROCLAIMED A
SET TIME AGAINST ME, TO CRUSH MY YOUNG MEN
(Lamentations 1:15 JPS), and THE WHOLE COM-
MUNITY BROKE INTO LOUD CRIES, AND THE PEOPLE
WEPT THAT NIGHT (Numbers 14:1 JPS).

Rabba said in the name of Rabbi Yoḥanan, That night
was Tisha b'Av. The Holy One, blessed be He, said,
You have wept without cause – I ordain [this day as a
day of] weeping for you throughout the generations!

The First . . . Temple [was] destroyed. As it is written, ON
THE SEVENTH DAY OF THE FIFTH MONTH – THAT WAS THE
NINETEENTH YEAR OF KING NEBUCHADNEZZAR OF BABYLON
– NEBUZARADAN, THE CHIEF OF THE GUARDS, AN OFFICER
OF THE KING OF BABYLON, CAME TO JERUSALEM. HE
BURNED THE HOUSE OF THE LORD (2 Kings 25:8–9 JPS), and
it is written, ON THE TENTH DAY OF THE FIFTH MONTH –
THAT WAS THE NINETEENTH YEAR OF KING NEBUCHADREZ-
ZAR OF BABYLON – NEBUZARADAN, THE CHIEF OF THE
GUARDS, CAME TO REPRESENT THE KING OF BABYLON IN
JERUSALEM. HE BURNED THE HOUSE OF THE LORD . . .
(Jeremiah 52:12–13 JPS). It was taught: **You cannot say it was
on the seventh, since it is written 'on the tenth'; you cannot
say it was on the tenth, since it is written 'on the seventh'.
What happened? Foreigners entered the Temple on the
seventh, and ate there and desecrated it on the seventh and
eighth; they set fire to it just before dark on the ninth, and it
burnt for a whole day,** as Scripture says: ALAS FOR US! FOR
DAY IS DECLINING, THE SHADOWS OF EVENING GROW LONG
(Jeremiah 6:4 JPS). This is what Rabbi Yoḥanan meant: Had I
lived in that generation I would have fixed [the commemoration]
on the tenth, for that is when most of the Sanctuary was
burnt; the [other] rabbis, however, thought it preferable [to
commemorate] the onset of calamity.

And how do we know that the Second [Temple was destroyed
on Tisha b'Av]? A baraita teaches, **Reward is allotted to a day
of innocence and punishment to a day of guilt.**

18. 30 days; it is usually only 29.

They said, The First Temple was destroyed on the eve of Tisha b'Av; it was a Saturday night at the end of the Sabbatical Year, in the priestly course of Jehoiarib, and the Levites were standing on their platform, singing. What were they singing? HE WILL MAKE THEIR EVIL RECOIL UPON THEM (Psalm 94:23 JPS); before they reached the words, ANNIHILATE THEM THROUGH THEIR OWN WICKEDNESS, the heathen [armies] entered and overpowered them. It was the same at [the destruction of the] Second [Temple].

Beitar was captured. Gemara.[19]

These anecdotes illustrate God's providence, and teach that the righteous of all nations can earn a place in the World to Come.[20] *The view ultimately prevailed that though a Jew must be ready to give up his life where the alternative is apostasy, martyrdom should not positively be sought.*

And the city [of Jerusalem] was ploughed over. It was taught: When the wicked Tinius Rufus destroyed the Temple, Rabban Gamaliel was sentenced to death.[21] **A legionary entered the House of Study and called out, That famous man is summoned! That famous man is summoned! Rabban Gamaliel heard and concealed himself. [The legionary] came to him in secret and asked, If I save you, can you bring me to the World to Come? He replied, Yes! Swear to me! [Rabban Gamaliel] swore to him. [The legionary] climbed up, threw himself from the roof and died, and as we have learned, if they issue a decree and one of them dies, the decree is cancelled. A heavenly voice was heard to proclaim, [That legionary] is destined for the World to Come!**

The rabbis taught: When the First Temple was destroyed, groups of young priests gathered, holding the keys of the Temple

19. That is, there is no scriptural basis. Both the capture of Beitar and the ploughing of the Temple Mount are associated with the Bar Kokhba Revolt (131–5). See Introduction, 'How the Talmud Started', p. xxii.
20. Cf. the story of Jesus and the centurion (Matthew 8:5–13).
21. Historically, this is implausible; Gamaliel II must have died well before the Bar Kokhba Revolt. Several inscriptions attest the presence of Tinius Rufus in Bet Shean (Scythopolis); he was governor of the province of Judaea when Hadrian visited the city in the spring of 130 CE. The Temple had been destroyed in 70; Hadrian had the site ploughed over and a pagan temple built there.

in their hands, and ascended to the Temple roof. They declared:
Lord of the universe! As we have failed in our duty as guardians,
we return the keys to You! They threw them up, and the Palm
of a Hand issued forth and received them; the [young priests]
then leaped into the fire. It was for them that Isaiah lamented:
THE 'VALLEY OF VISION' PRONOUNCEMENT. WHAT CAN
HAVE HAPPENED TO YOU THAT YOU HAVE GONE, ALL OF
YOU, UP ON THE ROOFS. O YOU WHO WERE FULL OF TUMULT,
YOU CLAMOROUS TOWN, YOU CITY SO GAY? YOUR SLAIN ARE
NOT THE SLAIN OF THE SWORD NOR THE DEAD OF BATTLE
(Isaiah 22:1–2 JPS); and the Holy One, blessed be He,
[lamented]: HE WAILED AND MOANED FOR THE MOUNTAIN
(Isaiah 22:5).[22]

*The tractate concludes with a discussion of Simeon ben
Gamaliel's remarkable observation on the celebration of Yom
Kippur and the fifteenth of Av:*

Rabban Simeon ben Gamaliel said, 15 Av and the Day of 30b
Atonement were Israel's most joyful days. Yom Kippur is
certainly [joyful], for it is a day of pardon and forgiveness, and
the day on which the second tablets were given [to Moses at
Sinai]. But what is [so special] about 15 Av?

Rav Yehuda said in the name of Shmuel, It is the day the
tribes were given permission to intermarry with one another.
On what did they base this? [On the verse:] THIS IS WHAT THE
LORD HAS COMMANDED CONCERNING THE DAUGHTERS OF
ZELOPHEHAD (Numbers 36:6 JPS) – [i.e. the restrictions on
which tribe they might marry into] apply to this generation only.

Rav Yosef said in the name of Rav Naḥman: It is the day that
the tribe of Benjamin was permitted to [re-]enter the congregation [of Israel, after it had been said], NOW THE MEN OF
ISRAEL HAD TAKEN AN OATH AT MIZPAH: 'NONE OF US
WILL GIVE HIS DAUGHTER IN MARRIAGE TO A BENJAMINITE'
(Judges 21:1 JPS). On what did they base this? [On the
expression] NONE OF US – none of *us* [will give his daughter],
but our children may.

22. The four Hebrew words are obscure, and have been translated to fit the context.
    See Introduction, 'Bible Translation', p. li.

Rabba bar bar Ḥana said in the name of Rabbi Yoḥanan: It is the day that those condemned to die in the wilderness ceased dying. A scholar said, [God's] word to Moses did not resume until those condemned to die in the wilderness ceased dying, as it is said, **WHEN ALL THE MEN OF WAR CEASED DYING, GOD SPOKE TO ME** (Deuteronomy 2:16) – the Word came to me [once more].

Ulla said, It is the day that Hoshea the son of Elah abolished the guards that Jeroboam son of Nebat had appointed to prevent Israelites from [going to Jerusalem to] celebrate the pilgrim festivals; he said, They may go where they please.[23]

31a

Rav Matna said, It is the day permission was given [by the Romans] to bury those slain at Beitar. For Rav Matna said, On the day permission was given to bury those slain at Beitar, [the rabbis] at Yavné instituted [the blessing], 'Who is good, and Who brings about good' [in the grace after meals] – 'Who is good', for the corpses did not putrefy, and 'Who brings about good', for it was possible to bury them.

Rabba and Rav Yosef both said, It was the day they used to stop chopping wood for the fires of the altar, for a baraita taught: **Rabbi Eliezer the Great says, They stop chopping wood from 15 Av onward, since the sun is getting weaker and [the wood] does not dry out [properly].** Rav Menashya said, They called it 'the day for breaking the chopper'.

After [15 Av] who adds, increases; who does not add, perishes. Perishes? Rav Yosef said, May his mother bury him![24]

For [on them] the girls of Jerusalem. The rabbis taught: **The king's daughter would borrow from the high priest's daughter, the high priest's daughter from the deputy high priest's daughter, the deputy high priest's daughter from the war priest's**

23. Jeroboam and Hoshea were both kings of the Northern Kingdom of Israel. Jeroboam had rebelled against Solomon's son, Rehoboam, and erected shrines at Dan and Bethel to rival the attraction at Jerusalem. 2 Kings 17:2 states that Hoshea, though displeasing to God, was not as bad as his predecessors; the rabbis read this as a hint that he 'abolished the guards'.
24. There is a play here on the words *yosef* ('increases') and *yaesef* ('perishes'); Rav Yosef fittingly clarifies. Rashi explains that as the nights get longer one should 'add' more time for the study of Torah, and live, rather than neglect Torah and die.

daughter, the war priest's daughter from an ordinary priest's daughter, and all Israel one from another, so that she who had none would not be embarrassed.

And all [the dresses] were immersed [for purification] – Rabbi Eliezer said, Even if they had been folded away in a box.

The girls of Jerusalem went out and danced among the vineyards. It was taught: Whoever had no wife went there. The well-connected girls said, Young man, etc.

The rabbis taught:

The beautiful ones would say: Look for beauty – wives are for beauty! The well-connected ones would say: Look for [a good] family – wives are for children! The ugly ones would say: Take a wife for the sake of heaven, but crown us with gold pieces!

Ulla Bira'a said in the name of Rabbi Eliezer: In time to come the Holy One, blessed be He, will make a dance for the righteous, and He will sit among them in the Garden of Eden. Each will point with his finger, as it is said, IN THAT DAY THEY SHALL SAY: THIS IS OUR GOD; WE TRUSTED IN HIM, AND HE DELIVERED US. THIS IS THE LORD, IN WHOM WE TRUSTED; LET US REJOICE AND EXULT IN HIS DELIVERANCE! (Isaiah 25:9 JPS).

TENTH TRACTATE
MEGILLA (PURIM)

The Hebrew word megilla ('scroll') here denotes the Book of
Esther. Five biblical books (Song, Ruth, Lamentations, Ecclesiastes, Esther) are referred to collectively as the Five Megillot; a
custom of medieval origin[1] allots the reading of each to a specific
liturgical occasion – the Song to Passover, Ruth to Shavuot,
Lamentations to the Ninth of Av, Ecclesiastes to Tabernacles
and Esther to Purim. The Talmud knows only of the reading of
Esther.

The feast of Purim is mentioned in Esther, but not in the five
books of the Torah; the rabbis therefore treat it as a rabbinic
rather than a biblical institution. Mordecai and the 'men of the
Great Synod', instituting the festival, are anachronistically seen
acting as a rabbinic court.

CHAPTER ONE

MISHNA:

2a The *megilla* is read on 11, 12, 13, 14 or 15 [Adar], neither
earlier nor later.

Cities that were walled in the days of Joshua read it on 15.
Villages and large towns read it on 14, but villages bring
forward [the reading] to [the previous] market day.[2]

How does this work out? If [14 Adar] fell on Monday,

---

1. Isserles, notes on *Shulḥan Arukh: Oraḥ Ḥayyim* 490, based on the commentary
   of the fourteenth-century Spanish liturgist David ben Joseph Abudarham.
2. Monday or Thursday.

villages and large towns read [the *megilla*] on that day, and walled [cities] on the following day. If it fell on Tuesday or Wednesday, villages bring forward [the reading] to the previous market day, large towns read it on that day, and walled [cities] on the following day. If it fell on Thursday, villages and large towns read [the *megilla*] on that day, and walled [cities] on the following day. If it fell on the eve of the Sabbath, villages bring forward [the reading] to the previous market day, and large towns and walled [cities] read it on that day. If it fell on the Sabbath, villages and large towns bring forward [the reading] to the previous market day, and walled [cities read] on the following day. If it fell on Sunday, villages bring forward [the reading] to the previous market day, large towns read it on that day, and walled [cities] on the following day.

GEMARA:

The *megilla* is read on 11. How do we know this? As we will shortly explain, the Sages leniently permitted villagers to bring forward [their reading] to the market day, so that they would supply their brothers in the towns with water and food.

[That wasn't the question.] What we meant was this: [The laws of Purim must] all have been instituted by the men of the Great Synod – for if you suppose that the men of the Great Synod instituted [only] 14 and 15 [Adar], how could the rabbis abrogate something instituted by the men of the Great Synod? Does not the Mishna teach, **A court cannot abrogate anything instituted by another court unless it exceeds [the first court] in learning and number?**[3] Clearly, then, all [the dates] were instituted by the men of the Great Synod, so where are they indicated [in the book of Esther]?

Rav Shemen bar Ahava said in the name of Rabbi Yoḥanan: Scripture says, **THESE DAYS OF PURIM SHALL BE OBSERVED *BI-Z'MANEIHEM* ['in their times']** (Esther 9:31) – many [different] times were ordained for them.

Isn't that expression demanded by the context?[4] If that [were all], Scripture could have said *z'man*

3. Mishna *Eduyot* 1:5 (see p. 536).
4. That chapter of Esther has already made clear that Purim is celebrated on 15 in walled cities and on 14 elsewhere.

('time'); *z'maneihem* [indicates] many times[, not just the two specified in the context].

[Surely] it is still required [for the context], since there are [several] different times?[5]

If so, it could have said *z'manam* ('their time'); *z'maneihem* [indicates] *all* the times [from 11 onward].

Perhaps it means many [more] times?

[No.] *Z'maneihem* is like *z'manam*; just as *z'manam* [covers] two days, so *z'maneihem* [covers] two [extra] days.

I might think [this includes] 12 and 13 [but not 11. This is not the case, for] as Rav Shmuel bar Isaac said, 13 is a public gathering anyway, so need not have been specified; here likewise, 13 is a public gathering and does not need to be specified.

I might think [it includes] 16 and 17. This cannot be the case either, for it is written, [these days] SHALL NOT PASS (Esther 9:27).

But Rabbi Shmuel bar Naḥmani noted, Scripture says, AS THE DAYS ON WHICH THE JEWS HAD RELIEF [FROM THEIR ENEMIES] (Esther 9:22) – days 'as the days' [, i.e. two days, namely] 11 and 12.

I might think [this includes] 12 and 13. [No. For] as Rav Shmuel bar Isaac said, 13 is a public gathering anyway, so did not need to be specified; here likewise, 13 is a public gathering and does not need to be specified.

I might think [it includes] 16 and 17. [No. For] as it is written, [these days] SHALL NOT PASS (Esther 9:27).

Why did Rabbi Shmuel bar Naḥmani not derive [the dates] from *z'maneihem*? Because he did not regard the difference between *z'manam* and *z'maneihem* as significant.

Why did Rav Shemen bar Ahava not derive

5.   There are two dates, 14 and 15, so a plural is required.

[the dates] from As the days? Because he
interprets that in the context of future generations.

Rabba bar bar Ḥana said in the name of Rabbi Yoḥanan,
[Our Mishna is] the unattributed opinion of Rabbi Aqiva, for
he interprets *z'man, z'manam, z'maneihem*; but the [majority]
of the Sages hold that the *megilla* is read only at its [proper]
time[, namely 14 and 15 Adar].

An objection was raised: **Rabbi Judah says, When is this
done? When the years are in order, and Israel dwell in their
land. But nowadays, since people focus on it, [the *megilla*] is
read only at the specified times [on 14 and 15].**[6] Whose opinion
is Rabbi Judah interpreting? It cannot be Rabbi Aqiva's, since
[Rabbi Aqiva] holds that even nowadays [villagers read it on an
earlier day]. So it must be that of the Sages [who oppose Aqiva,
and yet he states that] when the years are in order, and Israel
dwell in their land, we do read [on the advanced dates]. This
refutes Rabbi Yoḥanan's position.

Another version [of the preceding discussion]:

Rabba bar bar Ḥana said in the name of Rabbi Yoḥanan,
[Our Mishna is] the unattributed opinion of Rabbi Aqiva, for
he interprets *z'man, z'manam, z'maneihem*; but the [majority]
of the Sages hold that nowadays the *megilla* is read only at its
[proper] time, since people look towards it.

A baraita supports this: **Rabbi Judah says, When is this done?
When the years are in order, and Israel dwell in their land.
But nowadays, since people focus on it, [the *megilla*] is read
only at the specified times [on 14 and 15].**

Rav Ashi found [the statements attributed to] Rabbi Judah
contradictory, and [therefore] attributed the baraita to Rabbi
Yosé bar Yehuda[, arguing]: Did Rabbi Judah really say that
nowadays, since people look towards it, [the *megilla*] is read
only at the specified times? As against that, [the next Mishna   2b

6. Rabbi Judah is concerned with fixing the correct date for Passover. With the
    people scattered and communications unreliable, people count the days from
    Purim to Passover, and if Purim were held on 11 or 12, there would be confusion
    – Rashi.

states:] **Rabbi Judah said, Where does this apply? In places where [the villagers] enter [the towns] on Mondays and Thursdays, but where they do not enter on Mondays and Thursdays, [the *megilla*] is read only on the specified dates.** [That is,] in those places where [the villagers] enter [the towns] on Mondays and Thursdays, [the *megilla*] is read [on those days] even nowadays. The baraita [that says otherwise] must therefore be attributed to Rabbi Yosé bar Yehuda.

So because he has a problem with contradictory statements of Rabbi Judah, he attributes the baraita to Rabbi Yosé bar Yehuda? [Yes, for] Rav Ashi had learned that some taught the baraita in the name of Rabbi Judah, and some in the name of Rabbi Yosé bar Yehuda; as he found the statements [attributed to] Rabbi Judah contradictory, he reasoned that those who taught in the name of Rabbi Judah were incorrect, but those who taught in the name of Rabbi Yosé bar Yehuda were correct.

By the time the Mishna was compiled the influential Greek-speaking Jewish community of Egypt had declined dramatically. It would have been known, however, that Alexandrian Jews read the Torah in Greek rather than in the original Hebrew, and also that their text – the Greek Septuagint – differed in many details from the Hebrew text used by the rabbis.[7]

The rabbis were also aware of an ancient Hebrew script that differed markedly from that in their own scrolls. They refer to the ancient script as k'tav 'Ivri *('Hebrew script'), and to their own as* k'tav Ashuri *('Assyrian script'); nowadays, they are known respectively as palaeo-Hebrew and Aramaic. The rabbis attributed the adoption of* k'tav Ashuri *to Ezra, but how could even Ezra dare to change the 'Hebrew' script presumably given to Moses at Sinai?*

7. Modern scholars recognize three distinct textual traditions for the Hebrew Bible: the proto-Masoretic, from which the Masoretic text now in common use developed, and which was the text accepted by the rabbis of the Talmud; the Hebrew Septuagint-*Vorlage*, on which the Greek Septuagint was based; and the proto-Samaritan, from which the Samaritan Pentateuch was derived. See Tov, *Textual Criticism*.

Mezuza
The container holds a sheet of parchment on which
Deuteronomy 6:4–9 and 11:13–21 are written in Hebrew.

MISHNA:

The only difference [in law] between scrolls [on the one   8b
hand] and *tefillin* and *mezuzot* [on the other], is that scrolls
may be written in any language, whereas *tefillin* and *mezuzot*
may be written only in Assyrian [script]. Rabban Simeon ben
Gamaliel says, They only permitted scrolls to be written in
Greek[, and not in any other language apart from Hebrew].

GEMARA:

So they are the same with respect to sewing [the parchment]
with sinews, and defiling the hands.[8]

8. The expression 'defiles the hands' paradoxically defines what constitutes sacred
    Scripture (see introductory note to *Yadayim*, p. 714).

Scrolls may be written in any language. They objected: [Another Mishna states:] **Scripture written as Targum, or Targum written as Scripture,**[9] or [palaeo-]Hebrew characters, do not defile the hands. **Only that written in Assyrian characters, on a scroll, in ink[, defiles the hands].**[10]

9a   Rava said: There is no contradiction; one [Mishna refers to] our script, the other to their script.

Abbaye said to him, Are you suggesting that [the other Mishna] speaks of their script? If so, what is meant by **Scripture written as Targum, or Targum written as Scripture?** Even if someone wrote Scripture as Scripture or Targum as Targum [in the wrong script], the same [would apply], since the Mishna states [explicitly], **Only that written in Assyrian characters, on a scroll, in ink.**

But there is no contradicton, since one [Mishna is the opinion of] the Sages, and the other [is the opinion of] Rabban Simeon ben Gamaliel.

But if [it is] Rabban Simeon ben Gamaliel, he [permits] Greek!

Then there is no contradicton – one [Mishna speaks of] scrolls, the other of *tefillin* and *mezuzot*. The reason that *tefillin* and *mezuzot* are different is that it says, **AND THEY SHALL BE** (Deuteronomy 6:6), [meaning] they must be just they are[, namely in Hebrew].

But what **Targum written as Scripture** could there be [in *tefillin* and *mezuzot*]? In the Torah [itself] you have [the Aramaic words] *Y'gar Sahaduta* (Genesis 31:57), but what Aramaic is there here [in *tefillin* and *mezuzot*]?

So there is no contradiction – one [Mishna speaks of the] scroll [of Esther], the other of [other] scrolls. The reason that Esther is different is that it says, **AS THEY ARE WRITTEN, AND IN THEIR LANGUAGE** (Esther 9:27).

But what **Targum written as Scripture** is there [in Esther]? Rav Papa said, [The word *pitgam* in] **AND THE WORD [***PITGAM***] OF THE KING SHALL BE HEARD** (Esther 1:20); Rav Naḥman bar

9.   i.e. if the Hebrew words are written in Aramaic or vice versa.
10.   Mishna *Yadayim* 4:5.

Isaac said, [The word *y'qar* in] **ALL THE WOMEN SHALL GIVE HONOUR [*Y'QAR*] TO THEIR HUSBANDS** (Esther 1:20).

Rav Ashi said, That [Mishna] applies to other books, and it is the opinion of Rabbi Judah, for a baraita states: *Tefillin* **and** *mezuzot* **may only be written in Assyrian [characters], but our rabbis permitted Greek.**

But doesn't it say, **AND THEY SHALL BE** (Deuteronomy 6:6)?

Then say, **Other books may be written in any language, but our rabbis permitted Greek.**

Permitted? Does this imply that the first Tanna forbade [Greek]?

Rather, say, **But our rabbis only permitted them to be written in Greek.** Moreover, a baraita states: **Rabbi Judah says, Even when our rabbis permitted Greek, they permitted only the Torah Scroll to be written in Greek, on account of the matter of King Ptolemy.**

Starting with Ptolemy I Soter (c. 367–282 BCE) the Greek rulers of Egypt founded and maintained the great library of Alexandria, known as the Museum. This was intended to be an international library, incorporating not only all Greek literature but also translations into Greek from the other languages of the Mediterranean, the Middle East and India. The Greek translation of the Hebrew Scriptures known as the Septuagint, or Translation of the Seventy, may have found a place there.

The Letter of Aristeas, a pseudepigraphal work by an Alexandrian Jew, probably written in the mid-second century BCE to promote the cause of Judaism, is the earliest account of the translation of the Hebrew Scriptures by seventy-two scholars, drawn 'from the twelve tribes of Israel', and completed in seventy-two days.[11] Philo states that Ptolemy II Philadelphus, who ruled Egypt 285–246 BCE, sent to the High Priest in Jerusalem to commission a translation of the Jewish Law; Josephus

---

11.   *Letter of Aristeas*, 46–50, 307. There may be a literary connection with another story that gained circulation at about the same time, according to which seventy-two *grammatikoi* independently edited the work of Homer, the finest version, that of Aristarchus of Samothrace, being selected on the basis of a competition (James I. Porter, 'Hermeneutic Lines and Circles: Tristarchus and Crates on the Exegesis of Homer', in Lamberton and Keaney, *Homer's Ancient Readers*, pp. 67–8.)

tells the story too, clearly citing the Letter of Aristeas.[12] *None of these gives any inkling of a miracle in which seventy-two independent translators came up with identical modifications of the text; this element in the story appears to be a way of explaining known textual divergences, defending the doctrine of the perfect revealed Torah and demonstrating divine guidance of the affairs of men.*

The Gemara's narrative is tabulated here for convenience. 'Standard version' is a translation of the Masoretic Hebrew text, identical in these instances with that before the rabbis; 'Amended version' is a translation of the text as the rabbis allege the translators modified it. Three of the modifications agree with the extant Septuagint text (Genesis 2:2; Exodus 12:40; Numbers 16:15); the others seem motivated by apologetic and theological considerations.

For it was taught: **King Ptolemy gathered seventy-two elders, set them in seventy-two houses and did not disclose why he had put them there. He visited each one [separately] and said to him, Write out for me the Torah of your teacher, Moses!**

The Holy One, blessed be He, put counsel into the mind of each one, so that they were all of one opinion.[13] **This is what they wrote:**

	Standard version	Amended version
Genesis 1:1	In the beginning God created.	God created the beginning.[14]
Genesis 1:26	Let Us make man in Our image, after Our likeness.	I shall make man in an image and a likeness.[15]
Genesis 2:2	And [God] finished on the seventh day, and He rested on the seventh day.	And [God] finished on the sixth day, and He rested on the seventh day.[16]

12. Philo, *Life of Moses* 2:5–7; Josephus, *Antiquities* 12:2.
13. That is, they independently produced the identical text.
14. Nothing existed before God. Greek inflections prevent any ambiguity; the Septuagint follows the Hebrew precisely.
15. i.e. the translators avoided both the plural (God has no partner) and the anthropomorphism of suggesting that God has a human form.
16. This conforms to the Septuagint text; God did *not* work on the seventh day.

	Standard version	Amended version
Genesis 5:2	He created them male and female.	He created him[17] male and female.
Genesis 11:7	Let Us descend and confound their language.	I shall descend and confound their language.[18]
Genesis 18:12	And Sarah laughed inside herself.	And Sarah laughed among her relatives.[19]
Genesis 49:6	For in their anger they slew a man, and willingly they maimed an ox.	For in their anger they slew an ox,[20] and willingly they damaged the crib.
Exodus 4:20	So Moses took his wife and sons, and mounted them on an ass.	So Moses took his wife and sons, and mounted them on a people-carrier.[21]
Exodus 12:40	And the time that the Israelites lived in Egypt was four hundred and thirty years.	And the time that the Israelites lived in Egypt and other lands was four hundred and thirty years.[22]
Exodus 24:5	He sent some young men of the Israelites.	He sent some *za'tuté*[23] of the Israelites.

17. A midrash states that Adam was created hermaphrodite.
18. God has no partner.
19. It is apparently indecent to refer to a woman's 'inside', though the Septuagint was not so squeamish. *Qarov* ('relative') comes from the same root as *qerev* ('inside').
20. So the ancestors of the Jews were not murderers.
21. No one should think that Moses could not afford a horse or a camel – Rashi.
22. A chronological problem in Scripture led the rabbis to count the 430 years from the Covenant of the Pieces in the time of Abraham. Septuagint reads 'that the Israelites lived in the land of Egypt and the land of Canaan'.
23. The language, meaning and spelling of this word are obscure. Rashi suggests that it is a more dignified term than the Hebrew *na'aré* in verse 5, which could mean 'servants'; but as Tosafot point out, in that case they ought to have adjusted it to 'elders', as in verse 11. The Septuagint is untroubled, and corresponds precisely with the Hebrew *na'aré*.

	Standard version	**Amended version**
Exodus 24:11	He did not raise His hand against the leaders of the Israelites.	He did not raise His hand against the *zaʾtuté* of the Israelites.
Numbers 16:15	I have not taken the ass of any one of them.	I have not taken the desirable [possession][24] of any of them.
Deuteronomy 4:19	That the Lord your God has allotted to all the [other] nations.	That the Lord your God has allotted to give light to all the nations.[25]
Deuteronomy 17:3	And he went and worshipped other gods . . . that I did not command.	And he went and worshipped other gods . . . that I did not command [him] to worship.[26]

9b (marginal to Numbers row)

They also wrote 'the swift of foot' instead of 'the hare' [in the list of forbidden animals in Leviticus 11:6], since Ptolemy's wife was called 'Hare';[27] they did not want him to think, The Jews are mocking me by putting my wife's name in the Torah.

In the light of the perceived ideological conflict between Greece and Israel, the conclusion that follows is astonishing. It is a powerful endorsement of the beauty to be found in Greek culture, with the proviso that it be used to articulate the values of Israel.

Rabban Simeon ben Gamaliel says, They permitted scrolls

24. Perhaps again a prejudice against asses. However, the emendation is supported by the Septuagint; it reads *epithumēma*, 'object of desire', which presupposes a difference of just one root consonant in the Hebrew.

25. Without 'to give light' it might appear that God had allotted the sun, moon, stars, etc., to the other nations to worship.

26. The point may be similar to the preceding, though Rashi suggests that without the words 'to worship' it might have been inferred that God did not command the sun, moon, etc., to exist, and that they are independent Powers.

27. Ptolemy I, son of the nobleman Lagus, is sometimes known as Ptolemy Lagus, and his successors as Lagids. *Lagōs* is Greek for 'hare', and was not the name of any of Ptolemy's wives.

to be written only in Greek[, and no other language apart from Hebrew].

Rabbi Abbahu said in the name of Rabbi Yoḥanan, The law is in accordance with [the opinion of] Rabban Simeon ben Gamaliel. Rabbi Yoḥanan said, moreover, that Rabban Simeon ben Gamaliel based his opinion on a verse of Scripture: GOD WILL GRANT BEAUTY TO JAPHETH,[28] AND HE WILL DWELL IN THE TENTS OF SHEM (Genesis 9:27).

Perhaps Gomer and Magog[29] are meant? Rabbi Ḥiyya bar Abba said, Since it says WILL GRANT BEAUTY TO JAPHETH, it means that Japheth's beauty will dwell in the tents of Shem.[30]

Public prayer may be led by any competent male from the age of thirteen. However, an individual may be disqualified because he is improperly dressed, his pronunciation is unsatisfactory or he is a heretic. As the prayers were not rigidly fixed in the period of the Mishna, the rabbis were on their guard against prayer leaders who might introduce heretical ideas. Christians may well have tried to infiltrate their beliefs into the synagogue prayers, and this may underlie the Gospel's allegation (John 9:22, 12:42, 16:2) that they were driven out of the synagogue.

Zoroastrianism was the dominant religion in the Parthian and Sasanian Empires, and Gnostic cults that shared its belief in two Powers, one good and one evil, struggling for supremacy in the world, had spread through much of the Roman Empire by the time of the Mishna. Mishna and Gemara show how Jews reacted by insisting that a single Power, God, was responsible for all that happens, whether it appears to us good or bad.

The passage includes remarks on the rationality of the mitzvot *and a brief but illuminating comment attributed to Rabbi Ḥanina on free will and determinism.*

28. Several alternative translations do not fit here, e.g. 'God will enlarge Japheth.'
29. Descendants of Japheth, cf. Genesis 10:2. Javan, the eponymous ancestor of the Greeks, was another descendant (10:2, 4).
30. 'Grant beauty' and 'Japheth' are spelled exactly the same in Hebrew. There is no doubt that the beauty of Japheth is pre-eminently expressed through the culture of Javan (Greece).

CHAPTER FOUR

MISHNA:

24b   If someone says, I will not stand at the [prayer-]lectern[31] in coloured [garments], he may not do so even in white; [if he says,] I will not [lead prayer] wearing sandals, he may not do so even barefoot.

If someone makes his *tefillin* round, it is dangerous, and does not fulfil the *mitzva*. Placing them on his forehead or in the palm of his hand is the manner of sectarians. If he overlays them with gold or places them over his sleeve, this is the way of outsiders.[32]

GEMARA:

Why? We suspect that he is affected by heresy[, since he insists on something that is not required by the law].

If someone makes his *tefillin* round, it is dangerous, and does not fulfil the *mitzva*. Surely we have learned this [elsewhere], for a baraita states: **Square *tefillin* are a [requirement of the] law [received by] Moses at Sinai**, and Rava clarified that that applied to the stitching and the diagonal. Rav Papa said, Our Mishna [covers the additional case] where he made them like a Magus.[33]

MISHNA:

25a   'May the good bless You' is a form of heresy. 'Your mercy extends to the bird's nest; may Your name be mentioned for goodness!' or 'We give thanks! We give thanks!' – if anyone prays in that form, he should be silenced.

Anyone who interprets the scriptural verses about forbidden sexual unions metaphorically should be silenced.

If anyone interprets YOU SHALL NOT GIVE OF YOUR SEED TO PASS OVER TO MOLECH (Leviticus 18:21) as You shall

---

31. To lead prayers.
32. The difference between 'sectarians' and 'outsiders' is unclear, and the text uncertain. Rashi suggests the former were people who belittled rabbinic tradition and the latter simply followed their independent interpretations of Scripture.
33. Rav Papa's meaning is obscure. Possibly Magi (Zoroastrian priests) made amulets resembling *tefillin*.

not impregnate an Aramean woman, he should be firmly silenced.[34]

GEMARA:

Now, **We give thanks! We give thanks!** is clearly [unacceptable], for it looks as if [he is praying] to two Powers. **May Your name be mentioned for goodness!** is also [clearly unacceptable], for it sounds as if we should praise God for good things, but not for bad, and a Mishna states, **One should bless [God when] bad things happen just as one does for good [tidings].**[35] But what is wrong with **Your mercy extends to the bird's nest?**

Two Amoraim in the West, Rabbi Yosé bar Avin and Rabbi Yosé bar Zevida, debated this. One said, [It is wrong because] it implies favouritism in creation.[36] The other said, [It is wrong because] it implies that God's [only] attribute is mercy, whereas [His commandments] are decrees.[37]

Someone was leading the prayers in the presence of Rabba, and said, You have pity on the bird's nest – have pity on us! Rabba remarked, How beautifully this scholar knows how to appeal to his Master! Abbaye said, But doesn't the Mishna say you should silence him? Rabba was simply trying to sharpen Abbaye's wits.[38]

Someone leading the prayers in the presence of Rabbi Ḥanina said, Great, mighty, awesome, noble, strong and powerful God! Have you finished praising your Master? asked Rabbi Ḥanina. If not that the three epithets [we normally use in prayer] had been written by Moses in the Torah and fixed in prayer by the men of the Great Synod, we could not [dare to] say them, yet you say all that! It is as if a man were to have billions of gold pieces, and people praised him as possessing a few silver denarii; wouldn't that be an insult?

---

34. This statement may be directed against views expressed in the apocryphal Testament of Levi (14:6) and in Jubilees (30:7–10); the latter compares a father who gave his daughter in marriage to a non-Jew to a father who gave her to Moloch.
35. Mishna *Berakhot* 9:5 (48b). This is a rejection of Zoroastrian dualism.
36. As if to say, God has pity on birds but not on animals – Rashi.
37. God's attributes are beyond our understanding, and we cannot know the reasons for His commandments. This is peremptorily dismissed by Maimonides (*Guide* 3:48), who staunchly upholds the rationality of the commandments.
38. Rabba adopted Abbaye as a child and was his teacher.

Rabbi Ḥanina said, All is in the control of Heaven except the fear of Heaven, as it is said, AND NOW, O ISRAEL, WHAT DOES THE LORD YOUR GOD ASK OF YOU BUT TO FEAR HIM? (Deuteronomy 10:12).

Is the fear of Heaven just a small thing, then? Yes – for Moses our Teacher it was a small thing. If you ask someone for a large item and he has it, it is like a small thing to him; if you ask him for a small item and he doesn't have it, it is like a large thing to him.

Rabbi Zeira said, If someone says, *Shema! Shema!* it is like saying, We give thanks! We give thanks! [He gives the impression of serving two Powers.] They objected [to Rabbi Zeira]: **If someone says *Shema* and doubles it, it is improper** – improper, but you don't have to silence him. No objection – if he repeats word by word[, it is improper, but does not appear to be serving two Powers]; if he repeats verse by verse[, it is like serving two Powers, and he should be silenced].

Rav Papa said to Rava, Perhaps [he is only repeating the verse] because he didn't concentrate the first time and now he is concentrating. Do you treat Heaven like a [familiar] friend! retorted Rava – if he didn't concentrate, hit him with a hammer so he does concentrate![39]

Anyone who interprets the scriptural verses about forbidden sexual unions metaphorically should be silenced. Rav Yosef [gave as an example], If someone said that YOU SHALL NOT UNCOVER YOUR FATHER'S NAKEDNESS OR YOUR MOTHER'S NAKEDNESS (Leviticus 18:7), it meant you shouldn't reveal anything that might embarrass them.

If anyone interprets YOU SHALL NOT GIVE OF YOUR SEED TO PASS OVER TO MOLECH. It was taught in the School of Rabbi Ishmael: [**The Mishna has in mind someone who says that**] Scripture here speaks of an Israelite who had sex with a non-Israelite [woman] and engendered a child for idolatry.

---

39. i.e. a person should not be so lacking in the fear of God that he fails to concentrate.

ELEVENTH TRACTATE
MO'ED QATAN (MIDDLE DAYS OF FESTIVALS)

The festivals of Passover and Tabernacles last, respectively, for seven and eight days. Scripture designates the first and last days as 'holy gatherings' on which work, other than food preparation and the like, is forbidden. The days between – Hebrew Ḥol ha-Mo'ed, literally 'the unconsecrated [days] of the festival' – are sacred to a minor degree, and some kinds of work are forbidden on them. This tractate gives examples of what may or may not be done, though it does not formulate any underlying principle. Rashi says that the Torah delegated to the Sages to determine what kinds of work were allowed, and that they permitted anything that might cause significant financial loss if neglected, for instance, irrigating fields.

CHAPTER ONE

MISHNA:

You may irrigate a parched field on the intermediate days of a festival or in the sabbatical year, whether with an established spring or a newly flowing one, but you must not use rainwater or deep-well water.

You may not make circular depressions around vines [to retain moisture].

Rabbi Eleazar ben Azaria says, You may not make new irrigation channels in the sabbatical year, but the Sages say, You may make new irrigation channels in the sabbatical year, and you may repair damaged ones on the intermediate days of a festival. You may [also] repair damaged public water supplies and dig them out, repair paths, roads and immersion pools, do whatever the public needs, and mark burial sites; [officers of the court] may go out [to uproot] *kil'ayim*.

GEMARA:

Now surely if you are allowed to water from a newly flowing spring which might collapse [and involve heavy repairs], you would be allowed to water from an established one, which is unlikely to collapse[, so why mention the established one]? It was necessary, they say, to specify both. Had Mishna specified only a newly flowing spring I might have reasoned that [permission was given] here to irrigate a parched field, even though [the spring] might collapse, but it would not be permitted to irrigate a moist field; but if the spring was an established one, unlikely to collapse, you could irrigate even a moist field with it. Mishna therefore informs you that it makes no difference whether the spring is new or established, you may use it to water a parched field, but not a moist one.

How do we know that the [Mishna's] expression *beit ha-sh'laḥin* means 'parched'? The Targum of YOU WERE FAINT AND WEARY (Deuteronomy 25:18) is *v'at m'shalhi v'lai*.[1]

How do we know that *beit ha-ba'al* denotes a moist [literally, 'satisfied'] field? The verse FOR AS A YOUNG MAN TAKES SATIS-FACTION[2] WITH A VIRGIN (Isaiah 62:5) is rendered by the Targum, 'For as a young man is satisfied with a virgin, Your children will find satisfaction in You.'

Which Tanna is it who holds that [avoidance of] loss [is permitted on intermediate days,] but making profit is not?

Rav Huna says, It is Rabbi Eliezer ben Jacob, for [a later] Mishna states, **Rabbi Eliezer ben Jacob says, You may channel water from one tree to another, provided you do not irrigate the whole field.**

You may [indeed] infer from this that Rabbi Eliezer ben

---

1. i.e. the Aramaic translation of 'faint' has a similar root to the term the Mishna uses for the field.
2. The root of this word, like the one in the Mishna, is *B'L*, and, as in the name Baal, has to do with mastery; it also has a strong sexual connotation, and is often translated by a euphemism.

Jacob holds that [work merely] for profit is not allowed, but how do you know that he permits heavy work to avoid loss?

Rava Papa said, It is Rabbi Judah, for a baraita teaches: **If a spring erupts [on the intermediate days], you may use it to irrigate even a moist field, according to Rabbi Meir. Rabbi Judah says, You may only use it to irrigate a parched field that is ruined. Rabbi Eleazar ben Azaria says, You may do neither. Moreover, said Rabbi Judah, On the intermediate days, a man may not divert a channel of water to irrigate his vegetable garden or his ruined plot.**

> What does he mean by 'ruined'? If it is literally ruined, what is the point of irrigating it? Abbaye said, He means 'ruined' by [the failure of] its [original] spring, but another one has erupted; and to this Rabbi Eleazar responds, It makes no difference – whether or not [the original] spring has failed, he may not use a newly flowing spring.

How [does the baraita imply that Rabbi Judah holds that avoidance of loss is permitted on intermediate days, but making profit is not]? Perhaps when Rabbi Judah permits irrigating only a parched field, not a moist one, he [is speaking] of a newly flowing spring [and is worried that] it might collapse, but [in the case of] an established spring, which is unlikely to collapse, he would permit irrigation even of a moist field.   2b

If that is what you think, whose opinion does our Mishna accord with? [None.] So [we must conclude that] for Rabbi Judah, whether the spring is new or established, you may [irrigate] a parched field, but not a moist one. When the Mishna speaks of a newly flowing spring, this is to tell you how far Rabbi Meir [is prepared to] go – he permits you to irrigate even a moist field, and even with a newly flowing spring.

The Sages forbade shaving and laundering during the festival, in order to ensure that people did these things in advance and looked their best when the festival began. Certain categories – for instance, a person released from imprisonment, one who returned from a long journey or one whose period of mourning ended as the festival began – were permitted to shave on the intermediate days, since it was not possible for them to do so earlier.

As the topic of mourning was mentioned, the editors chose to review the laws here, since they are nowhere systematically presented in the Mishna. Leviticus sets out the list of relatives for whom one is obliged to mourn, and there is mention of mourning for prominent leaders such as Jacob (Genesis 50:1–14), Aaron (Numbers 20:29) and Moses (Deuteronomy 34:8), but the Torah has little to say on mourning procedures for ordinary people.

The most intense period of mourning is the seven days (shivʿa) beginning with the day of burial; the common Jewish expression 'to sit shivʿa' refers to this period, when the mourners sit on the ground or on low stools or and are visited by those offering condolence. This is followed by shʾloshim ('thirty' – the thirty days include the first seven), a time of less intense mourning. Parents are mourned for twelve months.

This Mishna deals with the conflict that arises when a period of private mourning clashes with a festival. The sugya on mourning is somewhat loosely constructed, perhaps because there is so little foundation in Scripture; the rules evolved as social custom rather than law, and several Tannaim take positions at variance with the Mishna. In accordance with Shmuel's principle (19b) that, in respect of the laws of mourning, the decision goes according to the more lenient authority, it is decided that so long as the period of shivʿa or shʾloshim commenced before the festival, the festival cancels it.

CHAPTER THREE

MISHNA:

19a   **If someone buries his dead three days prior to a pilgrim festival, the law of *shivʿa* ceases to apply to him; if eight days [prior to the festival], the law of *shʾloshim* does not apply.**

The principle is,[3] Shabbat is counted [as a day of mourning even though outward signs of mourning are forbidden] and

---

3.   Literally, 'for they say'.

does not cut short [the period of mourning]; festival days cut short [the period of mourning], but are not counted [towards a period of mourning].

Rabbi Eliezer said, Since the destruction of the Temple, Shavuot is [in this respect] like the Sabbath. Rabban Gamaliel says, Rosh Hashana and Yom Kippur are like pilgrim festivals [in this respect]. The [majority of] Sages, however, say, [The law] is according to neither, but Shavuot is like a pilgrim festival, and Rosh Hashana and Yom Kippur are like the Sabbath.

GEMARA:

The rabbis taught: A man must mourn for all those [relatives] specified in the Priestly Code[4] for whom a *Kohen* is obliged to defile himself. They are: wife, father, mother, brother, [virgin] sister, son and daughter. [The rabbis] added: Maternal brother, maternal virgin sister, married sister whether paternal or maternal.

20b

Rabbi Aqiva says, Just as he mourns for them, he mourns for their 'seconds';[5] but Rabbi Simeon ben Eleazar says, The only 'seconds' he mourns for are his son's son and his father's father. The [other] Sages say, Whoever he mourns *for*, he mourns *with*.[6]

Doesn't what the Sages say come to the same as what [Rabbi Aqiva] says? The difference [between them] is, that [the Sages rule that he should mourn only] if he is in the same house [as the principal mourner, whereas Rabbi Aqiva rules that he should mourn irrespective]. This is like what Rav told his son Ḥiyya, and Rav Huna told his son Rabba: When you are with her[7] observe the mourning [rites]; when you are not with her don't observe the mourning [rites].

A son of Mar Uqba's mother-in-law died, so he decided to observe *shiv'a* and *sh'loshim* for him. Rav Huna paid [Mar

4. 'Code' here refers to Leviticus 21 and 22 only. The relatives for whom a *Kohen* must defile himself by burying them (contact with a corpse defiles) are listed in 21:2–3.
5. Father's father, son's son, daughter's son, sister's son – Rashi.
6. e.g. if his father's father dies, he mourns together with his father.
7. Your wife, as she is in mourning for her relative.

Uqba] a visit. Will you eat *tzuranaita?*[8] [he asked.] When they said [you should observe mourning] out of respect to your wife, that was only if your father-in-law or mother-in-law [died], as a baraita teaches: **If someone's father-in-law or mother-in-law died, he may not oblige his wife to make up with kohl or rouge, but should overturn the couch and observe the mourning [rites] with her. The same goes for her – if her father-in-law or mother-in-law died, she should not make up with kohl or rouge, but should overturn the couch and observe the mourning [rites] with him.**

But another baraita states: **Even though they said he may not oblige his wife to make up with kohl or rouge, she may pour out his cup, make his bed and wash his face, hands and feet.** Isn't this a contradiction? It must be that one [baraita] [deals with a case where] his father-in-law or mother-in-law [died], and the other where some other relative had died. That is proof.

Another baraita states [explicitly]: **When they said [you should observe mourning] out of respect to your wife, that was only if your father-in-law or mother-in-law [died].**

The son of Amemar's son died, and [Amemar] rent [his garments] over him. When [Amemar's] son arrived, [Amemar] again rent [his garments]. Then [Amemar] realized that he had rent [his garments] sitting, so he got up and rent them [again] standing.

Rav Ashi [then] asked Amemar, What basis is there for standing to rend [garments]?

[He replied:] **THEN JOB STOOD UP AND RENT HIS ROBE** (Job 1:20).

21a   [Ashi:] In that case, [what about] **AND HE STANDS AND SAYS, I DON'T WISH TO MARRY HER** (Deuteronomy 25:8)? [Must he stand to proclaim his refusal?] A baraita states, **Whether sitting, standing or lying down.**

[Amemar] replied, [Deuteronomy] does not say

---

8.   A word of uncertain etymology (Sokoloff, *Babylonian*), but evidently food for mourners – Rashi.

AND HE STOOD; Job says HE STOOD UP AND RENT
HIS ROBE.

Rami bar Ḥama commented: What basis is there
for standing to rend [garments]? JOB STOOD UP AND
RENT HIS ROBE. Perhaps [Job] did something beyond
[the normal requirement]? [Indeed, you have to say
Job's behaviour was excessive,] otherwise HE CUT OFF
HIS HAIR (Job 1:20) [would have to be applied literally,] too.

So [we derive it] from here: THE KING AROSE AND RENT
HIS GARMENT (2 Samuel 13:31). [No.] Perhaps [David] did
something beyond [the normal requirement]? [Indeed, you have
to say David's behaviour was excessive,] otherwise AND HE LAY
UPON THE GROUND (2 Samuel 13:31) [would have to be applied
literally,] too. However, a baraita states, If he sat on a couch, a
chair, a teacher's chair or the floor,[9] he has not complied with
the law – and Rabbi Yohanan said, [This is] because he has not
complied with the rule to overturn the couch.

Rami bar Ḥama replied: [Scripture means that David lay on
the upturned couch] as if on the ground.

The rabbis taught: These are the things a mourner must
not do: work, washing, anointing, sexual intercourse, wearing
shoes. He must also not read Torah, Prophets or Hagiographa,
or study Mishna, Midrash, *halakhot*, Talmud or *aggada*. However, if the public are dependent on him [for learning], he may
do so; when Rabbi Yosé's son died in Sepphoris, he attended
the House of Study and expounded [Torah] throughout the
day.

Rabba bar bar Ḥana suffered a bereavement. He thought he
should not go out [to deliver] the lesson, but Rabbi Ḥanina
reminded him, If the public are dependent on him [for learn-
ing], he may do so. He thought it would be all right to appoint
an assistant [to deliver the lecture], but Rav said to him, A
baraita teaches, So long as he does not appoint an assistant. So
what could he do? He acted similarly to what is reported in a

---

9.   There are variant readings here, and an obscure word, translated (following Jastrow,
      Dictionary) as 'teacher's chair'.

baraita: **A son of Rabbi Judah bar Ilai died. He [nevertheless] entered the House of Study. Rabbi Ḥanania ben Aqavia came and sat next to him. He whispered [the lecture] to Rabbi Ḥanania ben Aqavia; Rabbi Ḥanania ben Aqavia [rehearsed it] to the assistant and the assistant delivered it to the public.**

TWELFTH TRACTATE
ḤAGIGA (THE FESTIVAL SACRIFICE)

NONE SHALL APPEAR BEFORE ME EMPTY-HANDED ... THREE TIMES A YEAR ALL YOUR MALES SHALL APPEAR BEFORE THE SOVEREIGN, THE LORD. (Exodus 23:15, 17 JPS)

THREE TIMES A YEAR – ON THE FEAST OF UNLEAVENED BREAD, ON THE FEAST OF WEEKS, AND ON THE FEAST OF BOOTHS – ALL YOUR MALES SHALL APPEAR BEFORE THE LORD YOUR GOD IN THE PLACE THAT HE WILL CHOOSE. THEY SHALL NOT APPEAR BEFORE THE LORD EMPTY-HANDED. (Deuteronomy 16:16 JPS)

The rabbis understood that these passages mandated two distinct offerings: a burnt-offering associated with 'appearing before the Lord', and a peace-offering in celebration of the festival.

The pilgrim festivals (Pesach, Shavuot, Sukkot) were popular, joyful occasions. Philo, early in the first century, described the scene vividly:

Countless multitudes from countless cities come, some over land, others over sea, from east and west and north and south at every feast. They take the Temple for their port as a general haven and safe refuge from the bustle and turmoil of life and there they seek to find calm weather and, released from the cares whose yoke has been heavy upon them from their earliest years, to enjoy a brief breathing-space in scenes of genial cheerfulness.[1]

1.   Philo, *Special Laws* 1:69f. (Loeb edn.)

The Mishna appears to say that only those who are male, adult, free, healthy and sane are obliged to 'appear before the Lord'. The Gemara tests the limits of these categories. Two cases are of broader interest. The 'half slave and half freedman' is a classical legal dilemma, and we are reminded that it is an intolerable status, finally outlawed. The deaf-mute throws light on rabbinic attitudes to disability;[2] almost two thousand years were to pass before effective methods were devised to communicate with and educate such people.

CHAPTER ONE

MISHNA:

2a   All are obliged to appear [before the Lord in Jerusalem with an offering[3] at the three pilgrim festivals] except a deaf-mute, an imbecile, a child, a person of undetermined sex, a hermaphrodite, women, slaves who have not been freed, the lame, the blind, the sick, the elderly or anyone incapable of ascending [to Jerusalem] on foot.

Who is a child [for this purpose]? The School of Shammai say, One who can't ride on his father's shoulders and ascend to the Temple Mount in Jerusalem; the School of Hillel say, Anyone who can't hold his father's hand and ascend to the Temple Mount in Jerusalem, as it is said, THREE FOOT[-FESTIVALS][4] (Exodus 23:14).

The School of Shammai say, The appearance-offering must be [worth at least] two silver pieces, and the festival peace-offering one silver *maʿa*; the School of Hillel say, The appearance-offering must be [worth at least] one silver *maʿa*, and the festival peace-offering two silver pieces.

2. For a general study of rabbinic attitudes to disability, see Marx, *Disability*.
3. This is the interpretation of the Tosafot; Rashi leaves open the question of whether an offering is implied at this point.
4. The Hebrew *regel*, 'foot', stands for 'pilgrim festival', since most pilgrims would arrive in Jerusalem on foot. The word is interpreted here as limiting the obligation to attend to those able to walk.

GEMARA:

[**All are obliged to appear.**] Who[, in addition to those specified,] is included in **all**? Someone who is half slave and half freedman.

According to Ravina, who holds that anyone who is half slave and half freedman is exempt from 'appearance', who else is included? Someone who was lame on the first day [of the festival] but cured on the second day.

That is all very well in the view of those who hold that each of the days of the festival may compensate for any of the others, but in the view of those who hold that the later days are a replacement for the first, who is included by **all**?[5] Someone who was blind in one eye.

This would not accord with the opinion of the Tanna in the baraita which states: **Yoḥanan ben Dahavai said in the name of Rabbi Judah, A man who is blind in one eye is exempt from 'appearance', as it is said, HE SHALL APPEAR** (Exodus 23:17) – **just as He comes to see, with two eyes, so shall he appear, with two eyes.**[6]

Alternatively, it is as we said previously, and as to Ravina's question, that is no problem, for one opinion accords with the original Mishna, and the other with the final Mishna. The Mishna states, **The School of Hillel say, Someone who is half slave and half freedman serves his master for a day and himself for a day. The School of Shammai said to them, You have** 26 **provided for his master, but not for himself. He cannot marry a slave-woman, nor can he marry a free woman. Should he remain unmarried? Surely [not, for] the world was created TO BE FRUITFUL AND MULTIPLY** (Genesis 1:28), **as it is said, HE DID NOT CREATE IT A WASTE, BUT FORMED IT FOR HABITATION** (Isaiah 45:18 JPS). **So, in the interest of social justice,[7] his master must be forced to free him [completely] by**

5. In this view, someone who was lame on the first day would be exempt and 'appearance' on the second day would be pointless, seeing that it would serve only to make up for the first day, on which he had no obligation.

6. In unvocalized biblical Hebrew the passive *yera'eh*, 'he shall be seen (appear)', is spelled exactly the same as the active *yir'eh*, 'he shall see'.

7. This is a very free rendition of the Hebrew *mipnei tiqqun ha-'olam*, 'to put the world right'.

writing an acknowledgement of debt to him for half his value. The School of Hillel revised their opinion and ruled as the School of Shammai.[8]

Except a deaf-mute,[9] **an imbecile, a child.** The Mishna lists the *ḥeresh* together with the imbecile and the child – just as the imbecile and the child lack understanding, so the *ḥeresh* [referred to here] is one who lacks understanding. This confirms what the Mishna says [elsewhere], **Whenever the Sages use the term *ḥeresh*, they mean one who neither hears nor speaks.**[10] It follows that someone who speaks but cannot hear, or who can hear but does not speak, is obliged to appear [before the Lord in Jerusalem]. This is what a baraita teaches: **One who speaks but cannot hear is a *ḥeresh*; one who hears but cannot speak is an *'illem*.** Both[, in the eyes of the law,] are of sound mind in every respect.

> How do we know that someone who speaks but cannot hear is called *ḥeresh*, and who can hear but not speak is called *'illem*? From the verse, FOR I AM AS A ḤERESH WHO DOES NOT HEAR, AND AS AN 'ILLEM WHO DOES NOT OPEN HIS MOUTH (Psalm 38:14). Alternatively, from the popular idiom, 'He is lost for words.'[11]

[We just interpreted our Mishna to mean that] someone who speaks but cannot hear, or who can hear but does not speak, is obliged [to appear before the Lord in Jerusalem]. But a baraita teaches, **Someone who speaks but cannot hear, or who can hear but not speak, is exempt!**

Ravina – some say it was Rava – said, The Mishna is incomplete. What it means to say is, **All are obliged to appear [before the Lord in Jerusalem at the three pilgrim festivals] except a deaf-mute. If he speaks but cannot hear, or hears but does not speak, he is exempt from appearing [before the Lord], but though exempt from appearing, he**

---

8.   Mishna *Eduyot* 1:13.
9.   Hebrew *ḥeresh* can mean 'deaf' or 'deaf-mute'.
10. Mishna *Terumot* 1:2.
11. The Aramaic idiom is literally, 'His words are taken from him.' It is unclear what this is meant to prove; Rashi interprets it as an acrostic.

is obliged to rejoice [on the festival. However,] if he can neither hear nor speak, or is an imbecile or a child . . . he is exempt even from the obligation to rejoice, seeing that he is exempt from all the *mitzvot* of the Torah.

A baraita says this too: **All are obliged to appear** [before the Lord in Jerusalem at the three pilgrim festivals] **and to rejoice, except a** *ḥeresh* **who speaks but cannot hear, or who hears but does not speak,** [for] **he is exempt from appearing; but** [even though] **he is exempt from appearing, he is obliged to rejoice. One who neither hears nor speaks, or an imbecile or a child, is exempt even from rejoicing, since he is exempt from all** *mitzvot* **of the Torah.**

3a

What difference is there [between 'appearing' and rejoicing,] that though they are exempt from appearing they are obliged to rejoice? The same expression, 'appear', is used in connection with *haqhel*,[12] as it is written, **ASSEMBLE ALL THE PEOPLE – MEN, WOMEN AND CHILDREN** (Deuteronomy 31:12), and **WHEN ALL ISRAEL COMES TO APPEAR BEFORE THE LORD YOUR GOD** (Deuteronomy 31:11). How do we know [that the deaf-mute is exempt from] that [obligation]? For it is written, **IN ORDER THAT THEY SHOULD HEAR AND IN ORDER THAT THEY SHOULD LEARN** (31:12), and a baraita interprets: **IN ORDER THAT THEY SHOULD HEAR** excludes one who speaks but does not hear; **IN ORDER THAT THEY SHOULD LEARN** excludes one who hears but does not speak.

Do you mean to say that someone who is unable to speak cannot learn? What about those dumb men, sons of Rabbi Yoḥanan ben Gudgada – or some say, sons of Rabbi Yoḥanan's sister – [who lived] in the neighbourhood of Rabbi (Judah ha-Nasi)? Whenever Rabbi entered the House of Study they went and sat before him, nodded their heads and moved their lips. Rabbi prayed for them and they were healed, and it was found that they had mastered the laws, *Sifra*, *Sifré*, and all Talmud![13]

12. The ceremony of the Sabbatical Year at which the king reads the Torah to the assembled nation.
13. *Sifra* and *Sifré* are *halakhic midrashim*. 'Talmud' is used here of the activity of interpretation of Torah, not as the name of a book.

Mar Zutra said, Read [the verse], IN ORDER THAT THEY
SHOULD TEACH.[14]

Rav Ashi said, Scripture must [in any case] mean, IN ORDER
THAT THEY SHOULD TEACH. If you suppose that it means IN
ORDER THAT THEY SHOULD LEARN, and that those who can't
hear can't learn, that could have been inferred from IN ORDER
THAT THEY SHOULD HEAR. So there is no doubt that it means
IN ORDER THAT THEY SHOULD TEACH.

*Next comes one of very few instances in Mishna and Talmud
where there may be some reference to esoteric teachings. There
were undoubtedly circles of Jewish mystics contemporary with
the rabbis; the surviving* Heikhalot *literature graphically
describes the 'journeys' of adepts through heavenly palaces
towards the Holy Presence.[15] However, the Talmud scarcely if
ever refers to them; perhaps the rabbis had reservations about
this kind of activity, particularly if they were mindful of Gnostic
doctrines which downgraded the God of the Scriptures to a
demiurge. As time went on the names of certain Tannaim,
especially Aqiva and Simeon ben Yohai, became associated with
mystical practices, but historians are sceptical of such attributions.*

The terms maʿasé bʼreshit *(the work of Creation – Genesis 1)
and* maʿasé merkava *(the work of the Chariot – Ezekiel 1) used
in this Mishna assumed importance in later Jewish mystical
teaching, and were appropriated by the medieval Kabbalists for
their speculations. At the other extreme, Maimonides interpreted them as physics and metaphysics respectively.*

'The Other' (Hebrew: Aher) *in the Gemara is Elisha ben*

---

14. In unvocalized biblical Hebrew *yilmʼdu* ('they shall learn') and *yʼlammedu* ('they
    shall teach') are spelled exactly the same. Mar Zutra accepts that dumb people can
    learn; however, since they are unable to speak they cannot teach.
15. *Heikhal* means 'palace'; some *heikhalot* hymns are translated in Carmi, *Hebrew
    Verse*, pp. 195–201. On *Hekhalot* and *Merkava* mysticism, see Scholem, *Gnosti-
    cism* and Schäfer, *Hekhalot*. On the relationship between Hermetism, Jewish
    Gnosticism and the Roman and Greek Eucharists, see Gilles Quispel, 'The *Asclep-
    ius*', in van den Broek and Hanegraaff, *Gnosis,*, pp. 69–78. See also 2 Corinthians
    12:1–4.

Avuya, a second-century Tanna who became the prototypical heretic in rabbinic literature. No one knows precisely what form his deviation took, or indeed if he was a heretic at all; some early rabbinic texts treat him as a perfectly ordinary member of his class.[16] Comparison with other versions suggests that this highly developed narrative is a conflation of several anecdotes, possibly relating to different individuals, and treating not only of sin and heresy, but of master/disciple relationships, relations between angels and humans, the virtue of Torah learning, and the redemption of sinners.

Alon Goshen-Gottstein has reassessed the significance of the Elisha ben Avuya stories. How are we to interpret the key story, told in outline in the Tosefta, of the rabbis who entered the 'garden', or orchard? Is it an account of a mystical 'journey' (the traditional view, supported by G. G. Scholem), a parable about four kinds of Torah scholar (E. E. Urbach) or a 'typological' narrative (Goshen-Gottstein's preferred view).[17]

CHAPTER TWO

MISHNA:

The [section of the Torah concerning] forbidden sexual liaisons should not be expounded in the presence of three, nor the Creation in the presence of two, nor the Chariot in the presence of one, unless he is wise and able to understand it on his own.   11b

Whoever contemplates four topics, it would be better had he never been born. These are they: What is above, what is below, what is in front and what is behind.

And whoever does not show concern for the honour of the One to Whom he belongs,[18] it would be better had he never been born.

GEMARA:

The rabbis taught: **Four entered the Garden[19] – Ben Azzai,**   14b

16.   e.g. *Avot de Rabbi Nathan* 4:20; *Mo'ed Qatan* 20a.
17.   Goshen-Gottstein, *Sinner and the Amnesiac*, pp. 48–54.
18.   God. Literally, 'his owner'.
19.   Hebrew *pardes* is a garden or enclosure, often an orchard, and here by analogy the heavenly garden. It should not be confused with later ideas of paradise.

Ben Zoma, The Other[20] and Rabbi Aqiva. Rabbi Aqiva said to them, When you reach the stones of pure marble do not say, Water! Water! For it is said, HE WHO SPEAKS FALSEHOOD SHALL NOT BE FIRM IN MY SIGHT (Psalm 101:7).

Ben Azzai gazed and died. Of him Scripture says, THE DEATH OF HIS FAITHFUL ONES IS GRIEVOUS IN THE LORD'S SIGHT (Psalm 116:15 JPS).

Ben Zoma gazed and went mad. Of him Scripture says, IF YOU FIND HONEY, EAT ONLY WHAT YOU NEED, LEST, SURFEITING YOURSELF, YOU THROW IT UP (Proverbs 25:16 JPS).

The Other cut down the plants.[21]

Rabbi Aqiva emerged in peace.

They asked Ben Zoma, Is it permissible to castrate a dog? He replied, AND YOU SHALL NOT DO THAT IN YOUR LAND (Leviticus 22:24) – [Wherever you are,] do none of those things [that idolaters do] in your land!

They asked Ben Zoma, If a virgin becomes pregnant may the High Priest marry her?[22] Do we take into consideration Shmuel's claim that it is possible to have sexual intercourse with a virgin several times without [causing a discharge of] blood, or is what Shmuel claimed abnormal? He replied,[23] What Shmuel claimed is abnormal; we do, however, consider that she might have become pregnant in a bathtub [while still a virgin]. But didn't Shmuel state that if semen does not shoot like an arrow it cannot impregnate? [Answer: Although it did not enter her until it was in the bathtub,] it shot like an arrow [when] originally [produced].

The rabbis taught: **Rabbi Joshua ben Ḥanania was standing on a step on the Temple Mount.**[24] Ben Zoma saw him but

---

20. The Tosefta and Yerushalmi versions use Elisha's name. See Goshen-Gottstein, *Sinner and the Amnesiac*, p. 207.

21. Several commentators take this to mean that he abandoned the roots of faith, but comparison with the Yerushalmi suggests that it means that he led young people away from Torah (Goshen-Gottstein, *Sinner and the Amnesiac*, p. 207).

22. Leviticus 21:13 states that a High Priest may only marry a virgin. Perhaps there is a veiled comment here on the Christian doctrine of the virgin birth.

23. This is a fictional debate; Ben Zoma could not have commented on a claim made by Shmuel two generations later.

24. Some versions have the conversation take place at the Temple, which is an anachronism.

did not stand. What are you up to, Ben Zoma? enquired [Joshua].

He replied, I was looking at where the upper and lower waters join, and there was not more than three finger-breadths between them, as it is said, THE SPIRIT OF GOD HOVERED OVER THE SURFACE OF THE WATERS (Genesis 1:2) – like a dove that hovers over her young without touching them.

Said Rabbi Joshua to his disciples: Ben Zoma is still out [of his mind]. When did the spirit of God hover over the surface of the waters? On the first day. But the separation [between upper and lower waters] was on the second day, as it is written, AND HE SEPARATED THE WATERS FROM THE WATERS (Genesis 1:6).[25]

> By how much[, then]? Rav Aḥa bar Jacob said, A hairsbreadth. The [other] rabbis said, Like the space between the planks [of a bridge]. Mar Zutra – some say Rav Assi – said, Like two cups pressed together.

The Other cut down the plants. Of him Scripture says, Don't let your mouth bring you into disfavour (Ecclesiastes 5:5 JPS).

What was that? He saw Metatron,[26] to whom permission had been given to sit and write down the merits of Israel. [The Other] reflected, I learned that Above, there is no sitting, no striving, no back of the neck,[27] no tiredness. Perhaps, God forbid, there are two Powers?

They took Metatron out and struck him sixty blows[28] of fire. Why did you not stand up when you saw him? they asked.

[Metatron] was given authority to erase the merits of The

---

25. 'Rabbi Yosé says, The *Shekhina* never descended to earth, nor did Moses or Elijah ever ascend to heaven' (*Sukka* 5a). The rabbis polemicized against any confusion of the human and the divine, such as the apotheosis of kings or the notion that Jesus was the incarnation of God.

26. A very important angel, variously identified as the Prince of the Presence, the Archangel Michael or Enoch after his ascent into heaven. The name is obviously derived from the Greek *meta thronou* ('with the [divine] throne'); its numerical equivalence (314) with Hebrew *Shaddai* ('the Almighty') was noted by Kabbalists.

27. Angels have faces in all directions – Rashi.

28. Sperber, *Dictionary*, p. 21, denies that *pulsa* is the Latin *pulsus*, but notes the expression 'scourges of fire' in the Gnostic *Book of Thomas the Contender*. Presumably, other angels scourged and questioned Metatron.

Other, and a heavenly voice proclaimed, RETURN, O BACK-SLIDING CHILDREN (Jeremiah 3:14), but not The Other!

[The Other] thought, Since I have now been excluded from that world, I shall go and enjoy myself in this world! The Other turned to evil.

He found a prostitute and propositioned her. She said, But aren't you Elisha ben Avuya? [So] he uprooted a radish from the meadow on the Sabbath and gave it to her. She thought, He must be another.

After The Other turned to evil he asked Rabbi Meir, What is the meaning of GOD MADE THIS CORRESPONDING TO THAT (Ecclesiastes 7:14)?

[Rabbi Meir] replied: Whatever the Holy One, blessed be He, created, He created its complement: He created mountains, He created hills; He created seas, He created rivers.

The Other responded, This is not what your master, Aqiva, taught, but: He created the virtuous, He created the wicked; He created the Garden of Eden, He created Gehinnom. Each person has two portions. When the virtuous is found in the right, he receives his portion together with that of the wicked in the Garden of Eden; when the wicked is found guilty, he receives his portion together with that of the virtuous in Gehinnom.

Rav Mesharshya said, Where is this [thought to be found] in Scripture? Of the virtuous it is written, ASSUREDLY, THEY SHALL HAVE A DOUBLE SHARE IN THEIR LAND (Isaiah 61:7 JPS); of the wicked it is written, AND SHATTER THEM WITH DOUBLE DESTRUCTION (Jeremiah 17:18 JPS).

After The Other turned to evil he asked Rabbi Meir, What is the meaning of, GOLD OR GLASS CANNOT MATCH ITS VALUE, NOR VESSELS OF FINE GOLD BE EXCHANGED FOR IT (Job 28:17 JPS)?

He replied, This refers to the words of Torah, which are as hard to acquire as vessels of gold and fine gold, but as easy to smash as glass.

The Other responded, That is not what your master, Aqiva, taught, but: Just as there is remedy for vessels of gold and glass that have been broken, so is there remedy for the learned after they have gone astray.

[Meir:] In that case, repent!

[The Other:] But I heard from behind the partition,[29] RETURN, O BACKSLIDING CHILDREN, but not The Other!

The rabbis taught: The Other was riding a horse on the Sabbath, and Rabbi Meir was walking behind to learn Torah from him. [The Other] said, Meir, turn back! I can tell from the paces of the horse that you have reached the Sabbath limit.

Then you turn back,[30] too! said Meir.

[The Other:] Have I not told you? I heard from behind the partition, RETURN, O BACKSLIDING CHILDREN, but not The Other!

[Meir] took hold of him and led him into the House of Study.

Recite your verse to me! said [The Other] to a child.

[The child] recited: THERE IS NO PEACE, SAYS THE LORD, FOR THE WICKED (Isaiah 48:22).

[Meir] led him into another House of Study.

Recite your verse to me! said [The Other] to a child.

[The child] recited: THOUGH YOU WASH WITH NATRON AND USE MUCH LYE, YOUR GUILT IS INGRAINED BEFORE ME (Jeremiah 2:22 JPS).

[Meir] led him into another House of Study.

Recite your verse to me! said [The Other] to a child.   15b

[The child] recited: AND YOU, WHO ARE DOOMED TO RUIN, WHAT DO YOU ACCOMPLISH BY WEARING CRIMSON, BY DECKING YOUSELF IN JEWELS OF GOLD, BY ENLARGING YOUR EYES WITH KOHL? YOU BEAUTIFY YOURSELF IN VAIN, ETC. (Jeremiah 4:30 JPS).

He led him to another House of Study, to thirteen in all, and all [the children] recited verses of this kind.

To the last one, [The Other] said, Recite your verse!

[The child] recited: AND TO THE WICKED, GOD SAID: 'WHO

---

29. Separating this world from the heavenly world beyond.
30. i.e. repent of your evil ways.

ARE YOU TO RECITE MY LAWS, AND MOUTH THE TERMS OF MY COVENANT' (Psalm 50:16 JPS).

The child stuttered, and it sounded as if he said, And to Elisha, God said . . .[31] Some say, [The Other] had a knife and killed him; some say, [The Other] said, If I had a knife I would have killed him.

When The Other died they[32] said, He cannot be sentenced [to punishment], nor can he be admitted to the World to Come. He cannot be sentenced [to punishment] since he has engaged in [the study of] Torah; he cannot be admitted to the World to Come since he has sinned.

Rabbi Meir said, Better they should sentence him [to punishment], so that [when his sin is purged] he can be admitted to the World to Come. When I die I shall make [sure that] smoke arises from his grave.[33]

When Rabbi Meir died smoke arose from the grave of The Other.

Rabbi Yoḥanan said, What kind of heroism is it to burn one's master? He was one of us – are we incapable of saving him? If I were to take him by the hand, who could get him away from me? When I die I will snuff out the smoke from his grave.

When Rabbi Yoḥanan died the smoke ceased from the grave of The Other. The eulogist said [of Rabbi Yoḥanan], Even the keeper of the gate[34] did not stand in your way, O Master!

The Other's daughter came to Rabbi (Judah ha-Nasi) and asked for alms.

Whose daughter are you? he asked.

I am the daughter of The Other, she replied.

He said to her, Is his seed still in the world? Is it not written, **HE HAS NO SEED OR BREED AMONG HIS PEOPLE, NO SURVIVOR WHERE HE ONCE LIVED** (Job 18:19 JPS)?

---

31. *La-rasha'* ('to the wicked') and *L'Elisha* (to Elisha) might have sounded similar when pronounced indistinctly. The parallel account in the Yerushalmi, though different in many details, attributes the murder of disciples to Elisha.

32. The angelic 'judges' in the world beyond the grave.

33. Elisha will be punished for his sin by being burnt, and when the sin is purged he will be able to enter the World to Come.

34. The gate of Gehinnom. Rabbi Yoḥanan descended to Gehinnom and brought Elisha out [to enter the World to Come] – Rashi.

She said to him, Think of his learning, not of his deeds.

At that moment fire came down [from heaven] and singed Rabbi's bench.[35]

Rabbi lamented, If this is [what happens] to those who are disgraced by [Torah], how much more so will [wonderful things] happen to those honoured through it.

How could Rabbi Meir study Torah at the feet of[36] The Other? Did not Rabba bar bar Ḥana say in the name of Rabbi Yoḥanan, What is the meaning of FOR THE LIPS OF A PRIEST GUARD KNOWLEDGE, AND MEN SEEK TORAH FROM HIS MOUTH; FOR HE IS AN ANGEL OF THE LORD OF HOSTS (Malachi 2:7)? If he is like an angel of the Lord of Hosts, seek Torah from his mouth; but if [he is] not [like an angel of the Lord of Hosts], do not seek Torah from his mouth!

Resh Laqish said, Rabbi Meir found a verse of Scripture to interpret [in justification of his action]: INCLINE YOUR EAR AND LISTEN TO THE WORDS OF THE SAGES; PAY ATTENTION TO MY WISDOM (Proverbs 22:17 JPS) – it doesn't say 'Pay attention to *their* wisdom' but 'Pay attention to *my* wisdom.'

Rav Ḥanina said, [he could have inferred it] from this verse: TAKE HEED, LASS, AND NOTE, INCLINE YOUR EAR: FORGET YOUR PEOPLE AND YOUR FATHER'S HOUSE (Psalm 45:11 JPS).

Isn't there a contradiction between the verses? No, there is no contradiction; [Proverbs and Psalms are addressed to] a great person, [Malachi] to a lesser one.

When Rav Dimi came [to Babylon] he said, In the West they say, Rabbi Meir ate the date and threw away its skin.

Rava expounded: I WENT DOWN TO THE NUT GROVE TO SEE THE BUDDING OF THE VALE (Song 6:11 JPS). Why are the Sages compared to a nut? It is to teach you that just as a nut may be covered with mud and dirt, but [the fruit] inside is not spoiled, so a Sage may have turned astray, but the Torah [within him] is not spoiled.

The following brief anecdote is a dramatization of the previous statement. A final tiny, but fearlessly anthropomorphic,

35. A divine intervention earned by Elisha's learning.
36. Literally, 'from the mouth of'.

paragraph epitomizes rabbinic teaching on the 'divine pathos' –
God's fellow-suffering with humanity:

Rabba bar Shila met Elijah [the prophet].[37] He asked, What
is the Holy One, blessed be He, doing?

[Elijah] replied, He is rehearsing the discourse in the name
of each of the rabbis, but not in the name of Rabbi Meir.

[Rabba bar Shila:] Why [is that]?

[Elijah:] Because [Rabbi Meir] learned his discourse from
The Other.

[Rabba bar Shila:] Rabbi Meir found a pomegranate; he ate
the fruit and threw away the husk.

[Elijah:] Now [the Holy One, blessed be He] will say, My
son Meir says . . .

What does the Divine Presence say when anyone suffers? My
head is heavy; My arm is heavy. If that is how the Holy One,
blessed be He, is distressed for the blood of the wicked, how
much more so [is He distressed] when the blood of the righteous
is shed.

---

37. Elijah did not die, but occasionally visits and instructs the wise.

THIRD ORDER

NASHIM (WOMEN)

INTRODUCTION

Five of the seven tractates comprising this Order regulate the status and rights of women. A girl up to the age of twelve is under her father's authority, a married woman is under her husband's authority, a single adult woman is independent; Mishna defines ways in which changes of women's status take place.

The remaining two tractates deal with vows, and with few exceptions their contents apply equally to both men and women. The Gemara (Sota 2a; see Chapter One) suggests that Nedarim *is included since the previous tractate,* Ketubot, *touched upon matters involving vows;* Nedarim *is naturally followed by* Nazir, *since they both concern vows, and* Nazir *by* Sota, *with which it is juxtaposed in Numbers 5 and 6.*

The Order commences with the longest tractate and ends with the shortest, with the paradoxical result that Gittin *(divorce) precedes* Qiddushin *(betrothal), and the most complex,* Yevamot, *is placed first.*

FIRST TRACTATE
YEVAMOT
(SISTERS-IN-LAW)

WHEN BROTHERS DWELL TOGETHER AND ONE OF THEM DIES AND
LEAVES NO SON, THE WIFE OF THE DECEASED SHALL NOT BE
MARRIED TO A STRANGER, OUTSIDE THE FAMILY. HER HUSBAND'S
BROTHER SHALL UNITE WITH HER: HE SHALL TAKE HER AS HIS
WIFE AND PERFORM THE LEVIR'S DUTY. THE FIRST SON THAT SHE
BEARS SHALL BE ACCOUNTED TO THE DEAD BROTHER, THAT HIS
NAME MAY NOT BE BLOTTED OUT IN ISRAEL. BUT IF THE MAN
DOES NOT WANT TO MARRY HIS BROTHER'S WIDOW, HIS
BROTHER'S WIDOW SHALL APPEAR BEFORE THE ELDERS IN THE
GATE AND DECLARE, 'MY HUSBAND'S BROTHER REFUSES TO ESTAB-
LISH A NAME IN ISRAEL FOR HIS BROTHER; HE WILL NOT PERFORM
THE DUTY OF A LEVIR.' THE ELDERS OF HIS TOWN SHALL THEN
SUMMON HIM AND TALK TO HIM. IF HE INSISTS, SAYING, 'I DO
NOT WANT TO MARRY HER', HIS BROTHER'S WIDOW SHALL GO UP
TO HIM IN THE PRESENCE OF THE ELDERS, PULL THE SANDAL OFF
HIS FOOT, SPIT IN HIS FACE AND MAKE THIS DECLARATION: THUS
SHALL BE DONE TO THE MAN WHO WILL NOT BUILD UP HIS
BROTHER'S HOUSE! AND HE SHALL GO IN ISRAEL BY THE NAME OF
'THE FAMILY OF THE UNSANDALLED ONE'. (Deuteronomy 25:5–10
JPS)

*These laws are expounded in such a way as to define, in
accordance with rabbinic interpretation, the extent of permitted
and forbidden relationships between men and women; in other
circumstances, a man may not marry his brother's (ex-)wife
(Leviticus 18:16).*

*In principle, a man might marry his deceased brother's widow
as mandated in Deuteronomy even if he was already married,*

*though polygamy was certainly uncommon among Jews after
biblical times. Roman law punished bigamy, but the Roman
authorities may have tolerated Jewish polygamy in Palestine in
the period of the Mishna.[1]*

*The Gemara (39b) records the opinion of Abba Saul that
ḥalitza (the ceremony of removal of the sandal) should 'nowadays' be performed in preference to actually marrying the
sister-in-law, but the matter was still in dispute in the Middle
Ages and was to have serious repercussions on the English
Reformation. In 1530 King Henry VIII sought support from
Jewish sources in Italy to invalidate his levirate marriage with
Catherine of Aragon; rabbis advising Pope Clement VII, who
was under pressure not to permit Henry to set Catherine aside,
had little difficulty in demonstrating that the marriage was in
accordance with both biblical precedent and current Sefardic
Jewish practice.[2]*

*A man may not marry two living sisters (Leviticus 18:18).
Therefore, if the deceased brother's wives included his brother's
wife's sister (two brothers married two sisters), the surviving
brother could not implement the levirate marriage. In general,
if the widow was a woman whom the brother-in-law would
have been forbidden to marry even had she not been married to
his brother, he may not marry her after his brother's death;
moreover, she exempts any co-wives from the obligation. The
opening Mishna tells us that fifteen female relatives fall into this
category.*

*The more outlandish cases discussed in this tractate, including
several of those listed in the opening Mishna, are not actual case
law, but hypothetical constructs devised to test the limits of
law; indeed, in 35a the Gemara itself expresses surprise at the
suggestion that a certain case actually occurred.*

1.   A. M. Rabbello, 'Jewish and Roman Jurisdiction', in Hecht, Jackson, Passamanek,
     Jewish Law, p. 156, notes that from 393 it was expressly forbidden (*Code of
     Justinian* 1.9.7). The Palestinian Rabbi Ammi forbade polygamy *c.* 300, whereas
     the Babylonian Rava permitted it (*Yevamot* 65a).
2.   D. Katz, *Jews in England*, pp. 15–48. Henry ordered a copy of the Talmud but
     failed to pay the binders; it passed to the Westminster Library, where it was
     studied by John Selden, and is now in the possession of the Valmadonna Trust.

CHAPTER ONE

MISHNA: 2a

Fifteen women exempt their co-wives and co-wives of their co-wives ad infinitum from *yibbum* and *ḥalitza*, and these are they: [the surviving brother's] daughter, his daughter's daughter, his son's daughter, his wife's daughter [from another marriage], her son's daughter, her daughter's daughter, his mother-in-law, his mother-in-law's mother, his father-in-law's mother, his maternal sister, his mother's sister, his wife's sister, his maternal brother's wife, the wife of a brother who was not   2b
in his world[3] and his daughter-in-law – these exempt their co-wives and co-wives of their co-wives ad infinitum from *yibbum* and *ḥalitza*.

If, however, any of these had protested,[4] been divorced [prior to her husband's death] or was found to be sterile, the co-wives are permitted [to marry the brother]; but you cannot say of his mother-in-law, her mother or his father-in-law's mother that they are found to be sterile or that they have 'protested'.

The next selection affords an opportunity to see how the Talmud is read by those who seek to apply Torah law to contemporary practice. Rabbi Moshe Feinstein (1895–1986), a leading Orthodox halakhic authority in New York, was asked whether a woman advised by doctors that her life might be endangered by pregnancy might make use of a 'pad' during intercourse to avoid conception; he not only permits this but recommends it, arguing that the debate between Rabbi Meir and the Sages concerns only the 'three women' specified, where the danger is minimal, and it is proper to rely on heaven's mercy; but where the danger is significant, as in this case, all would agree that contraception should be used. The questioner presumably had in mind a diaphragm (though Feinstein does not make this clear). Feinstein

3. i.e. who died before he was born.
4. If a girl was married off with her consent by her mother or brothers when she was a minor, she had a right to protest on reaching adulthood, retrospectively invalidating the marriage. (A marriage contracted by them against her will has no validity.)

follows Rashi's interpretation of mokh ('pad') as some material placed in the vagina prior to intercourse to absorb or obstruct semen. Rashi's grandson Jacob Tam, however, maintained that it was a swab used to remove semen following intercourse; some halakhic authorities therefore ban barrier contraception altogether.[5] The approach of the halakhists is purely textual; they do not investigate historically what contraceptives might have been known to the rabbis of the Talmud. Oral contraception raises other issues; it is discussed below, 65b. Though Rav in Babylonia and Rabbi Eleazar in Palestine both ruled, 'It is forbidden for a man to give his under-age daughter in marriage' (Qiddushin 41a), child marriages remained a fact of Jewish life until the late Middle Ages; it is in that context that sex with minors figures.

GEMARA:

Rav Assi suggests that the co-wife of a sterile woman is forbidden to marry the deceased husband's brother. An objection is raised:

12a   The Mishna stated: **If, however, any of these had protested, been divorced [prior to her husband's death] or was found to be sterile, the co-wives are permitted [to marry the brother].**

No problem! [Rav Assi's statement applies] where he knew [she was infertile when he married her,] the [Mishna] applies where he did not know; this is precisely indicated, since the Mishna says **was found to be sterile** rather than **was sterile**.

12b   Rava ruled, The law is that the co-wife of a sterile woman is permitted [to marry the deceased husband's brother], even if [the deceased brother] knew she was sterile at the time he married her, and [this goes] even for the sterile co-wife of his own daughter. But doesn't the Mishna state, **was found to be sterile?** [Rava would say,] Read [instead,] **was sterile**.

When Ravin arrived he said in the name of Rabbi Yoḥanan, Whether [the widow] is the co-wife of a 'protester', the co-wife of a sterile woman or the co-wife of a woman her husband

5.   Feinstein, *Igrot Moshe*, 3:43 (pp. 152f.).

had divorced and remarried,[6] she is permitted to marry [the brother-in-law].

Rav Bibi taught in the presence of Rav Naḥman, **Three women may have intercourse with [the use of] a pad: a minor, a pregnant woman and a lactating woman. A minor [is permitted to use a pad] in case she becomes pregnant and in case she dies; a pregnant woman in case she damages the foetus;**[7] **a lactating woman in case she [becomes pregnant again,] is forced to wean her baby, and it dies. Who is a minor? A girl from eleven years and a day to twelve years and a day old; if she is younger or older than that she should have intercourse in the normal way, says Rabbi Meir. The Sages, however, say that all of them should have intercourse in the normal way, and heaven will have mercy, as it is said, THE LORD PROTECTS THE SIMPLE** (Psalm 116:6 JPS).

Now, since it says **in case she becomes pregnant and in case she dies**, it follows that there are minors who become pregnant but do not die. If that is so, there could be a mother-in-law who has 'protested',[8] yet the Mishna states, **but you cannot say of his mother-in-law, her mother or his father-in-law's mother that they are found to be sterile or that they have 'protested'**!

Understand the baraita [to say], **in case she becomes pregnant and dies**. For Rabba bar Livai stated, These are limits. Below the limit she will not become pregnant at all; within these limits she will die and the foetus will die; above the limit she will live and the foetus will live.

Surely this cannot be so, for Rabba bar Shmuel taught [explicitly], **You cannot say of his mother-in-law, her mother or his father-in-law's mother that they are found to be sterile or that they have 'protested', for they have already given birth.** The baraita therefore must mean **in case she becomes pregnant and in case she dies**.

Then the problem remains!

6.   i.e. illegally remarried. A husband may remarry his divorced wife only if she has not meanwhile been married to another man (cf. Deuteronomy 24:1–4).
7.   Literally, 'in case she makes the foetus [into a] sandal'.
8.   She could have given birth before the age of eleven, and 'protested' on reaching her majority at twelve.

Rav Safra answered, Children[9] are a sign [that she is no longer a minor, irrespective of age]. Some say, Children are superior to signs [of puberty as evidence of adulthood].

The anecdotes about Hillel and Shammai in Shabbat *31a indicate a strongly encouraging attitude towards converts, but the baraita below suggests caution, perhaps necessary when converts to Judaism lapsed and slandered Jews to the occupying authorities, or if they joined Christian or heretical sects and made a nuisance of themselves. This may be what lies behind Rabbi Ḥelbo's caustic yet ambivalent comparison of converts to a 'scab'.[10]*

CHAPTER FOUR

GEMARA:

47a   The rabbis taught: When someone nowadays presents himself for conversion, we say to him: Why do you wish to convert? Are you not aware that nowadays Israelites are careworn, stressed, despised, harassed and persecuted? If he responds, 'I know, and I [feel] unworthy [to share their troubles]', we accept him at once. We instruct him in some of the easy *mitzvot* and some of the hard ones, and inform him of the sin [incurred through neglect] of *leqet, shikh'ḥa, pe'ah* and the poor tithe, and of the punishment for [infringing] the commandments. We say to him, 'Be aware that before you reached this stage you were not liable to *karet* for eating prohibited fats, nor to stoning for breaking the Sabbath; now, if you eat prohibited fats you are liable to *karet*, and if you break the Sabbath you are liable to stoning.'

Just as we inform him of the punishment for [infringing] the commandments, we inform him of the reward [for obedience]. We tell him, 'You should know that the world is made for the righteous, but that Israel nowadays cannot

9.   i.e. giving birth.
10. On proselytism in the rabbinic period, see Goodman, *Mission*; for a broader appreciation of conversion in rabbinic teaching, see Finkelstein, *Conversion*.

endure either too much well-being or too much suffering.' We don't [alarm him] excessively, nor do we enter into too much detail.

If he accepts, we circumcise him at once; if strips [of foreskin] are left that invalidate the circumcision, this is corrected.[11] When he has recovered, he is immersed in the pool without delay. Two learned men stand nearby, reminding him of some of the easy *mitzvot* and some of the hard ones. As soon as he emerges and dries himself, he is an Israelite in all respects.

If [the convert] is a woman, women support her in water up to her neck, and two learned men stand outside, reminding her of some of the easy *mitzvot* and some of the hard ones. The same procedure applies to a proselyte as to a slave who is being freed;[12] both proselyte and slave may immerse in any [pool that is valid for purification of] a menstruant; moreover, whatever is an impediment [to immersion][13] is an impediment [equally] for proselyte, slave and menstruant.

A teacher said: If someone presents himself nowadays for conversion we say to him: Why do you wish to convert? . . . We instruct him in some of the easy *mitzvot* and some of the hard ones. What is the reason for this? [It is] so that if he wishes to leave he may [easily do so], for Rabbi Ḥelbo said, Proselytes are as bad for Israel as a scab, as it is written, AND STRANGERS SHALL JOIN THEM AND SHALL CLEAVE TO THE HOUSE OF JACOB (Isaiah 14:1 JPS).[14]

And inform him of the sin [incurred through neglect] of *leqet, shikh'ḥa, pe'ah* and the poor tithe. Why? Rabbi Ḥiyya bar Abba said in the name of Rabbi Yoḥanan, Because Noahides

---

11. Literally, 'we circumcise a second time'.
12. On receiving his freedom a non-Israelite slave automatically becomes an Israelite.
13. i.e. anything that physically interposes between the water and the bather.
14. The Hebrew *v'nisp'ḥu* ('they shall join') is derived from the same root as *sapaḥat* ('scab' – an attachment to the skin), one of the symptoms of the affliction ('leprosy') described in Leviticus 13. By citing a verse that clearly regards conversions as a blessing, Rabbi Ḥelbo gives a double edge to his remark; it is in any case contradicted by Rabbi Meir's comment that 'even a Gentile who engages in the study of Torah is like the High Priest' (*Bava Qama* 38a; see p. 434).

are executed for the theft of even less than a *peruta*, and cannot [avoid punishment by] restoring [the stolen property].[15]

We don't [alarm him] excessively, nor do we enter into too much detail. Rabbi Eleazar said, Where do we find this in Scripture? It is written [of Ruth], **WHEN [NAOMI] SAW HOW DETERMINED SHE WAS TO GO WITH HER, SHE CEASED TO ARGUE WITH HER** (Ruth 1:18 JPS). [Naomi said,] We are forbidden to cross the Sabbath boundaries; [Ruth replied:] **WHEREVER YOU GO, I WILL GO.** We are forbidden to remain alone with men; [she replied:] **WHEREVER YOU LODGE, I WILL LODGE.** We have 613 commandments [to keep]; **YOUR PEOPLE SHALL BE MY PEOPLE.** We must not worship idols; **AND YOUR GOD IS MY GOD.** We have four kinds of death sentence; **WHERE YOU DIE, I WILL DIE.** The court has two graveyards [for criminals]; **AND THERE I WILL BE BURIED** (Ruth 1:16, 17).

If he accepts, we circumcise him at once. Why? One does not delay a *mitzva*.

If strips [of foreskin] are left that invalidate the circumcision, this is corrected. This is to comply with the Mishna, which states: **The following strips [of foreskin] invalidate the circumcision: flesh that covers the majority of the glans; if these are not removed he may not eat *teruma*.**[16] Rabbi Jeremiah bar Abba said in Rav's name, [This means] flesh that covers most of the glans lengthwise.

When he has recovered, he is immersed in the pool without delay. When he has recovered, but not before he has recovered. Why is this? Because water irritates the wound.

Two learned men stand nearby . . . But didn't Rabbi Ḥiyya say in the name of Rabbi Yoḥanan, A proselyte requires three [assessors]? [Indeed,] Rabbi Yoḥanan instructed his Tanna, Say 'three'![17]

As soon as he emerges and dries himself he is an Israelite in

15. We explain that when he is no longer a Noahide but an Israelite he will be subject to laws with clearly defined limits (theft is not a capital offence, it is actionable only if exceeding a *peruta* in value and there is the possibility of redress); nevertheless, depriving the poor of their due is a grievous offence before God.

16. Mishna *Shabbat* 19:6 (137a).

17. That is, he adjusted the text of the baraita to fit his opinion that three were required.

all respects. How does this affect the law? If he reverts, and then marries an Israelite woman, he has the status of an apostate Israelite and any marriage he contracts is valid.

The same procedure applies to a proselyte as to a slave who is being freed. You would assume this means with regard to formally committing himself to the *mitzvot*.[18] As against that [assumption, a baraita states]: **To whom does this apply? To a proselyte. But a slave who is being freed does not need to make a formal commitment to the *mitzvot*.**

Rav Sheshet said, No problem! One is the opinion of Rabbi Simeon ben Eleazar, the other the opinion of the [majority of] Sages. A baraita states: **SHE SHALL WEEP FOR HER FATHER AND HER MOTHER** (Deuteronomy 21:13)[19] – **When does this apply? If she has not accepted [the *mitzvot*]. But if she has accepted, she immerses herself and is permitted to [marry her captor] immediately. Rabbi Simeon ben Eleazar says, Even if she has not accepted [the *mitzvot*], she is immersed to establish her slave status, then immersed again to free her, and when he has freed her he is immediately permitted [to take her as his wife].** 48a

CHAPTER SIX

MISHNA:

A man should not desist from BE FRUITFUL AND MULTIPLY (Genesis 1:28) **unless he has children. The School of Shammai say, Two males; the School of Hillel say, One male and one female, as it is said, MALE AND FEMALE HE CREATED THEM** (Genesis 1:27). 61b

GEMARA:

So if he has children, he may desist from **BE FRUITFUL AND MULTIPLY**, but not from having a wife. This confirms what Rav Naḥman said in Shmuel's name, for he said, Even though a

18. Literally, 'accepting the yoke of the *mitzvot*'.
19. The topic is the beautiful woman taken captive in war.

man has many children, he should not be without a wife, as it is said, IT IS NOT GOOD FOR MAN TO BE ALONE (Genesis 2:18).

But some say, If he has children, he may desist from BE FRUITFUL AND MULTIPLY, and also from having a wife. Does this contradict what Rav Naḥman said in Shmuel's name? No. If he has no children, he should marry a wife who can bear children, but if he already has children, he may marry a wife who cannot bear children.

> There is a difference [in law between these two views, since in the first view] he may sell a Torah Scroll [if necessary to marry a wife who can bear] children[, even if he already has children, whereas in the second view he may not].

The School of Shammai say, Two males. What reason do the School of Shammai have [for this]? They learn it from Moses, for it is written AND THE SONS OF MOSES WERE GERSHOM AND ELIEZER [after which he separated from his wife] (1 Chronicles 23:15).

And the School of Hillel? They learn from the way the world was created.[20]

Why don't the School of Shammai learn from the way the world was created? [Because] you cannot infer what is possible from what is impossible.

Why don't the School of Hillel learn from Moses? They would say, Moses acted on his own initiative [rather than in accordance with the law], as a baraita teaches:

Moses did three things on his own initiative, and his judgement conformed with the judgement of the Omnipresent: he separated from his wife, he smashed the tablets [of stone] and he added a day.

> **He separated from his wife.** On what did he base this?[21] If Israel, with whom the *Shekhina* spoke only briefly and at a designated time, were instructed DO NOT APPROACH A WOMAN (Exodus 19:15), how much

62a

---

20. i.e. Adam and Eve.
21. Literally, 'What did he interpret?'

more should I, who must be prepared for the Word constantly, with no designated time[, avoid contact with women]! And his judgement conformed with the judgement of the Omnipresent, for it is written, GO, SAY TO THEM, 'RETURN TO YOUR TENTS.'[22] BUT YOU REMAIN HERE WITH ME (Deuteronomy 5:27–8 JPS).

He smashed the tablets [of stone]. On what did he base this? He reasoned, If, in the case of the Passover lamb, which is just one of the 613 commandments, the Torah rules, NO STRANGER SHALL EAT IT (Exodus 12:43), how much more so should I decline to set the whole Torah before Israel, now that they have apostasized?[23] And his judgement conformed with the judgement of the Omnipresent, for it is written, WHICH YOU HAVE BROKEN (Exodus 34:1), and Resh Laqish said this means that the Holy One, blessed be He, said to Moses, 'Thank you for breaking them.'[24]

He added a day. On what did he base this? It is written, SANCTIFY THEM TODAY AND TOMORROW (Exodus 19:10). He understood 'today like tomorrow', i.e. just as tomorrow includes its eve, so does today include its eve, but as today's eve has already passed, [God] must mean two days excluding today. And his judgement conformed with the judgement of the Omnipresent, for the *Shekhina* did not come to rest [on Israel] until the Sabbath.

A baraita teaches: Rabbi Nathan says, The School of Shammai say, Two males and two females; the School of Hillel say, One male and one female.

Rav Huna said, In Rabbi Nathan's version, what reason do the School of Shammai have? It is written, THEN SHE BORE HIS BROTHER ABEL (Genesis 4:2)

22. Understood as 'your homes', i.e. resume relations with your wives.
23. By worshipping the golden calf.
24. There is a play on words here between *asher shibbarta* ('which you have broken') and *y'yasher (koḥakha) she-shibarta* ('thank you for breaking').

– Abel and his sister, Cain and his sister[25] – and [afterwards] it is written, FOR GOD HAS GRANTED ME ANOTHER SEED IN PLACE OF ABEL, FOR CAIN KILLED HIM (Genesis 4:25). But the others say [Eve] was just expressing gratitude.

Another baraita teaches: **Rabbi Nathan says, The School of Shammai say, One male and one female; the School of Hillel say, One male or one female.**

Rava said, On this version of Rabbi Nathan, what reason do the School of Hillel have? It is written, HE DID NOT CREATE IT A WASTE, BUT FORMED IT FOR SETTLEMENT (Isaiah 45:18), and [even one male or one female] is 'settlement'.

It was taught: If he had children when he was an idolater and was afterwards converted, Rabbi Yoḥanan says, Since he has produced children he has fulfilled BE FRUITFUL AND MULTIPLY; Resh Laqish says he has not fulfilled BE FRUITFUL AND MULTIPLY, since a convert is like a newborn child.

In this they follow a consistent line, for it was taught: If he had children when he was an idolater and afterwards converted, Rabbi Yoḥanan says, [The first-born son subsequent to his conversion] does not have first-born rights of inheritance, since [the father already] had a FIRST-FRUIT OF HIS VIGOUR (Deuteronomy 21:17); Resh Laqish says, [The first-born son subsequent to his conversion] does have first-born rights of inheritance, since a convert is like a newborn child.

Both cases need [to be stated]. If we knew only the former, we would think that Rabbi Yoḥanan held that point of view only with regard to BE FRUITFUL AND MULTIPLY, since BE FRUITFUL AND MULTIPLY applied even before conversion,[26] but in the matter of first-born inheritance he would agree with Resh Laqish; if we knew only the latter case, we would think that is where Resh Laqish held his view, but he would

25. The Hebrew objective particle *et* is interpreted as 'with': with each male a female twin was born.

26. It is addressed to Adam and Eve, representative of all humanity, not specifically to Israel.

agree with Rabbi Yoḥanan in the former case. Therefore, both need [to be stated].

Rabbi Yoḥanan objected to Resh Laqish: AT THAT TIME,
KING BERODACH-BALADAN SON OF BALADAN OF BABYLON
SENT (2 Kings 20:12 JPS). [Resh Laqish replied,] While they
remain idolaters they retain family relationships, but once they
are converted they lose them.

*Much discussion follows on the children of slaves, on children
who die, on whether grandchildren make up the number, and
like matters. The Mishna is then challenged on the basis of a
statement by Rabbi Joshua.*

Our Mishna does not accord with [the opinion of] Rabbi   62b
Joshua, for a baraita teaches: Rabbi Joshua says, If a man
married in his youth, let him marry in old age; if he fathered
children in his youth, let him father children in his old age, as
it is said, SOW YOUR SEED IN THE MORNING, AND DON'T HOLD
BACK YOUR HAND IN THE EVENING, SINCE YOU DON'T KNOW
WHICH IS GOING TO SUCCEED, THE ONE OR THE OTHER, OR IF
BOTH ARE EQUALLY GOOD (Ecclesiastes 11:6 JPS).

Rabbi Aqiva says, If you learned Torah in your youth, learn
Torah in your old age; if you raised disciples in your youth,
raise disciples in your old age, as it is said, SOW YOUR SEED
IN THE MORNING, AND DON'T HOLD BACK YOUR HAND IN
THE EVENING.

They say, Rabbi Aqiva had ten thousand pairs of
disciples, from Gabbath to Antipatris,[27] and they all
died in one period because they did not treat one
another with respect. The world was [then] desolate,
until Rabbi Aqiva approached our rabbis in the south[28]
and taught them – Rabbi Meir, Rabbi Judah, Rabbi
Yosé, Rabbi Simeon and Rabbi Eleazar ben Shamua –
and it was they who preserved Torah at that time.[29]

27. Gabbath has been identified as Gibbethon (Joshua 21:23) in the north, or else a
     town on the southern border of Judaea. Antipatris (now Kefar Saba) is north-west
     of Jerusalem. On rabbinic place names in Palestine, see Reeg, *Ortsnamen*.
28. Judaea, south of Galilee.
29. The historical background is generally thought to be the Second Revolt against
     Rome, in 131–5 CE. Aqiva had supported the uprising, which failed with heavy
     loss of life. There are several versions of his story and his successive sets of disciples,

> It was taught: They all died between Pass-
> over and Pentecost.
> Rav Ḥama bar Abba – or some say Ḥiyya
> bar Avin – said, They all died an evil death.
> What was that? Askara.[30]

Rav Matna said, The *halakha* goes according to Rabbi Joshua.
*There follows a collection of sayings in praise of marriage, and
advice about marriage; Michael Satlow has sensitively analysed
the concept of marital love in rabbinic literature. The positive
rabbinic attitude accords well not only with the earlier Roman
tradition but also with Sasanian Zoroastrian mores; it contrasts
with that of Christians in the Sasanian Empire, who felt under
considerable pressure to modify their traditions of asceticism
and celibacy in order to accommodate themselves to Sasanian
society. Isaiah Gafni has shown how differences in attitude
to marriage between Palestinian and Babylonian rabbis reflect
attitudes in the ambient societies.*[31]

Rabbi Tanḥum said in the name of Rabbi Ḥanilai: If a man
has no wife, he is without joy, without blessing and without
good. He is without joy, for it is written, **AND REJOICE WITH
YOUR HOUSEHOLD**[32] (Deuteronomy 14:26 JPS); without
blessing, for it is written, **THAT A BLESSING MAY REST UPON
YOUR HOME** (Ezekiel 44:30 JPS); and without good, for it is
written, **IT IS NOT GOOD FOR MAN TO BE ALONE** (Genesis 2:18
JPS).

In the West they say, Without Torah, without a [protective]
wall. Without Torah, for it is written, **FOR MY HELP IS NOT**

---

implying that he survived to take part in the rebuilding of Jewish life in Palestine
after 135. As against this, the story of Aqiva's martyrdom recounted in *Berakhot*
61b seems to suggest that he did *not* survive the Hadrianic persecutions. Amit ('Rabbi
Aqiva's Disciples', p. 266) argues that the story of his disciples is 'a Palestinian
amoraic tradition which was constructed in much the same way as later Babylonian
aggadic traditions, and has no historical import'.

30. Meaning uncertain; Sokoloff, *Babylonian*, relying on Preuss, renders 'diphtheria'.
31. Satlow, ' "One who loves" '; Erhart, 'Canon Law', pp. 118–23; Gafni, *Yehudei
Bavel*, Appendix 2, pp. 266–73, and 'Institution'. On rabbinic attitudes to asceticism, see Diamond, *Holy Men*.
32. This and subsequent interpretations depend on the identification of 'household',
'home' or 'tent' with 'wife'.

WITH ME, MY STRENGTH[33] IS TAKEN FROM ME (Job 6:13 JPS); without a [protective] wall, for it is written, A WOMAN SURROUNDS A MAN (Jeremiah 31:22).

Rava bar Ulla said, Without peace, for it is written, YOU WILL KNOW THAT THERE IS PEACE IN YOUR TENT; WHEN YOU VISIT YOUR HOME YOU WILL NOT FAIL (Job 5:24).

Rabbi Joshua ben Levi said, If anyone knows his wife is God-fearing but does not visit[34] her, he is called a sinner, as it is said, YOU WILL KNOW THAT THERE IS PEACE IN YOUR TENT; WHEN YOU VISIT YOUR HOME.

Rabbi Joshua ben Levi said, A man should visit his wife when he is about to set off on a journey, as it is said, YOU WILL KNOW THAT THERE IS PEACE IN YOUR TENT; WHEN YOU VISIT YOUR HOME.

Is that derived from [this verse]? Surely it follows from YOUR URGE SHALL BE FOR YOUR HUSBAND (Genesis 3:16 JPS)? Rav Yosef said, [Joshua ben Levi's verse] is required for a situation when [the husband sets off] close to the time her period is due. How close [to that time is it still permitted to have intercourse]? Rava said, A whole night or day.

This applies [if he is setting off] on an optional [journey], but if for a *mitzva* he would be preoccupied.[35]

The rabbis taught: Of one who loves his wife as himself, honours her more than himself, guides his sons and daughters in the right way, and marries them off as soon as they reach maturity, Scripture says, YOU WILL KNOW THAT THERE IS PEACE IN YOUR TENT.

Of one who loves his neighbours, brings close his relatives, marries his sister's daughter[36] and lends to the poor in their   63a

---

33. 'Help' is wife (cf. Genesis 2:18); 'strength' is Torah.
34. A euphemism for sexual intercourse. A God-fearing wife would not take the initiative; it is the husband's responsibility to see that her sexual needs are understood and attended to.
35. Rashi observes that it is unclear whether preoccupation with the *mitzva*, for example, the redemption of captives, exempts him from his marital obligation, or whether fulfilment of his marital duties might distract him from the *mitzva*.
36. A man may marry his niece, but a woman may not marry her nephew (derived from Leviticus 18:14 and 20:20).

time of need, Scripture says, THEN, WHEN YOU CALL, THE
LORD WILL ANSWER; WHEN YOU CRY, HE WILL SAY, HERE
I AM (Isaiah 58:9 JPS).

Rabbi Eleazar said, A man who has no wife is no man, for it
is said, MALE AND FEMALE HE CREATED THEM . . . AND
CALLED THEM MAN[37] (Genesis 5:2 JPS).

Rabbi Eleazar also said, A man who has no land is no man,
for it is said, THE HEAVENS BELONG TO THE LORD, BUT THE
EARTH HE GAVE OVER TO MAN (Psalm 115:16 JPS).

Rabbi Eleazar also said, What is the meaning of I WILL MAKE
HIM A HELPER K'NEGDO[38] (Genesis 2:18)? If he merits it, she
helps him; if not, she is against him.

> Rabbi Yosé met [the prophet] Elijah.[39] [Rabbi Yosé
> asked,] It is written, I SHALL MAKE HIM A HELPER;
> in what way does a woman help a man? [Elijah] replied,
> A man brings home wheat. Does he chew it [as it is]?
> He brings home linen. Does he wear [unwoven] linen?
> Does she not bring light to his eyes and [enable him]
> to stand on his feet?

Rabbi Eleazar also said, What is the meaning of 'THIS ONE
AT LAST IS BONE OF MY BONES AND FLESH OF MY FLESH'
(Genesis 2:23 JPS)? It teaches that Adam [attempted to] copulate
with every beast, but did not find satisfaction until he came
upon Eve.

Rabbi Eleazar also said, What is the meaning of ALL
FAMILIES OF THE EARTH SHALL BE BLESSED THROUGH YOU
(Genesis 12:3 JPS)? The Holy One, blessed be He, said to
Abraham, I have two good shoots to graft on to you, Ruth of
Moab and Naamah of Ammon.[40]

ALL FAMILIES OF THE EARTH. Even families who

37. Hebrew *Adam*, 'human'.
38. The Hebrew *k'negdo* can mean either corresponding to or opposite (against). In
the Talmud, the sentence is followed by an alternative reading which implies that
the word might be pronounced in two different ways corresponding to these
meanings.
39. Elijah was 'transported' to heaven about a thousand years earlier, but every now
and then he 'appears' to someone deserving of special enlightenment.
40. Naamah the Ammonite was the mother of Rehoboam (1 Kings 14:21), hence an
ancestress of the House of David.

live on the land are blessed only on account of Israel;[41] **ALL FAMILIES OF THE EARTH**. Even ships that sail from Gaul to Spain are blessed only on account of Israel.

Rabbi Eleazar also said, Men of all occupations will [one day] stand upon the land,[42] as it is said, **AND ALL THE OARSMEN AND MARINERS, ALL THE PILOTS OF THE SEA, SHALL COME DOWN FROM THEIR SHIPS AND STAND ON THE GROUND** (Ezekiel 27:29 JPS).

Rabbi Eleazar also said, No occupation is more lowly than [work on] the land, as it is said, [**THEY**] **SHALL COME DOWN**.

Rabbi Eleazar saw men sowing cabbage in a field. He said to them, Even if you [sow] the whole length, you would be better off to engage in commerce.

Rav was walking through a field of corn, and saw it waving in the wind. He said, Wave all you like! To engage in commerce is better!

Rava said, [Invest] 100 *zuz* in commerce, and you will have meat and wine every day; 100 *zuz* in agriculture, and you will get salt and weeds. Not only that, but you will lay your crops on the ground and get involved in disputes with people.

Rav Papa said, Sow [crops for your household] and don't buy; even if the cost is the same, [that which you grow is receptive to] blessing. Sell before you become poor[, so that you can trade and so avoid impoverishment] – but only your carpets, not your clothes, which you may be unable to replace. Stop up a hole rather than plastering it over. Plaster over rather than rebuild; whoever builds gets poor. Be quick to sell land, but cautious in acquiring a wife. Go down a step for a wife, up a step for a best friend.[43]

Rabbi Eleazar ben Avina said, Punishment is visited upon the world only on account of Israel, as it is said, **I WIPED OUT NATIONS: I TURNED THEIR THOROUGHFARES INTO RUINS, WITH NONE PASSING BY; THEIR TOWNS LIE WASTE WITHOUT**

41. i.e. through Abraham.
42. They will have to leave their occupations in order to plough and harvest – Rashi.
43. A wife from a higher social class may despise you; a friend from a higher social class will help you.

PEOPLE, WITHOUT INHABITANTS. AND I THOUGHT THAT SHE WOULD FEAR ME, WOULD LEARN A LESSON (Zephaniah 3:6–7 JPS).

Rav was taking leave of Rabbi Ḥiyya. [Rabbi Ḥiyya] said to him, May God save you from that which is worse than death! He looked carefully and found, **Now, I FIND WOMAN MORE BITTER THAN DEATH** (Ecclesiastes 7:26 JPS).

Rav's wife annoyed him. If he said, Prepare beans, she prepared lentils; [Prepare] lentils, she prepared beans. When his son Ḥiyya grew up he reversed [the instructions he passed on to his mother]. [Rav] said, Your mother has improved. Ḥiyya said, I reversed [the instructions]. [Rav] said, That's what people [mean when they] say, 'The one who comes from you teaches you.' [But] don't do it, for it says, **THEY HAVE TAUGHT THEIR TONGUE TO SPEAK LIES, THEY WEARY THEMSELVES TO COMMIT INIQUITY** (Jeremiah 9:4).

Rabbi Ḥiyya's wife used to annoy him. If he found anything [of value] he would wrap it in his *sudar* and bring it to her. Rav said, But doesn't she annoy you? He replied, Isn't it enough for us that they bring up our children and save us from sin!

63b

Rav Yehuda was teaching his son Isaac [the verse,] **Now, I FIND WOMAN MORE BITTER THAN DEATH.** Like whom? asked [the boy]. Like your mother[, he replied]. But didn't Rav Yehuda also teach his son Isaac [the verse,] **LET YOUR FOUNTAIN BE BLESSED; FIND JOY IN THE WIFE OF YOUR YOUTH** (Proverbs 5:18 JPS)? Like whom? asked [the boy]. Like your mother[, he replied]. [No contradiction here:] she would quarrel with him, but easily make it up with a word.

What is a bad wife like? Abbaye said, She sets the table and also sets her mouth [against him]; Rava said, She sets the table and turns her back on him.

Rabbi Ḥama bar Ḥanina said, When a man marries, his sins are stopped up,[44] as it is written, **HE WHO HAS FOUND A WIFE HAS FOUND HAPPINESS, AND HAS WON THE FAVOUR OF THE LORD** (Proverbs 18:22).

In the West, when a man married they would ask, Found or

44. Forgiven.

find? Found – HE WHO HAS *FOUND* A WIFE HAS FOUND
HAPPINESS; or Find – I *FIND* WOMAN MORE BITTER THAN
DEATH?

*The sugya continues for a page or so in like vein. Unfortunately,
the wives of the Sages left no record of what they felt about
their husbands.*

The first mitzva *in the Torah is procreation* – BE FRUITFUL
AND MULTIPLY. *Producing children carries more risks for
women than for men. Can anyone be subject to a* mitzva *that
involves risk of death? Note Rabbi Ḥiyya's wife, Judith's
recourse to an oral contraceptive.*

MISHNA:

Men are commanded to BE FRUITFUL AND MULTIPLY;   65b
women are not. Rabbi Yoḥanan ben Baroqa says, Of both it
states, AND GOD BLESSED THEM, AND GOD SAID TO THEM,
BE FRUITFUL AND MULTIPLY AND FILL THE EARTH (Genesis
1:28).

GEMARA:

How do we know that [men and not women are commanded
to be fruitful and multiply]? Rabbi Ila'a said in the name of
Rabbi Eleazar ben Simeon, Scripture says FILL THE EARTH AND
SUBDUE IT (Genesis 1:28) – it is normal for men to subdue, not
women.

To the contrary, 'subdue' [is plural – it] means both!

Rav Naḥman bar Isaac said, It is written defectively.[45]

Rav Yosef said, [The inference is made from the words
addressed to Abraham:] 'I AM ALMIGHTY GOD – BE FRUITFUL
AND MULTIPLY' (Genesis 35:11).[46]

Something else that Rabbi Ila'a said in the name of Rabbi
Eleazar ben Simeon: Just as it is a *mitzva* to say something that
will be listened to, it is a *mitzva* not to say something that will
not be listened to. Rabbi Abba said, [More than that, it is] a
duty, as it is said, DO NOT REBUKE A SCOFFER, FOR HE WILL
HATE YOU; REPROVE A WISE MAN, AND HE WILL LOVE YOU
(Proverbs 9:8 JPS).

---

45. The letter *vav* which indicates the plural is lacking.
46. This imperative is unambiguously singular.

Rabbi Ila'a also said in the name of Rabbi Eleazar ben Simeon:
It is permitted to dissemble in the interest of peace, as it is
written [of the brothers of Joseph], 'BEFORE HIS DEATH YOUR
FATHER LEFT THIS INSTRUCTION . . . SAY TO JOSEPH, "FOR-
GIVE, I URGE YOU, THE OFFENCE AND GUILT OF YOUR
BROTHERS . . ."' (Genesis 50:16 JPS). Rabbi Nathan said, It is
a *mitzva* [to do so], as it is said, AND SAMUEL SAID, 'HOW
CAN I GO? IF SAUL HEARS, HE WILL KILL ME' (1 Samuel 16:2).[47]
[Likewise,] it was taught in the School of Rabbi Ishmael, Great
is peace! Even the Holy One, blessed be He, dissembled – first,
it is written, [SARAH LAUGHED TO HERSELF SAYING: '. . . AM
I TO HAVE ENJOYMENT –] WITH MY HUSBAND SO OLD?' but
then, [when the angel reported it to Abraham, he said,] WHY
DID SARAH [LAUGH, SAYING,] 'SHALL I IN TRUTH BEAR A
CHILD, OLD AS I AM?' (Genesis 18:12, 13 JPS).

Rabbi Yohanan ben Baroqa says. It was taught [of] Rabbi
Yohanan and Rabbi Joshua ben Levi: One said, The *halakha* is
according to Rabbi Yohanan ben Baroqa; the other said, The
halakha is not according to Rabbi Yohanan ben Baroqa.

[Here is] proof that it was Rabbi Yohanan who said, The
halakha is not [according to Rabbi Yohanan ben Baroqa]. Rabbi
Abbahu was sitting and stated in the name of Rabbi Yohanan
that the *halakha* was [according to Rabbi Yohanan ben Baroqa,]
but Rabbi Ammi and Rabbi Assi averted their faces from him
[in disapproval]. (Some say it was Rabbi Hiyya bar Abba who
said it, and Rabbi Ammi and Rabbi Assi averted their faces.)

Rav Papa commented, If it was Rabbi Abbahu who
said it, they refrained from saying anything to him out
of deference to Caesar,[48] but if it was Rabbi Hiyya bar
Abba, why didn't they tell him that that was not what
Rabbi Yohanan said?

What happened [in the end]?

A proof – Rabbi Aha bar Hanina reported that Rabbi Abbahu
said in Rabbi Assi's name, A case[49] was submitted to Rabbi

47. God then supplied Samuel with an excuse to make to Saul.
48. Abbahu was in good standing with the Roman administration, so Ammi and Assi
    would not dare challenge him.
49. A woman sued for divorce on the grounds of the husband's impotence.

Yoḥanan in the synagogue of Caesarea, and he ruled that [the husband] must grant her a divorce and pay her *ketuba*. Now if you say she is not commanded [to 'Be fruitful and multiply'], why award her the *ketuba*? Perhaps she had [an additional claim,] like the woman who appeared before Rabbi Ammi; when she claimed the *ketuba* [Rabbi Ammi first refused, saying], Go away! You are not commanded [to 'Be fruitful and multiply']! She said, And what am I to do in my old age? If that is how things are, said [Rabbi Ammi], we must enforce [payment].

A woman came before Rav Naḥman [with a similar claim], and he replied, You are not commanded [to 'Be fruitful and multiply']! She said, And don't I need a stick in my hand and a spade to bury me? If that is how things are, said [Rav Naḥman], we must enforce [payment].

[Rabbi Ḥiyya's sons] Judah and Hezekiah were twins; one of them was fully formed at the end of nine months [pregnancy], the other at the beginning of seven. Rabbi Ḥiyya's wife, Judith, suffered greatly in childbirth. She changed her clothes, came before him [incognito] and asked, Are women commanded to be fruitful and multiply? No, he replied. She went and drank a potion of sterility. [Much later on,] the story came out. He asked her, Then how did you bear me more children (for the teacher said, Judah and Hezekiah were brothers, Pazi and Tavi were sisters)?[50]

66a

Aren't they commanded [to 'Be fruitful and multiply']? Didn't Rav Aḥa bar Qatina say in the name of Rabbi Isaac, A certain woman was half free and half slave, so they forced her master to free her? Rav Naḥman bar Isaac said, That was [not to enable her to marry and have children, but] because [people] were treating her as a prostitute.

Chapter Ten addresses a serious social problem arising from strict application of the law. A married woman may not remarry unless the first husband dies or divorces her, but what if he goes

---

50. Judith's daughters were younger than Judah and Hezekiah; if she drank the potion, how could she bear more children?

*missing, perhaps on a journey abroad? Normal laws of evidence
would require testimony of his death from two independent
adult, male witnesses. Such evidence may not be available, and
the woman would become an* aguna *('chained woman'), unable
either to remarry or to claim her* ketuba *from the missing husband's estate. The rules of evidence were therefore relaxed, so
that indirect evidence, and the testimony of women and slaves,
could be accepted.*

*This much was agreed by all, but its theoretical underpinning
is far from clear, and is the theme of this* sugya. *David Kraemer
writes, 'The Gemara, in its reference to various sources and
authorities, compromises their authority and makes their voice
essentially secondary to its own.'*[51] *There is some truth in this,
though what emerges from the present* sugya *is the firmness of
Tannaitic law as contrasted with the inconclusive theoretical
structures of the Amoraim.*

CHAPTER TEN

MISHNA:

87b   A woman's husband went abroad, [a witness[52]] came and
told her he had died, she remarried, and then her [first] husband returned. She must leave both [husbands], she needs a
bill of divorce from each and has no claim on either for the
ketuba, for income on her investments, for maintenance or for
old clothes;[53] even if she helped herself to these things from
either husband she must return them; any child she bears from
either is a *mamzer*; and [if either husband is a *Kohen*] he may
not defile himself to bury her. [For their part, neither husband
has a claim on] anything she finds, on the proceeds of any
work she does, nor can either annul her vows. If she was an
Israelite she is disqualified from marrying a *Kohen*; if she was

51. Kraemer, *Mind*, p. 138. On pp. 108–9 he discusses a parallel *sugya*, citing Shamma
    Friedman's analysis.
52. Although the Mishna has a plural verb, the Gemara establishes that it is dealing
    with a case where only one witness was involved.
53. Thus Rashi. Alfasi and others think that what is meant is that she cannot claim
    compensation for property of hers that has declined in value.

a Levite she may no longer eat tithes; if she was of a priestly family she may no longer eat *teruma*. Neither husband's heirs inherit her *ketuba*. If either husband dies his brothers may not marry her, but must perform *ḥalitza*.

Rabbi Yosé says, She may claim her *ketuba* from the estate of the first husband.

Rabbi Eleazar says, The first husband has a right to what she finds and to the proceeds of her work, and can annul her vows.

Rabbi Simeon says, If a brother of the first husband [following the death of the latter] marries her or performs *ḥalitza*, this exempts her co-wife [from the obligation to marry or receive *ḥalitza* from him]; [moreover,] any child she bears from [the first husband] is not a *mamzer*.

If [two witnesses testified to her husband's death, so] she remarried without [requiring special] permission, she may return [to the first husband].

If she remarried with the court's permission, she must [nevertheless] leave [the second husband], but she is exempt from bringing a sacrifice [for the sin of adultery]; if she had remarried without the court's permission, she must leave [the second husband], and is obliged to bring a sacrifice. The court's power suffices to exempt her from sacrifice.

If the court gave her permission to remarry, but she went and committed fornication [and then her husband returned], she must bring a sacrifice, for the court only permitted her to marry[, not to commit fornication].

GEMARA:

The end of the Mishna states, **If she remarried without [requiring special] permission, she may return [to the first husband]**; that is, she remarried on the evidence of two witnesses. This implies that the first part of the Mishna [speaks of a case where she required the court's permission because there was only] one witness [to his death]. From this [it appears that] a single witness is believed. [Indeed, another] Mishna[54] states [explicitly], **It became accepted practice to authorize marriages**

54. *Yevamot* 122a.

[on the basis of] one witness citing another, a woman citing another woman, or a woman citing a male or female slave. So we see that a single witness is believed.

Likewise[, in another context], a Mishna[55] states, **If one witness says, You ate forbidden fat, but [the accused] says I didn't, he is exempt [from the obligation to bring a sin-offering]**. The reason [for the exemption] is that he denies [the accusation]; had he remained silent, [the witness] would have been believed. So you see that the Torah gives credence to a single witness.

What is the basis for this?

[It is inferred from] a baraita: OR THE SIN OF WHICH HE IS GUILTY BECOMES KNOWN TO HIM (Leviticus 4:28) – **not that others make it known to him[, but he realizes it himself]. Do you think he would be exempt [from the obligation to bring a sin-offering if there was a witness] and he did not contradict [the witness]? [This is not so, therefore the Torah writes,]** BECOMES KNOWN TO HIM, **[meaning,] however [he finds out].**

How could this be? If two witnesses came and he contradicted them, why should we need Scripture [to tell us that their testimony would be accepted]? So [the baraita must have in mind a case where only] one [witness is involved, and it tells us that] if [the accused] contradicts [the witness, the accused] is believed[, but otherwise the witness is believed]. This demonstrates that a single witness is believed.

But perhaps it is not because the witness is believed, but because the accused is silent, and silence is like an admission [of guilt]? Indeed, this seems the case, since the latter part of the Mishna says, **If two [witnesses] said, You ate forbidden fat, and he denies it, he is exempt [from the obligation to bring a sin-offering], but Rabbi Meir says he is obliged [to bring a sin-offering]. Rabbi Meir says this follows a fortiori; if two witnesses have power to convict of a capital offence, which is serious, how much more do they have power to oblige someone to bring a sin-offering, which is [relatively] minor!** [The other rabbis replied to Meir:] But he could claim, I [committed the

offence] on purpose[, in which case he would not bring a
sin-offering, since that atones only for accidental sins].

Then why do the rabbis oblige him to bring a sin-offering in   88a
the first case[, seeing he could exempt himself on the grounds
that he had committed the offence deliberately]? Could it be
because he is believed [against the witness]? [No!] The rabbis
exempt him from a sin-offering where he contradicts two witnesses, even though we believe them [rather than him; the reason
for the exemption is therefore not that we believe him]. It must
be because he is silent, and silence is like an admission [of guilt].

[So the question of whether a single witness is believed is
irrelevant. The Mishna's statement] is based on reason. [The
case is] like that of a lump of meat, where there is doubt as to
whether it is forbidden or permitted fat, and a witness testifies
that he knows for certain it is permitted fat; [in such a case] he
is believed.

> How can you compare [the two]? In the [meat] case
> no prohibition has been previously established; in our
> Mishna case we know that she was a married woman,
> and 'matters of nakedness'[56] require two witnesses.

Then compare [the Mishna] to [the case of] a piece of meat
that is known to be forbidden fat, and a single witness testifies
that it is permitted fat; he would not be believed!

> How can you compare [the two]? In the [meat]
> case, even if a hundred witnesses were to testify that it
> was permitted fat, they would not be believed. In our
> Mishna, since if two came they would be believed, one
> also is believed, just as we find with *tevel, heqdesh* and
> *qonamot*.[57]

*Proofs that the Torah accepts the testimony of a single witness
for* tevel, heqdesh *and* qonamot *are offered, but rejected as
unsound. This leaves the Gemara to find some other justification
for relaxing the rules of evidence in the woman's favour.*

56. Sexual offences and marital status.
57. *Tevel* is produce from which tithes and/or *teruma* have not been set aside; *heqdesh*
is property dedicated for Temple use, whether as sacrifices, or as property that
may be sold and the proceeds added to the Temple funds; *qonam* is a type of vow
(*Nedarim* 16a; see p. 355).

Rabbi Zeira says, Because of the stringencies imposed on her at the end [if the first husband returns], we make it easier for her at the beginning [by not requiring the normal rigorous standards of evidence].

Then don't impose the stringencies [should things go wrong], and don't make it easy [for her to remarry]!

The rabbis [preferred to] make it easy [for her to remarry], so that she should not become an *aguna*.

SECOND TRACTATE
KETUBOT (MARRIAGE ENTITLEMENTS)

The rabbis were concerned to ensure the stability and quality of marriage, and the ketuba ('written [document]') was a valuable tool to this end. It placed a binding responsibility on the husband for the maintenance of his wife and her children, which in normal circumstances would continue even if he were to divorce her; as it was backed by a charge on his property, he would not lightly resort to divorce. Should she, however, be guilty of some serious marital misdemeanour the court could strip her of her financial rights under the ketuba. The shaping of the ketuba was attributed to the semi-legendary first-century BCE Pharisee Simeon ben Shetaḥ;[1] the attribution underlines the rabbis' conviction that the institution was ancient and authoritative though not biblical.

In 1961 the Israeli archaeologist Yigael Yadin identified a bundle of papyrus scrolls found in a cave on the west coast of the Dead Sea as the personal documents of a Jewish woman named Babatha, from roughly 94–132 CE; among them is an early form of ketuba, written in Aramaic, and pledging 400 rather than the standard 200 zuz. The text closely resembles that established by the rabbis; Babatha and her husband have both signed on the verso, before the witnesses. A still older Aramaic marriage document precisely dated to Seleucid year 136 (= 176 BCE) was found among Edomite documents at Maresha in the 1980s; it has much of the terminology that is

---

1. Tosefta *Ketubot* 12:1; Bavli *Shabbat* 14b and *Ketubot* 82b. On Simeon ben Shetaḥ, see Neusner, *Rabbinic Traditions*, pp. 86–141.

found in the rabbinic ketuba *and was probably common Aramaic law.*[2]

Marriage in the Talmudic period was a private, secular transaction, requiring neither judge nor rabbi,[3] *though it carried serious financial and religious consequences for both husband and wife. It was not a 'sacrament' administered by religious authorities, but it increasingly acquired deep religious symbolism when the notion of God and Israel as bride and groom took hold late in the Talmudic period.*[4]

CHAPTER ONE

MISHNA:

2a **Virgins are married on Wednesdays and widows on Thursdays. The court sits twice a week in towns, on Mondays and Thursdays; should the [groom wish to lodge] a complaint [that the bride is not a] virgin, he may arise early to [attend] the court.**

GEMARA:

Rav Yosef reported that Rav Yehuda said in the name of Shmuel, Why did they say that virgins should be married on Wednesdays? Because the Mishna states, **If the time [stipulated for the wedding] came and she had not yet been taken as wife, she eats his [food] and [if he is a** *Kohen* **she acquires the right to] eat** *teruma.*[5] Is he obliged to provide her with food [immediately] if the [stipulated] time falls on a Sunday? [No,] since our Mishna states, **Virgins are married on Wednesdays.**[6]

Rav Yosef commented, By the Lord of Abraham! [Shmuel] derived something taught from something not taught!

---

2. The Babatha documents are in Yadin, *Cave of Letters,* pp. 118–41; the Edomite document in E. Eshel and Kloner, 'Aramaic Ostracon'.
3. *Yevamot* 22a, *'erva la-kol m'sura.*
4. Satlow, 'Slipping Toward'.
5. *Ketubot* 57a. A virgin bride would be allowed twelve months to prepare her trousseau; then, even if the wedding had not yet taken place, the bridegroom was obliged to support her.
6. Consequently, his obligation to provide for her commences only on the Wednesday following completion of the stipulated period.

What is taught and what is not taught? Surely both
are taught! [Rav Yosef must have meant] he derived
something taught explicitly from something not taught
explicitly.

So if the report was correct, Shmuel must have meant as
follows: Why did they say that virgins should be married on
Wednesdays? The Mishna says that it is in case the [groom
should wish to lodge] a complaint [that the bride is not a]
virgin; he may arise early to [attend] the court. Then let her be
married on Sunday[, since he could attend the Monday sitting]!
[This is not possible;] the Sages were anxious for the welfare
of the daughters of Israel[, and so decreed] that [husbands] should
exert themselves for three days – Sunday, Monday and Tuesday
– preparing the [wedding] feast, and then marry on Wednesday.
So as Mishna states that the Sages were so anxious for the welfare
of the daughters of Israel, when it [says further,] **If the time
[stipulated for the wedding] came and she had not yet been
taken as wife, she eats his [food] and [if he is a *Kohen* she
acquires the right to] eat *teruma*,** [it follows that] if the time
elapsed on Sunday he is not obliged to provide her with food,
since he could not marry her [until Wednesday].

[Rav Yosef continued:] It follows that if he fell sick, or she
fell sick, or her period commenced, that he is not obliged to
provide her with food[, since the wedding would legitimately
be delayed].

Some put this into question form: What if he fell sick? Do
we say that the reason [he does not have responsibility to provide
for her if the stipulated period ended on a Sunday] is force of
circumstances, and [sickness] likewise is force of circumstances?
Or do we say that there the duress arises through a rabbinic
decree, but here there is no [decree, just a personal accident]?
Even if you grant that if he fell sick [and had to postpone the
wedding], he nevertheless becomes responsible to provide for
her, what if *she* fell sick? Can he say, I'm standing here [ready
to wed], or can she say, Your field is spoiled![7] Even if you grant

7.   Can he argue that she is holding up the wedding, and he cannot be held responsible
     for the consequences? Or can she say, Hard luck – you've got me for better or for
     worse, so feed me!

that [if she fell sick] she can say, Your field is spoiled, what if
her period commenced then? If it was her regular period she
certainly cannot say, Your field is spoiled; the question would
only arise if it was not the time of her regular period. As it is
not the time of her regular period, can she argue, Your field is
spoiled, or [do we say that] since some women have irregular
periods, it is no different from a regular period?

Rav Aḥai suggested an answer. [Mishna says,] **If the time
[stipulated for the wedding] came and she had not yet been
taken as wife, she eats his [food] and [if he is a Kohen she
acquires the right to] eat *teruma*.** It does not say, **If he did not
marry**, but **If she had not been taken as wife.** Now what
circumstances [does that Mishna envisage]? If she [is the one
who] prevents [the wedding from taking place], why should she
[acquire the right] to eat food and *teruma*? [The Mishna must
have in mind that] she suffers duress; nevertheless, it states: **She
eats his [food] and [if he is a Kohen she acquires the right to]
eat *teruma*.**

Rav Ashi said, I still say that she does not [acquire the right
to] eat unless the delay is his fault. The Mishna might indeed
have said 'If he did not marry', but since the first part is speaking
of her, the latter part also speaks of her [as the subject].

Rava said, The law [of duress] is different when it comes to
divorce.

Rava, we see, holds that duress is not [a valid plea] when it
comes to [compliance with conditions attached to a] divorce.
From where does Rava derive that? Could it be from the Mishna
that states, **[If a man hands a *get* to his wife, saying 'This
is your *get* on condition that I fail to return within twelve
months', and he dies within twelve months, it is not a [valid]
*get*** [8] – i.e. if he dies it is not valid, but if he falls sick it is? But
perhaps it would be invalid if he fell sick, and the Mishna is
simply making the point that a *get* cannot take effect after the
[husband's] death.

No *get* after the death [of the husband]? The Mishna stated
that previously: **[If he says,] This is your *get* when I die, or**

This I your *get* when this [terminal] sickness [is over], or This is your *get* after my death, he has said nothing.

Perhaps it is to exclude the opinion of 'our rabbis', for a baraita comments, But our rabbis permitted her to marry [without obtaining *ḥalitza* from a surviving brother].[9]

Who are 'our rabbis'? Rav Yehuda said in the name of Shmuel, The court who permitted oil.[10] They accepted the opinion of Rabbi Yosé, who said that the date in the *get* demonstrates [that it is intended to take effect immediately, subject to eventual fulfilment of the condition].

Then perhaps [Rava bases his opinion] on the end of the Mishna: [If he says, The *get* comes into effect] immediately if I don't return within twelve months, and he dies, it is valid – if he dies, [but does he mean the same to apply] if he fell sick? Perhaps he means only if he dies, since he does not want [his wife] to pass to his brother.[11]

Perhaps [Rava bases his opinion] on this [precedent]: A man said, If I don't return within 30 days, this is a *get*. At the end of 30 days he arrived, but was held up [on the wrong side of the river] by the ferry. He [called across], I'm coming! I'm coming! Shmuel said, That is not 'coming'.[12] Perhaps a foreseeable duress is different; he should have set an [appropriate] condition but did not do so, so he has caused his own loss.

Rava has his own reason for ruling [that there is no plea of duress in divorce]. It is [in the interest of both] virtuous and loose women. [It is in the interest] of virtuous women, because if you rule that a *get* is invalid [when a condition remains unfulfilled owing to duress], it could happen that there was no duress but she thought there was, and so she remains an *aguna*; [it is in the interest] of loose women, because if you rule that a   3a

---

9. 'Our rabbis' differed from the Mishna since they interpreted a statement such as 'This is your *get* when I die' to mean that the *get* took effect immediately, subject to the husband's death.

10. i.e. the court of Judah II (Judah Nesia), grandson of Judah ha-Nasi, who held the patriarchate from about 225 to 250, moving its seat from Sepphoris to Tiberias.

11. i.e. he is acting in the interest of his widow, so that she should be free to marry whom she wishes.

12. The *get* takes effect against his will even though he was kept away only by duress. This supports Rava's contention that there is no plea of duress for divorce.

get is invalid [when a condition remains unfulfilled owing to duress], it could happen there was duress but she thought there was none, so she remarried, and the *get* is invalid and her children are [consequently] *mamzerim*.

The next section touches on what is still one of the most sensitive issues in rabbinic law. Divorce is essentially a private procedure; a man delivers a bill of divorce to his wife in the presence of witnesses. How can a court dissolve a marriage, as it may well wish to do to save a woman from becoming an aguna? *We see that the Sages were prepared to take drastic measures.*

So can there be a situation in which a *get* is invalid in Torah law, yet in the interest of 'virtuous and loose women' the married woman [who receives it] is authorized to marry someone else?

Yes. When a man betroths a woman he does so 'in accordance with the intention of the rabbis', and the rabbis [retrospectively] confiscate his betrothal token[13] [thereby invalidating the first marriage].

Ravina asked Rav Ashi: That is all very well if he betrothed her with money. What if he betrothed by cohabitation?[14] [He replied:] The rabbis declared his cohabitation an act of prostitution.

Chapters Four and Five deal with the text and content of the ketuba.

CHAPTER FOUR

MISHNA:

51a   If [the husband] did not write a *ketuba*, a virgin may nevertheless claim 200 *zuz* and a widow 100, since it is a condition [of marriage] laid down by the court.

If he wrote 'a field worth a *maneh*' instead of '200 *zuz*', and failed to write, 'All my property is pledged to your *ketuba*', he

---

13. Nowadays a ring, though in the Talmudic period it could have been money, or goods worth more than a *peruta*.
14. Mishna *Qiddushin* Chapter One (see p. 400).

is still fully liable, since it is a condition [of marriage] set by the court.

If he did not write, 'Should you be taken captive I will ransom you and take you back as my wife' – or in the case of a *Kohen*, 'Should you be taken captive I will ransom you and return you to your home' – he is still fully liable, since it is a condition [of marriage] set by the court.

If she is taken captive he must ransom her; he may not say, 'Here is your *get* and your *ketuba* [money]; ransom yourself.'

If she falls sick he must pay her medical expenses, but he may say, 'Here is your *get* and your *ketuba* [money]; heal yourself.'

GEMARA:

Whose opinion is [the Mishna's opening statement]? It is Rabbi Meir's, for he says, If anyone [commits] less than 200 for a virgin, or a *maneh* for a widow, it is as if he is committing fornication; whereas Rabbi Judah said, If he wishes, he may write a document for 200 for a virgin, and she writes, I have received a *maneh* from you; for a widow he may write a *maneh*, and she writes, I have received 50 [*zuz*] from you.[15]

But the [second] part [of our Mishna] must be Rabbi Judah's opinion[, since it states], If he wrote 'a field worth a *maneh*' instead of '200 *zuz*', and failed to write, 'All my property is pledged to your *ketuba*', he is still fully liable, since it is a condition [of marriage] laid down by the court.

It is Rabbi Judah who holds that [missing] guarantees [are treated] as scribal errors [and enforced by the court regardless], whereas Rabbi Meir holds that [missing] guarantees are not [treated as] scribal errors [and cannot be enforced]. For a Mishna states: **If someone found bills of debt with property mortgaged to the debt, he should not return them [to the lender, even with the borrower's agreement], since the court may enforce payment [from the mortgaged property]. If property is not mortgaged to the debt, he should return them to the lender, since the court cannot enforce payment [from the mortgaged** 51b

---

15. That is, he may by arrangement with his wife commit only half the stipulated sum.

property]. **This is the opinion of Rabbi Meir, but the Sages say he should not return the documents in either case, for the court may enforce payment [from the property even though it is not explicitly mortgaged].**[16]

The first part of the Mishna must be [according to] Rabbi Meir, and the last part [according to] Rabbi Judah. For if you think that the whole Mishna is [according to] Rabbi Meir, and he distinguishes between a *ketuba* and [commercial] documents, surely he does not! A baraita states: **Five can claim from unencumbered**[17] **property** [only]. **They are: produce; improvements to produce; one who takes on responsibility for maintaining his wife's son or daughter** [by a previous husband]; **a bill of debt which lacks a guarantee; a *ketuba* which lacks a guarantee.** Now, whom do we know who holds that [missing] guarantees are not [treated as] scribal errors? Rabbi Meir! Yet he includes a *ketuba*[, so clearly he makes no distinction between a *ketuba* and any other document].

You could say [our Mishna] is [according to] Rabbi Meir, or you could say it is [according to] Rabbi Judah.

You could say it is [according to] Rabbi Judah: there she writes 'I have received'; here she does not write 'I have received.'

Or you could say it is [according to] Rabbi Meir: when it says, 'He is still fully liable', it means [he is liable to pay] out of unencumbered property.

CHAPTER FIVE

MISHNA:

54b   **Though they said a virgin is entitled to 200 [*zuz*] and a widow to a *maneh*, if [the husband] wishes to add, he may add even 100 *maneh*.**

16. Mishna *Bava Metzi'a* 1:6 (12b). The fear is that the lender and the borrower may have connived to collect the debt from a third party who had meanwhile purchased the mortgaged property.
17. Literally, 'free'.

If she is widowed or divorced, whether betrothed or married, she collects the whole [sum].

Rabbi Eleazar ben Azaria says, If married, she collects the whole; if betrothed, a virgin collects 200 and a widow a *maneh*, for he only wrote [the additional sum into the settlement] on the understanding that he would marry her.

Rabbi Judah says, If he wishes, he may write a document for 200 for a virgin, and she writes, I have received a *maneh* from you; for a widow he may write a *maneh*, and she writes, I have received 50 [*zuz*] from you.

Rabbi Meir says, If anyone [commits] less than 200 for a virgin, or a *maneh* for a widow, it is as if he is committing fornication.

GEMARA:

[Isn't it] obvious [that a husband may increase his wife's marriage settlement]? [No. If this had not been stated,] I might have thought that the rabbis instituted a fixed sum, in order not to embarrass anyone who does not have more; [Mishna therefore] informs us [that this is not the case].

If [the husband] wishes to add. The Mishna does not say he wishes to *write* but he wishes to *add*. This supports the view of Rabbi Aivu in the name of Rabbi Yannai, that conditions attached to the *ketuba* [take effect] as [if they are part of] the *ketuba* [itself].

This carries implications for a woman who sells [her *ketuba*]; for one who waives [her *ketuba*]; for one who refuses her marital obligations;[18] for one who detracts from [her *ketuba*];[19] for one who transgresses the law; [where the value of the property pledged to the *ketuba*] increases; for oaths; with regard to the [remission of debts in the] sabbatical year; for a man who makes over all his property to his children; for claims from real estate or from inferior-quality [land]; for [claims arising in] the period the bride remains in her father's

18. Literally, 'who rebels'.
19. i.e. helps herself, while still married, to part of the entitlement.

house; and for [the claims] of male children on the
ketuba [if their mother died before collecting it].

It was taught, [concerning] male children [who claim] the
ketuba [from their mother's estate]:

> The [scholars of] Pumbedita say, They may not
> claim from property on which there is a lien, [for]
> Mishna teaches [that the correct wording of the *ketuba*
> is] 'they shall inherit'.

> The [scholars of] Mata Meḥasya say, They may
> claim from property on which there is a lien, [for]
> Mishna teaches [that the correct wording of the *ketuba*
> is] 'they shall take'.

> > The law is, They may not claim from
> > property on which there is a lien, [for]
> > Mishna teaches [that the correct wording of
> > the *ketuba* is] 'they shall inherit'.

If [the father had designated] chattels [for payment of the
ketuba], and they are available, [the orphans may take the chattels
in payment] without an oath. If the chattels are not available:

> The [scholars of] Pumbedita say, [The orphans may
> collect from the estate] without an oath [that, to their
> knowledge, their mother had not already helped
> herself].

> The [scholars of] Mata Meḥasya say, [The orphans
> may collect from the estate only] with an oath [that, to
> their knowledge, their mother had not already helped
> herself].

> > The law is, [The orphans may collect from
> > the estate] without an oath [that, to their
> > knowledge, their mother had not already
> > helped herself].

If [the father] had specified land [for payment of the *ketuba*]
by its four boundaries, [the orphans may take possession of the
land] without an oath [that, to their knowledge, their mother
had not already taken possession of something else as security].
If he specified only one boundary:

> The [scholars of] Pumbedita say, No oath [is
> required].

The [scholars of] Mata Meḥasya say, An oath [is
required].

The law is, No oath [is required].

If [someone] said to witnesses, Write and sign [a document]
and give it to [the other party], then if they made a *qinyan*,[20]
they do not [subsequently] need to refer back to him [before
signing]. If no *qinyan* was made:

The [scholars of] Pumbedita say, He does not need
to refer back to him.

The [scholars of] Mata Meḥasya say, He needs to
refer back to him.

The law is, He needs to refer back to him.

Rabbi Eleazar ben Azaria says, etc. It was taught, Rav and
Rabbi Nathan: One of them said, The law is according to Rabbi
Eleazar ben Azaria; the other said, The law is not according to
Rabbi Eleazar ben Azaria.

There is proof that it was Rabbi Nathan who said,
The law is according to Rabbi Eleazar ben Azaria.
There is evidence that Rabbi Nathan [was prepared
to] judge on the basis of a conjecture, since Rabbi
Nathan said, The law is according to Rabbi Simeon
Shezuri with respect to [instructions given by a] mor-
tally sick person and with respect to *teruma* from the
levitical tithe of doubtfully tithed produce.[21]

But doesn't Rav, also, accept conjecture? For it was
taught: They say in Rav's School in Rav's name, of a
gift made by a dying person, and in which a *qinyan* is
written, 'He has given it two horses to ride';[22] but
Shmuel said, I don't know how to judge this.

'They say in Rav's School in Rav's name,
"He has given it two horses to ride."' It is
like the gift of a well person, and also like a

20. If they formally ratified the procedure.
21. Both cases depend on conjecture by the court as to the true intentions of the agent
who cannot be questioned.
22. A gift made in anticipation of death does not require a *qinyan*, but one made in
good health does, since if there is no *qinyan* the donor may change his mind.
Here the donor has ensured the validity of his gift in two ways.

gift in anticipation of death. It is like the gift of a well person, in that if he recovers he cannot change his mind; and it is like a gift in anticipation of death, in that if he said, What I have borrowed should go to so-and-so, then what he borrowed must go to so-and-so [even if he recovers].

'But Shmuel said, "I don't know how to judge this."' Perhaps [the testator's] intention was that [the gift] would be acquired on [the strength of] the document [rather than merely through the pronouncement of a dying man]; a document, however, cannot take effect posthumously.

So it seems that both of them accept conjecture. For the one who says, [The] law [is according to Rabbi Eleazar ben Azaria,] this is all right. For the one who says, [The] law [is not according to Eleazar ben Azaria,] here, too, conjecture [is involved], namely that [the bridegroom increases the settlement] in order to demonstrate his feelings,[23] and he has demonstrated his feelings.

Rav Ḥanina sat before Rabbi Yannai and said, the law is according to Rabbi Eleazar ben Azaria. [Rabbi Yannai] said to him, Go read your verse outside![24] The law is not according to Rabbi Eleazar ben Azaria.

Rav Yitzḥaq ben Avdimi said in the name of our master,[25] the law is according to Rabbi Eleazar ben Azaria.

Rav Naḥman said in the name of Shmuel, The law is according to Rabbi Eleazar ben Azaria; but Rav Naḥman for his own part said the law is not according to Rabbi Eleazar ben Azaria. [However,] the [scholars of] Nehardea said in the name of Rav Naḥman, The law is according to Rabbi Eleazar ben Azaria, and

23. Literally, 'to bring near his mind'.
24. 'Tell it to the marines!' – You are talking nonsense.
25. Rav – Rashi.

even though Rav Naḥman[26] uttered a curse, saying so-and-so should befall any judge who judged according to Rabbi Eleazar ben Azaria, the law is according to Rabbi Eleazar ben Azaria.

The decision in practice goes according to Rabbi Eleazar ben Azaria.

The ketuba is entirely concerned with a husband's responsibilities towards his wife. What are her responsibilities?

MISHNA:

These are the things a woman must do for her husband: [she must] grind, bake bread, wash clothes, cook, nurse her children, make his bed and knit wool.   59b

If she brings one maid-servant with her, she need not grind, bake or wash clothes. If she brings two, she need not cook nor nurse her children; three, she need not make his bed nor knit; four, she may sit upon a throne!

Rabbi Eliezer says, Even if she brings a hundred maid-servants with her, she should [still] knit, because idleness leads to wickedness. Rabban Simeon ben Gamaliel said, [Likewise,] if a husband made his wife swear not to knit, he should divorce her[27] and pay her the *ketuba*, because idleness leads to madness.

GEMARA:

Must *she* grind? [Surely, the watermill does this – Rashi.] Rather, she must attend to the grinding; alternatively, she may use a handmill.

The Mishna does not accord with Rabbi Ḥiyya's [view], for Rabbi Ḥiyya taught: Wives are for beauty; wives are for [bearing] children, and he taught: Wives are for ornament, and he taught: If you want to make your wife radiant, buy her silk garments, and if you want to give your daughter a fair complexion, give her chicken to eat and milk to drink when she reaches puberty.[28]

26. Rabbi Shmuel Strasun ('Rashash', 1794–1872) suggests that this is Naḥman bar Abba, and the preceding one is Naḥman bar Isaac; perhaps he overlooks the irony of the passage.
27. i.e. she can claim divorce with full settlement.
28. Rabbi Ḥiyya does not dispute that she may knit; she should, however, avoid activities such as grinding, baking and nursing that might compromise her beauty (Tosafot).

Nurse her children. Is this Mishna contrary to [a ruling of] the School of Shammai? Tosefta teaches: **If she swore not to suckle her child, the School of Shammai say, She removes her nipple from its mouth; the School of Hillel say, He may force her to nurse it** [notwithstanding the oath]. **If she is divorced** [from the father of the child,] **he cannot force her, but if** [the baby] **recognizes her** [and refuses to suckle from anyone else, the ex-husband] **must pay her, and force her to nurse, in case of danger** [to the baby].

[The Mishna] may accord even with the School of Shammai. [Tosefta] deals with a case where she vowed, and he confirmed the vow, so he 'puts a finger between her teeth',[29] whereas the School of Hillel hold that she has put a finger between her own teeth.

Then why don't [the Schools] debate the plain [case of a woman who vowed against the provisions of the] *ketuba*? Moreover, a baraita states: The School of Shammai say that she need not suckle. So it makes more sense [to conclude] that the Mishna is not in accordance with the School of Shammai.

If [the baby] **recognizes her** [and refuses to suckle from anyone else]. To what age? Rava said that Rabbi Yirmiya bar Abba said in Rav's name, Three months, but Shmuel said, Thirty days; Rabbi Isaac said in the name of Rabbi Yoḥanan, Fifty days.

Rav Shimei bar Abbaye said, The law is according to what Rabbi Isaac said in the name of Rabbi Yoḥanan.

Now both Rav and Rabbi Yoḥanan assessed the child according to its development, but did Shmuel's ruling correspond to reality? When Rami bar Ezekiel came he said, Take no notice of the rules my brother stated in Shmuel's name. What Shmuel said was, At whatever age [the baby] recognizes her. A woman came before Shmuel and he asked Rav Dimi bar Yosef to put her to the test. He seated her among rows of women and passed the baby around. When [the baby] reached her it gazed at her, even though she averted her eyes from him.[30] Raise your eyes and take your child, he said.

29. He has placed himself at a legal disadvantage by confirming the vow; otherwise, he could force her to suckle, as the Mishna indicates.
30. This is not a mother who claims her baby, but one who refuses to suckle it.

How does a blind baby know [its mother]? Rav Ashi said, By smell and taste.

The rabbis taught: A baby sucks for twenty-four months; after that it is like sucking a 'swarming creature'.[31] This is Rabbi Eliezer's opinion, but Rabbi Joshua says, He may continue to suck until four or five years old, but if he stopped after twenty-four months and then restarted, it is like sucking a 'swarming creature'.

A scholar said, From then on it is like sucking an 'abomination'.

An objection was raised [to the notion that breast milk was like 'an abomination']: Is the milk of bipeds unclean? You might reason that if [the Torah] is lenient with animals, permitting contact, but is nevertheless strict with their milk,[32] in the case of humans, who can defile by contact, would it not be strict with their milk? That is why it says, AND THE CAMEL, THOUGH IT CHEWS THE CUD . . . IS UNCLEAN (Leviticus 11:4) – It is unclean, but the milk of bipeds is not unclean, but clean. Perhaps I should make an exception only of the *milk* of bipeds, since milk of only some animals is forbidden,[33] but not their blood, since the blood of all animals is forbidden? That is why it says, AND THE CAMEL, THOUGH IT CHEWS THE CUD . . . IS UNCLEAN – [The camel] is unclean; the blood of bipeds is not unclean, but clean. Rav Sheshet added, There is not even a *mitzva* to avoid it!

No contradiction. One [ruling applies] if [the milk] has left [the breast], the other if it has not.

The opposite applies to blood, as a baraita teaches: If there was blood on a loaf, he must scrape it off before eating; if the blood was still between his teeth, he need not worry about sucking it down.

A teacher said: Rabbi Joshua said, He may continue to suck [at the breast] until he is four or five years old. But didn't Rabbi Joshua say, Until he carries his bag on his shoulder? Both come to the same thing.

31. i.e. something not *kasher*: cf. Leviticus 11:29.
32. Someone who has contact with, e.g. a camel, is not thereby rendered unclean; but its milk is forbidden.
33. Literally, 'it is not equal for all'. The interpretation follows Rashi.

Rav Yosef said, The *halakha* is according to Rabbi Joshua. *Among the wife's rights in marriage is a right to sex. But what if the husband took an oath not to derive pleasure from his wife, or had some occupation which kept him away from home for lengthy periods, or wished to go away to study?*

MISHNA:

61a   If someone swore that he would not have sex with his wife, the School of Shammai say, [The limit is] two weeks; the School of Hillel say, One week. Disciples may leave home to study [even] without their wives' agreement for [up to] thirty days.

Times [set] by the Torah for frequency of intercourse are: for idlers,[34] daily; for [agricultural] workers, twice a week; donkey drivers, once a week; camel drivers, once in 30 days; sailors, once in 6 months, according to Rabbi Eliezer.

GEMARA:

62b   What is the frequency for disciples? Rav Yehuda said in the name of Shmuel, From Sabbath eve to Sabbath eve.[35]

[HE IS LIKE A TREE PLANTED BY STREAMS OF WATER,] WHICH YIELDS ITS FRUIT IN SEASON (Psalm 1:3 JPS). Rav Yehuda – some say Rav Huna and some say Rav Naḥman – said, This is one who has intercourse with his wife each Sabbath eve.

Yehuda the son of Rabbi Ḥiyya was the son-in-law of Rabbi Yannai. He went to study under Rav, and returned home each evening; when he arrived home he would see in front of him a pillar of fire. One day he was absorbed late in his studies. When the sign did not appear, Rabbi Yannai said, Overturn the bed;[36] if Yehuda was alive he would not have neglected his marital duty. It was AS AN ERROR COMMITTED BY A RULER (Ecclesiastes 10:5 JPS); [Yehuda] died.

---

34. An obscure term, discussed by the Gemara (62a).
35. Sex on Shabbat had been forbidden by some Jewish teachers; Jubilees 50:8 classes it as a capital offence. Michael Corinaldi, 'Karaite Halakha' in Hecht, Jackson, Passamanek, *Jewish Law*, p. 262, reports a recent case in which a Karaite court cited marital relations on the Sabbath as a contributory factor in a wife's plea for divorce.
36. As a sign of mourning. Presumably Yannai was joking; but a great man should be more careful.

Rabbi (Judah ha-Nasi) was arranging his son's marriage to the daughter of Rabbi Ḥiyya. When he was about to write the *ketuba*, the girl died. He said, God forbid! Something must be wrong [with the family]! They sat and examined the families' records and found that Rabbi was descended from Avital[, the wife of King David,] through Shefatia, whereas Rabbi Ḥiyya was descended from Shamma, David's brother.[37]

He then set about marrying his son to a daughter of Rabbi Yosé ben Zimra. They agreed that [the son] should spend twelve years in study. When they brought [the bride] before him, [the young man] said, Let it be six years! They brought her again; he said, Let me marry her first, then go and study! He was ashamed [to admit this] to his father. His father said, My son, you understand your Creator! First He said, BRING THEM AND PLANT THEM [IN THE MOUNTAIN OF YOUR INHERITANCE] (Exodus 15:17); but then he said, LET THEM MAKE ME A SANCTUARY AND I WILL DWELL AMONG THEM (Exodus 25:8).[38] He went away and studied for twelve years. By the time he returned, his wife was no longer able to bear children. Rabbi said, What shall we do? Should he divorce her? They will say, This poor woman waited twelve years in vain! Should he take an additional wife? People will say, This is his wife, and this is his harlot! So he prayed for her, and she recovered.

After the wedding of Rabbi Simeon ben Yoḥai, Rabbi Ḥanania ben Ḥakhinai went off to study. [Rabbi Simeon] said, Wait for me to come with you; but he didn't wait. He went and studied for twelve years, by which time the roads in the town had changed and he couldn't find his way home. He sat down by the riverbank and heard people calling, 'Ḥakhinai's daughter! Ḥakhinai's daughter! Fill your apron and come along!' She must be one of the family, he reasoned. He followed her, and found his wife sitting and sifting flour. When she saw him,

37. Rabbi's family, being of the royal line, would not marry with the family of Shimma. The printed Talmud text has Shimei (2 Samuel 16:7) instead of Shamma (1 Samuel 16:9) or Shim'a (1 Chronicles 2:13), but this is clearly an error.

38. God first 'planned' to settle the Israelites in the Land, and after a period of preparation He would 'consummate' his relationship with them by allowing a Temple to be built for His Presence; but He relented and set His Presence among them in the desert, so that they should not have to wait.

[she had such a shock that] she expired. He [protested], Lord of the Universe! Is that the reward for this poor woman! He prayed for her and she recovered.

Rabbi Ḥama bar Bissa passed twelve years in the House of Study. When he [was ready to] return, he said, I'll not do what the son of Ḥakhinai did! He remained in the House of Study and sent a message home. His son, Oshaya, came and sat before him [incognito – Rashi]. [Rabbi Ḥama] questioned him, and found his grasp of learning was brilliant. He became despondent, and thought, If I had stayed at home I could have [brought up] a son like this! He went home, and his son followed. [Rabbi Ḥama] stood, thinking [the unknown young man] was going to question him. His wife said to him, Does a father stand in the presence of his son? Rami bar Ḥama commented on the verse, THE THREEFOLD CORD WILL NOT EASILY BE BROKEN (Ecclesiastes 4:12) – This applies to Rabbi Oshaya the son of Rabbi Ḥama bar Bissa.

Rabbi Aqiva was Ben Kalba Sabua's shepherd. Ben Kalba Sabua's daughter saw that he was a man of virtue and excellence. She said, If I marry you, will you study? He said, Yes. She married him in secret and sent him on his way. When her father heard he threw her out of his house and swore that she should not benefit in any way from his wealth. Aqiva went to study for twelve years. When he came back he brought with him 12,000 disciples. He overheard an old man ask his wife, Why do you carry on like a living widow? She replied, If he would listen to me, he would study for another twelve years! [Aqiva] reflected, Then I have her permission [to continue my studies]; so he went and studied for another twelve years. When he returned he brought with him 24,000 disciples. His wife heard [he was coming] and went out to meet him. Her neighbours said, Borrow some [nice] clothes to cover yourself with! She replied, THE RIGHTEOUS MAN KNOWS THE SOUL OF HIS BEAST (Proverbs 12:10). When she reached him, she fell on her face and kissed his feet. His servants tried to push her away, but he said, Leave her! All that we have we owe to her! Her father heard that a great man had come to town. He said, I will go and see whether he can absolve my vow. [Aqiva] said, Did you intend

63a

your vow [to apply should your son-in-law be] a man of great [learning]? He replied, [My vow was not meant to stand] even if he would learn one chapter or one law. I am he, said Aqiva. [Ben Kalba Sabua] fell on his face and kissed [Aqiva's] feet, and made over half his fortune to him.

Rabbi Aqiva's daughter did the same for Ben Azzai. That's why they say, Sheep follows sheep;[39] like mother like daughter.

Certain offences committed by a wife lead to her forfeiting her financial rights under the ketuba; *conversely, some offences committed by the husband allow her to sue for divorce. Though in rabbinic law divorce is formally effected by the husband, not by the court, there are several situations in which a court will coerce the husband to divorce his wife and to pay her the* ketuba.

CHAPTER SEVEN

MISHNA:

These [women must] leave [the marriage] without *ketuba*: 72a those who transgress the law of Moses and the Jewish[40] people. What [constitutes transgressing] the law of Moses? If she gives him untithed food to eat, or cohabits with him during menstruation, or neglects to set aside *ḥalla* [from the dough], or makes vows and fails to keep them. What [constitutes transgressing] the law of the Jewish people? If she goes out with her hair uncovered, or spins in a public place,[41] or converses with [strange] men in the street. Abba Saul adds, If she belittles [her husband's] parents in his presence. Rabbi Tarfon adds, If she is loud-voiced. What is 'loud-voiced'? If she talks so loudly in her own house that her neighbours hear her.

MISHNA:

[The court] coerces these men to divorce:[42] If his skin is 77a

39. Rabbi Aqiva's wife was called Rachel, which is Hebrew for sheep.
40. This is one of the rare occasions the Mishna uses *yehudit* 'Jewish' rather than *Israel*. See Introduction, ' "Israel", "Jew", "Palestine" '.
41. She would bare her arms.
42. That is, if the wife finds them unacceptable.

diseased, if he has a nasal polyp, if he is a dog-dung collector, a bronze refiner or a tanner, whether or not this was the case when they married. Rabbi Meir said, In all these cases, even if he made the situation clear to her before they married, she can say, I thought I could stand it, but now I can't! The Sages say, She has to accept the [agreed] situation except in the case of the skin disease, because his flesh putrefies.

A tanner in Sidon died, leaving a brother who was also a tanner. The Sages said, She can [refuse to marry her brother-in-law, and] say, I could accept your brother, but I cannot accept you.

The next passage is of interest for its application to bankruptcy law. Because it gives so few numerical examples, there is considerable divergence among the early authorities as to the principles on which the calculations are based. This has attracted the attention of modern mathematicians. Robert J. Aumann and Michael Maschler argue that in this passage, 'For three different bankruptcy problems, the . . . Talmud prescribes solutions that equal precisely the nucleoli of the corresponding coalitional games';[43] this means simply that Aumann and Maschler can produce the same numerical results as the Mishna by an algorithm that treats the three widows (or debtors in the bankruptcy case) as forming successive coalitions to divide the estate, rather than dividing it proportionately according to their claims. Aumann was awarded the Nobel Prize for Economics in 2005 with a citation 'for having enhanced our understanding of conflict and cooperation through game-theory analysis'; no Nobel prize is awarded for Talmud or, more surprisingly, for Mathematics.

Neither this nor the succeeding Mishna should be taken as evidence of polygamy. They are abstract exercises devised to demonstrate the principles of bankruptcy law where there are competing claims against a limited estate. As Rashi observes, our Mishna assumes that all the claims were incurred simultaneously, so none has chronological priority.

43.   Aumann and Maschler, 'Game Theoretic Analysis', p. 195.

CHAPTER TEN

MISHNA:

[Suppose] a man with three wives died. The *ketuba* of one   93a
was 100 [*zuz*], of one 200, and of one 300. If [only] 100 [*zuz*
remained in his estate], they divide it equally. If there were
200, the one with a *ketuba* for 100 takes 50, and those with
[*ketubot* for] 200 and 300 take three gold pieces[44] each. If there
were 300, the one with a *ketuba* for 100 takes 50, the one with
a *ketuba* for 200 takes 100, and the one with a *ketuba* for 300
takes six gold pieces.

The same applies to three who invest money in a venture;[45]
this is how they divide the [end sum], according to whether it
has decreased or increased.

GEMARA:

The one with a *ketuba* for 100 takes 50. Surely she should
take 33⅓[, seeing that the three of them have equal claims on the
first 100]?

Shmuel said, [She takes 50] only if [the wife with a *ketuba*]
for 200 had written to her, I will not dispute [the first] 100 with
you.

But if [we are dealing with a case] like that, why does the
latter part [of the Mishna] say, **The one with a *ketuba* for 200
takes 100, and the one with a *ketuba* for 300 takes six gold
pieces?** The first wife could say to the second, You relinquished
your right [with regard to the first 100]!

[The second wife] could reply to [the first], I said I would
not dispute; I did not relinquish my right.

**If there were 300, the one with a *ketuba* for 100 takes 50,
the one with a *ketuba* for 200 takes 100** – [Why?] Surely she
can claim [only] 75?

Shmuel said, [The second takes 100] only if [the wife with a
ketuba] for 300 had written to both the one with 100 and the
one with 200, I will not dispute [the first] 100 with you.

---

44. One gold piece is worth 25 *zuz*.
45. Literally, 'put money in a purse'.

Rav Yaakov of Nehar Peqod said in the name of Ravina, The middle [case in the Mishna is a case of] two [successive] claims, and the last is also [a case of] two [successive] claims. The middle concerns two [successive] claims; 75 [*zuz*] became available first, then 125 on a [subsequent] occasion. The last concerns two [successive] claims; 75 [*zuz*] became available first, then 225 on a [subsequent] occasion.

It was taught: **This is the Mishna of Rabbi Nathan, but Rabbi says, I do not agree with Rabbi Nathan's opinion on this; they divide the estate equally.**

The same applies to three who invest money in a venture.
93b   Shmuel said, If two contributed, one 100 and one 200, the profit is shared [equally between them].

Rabba said, Shmuel's ruling is plausible [where they invest in] an ox to plough and they use it to plough. [However,] if they [invest in] an ox to plough, but it is slaughtered [for food], each takes in proportion to what he has invested. But Rav Hamnuna said, Even if they [invested in] an ox to plough and then slaughtered it [for food], they share the profit equally.

An objection was raised: **If two contribute to a project, one 100 and the other 200, the profit is shared equally.**[46] Isn't this [a case where they invested in] an ox to plough, but it was slaughtered [for food], and so refutes Rabba's [comment]? No. It concerns [a case where they invested in] an ox to plough, and they used it to plough. But what [happens] if they [invested in] an ox to plough, and then slaughtered it [for food]? Does each take in proportion to what he has invested? In that case, why does the latter part read: **If each bought [an ox**[47]**] with his own money and they combined them, each gets back in proportion to what he contributed?** It should make the distinction [explicit], and state, When does this apply? If the oxen were for ploughing and they used them for ploughing; but if the oxen were for ploughing and they [subsequently] slaughtered them

46. This sentence, and the 'latter part' cited below, are from the parallel passage in the Tosefta.
47. Of different value – Rashi.

for food, each takes according to what he has contributed. [Indeed,] this is what it means: This is where the oxen were for ploughing and they used them for ploughing, but if the oxen were for ploughing and they [subsequently] slaughtered them for food, it is as if each bought [an ox] with his own money and they combined them, and each gets back in proportion to what he has contributed.

The Mishna said: **The same applies to three who invest money in a venture; this is how they divide the [end sum], according to whether it has decreased or increased.** Doesn't this mean[, literally,] that there is less money or more money? Rav Naḥman said in the name of Rabba bar Abuha, No; **increased** means authentic *zuzim*; **decreased** means debased *istiras*.

Politics, religion and matrimonial law meet in the next extract. Mishna is clearly concerned to establish the primacy of the Land of Israel; the Babylonian Yehuda bar Ezekiel seeks the primacy of Torah.

After some technical clarifications the Gemara presents collections of sayings illustrating attitudes to the Land of Israel. The first is dramatized as a conversation between Rav Yehuda bar Ezekiel and Rabbi Zeira, when the latter decided to emigrate from Babylonia to Israel; in its present literary form it expresses ongoing rivalries between the two centres of Jewish life. Yosé bar Ḥanina's 'three oaths', including 'that they shall not go up in military formation', have frequently been cited by religious opponents of political Zionism; Zionists have been happier with the views of Rabbi Eleazar, a devoted advocate of the Land.

CHAPTER THIRTEEN

MISHNA:

110b   All – both men and women – may raise to the Land of
Israel, and none may bring down [from there]. All may elevate
to Jerusalem, and none may bring down.[48]

If [a man] took a wife in the Land of Israel and divorced
her in the Land of Israel, he must pay the *ketuba* in the
currency of the Land of Israel. If he took a wife in the Land
of Israel and divorced her in Cappadocia, he may pay the
ketuba in the currency of the Land of Israel. If he took a wife
in Cappadocia and divorced her in the Land of Israel, he must
pay the *ketuba* in the currency of the Land of Israel, but
Rabban Simeon ben Gamaliel says he may pay in the currency
of Cappadocia. If he took a wife in Cappadocia and divorced
her in Cappadocia, he must pay the *ketuba* in the currency of
Cappadocia.

GEMARA:

The rabbis taught: A person should always dwell in the Land
of Israel, even in a town where the majority of inhabitants are
idolaters; he should not dwell outside the Land, even in a town
where the majority are Israelites. For if you dwell in the Land
of Israel, it is as if you have a God, whereas if you dwell outside
the Land, it is as if you have no God, as it is said, To GIVE
YOU THE LAND OF CANAAN AND TO BE YOUR GOD (Leviticus
25:38). So does no one who lives outside the Land have a
God? [Surely they do,] but what is meant is that if you dwell
outside the Land, it is as if you serve idols, as David said, FOR
THEY HAVE DRIVEN ME OUT TODAY, SO THAT I CANNOT HAVE
A SHARE IN THE LORD'S POSSESSION, BUT AM TOLD, 'GO
AND WORSHIP OTHER GODS' (1 Samuel 26:19 JPS) – so it
means that if you dwell outside the Land it is as if you serve
idols.[49]

Rabbi Zeira wanted to go up to the Land of Israel, so he tried

48. That is, either party has a right to insist that the other move with them to the
Land or to Jerusalem, but neither can insist on leaving.
49. Tosefta *Avoda Zara* 5.

to evade Rav Yehuda, for Rav Yehuda said, Whoever goes up from Babylonia to the Land of Israel transgresses a positive commandment, as it is said, **THEY SHALL BE BROUGHT TO** iiia **BABYLON, AND THERE THEY SHALL REMAIN, UNTIL I TAKE NOTE OF THEM – DECLARES THE LORD** (Jeremiah 27:22 JPS).

And Rabbi Zeira? The verse refers to sacred vessels[, not to people].

And Rav Yehuda? There is another verse: **I ADJURE YOU, O MAIDENS OF JERUSALEM, BY GAZELLES OR BY HINDS OF THE FIELD: DO NOT WAKE NOR ROUSE [MY] BELOVED UNTIL SHE PLEASE!** (Song 2:7).

And Rabbi Zeira? That [verse indicates] that [the people of Israel] should not go up in military formation.[50]

And Rav Yehuda? Another verse repeats, **I ADJURE YOU** (3:5).

And Rabbi Zeira? He uses the verse as Rabbi Yosé does, for Rabbi Yosé bar Ḥanina asked, What were the three oaths (Song 2:7, 3:5, 8:4)?[51] One, that Israel should not go up in military formation; one, that the Holy One, blessed be He, made Israel swear not to rebel against the nations; one, that the Holy One, blessed be He, made the nations swear not to oppress Israel too harshly.

And Rav Yehuda? It is written, **DO NOT WAKE NOR ROUSE [MY] BELOVED UNTIL SHE PLEASE!** (Song 8:4).[52]

And Rabbi Zeira? He needs [the extra verse to cover] what Rabbi Levi said: Why are there six oaths? The three we have mentioned, and in addition that [Israel] should not reveal the end, nor delay the end, nor reveal the secret to the nations.

I ADJURE YOU ... BY GAZELLES OR BY HINDS OF THE FIELD. Rabbi Eleazar said, The Holy One, blessed be He, said to Israel: If you keep my oath, it will be well; but if you do not, I shall permit your flesh [to be consumed] as [the flesh of] the gazelles and hinds of the field!

Rabbi Eleazar said, Whoever lives in the Land of Israel lives without sin, as it is said, **AND NONE WHO LIVES THERE SHALL**

---

50. Literally, 'in a wall'; perhaps it is analogous with the Latin *vallum*, a wall or fortification.
51. Song 5:8 also has 'I adjure', but not 'do not awaken'.
52. This covers the third oath.

SAY, 'I AM SICK'; IT SHALL BE INHABITED BY FOLK WHOSE
SIN HAS BEEN FORGIVEN (Isaiah 33:24 JPS).

Rava said to Rav Ashi, We [in Babylon] apply the
verse to those who suffer.

Rav Anan said, Whoever is buried in the Land of Israel, it is
as if he is buried beneath the altar; in one place it is written,
MAKE ME AN ALTAR OF EARTH (Exodus 20:21), and in another,
AND HIS EARTH WILL CLEANSE HIS PEOPLE (Deuteronomy
32:43).[53]

Ulla used to travel to the Land of Israel [from Babylonia],
but died outside the Land. When this was reported to Rabbi
Eleazar he said, Thou art Ulla! YOU YOURSELF SHALL DIE ON
UNCLEAN SOIL (Amos 7:17 JPS). They said to [Rabbi Eleazar],
But his coffin has come!

Being absorbed [in the Land] in death is not comparable
with being absorbed [in the Land] in life, responded Rabbi
Eleazar.

A man [living in the Land had a brother who died childless,
leaving a widow in] Bei Ḥoza'a[, north-east of Basra]. Shall I go
down and take her as wife? he asked Rabbi Ḥanina. [Rabbi
Ḥanina] retorted, His brother married an idolater[54] – blessed be
the Omnipresent who slew him! Should you follow him?!

Babylonian Jews could not deny the pre-eminence of the Land
of Israel – the Bible and the Mishna make it clear – but they
sought special status for the area in which they lived on the
grounds of both Torah learning and family purity.

Rav Yehuda said in the name of Shmuel, Just as it is forbidden
to leave the Land of Israel, it is forbidden to leave Babylonia to
go to other lands.

Rabba and Rav Yosef both [added], Even to go from
Pumbedita to Bei Kubi.

The topic continues for some pages, with often passionate

---

53. The last verse is more correctly translated, 'And cleanse the land of His people'
    (JPS) or 'And will be merciful unto his land, and to his people' (KJV), but neither
    is how the rabbis understood it.

54. Printed editions have *kutit*, 'a Samaritan', probably because censors insisted on
    replacing *goya*, 'a Gentile'. The widow was certainly Jewish, or the problem would
    not have arisen; Rabbi Ḥanina is merely being offensive.

sayings relating to the beauty, fruitfulness and sanctity of the Land. The final tribute is assigned to a Babylonian, Rav:

Rav Ḥiyya bar Ashi said in the name of Rav: Even the non-fruiting trees of the Land of Israel will one day yield fruit, as it is said, [FEAR NOT, O BEASTS OF THE FIELD, FOR THE PASTURES IN THE WILDERNESS ARE CLOTHED WITH GRASS.] THE TREES HAVE BORNE THEIR FRUIT; FIG TREE AND VINE HAVE YIELDED THEIR STRENGTH (Joel 2:22 JPS).[55]

112b

---

55. The interpretation depends on contrasting 'trees', i.e. non-fruiting trees, with 'fig tree and vine'.

THIRD TRACTATE
NEDARIM (VOWS)

An oath (Hebrew shavu'a*) is a personal commitment to do or not do something; a vow (Hebrew* neder*) is a ban placed on an object or activity, though the term is sometimes used more broadly.*

Certain features are common to both: an oath or vow does not take effect unless it is expressed clearly and the wording matches the intention of the person who made it; once properly made, it is fully binding; in certain circumstances an oath or vow can be absolved by a court or by an expert scholar, and a pretext must be found to establish that it had been made under a misapprehension and that the person who made it now regrets having done so.

CHAPTER TWO

MISHNA:

16a   In those respects[1] oaths are stricter than vows. In what way are vows stricter than oaths? If someone said, *Qonam*,[2] I won't make a *sukka* or a *lulav*, or, I won't put on *tefillin*, if he formulated it as a vow it takes effect, but if as an oath it does not, because you cannot swear an oath contrary to a *mitzva*.

GEMARA:

16b   In what way are vows stricter than oaths? Rav Kahana

---

1. Discussed earlier in the tractate.
2. The Gemara queried earlier (10a) whether this and other terms the Mishna lists as 'handles' for making vows are foreign words, or expressions devised by the Sages to avoid the use of God's name; *qonam* could be a variant of *qorban* 'sacrifice'.

reported that Rav Giddel said in Rav's name (but Rav Tavyumi reported that he said it in Shmuel's name), How do we know that you cannot swear an oath contrary to a *mitzva*? The Torah says, **HE SHALL NOT BREAK *HIS* WORD** (Numbers 30:3) – he may not break his word for *his* affairs, but he must break [his word] for the affairs of Heaven.

Then why should vows be different [from oaths]? Surely, just as it says, **IF A MAN MAKES A VOW TO THE LORD . . . HE SHALL NOT BREAK HIS WORD**, it says, **OR SWEARS AN OATH, HE SHALL NOT BREAK HIS WORD**!

Abbaye explained: A vow is if he said, All benefit from a *sukka* is forbidden to me; an oath is if he said, I swear I will not benefit from a *sukka*!

Rava objected, Are *mitzvot* given for [personal] benefit? Rather, said Rava, a vow is if he said, Sitting in a *sukka* is forbidden to me; an oath is if he said, I swear I will not sit in a *sukka*![3]

Is that where we derive it from? Surely it is from another verse, as a baraita states: **Could it be that if someone swore to act contrary to a *mitzva*, but failed to act contrary to it, he would be held liable for breaking his oath? Scripture says, To DO EITHER BAD OR GOOD** (Leviticus 5:4) – **just as 'doing good' refers to what is optional,[4] so 'doing bad' refers to what is optional; this excludes one who swears to ignore a *mitzva*, but does not ignore it, since he has no option.**   17a

[Both verses are needed:] one exempts him from the reparation-offering for [breaking his] oath, the other invalidates the oath.

If it is evident that someone who uttered a form of words that could constitute a vow did not really mean what he said – in the rabbinic phrase, 'his mind and his mouth are not at one' –

---

3. Both Abbaye and Rava distinguish between a vow, which bans use of an *object* and so indirectly prevents whoever made the vow from fulfilling the *mitzva*, and an oath, which would bind the *person* to act contrary to the way the *mitzva* tells him to. This is akin to the Roman law distinction between *actio in rem* and *actio in personam*.

4. 'Good' and 'bad' here relate only to actions neither commanded nor forbidden by the Torah.

the vow is not valid. Several instances of this are discussed in Chapter Three.

CHAPTER THREE

MISHNA:

20b The Sages declared four vows non-binding: challenging vows; nonsense vows; accidental vows; vows made under duress.

What is a 'challenging vow'? Someone is selling an object, and he says, *Qonam*, I won't part with it for less than a *sela*; the other says, *Qonam*, I won't give you more than a *sheqel*.[5]

21a They may reach agreement on three denarii[, and are not bound by the apparent vow].

GEMARA:

The Sages declared four vows non-binding. Rabbi Abba bar Memel said to Rabbi Ammi, You told us in the name of Rabbi Judah Nesia that the Mishna of the four vows was the opinion of Rabbi Judah in the name of Rabbi Tarfon, who said, **Neither is a Nazirite, since [a vow of] naziriteship must be unconditional.**[6]

Rava said, It could even be the view of the Sages [who disagree regarding the Nazirites: our Mishna] does not say 'they agreed' but 'they may reach agreement'.[7]

Ravina asked Rav Ashi, If one trader had vowed more than a *sela* and the other offered less than a *sheqel*, would the vow stand, or is it still a 'challenge'?

[Rav Ashi replied,] The Mishna teaches this: **If [a man] was pestering his friend to come to a feast, and the friend said, *Qonam* that I enter your house or taste [even] a drop of cold**

5. A *sela* is four denarii, a *sheqel* two.
6. Tosefta *Nazir* 3:11; the case concerns two men who each declared himself a Nazirite on condition that the other was. Abba bar Memel thinks that the traders' vows are invalid because each is conditional on the other's reaction.
7. Rava thinks that the traders' vows are invalid since neither really means what he says – 'I won't let it go for less than a *sela*' really means 'I'll compromise at three denarii.'

water!, he may [nevertheless] enter the house and have a cold drink, for he only meant he would not eat or drink [at the feast].[8] Why so? Surely he said, 'even a drop of water'? But that is how people talk. Similarly,[in the case of the traders,] that is how people talk.

[Ravina objected:] How can you compare [the two cases]? In the case of the water, the righteous say little but do much.[9] [As for traders,] there is doubt: when they say 'more than a *sela*' or 'less than a *sheqel*', are they just challenging [each other], or do they really mean it, so that it is a [proper] vow?   21b

Rav Yehuda said in the name of Rav Assi, These four kinds of vow have to be absolved by a scholar. When he repeated this in the presence of Shmuel, [Shmuel] exclaimed, The Mishna states **The Sages declared four vows non-binding**; how can you say that they require absolution by a scholar?

Rav Yosef taught this *sh'ma'ta* as follows: Rav Yehuda said in the name of Rav Assi, These four kinds of vow are the only kinds that may be absolved by a scholar. He holds that the scholar may not [himself] propose a pretext [for the enquirer to express regret and seek absolution of the vow].[10]

Against Rav Yosef's interpretation, the Gemara adduces several instances of Sages who suggested pretexts to people who had requested absolution. It becomes clear that the Sages frowned on the practice of making vows.

Someone came to Rav Huna [seeking to absolve a vow]. Are you still of the same mind [as when you made it]? asked [Rav Huna]. No, replied the man, and [Rav Huna] absolved him.

Someone came to Rabba, the son of Rav Huna[, seeking to absolve a vow]. Would you have made the vow if ten men had appeased you at that time? asked [Rabba]. No, replied the man, and [Rabba] absolved him.

A baraita states: **Rabbi Judah says, You ask a man [who seeks absolution for a vow] whether he is of the same mind [as when**

8. *Nedarim* 63b.
9. The 'righteous' host would have said, 'Come and have a drop of water and a bite to eat', meaning 'join in the feast'; the guest would have responded in like vein.
10. That is, the initiative must come from the person who seeks absolution; the scholar should not put words in his mouth.

he made it]; if he says No, you absolve him. **Rabbi Ishmael, the son of Rabbi Yosé, says, You ask a man [who seeks absolution for a vow] whether he would have made the vow if ten men had appeased him at [the time he made it]; if he says No, you absolve him.**

Someone came to Rabbi Assi [seeking to absolve a vow]. Do you regret [having made it]? asked [Rabbi Assi]. Yes, replied the man, and [Rabbi Assi] absolved him.

Someone came to Rabbi Eleazar [seeking to absolve a vow]. Did you really want to make a vow? asked [Rabbi Eleazar]. No, replied the man, if they hadn't been threatening me, I wouldn't have wanted to; [Rabbi Eleazar] said, Then let it be as you [really] wished!

A woman imposed a vow on her daughter, then came before Rabbi Yoḥanan [seeking to absolve it]. [He said to her,] If you had realized that your neighbours would have thought, 'Had she not seen something untoward in her daughter she would not have imposed a vow on her', would you have done so? No, she replied, and he absolved her.

The son of Rabbi Yannai the Elder's daughter went to him [to seek absolution from a vow]. Would you have vowed[, asked Rabbi Yannai,] if you knew that they would open your account book [in Heaven] and investigate all your deeds?[11] No, replied [the grandson], and [Rabbi Yannai] absolved him.

Rabbi Abba asked, On what verse is that based? AND AFTER VOWS TO MAKE ENQUIRY (Proverbs 20:25).

Although Rabbi Yannai accepted that pretext, we do not, nor do we accept the other pretext offered by Rabba bar bar Ḥana in the name of Rabbi Yoḥanan [on the basis of] a baraita that states: **Rabban Gamaliel absolved an old man [from his vow on the pretext that]** HE WHO UTTERS IS LIKE THRUSTS OF THE SWORD, BUT THE WORDS OF THE WISE HEAL (Proverbs 12:18) – **Whoever utters [a vow] deserves to be pierced by a sword, but the words of the Sages heal.**

Nor do we accept the pretext in this baraita: Rabbi Nathan

---

11. By binding himself with a vow he implies that he already keeps the whole Torah, and needs to add to it; Heaven would question his excessive piety.

says, **He who makes a vow is as one who builds a forbidden altar,**[12] **and if he fulfils it, it is as if he sacrificed thereon.**[13]

The first part of that statement is acceptable as a pretext. Abbaye said, The latter part is acceptable as a pretext; Rava said, It is not.

> This is how Rav Kahana taught this *sh'ma'ta*, but Rav Tavyumi taught it as follows: The latter part of that statement is not acceptable as a pretext. Abbaye said, The first part is acceptable as a pretext; Rava said, It is not.
>
> [Nevertheless,] the *halakha* is that neither the former nor the latter part is acceptable as a pretext.

Nor do we accept as a pretext what Shmuel said, for Shmuel said, Even if he fulfils [his vow] he is called wicked. Rabbi Abbahu asked, On what verse is that based? IF YOU CEASE MAKING VOWS YOU WILL BE FREE FROM SIN (Deuteronomy 23:23), and the same expression occurs in THERE THE WICKED CEASE THEIR TUMULT (Job 3:17).

Rav Yosef said, We find the same [thought] in a Mishna: **If he said, Like a vow of the wicked, this is valid, whether for an oath, [dedication of] a sacrifice or Nazirite status; if he said, Like a vow of the virtuous, he has said nothing.**[14]

In certain circumstances a woman's vow may be anulled by her father or husband, depending on whether she is a minor (under the age of 12), an adult (from 12½) or a na'ara, (the stage in between). So long as she is a minor in her father's home she is under his authority, and he may cancel her vows (Numbers 30:4–6); when she marries, she passes to the authority of her husband, who may cancel vows (Numbers 30:7–9); an adult single woman has full control of her own vows. Rabbinic

---

12. Literally, 'a high place'. Once Jerusalem was chosen it was forbidden to offer sacrifices elsewhere.

13. These pretexts are rejected by the later authorities (Savoraim or perhaps Geonim) because they are too frightening – no one would dare to deny them – Rashi.

14. Because the virtuous don't vow. There is a slight confusion in the text here, which does not exactly match the Mishna (9a).

interpretation limits the type of vows that a husband can annul to two categories: self-denial and 'matters between him and her', that is, matters that would interfere with the marriage.

CHAPTER ELEVEN

MISHNA:

These are the vows [a husband] can annul: vows of self-denial, such as 'I will not wash myself' or 'I will wash myself',
'I will not beautify myself' or 'I will beautify myself.' Rabbi Yosé said, Those are not vows of self-denial, but these are: if she said, 'Produce of the whole world is *qonam* to me', he can annul it, but if she said, 'Produce of this area is *qonam* to me', he must provide her with produce from elsewhere. If she said, 'Produce of this grocer is *qonam* to me', he cannot annul it, but if all his provision was from there, he can annul [the vow] – this is Rabbi Yosé's view.

GEMARA:

He can annul vows of self-denial, but not vows that do not involve self-denial. But a baraita states: BETWEEN MAN AND WIFE, BETWEEN SON AND DAUGHTER (Numbers 30:17) – This teaches that a husband can annul vows concerning matters between him and her.[15]

They explained, He can annul both kinds. He can annul vows of self-denial permanently, but if self-denial is not involved he can annul while she is under his authority, but the vow comes into force if he divorces her. [This applies to] vows concerning matters between him and her that do not involve self-denial, but if they involve self-denial the vow does not take effect [at all].

Is it indeed the case that matters that do not involve self-denial take effect when he divorces her? Surely a Mishna states, **Rabbi Yoḥanan ben Nuri says, He should annul, in case he divorces**

---

15. That is, not necessarily matters involving self-denial.

her and she remains forbidden to him,[16] from which you see that even if he divorces her, if he previously annulled the vow the annulment remains in force.

They explained, He can annul both kinds. He can annul vows of self-denial both in respect of himself and in respect of others, but if self-denial is not involved he can annul in respect of himself but not in respect of others.

16. The Mishna (85a) deals with vows that prevent her fulfilling the normal responsibilities of a wife. He may intend to divorce her, and so would not bother annulling the vow; Yoḥanan ben Nuri advises him to annul in case he later wishes to remarry her.

FOURTH TRACTATE
NAZIR (THE NAZIRITE)

The Nazirite (Hebrew nazar, *'to abstain from', or 'to consecrate oneself to') left his hair uncut, abstained from produce of the grapevine and avoided contact with corpses (Numbers 6:1–21). In biblical times the Nazirite, like holy persons in other Middle Eastern cultures, was a charismatic figure who held his status for life, e.g. the warrior-leader Samson (Judges 13–16). By the late Second Temple period lifelong naziriteship, like the 'naziriteship of Samson', was the exception; the normal period was thirty days, on completion of which sacrifice was offered.*

Little is known about the number or role of Nazirites in Jewish society in the late Second Temple period, though they feature occasionally in Apocrypha (1 Maccabees 3:49), possibly in the New Testament (Acts 21:24), and are mentioned by other ancient authors.[1] Similar vows persisted after the Temple was destroyed in 70, but the system could not operate properly without sacrifice; it was not practised in Babylonia.

Eleazar Kappar, a contemporary of Judah ha-Nasi, stigmatizes the Nazirite as a sinner, though it is not certain that his remark was intended to apply to all Nazirites (3a); this parallels the disfavour with which several rabbis regarded vows in general (Nedarim 22). Maimonides, writing in an Islamic milieu, found value in the practice: 'The reason for naziritism is most manifest; it consists in bringing about abstinence from drinking wine, which has caused the ruin of the ancients and the moderns.'[2]

---

1. Many of the relevant texts have been edited by Chepey, *Nazirites*.
2. Maimonides, *Guide*, 3:48, pp. 600–601.

The passage selected illustrates what David Kraemer calls the 'fictional argumentation' of the Stamaim.[3] Clearly, it is not a verbatim report of a debate, and there are two versions of what the original disagreement was – one anonymous and the other attributed to Mar bar Rav Ashi. As often in Gemara, a contrived question is used as a searchlight to illumine different facets of a topic and the whole worked into a stylized composition; only part is translated here.

CHAPTER THREE

MISHNA:

If someone was in a graveyard when he vowed to be a Nazirite, even if he stays there for thirty days they do not count [towards his naziriteship], nor does he offer a sacrifice to atone for his defilement[, since his naziriteship has not yet commenced]. If he left [the graveyard, purified himself,] and then re-entered, the days [he has observed] count [towards his naziriteship], and he must offer a sacrifice to atone for his defilement. Rabbi Eliezer says, Not if he re-entered on the same day [as he purified himself], since the Torah says, AND THE FIRST DAYS SHALL BE VOID (Numbers 6:12).

16b

GEMARA:

It was taught: If someone was in a graveyard when he vowed to be a Nazirite, Rabbi Yoḥanan says, The vow comes into being; Resh Laqish says, It does not.

Rabbi Yoḥanan says, The vow comes into being: it hangs in abeyance, and takes effect following purification.

Resh Laqish says, The vow does not come into being: only if he reaffirms the vow [following purification] does it [come into being and] take effect.

Rabbi Yoḥanan objects to Resh Laqish: **If someone was in a graveyard when he vowed to be a Nazirite, even if he stays there for thirty days they do not count [towards his naziriteship], nor**

3.   Kraemer, *Mind*, pp. 87–9.

does he offer a sacrifice to atone for his defilement – he doesn't offer a sacrifice, but the vow takes effect.

[Resh Laqish] replies: He is not in the category [subject to] defilement, therefore he does not offer a sacrifice.

Rabbi Yoḥanan objects: **If someone was unclean and vowed to be a Nazirite, he must not cut his hair, drink wine or defile himself for the dead; if he cuts his hair, drinks wine, or defiles himself for the dead, he is liable to forty lashes.**[4] If you agree that the vow comes into being, that explains why he is liable to flogging; but if the vow did not exist, why should he be liable to flogging?

17a   [Resh Laqish replies:] What case is this? [It is] where he has gone out[, purified himself] and re-entered.

Rabbi Yoḥanan objects: [A baraita states:] **The only difference between an unclean person who vowed to be a Nazirite and a clean person who was defiled is that the unclean person who vowed to be a Nazirite may count the seventh day [of purification] towards his naziriteship, but the clean person who was defiled may not count the seventh day [of purification] towards his naziriteship.** If you assume that the vow has not come into being, why should the [first days] count?

Mar bar Rav Ashi said, [Rabbi Yoḥanan and Resh Laqish] agree that the vow comes into being; they disagree with regard to flogging. Rabbi Yoḥanan holds that since the vow comes into being, he is liable to flogging; Resh Laqish holds it comes into being, but he is not liable to flogging.

Rabbi Yoḥanan objects to Resh Laqish: **If someone vowed to be a Nazirite while he was in a graveyard, even if he stays there for thirty days they do not count [towards his naziriteship], nor does he offer a sacrifice to atone for his defilement** – he doesn't offer a sacrifice, but he is liable to flogging.

[Resh Laqish replies:] It would have been accurate for the Tanna to state that he is not liable; however, since the Mishna goes on to say, **If he left [the graveyard, purified himself,] and then re-entered, the days [he has observed] count [towards his naziriteship], and he must offer a sacrifice to atone for his**

---

4. Tosefta *Nazir* 2:9.

defilement; the first part said, **He does not offer a sacrifice to atone for his defilement** [and omits the reference to flogging].

A proof: **The only difference between an unclean person who vowed to be a Nazirite and a clean person who was defiled is that the unclean person who vowed to be a Nazirite may count the seventh day [of purification] towards his naziriteship, but the clean person who was defiled may not count the seventh day [of purification] towards his naziriteship** – [it follows] that with respect to flogging both are equal.

[Resh Laqish replies:] No. They are equal with regard to haircutting, but not with regard to flogging. Why, then, does the baraita not mention flogging? Because it deals with [matters which are] to his advantage, not to his disadvantage.

A proof: **If someone was unclean and vowed to be a Nazirite, he must not cut his hair, drink wine or defile himself for the dead; if he cuts his hair, drinks wine or defiles himself for the dead, he is liable to forty lashes.** That certainly refutes [Resh Laqish's view].

FIFTH TRACTATE
SOTA
(THE WAYWARD WIFE)

Numbers 5:11–31 sets out a procedure for trial by ordeal of a wife suspected by her husband of adultery. It had become obsolete by the rabbinic period, but the rabbis nevertheless expounded it in detail, bringing it as far as possible into line with other provisions of Torah and deriving lessons from it. The procedure, inconsistent as it appears to be with standard rules of evidence, is explained as a kind of talion ('like for like' punishment), a theme developed at great length in the Tosefta.

CHAPTER ONE

MISHNA:

2a   Rabbi Eliezer says that if someone issues a jealous warning to his wife he must do so in the presence of two witnesses, but he may oblige her to drink the bitter waters on the testimony of one witness, or himself. Rabbi Joshua says that if someone issues a jealous warning to his wife, he must do so in the presence of two witnesses, and he may oblige her to drink the bitter waters only on the testimony of two witnesses.

How does he 'issue a jealous warning'? If he said to her in the presence of two witnesses, Do not speak with so-and-so, and she spoke with him, she is still permitted to her husband, and [if he is a *Kohen* she is] permitted to eat *teruma*. If she secluded herself with [the subject of the warning] and remained with him long enough for defilement, she is prohibited to her husband and forbidden to eat *teruma*; should [the husband] die [childless, leaving a brother], she must accept *ḥalitza* and not marry the brother.

GEMARA:

Now, the Tanna has just dealt with the Nazirite; why does he follow this with the wayward wife? It is as a baraita states: **Rabbi said, Why does the Torah place the law of the Nazirite next to that of the wayward wife? It is to teach you that whoever sees the disgrace of the wayward wife will swear not to drink wine!**

Then why not put *Sota* before *Nazir* [in the order they occur in Scripture]? The Tanna dealt with *Ketubot*, in the course of which he touched upon matters involving vows; this led to *Nedarim*, so then he dealt with the Nazirite, a similar topic, and then with *Sota*, as Rabbi explained.

If someone issues a jealous warning. 'If' implies that it is preferable that he should not do it – our Tanna must hold that it is not proper to issue a jealous warning.

Rav Shmuel bar Isaac said, When Resh Laqish commenced [teaching] *Sota*, he used to say, [Heaven] makes a match for a man according to his deeds, as it is said, THE ROD OF THE WICKED SHALL NOT REST UPON THE LOT OF THE RIGHTEOUS (Psalm 125:3 KJV).

Rabba bar bar Ḥana said in the name of Rabbi Yoḥanan, It is as hard [for Heaven] to make matches as to split the Red Sea, as it is said, GOD SETTLES THE SOLITARY IN A HOME, HE BRINGS OUT THE PRISONERS AT A PROPITIOUS TIME (Psalm 68:7).[1]

Is this so? Didn't Rav Yehuda say in the name of Rav, Forty days before a child is formed[2] a heavenly voice proclaims: So-and-so's daughter is for so-and-so; So-and-so's house is for so-and-so; So-and-so's field is for so-and-so! No contradiction. [Rav] spoke of a first marriage, [Rabbi Yoḥanan] of a second.

Rabbi Eliezer says . . . he may oblige her to drink the bitter waters on the testimony of one witness, or himself. Rabbi Joshua says . . . he may oblige her to drink the bitter waters

---

1. I follow Rashi's interpretation of the verse in this context; most versions translate differently.
2. 'Formation' lies somewhere between conception and birth.

only on the testimony of two witnesses. They argue only about jealousy and concealment, but they agree that one witness would suffice [as evidence of] defilement, and [indeed] the Mishna states, **If one witness states, I saw that she was defiled, she does not drink [the bitter waters].**[3] What basis is there in Scripture for saying that a single witness is sufficient?

The rabbis taught: AND THERE IS NO WITNESS AGAINST HER (Numbers 5:13) – Scripture means that there are not two witnesses. Or could it mean that there is not even one? It states, A SINGLE WITNESS SHALL NOT RISE UP AGAINST ANYONE (Deuteronomy 19:15). Now, if it just said A WITNESS, would I not have understood that it meant A SINGLE WITNESS? What does the word 'single' add? It establishes the general principle that wherever the Torah says 'witness' it means two, unless it specifies that it means one. Therefore here, when the Torah says, AND THERE IS NO WITNESS AGAINST HER, it means that if there are not two, only one, AND SHE WAS NOT FORCED (Numbers 5:13), she is forbidden [to her husband].

So it seems that the requirement for a single witness derives from [the verse in Deuteronomy], and that otherwise you might have thought that AND THERE IS NO WITNESS AGAINST HER meant 'not even a single witness'. But if there was not even one witness, how could she be forbidden? The verse would still be necessary, for [without it] you might have thought that when it says AND THERE IS NO WITNESS AGAINST HER it means 'a single witness cannot be trusted against her'. Not trusted against her? Do we need two witnesses? If that is the case the verse need have said nothing, since we could have inferred by analogy with monetary law, just as we do in laws of evidence throughout the Torah[, that two witnesses are needed]. It is still necessary to state the matter explicitly; you might have thought that *Sota* would be different, since there is the contributory factor that he has warned her and she has nevertheless secluded herself [with the accused], and so a single witness should be trusted against her.

Then does this imply that despite the single witness she remains permitted? Is it not written, AND SHE WAS NOT

<hr>

3. *Sota* 31a. She is only made to drink if there is no evidence as to actual defilement.

2b

FORCED, which implies that she is forbidden on the testimony of the single witness? The verse is still needed, since without it you might have thought that only two witnesses are trusted, not a single one, and that even if there are two witnesses we could not conclude **SHE WAS NOT FORCED**; it informs us that this is not the case.

Chapter Seven lists prayers and formal declarations that need or need not be said in 'the holy tongue'. Among those that must be said in Hebrew are the priest's address to the wayward wife (Numbers 5:19–22) and the priestly blessing. There is no longer a functioning Jewish priesthood, but many families still claim descent in the male line from Aaron, and are known as Kohanim *(singular:* Kohen*); they retain vestigial duties and privileges including conveying the priestly blessing in the Synagogue, daily in Israel and most Sefardic communities, but in Ashkenazic communities outside Israel only on Festival days.*

THE LORD SPOKE TO MOSES: SPEAK TO AARON AND HIS SONS: THUS SHALL YOU BLESS THE PEOPLE OF ISRAEL. SAY TO THEM:

THE LORD BLESS YOU AND PROTECT YOU! THE LORD DEAL KINDLY AND GRACIOUSLY WITH YOU! THE LORD BESTOW HIS FAVOURS UPON YOU AND GRANT YOU PEACE!

THUS THEY SHALL LINK MY NAME WITH THE PEOPLE OF ISRAEL, AND I WILL BLESS THEM. (Numbers 6:22–7 JPS)[4]

CHAPTER SEVEN

MISHNA:
How is the priestly blessing enacted?
Outside the Temple it is recited as three blessings; within the Temple as a single blessing.
Within the Temple the Name [of God] is pronounced as

37b

---

4.   A version of the priestly blessing dated to about 600 BCE is the oldest biblical text to have been recovered by archaeologists (Tov, *Textual Criticism*, p. 118).

38a written; outside the Temple [only] a substitute name is used.

Outside the Temple the *Kohanim* lift their hands to the level of their shoulders; within the Temple [they lift them] above their heads, except for the High Priest, for he may not lift his hands above the [golden] frontlet.[5] Rabbi Judah says the High Priest may lift his hands above the frontlet, as it is written, AARON LIFTED HIS HANDS TOWARDS THE PEOPLE AND BLESSED THEM (Leviticus 9:22 JPS).

GEMARA:

The rabbis taught: THUS SHALL YOU BLESS – in the holy tongue. You say 'in the holy tongue', but perhaps it may be done in any language? [No, for] here it says, THUS YOU SHALL BLESS, and there it says, THESE SHALL STAND ON MOUNT GERIZIM TO BLESS (Deuteronomy 27:12); just as there [it was done] in the holy tongue, so here [it must be done] in the holy tongue. Rabbi Judah says, [That argument] is not required, for it says THUS, [which implies] that they must say it in [precisely] these words.

Another baraita teaches: THUS SHALL YOU BLESS – standing. You say 'standing', but perhaps it may be done sitting? [No, for] here it says, THUS SHALL YOU BLESS, and there it says, THESE SHALL STAND ON MOUNT GERIZIM TO BLESS; just as there they stood, so here they must stand. Rabbi Nathan says, [That argument] is not required, for it says, TO SERVE HIM, AND TO BLESS IN HIS NAME (Deuteronomy 10:8) – just as service requires standing, so blessing requires standing; and we know that service requires standing, since it states [explicitly], TO STAND [BEFORE THE LORD, TO SERVE HIM].

Another baraita teaches: THUS SHALL YOU BLESS – lifting the hands. You say 'lifting the hands', but perhaps it may be done without lifting the hands? [No, for] here it says, THUS SHALL YOU BLESS, and there it says, AARON LIFTED HIS HANDS TOWARDS THE PEOPLE AND BLESSED THEM (Leviticus 9:22 JPS); just as there he lifted his hands, so here they must lift their hands.

5.   The frontlet is described in Exodus 28:36–8, 39:30–31 and Leviticus 8:9.

Rabbi Jonathan had a problem [with this analogy, since you could argue]: Just as there, when [Aaron] the High Priest [officiated], it was the New Moon and it was a sacrifice on behalf of the public, so here[, for the priestly blessing, there should be a requirement for] the High Priest, the New Moon, and a public sacrifice.[6]

Rabbi Nathan says, [That argument] is not required, for it says, HE AND HIS SONS FOR ALL TIME (Deuteronomy 18:5) – his sons are compared with him; just as he must lift his hands [in blessing,] so must his sons lift their hands in blessing; moreover, it says FOR ALL TIME, and blessing is like [other forms of] service.

Further baraitot are adduced to demonstrate that the priestly blessing must be pronounced with the four-lettered Name of God in the Temple, though with a substitute name elsewhere; that proselytes, women and slaves are included in the blessing; that priests and people must face each other; and that the blessing must be pronounced aloud. Abbaye makes the point that only if two or more Kohanim *are present should they be formally summoned to bless. A collection of Joshua ben Levi's sayings, mostly about the priestly blessing, follows:*

Rabbi Joshua ben Levi said, How do we know that the Holy One, blessed be He, longs for the priestly blessing? [We learn this from] what is said, THUS THEY SHALL LINK MY NAME WITH THE PEOPLE OF ISRAEL, AND I WILL BLESS THEM (Numbers 6:27 JPS). 38b

Rabbi Joshua ben Levi also said, Every priest who blesses will himself be blessed, as it is said, I WILL BLESS THOSE WHO BLESS YOU (Genesis 12:3 JPS).

Rabbi Joshua ben Levi also said, Every *Kohen* who does not ascend the *dukhan*[7] transgresses three positive commandments: THUS SHALL YOU BLESS, SAY TO THEM and THEY SHALL LINK MY NAME.

Rav observed, One may suspect that he is the son

---

6. Rabbi Jonathan's question, an interpolation in the baraita, remains unanswered.
7. The platform on which the *Kohanim* stand to bless the people.

of a divorcee [married to a *Kohen*] or of a woman who
has received *ḥalitza* [and is married to a *Kohen*].[8]

Rabbi Joshua ben Levi also said, Every *Kohen* who does not
ascend [the *dukhan*] at the blessing of service[9] should not ascend
[later], as it is said, **AARON LIFTED HIS HANDS TOWARDS THE
PEOPLE AND BLESSED THEM; AND HE STEPPED DOWN AFTER
OFFERING THE SIN-OFFERING, THE BURNT OFFERING AND
THE OFFERING OF WELL-BEING** (Leviticus 9:22 JPS) – just as
there [blessing was associated with] service, so [whenever the
priestly blessing is recited, it is associated with] service.

> Can this be right? Did not Rabbi Ammi and Rabbi
> Assi ascend [after the blessing of service]? [Not really.]
> Rabbi Ammi and Rabbi Assi left their place[10] before,
> but did not reach [the *dukhan* until afterwards]. As
> Rabbi Oshaya taught, [Rabbi Joshua ben Levi's com-
> ment] only applies if [the *Kohen*] has not left his place
> [during the blessing of service], but so long as he has
> left his place, he may ascend.
>
>> Likewise the Mishna states, **If he is confi-
>> dent that he can lift his hands and return to
>> [leading] the prayer, he may do so.**[11] We
>> questioned this[, seeing that he did not
>> ascend as required during the blessing of
>> service, and the answer was given that] he
>> moved a little [in preparation to ascend]; here
>> too, [Rabbi Ammi and Rabbi Assi] moved a
>> little [in preparation to ascend].

Rabbi Joshua ben Levi also said, The cup of blessing [at grace
following a meal] should be handed to a generous person, as it
is said, **THE GENEROUS MAN IS BLESSED, FOR HE GIVES OF
HIS BREAD TO THE POOR** (Proverbs 22:9 JPS); read not **IS
BLESSED** but **SHALL BLESS.**

---

8. In both cases, he would have forfeited the privileges of priesthood.
9. The first blessing of the three that conclude the *Amida* prayer; it recalls the Temple
    service. The proof-text from Leviticus demonstrates that Aaron completed the
    'service', i.e. the sacrifices, before commencing the blessing.
10. Literally, 'moved their legs'.
11. Mishna *Berakhot* 5:4.

Rabbi Joshua ben Levi also said, How do we know that even birds can tell who is miserly? It is written, IN THE EYES OF EVERY WINGED CREATURE THE OUTSPREAD NET MEANS NOTHING (Proverbs 1:17 JPS).[12]

Rabbi Joshua ben Levi also said, If you benefit from a miserly person you transgress a prohibition, for it is said, DO NOT EAT OF A STINGY MAN'S FOOD; DO NOT CRAVE FOR HIS DAINTIES. HE IS LIKE ONE KEEPING ACCOUNTS; 'EAT AND DRINK,' HE SAYS TO YOU, BUT HE DOES NOT REALLY MEAN IT (Proverbs 23:6–7 JPS).

Rabbi Joshua ben Levi also said, The [ceremony of the] calf whose neck is broken[13] is the result of meanness, as it is said, OUR HANDS DID NOT SPILL THIS BLOOD (Deuteronomy 21:7). [Now,] would anyone have thought that the elders of the court had shed blood? [Obviously not. What they mean by the declaration is, It was not the case that the victim] entered our territory and we sent him off, or that we saw him and let him go; [i.e. it was not the case that] he entered our territory and we let him go without food, or that we saw him and allowed him to depart without someone to accompany him [on his journey].

Rav Ada said in the name of Rabbi Simlai, If all present in the Synagogue are *Kohanim*, they ascend [to the platform to bless].

Whom do they bless? Rabbi Zeira said, Their brothers in the fields.

How can that be? Didn't Abba the son of Rav Minyamin bar Ḥiyya say that people behind the *Kohanim* are not included in the blessing? No problem. If they are [absent because] under duress, they are included [in the blessing]; if there is no duress, not.[14]

But didn't Rav Shimi of Shiḥori teach, If all present in the

12. The relevance of the proof-text is not obvious. Rashi suggests that Proverbs 22:9 refers to miserly people, and that this verse means that birds refuse to eat from the nets they spread.

13. See p. 377.

14. 'Behind' means 'invisible to'. People at work in the fields are 'under duress'; people who are in the Synagogue but wantonly place themselves behind the *Kohanim* are not.

Synagogue are *Kohanim*, some ascend [to the platform to bless] and some [remain in their places and] respond, Amen? No problem. If ten are left [they stay in their place], but if there are not ten left[, they all ascend].

Let's look more closely at the statement of Abba the son of Rav Minyamin bar Ḥiyya that people who are behind the *Kohanim* are not included in the blessing. Obviously, tall people in front of short people would be no barrier, and the prayer-lectern is no barrier, but what about a partition? There is proof [that a partition constitutes no barrier], for Rabbi Joshua ben Levi said, Even a wall of iron cannot separate Israel from their Father in Heaven!

After further interpolations we return to Joshua ben Levi's rulings on the priestly blessing:

39a   Rabbi Joshua ben Levi also said, The *Kohen* may not raise his hands in blessing until he has washed them, as it is said, **RAISE YOUR HANDS IN HOLINESS, AND BLESS THE LORD** (Psalm 134:2).

Rabbi Eleazar ben Shamua's disciples asked him, How is it that you have lived so long? He replied: I have never used the synagogue as a shortcut; I have never stepped over the heads of the holy people;[15] and I have never raised my hands for [the priestly] blessing without [pronouncing] the benediction.

What benediction? Rabbi Zeira said in the name of Rav Hisda, [Blessed are You, Lord our God, King of the universe,] Who has invested us with the holiness of Aaron and commanded us to bless Your people Israel with love.

The priest and officers who addressed soldiers before battle were to do so only in Hebrew. This leads, in Chapter Eight, to a discussion of war, its justification and conduct. This brief section is the foundation for the rabbinic distinction between three

15.   He either arrived early or sat outside to avoid trampling over the students to reach his place – Rashi.

kinds of war: milḥemet ḥova *(obligatory war, restricted to the wars of the original conquest);* milḥemet reshut *(discretionary war, possible only on the authority of Sanhedrin, Urim and Tummim); and defensive, possibly including pre-emptive, war.*[16]

CHAPTER EIGHT

MISHNA:

AND THE OFFICERS SHALL CONTINUE TO ADDRESS THE PEOPLE[: 'ANY AMONG YOU WHO IS AFRAID OR FAINT-HEARTED SHALL RETURN HOME, AND NOT DEMORALIZE HIS BROTHERS'] (Deuteronomy 20:8). Rabbi Aqiva says, AFRAID OR FAINT-HEARTED is to be taken in its plain sense, of one who cannot bear the tensions of war or the sight of a drawn sword. Rabbi Yosé the Galilean says, AFRAID OR FAINT-HEARTED means one who is afraid because he has sinned; the Torah affords him the opportunity to depart among all the others.[17] Rabbi Yosé says, AFRAID OR FAINT-HEARTED means a High Priest married to a widow, a divorcee or a woman who has received *ḥalitza* married to an ordinary *Kohen*, a *mamzeret* or *netina* to an Israelite, an Israelite woman to a *mamzer* or *natin*[18] ... This applies only in a discretionary war,[19] but in an obligatory war all must go, even the groom from his chamber and the bride from her canopy. Rabbi Judah said, This applies only in a *mitzva* war, but in an obligatory war all must go, even the groom from his chamber and the bride from her canopy.

44a

44b

GEMARA:

In what way do Rabbi Yosé and Rabbi Yosé the Galilean

16. For a fuller treatment of the ethics of war in Judaism, see Ravitsky, 'Prohibited Wars', and Solomon, 'Ethics of War'. Urim and Tummim are the High Priest's oracle (Exodus 28:21, 30; Judges 20; 1 Samuel 10; *Yoma* 73).
17. That is, with the newly betrothed, or those who have built a new house or planted a vineyard (verses 5–7); the faint-hearted need not be embarrassed at departing, since people may assume he belongs to one of the other groups.
18. These are relatively minor infringements of marriage law: see *Qiddushin*, pp. 410–11.
19. 'Discretionary' means the discretion of the authorities, however they are defined, not that of the individual.

differ? They differ with regard to offences against rabbinic law.

According to which of them is this baraita: **Even if someone spoke between putting on one *tefilla* and the other,**[20] **it is accounted a sin, and he should return from the ranks of the army**? This accords with the view of Rabbi Yosé the Galilean. And according to whom is this teaching of the rabbis: **If he shrinks back at the sound of the trumpet or the clash of shields, or urine drips on his knees when swords flash, he should return [from the ranks]**? Would this be according to Rabbi Aqiva rather than Rabbi Yosé the Galilean?[21] Even Rabbi Yosé the Galilean would agree [that such a man should return from the lines], since Scripture says, AND NOT DEMORALIZE HIS BROTHERS.

This applies only in a discretionary war. Rabbi Yoḥanan said: The rabbis' 'discretionary war' is equivalent to Rabbi Judah's '*mitzva* war'.

Rava said: All agree that Joshua's war of conquest was obligatory and the expansionist wars of David were discretionary, but they differ with regard to [the status of] a pre-emptive war intended to prevent idolaters from attacking them; one calls it a '*mitzva* war', the other calls it a discretionary war. The difference would be with regard to someone who was engaged in another *mitzva* [– he could claim exemption from a defensive war].

The final chapter focuses on a biblical institution which, like that of Sota itself, was obsolete by the rabbinic period, namely the ceremony of breaking the calf's neck:

IF, IN THE LAND THAT THE LORD YOUR GOD IS ASSIGNING TO YOU TO POSSESS, SOMEONE SLAIN IS FOUND LYING IN THE OPEN, THE IDENTITY OF THE SLAYER NOT BEING KNOWN, YOUR ELDERS AND MAGISTRATES SHALL GO OUT AND MEASURE THE DISTANCES FROM THE CORPSE TO THE NEARBY TOWNS. THE ELDERS OF THE TOWN NEAREST TO THE CORPSE SHALL THEN TAKE A HEIFER

20. That is, between putting on the hand and head *tefillin* – a comparatively trivial sin.
21. The questioner assumes that the terrified conscript is free from sin.

WHICH HAS NEVER BEEN WORKED, WHICH HAS NEVER PULLED A YOKE; AND THE ELDERS OF THAT TOWN SHALL BRING THE HEIFER DOWN TO AN EVERFLOWING WADI, WHICH IS NOT TILLED OR SOWN. THERE, IN THE WADI, THEY SHALL BREAK THE HEIFER'S NECK ... THEN ALL THE ELDERS OF THE TOWN NEAREST TO THE CORPSE SHALL WASH THEIR HANDS OVER THE HEIFER WHOSE NECK WAS BROKEN IN THE WADI. AND THEY SHALL MAKE THIS DECLARATION: 'OUR HANDS DID NOT SHED THIS BLOOD, NOR DID OUR EYES SEE IT DONE. ABSOLVE, O LORD, YOUR PEOPLE ISRAEL ...' THUS YOU WILL REMOVE FROM YOUR MIDST GUILT FOR THE BLOOD OF THE INNOCENT, FOR YOU WILL BE DOING WHAT IS RIGHT IN THE SIGHT OF THE LORD. (Deuteronomy 21:1–4, 6–9 JSP)

It would have been unthinkable for the rabbis to abolish a law of the Torah, so the discontinuation of the ancient institution was justified instead on the basis of the declining standards of the people – in the case of sota *on the notion that men were now as immoral as women!*

Reflection on the decline of the generations leads to the 'rabbinic apocalypse' which ends the chapter.[22]

CHAPTER NINE

MISHNA:

If the murderer was found before the calf's neck was broken, [the calf] may go away and pasture among the flock; if after the calf's neck was broken, it is buried in its place, since it was brought [to atone] in a situation of doubt, and it has atoned for the doubt and departed. If the calf's neck was broken and the murderer was subsequently found, he is [nevertheless] executed.   47b

If one witness said, I saw the murderer, and another said, You did not, or one woman said, I saw the murderer, and another said, You did not, the calf's neck was broken.

---

22. Numerous textual variants have been ignored, and I follow the convention of the
     Vilna edition as to where Mishna ends and Gemara begins.

If one witness said, I saw the murderer, and two said, You did not, the calf's neck was broken.

If two witnesses said, We saw [the murderer], and one said, You did not, the calf's neck was not broken.

When murderers increased, they suspended [the ceremony] of breaking the calf's neck. [This was] in the time of Eliezer ben Dinai, also known as Teḥina ben Parisha, or Son of a Murderer.

When [male] adulterers became numerous, the bitter waters ceased, and it was Yoḥanan ben Zakkai who stopped them, in accordance with the verse, I WILL NOT PUNISH THEIR DAUGHTERS FOR FORNICATING, NOR THEIR DAUGHTERS-IN-LAW FOR COMMITTING ADULTERY; FOR THEY THEMSELVES TURN ASIDE WITH WHORES AND SACRIFICE WITH PROSTITUTES (Hosea 4:14 JPS).

After the death of Yosé ben Yoezer of Tzereda and Yosé ben Judah of Jerusalem, the 'clusters' ceased, as it is said, [I AM BECOME LIKE THE LEAVINGS OF A FIG HARVEST . . .] THERE IS NOT A CLUSTER TO EAT, NOR A RIPE FIG I COULD DESIRE (Micah 7:1 JPS).[23]

Yoḥanan the High Priest stopped the tithe declaration and abolished the awakening call and the knockers. Until his day hammers had been heard in Jerusalem and no one had to enquire about *demai*.[24]

MISHNA:

48a   When the Sanhedrin ceased [functioning], song ceased in the house of feasting, as it is said, THEY DRINK THEIR WINE WITHOUT SONG; LIQUOR TASTES BITTER TO THE DRINKER (Isaiah 24:9 JPS).

When the early prophets died, the Urim and Tumim ceased.

When the Temple was destroyed, the *shamir* and the 'dripping of the honeycomb' were lost and men of faith disappeared from Israel, as it is said, SAVE, O LORD, FOR THE FAITHFUL ARE NO MORE! (Psalm 12:1). Rabban Simeon ben Gamaliel says, Rabbi Joshua testified that from the day the Temple was

23. The 'clusters' are groups of learned and pious men.
24. Mishna Ma'aser Sheni 5:15 (see p. 80).

destroyed there had been no single day without its curse, that dew had not fallen as a blessing and that fruit had lost its flavour; Rabbi Yosé added, Even the juice had gone from the fruit. Rabbi Simeon ben Eleazar says, [Neglect of] purity removed the taste and the smell, and [neglect of] tithing removed the fat from the corn. The Sages say, Immorality and witchcraft destroyed everything.

MISHNA:

In the war of Vespasian they decreed that bridegrooms should not wear crowns, and that the *erus*[25] should not be played. In the war of Titus they decreed that brides should not wear crowns, and that a man should not teach his son Greek. In the last war[26] they decreed that a bride should not go about town in a palanquin, but our rabbis [later] permitted a bride to go about town in a palanquin.

49a

With the death of Rabbi Meir, makers of parables ceased; with the death of Ben Azzai, diligent students ceased; with the death of Ben Zoma, preachers ceased; with the death of Rabbi Aqiva, the honour of Torah ceased; with the death of Rabbi Ḥanina ben Dosa, men of [wonderful] deeds ceased; with the death of Rabbi Yosé Qatonta, piety ceased – they called him Qatonta because he was the least (*qaton*) of the pious; with the death of Rabbi Yoḥanan ben Zakkai, the radiance of wisdom ceased; with the death of Rabban Gamaliel the Elder, the honour of Torah ceased, and purity and abstinence were no more; with the death of Rabbi Ishmael ben Phoebus, the radiance of priesthood ceased; with the death of Rabbi [Judah ha-Nasi], humility and the fear of sin ceased.

GEMARA:

The rabbis taught: Rabbi Pinḥas ben Yair says, Since the Temple was destroyed *ḥaverim* and free men cover their heads in shame and men of [great] deeds are diminished, while violent and persuasive men prevail, and no one enquires or seeks or asks. In whom, then, can we put our trust? In our Father in Heaven!

25. Uncertain. Possibly 'a small, brightly adorned hand-drum, used at weddings' (Sendrey, *Music*, p. 413).
26. The Bar Kokhba Revolt.

Rabbi Eliezer the Great says, Since the Temple was destroyed the Sages have been reduced to elementary teachers, the elementary teachers to supervisors, the supervisors to common people, while the common people become weaker and weaker, and no one enquires or seeks or asks. In whom, then, can we put our trust? In our Father in Heaven!

49b

In the footsteps of the Messiah[27] insolence will increase, [unworthy] people will pursue honours,[28] the vine will yield fruit but wine will be expensive, the government will turn to heresy,[29] none will rebuke, the council chamber will become a brothel, Galilee will be destroyed and Gabla laid waste, country people will wander from town to town and find no favour, the learning of the scribes will deteriorate, sin-fearers will be despised and truth will be concealed, the young will shame the old, elders will stand before children, SON SPURNS FATHER, DAUGHTER RISES UP AGAINST MOTHER, DAUGHTER-IN-LAW AGAINST MOTHER-IN-LAW – A MAN'S OWN HOUSEHOLD ARE HIS ENEMIES (Micah 7:6 JPS), the faces of the generation are the faces of dogs, no son is ashamed before his father. In whom, then, can we put our trust? In our Father in Heaven!

The next paragraph concludes this tractate in the Mishna, but in the Bavli comes with slightly different wording in Avoda Zara *20b; here, as against the general decline presaging the Messiah, it offers the individual a path to spiritual progress prior to the final redemption. The Italian Rabbi Moshe Ḥayyim Luzzatto (1707–46) used it as the framework for his still popular ethical classic* Mesilas Yesharim *('Path of the Upright').*

Rabbi Pinḥas ben Yair says: Enthusiasm [for God's commandments] leads to cleanness, cleanness to purity, purity to abstinence, abstinence to holiness, holiness to humility, humility

---

27. i.e. the period prior to his arrival.
28. This is one of several obscurities in this paragraph, which is lacking in many manuscripts. The notion of society disintegrating prior to the arrival of the Messiah is well developed in 2 Baruch 27–30, and there are Christian parallels in Mark 13:12 and *Didache* 16. Cf. also Hesiod, *Works and Days*, lines 170–201.
29. If this is a reference to the Edict of Milan in 313, the passage is a late addition to the Mishna.

to the fear of sin, the fear of sin to piety, piety to spirituality,[30] spirituality to the resurrection of the dead, and the resurrection of the dead will be brought by Elijah, may he be remembered for good!

30. Literally, 'holy spirit'.

SIXTH TRACTATE
GITTIN (DIVORCE)

Reflections on the personal, social and religious significance of divorce figure in aggadot *scattered through the Talmud, and in the final pages of this tractate there is discussion of what we might call the 'moral issue' of the desirability or otherwise of divorce. Where* Ketubot *dealt with conditions under which divorce is permissible or mandatory, most of* Gittin *is concerned with procedural questions on the writing and delivery of the bill of divorce.*

The non-biblical Hebrew term get *(plural:* gittin), *used by the rabbis for a bill of divorce, can refer also to commercial documents and the document manumitting a slave.*

The laws of divorce are derived from Deuteronomy 24:1–4. This literal translation of the first verse is arranged to indicate points of law arising from each expression:

IF A MAN TAKES A WIFE	*How the status of marriage is established*
AND HAS INTERCOURSE WITH HER	*Cohabitation may establish marriage*
IT SHALL BE	
IF SHE DOES NOT FIND FAVOUR IN HIS EYES	*Grounds on which a man might divorce*
FOR HE HAS FOUND NAKEDNESS OF WORD IN HER	*Grounds on which a man might be obliged to divorce*
HE SHALL WRITE	*There must be a document written by the husband or his agent*

FOR HER	*It must be written for a specific woman*
A SCROLL OF	*The object on which it is written must be movable*
SEVERANCE	*The divorce must be unrestricted*
AND PUT IT	*The* get *must be delivered*
IN HER HAND	*It must be received by or on behalf of the woman*

AND SEND HER FROM HIS HOUSE

The divorce process is by definition the release of a woman by a man. This would normally take place on the man's initiative, with or without the prior agreement of the court, but proceedings might also be initiated by the court, whether or not at the behest of the wife, as in Ketubot 77a (see pp. 345–6).

Though in some matters the law may determine a situation retrospectively, a legal device known as berera ('choice'), this cannot happen with gittin; unless both husband and wife were consciously and unambiguously specified at the time of writing, the get is invalid even though the names are correct.

CHAPTER THREE

MISHNA:

A *get* that is not written for a specific woman is invalid.   24a
How does this work?

If a man was walking along the street and heard scribes dictating, Such-and-such a man divorces such-and-such a woman of such-and-such a place, and he thought, That is my name, and that is my wife's name, [the *get* they write] is not valid for him to divorce with.

Moreover, if a man wrote [a *get*] to divorce his wife and changed his mind, and another man of that town found it and said to him, My name is the same as yours, and my wife's name is the same as your wife's, it is not valid for [the second man] to divorce with.

Moreover, if a man had two wives with the same name, and wrote the *get* to divorce the elder, he may not divorce the younger with it.

Moreover, if a man instructed the scribe, Write! I will give it to whichever [of my wives] I decide, it is not valid for him to divorce with.

GEMARA:

A man wrote [a *get*] to divorce his wife and changed his mind. So what is the first [statement in the Mishna] about? Rav Papa says, It is about scribes who are busy learning [how to write a *get*]. Rav Ashi says, You can infer this from the precise wording of the text, since it says **scribes dictating**, not **scribes reading**. That proves it.

What does [the Mishna] mean by **Moreover**? They taught in the School of Rabbi Ishmael: **Not just** [a *get*] that was not written to divorce with, but even one that was written to divorce with is invalid; not just one that was not written for this man to divorce with, but even one that was written for him to divorce with is invalid; not just one that was not written to divorce this [wife] with, but even one that was written to divorce this [wife] with is invalid. Why is this so? If [Scripture] had written HE SHALL PUT A SCROLL OF SEVERANCE INTO HER HAND, I might have thought this would exclude the first case, where [the scroll] is not written for severance [but simply for practice], but if someone wrote it to divorce his wife and then changed his mind, [and another man used it,] it would be valid, since it was written for severance; hence the Torah writes AND HE SHALL WRITE. If it had only written AND HE SHALL WRITE, I might have thought this excluded the case where [the husband himself] did not write it, but if he had two wives, and he wrote it himself, I would think it was valid [notwithstanding the fact that he had originally intended it for the other wife]; therefore the Torah states FOR HER, [meaning] with this [wife] in mind. Why is the final case [included]? It is to inform us of the principle of *ein berera* [no retrospective determination].

Moreover, if [a man] had two wives with the same name, and wrote the *get* to divorce the elder, he may not divorce the younger with it.

[This implies] that he may not divorce the younger, but he may divorce the elder. Rava said, It follows that if there are two men called Joseph ben Simeon in a town, they may serve debit notes to other people[, even though it is unclear which of them has issued the note]. Abbaye said to him, If you interpret like that, the first case in the Mishna – **That is my name, and that is my wife's name, it is not valid for him to divorce with** – would likewise imply that the second man could not divorce with it but the first could, yet we have said, **Nor can anyone else serve a debit note to them**. So what can we say? [A note may be served] in accordance with the opinion of Rabbi Eleazar, who holds that the witnesses of delivery effect the transaction; here, too, [i.e. where the first husband delivers the *get* to his wife,] there are witnesses to the delivery, [so the process is valid] according to Rabbi Eleazar.

Rav said, All [*gittin* listed in the Mishna] except the first disqualify from the priesthood;[1] but Shmuel said, Even the first disqualifies.

Shmuel follows his [usual line of] reasoning, for Shmuel said that wherever the Sages of the Mishna referred to a *get* as invalid, they meant invalid and disqualifies; wherever they referred to a *halitza* as invalid, they meant invalid and disqualifies from the brothers.[2]

In the West they said in the name of Rabbi Eleazar, 'Left' and 'night' are invalid and disqualify; 'minor' and 'sock' are invalid but do not disqualify.[3] Zeiri said, None of them disqualifies except the last; Rav Assi, similarly, said, None of them disqualifies except the last. And Rabbi Yoḥanan said, Even the last does not disqualify.   25a

1. If a woman receives any of the *gittin* that the Mishna lists as invalid, other than the first instance, she is regarded as a divorcee and may not marry a *Kohen* – Rashi.
2. That is, although the *halitza* is invalid and has to be done again, she is no longer permitted to marry any of the brothers.
3. If the sister-in-law removes the levir's left shoe, or removes the correct one at night, or if he is a minor or she removes a sock rather than a shoe, the *halitza* is invalid (*Yevamot* 104a).

Rabbi Yoḥanan follows his [usual line of] reasoning, for Rav Assi said in the name of Rabbi Yoḥanan that brothers who divide [their inheritance] are like buyers, and must return [the property] to one another in the Jubilee year.

Both cases are needed. For if Rabbi Yoḥanan had stated his opinion only in [the divorce] case, I might have thought that *berera* does not operate here since we require [a *get* to be written] FOR HER, [meaning] with this one in mind; but [in the inheritance case, I would have thought that] the Torah required [real estate] purchases to be returned [to their original owners] in the Jubilee year, but not inheritance or gifts. Had he stated his opinion only with regard to fields [inherited by brothers], I might have thought it was a [mere] stringency, or that it was to restore the status quo [where the heritage had a single owner – Rashi], but that would not apply [in the divorce case]. Therefore, both statements are needed.

Rav Hoshaya asked Rav Yehuda, What if he said to the scribe, Write [a *get* for me]! I will give it to whichever [of my wives, each of whom has the same name,] comes through the door first?

He replied, [The answer to that is implied in] our Mishna: **Moreover, if he instructed the scribe, Write! I will give it to whichever one I decide, it is not valid for him to divorce with**. From this it follows that *berera* does not operate[, that is, the law does not determine retrospectively which wife was intended].

[Hoshaya] raised an objection [to this from another Mishna]: **If someone said to his sons, I will slaughter the paschal lamb on behalf of whichever of you arrives first in Jerusalem, when the first son arrives – his head and most of his body – he gains the right to a share in the lamb, and acquires rights on behalf of his brothers.**[4]

[Rav Yehuda] replied, Hoshaya, my son! What has the paschal lamb to do with divorce? With regard to [the Mishna concerning the paschal lamb], it was taught, **Rabbi Yoḥanan said: [This is a case where the father intended] to encourage them to observe**

4. That is, *berera* operates to establish retrospectively that this son acquired the right from the moment of slaughter – Rashi. Only those designated at the time of slaughter may eat the lamb.

the commandments. Careful inspection of the text also shows this, for it said, **When the first son arrives – his head and most of his body – he gains the right to a share in the lamb, and acquires rights on behalf of his brothers.** Now, if you say that the father had designated them previously [as participants], that is all right; but if he designated them only after slaughtering [the lamb], how could they be numbered [among the participants]? Does not the Mishna teach, [**People**] **may be designated and may withdraw** [only] **up to the time** [the lamb] **is slaughtered?**

A baraita supports this: **It once happened that the girls arrived before the boys, for the girls were eager and the boys indolent.**

Abbaye said, [Rav Hoshaya] enquired about a case where the outcome was dependent on an external factor, but [Rav Yehuda] replied with a case where the outcome depended on the [the agent's] own action, and then [Rav Hoshaya] responded with a case dependent on an external factor![5]

Rava responded, What is the problem? Perhaps one who accepts [the principle of] *berera* maintains it irrespective of whether the outcome depends on external factors or on [the agent's] own action, and one who accept *berera* rejects it irrespective of whether the outcome depends on external factors or on [the agent's] own action.

Rav Mesharshya said to Rava, Surely Rabbi Judah does not accept *berera* in a case where the outcome depends on [the agent's] own action, but does accept *berera* in a case where the outcome depends on external factors. For a baraita teaches: **One who purchases wine from Samaritans should declare: two *logs* which I shall separate are *teruma*, ten are first-tithe and nine are second-tithe, and he may then redeem** (the second-tithe – Rashi) **and drink immediately. So says Rabbi Meir, but Rabbi Judah, Rabbi José and Rabbi Simeon forbid it.** [From this it appears that Rabbi Judah does not allow the portions set aside

25b

---

5.   Kraemer, *Mind*, pp. 64–5, cites this passage to demonstrate that Amoraim of the middle generations, such as Abbaye, intentionally preserved their argumentation and that of their predecessors, contrary to Halivni's view that intentional preservation was an innovation of the Stammaim.

as tithes to be determined retrospectively by *berera*, and in this case it is the agent himself who would determine which portions to set aside. On the other hand, in a case in which the outcome depends on] external factors, [Rabbi Judah] does accept *berera*, for the Mishna states [of a woman whose husband has delivered a *get* to her on condition that he dies from his current sickness, that is, an external factor]: **What is her status during that period? Rabbi Judah says, she is in all respects a married woman, but when [her husband] dies the *get* operates [retrospectively].**

Ravina said to Rava: Surely Rabbi Simeon does not accept *berera* in a case where the outcome depends on [the agent's] own action, but does accept *berera* in a case where the outcome depends on external factors. The case where the outcome depends on his own actions is the one just cited. The case where the outcome depends on external factors occurs in a baraita: [**If a man says,**] **I will have intercourse with you [to betroth you as my wife] on condition that [my] father agrees [to your becoming my wife], she is betrothed [to him by this act]; Rabbi Simeon ben Judah said in the name of Rabbi Simeon, If the father agrees she is betrothed; if not, not.**

26a

[Rava] said to [Ravina], Neither Rabbi Judah nor Rabbi Simeon distinguishes between [a case conditional on] the agent's own decision, and [one conditional on] external factors; they apply [the principle of] *berera* [to both]. The reason [that Rabbi Simeon demurs in the case of tithing] is [not to do with *berera*, but simply] in case the jar breaks, so the person [would be unable to fulfil the condition and] would retrospectively be [guilty of] drinking untithed produce. [Rabbi Meir] said to them, When it breaks[, we will worry about it]![6]

6.   But there is no need to worry about that contingency, since it is unlikely – Rashi.

CHAPTER FIVE

MISHNA:

In the time of the war slain,[7] there were no *sicarii*[8] in Judaea; 55b
since the time of the war slain, there have been *sicarii* in
Judaea.

How does [the law operate]? If someone purchased [land]
from a *sicarius* and then from the [rightful] owner, the sale is
void;[9] if he purchased from the [rightful] owner and then from
the *sicarius*, the sale is valid.

[Likewise], if he purchased [land] from the husband and
then from the wife, the sale is void;[10] if he purchased from the
wife and then from the husband, the sale is valid.

This was the original Mishna. A later court decreed that if
someone buys [land] from a *sicarius*, he must pay the [rightful]
owner a quarter [of its value by way of compensation]. This is
only if the [rightful] owner is not in a position to buy [back
the land himself], but if he is in the position [to do so], he has
priority over anyone else.

Rabbi [Judah ha-Nasi] convened a court that voted that if
land had remained in the possession of the *sicarius* for twelve
years, whoever then purchased it had the right to retain it, on
condition that he pay the [rightful] owner a quarter [of its value].

GEMARA:

If there were no *sicarii* during the time of the war slain, how
come there were *sicarii* after the time of the war slain? Rav
Yehuda said, The Mishna means that during the time of the
war slain, the law regarding *sicarii* did not operate[, but after
the time of the war slain, it became operative]. As Rabbi Assi
said, There were three [successive] decrees: The first was whoever
does not kill [a Jew] will be killed; the middle was whoever kills

7. Reference uncertain. Rashi says it refers to 'the war of Titus', i.e. the First Revolt.
8. Latin *sicarius*, 'dagger man', 'murderer' – used here of terrorists who appropriated
   land by threatening to kill, or more specifically of the Zealots (see n. 21).
9. This is because the rightful owner may not have agreed to the sale.
10. She may not have agreed to the sale of land mortgaged to her *ketuba* or land to
    which she had a personal claim.

[a Jew] will receive four *zuz*; the last was whoever kills [a Jew] will be killed. Under the first and middle decrees, a Jew would agree to relinquish his property rather than lose his life; under the final decree he would think, Let him take the land now, but then I will sue him in court.

These references to the troubled times of the Great Revolts lead to a narrative interpreting the events surrounding the Destruction of the Second Temple in 70. The complex literary structure of which the first part is given here cannot have achieved its present form until the fifth or sixth century; its historical value is limited, but it throws light on the formation of rabbinic memory and of rabbinic attitudes to sin, suffering and the outside world.

Rabbi Yoḥanan said, What is the meaning of the verse, **HAPPY IS THE MAN WHO IS ANXIOUS ALWAYS, BUT HE WHO HARDENS HIS HEART FALLS INTO MISFORTUNE** (Proverbs 28:14 JPS)? Jerusalem was destroyed through Qamtza and Bar Qamtza;[11] Tur Malka[12] was destroyed on account of a cock and a hen; Beitar was destroyed because of a carriage shaft.

Jerusalem was destroyed through Qamtza and Bar Qamtza – A man had a friend called Qamtza and an enemy enemy called Bar Qamtza. He made a feast and sent his servant to invite Qamtza. The servant went but fetched Bar Qamtza [in error]. When the man came and found [Bar Qamtza] there, he exclaimed, Aren't you my enemy? What are you doing here? Get up and go! [Bar Qamtza] said, Since I am here, let me stay, 56a and I will pay for whatever I eat or drink. No, said he. Then I will pay for half of your feast. No! I'll pay for the whole feast. No! He took [Bar Qamtza] by the arm and threw him out. Bar Qamtza reasoned, Rabbis[13] were sitting there and didn't intervene; evidently they approve [of what he did]; I shall denounce them to the [Roman] government. So he went and told Caesar, The Jews are plotting a revolt against you!

11. Unknown persons. *Qamtza* is a locust.
12. 'Royal Mountain'. Not identified, though Targum Pseudo-Jonathan to Judges 4:5 gives the name to Mount Ephraim.
13. A parallel account in Midrash *Eikha Rabbati* 4:3 specifies that Rabbi Zechariah ben Eukylos was there and failed to intervene.

What proof do you have? asked [the Roman].

Send them [an animal for] sacrifice, he said, and you will see whether they offer it.

[The Roman] dispatched [Bar Qamtza] with a three-year-old calf, but on the way [Bar Qamtza] made a blemish in its lip – some say a spot in its eye – a place which constitutes a blemish for us but not for them.

The rabbis had a mind to offer it [nevertheless], for the sake of peace with the government, but Rabbi Zechariah ben Eukylos objected, People will say that blemished animals are being offered on the altar! They thought of putting [Bar Qamtza] to death, but [again] Rabbi Zechariah objected, People will say that you can be executed for causing a blemish to a sacred animal!

Rabbi Yoḥanan reflected, The reticence of Rabbi Zechariah ben Eukylos destroyed our home, burnt down our Temple and exiled us from our land!

He sent [a communication] about them to Nero Caesar.[14] When [Nero] arrived he shot an arrow to the east and it fell in Jerusalem; to the west and it fell in Jerusalem; in all four directions and it fell [towards] Jerusalem. He said to a child, What verse [of Scripture] did you learn today? [The child] replied, I WILL WREAK MY VENGEANCE ON EDOM[15] THROUGH MY PEOPLE ISRAEL (Ezekiel 25:14 JPS). He thought, The Holy One, blessed be He, wants to destroy His House, and will then wash his hands of whoever has done it [for Him]! He fled, converted and was the ancestor of Rabbi Meir.

He reported on them to Vespasian.[16] Vespasian came and lay siege [to Jerusalem] for three years.

Three wealthy men were [in Jerusalem]: Nicodemus ben Gorion, Ben Kalba Savu'a and Ben Tzitzit he-Keset.

14. The Roman official sent to Caesar. Nero was emperor 54–68 CE, so was certainly in power when the Revolt began. Equally certainly he did not travel to Palestine and convert to Judaism, though there is some mystery about his death; Suetonius, *Twelve Caesars*, says he stabbed himself in the throat with a dagger, but Tacitus, *Histories*, alleges that he fled to Greece, where the governor of Cythnos had him executed in 69.

15. In rabbinic symbolism, Edom is Rome.

16. Titus Flavius Vespasianus, founder of the Flavian dynasty, was emperor 69–79 CE.

Nicodemus ben Gorion was so called because the sun shone for him;[17] Ben Kalba Savu'a was so called because whoever entered his house hungry as a dog left it replete;[18] Ben Tzitzit he-Keset was so called because the fringes of his garments trailed along cushions – some say, because his cushion was [set] among the great of Rome.[19]

One of them said, I can provide wheat and barley [to withstand the siege]; one said, [I can provide] wine, salt and oil; and one said, [I can provide] firewood. They had sufficient stores [between them] to last twenty-one years.

The rabbis esteemed the provider of firewood most highly [of the three]. Rav Ḥisda entrusted his servant with all his keys, but not with [the key] to the firewood [store]; for, said Rav Ḥisda, a storehouse of wheat requires sixty storehouses of firewood [as fuel].[20]

There were Zealots[21] [in the city]. The rabbis said, Let us go and make peace with [the Romans], but the Zealots wouldn't let them. Rather, they said, let us make war against them! The rabbis said, It will not work. [So the Zealots] went and set fire to the stores of wheat and barley,[22] causing a famine.

Martha the daughter of Boethus was one of the wealthiest women in Jerusalem. She sent a messenger to buy some fine flour, but it was sold out. The messenger reported that there was no fine flour, only white, so she sent for white, but meanwhile white was sold out. The messenger reported that there was no white

17. This is a play between Greek Nicodemos and Hebrew *naqad* (to pierce or shine); the allusion is to a story in *Ta'anit* 20a.
18. Aramaic *kalba*, 'dog' and *savu'a*, 'satisfied'.
19. Hebrew *tzitzit*, 'fringe' and *keset*, 'cushion'.
20. Sokoloff, *Babylonian*, entry on *k'laka*.
21. A sect, known also from Josephus and possibly from some of the Dead Sea Scrolls, which was implacably hostile to Rome and to Roman sympathizers among the Jews. Some of them were allegedly involved in terrorism, and they may well be the *sicarii* of our Mishna. The actual term used here (the vocalization is uncertain) is *biryonei*, derived, according to Sokoloff, *Babylonian*, from the Akkadian *bārāmū*, 'rebel'.
22. In order to force a confrontation with Rome. See Tacitus, *Histories* 5:12.

flour, only low grade,[23] so she sent for low grade, but meanwhile low grade was sold out. The messenger reported that there was no low grade flour, only barley flour, so she sent for barley flour, but meanwhile barley flour was sold out. She put on her shoes and said, I will go and see [for myself] whether I can find anything to eat! A cowpat stuck to her foot and she died. Rabban Yohanan ben Zakkai applied to her [the verse], AND SHE WHO IS MOST TENDER AND DAINTY AMONG YOU, SO TENDER AND DAINTY THAT SHE WOULD NEVER VENTURE TO SET A FOOT ON THE GROUND (Deuteronomy 28:56 JPS). Others say she ate the [cast-off] figs of Rabbi Zadok and became sick and died. As she was dying she brought out all her silver and gold, and threw it in the street, saying, What use is this to me? That is as it is written, THEY SHALL THROW THEIR SILVER INTO THE STREETS[, AND THEIR GOLD SHALL BE TREATED AS SOMETHING UNCLEAN. THEIR SILVER AND GOLD SHALL NOT AVAIL TO SAVE THEM] (Ezekiel 7:19 JPS). (Now Rabbi Zadok had fasted forty years, [praying] that the Temple should not be destroyed, and when he ate the food could be seen passing through him.[24] When he was recovering they brought him figs; he sucked out the juice and threw the rest away.)

Abba Sikkara, leader of the Zealots, was the son of Rabban Yohanan ben Zakkai's sister. [Yohanan] sent for him to come in secret. [When] he arrived, [Yohanan] said to him, How long are you going to carry on like this and kill everyone by famine? [Abba Sikkara] replied, What can I do? If I say anything, [my followers] will kill me!

[Yohanan said,] If only I could get out [of Jerusalem], I might be able to save something.

[Abba Sikkara said,] Put about a rumour that you are sick, and let people come and enquire about you. Then fetch some

23. Middle Iranian *xushkar* (Sokoloff, *Babylonian*, entry on *kushkar*).
24. Literally, 'from outside'.

decaying material, spread it over you and have it said that you
have died. Let your disciples carry you, but no one else, since
they may notice that a living body is lighter than a corpse.[25]

He did so. Rabbi Eliezer bore him on one side, and Rabbi
Joshua on the other. When they arrived at the gate, the [Zealots
on guard] wanted to pierce [the bier with a sword]; the [disciples
objected: The Romans] will say, They pierced their Master.
[The Zealots then] wanted to jostle [the bier]; the [disciples
objected: The Romans] will say, They jostled their Master.

They opened the gate.

When [Rabbi Yoḥanan] arrived [in Vespasian's] presence, he
said, Hail, O King! Hail, O King!

[Vespasian:] You are deserving of death on two counts! First,
I am not the king, and you have addressed me as king.[26] Second,
if I were the king, why did you not come to pay your respects
earlier?

56b   [Yoḥanan:] You say that you are not the king, but you
certainly are king; for if you were not king, Jerusalem could not
fall into your hands, as it is written, THE LEBANON SHALL
FALL BY A MIGHTY ONE (Isaiah 10:34). A MIGHTY ONE implies
a king, as it is written, HIS MIGHTY ONE SHALL BE OF HIS
OWN (Jeremiah 30:21); LEBANON refers to the Temple, as it is
written, THIS GOOD MOUNTAIN AND THE LEBANON (Deuteronomy 3:25). As to your asking if you were king, why did I
not come to pay my respects earlier; [that is because] the Zealots
among us would not let me come until now.

[Vespasian:] If you had a barrel of honey and a snake was
after it, would you not smash the barrel to get rid of the snake?[27]

[Rabbi Yoḥanan] fell silent.

Rav Yosef, or perhaps Rabbi Aqiva, commented,
WHO TURN SAGES BACK AND MAKE NONSENSE OF

---

25. The story of Yoḥanan ben Zakkai's escape from Jerusalem, his interview with
    Vespasian and his prophecy that Vespasian was destined for imperial power, has
    remarkable similarities with Josephus' account of his own escape from Galilee to
    the Roman lines and his conversations with Vespasian (Josephus, Wars 3:341;
    392–408; 4:622–9).
26. Thereby commiting treason against the real emperor.
27. Just so, you could have knocked down or set fire to the wall to get rid of the
    Zealots.

THEIR KNOWLEDGE (Isaiah 44:25 JPS). He should
have said, We fetch tongs, seize the snake and kill it,
and leave the barrel [unharmed].[28]

Meanwhile, a messenger arrived from Rome: Arise! Caesar is
dead, and the great men of Rome want to make you leader!

[Vespasian] had put on one boot. He wanted to put the other
on but it wouldn't fit; he tried to remove the first but it wouldn't
come off. He said, What is going on?

[Yoḥanan] said, Don't worry! You have received good news,
as it is written, **GOOD NEWS PUTS FAT ON THE BONES** (Proverbs
15:30 JPS).

[Vespasian:] So what should I do?

[Yoḥanan:] Bring someone you dislike and let him pass before
you, as it is written, **DESPONDENCY DRIES UP THE BONES**
(Proverbs 17:22 JPS).

[Vespasian] did [as advised] and it worked.

[Vespasian:] As you are so clever, why did you not come to
see me until now?

[Yoḥanan:] Didn't I tell you?

[Vespasian:] And didn't I tell you? [Anyway,] I am leaving
now, and I will send someone else [to continue the siege].[29]
What would you like me to grant you?

[Yoḥanan:] Give me Yavné and its Sages; spare the family of
Rabban Gamaliel; and provide doctors for Rabbi Zadok.

Rav Yosef, or perhaps Rabbi Aqiva, commented,
**WHO TURN SAGES BACK, AND MAKE NONSENSE OF
THEIR KNOWLEDGE** (Isaiah 44:25 JPS). He should
have said, Leave us alone this time! But [Yoḥanan]
thought, He might not grant that, and I would have
achieved nothing.

*In the time of the Mishna, marriage and divorce were private
procedures; provided they were correctly carried out, the court*

28. Likewise, we could have handed you an undamaged city – Rashi.
29. Immediately on being proclaimed emperor in 69, Vespasian gave his son Titus
charge of the Jewish war. The Arch of Titus, still standing at the entrance to the
Roman Forum, commemorates his victory.

would recognize what had been done as binding on the parties. That is why the Schools argued about what advice should be given to someone contemplating divorce: whether *to divorce is a moral issue rather than a legal one. Later Jewish Law removed divorce from the private sphere; since the Middle Ages it can only be carried out through a* bet din, *or religious court.*

For the Shammaites, only adultery offers a moral justification for divorce; for the Hillelites and Aqiva (who, incidentally, was celebrated for his devotion to his wife), even a minor annoyance would suffice. Though proof-texts are supplied for both sides, it is clear that the debate runs deeper: the Shammaites emphasize the sanctity and seriousness of marriage, and the Hillelites the quality of the relationship – when love is no longer strong enough to overcome a minor kitchen disaster, or a man begins to think of other women as more beautiful than his wife, the marriage is already in jeopardy.

There is no evidence that any rabbinic authority banned divorce, in the way some Christians believe that Paul did. Though scholars have suggested, on the basis of a passage in the Damascus Document (4:20b–5:6a), that there is precedent in the Qumran community for an outright ban on divorce, further Dead Sea Scrolls research has cast doubt on this; at most Qumran halakha *may have outlawed 'remarriage subsequent to divorce as long as the former spouse was still living'.*[30]

CHAPTER NINE

MISHNA:

90a   The School of Shammai say, A man should not divorce his wife unless she has been unfaithful, as it is said, FOR HE HAS FOUND NAKEDNESS OF WORD[31] IN HER (Deuteronomy 24:1); but the School of Hillel say, Even if she overcooked his food,

---

30. Shemesh, 'Matrimonial Law', 246, 248. On the relationship between Qumran *halakha* and early rabbinic *halakha*, see Noam, 'Divorce in Qumran'.

31. This is a strictly literal translation. JPS has 'something obnoxious', KJV has 'some uncleanness'; these are correct translations, but insufficiently literal to support the interpretation of the Schools. The Hillelites interpret as 'anything untoward'; Hebrew *davar* can mean 'word' or 'thing'.

as it is said, FOR HE HAS FOUND NAKEDNESS OF WORD IN
HER. Rabbi Aqiva says, Even if he finds another more beautiful
than she, as it is said, IF SHE DOES NOT FIND FAVOUR IN HIS
EYES (Deuteronomy 24:1).

GEMARA:

It was taught: The School of Hillel said to the School of
Shammai, Does it not say, WORD? The School of Shammai
replied, But does it not say NAKEDNESS? The School of Hillel
responded, If it said NAKEDNESS, but did not say WORD, I
might think that she should go on account of adultery[32] but
not on account of anything [less]; therefore, it says WORD. But
if it said WORD and did not say NAKEDNESS, I would think
that if [she is divorced] on account of [some small] thing, she
would be permitted to marry another man, but if [she is
divorced] on account of adultery, she would not be permitted
to marry another man.

What use do the School of Shammai make of WORD? WORD
occurs here, and it occurs also in: A WORD[33] SHALL STAND BY
THE TESTIMONY OF TWO WITNESSES OR BY THE TESTIMONY
OF THREE WITNESSES (Deuteronomy 19:15). Just as there [at
least] two witnesses are required, so here two witnesses are
required.[34]

And the School of Hillel? It does not say NAKED-
NESS [PROVED] *BY* WORD. And the School of Shammai? Nor does it say NAKEDNESS *OR* WORD. And
the School of Hillel? That is [precisely] why it says
NAKEDNESS OF WORD – it means 'either nakedness or
word' [that is, either adultery or a lesser matter].

Rabbi Aqiva says, Even if he finds another more beautiful
than she. What is [the basis of his] dispute [with the Schools]?
It is [the point] Resh Laqish [made], for Resh Laqish said, *Ki*
has four different meanings: 'if', 'perhaps', 'but', 'since'.[35] The
School of Shammai hold [that the verse,] IT SHALL BE, IF SHE

---

32. Literally, 'nakedness'.
33. Usual translation: 'matter'.
34. That is, he should not divorce without adequate evidence of adultery.
35. Precise translation is not possible, e.g. the word *ki* translated 'since' could just as
    well be translated 'for' or 'because'; see also *Rosh Hashana* 3a (see p. 239).

**DOES NOT FIND FAVOUR IN HIS SIGHT, *KI* HE HAS FOUND
NAKEDNESS OF WORD IN HER,** [should be read] ***SINCE* HE HAS
FOUND NAKEDNESS OF WORD IN HER,** but Rabbi Aqiva takes
it to mean **OR *IF* HE HAS FOUND NAKEDNESS OF WORD IN
HER.**

Rav Papa asked Rava, What [is the situation if he wants to
divorce her but] finds neither 'nakedness' nor 'word'? [Rava
replied,] Since the Torah reveals regarding a rapist, **HE CAN
NEVER HAVE THE RIGHT TO DIVORCE HER** (Deuteronomy
22:29 JPS) – as long as he lives he must take her back[36] – the
Torah reveals in that case [that he has no power to divorce], but
in this case what he has done is done.[37]

Rav Mesharshya asked Rava, What if a man has decided to
divorce his wife and she is still living with him as man and wife?
[Rava] recited the verse, **DO NOT DEVISE HARM AGAINST YOUR
FELLOW WHO LIVES TRUSTFULLY WITH YOU** (Proverbs 3:29
JPS).

A baraita taught: **Rabbi Meir used to say, Just as people's
attitudes to food vary, so do their attitudes to women. There
are men who, if a fly falls into their cup, throw it out and
don't drink [the contents of the cup]; Pappos ben Judah was
like this with women – he locked his wife in whenever he went
out. Then there are those who, if a fly falls into their cup,
throw it out but drink [the contents of the cup]; this is what
most men are like – he leaves her to talk with her brothers and
her male relatives. And there are men who, if a fly falls into
the food in their dish, suck it and eat it; this is the way of a
bad man, who sees his wife go out with her head uncovered,**
90b   **spin threads in the marketplace, [wear garments] open on both
sides[38] and bathe with men.** (Bathe with men? [Surely not –
but] bathe in a place where men bathe.[39]) **It is a duty to divorce**

36. i.e. he has a lifelong responsibility for her.
37. The divorce would take effect, even though he had no cause for complaint against
his wife. Subsequent Jewish law forbade divorce without the woman's consent
other than where ordered by the court.
38. Opposite her elbows, like the Edomite (Christian) women in France whose bare
sides are visible – Rashi.
39. Cassius Dio, *Roman History* 69.8.2, writes of Hadrian on a particular occasion,
'And further, he commanded them (men and women) to bathe separately'.

such a woman, as it is said, FOR HE HAS FOUND NAKEDNESS OF WORD IN HER ... HE SHALL SEND HER AWAY FROM HIS HOUSE (Deuteronomy 24:1). AND [IF] SHE GOES AND BECOMES THE WIFE OF ANOTHER MAN (24:2) – Scripture calls him 'other', as if to say, he is not the equal of the first [husband], for [the first husband] sent a bad woman out of his house, but this one took a bad woman into his house. If the second [husband proves] worthy, he will send her away [too], as it is said, AND [IF] THE LATTER MAN HATES HER ... AND SENDS HER FROM HIS HOUSE (24:3); but if not, she will bury him, as it is said, OR IF THE LATTER MAN DIES (24:3) – he deserves to die, for [the first husband] sent a bad woman out of his house, but this one took a bad woman into his house.

FOR I DETEST DIVORCE[40] [– SAID THE LORD, THE GOD OF ISRAEL] (Malachi 2:16 JPS). Rav Yehuda said, If you hate her, send her away; Rabbi Yohanan said, He who divorces is to be hated. But they did not disagree; one statement was about a first marriage, the other about a second. For Rabbi Eleazar taught, When someone divorces his first wife, even the altar sheds tears, as it is said, AND THIS YOU DO AS WELL: YOU COVER THE ALTAR OF THE LORD WITH TEARS, WEEPING, AND MOANING, SO THAT HE REFUSES TO REGARD THE OBLATION ANY MORE AND TO ACCEPT WHAT YOU OFFER. BUT YOU ASK, 'BECAUSE OF WHAT?' BECAUSE THE LORD IS A WITNESS BETWEEN YOU AND THE WIFE OF YOUR YOUTH WITH WHOM YOU HAVE BROKEN FAITH, THOUGH SHE IS YOUR PARTNER AND COVENANTED SPOUSE (Malachi 2:13–14 JPS).[41]

---

40. Though the roots of the words 'detest' and 'divorce' are clear, the syntax is not.
41. Eleazar understands Malachi's metaphor of unfaithfulness to God; however, the metaphor would lose all force if not literally true that it was a bad thing to break faith with the 'wife of one's youth'.

SEVENTH TRACTATE
QIDDUSHIN (BETROTHAL)

How does a woman's legal status change from single to married? How is she 'transferred' from one family to another? Most of this tractate is concerned with the legal process called qiddushin *or* erusin *(betrothal) by which the change is effected. This leads to a general discussion of modes of acquisition and transfer by principals and agents, and of imposed and implied conditions of contract.*

It is always a man who effects qiddushin, *but he cannot do this without the woman's free consent. The only exception to this is that a father may, under biblical law, contract a marriage for his minor daughter; as we have seen, the rabbis attempted to ban child marriages, but failed.*[1]

Other matters of family law dealt with include reciprocal responsibilities of parents and children, degrees of propinquity, and the personal status of Kohanim, *converts and other groups.*

CHAPTER ONE

MISHNA:

2a   A wife is acquired in three ways: by money, by document or by sexual intercourse.

Money – The School of Shammai say, A denarius, or [goods] worth a denarius; the School of Hillel say, A *peruta*, or [goods]

1.   Introductory note to *Yevamot* 12a (see p. 304).

worth a *peruta*. How much is a *peruta*? One-eighth of an Italian *as*.[2]

She acquires her [independence] by divorce or by her husband's death.

A sister-in-law is acquired [as wife by her deceased husband's brother] by intercourse, and acquires her [independence] by *halitza* or by the brother-in-law's death.

The Gemara exploits an apparent verbal quibble to cast light on several important aspects of the topic, not least the need for a woman's free consent.

GEMARA:

A wife is acquired. Why does Mishna say here, **A wife is acquired**, whereas [at the beginning of Chapter Two] it says, **A man effects *qiddushin*?** It is because it has to mention money. The validity of money [for effecting *qiddushin*] is derived by word analogy from [Abraham's purchase of] the field of Efron – in one place it is written, IF A MAN TAKE A WIFE (Deuteronomy 22:13), and in another, I GIVE YOU MONEY FOR THE FIELD; TAKE IT FROM ME (Genesis 23:13) – and 'taking' signifies acquisition, for it is written, THE FIELD THAT ABRAHAM ACQUIRED (Genesis 49:30). Alternatively, [it may be derived from] LET THEM ACQUIRE FIELDS FOR MONEY (Jeremiah 32:44). This it why it says, **A wife is acquired.**   2b

Then let [Chapter Two] commence, **A man acquires!** [Chapter One opens] with a Torah expression[, *qana*, 'acquire'], but the later Mishna uses a rabbinic expression.

What does the rabbinic expression [*qiddushin*] mean? It means that she is now forbidden to all [other men], just as *heqdesh* [is forbidden].[3]

Our Mishna could have said, **A man acquires.** [However, since] the the Mishna continues by saying, **She acquires her [independence]**, and in that context she is the Tanna's subject, she is made the subject at the beginning too.

2.   That is, 144 *perutot* = 1 denarius (see Appendix III). The use of wedding rings by Jews is not attested prior to the Middle Ages.
3.   Sacred property. *Qiddushin* and *heqdesh* derive from the root QDSH, meaning 'sacred', 'reserved'.

Then might it not have said, **A man acquires . . . A man gives . . .**? This would not work, since [one way she may acquire her independence is by] the death of the husband; he does not 'give' this, Heaven does!

Alternatively, you could argue that had [Mishna] said, **A man acquires . . .**, you might have thought [that this would be the case] even without her consent; so it says, **A wife is acquired . . .**, [implying] with her consent, not against her will.

The next selection concerns mutual responsibilities within the family, defined in terms of the mitzvot.

MISHNA:

29a   *Mitzvot* of the son on the father,[4] men are obliged [to observe] but women are exempt from [observing].

Mitzvot of the father on the son are obligatory upon both men and women.

All positive *mitzvot* that are time dependent, men are obliged [to observe] but women are exempt from [observing].

All positive *mitzvot* that are not time dependent are obligatory upon both men and women.

All negative *mitzvot*, whether or not time dependent, are obligatory upon both men and women, except for DO NOT ROUND THE CORNERS OF YOUR HEAD (Leviticus 19:27), DO NOT DESTROY THE CORNERS OF YOUR BEARD (Leviticus 19:27) and DO NOT DEFILE YOURSELVES FOR THE DEAD (Leviticus 21:1).[5]

GEMARA:

What is the meaning of *Mitzvot* **of the son on the father**? If you say [it means] a son's obligations towards his father, [how can it then say] **men are obliged but women are exempt**? [Daughters also have duties towards their parents, for] does not a baraita teach: MAN – **I would know only that a man [ought to respect his father and mother]; how do I know that a woman**

---

4.   This translation deliberately reproduces the ambiguity of the original. Are 'commandments of the son on the father' responsibilities of the son towards the father or of the father towards the son? Are 'son' and 'father' gender-determined terms, or inclusive terms for 'child' and 'parent'?

5.   The first two are physically inappropriate for women; priestly restrictions, to which category the third belongs, apply only to men.

[must do likewise]? When it says, [EVERY] MAN SHOULD RESPECT HIS FATHER AND MOTHER (Leviticus 19:2), [at least] two[, male and female, are addressed, as the verb 'respect' is in the plural].

Rav Yehuda says, What it means is, *mitzvot* that the father must perform for his son. This we have learned, for the rabbis taught: A father is obliged to circumcise his son, to teach him Torah, to find him a wife and to teach him a trade; some say he is also obliged to teach him to swim. Rabbi Judah says, If a man fails to teach his son a trade, he teaches him theft.[6]

[How can Rabbi Judah say,] He teaches him theft!
Does he really teach him to steal? [No, but] it is as if he teaches him to steal, [since if he knows no trade he will be driven to rob people in order to eat – Rashi].

Scriptural basis for the obligations, and for women's exemption.

To circumcise his son. What is the scriptural basis for this? It is written, ABRAHAM CIRCUMCISED ISAAC HIS SON (Genesis 21:4). If the father does not circumcise him, responsibility for circumcising him devolves upon the court, as it is written, EVERY MALE AMONG YOU MUST BE CIRCUMCISED (Genesis 17:10). If the court does not circumcise him, responsibility for circumcising devolves upon himself, for it is written, AND ANY UNCIRCUMCISED MALE WHO HAS NOT CIRCUMCISED THE FLESH OF HIS FORESKIN SHALL BE EXCLUDED [FROM HIS PEOPLE] (Genesis 17:14).

How do we know that [the mother] is not responsible [for circumcising her son]? Since it is written, As GOD COMMANDED HIM (Genesis 21:4) – him, not her.

We find [that this was the case] at the time [God spoke with Abraham]. How do we know [that it applies throughout] the generations? It was taught in the school of Rabbi Ishmael: Wherever the Torah uses the expression *tsav* (command), it [conveys] an exhortation for that time and for the generations [to come]. That it is an exhortation [is inferred from the verse about Joshua], for it is written, COMMAND JOSHUA, STRENGTHEN AND ENCOURAGE HIM (Deuteronomy 3:28).

6. Tosefta to this tractate.

[That it is] for that time and for the generations [to come, we derive from] the verse, FROM THE DAY THAT THE LORD COMMANDED AND ONWARD THROUGH YOUR GENERATIONS (Numbers 15:23).

To redeem him. What is the scriptural basis for this? It is written, OF HUMANS, YOU SHALL REDEEM ALL YOUR FIRST-BORN SONS (Exodus 13:13). And if his father did not redeem him, he is obliged to redeem himself, as it is written, YOU SHALL SURELY REDEEM[7] (Numbers 18:15).

And how do we know that [the mother] is not responsible [for redeeming her son]? The word written is *TIFDÉ* ('redeem'), which may be read *TIPADÉ* ('shall be redeemed');[8] [this implies that] whoever is obliged to redeem himself may be obliged to redeem another, but whoever is not obliged to redeem him/herself is not obliged to redeem another.

Then how do we know that [a woman] is not obliged to redeem herself? Since *TIFDÉ* ('redeem') is written, which may be read *TIPADÉ* ('shall be redeemed'), [implying that] whoever is obliged to redeem another is obliged to redeem himself, but whoever is not obliged to redeem another is not obliged to redeem himself.

And how do we know that no one else is obliged to redeem her? Scripture says, OF HUMANS, YOU SHALL REDEEM ALL YOUR FIRST-BORN SONS (Exodus 13:13) – sons, not daughters.

Priorities

The rabbis taught: [If] he [needs] to be redeemed, and his son [needs to be redeemed, and there is only enough money available to redeem one of them], he has priority over his son. Rabbi Judah says, His son has priority over him, since the *mitzva* of redeeming his son rests upon him, and he has a duty to redeem his son.[9]

29b   Rav Yirmiya said, All agree that if no more than five

7.   Biblical Hebrew duplicates the verb for emphasis; the rabbis interpret this as indicating two different situations: one in which the father is responsible, the other in which the son is.

8.   The Hebrew consonants may be read either way.

9.   That is, the obligation arises in two ways; through the son, who has a claim on the father to redeem him, and through the father, who has a duty to redeem his son.

selas[10] is available, he has priority over his son. Why? Because a personal *mitzva* takes priority. They differ [only about a situation] where five *selas* are pledged [to someone else] and five are unencumbered. Rabbi Judah holds, A loan written in the Torah is as if it is written in a document.[11] He redeems his son with the five [unencumbered *selas*], and the *Kohen* reclaims the pledged *selas* as redemption for the father. The [other] rabbis hold, A loan written in the Torah is not as if it is written in a document; therefore, his own *mitzva* takes priority [that is, he redeems himself with the unencumbered *selas* and cannot redeem his son].

The rabbis taught: **[If he does not have enough money to] redeem his son and to [purchase offerings and] ascend [to Jerusalem] for the festival, he should redeem his son and then ascend for the festival. Rabbi Judah says, He should ascend for the festival and then redeem his son, for [celebration of the festival] is a transient *mitzva*, but [the redemption] is not a transient *mitzva*[, since it can be carried out at a later date].**[12] Now Rabbi Judah gave a [satisfactory] reason [for his opinion], but what is the rabbis' reason? [It is that] Scripture [first] says, YOU SHALL REDEEM ALL YOUR FIRST-BORN SONS and [only] then says, NONE SHALL APPEAR BEFORE ME EMPTY (Exodus 34:20).

The rabbis taught: **How do we know that if someone had five [first-born] sons from five wives, he has to redeem all of them? That is what is meant by, YOU SHALL REDEEM ALL YOUR FIRST-BORN SONS.**[13] Isn't this obvious, since Scripture relates it to WHO OPENS THE WOMB (Exodus 34:19)? You might have thought that we should infer [the meaning of] first-born from the first-born in inheritance; just as there it is THE BEGINNING OF HIS STRENGTH (Deuteronomy 21:17), [that is, the first

10. Numbers 18:16 sets the redemption money at five *sheqalim*.
11. The *Kohen*'s claim for the father's redemption money is a debt imposed by the Torah, therefore it is as if written in a document. Since it arose at the time the father himself ought to have been redeemed, i.e. when he (the father) was thirty days old, it predates and therefore has priority over debts he incurs subsequently.
12. Tosefta *Bekhorot* 6:3.
13. *Mekhilta d'Rabbi Ishmael: Pisḥa* 18, section *v'khol peter*.

child born to the father,] so here it is the first-born of his strength; it lets you know that that is not the case.

Torah Study

To teach him Torah. How do we know this? It is written, **YOU SHALL TEACH THEM TO YOUR SONS** (Deuteronomy 11:19).[14] And if his father hasn't taught him, he must teach himself, as it is written, **AND YOU SHALL LEARN** (Deuteronomy 5:1).

How do we know that [the mother] is not obliged [to teach her son]? Because it is written, **YOU SHALL TEACH THEM TO YOUR SONS** and [also] **AND YOU SHALL LEARN**; [this implies that] whoever has a duty to learn has a duty to teach, but whoever is not obliged to learn is not obliged to teach.

Then how do we know that she is not obliged to teach herself? Because it is written, **YOU SHALL TEACH THEM TO YOUR SONS** and [also] **AND YOU SHALL LEARN**; [this implies that] whoever others are obliged to teach has a duty to teach himself, but whoever others are not obliged to teach has no duty to teach himself.

So how do we know that others are not obliged to teach her? Scripture says, **YOU SHALL TEACH THEM TO YOUR SONS** – your sons, not your daughters.

More questions of priority, and some anecdotes.

The rabbis taught: **[If] he [needs] to learn, and his son [needs] to learn, he has priority over his son. Rabbi Judah says, If his son is smart and retains what he has learned, his son takes precedence.**[15]

This is like what happened to Rav Jacob, the son of Rav Aḥa bar Jacob. His father sent him to study under Abbaye. When he arrived, [his father] saw that he wasn't very bright,[16] so he said, It is better for me [to study] than you; go back home, and I will attend. Abbaye heard that [Rav Aḥa] would be coming. Now,

14. The usual translation is 'children'; however, it is evident later that the rabbis do not read the term inclusively.
15. Variant readings in this paragraph have been ignored. This citation and the next are from Tosefta *Bekhorot* 6.
16. Literally, 'his topics were not sharp'.

there was a demon in [the neighbourhood of] Abbaye's academy [that was so dangerous] that people were injured even when they went about in pairs in the daytime. [Abbaye] said to [the students], Don't offer hospitality to [Aḥa] – for perhaps, [if he stays at the academy,] a miracle will happen.[17] [Aḥa therefore] spent the night at the academy. The demon appeared to him as a seven-headed monster; each time [Aḥa] bowed [in prayer], one head fell off [the monster]. In the morning [Aḥa protested] to them, If a miracle hadn't happened, my life would have been in danger! The rabbis taught: **To learn Torah, and to marry – first learn Torah and then marry. But if he cannot [control his sexual impulse] without a wife, he should first marry and then learn Torah.** Rav Yehuda said in the name of Shmuel, The law is, a man should marry first and then learn Torah. Rabbi Yoḥanan exclaimed, A millstone around his neck, and [you expect him to] engage in Torah! But there was no [real] disagreement between them; one [ruled] for us, and one for them.[18]

Rav Ḥisda commended Rav Hamnuna highly to Rav Huna, [saying that] he was a great man. [Rav Huna] said, When you come across him, bring him to me. When [Hamnuna] came, [Rav Huna] observed that he was not wearing a *sudar*. Why are you not wearing a *sudar*? he asked. Because I am not married. [Rav Huna] turned away from him and said, Don't see me again until you are married! [In this,] Rav Huna was following his [customary] opinion, for he said, [If a

---

17. That is, Abbaye wanted to force Aḥa to stay overnight at the academy, as he was confident that Aḥa was such a holy man that he could rid them of the demon.
18. 'Us' are Babylonians for whom Shmuel gives his ruling; 'them' are Palestinians, for whom Rabbi Yoḥanan gives his. Rashi explains that since the Babylonians went away from home to study, in the Land of Israel, they might marry first 'to overcome their impulses', but would be free from domestic responsibilities while they were away; the Palestinians, on the other hand, remained at home to study, and if married would have a 'millstone around their neck'.

man reaches] twenty and has not married, all his days will be [spent] in sin. Do you think [he really meant] sin? [No, he meant] all his days will be [spent] in sinful thoughts.

Rava said – and the same was taught in the school of Rabbi Ishmael – Up to the age of twenty, the Holy One, blessed be He, sits and waits [to see] when [a man] will marry; once he reaches twenty and has not married, [God] says, May his soul perish!

Rav Ḥisda said, The reason I excel my colleagues is that I married at sixteen. Had I married at fourteen, I would have said to Satan, An arrow in your eye![19]

30a

CHAPTER TWO

MISHNA:

41a

A man may effect *qiddushin* personally or through an agent; a woman may accept *qiddushin* personally or through an agent.

A man may effect *qiddushin* for his pubescent[20] daughter personally or through an agent.

GEMARA:

If he can effect *qiddushin* through an agent, does it need to say he can do it himself? Rav Yosef said, Better to do a *mitzva* yourself than to do it through an agent, as we find [in connection with the Sabbath], Rav Safra singed a [sheep's] head; Rava salted the fish.[21]

Some say, It is forbidden [to effect *qiddushin* through an agent], as Rav Yehuda said in the name of Rav. For Rav Yehuda

---

19. That is, he would have gained sufficient control over his evil impulse to challenge Satan with confidence.
20. Hebrew *na'ara* 'girl', used of a girl in the first half of her thirteenth year, when she is no longer a minor but not yet an independent adult.
21. *Shabbat* 119a (see pp. 119–20). Getting married is a *mitzva*, just as observing Shabbat is; personal involvement is important.

said in the name of Rav, A man should not effect *qiddushin* without seeing the woman, for he may discover something unpleasant about her and she will be distasteful to him, and the Torah says, YOU SHALL LOVE YOUR NEIGHBOUR AS YOURSELF (Leviticus 19:18).

[On this view,] Rav Yosef must have been commenting on the later part of the Mishna, **A woman may accept *qiddushin* personally or through an agent.** If she can accept *qiddushin* through an agent, doesn't it go without saying that she can do it herself? Rav Yosef said, Better for her to do a *mitzva* herself than to do it through an agent, as we find [in connection with the Sabbath], Rav Safra singed a [sheep's] head; Rava salted the fish. But she would not be prohibited [from recourse to an agent], as Resh Laqish observed; for Resh Laqish [cited the Aramaic proverb]: 'Better to live with two bodies than to be a widow.'[22]

A man may effect *qiddushin* for his pubescent daughter. Pubescent, but not minor. This supports Rav's view, for Rav Yehuda said in the name of Rav, A man is forbidden to accept *qiddushin* on behalf of his daughter until she is old enough to say, I like this one [and not that].

How do we know that agents may be used? A baraita states: HE SHALL SEND teaches that he may appoint an agent; HE SHALL SEND HER teaches that she may appoint an agent; HE SHALL SEND and HE SHALL SEND HER[23] [together teach] that the agent may appoint a [further] agent.

That covers divorce, but how do we know [that it applies to] *qiddushin* too? You might say that we could infer it from divorce. Although divorce takes effect even against her will [unlike marriage], you could compare coming-in-to-being to exiting, arguing that just as an agent can effect exiting, so he can effect coming-in-to-being.

But then what about this Mishna? **If someone instructs his agent, Go, set aside *teruma* for me, the agent should set aside *teruma* [in the proportion] the owner usually does; if he doesn't**

22. Better any husband than none at all.
23. The word interpreted is in Deuteronomy 24:1; Hebrew *v'shilḥah* 'and he shall send her' could be read *v'shalḥa* 'and she shall send'. The verse is about divorce.

know the owner's habit, he should set aside one fiftieth. If he
41b set aside ten per cent more or less, the *teruma* is valid.[24] What
is that based on? Should you suggest, on divorce, [we would
object that] divorce is a secular matter. [It is derived from the
words,] So SHALL YOU ALSO SET ASIDE ... (Numbers 18:28)
– 'also' includes an agent.

Why does the Torah not write agency only in [connection
with] *teruma*, and then we could infer the other cases from it?
Because designating *teruma* is merely a mental process.

Then what about this Mishna? **A group lost their Passover
[lamb], and they asked someone to find it and slaughter it for
them, and he went and did so; [meanwhile,] they bought one
and slaughtered it themselves. If his was slaughtered first, he eats
it, and they eat and drink with him.**[25] What is that based on?
Should you suggest, [it follows from] the other [cases], [we would
object that] in relation to a sacrifice [even *teruma* is] secular.

It is as Rabbi Joshua ben Qorha said, **How do we know that
a man's agent is as himself? It is written, AND ALL THE
CONGREGATION OF ISRAEL SHALL SLAUGHTER IT IN THE
AFTERNOON (Exodus 12:6). But surely only one person slaughters it [on behalf of the party]? From this you see that a man's
agent is as himself.**

CHAPTER FOUR

MISHNA:
69a **Ten lineages came up from Babylon: *Kohen*,[26] Levi, Israel,
ḥalal, proselyte, freedman, *mamzer*,[27] *natin*, *sh'tuqi* and *asufi*.**

24. Mishna *Terumot* 4:4.
25. Mishna *Pesaḥim* 9:9 (98b).
26. Hebrew uses adjectives for lineages. As English adjectives are lacking for most, I
have used singular nouns. Some, e.g. *ḥalal*, have no English equivalent.
27. *Mamzer* is often translated 'bastard'; however, the child of unmarried parents is
not a *mamzer*, provided there was no legal obstacle to the parents marrying. A
mamzer is the child of a relationship which could in no circumstances be permitted,
for instance the child of an incestuous union, or of a man by a woman married to
someone else.

Kohen, Levi, Israel are permitted [to marry] one another.

Levi, Israel, *ḥalal*, proselyte, freedman are permitted [to marry] one another.

Proselyte, freedman, *mamzer*, *natin*, *sh'tuqi* and *asufi* are permitted [to marry] one another.

A *sh'tuqi* ['silent one'] is one who knows his mother but not his father.

An *asufi* ['gathered one' – foundling] is one who was gathered from the street and knows neither his father nor his mother.

Abba Saul called the *sh'tuqi b'duqi*.

GEMARA:

Ten lineages came up from Babylon. Why does [the Mishna] say came up from Babylon rather than went to the Land of Israel? It is to give incidental information, as it was taught: YOU SHALL ARISE AND ASCEND TO THE PLACE THE LORD YOUR GOD CHOOSES (Deuteronomy 17:8): this teaches that the Temple is higher than the rest of the Land of Israel, and the Land of Israel is higher than all other lands.

The Temple is certainly higher than the rest of the Land of Israel; that is why it is written, IF THERE ARE DISPUTES WITHIN YOUR GATES YOU SHALL ARISE AND ASCEND TO THE PLACE (Deuteronomy 17:8). But how do we know that the Land of Israel is higher than all other lands? It is written: SEE, A TIME IS COMING, DECLARES THE LORD, WHEN IT SHALL NO MORE BE SAID, 'AS THE LORD LIVES, WHO BROUGHT UP THE ISRAELITES FROM THE LAND OF EGYPT', BUT RATHER, 'AS THE LORD LIVES, WHO BROUGHT UP AND LED THE OFFSPRING OF THE HOUSE OF ISRAEL FROM THE NORTHLAND AND FROM ALL THE LANDS TO WHICH I HAVE BANISHED THEM' (Jeremiah 23:7–8).

Why does the Mishna say came up from Babylon rather than came up to the Land of Israel? It is in support of [the statement of] Rabbi Eleazar, for Rabbi Eleazar said, Ezra did not come up from Babylon until he had sifted it like fine flour.[28]

69b

28. That is, he had thoroughly investigated the family lineages of those he brought with him.

It was taught: Abbaye said, The Mishna reads, **They came up**, [that is] of their own accord. Rava said, The Mishna reads, **They brought them up** [against their will].

[Abbaye and Rava] disagree with regard to [the statement of] Rabbi Eleazar, who said, **Ezra did not come up from Babylon until he had sifted it like fine flour**; Abbaye rejects Rabbi Eleazar's statement, while Rava accepts it. Or perhaps they both accept Rabbi Eleazar's statement, but disagree on this: one of them holds that Ezra sorted the people out, and then they came up [to the Land of Israel] of their own accord, while the other holds that [Ezra] coerced them into coming up.

Now according to the one who says [the Mishna reads], **They came up**, that is what Rav Yehuda said in the name of Shmuel: All lands are dough[29] compared with the Land of Israel, but the Land of Israel is dough compared with Babylon. But according to the one who says [the Mishna reads], **They brought them up**, surely they would have known [their lineages, so the lineages of the Land of Israel would be as pure as those of Babylon]? That generation would have known, but later generations may not have done.

According to the one who says [the Mishna reads], **They came up**, that is [the meaning of the verse], **THESE I ASSEMBLED BY THE RIVER THAT ENTERS AHAVA, AND WE ENCAMPED THERE FOR THREE DAYS. I REVIEWED THE PEOPLE AND THE PRIESTS, BUT I DID NOT FIND ANY LEVITES THERE** (Ezra 8:15 JPS). But according to the one who says [the Mishna reads], **They brought them up**, surely they would have taken care [to ensure that Levites were included]? They would have taken care to disqualify those who were unfit, but not [to coerce] the fit.

***Kohen*, Levi, Israel.** How do we know that [people of these lineages] came up [from Babylon to the Land of Israel]? Because it is written: **THE PRIESTS, THE LEVITES AND SOME OF THE PEOPLE, AND THE SINGERS, GATEKEEPERS, AND THE**

29. Other lands are of mixed lineage, as opposed to the 'fine flour', or pure lineage, of Babylonia. Rashi: 'like dough, in which sourdough, water, flour, salt and bran are mixed'.

NETINIM[30] TOOK UP RESIDENCE IN THEIR TOWNS (Ezra 2:70 JPS).

Ḥalal, proselyte, freedman. How do we known that *ḥalalim* [came up]? It was taught: **Rabbi Yosé says, Customary status is a great thing! For it is written: OF THE SONS OF THE PRIESTS, THE SONS OF HABAIAH, THE SONS OF HAKKOZ, THE SONS OF BARZILLAI WHO HAD MARRIED A DAUGHTER OF BARZILLAI AND TAKEN HIS NAME – THESE SEARCHED FOR THEIR GENEALOGICAL REORDS, BUT THEY COULD NOT BE FOUND, SO THEY WERE DISQUALIFIED FOR THE PRIESTHOOD. THE TIRSHATHA[31] ORDERED THEM NOT TO EAT OF THE MOST HOLY THINGS UNTIL A PRIEST WITH URIM AND THUMMIM SHOULD APPEAR** (Ezra 2:61–3 JPS). He said to them, Remain in your customary status. What did you eat in exile? Priests'-due.[32] Here also [in the Land of Israel, even though rejected from the priesthood,] you may eat priests'-due[, but not 'the most holy things', that is, the meat of sacrifices].

Now, according to the opinion of the one who says, They promote from priest's-due to lineage,[33] these families who have been eating priests'-due will be [incorrectly] promoted! [No. This would not happen, as] the presumption in their favour is weak.

[But if they are not accorded full priestly status,] what [did Rabbi Yosé mean by saying] customary status is a great thing! Previously they could eat only priests'-due of rabbinic status;[34] now they may eat priests'-due of biblical status.

An alternative answer – They may continue to eat that which is priests'-due by rabbinic ordinance, but

30. I have substituted a transliteration of the Hebrew term for JPS 'temple servants' to make sense of the sequel.
31. The title is applied to Nehemiah (Nehemiah 10:2); here it is more likely to refer to a Persian official, though rabbinic tradition consistently identifies Tirshatha as Nehemiah.
32. Literally, 'Holy things [that are eaten] in the provinces'. This is taken to refer to *teruma*, since *Kohanim* were permitted to eat it outside the Temple and they could therefore receive it in Babylon as well as in the Land of Israel.
33. That is, if it can be established that a family has been receiving priests'-due, they are accorded the full privileges of priestly lineage.
34. That would be the status of priests'-due in Babylon.

not that which the Torah decrees as such. We only **promote from priests'-due to lineage** on the basis of [a customary right] to eat priests'-due of biblical status; we do not promote on the basis of [a customary right] to eat priests'-due of [merely] rabbinic status.

In that case,[35] what [did Rabbi Yosé mean by saying,] Customary status is a great thing! Previously, [when they ate priests'-due of rabbinic status in Babylon,] there was no need for concern that they might eat priests'-due of biblical status [without entitlement, since there was none in Babylon]; now, even though there is concern that they might eat priests'-due of biblical status [without entitlement], they may continue to eat priests'-due of rabbinic status though not that of biblical status.[36]

But isn't it written, **THE TIRSHATHA ORDERED THEM NOT TO EAT OF THE MOST HOLY THINGS** (Ezra 2:63), [implying that] they were not to eat of the *most* holy things, but might eat other [holy] things? This is what ['most holy' – literally, 'holy of holies'] means: nothing that is called 'holy', and nothing that is called 'holies': nothing that is called 'holy', as it is written, **NO LAY PERSON SHALL EAT OF THE HOLY THINGS** (Leviticus 22:10); and nothing that is called 'holies', as it is written, **IF A PRIEST'S DAUGHTER MARRIES A LAYMAN, SHE MAY NOT EAT OF THE HOLY THINGS** (literally, 'holies' – Leviticus 22:12) – a scholar said that this means she must not eat that which is removed from the holy things.[37]

70a

Proselyte, freedman. How do we know [that they came up]? Rav Ḥisda says, Since Scripture says, [**THE CHILDREN OF ISRAEL WHO HAD RETURNED FROM THE EXILE, TOGETHER**

---

35. Since they would be given no new privilege.
36. Their established status enables them to retain a privilege they would otherwise have been denied.
37. The breast and the thigh [of sacred offerings – Leviticus 7:30, 32] – Rashi.

WITH] ALL WHO JOINED THEM IN SEPARATING THEMSELVES
FROM THE UNCLEANLINESS OF THE NATIONS OF THE LANDS
TO WORSHIP THE LORD GOD OF ISRAEL (Ezra 6:21).[38]

Mamzer. How do we know [that *mamzerim*, too, returned
from Babylon]? Because it is written: WHEN SANBALLAT THE
HORONITE AND TOBIAH THE AMMONITE SLAVE[39] HEARD
(Nehemiah 2:10), and it is written [of Tobiah], MANY IN
JUDAH WERE HIS CONFEDERATES, FOR HE WAS A SON-IN-LAW
OF SHECANIAH SON OF ARAH, AND HIS SON JEHOHANAN
HAD MARRIED THE DAUGHTER OF MESHULLAM SON OF
BERECHIAH (Nehemiah 6:18 JPS).

> [Evidently,] he holds that if an idolater or a slave
> cohabits with an Israelite woman, the child is a
> *mamzer*.[40] But what proof do we have according to
> those who hold that if an idolater or a slave cohabit
> with an Israelite woman, the child is legitimate? And
> anyway, how do we know that [Tobiah and Jeho-
> hanan] produced children [from their Israelite wives]?
> Perhaps they had no children. Moreover, [even if they
> did,] how do we know that they 'came up' [from
> Babylon] with them? Perhaps they had them [in the
> Land of Israel].

So [we must prove it] from here: THE FOLLOWING WERE
THOSE WHO CAME UP FROM TEL MELAH, TEL-HARSHA,
CHERUB, ADDON AND IMMER – THEY WERE UNABLE TO
TELL WHETHER THEIR FATHER'S HOUSE AND DESCENT WERE
ISRAELITE [Nehemiah 7:61 JPS]. TEL-MELAH ('salt mound') –
these are people whose behaviour was like that of Sodom, which
was turned to a mound of salt; TEL-HARSHA ('mound of
silence'[41]) – this is one who calls Daddy! and his mother silences
him; THEY WERE UNABLE TO TELL WHETHER THEIR FATHER'S

---

38. Proselytes and freed slaves were by definition of non-Israelite origin.
39. JPS translates 'servant', which would miss the point here.
40. The proof that *mamzerim* came from Babylon depends on showing that Tobiah
    and his son, who had the status of slaves, arrived in the Land of Israel with children
    they had produced from Israelite wives in Babylon.
41. A much more likely derivation is 'wooded mound', but the same Hebrew root is
    involved; it also means 'to plough', as is seen below.

HOUSE AND DESCENT WERE ISRAELITE – this is the *asufi* ('foundling'), gathered from the street. **CHERUB, ADDON AND IMMER** – the Lord [*adon*] says [*amar*], I said Israel would be esteemed by Me as cherubs, but they have made themselves like leopards;[42] Rabbi Abbahu said, Even though they have made themselves like leopards, I esteem them as cherubs.

Rabba bar bar Ḥana said, When anyone takes an unsuitable[43] wife, Scripture accounts it as if he had ploughed over the whole world and sown it with salt, as it is said, **THE FOLLOWING WERE THOSE WHO CAME UP FROM TEL MELAH, TEL-HARSHA**[44] (Nehemiah 7:61 JPS).

Rabba bar Rav Ada said in the name of Rav: If someone marries for money, he will have ill-behaved children, as it is said, **THEY HAVE BROKEN FAITH WITH THE LORD, [SO] HAVE BEGOTTEN STRANGE CHILDREN** (Hosea 5:7 JPS). Should you think the money will escape, it continues, **THEREFORE, THE NEW MOON SHALL DEVOUR THEIR PORTION**; should you think his portion but not hers, it states [clearly], **THEIR PORTION**; should you think [it will take] a long time, it states [clearly], **THE NEW MOON**.

How does it indicate that? Rav Naḥman bar Isaac said, A moon comes, a moon goes, and their money is lost.

Rabba bar Rav Ada also said (though some say it was Rabbi Sala in the name of Rav Hamnuna): When anyone marries an unsuitable wife, Elijah binds him and the Holy One, Blessed be He, whips him. A Tanna taught: **Concerning all of them,**[45] **Elijah writes and the Holy One, blessed be He, signs: Woe to anyone who disqualifies his seed, who pollutes his family or who marries an unsuitable wife; Elijah will bind him and the Holy One, blessed be He, will whip him.**

The Babylonian rabbis strove to ensure the 'pure lineage' of the Jews under their control, so much so that an area of Meso-

---

42. Many spots, a metaphor for mixed lineage. 'Cherub' and 'leopard' are collective singular.
43. Legally unsuitable, i.e. forbidden.
44. Rabba bar bar Ḥana reads *harsha* as a derivative of the verb *harash*, to plough.
45. *Kohen*, Levi and Israelite – Rashi.

potamia was declared the 'area of pure lineage'.[46] *This did not mean that other persons could not be Jews; converts were welcomed, and* mamzerim *and other 'inferior' lineages retained their status as Jews.*

The following anecdote illustrates the association of pure lineage with moral behaviour, and also the extreme length some rabbis were prepared to go to to ensure what they considered pure lineage, often in the face of public opposition. A sub-theme of the story, related with a touch of humour, is the 'putting down' of Rav Naḥman by Yehuda bar Ezekiel. Richard Kalmin has disputed Jacob Neusner's contention that Rav Naḥman is being criticized on account of his association with the Exilarch.[47] *As the story would have been redacted in Pumbedita (Rav Yehuda's place) or possibly Sura long after the events, it may be intended to demonstrate the superiority of learning in those academies; it is unlikely that Naḥman, the disciple and successor of Shmuel, would be as ignorant of his master's teachings as the story suggests. Another subtext is the negative rabbinic attitude to the Hasmonean dynasty.*

Whoever questions the pedigree of others and never speaks well [of people] is himself disqualified. Shmuel said, He casts doubt on others by what is his own failing.

A man from Nehardea went to a butcher in Pumbedita and demanded meat. [The butcher] said to him, Wait until I have weighed [the meat] for Rav Yehuda bar Ezekiel's servant, and then I'll serve you.

The man [complained], Who is this Yehuda bar Shviskel[48] that he should take precedence and be served before me?

They told Rav Yehuda about this. He placed the man under ban. They said, [That man is always] calling people slaves. [Rav Yehuda] proclaimed that [the man] was a slave.

The man procured a summons for [Rav Yehuda] to appear before the court of Rav Naḥman, and delivered the summons.

46. See Oppenheimer, *Rome and Babylon*, pp. 339–55. Oppenheimer and Lecker argue on p. 343 that the boundary corresponded to that of a Sasanian administrative district.
47. Kalmin, *Sages, Stories*, pp. 30–31.
48. A contemptuous corruption of the name.

Rav Yehuda then went to Rav Huna,[49] and said, Shall I go or not?

Rav Huna said, You are not obliged to go, for you are a great man, but out of respect for the Exilarch[50] please go.

When [Rav Yehuda] arrived [at Rav Naḥman's place], he found him building a parapet. He said, Does Your Eminence[51] not accept what Rav Huna bar Idi said in Shmuel's name, that once a man is appointed leader of the community he should not engage in [manual] labour in the presence of three?

I am just making a little *gunderita*,[52] replied Rav Naḥman.

Then surely you should call it *ma'aqé* as the Torah does, or else *meḥitza* as the rabbis do!

Pray be seated on the *qarpeta*!

Why not *safsal* as the rabbis call it, or *itztaba* as it is commonly known?

Have an *etronga* to eat!

Said Rav Yehuda, Shmuel said that anyone who says *etronga* has one part in three of pride. Either *etrog* as the rabbis call it, or *etroga* as it is commonly called.

[Then] drink an *inbaga* [of wine]!

Don't you like *ispargos* as the rabbis call it, or *anapaq*[53] as it is commonly called?

Donag will bring us the drinks.

[Rav Yehuda objected,] Shmuel said one should not make use of a woman.

She's only a girl.

But Shmuel was explicit, You should not make use of women at all, whether old or young!

Would you [care to] send your compliments to Yalta?[54]

---

49. Rav Huna was in Sura; perhaps messengers relayed the question.
50. Literally, 'for the house of the Nasi'; Rav Naḥman was the Exilarch's son-in-law.
51. Or simply 'Sir' – but there is irony in Rav Yehuda's conversation.
52. A small fence. Terms are left in Aramaic since the conversation now hinges on the issue of appropriate terminology; Rav Yehuda teases Rav Naḥman for his use of 'posh' language. Rav Naḥman apparently ignores this and is not deflected from his duty as host.
53. *Qarpeta* is Greek *krabatos*, Latin *grabatus*, 'couch'; *ispargos* is a blend of wine and asparagus; *anapak* in Middle Persian is 'unmixed [wine]'.
54. The wife of Rav Naḥman, and daughter of the Exilarch.

[Rav Yehuda again objected:] Shmuel said, A woman's voice is nakedness!

You can use a messenger!

But Shmuel said, Do not send your greeting to a woman, 70b even through her husband!

[Yalta] sent [a message to her husband, Naḥman]: Let him go, so he doesn't make you look like an ignoramus!

Rav Naḥman said, Sir, what is it that brings you here?

He replied, I received a summons from you.

[Rav Naḥman:] But Sir, I don't even fathom your speech! Why would I send you a summons?

[Rav Yehuda] produced the summons from his cloak and showed him, saying, This is the summons, and here is the man!

Said [Rav Naḥman]: Since you have come, set out your case. Let no one say the rabbis show favours to one another! Why did you excommunicate that man?

[Yehuda:] Because he insulted an officer of the court![55]

[Naḥman:] Then why didn't you [merely] have him lashed? Rav used to lash anyone who insulted an officer of the court.

[Yehuda:] I did better than that.

[Naḥman:] Why did you proclaim that he was a slave?

[Yehuda:] Because he habitually declared that other people were slaves; [the rabbis] taught that whoever questions the pedigree of others and never speaks well [of people] is himself disqualified. Shmuel said, He casts doubt on others by what is his own failing.

[Naḥman:] Shmuel may have said that we should suspect [that such a person is projecting his own defect on others], but surely he did not say we should proclaim it [as a fact]!

While this was happening,[56] the plaintiff arrived, and said to Rav Yehuda, Do you call me a slave, I who come from the royal house of the Hasmoneans?

55. Literally, 'an agent of the rabbis'.
56. The Talmud's dramatic use of the Aramaic expression *ad'hakhi* ('while this was happening', or 'just then') is examined by L. Jacobs, *Structure and Form*, pp. 95–9, with reference to *Menaḥot* 37, *Ketubot* 67b and *Yevamot* 105, but he does not cite this passage.

[Rav Yehuda] replied, Shmuel said that anyone who claims descent from the Hasmoneans is a slave.

[Rav Naḥman intervened:] Do you not agree, Sir, with what Rabbi Abba said that Rav Huna said in the name of Rav, that if a scholar issues a ruling prior to the event you listen to him, but if [after the event] you do not?[57]

[Rav Yehuda] replied, Rav Matna holds the same as I [and stated it independently].

[Now] Rav Matna has not been seen in Nehardea for thirteen years; that day he arrived [in town]. [Rav Yehuda] said to him, Do you remember, Sir, what Shmuel said when he was standing with one leg on the riverbank and one leg on the ferry?

He replied, This is what Shmuel said, Anyone who claims descent from the Hasmoneans is a slave, for none was left of them except for a girl who climbed on the roof and shouted, 'Whoever says I am of the Hasmoneans is a slave!', then fell from the roof and died.

So they proclaimed the man a slave.

That day many marriage agreements were torn up in Nehardea.

When [Rav Yehuda] emerged, [the Nehardeans] came after him to pelt him with stones. He said to them, Silence, if you will! But if not, I shall publicize what Shmuel said about you: There are two clans in Nehardea, the Doves and the Ravens, and the sign is, the clean is clean, the unclean unclean![58] [So] they threw away their stones, blocking the Royal Canal.

57. The judge may have been influenced by the case in hand. Rav Yehuda has in this instance reported Shmuel's ruling that self-proclaimed Hasmoneans are slaves only after the event has taken place, so he can be suspected of bias; Rav Matna arrives with an independent statement of the law.

58. The dove is a *kasher* bird, the raven not; the Dove family are of pure descent, the Ravens not.

FOURTH ORDER

NEZIQIN (DAMAGES)

INTRODUCTION

*Jews lacked full juridical autonomy throughout the period of formation of the Mishna and the Babylonian Talmud. In Hellenistic Egypt the Ptolemies issued edicts (*diagrammata*) binding all their subjects equally; however, these left room for the operation of civic laws (*politikoi nomoi*), varying from city to city and from ethnic group to ethnic group, provided these contradicted neither the king's edicts nor equity (*gnome dikaiotate*). The Bible, in the Greek Septuagint version, functioned as the 'ancestral custom' or civic law of the Jews.*[1]

After Pompey's annexation of Judaea in 63 BCE, the inhabitants of Palestine became subject to the Roman ius gentium *(law of the nations). In principle, only individuals who gained Roman citizenship would have had access to the* ius civile *(citizen law), since the Roman 'principle of personality' restricted operation of the law of the state to its citizens (see* Bava Qama *Chapter Four). Jews were not alone in resenting subjection to 'foreign' law; Cicero wrote to Atticus in 50 BCE, 'I have followed Scaevola in many details, among them . . . that Greek cases are to be settled according to Greek law.'*[2]

A. M. Rabello has argued that at least until 70 CE the Roman governor left civil, though not criminal, justice in the hands of

1. J. M. Modrzejewski, 'Jewish Law and Hellenistic Legal Practice in the Light of Greek Papyri in Egypt', in Hecht, Jackson, Passamanek, *Jewish Law*, pp. 75–99.
2. Cicero, *Ad Atticum* 6.1.15 (tr. Winstedt, Loeb edn (1912), p. 430).

local Jewish institutions.[3] *In 212, about the time of compilation of the Mishna, Emperor Antoninus (Caracalla) extended Roman citizenship, and thus* ius civile, *to all free men in the Empire. But to accept Roman law would have been to reject the Torah and the traditional law of Israel; the rabbis under the leadership of Judah ha-Nasi therefore did their utmost to retain a measure of legal autonomy, and at the least to continue studying and interpreting Torah law in hope of the restoration of Jewish independence. To some extent Roman governors played along with this; during the third and fourth centuries they appear to have tolerated the resolution of civil disputes by religious authorities, Christian bishops as well as Jewish rabbis, and possibly even favoured it as relieving them of responsibility and contributing to social stability. In Sasanian Babylonia a similar situation prevailed, with perhaps greater autonomy allowed to Jews in criminal jurisdiction.*

The Talmud relates its civil and criminal law to biblical texts. However, the social and economic circumstances envisaged in biblical codes such as the Book of the Covenant (Exodus 20:19–23:33) are very different from those confronted in the Palestine of the Mishna or the Babylonia of the Bavli; the laws of Exodus would not, without development, serve adequately the needs of the later, more complex and more urbanized society. The gap is covered by a continuing process that not only modifies the plain meaning in some respects but interprets the casuistic laws of Exodus as instances of broad legal principles.

The 'goring ox' of Exodus 21:29 illustrates this process: **IF, HOWEVER, THAT OX HAS BEEN IN THE HABIT OF GORING, AND ITS OWNER, THOUGH CAUTIONED, HAS NOT CON-TROLLED IT, AND IT KILLS A MAN OR WOMAN — THE OX SHALL BE STONED AND ITS OWNER, TOO, SHALL BE PUT TO DEATH.** *In the light of the next verse and Numbers 35:21, the Sages commute the apparent death sentence on the owner to a 'ransom', or fine.*[4] *Then, they interpret the 'goring ox', or* qeren

3. A. M. Rabello, 'Jewish and Roman Jurisdiction', in Hecht, Jackson, Passamanek, *Jewish Law*, p. 144.
4. Mekhilta; *Bava Qama* 27a and *Sanhedrin* 15b.

('horn'), as a prototype for any possession that is subject to a court order of restraint, even though it is not normally a hazard.

The extent to which such interpretation is influenced by Roman, Greek or Near Eastern law systems and social mores is much debated. Some legal concepts, such as guardianship, have no biblical precedent, so that the rabbis were driven to use Greek terms such as epitropos *('guardian'),* hypothēkē *('deposit', 'pledge') or* diathēkē *('disposition', 'contract') to articulate them;[5] even an institution of undoubted Israelite origin, such as the* Bet Din ha-gadol *(the High Court), acquired a Greek name,* Sanhedrin.

5.   For Greek and Latin legal terms in the Talmud, see Sperber, *Dictionary*.

FIRST TRACTATE
BAVA QAMA
(THE FIRST GATE)

Bava Qama *contains the first ten chapters of what was originally one large tractate,* Neziqin *(damages, torts), covering civil and commercial law; for convenience this was divided into* Bava Qama *(The First Gate, or Division),* Bava Metzi'a *(The Middle Gate) and* Bava Batra *(The Last Gate). The First Gate covers classification of damage, personal injury, cattle rustling, return of stolen goods and tax farming. It opens with a discussion of the four main categories of damage, derived from Exodus 21–2.*

CHAPTER ONE

MISHNA:
There are four main categories of damage: Ox, pit, consumer[1] and fire. Ox is not like consumer, and consumer is not like ox; neither – seeing that they are living creatures – is like fire; none of these, that cause damage when they move, is like pit, which does not cause damage by moving. The common factor they share is that they are hazards, that you must keep them under control, and that if they cause damage, the person responsible for the damage must pay compensation from his best-quality land.
The carefully crafted opening sugya *explores the extent of each*

---

1. An obscure term, which the Gemara says refers to an animal grazing on someone else's produce.

category. First, it establishes that there are subcategories; Rav
Papa observes that the subcategories sometimes resemble the
main categories and sometimes do not. The Gemara then inves-
tigates each category, ostensibly to test Rav Papa's assertion
that there are subcategories that differ from the main ones, but
in fact to tease out the full range of torts. 'Consumer', according
to Shmuel, is better understood as 'tooth', that is, an animal
that eats produce to which the owner has no right; but according
to Rav, it refers to damage caused directly by a human being.

GEMARA:

3a   What are the subcategories of 'tooth'? If [the animal] scraped
herself against a wall for her satisfaction [and accidentally damaged it], or spoiled fruit while satisfying herself. The distinctive
features of 'tooth' are that [the animal] gets satisfaction while
causing damage, she is your property and you should keep her
under control; here, likewise, she gets satisfaction while causing
damage, she is your property and you should keep her under
control.

It seems, then, that the subcategories of 'tooth' are like 'tooth'.
Perhaps Rav Papa had 'foot' in mind. What are the subcategories
of 'foot'? If [the animal] caused damage with her body as she
was walking, or with her hair as she was walking, or with her
halter, or with the bell around her neck. The distinctive feature
of 'foot' is that it is a common occurrence, the animal is your
property and you should keep her under control; here, likewise,
it is a common occurrence, the animal is your property and you
should keep her under control.

So it seems that the subcategories of 'foot' are like 'foot'.
Perhaps Rav Papa had 'pit' in mind. What are the subcategories
of 'pit'? Perhaps the main category is a 10-palm deep pit, and
the subcategory is 9 palms deep. But neither 9 nor 10 is written in
Scripture! That is no problem, for Scripture says, THE CARCASS
SHALL BE HIS (Exodus 21:34), and the rabbis assume that [a
depth of] 10 would kill the animal, whereas 9 would injure but
not kill.

Then Rav Papa must have been thinking of someone who
left a stone, knife or other object in a public area, and it caused

damage. What category would that be? If he had relinquished ownership, both Rav and Shmuel would agree that it was 'pit'. If he had *not* relinquished ownership, then according to Shmuel, 3b who said that all [hazards left in a public place] are derived from 'pit', that is all right; but according to Rav, who said that all [hazards left in a public place] are derived from 'ox', it would be 'ox'. The distinctive features of 'pit' are that it is by nature a hazard, it is your property and you should keep it safe; here, likewise, it is by nature a hazard, it is your property and you should keep it safe.

So it seems that the subcategories of 'pit' are like 'pit'. Perhaps Rav Papa had 'consumer' in mind. But what is 'consumer'? According to Shmuel, who says it is 'tooth', we have already shown that the subcategories of 'tooth' are like 'tooth'. According to Rav, who says it is 'human being', what categories or subcategories are there? You might have thought that 'awake' is a main category, and 'asleep' a subcategory, but [there is no difference between them, since] a Mishna states: **Man is always [to be considered] under caution, whether awake or asleep.**[2] Perhaps phlegm or nasal mucus is a subcategory. In what way? If [they cause the damage] while in motion [through coughing or sneezing], that is the same as direct force; if they are at rest on the ground, both Rav and Shmuel would agree that this is 'pit'.

So it seems that the subcategories of 'consumer' are like 'consumer'. Perhaps Rav Papa had 'fire' in mind. What subcategories does 'fire' have? If you say, [for instance,] someone left a stone, knife or other object on the roof and it was swept off by a normal wind and caused damage, how would that be? If [it caused the damage] as it was moving, that is [the same as] 'fire'. The distinctive features of 'fire' are that an external force is needed [to spread it], it is your property and you should keep it safe; here, likewise, an external force is needed [to spread it], it is your property and you should keep it safe.

So it seems that the subcategories of 'fire' are like 'fire'.

2. *Bava Qama* 26a.

Perhaps Rav Papa had a subcategory of 'foot' in mind. But haven't we already said that the subcategories of 'foot' are like 'foot'? [Even so, there is the anomalous case of] half-compensation for pebble[-damage], which we know as a *halakha*.[3] In what respect is it a subcategory of 'foot'? It is because [if the damage exceeds the value of his animal,] he must pay the excess.

But isn't that a moot point? For Rava enquired, Is the half-compensation for pebble[-damage] limited to the value of the animal that caused the damage, or must [the owner] pay any excess? To Rava it is a moot point, but to Rav Papa it is obvious. Then why would Rava classify [this case] as a subcategory of 'foot'? It is because [the owner of the animal] would be exempt [if the damage occurred] in a public place.[4]

'Tooth' is derived from Exodus 22:4: **WHEN A MAN LETS HIS LIVESTOCK LOOSE TO GRAZE IN ANOTHER'S LAND . . . HE MUST COMPENSATE FOR THE DAMAGE DONE TO THAT FIELD OR VINEYARD.** *Now, if an animal grazes on my field, the animal and its owner benefit at my expense; but there are other situations where I benefit from someone's possessions without causing him any loss, even though I am doing this without his permission. Such situations are known in Western law systems as 'unjust enrichment', and in the Talmud as* ze nehene v'ze lo ḥaser *('one benefits but the other does not lose').*[5]

Ḥisda died around 309; Ammi, who emigrated from Babylonia to Palestine and became head of the academy at Tiberias c. 270, may have died before Ḥisda. This discussion is set around the year 300, when Rami bar Ḥama and Rava were young students.

3. A cow accidentally knocked some pebbles as she was walking, and they rolled and caused damage. *Halakha* here means 'law received by Moses at Sinai', that is, a law which is not in dispute, but lacks any basis in Scripture.
4. People may walk their animals in public areas provided they exercise reasonable caution.
5. On unjust enrichment in Jewish law, see *The Jewish Law Annual*, vol. 3 (Leiden: E. J. Brill, 1980); for a literary analysis of this *sugya*, see L. Jacobs, *Structure and Form*, pp. 56–64; on *ze nehene v'ze lo ḥaser* see Solomon, 'Concepts'.

CHAPTER TWO

MISHNA:

An animal is [regarded as] cautioned [not] to eat fruit and
vegetables . . . If she benefits, she repays as much as she has
benefited.[6]

GEMARA:

Rav Ḥisda said to Rami bar Ḥama, Weren't you in our
neighbourhood yesterday when some excellent questions were
asked?

What were they? he asked.

He replied: If someone lives on another's premises without
his knowledge, does he have to pay rent or not?

> What sort of case is this? If the premises are not for
> hire, and the occupier doesn't usually rent, then [the
> occupier] hasn't gained anything and the owner hasn't
> lost[, so there is no reason to pay rent]. But if the
> premises are for hire, and the occupier does usually
> rent, one has gained and the other has lost[, so it is
> obvious that rent should be paid]. The question, then,
> must refer to premises that are not for hire, and an
> occupier who usually pays rent. What happens [in this
> case]? Can [the occupier] say, What loss have I caused
> you [since you would not have hired out the premises]?
> Or can the [owner] say, You have benefited [by occu-
> pying the premises rent-free]?

He replied: It's our Mishna.

Which Mishna?

If you do me a service [I will explain].

He took his *sudar* and folded it up for him.[7]

19b

20a

20b

---

6. Even if the court has not warned the owner to prevent his animal eating other
    people's crops, the law treats him as cautioned, so he must pay full compensation
    for the food consumed.

7. Rami wants to establish that he is a mature scholar: Rav Ḥisda good-humouredly
    accedes to this by folding Rami's *sudar*, as a disciple would do for the master,
    even though Rav Ḥisda was senior, and possibly already his father-in-law.

[Rami] said: **If she benefits, she repays whatever benefit she had.**

> Rava observed: When someone has [God] on his side, he can get away with anything;[8] even though the case is unlike that in the Mishna, [Ḥisda] accepted [his analogy]. But [the Mishna deals with a case] where one benefits and one loses, [whereas in the case under discussion,] one benefits and the other does not lose.

>> So [what would] Rami bar Ḥama [have said to that]? [He would have responded:] You may assume that fruit [left] in a public place has been abandoned.[9]

A Mishna says: **If A borders B on three sides and fences off the first, second and third sides, [B] is not obliged [to contribute to the cost of the fence].**[10] From this you may infer that if A [surrounds B on four sides and] fences off the fourth side, B would be obliged [to pay his share]. It follows that if one benefits and the other loses nothing, the one who gains nevertheless has to pay [for the benefit].[11] [No,] this case is different, since [A] can say to [B], It was on your account that I built an extra fence.[12]

A proof. **Rabbi Yosé said: If the one whose [field] was surrounded fenced the fourth side [himself], he is held responsible for all of it.**[13] That is because it is he who is surrounded, but [if] the surrounder [bought the field on the fourth side and erected a fence there, the surroundee] would not be held responsible. From this you can infer that if one benefits and the other loses nothing, the one who gains is exempt from payment.

8.   Literally, 'he does not worry or feel [bad]'.
9.   The Mishna deals with an animal that eats food which was not fenced off from the public, so the victim cannot claim loss; even so, the animal's owner must compensate him.
10. *Bava Batra* 4b.
11. B has benefited from the fence that A constructed, but A has lost nothing by benefiting B since A would have fenced off his field anyway.
12. That is, A claims he has suffered loss on B's account, since had B's field not been there the enclosure would not have been necessary.
13. i.e. he must contribute his share towards the fences on the other three sides, seeing he has made it clear through his action that he wants to be enclosed – Rashi.

No; [perhaps this is different, since] he could say to him, I would have been satisfied with a cheaper fence.[14]

A proof. **If a house and its attic, each belonging to a different person, fell down, and the owner of the attic asked the owner of the house to rebuild, but he was unwilling to do so, the owner of the attic may rebuild the house and remain in it until [the owner of the house] pays his expenses.**[15] The owner of the house has to repay the [building] expenses of the attic owner, but [may] not [deduct] rent. From this you can infer that if one benefits and the other loses nothing, the one who gains is exempt from payment. No; this is different, since the house is pledged to the attic[, and so the attic owner has a right to live there pending agreement on rebuilding the house].

A proof. **Rabbi Judah says: Even this one, since he lives on another's premises [without his agreement], must pay rent.**[16] From this you can infer that if one benefits and the other loses nothing, the one who gains is obliged to pay. No; this is different, because of the blackening of the walls.[17]

They sent [the question as to whether a squatter, as defined above, must pay rent] to Rabbi Ammi.[18] He said, What has he done to him? What loss or damage has he caused him? Rabbi Ḥiyya bar Abba said: Let's consider this carefully.

They sent again to Rabbi Ḥiyya bar Abba. He said, Do they need to keep asking me? If I had found an argument, would I not have communicated it to them?

The model and context for the discriminatory legislation against 'idolaters' in this section are the Roman 'principle of personality', restricting the state law to its citizens, and the perceived rapacity of the occupying power.[19] *The Yerushalmi here reports*

14. Literally, 'protection for a *zuz*'. The surrounder, that is, has no interest in erecting a strong boundary around the enclosed field.
15. *Bava Metzi'a* 117a.
16. Ibid.
17. He pays for wear and tear of the new walls.
18. Presumably, that is, to Tiberias. Both Ammi and Ḥiyya bar Abba were native Babylonians, and were old and distinguished by this time.
19. Cicero arraigned Verres for ignoring the law enacted in Sicily in 131 BCE by Publius Rupilius (the *Lex Rupilia*): 'If a Roman citizen makes a claim on a Sicilian, a Sicilian judge is assigned; if a Sicilian makes a claim on a Roman citizen, a Roman citizen is assigned as judge' (*Contra Verres* 2:32). The experience of Jews would

Rabbi Abbahu's observation that the discrimination is 'according to their laws', and it notes that Rabban Gamaliel had said that any Jew who took advantage of this would nevertheless be guilty of 'profanation of the Divine Name'. Later Jewish authorities were considerably embarrassed by the text and at pains to rule it out of practical consideration. However, it contains some of the most positive rabbinic comment on the Gentiles, not least Rabbi Meir's remark that 'even a Gentile who engages in the study of Torah is like the High Priest'.

CHAPTER FOUR

MISHNA:

37b   If a Israelite's ox gored an ox belonging to the Temple or an ox belonging to the Temple gored a lay person's ox, he[20] is exempt [from payment of damages], for it is written, HIS NEIGHBOUR'S OX (Exodus 21:35) – not an ox belonging to the Temple.

If an Israelite's ox gored an idolater's ox, he is exempt [from payment of damages]; if an idolater's ox gored an Israelite's ox, he must pay full damages, whether or not the ox[21] has been cautioned.

GEMARA:

38a   **If an Israelite's ox gored an idolater's ox, he is exempt.** One way or the other! If HIS NEIGHBOUR is meant exclusively, an idolater whose ox gored an Israelite's ox should be exempt; if it is inclusive, an Israelite whose ox gored an idolater's ox should be liable!

Rabbi Abbahu said, Scripture says, HE STOOD, AND MEASURED THE EARTH; HE BEHELD, AND LOOSENED[22] THE

---

have been like that of Sicilians under Verres; Romans worked 'their' laws to their advantage.
20. The private owner or the Temple treasury.
21. That is, the owner has been cautioned to control his ox.
22. This phrase is usually translated 'drove asunder'; the root meaning is 'loosen', which in rabbinic Hebrew also means 'permit'.

NATIONS (Habakkuk 3:6) – [God] beheld that the nations disregarded the Seven Commandments[23] he had given them, so He permitted their property [to be appropriated by] Israel.[24]

Rabbi Yoḥanan derived it from here: HE REVEALED[25] FROM MOUNT PARAN (Deuteronomy 33:2) – [God] revealed their property to Israel.

A baraita likewise states: **If an idolater's ox gored an Israelite's ox, he must pay full damages, whether or not the ox has been cautioned, as it is said, HE STOOD, AND MEASURED THE EARTH; HE BEHELD, AND LOOSENED THE NATIONS, and also, HE REVEALED FROM MOUNT PARAN.**

Why the extra proof-text? In case you hold that HE STOOD, AND MEASURED THE EARTH is needed to support the interpretation of Rav Matna and Rav Yosef, [the baraita adds,] HE REVEALED FROM MOUNT PARAN.

What did Rav Matna say? Rav Matna said, HE STOOD, AND MEASURED THE EARTH; HE BEHELD, ETC. – What did He behold? He beheld that the nations disregarded the Seven Commandments He had given them, so He exiled them from their land. How does [Rav Matna] justify interpreting *va-yater* as 'exile'? We have VA-YATER THE NATIONS here, and there we have L'NATER WITH THEM ON THE EARTH (Leviticus 11:21), which the Targum translates as 'to leap with them on the ground'.[26]

What did Rav Yosef say? Rav Yosef said, HE STOOD, AND MEASURED THE EARTH; HE BEHELD, ETC. – What did He behold? He beheld that the nations disregarded the Seven Commandments He had given

---

23. *Sanhedrin* 56a (see pp. 506–10).
24. Since they ignored the commandment not to steal, they were not rightful owners of the property in their possession.
25. Usually translated 'shone forth'.
26. Exile is detachment ('leaping') from one's native land.

them, so He released them from them. Some
paradox! Do you mean to say that the sinner
profits [by his sin]! Mar the son of Rabana
explained, It means that now, even if they
keep them, they do not receive the reward.
Don't they? A baraita teaches: **Rabbi Meir
says, even a Gentile who engages in the
study of Torah is like the High Priest, for
it is written, KEEP MY JUDGEMENTS AND
MY STATUTES WHICH, IF A MAN DO, HE
SHALL LIVE BY THEM** (Leviticus 18:5); **it does
not say, Priests, Levites and Israelites, but
'man', from which you learn that even a
Gentile who engages in the study of Torah
is like the High Priest.** It was [explained],
They don't receive [as a great] a reward as
those who are commanded and fulfil, but
[only] as those who are not commanded and
fulfil, for as Rabbi Ḥanina said, **He who is
commanded and fulfils is greater than he
who is not commanded and fulfils.**[27]

The rabbis taught: The Roman government dispatched two
officials[28] to the Sages. Teach us your Torah! [they requested.]
They studied, revised and reviewed. When they left they said,
We have examined your Torah carefully and it is all true except
for this thing that you say: **If a Israelite's ox gored an idolater's
ox, he is exempt [from payment of damages]; if an idolater's ox gored an Israelite's ox, he must pay full damages,
whether or not the ox has been cautioned.** One way or the
other! If HIS NEIGHBOUR is meant exclusively, an idolater whose
ox gored an Israelite's ox should be exempt; if it is inclusive,
an Israelite whose ox gored an idolater's ox should be liable!
[However,] we will not inform the government of this.

27. This apparently paradoxical statement is intended to stress the privilege of obeying
     God's commandments with love.
28. The Gemara uses the Greek word *sardiotes* ('soldiers'), but was evidently referring
     to administrative officials. The incident is well explained by A. M. Rabello, 'Jewish
     and Roman Jurisdiction', in Hecht, Jackson, Passamanek, *Jewish Law*, p. 150.

The next passage elegantly combines halakha *and* aggada, *giving the lie to the notion that they are entirely distinct genres. It also affords an opportunity to sample the wisdom of the influential French Jewish philosopher Emmanuel Levinas (1905–95), who presented this reading at a colloquium of French-speaking Jewish intellectuals in 1975 on the theme of war. The citations woven into the text are from Levinas,* Talmudic Readings; *the reader may wonder where the Talmudic argument stops and Levinas introduces his own thoughts . . .*

CHAPTER SIX

MISHNA:

If someone lets a flame spread and it consumes wood, or 60a
stones, or earth, he is liable [for damages], as it is said, IF FIRE
BREAKS OUT AND SPREADS TO THORNS, AND A STACK IS
CONSUMED, OR STANDING CORN, OR [OPEN] FIELDS, HE WHO
STARTED THE FIRE MUST MAKE RESTITUTION (Exodus 22:5).

GEMARA:

Rava asked, Why does the Merciful One[29] specify thorns, stacks, standing corn and open fields? If the Torah specified only thorns, I might have thought that the Merciful One held him liable [only] for thorns, since it is common for them to catch fire and common for people to be careless [with them]; but fire is not common among stacks, nor are people commonly careless with them. If the Merciful One specified only stacks, I might have thought that the Merciful One held him liable [only] for stacks, for considerable [financial] loss [is incurred], but he would not be liable for [setting fire to] thorns, since the loss is small.

---

29. *Raḥmana* ('the Merciful One'), in Aramaic, is strictly speaking a designation of God, the giver of Torah. The Talmud frequently uses it to designate the Torah itself, so I have normally translated it as 'Torah'. Here it is translated literally to correspond with Levinas's French translation; in his commentary he expatiates on the significance of the relationship of the word with *raḥam*, the womb: 'a feminine element is stirred in the depth of this mercy' (*Talmudic Readings*, p. 183).

Why is standing corn mentioned? [To teach us that] just as standing corn is out in the open, so [he would be liable for] anything that is out in the open[, but not for concealed objects]. *Levinas notes that the generalization is 'a procedure characteristic of Talmudic exegesis' (Levinas, Talmudic Readings, p. 184); it is, indeed, the way in which the rabbis generated a complex and comprehensive legal system out of the limited case-law of the Bible.*

According to Rabbi Judah, who holds that [whoever lit the fire] is liable for [damage to] concealed objects, why is standing corn specified? It is to include anything that stands[, even animals].

On what do the [other] rabbis base liability for anything that stands? They base it on the expression OR STANDING CORN.

And Rabbi Judah? OR indicates separation.[30]

On what do the rabbis base separation? On [the expression] OR [OPEN] FIELDS.

And Rabbi Judah? As the Merciful One [needed to] write OR STANDING CORN, it [similarly] writes OR [OPEN] FIELDS.[31]

Why are open fields specified? To include lapping a furrow or scorching stones.

[In that case could not] the Merciful One [simply] have written [OPEN] FIELDS and the rest would follow? [No,] for if He had [simply] written [OPEN] FIELDS, I might have thought he would be liable for what is in the field but for nothing else, so [the other expressions] are necessary to let us know [that such is not the case].

'Fire, an elementary force to which other elementary forces will add themselves, multiplying damages beyond any rational conjecture! The wind adds whims and violences to it. And yet responsibility is not diminished . . . But are we speaking of war? Are we not in a time of peace? . . . Perhaps the elemental force of fire is already the intervention of the uncontrollable, of

30. i.e. you don't need to set fire to all four categories to be held liable.
31. i.e. it is a matter of literary style.

war. It does not annul responsibilities! ... Here the text ...
transforms its juridical truths into religious and moral ones'
(Levinas, Talmudic Readings, p. 185).

Rabbi Simeon bar Naḥmani said, Disaster comes to the world
only when the wicked are present, but it begins with the right-
eous, as it is said, IF FIRE BREAKS OUT AND SPREADS TO
THORNS – When does fire break out? When thorns are present.
But it first [consumes] the righteous, as it is said, A STACK IS
CONSUMED – it does not say AND CONSUMES A STACK, but A
STACK HAS BEEN[32] CONSUMED, meaning that the stack has
already been consumed.

Rav Yosef taught: What does Scripture mean by, NONE OF
YOU SHALL GO OUTSIDE THE DOOR OF HIS HOUSE UNTIL
MORNING [... THE LORD WILL PASS OVER THE DOOR AND
NOT LET THE DESTROYER ENTER AND SMITE YOUR HOME]
(Exodus 12:22, 23 JPS)? Once the Destroyer is authorized [by
God to destroy], he does not distinguish between the wicked
and the righteous. Not only that, he begins with the righteous,
as it is said, I WILL WIPE OUT FROM YOU BOTH THE RIGHT-
EOUS AND THE WICKED (Ezekiel 21:8 JPS).
'Social evil already contains within itself the uncontainable
forces of war ... The righteous are responsible for evil before
anyone else is ... because they have not been righteous enough
to make their righteousness spread and abolish injustice ... an
occurrence not entirely free of the will of rational beings ...
Another way: evil people bring war about ... Those who could
stop it would have been its first victims ... The reason of war
would end in unreason ... But perhaps in the end, the reason
of war consists in the very turning upside down of reason ...

Does the madness of extermination retain a grain of reason?
That is the great ambiguity of Auschwitz. That is the question.
Our text does not resolve it. It underlines it. Our text does not
resolve it because the answer here would be indecent, as all
theodicy probably is' (Levinas, Talmudic Readings, pp. 186,
187).

Rav Yosef wept: Is this what befalls the incomparable ones?

32. Biblical Hebrew does not distinguish between 'is consumed' and 'has been consumed'.

Abbaye [consoled] him: It is a blessing for them, as it is written,
THE RIGHTEOUS IS GATHERED IN BEFORE THE EVIL (Isaiah
57:1).[33]

*'Will Abbaye's consolation – that the righteous will have a
negative reward – stop the tears of Rav Joseph if Rav Joseph
suffers for others? ... Abbaye, who grants the saints the ignorance of the sufferings of others, is perhaps as pessimistic as Rav
Joseph, who weeps' (Levinas*, Talmudic Readings, *p. 188).*

60b   Rav Yehuda said in the name of Rav, A man should always
enter [his house] with **THAT IT WAS GOOD** (Genesis 1:4) [i.e.
while it is still light] and exit with **THAT IT WAS GOOD**, as it
says, **NONE OF YOU SHALL GO OUTSIDE THE DOOR OF HIS
HOUSE UNTIL MORNING** (Exodus 12:22 JPS).

*'The hour of the exterminating angel is night ... Interhuman
relations require the clarity of day; night is the very danger of a
suspended justice among human beings' (Levinas*, Talmudic
Readings, *p. 189).*

The rabbis taught: If plague breaks out in a town, gather in
your legs,[34] as it is said, **NONE OF YOU SHALL GO OUTSIDE
THE DOOR OF HIS HOUSE UNTIL MORNING**, and **GO, MY
PEOPLE, ENTER YOUR CHAMBERS, AND LOCK YOUR DOORS
BEHIND YOU** (Isaiah 26:20 JPS), and **THE SWORD SHALL DEAL
DEATH WITHOUT, AS SHALL THE TERROR WITHIN** (Deuter-
onomy 32:25 JPS).

*'There is infiltration of night into day ... The elemental, the
uncontrollable, is beyond the war which is still visible ... the
storm is sheer menace; one must go back home. If one has a
home ... There is no salvation except in the reentry into oneself.
One must have an interiority where one can seek refuge ...'
(Levinas*, Talmudic Readings, *pp. 188, 189).*

Why the additional verses? You might have thought
that [you only needed to stay indoors] in the night,
not in the day; therefore, he cites, **GO, MY PEOPLE,
ENTER YOUR CHAMBERS, AND LOCK YOUR DOORS
BEHIND YOU**. You might have thought that this is

---

33. i.e. the righteous dies first, and is thereby saved from trials and tribulations.
34. Stay at home.

only when there is no terror indoors, but if there is terror indoors it would be better to go out and sit in the company of others; therefore, he cites, **THE SWORD SHALL DEAL DEATH WITHOUT, AS SHALL THE TERROR WITHIN.**

'Do we not smell here . . . beyond all violence which still submits to will and reason, the odor of the camps? Violence is . . . beyond all morality. It is the abyss of Auschwitz or the world at war . . . Is the fact of Israel unique? Does it not have full meaning because it applies to all humanity?' (Levinas, Talmudic Readings, *pp. 190, 191).*

When plague threatened, Rava blocked the windows, as it is written, **FOR DEATH HAS CLIMBED THROUGH OUR WINDOWS** (Jeremiah 9:20 JPS).

'While outside it is the sword, inside it is terror. But one must go back inside . . . That inside in which there is fear is still the only refuge. It is the no-exit . . . This, for me, is the central passage of the entire text . . . the no-exit of Israel is probably the human no-exit. All men are of Israel . . . This interiority is the suffering of Israel as universal suffering' (Levinas, Talmudic Readings, *p. 191).*

The rabbis taught: When there is famine in town, scatter your legs,[35] as it is said, **THERE WAS A FAMINE IN THE LAND, AND ABRAM WENT DOWN TO EGYPT TO SOJOURN THERE** (Genesis 12:10 JPS), and **IF WE DECIDE TO GO INTO THE TOWN, WHAT WITH THE FAMINE IN THE TOWN, WE SHALL DIE THERE** (2 Kings 7:4 JPS).

Why the additional verse? You might have thought, this is only if there is no danger to life [in leaving the town], but where there is danger to life [outside, it is better to remain in town]; that it why it continues, **COME LET US GO OVER TO THE ARAMEAN CAMP; IF THEY SUSTAIN US, WELL, AND IF NOT, WE SHALL DIE [ANYWAY]** (2 Kings 7:4).

'At the time of external menace and internal terror . . . Go, even to the Syrians! . . . More can be hoped for from men that from

35. Run away.

that elemental thing – or from that Nothing – which famine symbolizes' (Levinas, Talmudic Readings, p. 192).

The rabbis taught: **When plague [strikes a] town, a man should not walk in the middle of the road, because the Angel of Death walks in the middle of the road, for since he is authorized [to strike], he walks boldly. When there is peace in town, do not walk at the side of the road, for since the Angel of Death is not authorized [to strike], he conceals himself [at the side] as he walks.**

'The violence which exterminates: there is no radical difference between peace and war, between war and holocaust … no radical difference between peace and Auschwitz … Evil surpasses human responsibility and leaves not a corner intact where reason could collect itself. But perhaps this thesis is precisely a call to man's infinite responsibility' (Levinas, Talmudic Readings, pp. 192, 193).

The rabbis taught: **When plague [strikes a] town, a man should not go alone to the assembly house,[36] for that is where the Angel of Death stores his weapons. But that is only if children do not learn there, or if ten men do not gather there for prayer.**

The rabbis taught: **If dogs whine, the Angel of Death is coming to town. If dogs are happy, the prophet Elijah is coming to town – but that is only if there is not a female among them.**

'Do not confuse eroticism and messianism' (Levinas, Talmudic Readings, p. 194).

Rabbi Ammi and Rabbi Assi were sitting in the presence of Rabbi Isaac the Smith. One asked, Sir, Tell us some *halakha*; the other asked, Sir, Tell us some *aggada*. He began with *aggada* but one of them objected; then he embarked on a *halakhic* topic and the other objected.

He said, [Then] let me tell you a parable. What is this like? A man had two wives, one young and one old; the younger one pulled out his white hairs, and the older one his black ones, so between them he became bald!

36. This word is usually translated 'synagogue'.

Halakha, the old woman, the traditionalist; Aggada, the young woman, the revolutionary. How are they to be reconciled? Rabbi Isaac is a blacksmith; 'he knows the peaceful handling of fire' (Levinas, Talmudic Readings, *p. 194).*

He went on, Since that is how it is, let me say something that should satisfy both of you equally. **IF FIRE BREAKS OUT AND SPREADS TO THORNS** – If it breaks out of its own accord, **HE WHO STARTED THE FIRE MUST MAKE RESTITUTION.** The Holy One, blessed be He, is saying, I am responsible for the fire I have lit; it is I who set fire to Zion, as it is said, **HE KINDLED A FIRE IN ZION WHICH CONSUMED ITS FOUNDATIONS** (Lamentations 4:11 JPS), and I will rebuild it with fire, as it is said, **AND I MYSELF, DECLARES THE LORD, WILL BE A WALL OF FIRE ALL AROUND IT, AND I WILL BE A GLORY INSIDE IT** (Zechariah 2:9 JPS).

[And the] *halakha*? The verse commences with damage to property and concludes with personal injury; this teaches that [a person is responsible for] fire damage on the same basis as [damage caused by shooting] arrows.

This is the blacksmith's lesson. 'The blacksmith, who knows the peaceful use of elemental forces, extends responsibility, pushed to its extreme, to the chaos of war, and no doubt, to the National-Socialist holocaust . . . Where is the glory of His presence among us, if not in the transfiguration of consuming and avenging fire into a protective wall, into a defensive barrier?' (Levinas, Talmudic Readings, *p. 196).*

Chapter Seven is mainly concerned with cattle rustling, and elaborates on Exodus 21:37. This leads to consideration of the risk of damage to crops by grazing animals. The conflict between pastoralists and settled agriculture is resolved in favour of settled agriculture; pasturing sheep or goats is forbidden throughout the Land of Israel, a draconian measure which, had it been enacted, would have put the biblical patriarchs out of business! However, the Gemara immediately restricts its provisions.

CHAPTER SEVEN

MISHNA:

79b   You may not raise sheep or goats[37] in the Land of Israel, but you may raise them in Syria[38] and in the uncultivated parts of the Land of Israel.

You may not raise chickens in Jerusalem on account of the sacrifices,[39] nor may *Kohanim* [raise them anywhere] in the Land of Israel, because [they may defile food that must be eaten in] purity.

You may not raise pigs anywhere.

You should not raise dogs unless they are kept on a chain.

You may not spread nets [to catch] doves unless you are [at least] 30 *ris* from any settlement.[40]

GEMARA:

The rabbis taught: You may not raise sheep or goats in the Land of Israel, but you may raise them in wooded areas of the Land of Israel; in Syria, you may raise them in inhabited areas, and it goes without saying that you may do so beyond the Land. Another baraita states: You may not raise sheep or goats in the Land of Israel, but you may raise them in the Judaean desert and in the desert that borders on Acre. Even though they said you may not raise sheep or goats, you may raise cattle, for [the Sages] would not enact a law that most people would be unable to keep; whereas sheep and goats can be brought from beyond the Land, it would not be possible to bring cattle. And even though they said you may not raise sheep or goats, you may hold them thirty days prior to a festival, or thirty days in advance of your son's [wedding] feast, provided you do not retain the last one for thirty days. You

---

37. Literally, 'small beasts', as opposed to 'large beasts' – oxen and cows.
38. Areas mainly in what is now southern Lebanon, and which in the time of the Mishna had a substantial Jewish population.
39. Chickens may pick up bones or other unclean items and defile the meat of the sacrifices.
40. The doves may be private property.

might have thought that if the festival has passed, but thirty days have not elapsed since you purchased [the animal], that you would be allowed to retain it for the [full] thirty days; but [this is not correct,] since once the festival has passed you may not retain it. **A butcher may purchase for slaughter, and** 80a **purchase and retain [until market day], provided he does not retain the last animal for thirty days [from the date of purchase, if that extends beyond market day].**

The Mishna's reference to pigs brings to mind an alleged incident of the fratricidal war between the rival High Priests Hyrcanus and Aristobulus, sons of Alexander Yannai and Alexandra Salome, which led to the annexation of Judaea by Pompey in 63 BCE; Hyrcanus was favoured by the Pharisees and Aristobulus by the Sadducees.[41] *The term 'Greek wisdom' here was interpreted by medieval opponents of philosophy as Greek philosophy; the philosophers, on the other hand, argued that philosophy was permitted, and that the 'Greek wisdom' which was banned was some form of cryptic communication used by Greeks to trick their enemies.*[42] *See* Megilla *9a (see pp. 268–9).*

You may not raise pigs anywhere. The rabbis taught: **When** 82b **the Hasmoneans fought one another, Hyrcanus was inside [the Temple] and Aristobulus outside. Once every thirty days, (Hyrcanus' followers) would let down money and [Aristobulus' followers] would send up [animals for] the daily sacrifice. An old man versed in Greek wisdom was present; he advised [Aristobulus' followers], So long as they keep up the Temple service they will not fall into your hands. The following day [those inside] let down the box of money, but [Aristobulus' followers] sent up a pig. When it got halfway up the wall it dug its claws into the wall, and the Land of Israel trembled, 400** *parasangs* **by 400** *parasangs.* **That is when they said: A curse on anyone who raises pigs, or who teaches his son Greek wisdom!** It was in connection with the same episode that we learned, **It happened that the Omer-sheaf was brought from**

---

41. The events are described by Josephus, *Antiquities* 14:5–13.
42. For an historical assessment of the alleged ban on Greek wisdom, see Lieberman, *Hellenism*, pp. 100–114.

Gagot Tz'rifim and the two loaves [for Shavuot] from the
Valley of Ein Sokher.[43]

Is Greek wisdom forbidden, then? A baraita states, **Rabbi
said, Why speak Syriac in the Land of Israel? [Rather, speak]
either the holy tongue or Greek!** Likewise, Rabbi Yosé said,
**Why speak Aramaic in Babylonia? [Rather, speak] either the
holy tongue or Persian!** They say, Greek language is one thing;
Greek wisdom is another.[44]

Is Greek wisdom forbidden, then? Surely Rav Yehuda
reported that Shmuel said in the name of Rabban Simeon ben
Gamaliel, MY EYES HAVE BROUGHT ME GRIEF OVER ALL THE
MAIDENS OF MY CITY (Lamentations 3:51 JPS) – **There were a
thousand children in my father's house; five hundred learned
Torah, and five hundred learned Greek wisdom, and none is
left except for me here and a son of my father's brother in Asia
[Minor]!**[45] They say, The family of Rabban Gamaliel were an
exception, since they were close to the government. This is as a
baraita teaches: **It is forbidden to shave the forehead since it is
an idolatrous practice, but they allowed Eupolemus to shave
his forehead since he was close to the government; likewise,
they permitted the family of Rabban Gamaliel to speak Greek
wisdom since they were close to the government.**

You should not raise dogs unless they are kept on a chain.
The rabbis taught: **You may not raise a dog unless it is kept on
a chain, but if you live in a border town you may raise one,
tie it up by day and release it at night.** A baraita states: Rabbi
Eliezer the Great says, He who raises dogs is like one who raises
pigs. What difference does that make? It is that he is included
in the curse.

Rav Yosef ben Manyumi said in the name of Rav Naḥman,
Babylon is like a border town[, so you may keep a dog]. This
was understood to refer to Nehardea.

43. Although these locations were some distance away from Jerusalem, and it was
    preferable to bring from nearby – Mishna *Menaḥot* 10:2 (64b).
44. Syriac and Aramaic are dialects of the same language; the 'holy tongue' is Hebrew.
45. Lieberman (*Greek*, p. 20) takes this to mean that 'five hundred men connected
    with the house of the Jewish patriarch devoted their time to the study of Greek
    literature', and adduces evidence that several Palestinian Sages were fluent in Greek
    and utilized Greek wordplay and popular sayings in their sermons.

Rabbi Dostai of Biri preached: **AND WHEN [THE ARK] CAME TO REST, HE WOULD SAY, RETURN, O LORD, TO THE MYRIADS AND THOUSANDS OF ISRAEL** (Numbers 10:36) – this teaches you that the *Shekhina* does not rest on less than 22,000 Israelites.[46] If there was one less, and a pregnant woman among them who could make up the number, and a dog barked and caused her to miscarry, it would have caused the *Shekhina* to depart from Israel!

It happened that a woman was on her way into a building to bake when a dog barked at her. The owner said, Don't be afraid, his teeth have been taken out! She said, Keep your favours, the child has already stirred!

Chapter Eight is a striking instance of creative interpretation of biblical law. Scripture says 'An eye for an eye', but what does this mean? The literal interpretation is firmly rejected in favour of the idea that it means proportionate compensation. This is analysed into five components.

CHAPTER EIGHT

MISHNA:
If someone injures another he is liable under five counts: injury, pain, medical, idleness (loss of earnings), embarrassment.   83b

How [do we assess] injury? If he blinded someone's eye, cut off his hand or broke his leg, we view [the victim] as a slave sold in the market; [the court] assesses what he would have been worth previously and what he is worth now.

How [do we assess] pain? If he burnt him on a spit, or [pierced him] with a nail, even [if he pierced] a fingernail, where it does not cause a [permanent] injury, we assess how much a man of that kind would be willing to accept to submit to that much pain.

Medical? If he injured him he is obliged to cure him. If the wound was infected by fungus,[47] then if this is a result of the wound he must pay [for treatment], but if it was not a result of the wound, he is not obliged [to pay] for treatment. If it healed but reopened repeatedly, he is obliged [to pay] for treatment, but if it healed completely, he is not obliged [to pay] for treatment.

Idleness? Seeing that he has already been compensated [under the first heading] for loss of the arm or leg, we assess [the injured party] as a cucumber guard.[48]

Embarrassment? This depends on [the status of] the one who caused the embarrassment and the one who is embarrassed.

GEMARA:

Why [do we compensate in this way]? Surely the Torah says, An eye for an eye (Exodus 21:24)? Perhaps it means literally an eye?

Don't entertain that thought! A baraita teaches, Could it be that if A blinded B's eye, [the court] blinds A's eye, or if A cut off B's hand, [the court] cuts off A's hand? [No.] That is why Scripture says, WHO STRIKES[49] A MAN . . . WHO STRIKES AN ANIMAL (Leviticus 24:17, 18); just as one who injures an animal pays compensation, so one who injures a man pays compensation. You could also argue that Scripture says, YOU MAY NOT ACCEPT A RANSOM FOR THE LIFE OF A MURDERER (Numbers 35:31 JPS) – you may not indeed accept a ransom for the life of a murderer, but you may accept a ransom for the life of one who has caused irreparable loss of limb.

WHO STRIKES – does this refer to WHO STRIKES AN ANIMAL SHALL MAKE RESTITUTION, WHO STRIKES A MAN SHALL BE PUT TO DEATH (Leviticus 24:21)? Surely this verse speaks of someone who kills [a man]! Then is it from here: HE WHO STRIKES AN ANIMAL SHALL PAY FOR IT, LIFE FOR LIFE (Leviticus

---

47. Literally, 'if plants grew on it'.
48. That is, he receives compensation for enforced idleness during his recuperation, but only at the rate for the light work he will be able to do subsequently.
49. Some English translations have 'kills', but this is questionable; the rabbis were aware of the ambiguity, as will appear shortly.

24:18), following which it says AND IF A MAN CAUSE
A DEFECT IN ANOTHER, AS HE DOES, SO SHALL IT
BE DONE TO HIM (Leviticus 24:19)? This [likewise]
refers not to a blow[, but to killing].

We may compare 'striking' in the two cases: just as
[injury caused by] 'striking' in the case of an animal
results in [liability to] compensation, so [injury caused
by] 'striking' in the case of a human being results in
[liability to] compensation.

But doesn't it say [explicitly], AND IF A MAN STRIKE
ANY PERSON HE SHALL BE PUT TO DEATH (Leviticus
24:17)?

*There is further inconclusive discussion on the interpretation of
biblical verses, but never any doubt as to the law: the remedy
for injury is monetary compensation, not the infliction of similar
injury on the defendant. The Gemara then cites and discusses
some Tannaitic sources.*

It was taught in a baraita: **Rabbi Dostai ben Yehuda says,
AN EYE FOR AN EYE – [this means] monetary compensation.
Do you think it means an actual eye, rather than monetary
compensation? Then what would you do if one had a large eye
and one had a small eye? How could you call that AN EYE FOR
AN EYE, seeing that they are not equal?**

If you say that in a case like this[, where the eyes
are unequal], you should accept compensation[, but if
the eyes are equal you should apply the verse literally,
this cannot be the case, since] the Torah says, THERE
SHALL BE ONE LAW FOR YOU (Leviticus 24:22) – a
law which is the same for all of you.

They said,[50] What is [Rabbi Dostai ben
Yehuda's] problem? [Why not say,] A has
taken the light from B's eye, so the Torah
says take the light from A's eye [irrespective
of size]? If you don't argue like this, how
could we execute a dwarf who killed a giant

84a

---

50. The subject of this verb is unidentified – presumably Amoraim of the fourth or a
later generation.

or a giant who killed a dwarf, seeing that the
Torah says, THERE SHALL BE ONE LAW FOR
YOU – a law which is the same for all of you?
[The point is,] he has taken a life, and the
Torah says his life should be taken; here,
likewise, A has taken the light from B's eye,
so the Torah says take the light from A's eye.

Another baraita says: **Rabbi Simeon ben Yoḥai said, AN EYE
FOR AN EYE** – [this means] **monetary compensation. Do you
think it means an actual eye, rather than monetary compensation? In that case, suppose a blind man knocked out someone's eye, or an amputee cut off a limb, or a lame person
lamed someone, how could you fulfil AN EYE FOR AN EYE? Yet
the Torah says, THERE SHALL BE ONE LAW FOR YOU – a law
which is the same for all of you!**

*After further discussion the Gemara reviews the five categories
of compensation; medical is given here. A significant theological
proposition emerges: far from being an interference with divine
justice, the scientific art of healing is a sacred duty, and the
patient must heed professional advice.*

85a   **Medical? If he hurt him he is obliged to cure him. If the
wound was affected by fungus . . .** The rabbis taught: **If fungus
infected [the wound] as a result of the blow, and the wound
was concealed, he must pay both the medical expenses and
compensation for idleness. If it was not a result of the blow, he
pays neither medical expenses nor compensation for idleness.
Rabbi Judah says, Even if it was a result of the blow, he pays
medical expenses but not compensation for idleness; but the
[majority of] Sages say, Both compensation for idleness and
medical expenses, [for] whoever must pay compensation for
idleness must also pay medical expenses, and whoever is
exempt from compensation for idleness is exempt from medical expenses.**

What is their argument based on?

Rabba says, I met the scholars of the academy[51] and they were

---

51. Or 'house'. On the term *bei rav* in this context, see Goodblatt, *Rabbinic Instruc-
     tion*, p. 116.

saying, This argument hinges on whether it is permissible for the injured party to bandage the wound; the majority hold that he may, but Rabbi Judah holds that he may not[, and is therefore himself responsible for causing the fungal growth by preventing air from getting to the wound]. [The assailant] is obliged to pay medical expenses, since the Torah duplicates the word, but not compensation for idleness, since that is not duplicated.[52]

But I said to them, If the victim is not allowed to bandage the wound, [the assailant] should not pay for the cure! Surely everyone agrees that he may bandage it, only not bandage it too tightly. Rabbi Judah holds that although [the victim] should not bandage it too tightly[, but negligently did so, the assailant] must pay medical expenses, since the Torah duplicates the word 'cure', but not compensation for idleness, since that is not duplicated. The majority hold that since 'cure' is duplicated, he must pay for idleness too, as it is juxtaposed [in the verse] with 'cure'; Rabbi Judah says, He does not have to pay compensation for idleness, since the Torah excludes this by [prefacing 'idleness' with] the term *raq* ('but', or 'only').

The majority understand *raq* to exclude the case where the fungus has arisen independently of the blow. The majority at the end [of the citation] say, **Whoever must pay compensation for idleness must also pay medical expenses, and whoever is exempt from compensation for idleness is exempt from medical expenses.** Why, in their view, does the Torah duplicate the word 'cure'? They require [the duplication to support] Rabbi Ishmael's interpretation: He must pay for the cure – from this [we learn] that a doctor is permitted to heal.[53]

The rabbis taught: **How do we know that if fungus infected [the wound] as a result of the blow and the wound was sealed,**

---

52. The reference is to Exodus 21:19. Biblical Hebrew conveys emphasis by duplication, e.g. by adding an infinitive to a finite verb; it does this in the phrase translated 'he must pay for his cure'. Sometimes this duplication is rendered in English by an adverb, e.g. 'he must certainly pay'.

53. We might otherwise have thought that if God brings a malady upon someone, that is His judgement and we may not interfere with His will.

he must pay both the medical expenses and compensation for idleness? [It is derived] from the verse, BUT HE MUST PAY FOR HIS IDLENESS AND MUST CURE HIM (Exodus 21:19). Would this be [the case] even if the fungus growth was not due to the blow? [No, for] it says *RAQ* ('but'). Rabbi Yosé bar Yehuda says, Even if it is due to the blow he is exempt, for it says *RAQ*.

Some say Rabbi Yosé bar Yehuda means entirely exempt, following the majority at the end [of the citation].

Others say he means exempt from [compensation for] idleness, but liable for medical expenses. In agreement with whose opinion [would this be? In agreement with] his father's.

A teacher commented: **Would this be [the case] even if the fungal growth was not due to the blow? [No, for] it says *RAQ*.** Do we need Scripture to tell us [that the assailant doesn't have to pay for injury] not due to the blow? [The verse is needed to cover cases] like that in the baraita:

If he contravened the doctor's instructions and ate honey or other sweet things that might aggravate the wound, so that the wound became *gargutani*, would [the assailant] be liable for medical expenses? [No, for] it says *RAQ*.

What does *gargutani* mean? Abbaye said, a twisted cicatrix.

How can you cure it? With alum, wax and resin.

If [the assailant] said, I'll cure it myself[, the victim may refuse, saying], You are like a lion crouching in wait for me!

If [the assailant] said, I'll fetch a doctor who will cure you for nothing[, the victim may refuse, saying], A doctor who cures for nothing is worth nothing!

If [the assailant] said, I'll fetch a doctor from far away[, the victim may refuse, saying], A doctor from far away is like a blind man![54]

If [the victim] said to [the assailant,] Give me the money! I'll

54. He will go away again and not care what happens to the patient.

heal myself! [the assailant may reply,] You may make a mistake, and I will get a bad reputation.[55]

The next Mishna selected is about honesty. It is forbidden to handle stolen goods or money; tax farmers ('publicans') are assumed to have robbed people. The Gemara raises two questions: By what authority does the state raise taxes? Shmuel's ruling that 'the law of the realm is [valid] law' is cited.[56] What should be done about 'idolaters' who themselves steal from Israelites; granted one should not actively steal from them, is one obliged to return their lost property? The text has been subjected to emendation by censors who misconstrued it as condoning theft from Gentiles.

CHAPTER TEN

MISHNA:
You may not change money either out of the tax coffers or through the tax farmers, nor may you accept charity from them; however, you may accept [their personal money] from their homes or the marketplace.

GEMARA:
They taught: **But you may give [the tax farmer] a denarius [that you are due to pay], and he may give you the change.**

The tax farmers. But did not Shmuel say, **The law of the realm is law**[, so the money in the coffers of the tax farmers is legitimate, not stolen]? Rav Ḥanina bar Kahana said in Shmuel's name, [The Mishna's case concerns] a tax farmer who has no fixed commission [but takes as much as he likes – Rashi]. In the School of Rabbi Yannai they said, [The Mishna's case concerns] a tax farmer who set himself up [without government authority].

Some understood [the discussion of Ḥanina and Yannai] in connection with [the following]: **It is**

---

55. The text here is confused, and is amended on the basis of *Shulḥan Arukh: Ḥoshen Mishpat* 420:20.
56. See Introduction, p. xxviii.

forbidden to wear mixtures of wool and linen even on top of ten garments in order to evade tax.[57] This Mishna does not accord with the view of Rabbi Aqiva, for a baraita teaches: **It is forbidden to evade tax. Rabbi Simeon said in the name of Rabbi Aqiva, It is permitted to evade tax.** Now, with regard to the prohibited mixture of wool and linen, they differ in this way: one holds it is permitted to act in such a way that an unintended result is produced,[58] while the other holds that it is forbidden to act in a way that an unintended result is produced. But how can it be permitted to evade tax, for did not Shmuel say, **The law of the realm is law?** It was [in response to this that] Rav Ḥanina bar Kahana said in Shmuel's name, [The Mishna's case concerns] a tax farmer who has no fixed commission, while in the School of Rabbi Yannai they said, [The Mishna's case concerns] a tax farmer who set himself up [without government authority].

Some understood [the discussion of Ḥanina and Yannai] in connection with [the following]: **One may vow**[59] **to a murderer, a violent robber or a tax farmer that the goods are priests'-due or royal property even though they are not priests'-due or royal property.** [It is understandable that one may vow to avoid a threat to one's life, but surely not to] a [mere] tax farmer? Did not Shmuel say, **The law of the realm is law?** It was [in response to this that] Rav Ḥanina bar Kahana said in Shmuel's name, [The Mishna's case concerns] a tax farmer who has no fixed commission, while in the School of Rabbi Yannai they said, [The Mishna's case concerns] a tax farmer who set himself up [without government authority].

57. Mishna *Kilayim* 9:2; the prohibition of combining wool and linen in clothing (*sha'atnez*) derives from Leviticus 19:19 and Deuteronomy 22:11. The Mishna is concerned with a discriminatory tax levelled on Jews only, which they can evade by dressing as non-Jews.
58. The Jew who briefly wears a garment of wool and linen to evade discriminatory taxes does not intend to benefit from the warmth of the clothing.
59. A vow does not involve swearing by the name of God.

The introduction to Chapter Four touched on the topic of con-
flicting jurisdictions: what happens when one litigant is a
Roman citizen and the other not? Jewish justices faced similar
problems.

Rav Ashi said, It is about an oppressive Canaanite,[60] as a
baraita teaches: **If a Jew and an oppressive Canaanite come to
law, if you can award the case to the Jew according to the laws
of Israel, do so and tell the Canaanite, 'This is our law'; if you
can award the case to the Jew according to Canaanite law, do
so and tell the Canaanite, 'This is your law'; and if not, use
devious means. This is the view of Rabbi Ishmael, but Rabbi
Aqiva said, You may not use devious means, because of the
sanctity of the [Divine] Name.** From this it appears that if not
for the sanctity of the [Divine] Name, Rabbi Aqiva would agree
that one might use [devious means].

Would [Rabbi Aqiva] really permit theft from a Canaanite?
[Surely not,] for it was taught: **Rabbi Simeon said, This is what
Rabbi Aqiva expounded when he came from Zefirin: How do
we know that it is forbidden to steal anything from a
Canaanite? It is written, AFTER HE HAS BEEN SOLD, HE MAY
BE REDEEMED** (Leviticus 25:48) – that is, [when a Hebrew
slave is redeemed from being a slave to a Canaanite,] they may
not simply remove him [without payment], nor cheat [the
Canaanite] over the payment, but **HE SHALL RECKON WITH
HIS OWNER** (Leviticus 25:50), that is, he must make a precise
calculation with the owner [of what is due, and pay accord-
ingly].

The next extract is about land theft, and the flight of Rav
Kahana to the Holy Land. If someone steals, he must restore
the stolen property to its owner or, if that is not possible, make
restitution. But what happens if a stolen field is confiscated
by the government or gangsters? The thief can hardly be held
responsible for something that would have been done irrespec-
tive of who was in possession of the field.

Shmuel may have ruled that the law of the realm was binding,
but the high taxes demanded by the Shah for his military

60. 'Canaanite' is a euphemism demanded by censors. Manuscripts vary.

operations, especially under Shapur II,[61] must have placed an intolerable burden on people; it would have been felt that tax evasion was legitimate, and disclosing other people's tax liabilities an act of disloyalty to the community.

MISHNA:

116b   **If A stole a field from B, and then gangsters took it [by force], then if this is a widespread problem,[62] [A] may say to [B], 'Here is your field before you.' But if an [independent] robber took it, [A] must provide [B] with another field.[63]**

GEMARA:

The Gemara clarifies the term loosely translated 'gangsters', then continues:

But if an [independent] robber took it, [A] must provide [B]. Does this mean someone who took [B's] land by force, but not everyone's land? [Surely] we would have inferred this from the previous statement, **If this is a widespread problem**[, implying that if it is not a widespread problem, he cannot say 'Here is your field before you']. It has to be [stated to cover a case where A did not appropriate the field himself,] but pointed it out [to a potential land robber]. Alternatively, we are considering a case where idolaters[64] forced him to show them [land they might appropriate], and he pointed out this particular plot of land.

A man revealed some piles of wheat at the Exilarch's [place to government agents]. He appeared before Rav Naḥman, who ordered him to pay compensation.[65] Rav Yosef was sitting behind Rav Huna bar Ḥiyya, and Rav Huna bar Ḥiyya before Rav Naḥman. Rav Huna bar Ḥiyya asked Rav Naḥman, [Is the payment true] legal compensation or a fine?

[Rav Naḥman] replied: [The answer to that follows from] the

---

61. See the *Acts of Simeon*, Recension B, section 4, for an account of how Shapur II handled fiscal matters with the Christian community through Simon, the Bishop of Seleucia-Ctesiphon. See also Brock, *Syriac Perspectives*, VI:4.

62. Literally, 'a scourge of the country'.

63. He does not need to make restitution, since he is no longer responsible for the loss of the field.

64. 'Royal agents' – Rashi.

65. Whether the government agents confiscated the wheat, or collected taxes the Jews were trying to evade, is unclear.

Mishna, since it states, [A] **must provide [B] with another field.**[66]

After [Rav Naḥman] left, Rav Yosef asked Rav Huna bar Ḥiyya, Why should it make any difference whether it is legal compensation or a fine?   117a

He replied, If it is legal compensation, you can use it as a precedent;[67] if it is a fine, you cannot.

How do you know you cannot use a fine as a precedent? A baraita states: **At first, they said [that only] one who pollutes and one who libates have to pay compensation, but then they changed their minds and added one who mixes.**[68] Yes, when they changed their minds; no, when they hadn't. Surely the reason is because it is a fine, and you cannot make inferences from a fine. No[, for perhaps] it was because [at first] they were only concerned with considerable loss, not with small loss,[69] but subsequently they were concerned with small loss, too.

How can this be? Did not Rabbi Avin's father teach: **At first, they said [that only] one who pollutes and one who mixes have to pay compensation, but then they changed their minds and added one who libates?** Yes, when they changed their minds; no, when they hadn't. Surely the reason is because it is a fine, and you cannot argue on the basis of a fine. No[, for perhaps] they first held the opinion of Rabbi Avin, and subsequently that of Rabbi Jeremiah. First, they held the opinion of Rabbi Avin, for Rabbi Avin said, If someone fired an arrow [on Shabbat] from beginning to end of four cubits, and in the course of its

66. That is, it is compensation.
67. Literally, 'you can learn from it'.
68. If someone pollutes *teruma*, rendering it unfit for the *Kohen* to eat, or pours out wine as a libation to an idol, rendering it unfit to drink, he must pay compensation even though the 'damage' is not physical. Similarly, if he mixes unconsecrated food with *teruma*, he decreases the value of the unconsecrated food, as only *Kohanim* may now eat it (*Gittin* 53).
69. The loss from pollution and libation is great, since the food or drink is useless; from mixing, the loss is small, since *Kohanim* may still consume it.

flight it ripped through material [causing damage], he is not liable [to pay compensation for the damage,] seeing that firing[70] [the arrow] is necessary for its landing and he has already incurred a capital penalty.[71] Later, however, they adopted the opinion of Rabbi Jeremiah, that as soon as [the offender] picks up [the wine] he comes into possession of it [and is therefore liable to compensation], but he only incurs the death penalty [for idolatry] when he pours it out.

Rav Huna bar Yehuda happened to be at Bei Evyonei,[72] and found himself in the presence of Rava, who asked him, Have any [interesting] cases come your way? He replied: A Jew was forced by idolaters to show them where someone else's property was [concealed]; the matter came before me and I made him pay up.

Then you will have to pay him back, responded [Rava], for it was taught: **If a Jew was forced by idolaters to show them where someone else's property was, he is exempt from compensation; if[, however,] he handled the goods himself, he is liable.**

Rabba observed, If he volunteered the information of his own accord, it is as if he had handled the goods himself.

A certain man was placed under duress by idolaters and revealed [to them] wine belonging to Rav Meri the son of Rav Pinḥas the son of Rav Ḥisda. They told him to help them carry it and he did so. When he was brought before Rav Ashi, he exempted him [from compensation]. The rabbis said to Rav Ashi, But are we not taught, **If he handled the goods himself, he is liable?** He replied, That is [if the robbers] had not

70. Literally, 'lifting'. You cannot transfer an object without (a) picking it up and (b) putting it down.

71. There is a legal principle that one cannot be liable to a death sentence and compensation on the same count. Both Sabbath-breaking and idolatry (e.g. pouring out libations to idols) are, according to the Bible, capital offences, though the rabbis did not carry out such sentences.

72. Literally 'in the house of the poor', but Rashi says it is the name of a place. B.-Z. Eshel, *Yishuvei*, p. 52, cites S. Funk's identification of it as Abjun, on the Tigris north of Mosul.

positioned him there, but if they had positioned him there, [it is as if] they had already burnt [the goods].

Rabbi Abbahu[73] objected to Rav Ashi: **If [the robber] said, Pass me that heap of sheaves or that bunch of grapes and he passed it to him, he is liable [to pay compensation].** What [situation] does that deal with? It is where they are on opposite banks of a river, as is proved by the expression **Pass me** rather than **Give me**.

Two men were quarrelling about a trap; one said, It's mine, and the other said, It's mine! One of them went and disclosed it to the royal guard.[74] Abbaye said, [He could defend himself by arguing,] I disclosed my own property! Rava said, Could he really? Rather, place him under ban until he submits to judgement.

Much in the following is incoherent or implausible. It is chronologically impossible that the young Rav Kahana should have fled Babylonia in the days of Rav, who died before 250, and come before an aged Yoḥanan, who was thriving in the 270s; the arrangement and behaviour of the disciples corresponds to that in the Babylonian academies, not that in Tiberias; and details such as a dignitary sitting upon a pile of carpets belong to the late Sasanian court rather than to third-century Galilee. Daniel Sperber has argued that the narrative in the form we have it is a literary construction devised in the sixth century to justify the claims of the Babylonian academies, particularly Rav's foundation at Sura, to superiority over their Palestinian counterparts; and he has drawn attention to the very different account in a Yemenite Midrash.[75]

A man who wanted to reveal [the whereabouts of] someone's straw came to Rav. Don't reveal it, don't reveal it! said Rav. [But the other] said, I *will* reveal it, I *will* reveal it! Rav Kahana, who was sitting in front of Rav, dislocated the man's windpipe.[76]

---

73. This cannot have been the well-known Rabbi Abbahu of Caesarea, who died well before Rav Ashi was born. The text is probably corrupt.
74. Middle Iranian *pāhrag-bān* (Sokoloff, *Babylonian*).
75. Sperber, 'Fortunate Adventures', pp. 83 and 100.
76. The reading here is very doubtful: Rashi interprets as 'broke his neck', but the Munich manuscript lacks the word for 'windpipe'. There are numerous variant readings.

Rav applied to [the man] the verse, **YOUR SONS LIE IN A SWOON AT THE CORNER OF EVERY STREET – LIKE AN ANTELOPE CAUGHT IN A NET** (Isaiah 51:20 JPS) – Just as no one has mercy on an antelope caught in a net, so one does not have mercy when the property of Israel has fallen into the hands of idolaters.[77]

Rav said to him, Kahana, until now we had the Persians who did not object to the shedding of blood; now we have the Greeks[78] who object to the shedding of blood and say, 'Murder! Murder!'[79] Get up and flee to the Land of Israel, and take it upon yourself not to question Rabbi Yohanan for seven years!

[Rav Kahana] went and found Resh Laqish sitting and preparing the day's lesson for the disciples.[80]

He said to them, Where is Resh Laqish?

They said, Why [do you ask]?

He said, This question, that question; this answer, that answer.

They told Resh Laqish.

Resh Laqish went and said to Rabbi Yohanan, A lion has arrived from Babylon! Take care, Sir, at tomorrow's session.

The next day [Kahana] was seated in the front row, facing Resh Laqish. [Rabbi Yohanan] introduced a topic, but [Kahana] asked no question, then [another] topic and [Kahana] asked no question. They moved him back row by row until he sat in the seventh row.

Rabbi Yohanan observed to Resh Laqish, The lion of whom you spoke has become a fox!

[Kahana prayed,] May it be [Your] will that these seven rows

77. Rav is justifying Kahana's violent reaction – Rashi.
78. If this is the correct reading, it is not merely incoherent but demonstrably wrong; most manuscripts read 'Greeks' before 'Persians'. There was indeed a major regime change in Babylonia in Rav's time, from Parthians to Sasanians, in 224, but it had nothing to do with Greeks, and it is unlikely that Parthians allowed Jews to carry out death sentences but Sasanians did not, or vice versa.
79. One possible interpretation of MRDYN. Neusner derives the word from Hebrew MRD 'rebel' (*Babylonia*, vol. 2, p. 31, cf. *Gittin* 56a), though Sperber, 'Fortunate Adventures', prefers Pahlavi *murd(an)*, death, or *mard*, man.
80. Some manuscripts add phrases to the effect that he did realize who Resh Laqish was.

may take the place of the seven years [of no questioning imposed on me] by Rav!

He arose and asked, Sir, will you repeat [the lesson] from the beginning?

[Rabbi Yoḥanan] introduced a topic, and [Kahana] questioned him; they moved [Kahana] forward a row. [Again, Rabbi Yoḥanan] introduced a topic, and [Kahana] questioned him. Rabbi Yoḥanan was sitting on seven carpets,[81] and they removed one from beneath him. [Again, Rabbi Yoḥanan] introduced a topic, and [Kahana] questioned him, until they removed all the carpets beneath Rabbi Yoḥanan and he sat on the floor.

Rabbi Yoḥanan was an old man and his eyelids were drooping.[82] He said to them, Raise my eyelids so I can see [Rav Kahana]. They raised them with a silver paint-stick. He noticed that [Kahana's] lips were parted and thought he was laughing at him. He was upset, and [Kahana collapsed and] died.[83]

The next day Yoḥanan said to the disciples, Did you see what that Babylonian did to me?

They said, But that is his [usual] appearance![84]

[Rabbi Yoḥanan] went to the cave [where Kahana had been buried] and saw that it was encircled by a snake. Snake, snake! he said. Open your mouth[85] and permit the master to visit the disciple! [The snake] did not open [its mouth]. Let the colleague visit the colleague! It still did not open its mouth. Let the disciple visit the master! It opened its mouth. [Rabbi Yoḥanan] prayed for Rav Kahana, and revived him. He said, Had I known that that was your usual [facial appearance], I would not have been upset. Now, Sir, come and join us!

He replied, If you will pray that I don't die again,[86] I will come; otherwise not, now that the time has passed.

117b

---

81. Middle Iranian *bistarak*, bedding or carpet (Sokoloff, *Babylonian*).
82. Sperber ('Fortunate Adventures', p. 90) draws attention to a tale the Arab historian al-Tabari (839–923) tells of an old Sasanian general called Wahriz whose lids drooped over his eyes; he had an aide hold up his eyelids to enable him to shoot and kill the Abyssinian king Masruk.
83. Kahana felt remorse at having caused such offence.
84. He was not laughing at you; his face is that way through an injury – Rashi.
85. Let go of your tail to permit entrance to the cave – Rashi.
86. In consequence of questioning you – Rashi.

[Rabbi Yoḥanan] roused him and got him up. He posed every question [he could think of] and [Rav Kahana] solved them all. That is why Rabbi Yoḥanan declared, They say it is yours, but it is theirs![87]

---

87. They say the Torah is the possession of the scholars of the Land of Israel, but the Babylonians are in reality the masters!

SECOND TRACTATE
BAVA METZI'A
(THE MIDDLE GATE)

This tractate covers: rival claimants, lost property, deposits, overcharging, interest, workers' rights and hired animals, bailees, borrowing and renting, sharecropping, wages and loans, and the first part of the laws of partnerships and neighbours.

There are four categories of bailees, that is, people who are responsible for looking after others' property.[1] What happens if the property is lost, damaged or stolen? Someone who is doing his friend a favour by looking after his things without payment would be called to account only if he had been demonstrably negligent; in other circumstances, he simply takes an oath that he has not misappropriated the goods, and is exempt from payment. What if he prefers, perhaps for religious reasons, to make restitution rather than take an oath, and subsequently the thief is caught? That is the case to which the following Mishna refers.

The Gemara's discussion on the transfer of rights is set in the academy of Rava at Meḥoza in the fourth century; Rami and Zeira III are his colleagues.

CHAPTER THREE

MISHNA:

If someone deposits an animal or object with a friend and 33b
it is stolen or lost, and [the depositor] is unwilling to take an

---

1. See pp. 478–80 and *Shavuot* 8:1.

oath [to the effect that he has not been negligent or actively
misappropriated the deposit], then – seeing that [the law is
that] one who looks after something without payment may
take an oath and go [free] – if the thief is caught, he [the thief]
must pay double, and if he has slaughtered and sold [the stolen
animal, he must pay] fourfold [for a sheep] and fivefold [for
an ox].[2] Whom does he pay? The one to whom the deposit
was [entrusted].

But if he takes the oath and does not pay, then if the thief
is caught, he must pay double, and if he has slaughtered and
sold [the stolen animal, he must pay] fourfold [for a sheep]
and fivefold [for an ox]. Whom does he pay? The [original]
owner of the deposit.

GEMARA:

Why does the Mishna specify [both] **animal** and **object**?
[Both are] necessary. If it had specified only animal, I might have
inferred that the owner transfers his right to double restitution to
the bailee only if the deposit was an animal, since it is a lot of
trouble to look after[3] [an animal]; but [if the deposit was an]
object that was not troublesome, he would not transfer [the
right to] double[restitution. If[, on the other hand, the Mishna]
had specified only objects, I might have inferred that the owner
transfers his right to double restitution to the bailee only if the
deposit was an object, since double restitution is not a high
multiple; but [if the deposit was an] animal, where if [the thief]
slaughtered and sold it, he would have to pay four- or fivefold
restitution, [the owner] would not transfer [his rights].
On the transference of rights.

Rami bar Ḥama objected, Surely a man cannot transfer what
does not yet exist! Even according to Rabbi Meir, who holds
that you can transfer what does not yet exist, this would only
be [something like] the fruit of the palm, which will [in the
natural course of events] come into existence,[4] but in the present

2. Double payment is stipulated in Exodus 22:10, and four- or fivefold in 22:27; this
    was dealt with in *Bava Qama* Chapter Seven.
3. Literally, 'to take it in and out'.
4. i.e. a man call sell the date crop before it has fruited.

case, who says [the deposit] will be stolen? Even if you could   34a
say it would be stolen, who says the thief will be caught? Even
if the thief is caught who says that he will [have to] pay [double]?
Perhaps he will confess and be exempt [from double restitution].

Rava [responded], It is as if [the owner] were to say[, when
entrusting his animal to the bailee], My cow will be yours
[retrospectively] from now, [subject to it] being stolen and your
agreeing to pay me for it.

Rabbi Zeira objected [to Rava's proposal]: If that were so,
then [the bailee would be entitled to] its offspring and its
shearings, so why does a baraita teach, **Except for its offspring
and its shearings**? So, said Rabbi Zeira, it is as if he were to say
[explicitly, My animal will be yours . . .], except for its offspring
and its shearings.

> How can he be so definite? [Because, we may pre-
> sume,] a man would [willingly] transfer a profit that
> comes from a external source, but not a profit that
> comes from the thing itself.[5]

Some say, Rava [responded to Rami's question]: It is as if he
were to say: My cow will be yours from the time it is stolen,
subject to your agreeing and paying me for it.

> What is the [practical] difference between these two
> versions of Rava's statement]? The difference lies [in
> the relevance of] Rabbi Zeira's question; alternatively,
> in [a case] where the animal is standing in a meadow
> [that is not on the bailee's premises].[6]

---

*Overcharging, cheating and insulting are all covered by the
Hebrew noun* ona'a, *and the verb* l'honot *from which it is
derived. A key scriptural text is:* **YOU SHALL NOT WRONG A
STRANGER OR OPPRESS HIM, FOR YOU WERE STRANGERS IN**

---

5. That is, he will sign over the right to excess restitution, but not that to offspring
    and shearings.
6. Rashi explains that the question of offspring and shearings would not arise if the
    bailee acquired ownership only at the time of the theft; if the cow was in a
    meadow, not on the bailee's premises, he could not at that moment legally acquire
    ownership.

THE LAND OF EGYPT *(Exodus 22:20 JPS); the verb 'wrong' in this translation is a rendering of* l'honot. *While the main theme is overcharging, the Mishna extends the concept of* ona'a *into the field of personal relationships.*

CHAPTER FOUR

MISHNA:

'Wronging' [*ona'a*] applies just as much to words as to commerce. You should not ask someone, How much is this article? when you have no intention of buying it. If someone was a penitent sinner, you should not say to him, Remember what you used to do! If he is a descendant of proselytes, you should not say to him, Remember what your ancestors did; as it is said, YOU SHALL NOT WRONG A STRANGER OR OPPRESS HIM (Exodus 22:20 JPS).

GEMARA:

The rabbis taught: YOU SHALL NOT WRONG A STRANGER OR OPPRESS HIM, FOR YOU WERE STRANGERS IN THE LAND OF EGYPT; Scripture [here] speaks of wronging [*ona'a*] in words. You say it is wronging by words, but perhaps it is wronging in money? When it says, WHEN YOU SELL PROPERTY TO YOUR NEIGHBOUR, OR BUY ANY FROM YOUR NEIGHBOUR (Leviticus 25:14), wronging in money is covered. To what, then, does YOU SHALL NOT WRONG ONE ANOTHER (25:14) refer? Surely to wronging by words.

What is meant by 'wronging by words'? If [the person addressed] was a penitent, you should not say to him, Remember your previous deeds! If he was a proselyte who has come to learn Torah, do not say to him, The mouth that has eaten carrion and torn meat, swarming and crawling creatures, now comes to learn Torah that issued from the mouth of the Almighty! If he has been subject to chastisements or sickness or the loss of children, do not talk to him as Job's friends spoke to Job: IS NOT YOUR PIETY YOUR CONFIDENCE, YOUR INTEGRITY YOUR HOPE? THINK NOW, WHAT INNOCENT MAN EVER PERISHED (Job 4:6, 7 JPS). If donkey drivers ask for fodder, do not send them to so-and-so the fodder merchant, when you know he has never sold any.

Rabbi Judah says, You should also not set your eyes on a purchase when you don't have the money; this is a matter in the mind [only], and of such matters it is written, YOU SHALL FEAR YOUR GOD (Leviticus 25:17).[7]

Rabbi Yohanan said in the name of Rabbi Simeon ben Yohai, Wronging by words is worse than wronging in money, [since] of the former it is said, YOU SHALL FEAR YOUR GOD, but not of the latter.

Rabbi Eleazar said, The one is with his body, the other [only] with his property.

Rabbi Shmuel bar Nahmani said, Restitution can be made for the one, but not for the other.

A Tanna taught in the presence of Rav Nahman bar Isaac: If anyone puts another to shame in public, it is as if he sheds blood.

[Rav Nahman bar Isaac] commented, You have put it well! As you can see, the red drains out of him and white takes its place!

Abbaye [once] asked Rav Dimi, What are they most careful about in the West? He replied, About putting people to shame, for Rabbi Hanina taught that all descend to Hell, bar three.

> All descend to Hell? [Surely not! What he meant was,] All descend to Hell and then return[8] except for three, who descend but do not ascend, and these are they: one who sleeps with another man's wife, one who puts another to shame in public and one who uses an offensive nickname for someone.
>
> > Surely using an offensive nickname is the same as putting someone to shame in public? [He meant,] Even if the person is used to [the nickname and does not take offence].

Rabba bar bar Hana said in the name of Rabbi Yohanan, It   59b

---

7.   Don't imagine that just because you take no action, God will not punish you.
8.   Rabbi Hanina seems to understand Hell as a place of purgation.

would be better for a man to have intercourse with someone who might possibly be a married woman than to put another to shame in public.

Where do we infer that from? It is from Rava's interpretation, for Rava interpreted the verse, BUT WHEN I STUMBLE, THEY GLEEFULLY GATHER; WRETCHES GATHER AGAINST ME, I KNOW NOT WHY; THEY TEAR AT ME WITHOUT END (Psalm 35:15 JPS). David declared to the Holy One, blessed be He: Lord of the Universe! It is clear to You that if they tore my flesh, my blood would not drip on to the ground. Not only that, but [even] when they study [the remote topics of] *Nega'im* and *Ohalot*,[9] they [taunt me], saying, David, what is the penalty for someone who has intercourse with another man's wife? I answer, He is executed by strangling, but [having repented] has a portion in the World to Come; but one who puts another to shame in public has no portion in the World to Come![10]

Mar Zutra bar Tovia said in the name of Rav (but some say it was Rav Ḥana bar Bizna in the name of Rabbi Simeon the Pious, and others that it was Rabbi Yoḥanan in the name of Rabbi Simeon bar Yoḥai), It is better for a man to throw himself into a fiery furnace than to shame another in public. On what do we base this? On Tamar, for it is written, AS SHE WAS BEING BROUGHT OUT, SHE SENT THIS MESSAGE TO HER FATHER-IN-LAW, 'I AM WITH CHILD BY THE MAN TO WHOM THESE BELONG' (Genesis 38:25 JPS).[11]

Rav Ḥinena the son of Rav Idi asked, What is [the meaning of 'one another' ('amito) in the phrase], YOU SHALL NOT WRONG ONE ANOTHER (Leviticus 25:14 JPS)? [Understand it

9.   Tractates in the Order *Tohorot*.
10. Rabbi Yoḥanan cannot have based his statement on Rava, who lived a century later. Possibly what is meant is that David slept with Bathsheba, who may have been Uriah's wife (*Shabbat* 56a); his sin was less than that of the men who continued to humiliate him publicly in later years.
11. She was prepared to be burnt to death rather than publicly humiliate Judah by naming him as the father.

as '*am she-it'kha*,] the 'people who are with you' in Torah and *mitzvot*[12] – do not wrong them.

Rav said, A man should be especially careful not to offend (*ona'a*) his wife; offence is all the more easily caused, since she is readily moved to tears.

Rabbi Eleazar said, On the day the Temple was destroyed the gates of prayer were closed, as it is written, AND WHEN I CALL OUT AND PLEAD, HE SHUTS OUT MY PRAYER (Lamentations 3:8). But though the gates of prayer are closed, the gates of tears are not closed, for it is written, HEAR MY PRAYER, O LORD; GIVE EAR TO MY CRY; DO NOT DISREGARD MY TEARS (Psalm 39:13 JPS).

Rav also said, Whoever follows his wife's [bad] advice falls into Hell, as it is written, INDEED, THERE WAS NEVER ANYONE LIKE AHAB, WHO COMMITTED HIMSELF TO DOING WHAT WAS DISPLEASING TO THE LORD, AT THE INSTIGATION OF HIS WIFE JEZEBEL (1 Kings 21:25 JPS).[13]

Rav Papa remarked to Abbaye, What about the popular saying, If your wife is small, bend down and listen to her?

No problem, One speaks of worldly matters, one of domestic; alternatively, one speaks of spiritual matters, the other of worldly.

Rav Ḥisda said, All gates are closed, but not that of *ona'a*,[14] as it is written, BEHOLD, THE LORD WAS STANDING ON A WALL CHECKED WITH A PLUMB LINE, AND A PLUMB LINE WAS IN HIS HAND (Amos 7:7).

Rabbi Eleazar said, [God] always metes out punishment

---

12. In keeping with the context, the commentator Yomtov of Seville (*c.* 1250–1330) interpreted 'people who are with you' to mean 'your wife'. Other commentators apply the phrase more generally, going so far as to exclude all but 'God-fearing people', quite narrowly defined (cf. Isserles's gloss on *Ḥoshen Mishpat* 228).

13. This complements Rav's previous statement by indicating that though a husband should treat his wife gently and with understanding, he should not necessarily do everything she says.

14. i.e. the prayer of the one unjustly wronged will be heard.

through an agent, except in the case of *ona'a*[, where He does it Himself], as it is written, **AND A PLUMB LINE WAS IN HIS HAND**.

Rabbi Abbahu said, There are three before whom the curtain[15] is never closed; [the perpetrators of] *ona'a*, robbery and idolatry: *ona'a*, as it is written, **AND A PLUMB LINE WAS IN HIS HAND**; robbery, as it is written, **LAWLESSNESS AND RAPINE ARE HEARD IN HER; BEFORE ME CONSTANTLY ARE SICKNESS AND WOUNDS** (Jeremiah 6:7 JPS); idolatry, as it is written, **THE PEOPLE WHO PROVOKE MY ANGER, WHO CONTINUALLY, TO MY VERY FACE[, SACRIFICE IN GARDENS AND BURN INCENSE ON TILES]** (Isaiah 65:3 JPS).[16]

Rav Yehuda said, A man should always take care [to ensure adequate provision] of grain in his house, for without adequate grain there is strife, as it is written, **WHO SETS AT PEACE YOUR BORDER, AND SATISFIES YOU WITH FAT WHEAT** (Psalm 147:14).

> Rav Papa commented, That is the meaning of the popular saying, When the jar is empty of barley, strife knocks at the door.[17]

Rav Ḥinena bar Papa [likewise] said, A man should always take care [to ensure adequate provision] of grain in his house, for Israel were called poor only on account of [lack of] grain, as it is said, **AFTER THE ISRAELITES HAD DONE THEIR SOWING, MIDIAN, AMALEK AND THE KEDEMITES WOULD COME UP AND RAID THEM; THEY WOULD ATTACK THEM, DESTROY THE PRODUCE OF THE LAND . . . ISRAEL WAS REDUCED TO UTTER POVERTY[18] BY THE MIDIANITES** (Judges 6:3–4, 6 JPS).

Rabbi Ḥelbo said, A man should always take great care to honour his wife; blessing is present in a man's home only

---

15. Hebrew *pargod*, from Greek *paragōdos*, itself derived from the Semitic root FRG, 'to divide'; here the curtain is the separation between the *Shekhina* and the heavenly host – Rashi.

16. All these proof-texts demonstrate God's direct, 'personal' concern with punishing wrongdoers.

17. This translation follows Jastrow, *Dictionary*, entry on *kada*, on the basis of the Munich manuscript.

18. JPS: 'misery'.

through his wife, as it is said, **Because of her, it went well with Abram** (Genesis 12:16 JPS).

> That is what Rava [meant when he] said to the people of Meḥoza, Honour your wives, so that you may prosper.

The next story was incorporated here because of its bearing on the seriousness of ona'a, *or verbal abuse, of which Rabbi Eliezer was a prime victim.*[19]

A Mishna says: **If he sliced [the oven] into rings and inserted sand between the rings, Rabbi Eliezer says, It is not susceptible to impurity; the [majority of] Sages say, It is susceptible.**[20] This is the 'Oven of 'Akhnai'.

59b

> What is 'Akhnai? Rav Yehuda said in the name of Shmuel, [It is so called because] they encircled it with words, like the [snake called] *'akhna*, and declared it [susceptible to] impurity.

It was taught: **On that day Rabbi Eliezer put forward every conceivable argument [to declare the oven pure], but they rejected all of them.**

He said, If the law accords with my opinion, let this carob tree validate it!

The carob tree shifted a hundred cubits from its place – some say, four hundred.

They said to him, A carob tree is no argument!

He then said, If the law accords with my opinion, let this stream prove it!

The water thereupon flowed backwards.

They retorted, A stream is no argument!

He then said, If the law accords with my opinion, let the walls of [this] House of Study] demonstrate it!

The walls began to cave in.

---

19. There has been much speculation on its theological implications, mostly without reference either to its context or to its literary history; among the more satisfactory interpretations are Halivni's in *Peshat & Derash*, pp. 107ff., and David Kraemer's literary analysis in *Mind*, pp. 120–24. The story is paralleled in part in Yerushalmi Mo'ed Qatan 3:1 (81c, d).
20. *Kelim* 5:10 and *Eduyot* 7:7.

Rabbi Joshua addressed them in protest: If the Sages debate among themselves on a point of *halakha*, what has this to do with you?

Out of respect for Rabbi Joshua, the walls did not collapse; out of respect for Rabbi Eliezer, they did not straighten but remained bent.

[Eliezer] then addressed [the Sages]: If the law accords with my opinion, let Heaven [itself] declare that I am right!

[At this,] a heavenly voice proclaimed, Why do you challenge Rabbi Eliezer, for the *halakha* accords with him in all matters!

Rabbi Joshua arose to his feet, and declared, IT IS NOT IN HEAVEN (Deuteronomy 30:12).

What does IT IS NOT IN HEAVEN mean? Rabbi Yirmiya said, Now that the Torah has been given on Mount Sinai we no longer pay attention to any heavenly voice, for at Mount Sinai the words, FOLLOW THE MAJORITY (Exodus 23:2), were written in the Torah.[21]

Rabbi Nathan met [the prophet] Elijah,[22] and asked, What did the Holy One, blessed be He, do when that happened? [Elijah] replied, He laughed, and said, My children have outvoted Me, my children have outvoted Me!

They say, On that day they brought all [the things] Rabbi Eliezer had declared pure and burnt them, then voted to place him under a ban. They then asked, Who will inform him [of the ban]? Rabbi Aqiva said, I will go [myself], for if anyone unsuitable informs him, he will destroy the world. What did Rabbi Aqiva do? He dressed in black, wrapped himself in black and sat at a distance of four cubits [from Rabbi Eliezer].

Why is today different from other days? asked Eliezer. [Aqiva] replied, Master, I am under the impression that your colleagues shun you! [Thereupon Eliezer himself] rent his garments,

21. In fact, 'Do not follow the majority (or "the great ones") to do evil.' This implies that you ought to follow the majority to implement the law correctly.
22. *Yevamot* 62b (see p. 313).

removed his shoes, slipped [from his seat] and sat upon the ground. His eyes filled with tears, [and as they did so] the world suffered; olives, wheat and barley all lost a third, and some say that even the dough that women were kneading spoiled.

It was taught: There was great distress that day; wherever Rabbi Eliezer set his eyes burnt.

[At that time] Rabban Gamaliel[23] was on board ship, and a wave rose up [ready] to drown him. He said, This must be on account of Rabbi Eliezer ben Hyrcanus. He got to his feet and declared, Lord of the Universe! You know that the action I took was not for my own honour, nor for the honour of my father's house, but for Your honour, that controversy might not spread in Israel! The sea ceased its threatening.

Rabban Gamaliel's sister, Imma Shalom, was Rabbi Eliezer's wife. From that episode onwards she would not let him fall on his face [in prayer, in case he prayed for her brother's downfall]. On one occasion the New Moon was due, and she was confused as to whether [the celebration lasted] one day or two – though some say she went to the door to give bread to someone in need – and she found that he had fallen on his face [in prayer while she was not attending]. Get up! she said, You have killed my brother! How do you know? he asked. She replied, I learned in my grandfather's house that all gates [of prayer] are closed except that of *ona'a*.

The rabbis taught: **He who wrongs the stranger transgresses three prohibitions, and who oppresses him transgresses two.**

Why the difference? In connection with wronging (*ona'a*), three prohibitions are written: YOU SHALL NOT WRONG A STRANGER (Exodus 22:20 JPS); WHEN A STRANGER RESIDES WITH YOU IN YOUR LAND, YOU SHALL NOT WRONG HIM (Leviticus 19:33 JPS); and YOU SHALL NOT WRONG ONE ANOTHER

23. The nature of Gamaliel's intervention is not made clear; the text appears to imply that Gamaliel had tried to rein in Eliezer. This pericope and the next are lacking in the Yerushalmi version.

(Leviticus 25:14 JPS) – this includes the stranger. In connection with oppression, too, three [prohibitions] are written: YOU SHALL NOT . . . OPPRESS HIM (Exodus 22:20 JPS); YOU SHALL NOT OPPRESS A STRANGER, FOR YOU KNOW THE FEELINGS OF THE STRANGER, HAVING YOURSELVES BEEN STRANGERS IN THE LAND OF EGYPT (Exodus 23:9 JPS); and DO NOT ACT TOWARDS THEM AS A CREDITOR (Exodus 22:24 JPS) – this includes the stranger. So, there is no difference; both [transgress] three prohibitions.

A baraita taught: **Rabbi Eliezer the Great says, Why does the Torah warn us in 36 places – some say in 46 places – [to show consideration for] the stranger? [It is] because they have a strong inclination to revert [to idolatrous ways].**[24]

What is the meaning of YOU SHALL NOT WRONG A STRANGER OR OPPRESS HIM, FOR YOU WERE STRANGERS IN THE LAND OF EGYPT (Exodus 22:20 JPS)? Rabbi Nathan says, Do not reproach your neighbour with a failing which you, too, have! That is [the meaning of] the popular saying, If you have a hanged man in your family, don't tell someone to hang a fish for you!

Words like 'usury' and 'increase' in the KJV of these verses impose alien interpretations on the biblical text. The Mishna builds its interpretation on the etymology of the words ('biting' and 'increase').

TAKE THOU NO USURY OF HIM, NOR INCREASE . . . THOU SHALT NOT GIVE HIM THY MONEY UPON USURY, NOR LEND HIM THY VICTUALS FOR INCREASE. (Leviticus 25:36, 37 KJV).

THOU SHALT NOT LEND UPON USURY TO THY BROTHER; USURY OF MONEY, USURY OF VICTUALS, USURY OF ANYTHING THAT IS LENT UPON USURY. UNTO A STRANGER THOU MAYEST LEND UPON USURY; BUT UNTO THY BROTHER THOU SHALT NOT LEND UPON USURY. (Deuteronomy 23:19, 20 KJV).

24. Rashi on *Horayot* 13a. The phrase ('because . . . revert') is obscure.

CHAPTER FIVE

MISHNA:

What is *neshekh* ['biting'] and what is *tarbit* ['increase']?[25]   60b
What is *neshekh*? If someone lends a *sela* for five denarii, or
two *seahs* of wheat for three, this is forbidden, since it 'bites'.
And what is *tarbit*? 'Increase' of fruit. How is this? Someone
paid one gold denarius per *kur* for wheat, that being the
[market] price [at the time of purchase], then the price rose to
30 [silver] denarii; [the purchaser] said to [the vendor], Deliver
my wheat, as I wish to sell it and buy wine; the [vendor]
replied, [Don't bother;] I'll treat your wheat as worth 30
[denarii] per *kur*, and let you have wine [for its value] – but
he has no wine [in stock].

GEMARA:

Since [the Mishna] abandons the topic of interest prohibited
by Torah law and proceeds to explain that forbidden by the
rabbis, it follows that in Torah law there is no difference between
neshekh and *tarbit*. But isn't it written, THOU SHALT NOT GIVE
HIM THY MONEY UPON USURY (*NESHEKH*), NOR LEND HIM
THY VICTUALS FOR INCREASE (*MARBIT*[26]) (Leviticus 25:37)?

Is it reasonable [to suppose] that there can be *neshekh* without
tarbit, and *tarbit* without *neshekh*?

How could there be *neshekh* without *tarbit*? Suppose A lent
B 100 [*zuz*] for 120, when at [the time of lending] a *danak* was
worth 100 and [at the time of repayment] a *danak* was worth
120.[27] There is [apparently] *neshekh*, for he 'bites' him by taking
back more than he gave, but not *tarbit*, for he has no profit,
since he lent a *danak* and he gets a *danak* back. [But this doesn't
work, for] in the last analysis [we must reckon either by the
initial exchange value or by the final exchange value]; if we go
by the initial exchange value, there is neither *neshekh* nor *tarbit*;

---

25. These two terms (or their cognates) are used in Leviticus (above) and in Proverbs
    28:8 to denote payment of interest; in Psalm 15:5 and in Deuteronomy (above)
    only *neshehkh* appears.
26. *Marbit* and *tarbit* are equivalent.
27. The problem is that the relative values of bronze and silver change.

if we go by the final exchange value, there are both *neshekh* and *tarbit*.

Further, how could there be *tarbit* without *neshekh*? Suppose A lent B 100 [*zuz*] for 100, when at [the time of lending] a *danak* was worth 100 and [at the time of repayment] a *danak* was worth 120. [This wouldn't work either, for] in the last analysis [we must reckon either by the initial exchange value or by the final exchange value]; if we go by the initial exchange value, there is neither *neshekh* nor *tarbit*; if we go by the final exchange value, there are both *neshekh* and *tarbit*.

Rava therefore [concluded] that you cannot find *neshekh* without *tarbit*, nor *tarbit* without *neshekh*. Scripture distinguishes them only to hold the transgressor responsible for transgressing two commandments.[28]

The rabbis taught: DO NOT LEND HIM YOUR MONEY ON INTEREST (*NESHEKH*), OR GIVE HIM YOUR FOOD ON INTEREST (*MARBIT*) (Leviticus 25:37)? I might think that *neshekh* applied only to money, and *tarbit* only to food. How do I know that *neshekh* applies to food, too? This is taught by the words NESHEKH OF FOOD (Deuteronomy 23:20). How do I know that *tarbit* applies to money, too? This is taught by the words NESHEKH OF MONEY (Deuteronomy 23:20); now [these words] cannot be meant to tell us that *neshekh* applies to money, since it has already said [at the beginning of the verse], DO NOT CHARGE YOUR BROTHER NESHEKH, so we must apply it to 'increase' of money.

This speaks only of the borrower. How do I know [that the prohibition applies] to the lender[, too]? The term *neshekh* is used of the borrower, and it is also used of the lender. Just as with *neshekh* of the borrower we do not distinguish between money and food, between *neshekh* and *ribit*,[29] so with *neshekh* of the lender we do not distinguish between money and food, between *neshekh* and *ribit*.

How do we know that everything[, not just money and food,] is included [in the prohibition]? It says, NESHEKH OF

61a

---

28. i.e. to emphasize the seriousness of the offence.
29. This is the more common form of the term *tarbit*, and is the usual Hebrew term for 'interest'.

ANYTHING ON WHICH INTEREST MAY BE CHARGED (Deuteronomy 23:20).

Nothing in the Torah is redundant, so why are interest, robbery and overcharging all specified? Do they not all amount to the same offence, misappropriation of another's property? Gemara demonstrates the fundamental coherence of the Torah's provisions and the heinousness of misappropriation of others' possessions.

Rava said, Why does the Torah contain a prohibition of interest, a prohibition of robbery and a prohibition of overcharging? Each of these must be [specified]. If the Torah had prohibited [only] interest, [I would not have inferred prohibitions of robbery and overcharging from it,] for it has a novel aspect, namely that the prohibition applies to the borrower [as well as to the lender who actually levies the charge];[30] if the Torah had prohibited [only] robbery, I would have thought this was on account of the element of force, and this does not apply to overcharging; if the Torah had prohibited [only] overcharging, I would have thought [that this was different,] since the person being overcharged might be unaware [of being overcharged], and so waive [the extra amount].

We cannot infer one from the other. Can we infer any one from the other two?

Which might we infer? Let the Torah not write a prohibition of interest, but infer it from the other two? But the others are done without [the victim's knowing] agreement, so how could we infer from this to interest, which [is charged *with* the knowing] agreement [of the borrower]?

[Then] let the Torah not write a prohibition of overcharging, but [allow us to] infer it from the other two? [This would fail, since we could object] that the others are not normal commerce.

[So] let the Torah not write a prohibition of robbery, but infer it from the other two, for how could you object? If you object that interest has a novel aspect, the inference may be

---

30. It would not make sense to prohibit the victim of robbery from being robbed or the purchaser from being overcharged.

made from overcharging[, which lacks a novel aspect]; if you object that in overcharging the buyer might be unaware [of being overcharged], and waive [the extra amount], the inference may be made from interest. The argument goes back and forth, neither is [exactly] like the other, but the common factor is that both involve taking what belongs to another; and on that basis we can infer that robbery [is forbidden].

They say, That is [indeed] right, so why the [express] prohibition of robbery? [Because] it refers to someone who withholds the wages of a hired worker. But surely withholding the wages of a hired worker is [itself expressly] mentioned in the Torah: **YOU SHALL NOT OPPRESS THE POOR AND NEEDY LABOURER . . . YOU MUST PAY HIS WAGES ON THE DUE DAY** (Deuteronomy 24:14, 15)? [It is repeated to make the transgressor] guilty of two offences. Then why not apply it to interest or overcharging, to make them double offences? We learn from the context; it is written in the context of the hired labourer.

Why does the Torah write **YOU SHALL NOT STEAL** (Leviticus 19:11)? It is as the baraita teaches: **YOU SHALL NOT STEAL** (Exodus 20:13) – **out of spite; YOU SHALL NOT STEAL** – [even] **in order to pay back double.**[31]

Rav Yeimar asked Rav Ashi, Why does the Torah [expressly] prohibit false weights[, seeing that this is already prohibited as a form of theft]? He replied, It is for people who submerge their weights in salt [to make them heavier]. But surely that is proper theft[? he asked]. [Rav Ashi replied,] The Torah prohibits submerging [weights] into salt[, even though he has not yet used the weights fraudulently].

The rabbis taught: **YOU SHALL NOT FALSIFY MEASURES OF LENGTH, WEIGHT OR CAPACITY (MESURA)** (Leviticus 19:35 JPS). **LENGTH** – this refers to land measure – don't measure for one in the summer and for another in the rainy season;[32] **WEIGHT** – don't dip your weights in salt; **CAPACITY** – don't make the liquid foam. Now can't we reason from minor to major? If the Torah insists on a correct *mesura*, which is a mere

---

31. That is, with the intention of making a gift to someone who is reluctant to accept one – Rashi.

32. Measurement was done with ropes, which could stretch more in the rainy season.

fraction of a *log*, how much more so would it care about a *hin*, a half-*hin*, a quarter-*hin*, a *log*, a half-*log* or a quarter-*log*![33]

Rava asked, Why does the Torah mention the Exodus from Egypt in connection with interest, the *tzitzit* ['fringes'] and weights? The Holy One, blessed be He, [thereby] declares, It is I who distinguished between the drop that was a first-born and the drop that was not,[34] and it is I who will punish whoever assigns his money to a non-Jew in order to lend it to an Israelite on interest, and whoever submerges his weights in salt, and whoever puts vegetable dye on his fringes and claims it is the [real] blue![35]

Ravina visited Sura-on-the-Euphrates.[36] Rav Ḥanina of Sura asked him, Why does the Torah mention the Exodus from Egypt in connection with [forbidden] swarming creatures (Leviticus 11:45)? He replied, The Holy One, blessed be He, [thereby] declares, It is I who distinguished between the drop that was a first-born and the drop that was not, and it is I who will punish whoever mixes the insides of forbidden fish with those of permitted fish and sells them to [a fellow-]Israelite. [Rav Ḥanina] responded, My problem is with the words WHO BROUGHT THEM UP (Leviticus 11:45); why is it just here that the Torah chooses to write WHO BROUGHT THEM UP? [Ravina] replied: It is as was taught in the school of Rabbi Ishmael. For it was taught in the school of Rabbi Ishmael: **If I had brought Israel up from Egypt for just this, that they refrain from defiling themselves with swarming creatures, it would have been worthwhile.** Rav Ḥanina: But is the reward for this greater than for [refraining from taking] interest, for [wearing] *tzitzit* or for correct weights! [Ravina] replied, Though the reward is not greater, it is more disgusting to eat such things.

---

33. That is, volume measurements in ascending order; the value of the *mesura* relative to the others is disputed.
34. Only God could know who were in fact the first-born.
35. The authentic blue dye was extracted from a mollusc.
36. A suburb of Sura, on the Euphrates rather than the Sura river (Obermeyer, cited by B.-Z. Eshel, *Yishuvei*, p. 196). Alternatively, the Sura above Zenobia.

CHAPTER SEVEN

MISHNA:

93a There are four bailees: one who looks after property without payment; one who borrows; one who receives payment [for looking after property]; and a hirer. The unpaid guardian takes an oath in all cases [of loss, and is exempt from restitution]; the borrower makes restitution in all cases; the paid guardian and the hirer take an oath if it has been broken, captured or died [through no fault of theirs, and are exempt from restitution], but make restitution if it has been lost or stolen.

GEMARA:

Who is the Tanna of the four bailees? Rav Naḥman said in the name of Rabba bar Abbuha, it is Rabbi Meir.

Rava asked Rav Naḥman, Is there anyone who doesn't hold that there are four bailees?

Rav Naḥman replied, What I meant to say was, Who is the Tanna who holds that the paid guardian and the hirer are subject to the same law[, and therefore there are only three categories of law]? Rabbi Meir.

But surely Rabbi Meir holds the opposite, for a baraita states: **How does the hirer pay? Rabbi Meir says, Like the unpaid guardian; Rabbi Judah says, Like the paid guardian.** Rabba bar Abbuha taught this the other way round. [Either way,] there are not four cases, but three. Rav Naḥman bar Isaac says, There are four cases, but [they fall within] three legal categories.

A shepherd was pasturing someone's flock on the riverbank, when a sheep slipped and fell in the river. He came before Rabba [for judgement] and was exempted. What more could he 93b have done? said Rabba, He guarded them as people guard! Abbaye asked: Then if he returned to town at the time that people return, would he be exempt? Yes[, replied Rabba]. And if he took a nap at the time people take naps, would he be exempt? Yes[, replied Rabba].

Abbaye objected, **A paid guardian is exempt only for contingencies such as, THE SABAEANS ATTACKED THEM AND**

CARRIED THEM OFF, AND PUT THE BOYS TO THE SWORD (Job 1:15 JPS). That applies only to the town's night-watchmen, replied [Rabba].

He objected, **How far does the responsibility of a paid guardian extend? As far as, SCORCHING HEAT RAVAGED ME BY DAY AND FROST BY NIGHT** (Genesis 31:40 JPS). That also applies only to the town's night-watchmen, [Rabba] responded. Then was our father Jacob a town night-watchman? No, but he was protesting to Laban, 'I have given your flocks extra protection, as if I were a town night-watchman.'

He[37] objected, **If a shepherd was in charge of the flock and left it to go into town and a wolf came and rent a sheep or a lion slashed one, we don't say, 'If he was there he could have saved it', but we assess the situation: if [, had he been there,] he would have been able to save it, he must pay; if [, had he been there,] he would not have been able to save it, he is exempt.** Doesn't this speak of a case where he returned to town at the time that people return? No, he returned to town at a time that people do not [normally] return. If that is the case, why should he be exempt? [Surely,] if someone is careless and an accident subsequently occurs, he is liable! Perhaps he returned to town because he heard a lion roar. If that was case, what is the point of assessing him? What else could he do? He should have gathered his fellow-shepherds and attacked the lion with sticks. In that case, why mention someone who guards for payment? Even if he was guarding for nothing he ought to do that, as a scholar said, If someone was looking after [another's animals] for nothing, and could have gathered his fellow-shepherds and attacked with sticks but didn't, he is liable. [There is a difference.] One who guards for nothing should not involve himself in any expense [by hiring others to help]; one who guards for payment should hire [others to help]. How much should he pay? Up to the value [of the animals]. But do we ever find that a paid guardian is responsible for accidents? He recoups the money from the owner of the animals. Rav Papa asked

---

37. It is not clear who this is.

Abbaye, If that's how it is, what advantage does [the owner] get from such an arrangement?[38] [It's still worth his while to get his own animals back, since] they are familiar with his ways; alternatively, it saves him the trouble [of purchasing new ones].

Rav Hisda and Rabba bar Rav Huna didn't agree with Rabba, for they said, The whole point of paying [someone to look after your animals] is to get extra security. Bar Ada the porter[39] was crossing a bridge at Naresh when one [cow?] pushed another and she fell in the river. He appeared before Rav Papa, who held him liable [to pay for the loss]. What could I have done? he asked. You should have taken them over one at a time, replied [Rav Papa]. [Bar Ada:] Are you telling me that your sister's child can get them over one at a time? [Rav Papa:] People before you have made the same complaint, but no notice was taken of them.[40]

Aibu deposited some flax at Ronia's, but Shevu stole it from [Ronia] and was identified as the thief. [Ronia] appeared before Rav Nahman, who obliged him to pay.

Does this conflict with [the ruling of] Rav Huna bar Avin, for Rav Huna bar Avin transmitted [the law that] if something was forcibly stolen and the thief was discovered, the one who was looking after [the object] without payment can choose whether to take an oath [and be exempt from restitution] or sue the thief; if he was receiving payment, he must [make restitution to the owner and] sue [the thief].

Rava [explained:] A gang[41] of robbers was there who would have backed up [Shevu] if anyone had made a fuss.[42]

38. There is no point in saving the animals if he has to pay out their full value to the guard who hired people to rescue them.
39. Alternative manuscript reading: 'of Sakola'.
40. Rav Papa rejects Bar Ada's plea that it is not practical to take the animals over the bridge one at a time.
41. Obscure term. Rashi thinks it is a government official.
42. Rav Nahman held that Ronia had been careless and was therefore responsible for the theft – Rashi.

THIRD TRACTATE
BAVA BATRA
(THE LAST GATE)

This tractate covers partnerships, neighbours, usucapio, *sale of property, buying and selling, inheritance, documents and contracts.*

When a partnership is dissolved, individual items can only be divided if each partner will receive a viable portion. Mishna states that sacred scrolls may not be divided; this leads the Gemara to speculate about the origin and classification of the books of Scripture.

Books of the Bible are classified in three groups: Torah, Prophets and Writings. The order of the books of Torah was settled long before the rabbinic period, but Hebrew Bibles now follow a slightly different order from that set out here for Prophets and Writings.

CHAPTER ONE

MISHNA:

A courtyard cannot be divided [between partners who are splitting up] unless there are [at least] four cubits [square] for each, nor a field unless each receives an area sufficient to sow nine *kabs*; Rabbi Judah says, Nine half-*kabs* each. A vegetable plot must be large enough for each to sow half a *kab*; Rabbi Akiva says, A quarter. A *torcularium*,[1] a peristyle,[2] a dovecote,

11a

1. Store room (Latin).
2. So Jastrow, *Dictionary*. The word *moran* does not occur elsewhere, and manuscripts vary.

a garment, a bath-place, an olive press and an irrigated plot
must have sufficient for each. The rule is, whatever retains its
name when it is split may be divided between them, but if it
will not retain its name it may not be divided. This is if they
do not agree. If they do agree, each may take a smaller part,
but they may not divide sacred scrolls even if they agree to
do so.

GEMARA:

14b   The rabbis taught: **The order of the [books of the] Prophets
is: Joshua, Judges, Samuel, Kings, Jeremiah, Ezekiel, Isaiah,
The Twelve.** But isn't Hosea first, since it is written, THE
BEGINNING OF GOD'S WORD TO HOSEA (Hosea 1:1)? Did He
speak to Hosea first? Surely there were many prophets between
Moses and Hosea? But, said Rabbi Yoḥanan, [the verse means
that] Hosea was the first of the four prophets who prophesied
at that time, namely Hosea, Isaiah, Amos and Micah. Then why
doesn't [the book of] Hosea come first? Since his prophesies are
included [among The Twelve] with those of the last prophets,
Haggai, Zechariah and Malachi, he is placed with them. Then
why not separate his book and put it first? Because it is so short
it could be lost [if written on a separate scroll].

Now wasn't Isaiah earlier than Jeremiah and Ezekiel? Why
not put him first?[3] Kings ends with destruction, Jeremiah is
all destruction, Ezekiel begins with destruction and ends with
consolation, and Isaiah is all consolation; therefore, they put
destruction with destruction and consolation with consolation.

**The order of [books in] the Writings is Ruth, Psalms, Job,
Proverbs, Ecclesiastes, Song of Songs, Lamentations, Daniel,
Esther, Ezra,[4] Chronicles.** According to those who say that Job
was written in the days of Moses, shouldn't it come first? [No,
since] it would not be appropriate to start with suffering. But
doesn't Ruth also contain suffering? Ruth's suffering had a
[constructive] purpose, as Rabbi Yoḥanan said, Why was she
called Ruth? Because from her was descended David, who

3.   This is the order in which the books now appear.
4.   Ezra and Nehemiah were regarded as one book.

'quenched the thirst'[5] of the Holy One, blessed be He, with songs and praises.

Who wrote [the books]? Moses wrote his book including the story of Balaam,[6] and also Job; Samuel wrote his book, Judges and Ruth; David wrote the Psalms with ten elders – Adam, Melchizedek, Abraham, Moses, Heman, Jeduthun, Asaph, and the three sons of Korah;[7] Jeremiah wrote his book, Kings and Lamentations; Hezekiah and his staff wrote Isaiah, Proverbs, Songs of Songs and Ecclesiastes; the men of the Great Synod wrote Ezekiel, The Twelve, Daniel and Esther; Ezra wrote his book and the genealogy of Chronicles up to his time.

15a

> This supports Rav, for Rav Yehuda said in the name of Rav, Ezra did not come up from Babylon until he had confirmed his own genealogy. Who completed it? Nehemiah the son of Hacaliah.

A scholar said, Joshua wrote his book and eight verses of the Torah.[8] A baraita supports the view that Joshua wrote eight verses of the Torah, for it says: **AND MOSES THE SERVANT OF THE LORD DIED THERE** (Deuteronomy 34:5) – is it possible that Moses wrote, **AND MOSES . . . DIED THERE**? But Moses wrote that far, and from there onwards Joshua wrote. This is the opinion of Rabbi Judah, but some say of Rabbi Nehemiah. Rabbi Simeon ben Yoḥai said, If the Torah scroll was lacking [even] one word, how could it possibly write, **TAKE THIS TORAH SCROLL** (Deuteronomy 31:26)? So, up to here the Holy One, blessed be He, spoke, and Moses repeated it and wrote it down; from this point onwards the Holy One, blessed be He, spoke, and Moses wrote it down in tears, as we find [with Jeremiah], And Baruch said to them, **HE RECITED ALL THESE WORDS TO ME BY MOUTH, AND I WROTE THEM IN INK ON A SCROLL** (Jeremiah 36:18).

5.   He derives the name Ruth from the root RWH, 'to saturate'.
6.   'His book' is the Torah, though his name is not attached to it. The events narrated in the story of Balaam (Numbers 22–4) were unknown to Israel, so Moses could only know about them by revelation from God.
7.   All except Adam, to whom tradition assigns Psalm 92 and Melchizedek, whose name possibly occurs in Psalm 110:4, are named in superscriptions. Abraham is discussed below.
8.   Deuteronomy 34:5–12, reporting the death of Moses.

Rabbi Joshua bar Abba reported that Rav Giddel said in Rav's name: The final eight verses of the Torah must be read by one person [and not divided]? According to whom [is this]? Surely according to Rabbi Judah, not Rabbi Simeon? It may even be according to Rabbi Simeon; since they are different, a special rule applies.

Joshua wrote his book . . . But isn't it written, AND JOSHUA THE SON OF NUN, THE SERVANT OF THE LORD, DIED (Joshua 24:29)? Eleazar finished it. But isn't it written, AND ELEAZAR THE SON OF AARON DIED (Joshua 24:33)? Pinḥas finished it.

Samuel wrote his book: But isn't it written, AND SAMUEL HAD DIED (1 Samuel 28:3)? Gad the seer and Nathan the prophet finished it.

David wrote the Psalms with ten elders: Why is Ethan the Ezrahite not listed? Rav said, Ethan the Ezrahite is Abraham – here is written, ETHAN THE EZRAHITE (Psalm 89:1), and there is written, WHO AROUSED RIGHTEOUSNESS IN THE EAST, AND SUMMONED IT TO HIS SERVICE (Isaiah 41:2)?[9] But it lists both Moses and Heiman, although Rav [similarly] said, Heiman is Moses – here is written HEIMAN (Psalm 87:1), and there is written, OF ALL MY HOUSE HE IS THE MOST FAITHFUL (Numbers 12:7)?[10] There were two Heimans.

Moses wrote his book, including the story of Balaam, and also Job: This supports Rabbi Levi bar Laḥma, for Rabbi Levi bar Laḥma said, Job lived in the time of Moses – here is written, O THAT MY WORDS WERE WRITTEN DOWN; WOULD THEY WERE INSCRIBED IN A RECORD (Job 19:23 JPS), and there is written, FOR HOW SHALL IT BE KNOWN THAT YOUR PEOPLE HAVE GAINED YOUR FAVOUR (Exodus 33:16 JPS)?[11] Then why not in the time of Isaac, for it is written, WHO, THEN, CAUGHT GAME (Genesis 27:33)? Or in the time of Jacob, for it is written, IF SO, DO THIS (43:11)? Or in the time of Joseph, for it is written, WHERE ARE THEY PASTURING (37:16)? No! [The com-

9. 'Ethan' is 'the strong or righteous one'; 'Ezrahite' could mean 'who came from the East', as Abraham did.
10. Another play on words: *ne'eman* (faithful) sounds like Heiman.
11. Both verses use the emphatic particle *eifo*. However, it is not an uncommon word, so objections are raised from other verses which contain the same particle.

parison with Moses is more apt, since] it is written of Job, WOULD THEY WERE INSCRIBED IN A RECORD, and Moses is referred to as 'the inscriber', for it is written, HE SAW A BEGINNING FOR HIMSELF, FOR THERE WAS CONCEALED THE PORTION OF THE INSCRIBER (Deuteronomy 33:21).[12]

Rava said, Job lived in the time of the spies – here is written, THERE WAS A MAN IN THE LAND OF UZ (*UTZ*) CALLED JOB (Job 1:1), and there is written, WHETHER THERE ARE ANY TREES (*ETZ*) (Numbers 13:20). How can you compare them? In one place it says *utz* and in the other *etz*! Moses was telling Israel, There is a certain man whose years are long like those of a tree, and who protects his generation like a tree.

A student sat before Rav Shmuel bar Naḥmani and said, Job never existed! [The story] is a parable! [Rav Shmuel bar Naḥmani] responded, Scripture had you in mind when it stated, THERE WAS A MAN IN THE LAND OF UZ CALLED JOB! Then what about, THE POOR MAN HAD NOTHING BUT A LITTLE SHEEP WHICH HE HAD BOUGHT AND WHICH WAS, ETC. (2 Samuel 12:3)? Did that happen? Surely not; it is a parable! Here likewise it is a parable. [If that were the case,] why mention his name and the name of his town?

Rabbi Yoḥanan and Rabbi Eleazar both said, Job was among those who returned from the [Babylonian] exile, and his House of Study was in Tiberias. An objection: **Job's years were from the time Israel went down to Egypt until the Exodus.** [No problem]. It means that he lived as long as from the time Israel went down to Egypt until the Exodus.   15b

Another objection: **Seven prophets prophesied to the nations of the world, and these are they: Balaam and his father, Job, Eliphaz the Temanite, Bildad the Shuhite, Zophar the Naamathite and Elihu the son of Barachel.**[13] Are you suggesting that Elihu the son of Barachel was not Israelite? Surely [he was, for] it is written, ELIHU THE SON OF BARACHEL THE BUZITE, OF THE FAMILY OF RAM (Job 32:2); he prophesied to the nations of the world[, but he himself was an Israelite]; Job,

12. The same Hebrew word means both 'inscriber' and 'law maker'. The verse is obscure, and in any case refers to the tribe of Gad; translations vary widely.
13. The implication is that none of them, Job included, was Israelite – Rashi.

likewise, prophesied to the nations of the world[, but he himself was an Israelite].

But didn't all the prophets prophesy also to the nations of the world? [They did, but] their prophecy was directed primarily to Israel; [these seven] directed their prophecy primarily to the nations of the world.

Another objection: There was one virtuous man among the nations of the world, and he was called Job. He entered the world only to receive his reward. When the Holy One, blessed be He, brought suffering on him, he began to curse and blaspheme. The Holy One, blessed be He, doubled his reward in this world so as to remove him from the World to Come.

[Job's identity] was a topic of dispute among the Tannaim. A baraita reads: Rabbi Eleazar said, Job lived IN THE DAYS WHEN THE JUDGES JUDGED (Ruth 1:1), for it is said, ALL OF YOU HAVE SEEN IT, SO WHY TALK NONSENSE? (Job 27:12 JPS). Which generation was a generation of nonsense? Surely, the generation when the judges judged! Rabbi Joshua ben Qorḥa says, Job lived in the days of Ahasuerus, for it says, NOWHERE IN THE LAND WERE WOMEN AS BEAUTIFUL AS JOB'S DAUGHTERS TO BE FOUND (42:15 JPS). In which generation did they seek out beautiful women? In the generation of Ahasuerus.

Why didn't he say the generation of David, for it is written, AND THEY SOUGHT A BEAUTIFUL MAIDEN (1 Kings 1:3)? That was only THROUGHOUT THE BORDERS OF ISRAEL, whereas [in the time of Ahasuerus they sought] throughout the world (Esther 2:2).

[The baraita continues:] Rabbi Nathan says, Job lived in the time of the Queen of Sheba, as it is said, SHEBANS[14] ATTACKED THEM AND CARRIED THEM OFF (Job 1:15); but the Sages say, It was in the time of Chaldeans, for it is said, THE CHALDEANS FORMED THREE COLUMNS (Job 1:17). Some say that Job lived in the days of Jacob and married Jacob's daughter, Dinah; [concerning Job's wife] it is written, YOU TALK LIKE AN ABHORRENT woman! (Job 2:10), and [of Dinah it is written]

14. The usual English name is 'Sabeans'.

HE HAD COMMITTED AN *ABHORRENCE* BY LYING WITH
JACOB'S DAUGHTER (Genesis 34:7).

*The sugya continues to speculate whether Job was an Israelite,
and whether, after the death of Moses, it is possible for a Gentile
to be a prophet. Then there is serious discussion of the character
of Job and of the identity and role of Satan (the Adversary) as
set out in the prologue to Job – the image presented of Satan
contrasts strongly with his portrayal in Christian literature. The
discussion, of which an extract follows, takes the form of a
running commentary on the opening chapters of Job.*

ONE DAY THE DIVINE BEINGS PRESENTED THEMSELVES   16a
BEFORE THE LORD, AND THE ADVERSARY (*SATAN*) CAME
ALONG WITH THEM. THE LORD SAID TO THE ADVERSARY,
'WHERE HAVE YOU BEEN?' THE ADVERSARY ANSWERED THE
LORD, 'I HAVE BEEN ROAMING ALL OVER THE EARTH' (Job
1:6–7 JPS). [Satan, the Adversary,] said: Lord of the Universe!
I have roamed the whole earth and found none to match your
servant Abraham. You said to him, EXPLORE THE LAND IN ITS
LENGTH AND BREADTH, FOR I AM GIVING IT TO YOU (Genesis
13:17), but when it was time to bury Sarah, he possessed no place
in which to bury her, yet he did not question Your attributes.

THE LORD SAID TO THE ADVERSARY, 'HAVE YOU NOTICED
MY SERVANT JOB? THERE IS NO ONE LIKE HIM ON EARTH,
A BLAMELESS AND UPRIGHT MAN WHO FEARS GOD AND
SHUNS EVIL! . . . HE STILL KEEPS HIS INTEGRITY; SO YOU
HAVE INCITED ME AGAINST HIM TO DESTROY HIM FOR NO
GOOD REASON' (Job 1:8; 2:3 JPS). Rabbi Yoḥanan said, Had
this not been written in Scripture, it would have been impossible
to say it – [it is as if someone] had incited God, and He had
allowed Himself to be incited.

A baraita says: [Satan] descends, misleads [people],
ascends, threatens and receives permission to take lives.

THE ADVERSARY ANSWERED THE LORD, 'SKIN FOR SKIN
– ALL THAT A MAN HAS HE WILL GIVE UP FOR HIS LIFE. BUT
LAY A HAND ON HIS BONES AND HIS FLESH, AND HE WILL
SURELY BLASPHEME YOU TO YOUR FACE.' SO THE LORD
SAID TO THE ADVERSARY, 'SEE, HE IS IN YOUR POWER; ONLY
SPARE HIS LIFE.' THE ADVERSARY DEPARTED FROM THE

PRESENCE OF THE LORD AND INFLICTED, ETC. (Job 2:4–7 JPS). Rabbi Isaac observed, Satan was in greater difficulty than Job; he was like a servant whose master tells him, Smash the barrel, but look after the wine!

Resh Laqish said: Satan, the Evil Inclination and the Angel of Death are one and the same.

The next sugya *has been carefully crafted to articulate in dialogue form the mutual responsibilities of neighbouring landowners. No one may say, 'This is my land so I shall do what I like on it'; care must be taken to avoid harm to adjoining property.*

CHAPTER TWO

MISHNA:

17a   You may not dig a pit next to your neighbour's pit, nor a trench or a cave or a stream of water or a fuller's ditch, unless you keep at least three palms away from your neighbour's wall, and plaster [the excavation].

You must keep olive waste, dung, salt, lime and rocks at least three palms from your neighbour's wall, or else[15] plaster [the side of the ditch].

You must keep seeds, the plough and urine at least three palms from your neighbour's wall, and [your] lower millstone three palms away, that is, four palms [as measured] from the upper millstone, and [you must keep your] oven three [palms away, as measured] from the base.

GEMARA:

17b   [The Mishna] starts [by saying you should keep your distance from your neighbour's] pit, but it finishes [by saying you should keep your distance from your neighbour's] wall. Surely it should say, Keep at least three palms from your neighbour's *pit*! Abbaye, though some say Rav Yehuda, said, Mishna means the wall of his pit. In that case, let it say, Keep at least three palms from

15. Tosafot read 'and' rather than 'or else'.

the wall of your neighbour's pit! [It puts it the way it does] to teach you that a pit wall is [assumed to be] three palms thick. This has consequences for buying and selling, as a baraita teaches: **If someone says to another, I sell you the pit with its wall, the wall must be three palms thick.**

It was taught: If someone wishes to dig a pit next to his boundary,[16] Abbaye says, He may, but Rava says, He may not. If the [neighbour's] field is suitable for digging pits, they agree that he may not [dig] next to the boundary. They disagree [in a situation] where the field is unsuitable for digging pits. Abbaye says, He may [dig next to the boundary], since [the field] is unsuitable for digging pits[, and his neighbour will not, therefore, wish to dig on his side of the boundary]; Rava says, He may not [dig next to the boundary], since the neighbour may say, Just as you changed your mind [about the suitability of the land for digging pits] and dug, so may I change my mind and dig.

Others say: [Abbaye and Rava] both agree that if the field is unsuitable for digging pits, he may [dig] next to the boundary. They disagree [in the circumstance] that the field *is* suitable for digging. Abbaye says, He may [dig] next to the boundary; even according to those rabbis who hold that a tree must be planted [not less than] twenty-five cubits away from a pit, that is because at the time he planted [the tree,] the pit was [already] there, but in our case, when he digs [on one side of the boundary], there is no pit [on the other side]. Rava[, however,] says, He may not [dig] next to [the boundary]; and even according to Rabbi Yosé who says, One may dig on his own side and the other may plant on his own side; that is only in the case where, when he plants, there are not yet roots that would damage the pit, but in our case he can [complain], Every spadeful that you dig out undermines my land.

The Mishna said: **You may not dig a pit next to your neighbour's pit.** The reason is that there is a pit [on your neighbour's side of the boundary]; [it follows that] if there is no pit [on his side], you may dig one next to [the boundary].

16. And the neighbour does not have a pit on his side of the boundary – Rashi.

On the view of those who say that [Abbaye and Rava] both agree that if the field is unsuitable for digging pits, he may [dig] next to the boundary, this is all right. But on the view of those who say that [Abbaye and Rava] disagree with regard to a field that is unsuitable for digging pits, [the Mishna] would be all right for Abbaye, but it presents a difficulty for Rava. Rava might reply, [as] Abbaye, or perhaps Rav Yehuda, said, that the Mishna means 'next to your neighbour's wall'.

Another version [of the preceding]. Abbaye, or perhaps Rav Yehuda, said that the Mishna means 'next to your neighbour's wall'. On the view of those who maintain that [Abbaye and Rava] agree that if the field is suitable for digging pits, he may not [dig] next to the boundary, the Mishna deals with a field that is suitable for digging pits. But according to those who say that [Abbaye and Rava] disagree with regard to a field that is suitable for digging pits, [the Mishna] would be all right for Rava, but it presents a difficulty for Abbaye. Abbaye might reply, The Mishna deals with a case where they both wanted to dig at the same time.

Here is proof [that Abbaye's assumption that the first one to dig a pit does not have to keep three palms from the boundary] is wrong: **In friable earth**[17] **each digs on his own side of the boundary, and each keeps three palms away [from the boundary] and plasters [the pit] with lime.**

[Abbaye could reply,] Friable earth is different.

> What did whoever made the statement have in mind? He needed to mention friable earth, since you might have thought that since the earth is friable [and the pits may easily collapse], more space should be required; he informs us [that this is not so].

Another proof: **You must keep olive waste, dung, salt, lime and rocks at least three palms from your neighbour's wall, or else plaster [the side of the ditch].** The reason is that he has a wall [that would be undermined if someone dug a pit right next to it]; it follows that if there was no wall, I may dig [a pit right] next to the boundary.

17.   Literally, 'rock that comes in the hands'.

No. Even if there is no wall, you may not dig [a pit right] next to the boundary. Then what does the Mishna tell us? [Simply] that these things are a danger to the wall.

Another proof: **You must keep seeds, the plough and urine, at least three palms from your neighbour's wall.** The reason is that he has a wall [that would be undermined if such things were put right next to it]; it follows that if there is no wall, I may put [these things right] next to the boundary.

No. Even if there is no wall you may not put [such things] next to the boundary. Then what does the Mishna tell us? [Simply] that damp things endanger the wall.

Another proof: **And [your] lower millstone three palms away, that is, four palms [as measured] from the upper millstone.** The reason is that he has a wall [that would be undermined if someone put a millstone next to it]; it follows that if there is no wall, I may put [my millstone] next to the boundary.

No. Even if there is no wall you may not place [a millstone] next to the boundary. Then what does the Mishna tell us? It tells us that vibration is bad for the wall.

Another proof: **And [you must keep your] oven three [palms away, measured] from the base.** The reason is that he has a wall [that would be undermined if someone put an oven next to it]; it follows that if there is no wall, I may put [my oven] next to the boundary.

No. Even if there is no wall you may not place [an oven] next to the boundary. Then what does the Mishna tell us? It tells us that hot air is bad for the wall.

Another proof: **You should not open a bakery or a dyer's shop under someone's warehouse.** The reason is that there is a warehouse; if there is no warehouse you could [open a bakery or a dyer's shop on the premises].

[No.] Human habitation is different. If you think carefully [you will see that this is so], for it was taught in this connection, **If a cowshed preceded the warehouse, it is permissible** [to install a bakery or dyers' shop].[18]

Another proof: **You may not plant a tree near [another's**

18. That is, the primary purpose of the building was not human habitation.

field], **unless you keep it four cubits away.** In connection with this it was taught, **They said four cubits, since that it how much you need to attend to the vine.**[19] The reason is that [space must be allowed] to cultivate the vine; [so] if not for the need to cultivate the vine, you could [plant a tree] next to [the boundary], even though its roots might cause damage.

[No.] What case are we talking about here? [It is a case] where there is stony ground [between the tree and the field, preventing the roots from spreading]. There is proof for this, for the Mishna[20] states: **If there was a fence between them, each one may [plant his tree] next to the fence.**

If so, what does the end of that Mishna mean: **If its roots extended to his neighbour's land, he must [prune them to] three palms deep so that they do not interfere with the plough.** If[, as you claim] there is stony ground between them, what would he be doing with the plough?

This is what it means: If there is no stony ground [between them] and its roots extended to his neighbour's land, he must prune them three palms deep so that they do not interfere with the plough.

Another proof: **A tree must be kept [at least] twenty-five cubits away from a pit.** The reason is that there is a pit; so if there is no pit, he would be allowed [to plant the tree nearer the boundary].

No. Even if there is no pit you may not [plant a tree] next to [the boundary]. Then what does the Mishna tell us? [Simply] that the roots of a tree may damage a pit up to twenty-five cubits away.

If so, why does [the Mishna] then say, **If the tree was there first, [the owner] does not have to cut it down**? If he is never allowed to plant near the boundary, how could that happen? It is as Rav Papa said [in another connection], Where the owner purchased it; here likewise, it is [a case] where the owner purchased [the tree].

19. The vine is considered a tree in this context.
20. *Bava Batra* 26a.

The Bible's laws of inheritance are set out in Numbers 27:8–11
and Deuteronomy 21:15–17. If a man dies leaving one or more
sons, the inheritance passes to them, the first-born receiving a
double portion; daughters are excluded. If there are daughters
but no sons, the daughters inherit; if he has no children, his
brothers inherit; if he has no brothers, the inheritance passes to
his father's brothers. In each case, descendants of the putative
heir take priority over the next eligible line; for instance, if there
were no sons, but a daughter who died leaving a child of either
sex, that child would take priority over the father's brothers.

The rabbis modified this in two ways. They put a charge
on the estate, prior to inheritance, to cover the ketuba *and*
maintenance of wife and daughters. In practice, this meant that
if the estate was small, the wife and daughters would benefit
and the sons receive nothing, a point made at the beginning
of Chapter Nine. And they distinguished, as Roman law did,
between intestate inheritance and inheritance where the
deceased had made a will. Since a modification expressly con-
trary to Scripture would ipso facto *be invalid (Bava Batra 126b),*
a will could not take the form 'I appoint A or B as my heir', if
A and B were not heirs designated by the Torah; instead, the
testator had to allocate gifts from his estate to take effect during
his lifetime.

See also Bekhorot *Chapter Eight.*

CHAPTER EIGHT

MISHNA:

The only differences between son and daughter with respect   122b
to inheritance are that a [first-born] son takes a double share
of the father's estate but not of the mother's, and that daugh-
ters are maintained out of the father's estate and not out of
the mother's.

GEMARA:

What does [the Mishna] mean by **The only differences**
between son and daughter? Is it telling us that [apart from
these differences] sons and daughters have the same rights of

inheritance? [Surely not, since] the Mishna [115a] has stated, **The son has priority over the daughter, and all his descendants have priority over the daughter!**

Rav Naḥman bar Isaac says, The point the Mishna is making is that both son and daughter inherit property due [to the father but not currently in his possession], as well as property [actually] in his possession.

> But that, also, has [already] been taught by the Mishna: **The daughters of Zelophehad took three portions in the inheritance [of the Land]: their father's share among those who had made the exodus from Egypt, and the [double] share he [would have] received among his brothers when they inherited the portion of their father Hepher.**[21] Moreover, why does our Mishna say, The *only* differences?

Rav Papa said, It means: Son and daughter alike inherit their father's double share as first-born.[22]

> But that, also, is implied in the Mishna [about the daughters of Zelophehad], since it states, **The [double] share he . . . inherited [from] their father**. And again, why does our Mishna say 'The *only* differences'?

Rav Ashi said, This is what it means: No difference whether a son among sons or a daughter among daughters, if [the father] said, Let this one inherit all my possessions! his words are binding.

> According to whom [would Rav Ashi's interpretation hold good]? According to Rabbi Yoḥanan ben Baroqa. But the Mishna states that [explicitly] later [130a]: **Rabbi Yoḥanan ben Baroqa says, If he [singled out as sole heir] someone who was qualified [by the Torah] to inherit from him, his words are binding, but if [singled out as sole heir] someone who was not qualified to inherit from him, his words are not**

---

21. The Mishna (116b) implies that the daughters of Zelophehad stood to inherit whatever Hepher, who outlived his first-born son Zelophehad, would have left him. See Numbers 27:1–11 and 36:1–12.

22. If the father A, who was a first-born, died in *his* father's lifetime, A's heir, whether son or daughter, would inherit the double share due to A – Rashbam.

binding. If you suggest that here Rabbi Yoḥanan ben Baroqa's opinion is given anonymously, [there is a rule that] when an anonymous ruling is followed by the same ruling in [the context of] a dispute, the *halakha* does not follow the anonymous ruling. And again, why does our Mishna say 'The *only* differences'?

So, said Mar bar Rav Ashi, [the Mishna] must mean this: son and daughter are equally [eligible to] inherit the mother's property and the father's property, except that the [first-born] son inherits a double share of his father's property but not of his mother's.

The rabbis taught: TO GIVE HIM A DOUBLE PORTION (Deuteronomy 21:17) – That is, double what [the other sons] each receive. But perhaps it means 'double' with respect to the whole estate? You might argue: His portion [when the estate is shared with] one [brother] is double, so his portion [when shared] with five [brothers] is double [what each receives]; or you might argue: Just as he receives a double portion [that is, two-thirds of the estate] when sharing with a single brother, so he receives a double portion [namely, two-thirds of the estate] when sharing with that received by [the other] five [together]. That is why it says, IT SHALL BE, ON THE DAY HE ALLOTS INHERITANCE TO HIS SONS (Deuteronomy 21:16) – the Torah includes each and every son in the inheritance, so you cannot interpret in the latter way, but only in the former. It also states: THE SONS OF REUBEN THE FIRST-BORN OF ISRAEL. (HE WAS THE FIRST-BORN; BUT WHEN HE DEFILED HIS FATHER'S BED, HIS BIRTHRIGHT WAS GIVEN TO THE SONS OF JOSEPH SON OF ISRAEL, SO HE IS NOT RECKONED AS FIRST-BORN IN THE GENEALOGY; THOUGH JUDAH BECAME MORE POWERFUL THAN HIS BROTHERS AND A LEADER CAME FROM HIM, YET THE BIRTHRIGHT BELONGED TO JOSEPH) (1 Chronicles 5:1–2 JPS) – birthright is mentioned for Joseph, and birthright is mentioned for the generations, so just as in Joseph's case birthright was double what each received, so throughout the generations birthright is double what each receives; for [Jacob said to Joseph:] I ASSIGN TO YOU ONE PORTION MORE THAN TO YOUR BROTHERS, WHICH

123a

I WRESTED FROM THE AMORITES WITH MY SWORD AND BOW (Genesis 48:22 JPS).

Did he indeed wrest it with his sword and his bow? Surely the Psalmist says, [DECREE VICTORIES FOR JACOB . . .] I DO NOT TRUST IN MY BOW; IT IS NOT MY SWORD THAT GIVES ME VICTORY (Psalm 44:5, 7 JPS)! 'My sword' denotes prayer; 'my bow' denotes supplication.

Why It also states? You might have thought that it supported the view of Rabbi Yoḥanan ben Baroqa [that someone may designate any of those eligible as a heir], therefore it cites, THE SONS OF REUBEN THE FIRST-BORN OF ISRAEL. And in case you should think that we could not draw an inference for the term *b'khora* [birthright] from the term *b'khorato* [his birthright], he cites [the explicit statement], THE BIRTHRIGHT BELONGED TO JOSEPH. You might ask, How do we know that Joseph himself received double? So he cites, I ASSIGN TO YOU ONE PORTION MORE THAN TO YOUR BROTHERS.

Rav Papa asked Abbaye, Perhaps he just assigned him an extra date palm? Abbaye replied, For you Scripture states, EPHRAIM AND MANASSEH WILL BE TO ME AS REUBEN AND SIMEON (Genesis 48:5).

FOURTH TRACTATE
SANHEDRIN (THE COURT)

This tractate, together with Makkot, *with which it was originally joined, deals with the constitution of courts, with court
procedure, including the vetting of witnesses and the assessment
of evidence, and with punishments. The tractate is in part historical recollection, in part reconstruction from biblical sources
and in part an idealized picture of what to expect in the days of
Messiah.*

*The New Testament Gospels carry diverse descriptions of a
trial of Jesus, allegedly by a court (Sanhedrin) presided over by
the High Priest; these are neither consistent among themselves
nor collectively consistent with rabbinic sources on court procedure.[1] Were there, as has been proposed by some scholars, two
Sanhedrins, one presided over by the High Priest and another by
a 'secular' judge? This seems unlikely. In any case, how do the
Mishna's rules, formulated almost two centuries later, relate to
the actual procedures early in the first century, in the time of
Jesus?*

*The Mishna assumes a single Sanhedrin in Jerusalem, presided
over by men such as Hillel and heading up a nationwide system
of lesser courts administering Torah law as received in the days
of Moses. Chapter One deals with the system of courts, ranging
from the local court of three judges which was competent to
judge non-capital cases, through the court of twenty-three which
could judge capital cases, to the Sanhedrin, or Great Court, of
seventy-one elders, which acted as a final court of appeal and
was empowered to make decisions of national importance. If*

1. See Cohn, *Trial*, and Winter, *Trial*.

*such a system ever functioned, it was a distant memory by the
time the Mishna was compiled.*

The Yerushalmi states: It was taught: **Forty years before the
Temple was destroyed [authority to judge] capital cases was
taken away [from the Jewish justices]; in the days of Simeon ben
Yohai, [authority to judge] monetary cases was taken away.**[2]

*Whether because rabbinic ordination lapsed, or because Jew-
ish jurisdiction was constrained by the Romans, arbitration
rather than strict justice became the norm in the Jewish courts,
despite the strenuous opposition of Rabbi Eleazar and perhaps
others; a similar development took place in Christian communities, whose members preferred arbitration before the bishop and
his associates to adjudication under 'pagan' Roman law.*[3]

CHAPTER ONE

MISHNA:

2a   **Monetary cases require three [judges]. Robbery and personal injury cases require three [judges]. Damages, half-
damages, double, fourfold and fivefold damages require three
[judges].**

Rape, seduction and slander[4] **require three [judges]. This is
the view of Rabbi Meir, but the [majority] Sages say that
slander requires a court of twenty-three, seeing that it can lead
to a capital charge.**

GEMARA:

6a   Rabbi Abbahu said, Everyone agrees that if two judged a
monetary case, their judgement is invalid.

Rabbi Abba objected to Rabbi Abbahu: **[If a single judge]
rendered judgement, pronounced the guilty innocent or the**

---

2. Yerushalmi *Sanhedrin* 1:1. The printed texts have Simeon ben Shetaḥ, though the
    parallel in 7:2 reads Simeon ben Yoḥai, which would place the loss of jurisdiction
    more appropriately in the days of Hadrian. Winter, *Trial*, pp. 110–30, argues
    persuasively that Jewish courts had capital jurisdiction at least until 70 CE.
3. Harries, 'Resolving Disputes'. Refer also to the introduction to this order.
4. Specifically, the accusation that a newly married woman was not a virgin, and by
    implication had committed adultery when betrothed (Deuteronomy 22:13–21).

innocent guilty, the pure impure or the impure pure, what he has done is done, and he must compensate out of his own pocket.[5] What case is that? It is where the litigants have accepted him as judge. If so, why should he pay compensation out of his own pocket? Because they said to him, Judge us [correctly] according to the law of Torah!

Rav Safra asked Rabbi Abba, What sort of mistake did he make? If it was a matter [decided by the] Mishna, did not Rav Sheshet say in the name of Rabbi Assi: If a judge made an error in a matter [decided by the] Mishna, the judgement must be cancelled?[6] It must, therefore, be a case where the error was a matter of weighing up opinions.

What is meant by 'weighing up opinions'? Rav Papa said, If for instance two Tannaim or two Amoraim had disputed the point, the *halakha* had not been decided either way, but the standard *sugya* was in accordance with one opinion and [this judge] followed the other, that would be [an error of] 'weighing up opinions'.

Was this a dispute between Tannaim? **Rabbi Meir says, Arbitration requires three assessors; the Sages say, One is enough for agreement.** Assume that they all compare arbitration to judgement: would not the argument be that [Rabbi Meir] requires three for judgement and the others hold that two suffice? No. Everyone agrees that three are needed for judgement; the dispute here is that [Rabbi Meir] compares arbitration to judgement, but the others do not compare arbitration to judgement.

Perhaps there are three [opinions of] Tannaim with regard to arbitration: one holds that three [assessors] are necessary, one that two suffice and one that only one is required? Rav Aḥa the son of Rav Iqa – some say Rav Yeimar the son of Shelemia – said, The [Tanna] who requires two [assessors] would [in

5. 'What he has done is done' implies that the judgement was valid, if incorrect: the judge must compensate for his error, but there is no retrial. See also *Bekhorot* 28 (see p. 629).
6. Literally, 'it reverts', i.e. any money that changed hands must be returned; since the status quo is restored and a retrial required, compensation is not relevant.

principle] be satisfied with one; he requires two [only to ensure that] there are witnesses.[7]

Rav Ashi said, You may infer from this that no *qinyan* is needed [to confirm] an arbitrated agreement, since if a *qinyan* were needed, why should anyone require three [assessors]? It would be enough to have two to effect the *qinyan*.

The *halakha* is [nevertheless] that an arbitrated agreement does need a *qinyan*.[8]

6b
The rabbis taught: **Just as judgement requires three, so arbitration requires three. Once judgement has been delivered, arbitration is not permissible.**

Rabbi Eleazar the son of Rabbi Yosé the Galilean says, It is forbidden to compromise; whoever makes a compromise sins, and whoever congratulates the compromiser insults [the law] – of such a one Scripture says, THE LORD DESPISES ONE WHO CONGRATULATES THE COMPROMISER (Psalm 10:3).[9] **Rather, let judgement pierce the mountain, as it is said, FOR JUDGEMENT IS OF GOD** (Deuteronomy 1:17).

Moses said, Let judgement pierce the mountain, but Aaron loved peace and pursued peace and reconciled men with one another, as it is said, THE LAW OF TRUTH WAS IN HIS MOUTH, AND INIQUITY WAS NOT FOUND ON HIS LIPS; HE WALKED WITH ME IN PEACE AND EQUITY, AND TURNED MANY AWAY FROM SIN (Malachi 2:6).[10]

Rabbi Joshua ben Qorḥa says, It is a *mitzva* to arbitrate, as it is said, JUDGE WITHIN YOUR GATES WITH TRUTH AND PEACEFUL JUDGEMENT (Zechariah 8:16) – surely, where there is judgement there is no peace,[11] and where there is peace there is no judgement – But what judgement really does offer peace? Arbitration!

7. The assessors may act as witnesses.
8. This sentence is presumably a later insertion, possibly Geonic.
9. The verse is obscure; other translations include 'The covetous blesseth himself when he praiseth the Lord.'
10. Some lines are omitted here; they interpret Psalm 10:3 in ways not relevant to this topic.
11. i.e. there is always an aggrieved party, whereas with arbitration both parties agree to the compromise, so none is aggrieved.

Local courts of three trying minor cases were often ad hoc groups of citizens.

CHAPTER THREE

MISHNA:

Monetary cases [are tried] by [a court of] three [judges].   23a
One [litigant] chooses one, the other [litigant] chooses one
and the two [together] choose another. This is Rabbi Meir's
opinion, but the [majority of] Sages say, The two judges
[together] choose another.

Each may reject the other's judge. This is Rabbi Meir's
opinion, but the [majority of] Sages say, Where does this
apply? If he has proof that [the judges] are related [to the
litigants] or [otherwise] unfit; but if they are fit, or certified as
competent by an [established] court, he cannot reject them.

Each may reject the other's witnesses. This is Rabbi Meir's
opinion, but the [majority of] Sages say, Where does this
apply? If he has proof that [the witnesses] are related [to the
litigants] or [otherwise] unfit; but if they are fit, he cannot
reject them.

GEMARA:

What is the meaning of **One [litigant] chooses one, the other
[litigant] chooses one and the two choose another?**[12] Are not
three [judges] sufficient? It means, When one chooses one court
and the other chooses a different court, they must choose a third
court together;[13] even the borrower can insist.

> Didn't Rabbi Eleazar say that [the Tannaim]
> allowed only the lender to insist, but the borrower is
> obliged to appear [before the court] in [the lender's]
> town? It must be as Rabbi Yoḥanan said, The Mishna
> is dealing here with *archai*[14] in Syria, but [the law]
> does not apply to expert courts. Rav Papa said, It could

12. The assumption at this point is that 'chooses one' means 'chooses one court'.
13. Neither can force the other to accept his choice of court – Rashi.
14. A Greek term for courts, here applied to Jewish courts inexpert in rabbinic law.

even refer to expert courts like those of Rav Huna and
Rav Ḥisda [which are both in the same town – Rashi[15]],
for he can say, I am not putting you to any trouble [by
requesting a hearing before the other court].

But the Mishna stated [explicitly], **The Sages say, The two
judges choose another.** If the meaning was as you have suggested,
how could it be that the courts, having each been rejected [by
a litigant], could choose a third? Also, how do you understand,
One [litigant] chooses *one*, the other [litigant] chooses *one*?
Surely what [the Mishna] means is the following: Each litigant
chooses a judge, and the two [together] choose a third.

What is the point of doing it that way? In the West they said
in the name of Rabbi Zeira, Since each chooses a judge and
between them they choose a third, true justice will ensue.

*Much of this tractate is devoted to the procedures associated
with capital punishment, which Scripture demands for a wide
range of offences. The occupying Romans reserved to themselves
the right to inflict capital punishment, but this alone would
not explain the rabbinic aversion, most strongly articulated in
Makkot 7a (see Chapter One (see pp. 520–21)). The extraordinary homily here indicates that the rabbis accepted in principle
that there were circumstances in which, given effective jurisdiction, criminals and sinners might be executed, but were acutely
aware of the need for careful scrutiny of the evidence; circumstantial evidence would not be acceptable.*

CHAPTER FOUR

MISHNA:

37a   **How do we impress on witnesses the gravity of the situation?[16] Witnesses in capital cases would be brought [before
the court] and alerted: Are you relying on conjecture? Did
someone tell you what another person said? Are you aware**

15. The Tosafot demur.
16. More literally, 'How do we frighten the witnesses?'

that we will question you in great detail? You should understand that capital cases are not like monetary cases. In monetary cases, the guilty party pays and is forgiven; in capital cases
his blood and the blood of his descendants for all time depends upon [the outcome]. We find with Cain, who killed
his brother, that Scripture says, YOUR BROTHER'S BLOODS
[plural] CRY OUT TO ME (Genesis 4:10) – not your brother's
blood [singular], but bloods, his blood and that of all his
descendants. (Another way to explain 'bloods' is that his blood
was spilled on sticks and stones.) Adam was created alone to
teach you that if anyone destroys one life,[17] Scripture reckons
it as if he had destroyed a whole world; conversely, if anyone
preserves one life, Scripture reckons it as if he had preserved a
whole world. [The creation of one common ancestor] also leads
to peace among people, for no man can say, My ancestor was
greater than yours. It also refutes heretics who say that there are
many Powers in heaven, and it demonstrates the greatness of
the Holy One, blessed be He – when a man mints several coins
in one mould, they emerge identical with one another, but
when the king of kings of kings,[18] the Holy One, blessed be He,
formed all men in the mould of Adam, none [exactly] resembled
another. Therefore a man should say, The world was created for
me![19] If[, on the other hand,] you should think, Why should we   37b
risk all this trouble? Scripture has said, AND HE IS A WITNESS
WHO SAW OR KNEW, AND IF HE DOES NOT TESTIFY HE INCURS
GUILT (Leviticus 5:1). Should you still say, How can we take
responsibility for this man's blood? Scripture says, THERE IS
JOY WHEN THE WICKED PERISH (Proverbs 11:10).

GEMARA:

The rabbis taught: What is meant by 'conjecture'? If you saw
someone enter a ruin and you ran after him and found him
with a sword in his hand dripping with blood and a slain man
in agony, you have seen nothing.[20]

---

17. The words 'of Israel' appear in some copies, but manuscript evidence as well as
    the sense of the passage suggest that this is a very late interpolation.
18. The Shah styled himself 'king of kings'; God is greater.
19. This should inspire him with a sense of gratitude and responsibility.
20. This is circumstantial and does not count as evidence.

A baraita states: **Rabbi Simeon ben Shetaḥ said, May I see consolation**[21] if I did not see a man pursue another into a ruin, and I ran after him and saw the sword in his hand dripping blood and a slain man in agony, and I said to him, You wicked man! Who killed this person? It was either you or me! But what can I do? The matter is not within my power, for the Torah states, HE IS PUT TO DEATH ON THE TESTIMONY OF TWO WITNESSES; [HE MUST NOT BE PUT TO DEATH ON THE TESTIMONY OF A SINGLE WITNESS] (Deuteronomy 17:6). He Who knows the thoughts of men will punish the one who slew his fellow!

They say, they had not departed the place before a snake came and bit [the murderer] and he died.

Two Mishnas are needed as the basis for the next Gemara extract, one of very few passages in the Talmud to refer explicitly to Jesus.[22]

CHAPTER SIX

MISHNA:

42b When the verdict was reached, they would take him out for stoning. The place of execution was close by the court, for it is said, TAKE OUT THE BLASPHEMER FROM THE CAMP (Leviticus 24:14).

[An officer] stands at the court door holding a flag, and a horseman remains within sight. If anyone says, I have something to say in his favour, [the officer] waves his flag and the horseman gallops to halt [the execution]. Even if [the accused] says, I have something to say in my favour, they bring him back, as many as four or five times, provided there is sense in what he says.

MISHNA:

43a If they find in his favour, they set him free, but if not, he is taken to be stoned.

---

21. A mild oath. The title 'Rabbi' for Simeon is an anachronism.
22. See Introduction, 'The Talmud and Christianity'.

A herald goes before him [and proclaims]: So-and-so is on his way to be stoned for such-and-such an offence, and so-and-so are the witnesses against him. Will anyone who knows anything in his favour come forward and plead for him!

GEMARA:

Abbaye said, [The herald] must also proclaim the day, the time and the place, for there may be someone who knows [that the witnesses were elsewhere] and can refute them.

A herald goes before him. Before him, but not earlier? Does not a baraita state: Jesus of Nazareth was hanged on Passover Eve. A herald went out for forty days [prior to the execution, proclaiming:] Jesus of Nazareth is to be executed by stoning for witchcraft and for leading Israel astray [to idolatry]. Will anyone who knows anything in his favour come forward and plead for him! They found nothing in his favour, so he was hanged on Passover Eve.

Ulla said, What sort of a question is that? Was Jesus of Nazareth a person for whom favourable arguments would be sought? He led people astray, and [of such a person] the Torah says, YOU SHALL NOT HAVE PITY NOR COVER UP FOR HIM (Deuteronomy 13:9). [Answer:] Jesus was [treated] differently since he was close to the government.

Roman law distinguished between ius civile, *the law applicable to Roman citizens, and* ius gentium, *the law applicable to* peregrini, *that is, to other free persons under Roman rule. Likewise, in Jewish law, there is a distinction between 'Israelites', that is, persons recognized as Jewish, and Gentiles, here called 'children of Noah'. The Talmud holds that Noahides are subject to a restricted range of law, known as the 'laws of Noah'; all human beings are descendants of Adam through Noah and therefore subject to the laws addressed to him (Genesis 2:16), as well as to God's covenant with Noah after the flood (Genesis 9).*[23]

The concept of Noahide law carries significant consequences

23. Theories of the origin and nature of 'Noahide law' are fully reviewed in Novak, *Image*.

for Jewish theology: it means that the essential Jewish 'mission'
is not to convert Gentiles to Judaism in its fullest form, but to
lead them to implement the Noahide commandments, a basic
programme for social justice in a spiritual setting; and it allows
for a positive evaluation of other religions, provided they
endorse the Noahide commandments.

The number and precise definition of the Noahide command-
ments are discussed here.

CHAPTER SEVEN

56a   The rabbis taught: **The children of Noah were given Seven**
Commandments: laws, blasphemy, idolatry, sexual immor-
ality, bloodshed, theft and [eating] the limb of a living [ani-
56b   **mal]. Rabbi Ḥanania ben Gamaliel says, Also blood of a living**
[animal]. Rabbi Ḥidqa says, Also castration [of animals]. Rabbi
Simeon says, Also witchcraft. Rabbi Yosé says, Noahides are
also forbidden to do whatever is listed in the passage about
witchcraft: [WHEN YOU ENTER THE LAND THAT THE LORD
YOUR GOD IS GIVING YOU, YOU SHALL NOT LEARN TO IMI-
TATE THE ABHORRENT PRACTICES OF THOSE NATIONS.] LET
NO ONE BE FOUND AMONG YOU WHO CONSIGNS HIS SON OR
DAUGHTER TO THE FIRE, OR WHO IS AN AUGUR, A SOOTH-
SAYER, A DIVINER, A SORCERER, ONE WHO CASTS SPELLS, OR
ONE WHO CONSULTS GHOSTS OR FAMILIAR SPIRITS, OR ONE
WHO ENQUIRES OF THE DEAD. FOR . . . IT IS BECAUSE OF
THESE ABHORRENT THINGS THAT THE LORD YOUR GOD IS
DISPOSSESSING THEM BEFORE YOU (Deuteronomy 18:9–12
JPS) – **He would not punish them if He had not forbidden**
them [such practices]. Rabbi Eleazar said, Also forbidden mix-
tures – Noahides are allowed to wear and sow forbidden
mixtures; they are only forbidden to crossbreed animals and
to graft trees [of different species].[24]

What [verse are the Noahide Commandments] based on?
Rabbi Yoḥanan said, They are derived from the verse, **AND**

24. This and some of the other baraitot cited are an expansion of Tosefta *Avoda Zara*
    Chapter 9. On forbidden mixtures see *Kil'ayim*.

THE LORD GOD COMMANDED THE MAN SAYING, 'FROM THE TREES OF THE GARDEN YOU MAY SURELY EAT' (Genesis 2:16) –

COMMANDED[25] refers to laws, as it is said, FOR I HAVE KNOWN HIM, THAT HE SHOULD COMMAND HIS SONS, ETC. (18:19).

THE LORD refers to [the prohibition of] blasphemy, as it is said, HE WHO PRONOUNCES THE NAME OF THE LORD SHALL BE PUT TO DEATH (Leviticus 24:16).

GOD refers to [the prohibition of] idolatry, as it is said, YOU SHALL HAVE NO OTHER GODS (Exodus 20:3).

THE MAN refers to bloodshed, as it is said, HE WHO SPILLS THE BLOOD OF MAN, BY MAN SHALL HIS BLOOD BE SPILLED (Genesis 9:6).

SAYING refers to sexual immorality, as it is said, SAYING, SHOULD A MAN SEND AWAY HIS WIFE AND SHE BECOMES [THE WIFE] OF ANOTHER MAN (Jeremiah 3:1).

FROM THE TREES OF THE GARDEN – but not from stolen [fruit].

YOU MAY SURELY EAT – but not of a limb [torn] from a living [animal].

When Rabbi Isaac came [to Babylonia], he reversed [two of the inferences. He said]: COMMANDED refers to idolatry; GOD refers to laws. GOD refers to laws, for it is written, THE OWNER OF THE HOUSE SHALL DEPOSE BEFORE GOD (Exodus 22:7 JPS). But how does COMMANDED suggest idolatry? Rav Ḥisda and Rav Avdimi [discussed this]: one of them said, THEY HAVE BEEN QUICK TO STRAY FROM THE PATH THAT I COMMANDED THEM[; THEY HAVE MADE THEM-SELVES A GOLDEN CALF] (Exodus 32:8); the other said, EPHRAIM IS OPPRESSED, CRUSHED BY INJUS-TICE, FOR HE HAS WILLINGLY PURSUED FUTILITY (Hosea 5:11). What difference does it make [which verse is invoked]? If a Gentile made an idol but did not worship it, according to the one who cites THEY HAVE MADE, he would be guilty; according to the one

25. Hebrew syntax places this verb first in the sentence.

who cites **THEY PURSUED**, he would not be guilty
unless he sought it out and worshipped it.

Rava asked, Does anyone actually hold
that if a Gentile made an idol but did not
worship it, he would be held guilty? A baraita
states, **With regard to idolatry, a Noahide is
held guilty for those offences for which an
Israelite, should he commit them, would be
put to death; he is not held guilty for those
offences for which an Israelite, should he
commit them, would not be put to death.**
What does this exclude? Surely it excludes
the case where the Gentile made an idol but
did not worship it. Rava Papa said, No; it
excludes embracing or kissing the idol. What
sort of embracing or kissing? If embracing or
kissing is the normal way [to worship the
idol], he would be liable to the death penalty;
what is excluded is embracing or kissing that
is not the normal way [to worship that idol].

Are Noahides really commanded about [civil and criminal]
laws? A baraita states: **Israel were given ten commandments at
Marah: the seven accepted by Noahides and in addition [civil
and criminal] laws, the Sabbath, and honouring father and
mother. Laws, as it is written, THERE HE GAVE THEM STAT-
UTES AND JUDGEMENTS, AND THERE HE TESTED THEM**
(Exodus 15:25); **the Sabbath and honouring father and mother,
for it is written, AS THE LORD YOUR GOD COMMANDED YOU**
(Deuteronomy 5:12 and 16); **and Rav Yehuda said that referred
to [what had taken place at] Marah.**

Rav Naḥman said in the name of Rabba bar Abbuha, [The
reference to additional laws at Marah] was needed to cover
courts and testimony and prior warning. If so, what is the
meaning of **in addition [civil and criminal] laws**[, seeing there
were no new laws]? So Rava said, It was needed to cover fines.
Even so, what is the meaning of **in addition laws**? So Rav Aḥa
bar Jacob said, It was needed to cover the commandment to
Israelites to set up courts in every city and every town.

But don't Noahides have to do that, too? A baraita states: **Just as Israel must set up courts in every city and every town, so must Noahides set up courts in every city and every town.**

Rava therefore said, This Tanna is of the School of Manasseh, who exclude blasphemy and laws, and include castration and mixtures. For it was taught in the School of Manasseh, **The children of Noah were given Seven Commandments: idolatry, sexual immorality, bloodshed, theft, the limb of a living [animal], castration and mixtures. Rabbi Judah says, Adam was given only the commandment against idolatry, as it is said, AND THE LORD GOD COMMANDED *ADAM*;**[26] **Rabbi Judah ben Bathyra says, [He was given] also [the commandment concerning] blasphemy; some say, Also laws.**

According to whom is the statement attributed to Rav Yehuda in the name of Rav: I AM GOD – do not revile Me; I AM GOD – do not exchange Me [for other gods]; I AM GOD – let fear of Me be upon you! It is according to 'some say'.[27]

If the Tanna of the School of Manasseh is interpreting [the verse], AND THE LORD GOD COMMANDED, he should have included the other [two commandments]; if he is not interpreting it, on what does he base [those he lists]? He does not interpret that verse, but bases each one on its own verse. Idolatry and sexual immorality derive from, AND THE EARTH WAS CORRUPT BEFORE GOD (Genesis 6:11); it was taught in Rabbi Ishmael's school that wherever corruption is mentioned, it refers to idolatry and sexual immorality – sexual immorality, for it is written, FOR ALL FLESH HAD CORRUPTED ITS WAY ON THE EARTH (Genesis 6:12); idolatry, for it is written, LEST YOU ACT CORRUPTLY AND MAKE IMAGES (Deuteronomy 4:16). (The others say that the verse merely explains the way of these things.) Bloodshed derives from the verse, HE WHO SPILLS THE BLOOD OF MAN, BY MAN SHALL HIS BLOOD BE SPILLED (Genesis 9:6). (The others say that the verse reveals how they are to be excuted.) Theft is derived from, I GRANT YOU EVERYTHING, AS THE

57a

---

26. *Adam* means 'the man'.
27. The statement, based on the word 'God' addressed to Adam, implies both the prohibition of blasphemy and obedience to the law – Rashi.

GREEN PLANTS (Genesis 9:3) – Rabbi Levi observed, As the [wild] green plants, not as the plants of a [private] garden. (The others say that this verse is to permit the consumption of meat.) [The prohibition of eating] a limb torn from a living animal is derived from the verse, **BUT YOU SHALL NOT EAT MEAT WITH ITS LIFE-BLOOD** (Genesis 9:4). (The others say that the verse permits [Noahides] to eat swarming creatures.) Castration, from the verse, **SWARM THOUGHOUT THE EARTH, AND INCREASE UPON IT** (Genesis 9:7). (The others say that the verse is simply a blessing.) Mixtures, from the verse, **FROM BIRDS, ACCORDING TO THEIR KIND** (Genesis 6:20). (The others say that that was just to ensure suitable company.)

Violence is not condoned for religious purposes, for instance to prevent Sabbath desecration or idolatry, but is mandatory if required to save a victim from an aggressor; sexual aggression, whether homosexual or heterosexual, is ranked with murder.

CHAPTER EIGHT

MISHNA:

73a   These are prevented[28] [from sin] even at the cost of their life: someone who is pursuing another to kill him, or a man who is pursuing another male or a betrothed woman [for sex];[29] but if someone is pursuing a beast [for sex], or intending to desecrate the Sabbath or to worship idols, you do not prevent them [from sin] at the cost of their life.

GEMARA:

The rabbis taught: **How do we know that if someone is pursuing someone else with the intent of killing that you may save him at the cost of [the pursuer's] life? This is what we learn from YOU SHALL NOT STAND BY YOUR BROTHER'S BLOOD** (Leviticus 19:16).

Is that what the verse is for? Surely it is for what a baraita

28. Literally, 'saved'.
29. These are the limiting cases; it is obvious that, for instance, a married woman should be rescued in similar circumstances.

teaches: **How do we know that if you see someone drowning in the sea, or about to be dragged away by a wild animal or attacked by robbers, that you should rescue him? This is what is meant by** You shall not stand by your brother's blood.[30]

That is correct. The question is, how do we know that you may rescue even at the cost of [the aggressor's] life? This is inferred a fortiori from the case of the betrothed girl: if, in the case of the betrothed girl, who stands only to have a stain on her reputation, the Torah says that you should save her at the cost of the aggressor's life, how much more [is this justified] where someone is about to kill another person?

But can you impose a penalty on the basis of a logical inference? [No.] It is an analogy: [To the girl you shall do nothing; she has committed no mortal sin.] For as when a man rises against his neighbour to slay him, just so is this matter (Deuteronomy 22:26). The verse comes to teach us something, but itself 'learns'. It compares a murderer to [someone who rapes] a betrothed girl; just as you may save the betrothed girl at the expense of the attacker's life, so you may save a [potential] murder victim at the expense of the attacker's life.

But how do we know [that you may save] the betrothed girl [at the expense of the attacker's life]? That is what was taught in the School of Rabbi Ishmael, for it was taught in the School of Rabbi Ishmael, And there was none to save her (Deuteronomy 22:27); **but if someone was in a position to save her, he could use any means [necessary].**

Further discussion leads on to the topic of martyrdom.[31]

Rabbi Yoḥanan said in the name of Rabbi Simeon ben Yehotzedeq, They voted conclusively in the upper chamber of Beit Nitzé in Lydda that if someone is threatened with death unless he disobeys a commandment of the Torah, he should transgress rather than submit to death, except in the cases of idolatry, sexual immorality and bloodshed.

74a

---

30. This literal translation fits better than 'Do not profit by the blood of your fellow' (JPS), or 'Neither shalt thou stand against the blood of thy neighbour' (KJV).
31. See also *Ta'anit* 29a (see p. 528).

Then he should not worship idols [even on pain of death]? But a baraita states: **Rabbi Ishmael said, How do we know that if they said to someone, Worship idols or be killed, he should worship and not be killed? It says, YOU SHALL LIVE BY THEM [My laws]** (Leviticus 18:5) – you shall not die by them. Would this be the case even if it was in public? [No!] That is why it says, YOU SHALL NOT PROFANE MY HOLY NAME, FOR I SHALL BE SANCTIFIED (Leviticus 22:32).

[The rabbis at Lydda] were following Rabbi Eliezer, as a baraita states: **Rabbi Eliezer says, YOU SHALL LOVE THE LORD YOUR GOD WITH ALL YOUR HEART, WITH ALL YOUR LIFE AND WITH ALL YOUR WEALTH**[32] (Deuteronomy 6:5) – **If it says WITH ALL YOUR LIFE, why does it say WITH ALL YOUR WEALTH, and if it says WITH ALL YOUR WEALTH, why does it say WITH ALL YOUR LIFE? For someone who values his life more than his property, it says, WITH ALL YOUR LIFE; for someone who values his property more than his life, it says, WITH ALL YOUR WEALTH.**

Sexual immorality and bloodshed [are forbidden on pain of death], as Rabbi said, for a baraita reads: **Rabbi says: FOR THIS MATTER IS AS WHEN A MAN RISES AGAINST HIS NEIGHBOUR TO SLAY HIM** (Deuteronomy 22:26). **What do we learn from [the case of] the murderer? The verse comes to teach us something, but itself 'learns'. It compares a murderer to [someone who rapes] a betrothed girl; just as you may save the betrothed girl at the expense of the attacker's life, so you may save a [potential] murder victim at the expense of the attacker's life; and it compares [someone who rapes] a betrothed girl to a murderer; just as you should be killed rather than commit murder, so should you be killed rather than [have sex with a] betrothed girl.**

How do we know that you should be killed rather than kill someone else? By reason. A man came before Rava and said, The mayor of my town ordered me to kill somebody, and [said] he would kill me if I didn't do it. Rava replied, You must let

---

32. The words translated 'life' and 'wealth' are often translated here as 'soul' and 'might' or 'strength'.

him kill you rather than you kill another person. What makes you think your blood is redder than the other's? Perhaps his blood is redder!

When Rav Dimi came [to Babylonia], he said in Rabbi Yohanan's name, All this is if it is not a time of official [persecution], but in times when the government is persecuting [Jews], you must be killed rather than transgress even a small *mitzva*.

When Rav Ravin came [to Babylonia], he said in Rabbi Yohanan's name, All this applies only in private, but if it is in public you must be killed rather than transgress even a small *mitzva*.

The final chapter (in the Mishna it is placed tenth) is a vast storehouse of aggada. It opens with the closest approach anywhere in classical rabbinic literature to a defined creed; Maimonides, in his Arabic Commentary on the Mishna composed around 1160, introduced at this point his influential Thirteen Principles of the Faith.

Several pages are devoted to the Messiah (mashiah means 'anointed'), a Davidic monarch who will preside over a world of peace and spirituality; he is not, as Christians understand him, an incarnation of God. The extract here occurs in the course of speculation as to when the Messiah is to be expected. The idea of a fixed framework of 6,000 or 7,000 years for the history of the world has roots in earlier Jewish literature; among Christians it led to the development of millenarianism.[33]

33.   The idea of a predetermined number of jubilee (fifty-year) cycles is found in Jubilees 1:29; 23:14–21, and of a temporary Messianic kingdom in 2 Baruch 24–27. 2 Enoch 33:1 states that the world will last 7,000 years, and the eighth millennium will be 'a time of no-counting, endless, with neither years nor months nor weeks nor days nor hours' (Charles, *Apocrypha*, p. 451). Revelation 20:6 predicts a thousand-year reign of Christ and his saints, and Augustine develops the idea for a Christian interpretation of history in *City of God* 22:30:5.

CHAPTER ELEVEN

MISHNA:

90a   All Israelites have a share in the World to Come,[34] as it is said, AND YOUR PEOPLE WILL ALL BE RIGHTEOUS; THEY WILL INHERIT THE LAND FOREVER: THE BRANCH THAT I HAVE PLANTED, THE WORK OF MY HANDS, OF WHOM I SHALL BE PROUD (Isaiah 60:21). But these have no share in the World to Come: one who denies that resurrection [of the dead] is [indicated] in the Torah; one who denies that the Torah is from Heaven; an Epicurean. Rabbi Aqiva says, Anyone who reads non-canonical writings. Also, anyone who casts spells on a wound, saying, I WILL PUT NONE OF THESE DISEASES I INFLICTED ON THE EGYPTIANS ON YOU, FOR I THE LORD AM YOUR HEALER (Exodus 15:26). Abba Saul says, Also anyone who utters[35] the four-lettered Name of God.

Three kings and four commoners have no share in the World to Come. The three kings are Jeroboam, Ahab and Manasseh, but Rabbi Judah said Manasseh does have a share in the World to Come, for it is said, HE PRAYED TO [THE LORD], AND HE GRANTED HIS PRAYER, HEARD HIS PLEA, AND RETURNED HIM TO JERUSALEM TO HIS KINGDOM (2 Chronicles 33:13 JPS); [the other rabbis said,] He restored him to his kingdom, but not to the World to Come. The four commoners are Balaam, Doeg, Achitophel and Gehazi.

GEMARA:

97a   It was taught in the School of Elijah: **The world is to last for 6,000 years; 2,000 desolate, 2,000 Torah and 2,000 of the**
97b   **Messiah. On account of our sins there have already elapsed those [years] that have elapsed.**[36]

---

34. That is, life after death.
35. Or 'meditates upon'. The four-lettered Name is the Name as written in the Bible but not pronounced other than by the High Priest in the Holy of Holies on the Day of Atonement.
36. The conventional Jewish calculation, based on the Tannaitic tract *Seder Olam*, starts 244 years later than the calculation published by Bishop Ussher in 1650 and familiar to Christians; on the Jewish calculation, the year 4000 from Creation

Elijah told Rav Yehuda, the brother of Rav Sala the Pious, The world will have not less than 85 Jubilee cycles, and the son of David will appear in the last one.[37] [Rav Yehuda] asked, At the beginning or the end [of the cycle]? He replied, I don't know. Will it be completed or not? I don't know.

> Rav Ashi said, What [Elijah] told him was: Don't expect [the Messiah] before this time, but from this time on, look out for him.

Rav Ḥanan bar Taḥlifa sent to Rav Yosef: I met a man carrying a scroll written in the holy tongue in Assyrian script.[38] I asked him where he got it from, and he told me he had been a Roman mercenary and found it in a storehouse in Rome. In it was written: 4,291 years after the creation of the world, the world will cease;[39] there will be wars among the sea-monsters, and the wars of Gog and Magog, and after that the days of the Messiah. The Holy One, blessed be He, will not renew His world until after 7,000 years.[40] (Rava's son, Rav Aḥa, said, The correct reading is 5,000 years.)

It was taught: **Rabbi Nathan said, This verse penetrates to the depths: FOR THERE IS YET A VISION FOR THE APPOINTED TIME; IT PUFFS AT THE END, AND DOES NOT DECEIVE; THOUGH HE TARRY, WAIT FOR HIM; BECAUSE HE WILL CER-TAINLY COME, HE WILL NOT DELAY** (Habakkuk 2:3).[41] It is not as our rabbis [thought], who interpreted, UNTIL A TIME, AND TIMES AND HALF A TIME (Daniel 7:25); nor as Rabbi Simlai [thought], who interpreted, YOU FED THEM WITH THE BREAD

---

would have coincided with 240 CE. The millenarian statement was probably formulated first, and the final comment added after 240 when the expected deliverance failed to materialize.

37. 85 Jubilees are 4,200 years, so around 440 CE.
38. *Megilla* 8b (see p. 268).
39. Or, 'will be orphaned'.
40. The text is clearly corrupt. However, apocalyptic scrolls of this type, notably some *Sybilline Oracles*, are included in the Jewish Pseudepigrapha, and a collection of them was indeed stored in Rome.
41. Habakkuk 2 is interpreted apocalyptically in the Dead Sea Scrolls. The word translated 'puff' to fit the wordplay that follows is generally translated 'speaks' (e.g. KJV); it derives from a root meaning 'to blow', and is used of boastful or exaggerated speech and also of breaking wind.

OF TEARS AND GAVE THEM PLENTIFUL TEARS TO DRINK
(Psalm 80:6); nor as Rabbi Aqiva [thought], who interpreted,
JUST A LITTLE, THEN I SHALL SHAKE THE HEAVENS, THE
EARTH, THE SEA AND THE DRY LAND (Haggai 2:6) – but the
first kingdom was 70 years, the second kingdom 52, and the
kingdom of Bar Koziba two and a half years.[42]

What does IT PUFFS AT THE END, AND DOES NOT DECEIVE
really mean? [It means:] may those who calculate the end time
puff [their last] breath! For they say, Since the appointed time
has come and [the Messiah] has not arrived, he will never come!
But keep up your hope, as it is said, THOUGH HE TARRY, WAIT
FOR HIM. Should you think, We await him, but he does not
await [us], Scripture says, AND THEREFORE WILL THE LORD
WAIT, THAT HE MAY BE GRACIOUS TO YOU, AND THEREFORE
WILL HE BE EXALTED[, THAT HE MAY HAVE MERCY UPON
YOU; FOR THE LORD IS A GOD OF JUDGEMENT; BLESSED ARE
ALL THEY THAT WAIT FOR HIM] (Isaiah 30:18). If we are
waiting for him and he is waiting for us, what stops him coming?
The [divine] Attribute of Justice stops him. If the Attribute of
Justice stands in the way, why do we wait [in hope]? In waiting
there is reward,[43] as it is said, BLESSED ARE ALL THEY THAT
WAIT FOR HIM.

Abbaye said, There are never fewer than thirty-six virtuous
men worthy to receive the *Shekhina* in each generation, as it is
written, BLESSED ARE ALL THEY THAT WAIT FOR HIM – the
numerical value of 'they that wait for' is thirty-six.

Can that be right? Didn't Rava say that the generation who
stand before the Holy One, blessed be He, is 18,000 strong,
as it is said, EIGHTEEN THOUSAND[44] ROUND ABOUT (Ezekiel
48:35)? No problem – [The thirty-six] behold Him as in a clear
glass, the 18,000 behold Him in a glass that is not clear.

But didn't Hezekiah report that Rav Yirmiya said in the name
of Rabbi Simeon bar Yoḥai, I have seen those who will ascend

---

42. Rashi cites his teacher's opinion that these short-lived ('just a little') kingdoms are
    periods of Jewish independence under, respectively, the Hasmoneans, Herod and
    Bar Koziba (Bar Kokhba); Aqiva supported Bar Kokhba's revolt.
43. Awaiting the Messiah is itself a virtue.
44. KJV inserts 'measures' and JPS 'cubits', but neither word is in the Hebrew.

and they are few; if there are a thousand, I and my son are among them; if a hundred, I and my son are among them; if only two, they are my son and I. No problem; these ascend to [the Divine Presence only] with permission; those [do not require] permission.

Rav said, All the end-times have passed, and the matter now depends only on penitence and good deeds; Shmuel said, Let it suffice for the mourner to mourn!

This is like [the dispute of] the Tannaim: **Rabbi Eliezer said, If Israel repent, they will be redeemed, and if not, they will not be redeemed. Rabbi Joshua responded, If Israel do not repent, they will not be redeemed, but the Holy One, blessed be He, will set over them a king whose decrees are as cruel as those of Haman, so they will repent and return to the good path.**

FIFTH TRACTATE
MAKKOT (FLOGGING)

The tractate opens with a case of false testimony:

**IF A MAN APPEARS AGAINST ANOTHER TO TESTIFY MALICIOUSLY
. . . IF HE HAS TESTIFIED FALSELY AGAINST HIS FELLOW, YOU
SHALL DO TO HIM AS HE INTENDED TO DO TO HIS FELLOW.**
(Deuteronomy 19:16, 18–19)

*If two pairs of witnesses give conflicting testimony, why pre-
fer the testimony of one pair over the other? Moreover, it may
not be possible to do to the witnesses what they schemed to
do to the accused; if, for instance, they testified that someone
claiming to be a* Kohen *was the son of a divorcee, hence
excluded from the priesthood, what punishment could you
inflict on a witness who was not a* Kohen? *Even if the witness
was a* Kohen, *would it be right to debar him from the priesthood, seeing that this punishment would affect his descendants
too?*

*The conflicting testimony problem was dealt with by confin-
ing the rule to a case that did not involve direct contradiction,
namely where the second pair of witnesses testified that the first
pair had been with them at another location at the time of the
alleged crime, so could not possibly have witnessed it; the first
pair are 'falsified' rather than 'contradictory' witnesses. The
second problem was addressed by imposing the punishment of
39 lashes on the false witness; much of the tractate reviews
offences for which this is the designated punishment.*

CHAPTER ONE

MISHNA:

How are falsified witnesses given the penalty they intended   2a
for the other? [If they said,] We testify that so-and-so is the
son of a divorcee or of a woman who has received *ḥalitza*,[1] we
do not say, Let them [have the status of] sons of a divorcee or
a woman who has received *ḥalitza* as they intended for the
other, but they receive 39 lashes.

[If they said,] We testify that so-and-so is [guilty of an
offence for which he is] liable for exile,[2] we do not say, Let
these be exiled in their place, but they receive 39 lashes.

GEMARA:

[Mishna said,] How are falsified witnesses given the penalty
they intended for the other? Surely it should have said, How
are falsified witnesses *not* given the penalty they intended for
the other! Moreover, Mishna says later,[3] But if they said to
them, How can you testify, seeing that you were with us in
such-and-such a place that day? that is how they are falsified.

The Tanna is referring to his previous statement, All falsified
witnesses [in capital cases] suffer the form of execution [they
had intended for the accused], except for falsified witnesses
[who have given false testimony] about the *Kohen*'s daughter
and the one who had intercourse with her.[4] [The Tanna is
telling us that] those falsified witnesses suffer a different death
penalty, and there are other falsified witnesses who do not suffer
a corresponding penalty at all, but receive lashes, namely, [If
they said,] We testify that so-and-so is the son of a divorcee
or a woman who has received *ḥalitza*, we do not say, Let them
[have the status of] sons of a divorcee or a woman who has
received *ḥalitza* as they intended for the other, but they receive
39 lashes.

1. Both, if sons of *Kohanim*, are debarred from the priesthood.
2. This would be a case of accidental homicide, as in Numbers 35:22–8; it is the
   theme of *Makkot* Chapter Two.
3. *Makkot* 5a.
4. *Sanhedrin* 89a, the 'previous statement' of the Mishna in its original arrangement.

How do we know that [that is the law]? Rabbi Joshua ben Levi explained, [It is] because the Torah says, **YOU SHALL DO TO HIM AS HE INTENDED TO DO TO HIS FELLOW** – to him, but not to his descendants. Then why not disqualify him alone, and not his descendants[, from the priesthood]? Scripture says, **AS HE INTENDED TO DO TO HIS FELLOW**, and that would not be [what he intended].

Bar Peda says, It can be argued a fortiori: if the man who creates a *ḥalal* does not become a *ḥalal* himself,[5] surely [witnesses] who intended to make someone a *ḥalal*, but failed to do so, do not become *ḥalalim* themselves! Ravina objected, If that was a valid argument, you would abolish the category of falsified witnesses! [For you could argue in general,] if someone who brought about death by stoning is not put to death by stoning, surely one who intended to bring about death by stoning but failed to do so should not be put to death by stoning![6] So the first argument[, of Joshua ben Levi,] is preferred.

2b

There was so much talk of capital punishment in Sanhedrin *that one might gain the impression it was a common occurrence. The Mishna corrects this.*

MISHNA:

7a

If sentence has been passed and the condemned man flees and is subsequently brought before the same court, they do not set aside the previous judgement.

Whenever two witnesses state, We testify that sentence was passed on so-and-so in such-and-such a court, and that A and B were the [prosecution] witnesses, [the accused] is executed [on that basis].

Sanhedrins operate both in the Land and outside the Land.

Any Sanhedrin that executes a capital sentence once in seven

5. If a *Kohen* produces a child from a divorcee, the child is a *ḥalal*, but the *Kohen* retains his priestly status.
6. One of the anomalies of the biblical law of falsified witnesses, as interpreted by the rabbis, is that if the death sentence had been carried out before the witnesses were falsified, they would not suffer that penalty, whereas if they were falsified before the sentence had been implemented, they would (*Makkot* 5b).

years is known as a brutal [Sanhedrin]; Rabbi Eleazar ben
Azaria says, Once in seventy years; Rabbi Tarfon and
Rabbi Aqiva say, Had we been in the Sanhedrin, no one
would ever have been put to death. Rabban Simeon ben
Gamaliel commented, They would have increased bloodshed
in Israel.

GEMARA:

The same court does not set aside its previous judgement.
Does this imply that another court would? [This conflicts with]
the later part of the Mishna, which says, **Whenever two witnesses state, We testify that sentence was passed on so-and-so
in such-and-such a court, and that A and B were the [pros-
ecution] witnesses, [the accused] is executed.** Abbaye said, That
is no problem; one law is for the Land, the other for outside it,
as a baraita teaches: **Rabbi Judah ben Dostai says in the name
of Rabbi Simeon ben Shetaḥ, If the condemned man fled from
the Land [of Israel] to elsewhere, the verdict on him is not set
aside; if he fled from elsewhere to the Land, the verdict is set
aside [and he is retried], on account of the merit of the Land
of Israel.**

**Sanhedrins operate both in the Land and outside the
Land.** How do we know that? The rabbis taught: SUCH SHALL
BE YOUR LAW OF PROCEDURE THROUGHOUT THE AGES IN
ALL YOUR SETTLEMENTS (Numbers 35:29 JPS) – from this we
learn that Sanhedrins operate both in the Land and outside
the Land. If so, why does it say, WITHIN YOUR GATES (Deuteronomy 17:8)? 'Within your gates' you must set up courts in
every district and in every town; outside the Land you must
set them up in every district, but not in every town.

**Any Sanhedrin that executes a capital sentence once in seven
years, etc.** They enquired, Is once in seventy years regarded as
brutal or as normal? No answer was given.

**Rabbi Tarfon and Rabbi Aqiva say, Had we been in the
Sanhedrin, etc.** How could they have ensured this? Rabbi
Yoḥanan and Rabbi Eleazar both said, They would have asked,
Did [the accused] kill a dying man or a sound one? If you claim
he was sound, perhaps the sword entered where [the victim]

had already been pierced.[7] How would they have handled a case involving sexual intercourse? Abbaye and Rava both said, [They] would have asked,] Did you see as kohl on a stick? How could the [other rabbis] ever judge such a case? As Shmuel said, With adulterers, when they appear to be committing adultery.[8]

There are several reports of Sages 'reducing' the Torah to its essential commandments. One was cited in Shabbat 31a *in the name of Hillel; Aqiva 'reduced' the Torah to* YOU SHALL LOVE YOUR NEIGHBOUR AS YOURSELF *(Leviticus 19:18) and Ben Azzai to the more universal* THIS IS THE BOOK OF THE STORY OF HUMANKIND *(Genesis 5:1).[9] In the following passage the focus is on* mitzvot. *There is a certain defensiveness with regard to the multiplicity of* mitzvot, *so often the butt of ridicule from Christians and pagans who regarded them merely as a burden. The late-third-century Rabbi Simlai's claim that there were 613 is followed by prophetic statements progressively reducing the commandments to Habakkuk's one; elsewhere, Simlai himself is reported as observing that the Torah begins and ends with loving-kindness (Sota 14a).*

Medieval commentators were uncomfortable with the notion that the number of commandments might be reduced; Rashi interprets the passage in the sense that succeeding generations were no longer able to cope with the full panoply. However, Samuel Edels (1555–1631) and others explain that the Sages were not saying that the excess had been abandoned, but rather that the underlying principles were summed up in the smaller number.

7. *Terefa*, literally 'torn'. This term is used of a human being or an animal which has a disease or injury from which it will inevitably die. What Rabbis Yoḥanan and Eleazar are saying is that Rabbis Tarfon and Aqiva would have avoided passing a death sentence by undermining the testimony of the prosecution witnesses.
8. It is not necessary to witness in intimate detail – 'as kohl on a stick'.
9. Sifra *Qedoshim* 2:4.

CHAPTER THREE

MISHNA:

Once they have submitted to flogging, all who would have   23a
been liable to *karet* are exempt from *karet*, as it is said, LEST
... YOUR BROTHER BE DEGRADED IN YOUR EYES (Deuteronomy 25:3) – once he has submitted to flogging, he is [again]
your brother; this is the opinion of Rabbi Ḥanania ben
Gamaliel. Rabbi Ḥanania ben Gamaliel said also, When a man
commits a sin, he casts away his life for it; how much more
so, then, will life be given to whoever performs a *mitzva*. Rabbi
Simeon says, You can learn that from one passage – [of those
who break the commandments it is written, ALL WHO DO ANY
OF THOSE ABHORRENT THINGS] – SUCH PERSONS SHALL BE
CUT OFF FROM THEIR PEOPLE (Leviticus 18:29 JPS), but [of
those who keep them,] it says, YOU SHALL KEEP MY LAWS   23b
AND MY RULES, BY THE PURSUIT OF WHICH MAN SHALL LIVE
(Leviticus 18:5 JPS); so whoever passively refrains from sin
receives a reward just as one who performs a *mitzva*.

[Similarly,] Rabbi Simeon the son of Rabbi [Judah ha-
Nasi] says, Scripture says, BE STRONG! DO NOT EAT THE
BLOOD, FOR THE BLOOD IS THE LIFE ... (Deuteronomy
12:23). Now, if you are rewarded for abstaining from blood,
which people find revolting, how much more so will you and
all future generations be rewarded for abstaining from theft
and from sexual immorality, which people find desirable and
tempting.

Rabbi Ḥanania ben Aqashya said, The Holy One, blessed
be He, wanted to give Israel [the opportunity for] merit,
therefore he gave them a Torah with numerous commandments, as it is said, THE LORD DESIRED, THAT HE MIGHT
VINDICATE HIM,[10] TO INCREASE AND GLORIFY THE TORAH
(Isaiah 42:21).

---

10. The phrase is obscure; most translators assume that 'him' refers to the suffering
servant, possibly Israel.

GEMARA:

Rabbi Simlai expounded: 613 *mitzvot* were declared to Moses
– 365 prohibitions corresponding to the 365 days of the solar
year, and 248 positive commandments corresponding to the 248
parts of a man's body.[11]

Rav Hamnuna said, [On] what verse [is this based]?
**MOSES COMMANDED TORAH TO US AS AN INHERIT-
ANCE** (Deuteronomy 33:4): the numerical value of [the
word] '*torah*' is 611; [in addition,] we heard I **AM** [**THE
LORD YOUR GOD**] and **YOU SHALL HAVE NO** [**OTHER
GODS BEFORE ME**] (Exodus 20:2, 3) directly from the
Almighty.

24a

When David came he reduced them to eleven, as it is written,
**A PSALM OF DAVID. LORD, WHO MAY SOJOURN IN YOUR
TENT, WHO MAY DWELL ON YOUR HOLY MOUNTAIN? HE
WHO LIVES WITHOUT BLAME, WHO DOES WHAT IS RIGHT,
AND IN HIS HEART ACKNOWLEDGES THE TRUTH; WHOSE
TONGUE IS NOT GIVEN TO EVIL, WHO HAS NEVER DONE HARM
TO HIS FELLOW, OR BORNE REPROACH ON ACCOUNT OF HIS
RELATIVE; FOR WHOM A CONTEMPTIBLE MAN IS ABHORRENT,
BUT WHO HONOURS THOSE WHO FEAR THE LORD; WHO
STANDS BY HIS OATH EVEN TO HIS HURT; WHO HAS NEVER
LENT MONEY AT INTEREST, OR ACCEPTED A BRIBE AGAINST
THE INNOCENT. THE MAN WHO DOES THESE THINGS SHALL
NEVER BE SHAKEN** (Psalm 15 JPS).

HE WHO LIVES WITHOUT BLAME – this is Abraham, of whom it is written, **WALK BEFORE ME AND
BE WITHOUT BLAME** (Genesis 17:1).

WHO DOES WHAT IS RIGHT – like Abba Ḥilkiah.

AND IN HIS HEART ACKNOWLEDGES THE TRUTH
– like Rav Safra.

WHOSE TONGUE IS NOT GIVEN TO EVIL – this is
our father Jacob, of whom it is written, **PERHAPS MY
FATHER WILL TOUCH ME AND I WILL SEEM TO HIM
A DECEIVER**[12] (Genesis 27:12).

11. Enumerated in Mishna *Ohalot* 1:8 (see p. 673).
12. The point is that Jacob was reluctant to deceive his father.

WHO HAS NEVER DONE HARM TO HIS FELLOW — who has not interfered in another's business.

OR BORNE REPROACH ON ACCOUNT OF HIS RELATIVE — this refers to one who brings his relatives close [to God].

FOR WHOM A CONTEMPTIBLE MAN IS ABHORRENT — this is [King] Hezekiah, who dragged his father's bones on a rope bier.

BUT WHO HONOURS THOSE WHO FEAR THE LORD — this is Jehoshaphat king of Judah, who would arise from his throne when he saw a man of learning, and embrace him and kiss him, and address him as My father! My father! My master! My master! My teacher! My teacher!

WHO STANDS BY HIS OATH EVEN TO HIS HURT — like Rabbi Yoḥanan who declared, I will fast until I get home.

WHO HAS NEVER LENT MONEY AT INTEREST — even to a non-Israelite.

OR ACCEPTED A BRIBE AGAINST THE INNOCENT — for instance, Rabbi Ishmael the son of Rabbi Yosé.[13]

THE MAN WHO DOES THESE THINGS SHALL NEVER BE SHAKEN — When Rabban Gamaliel came to this verse, he wept, saying, One who has done all these things will not be shaken, but if he has [omitted] any of them he *will* be shaken! They said to him, It does not say, **ONE WHO DOES *ALL* THESE THINGS**, but **ONE WHO DOES THESE THINGS** — any of them. [Indeed,] if you don't read it like that, what will you make of the verse, **DO NOT DEFILE YOURSELF WITH ALL THESE THINGS** (Leviticus 18:24)? Surely it does not mean that only someone who has contact with all these things is defiled, but not someone who has contact with only one of them! Here, likewise, it means any one of them.

---

13. *Ketubot* 105b records how he refused to act as a judge in a case involving a tenant who had done him some favours.

When Isaiah came he reduced them to six, as it is written,
**HE WHO WALKS IN RIGHTEOUSNESS, SPEAKS UPRIGHTLY,
SPURNS PROFIT FROM FRAUDULENT DEALINGS, WAVES AWAY
A BRIBE INSTEAD OF GRASPING IT, STOPS HIS EARS AGAINST
LISTENING TO INFAMY, SHUTS HIS EYES AGAINST LOOKING
AT EVIL [– SUCH A ONE SHALL DWELL IN LOFTY SECURITY]**
(Isaiah 33:15–16 JPS).

HE WHO WALKS IN RIGHTEOUSNESS – this is Abraham, of whom it is written, **FOR I HAVE KNOWN
HIM, THAT HE WILL COMMAND [HIS CHILDREN AND
HIS HOUSEHOLD AFTER HIM TO FOLLOW THE WAY
OF THE LORD AND TO PRACTISE JUSTICE AND
RIGHTEOUSNESS]** (Genesis 18:19).

SPEAKS UPRIGHTLY – he does not provoke his neighbour in public.

SPURNS PROFIT FROM FRAUDULENT DEALINGS – like Rabbi Ishmael ben Elisha.

WAVES AWAY A BRIBE INSTEAD OF GRASPING IT – like Rabbi Ishmael ben Yosé.

STOPS HIS EARS AGAINST LISTENING TO INFAMY – like Rabbi Eleazar ben Simeon, he does not remain silent when he hears a learned man insulted.

SHUTS HIS EYES AGAINST LOOKING AT EVIL – who like Rabbi Ḥiyya bar Abba avoids looking at the women when they are laundering.

[Then] came Micah and reduced them to three, as it is written, **HE HAS TOLD YOU, O MAN, WHAT IS GOOD, AND
WHAT THE LORD REQUIRES OF YOU: ONLY TO DO JUSTICE
AND TO LOVE GOODNESS, AND TO WALK MODESTLY WITH
YOUR GOD** (Micah 6:8 JPS).

TO DO JUSTICE – this refers to justice.

TO LOVE GOODNESS – this is the practice of loving-kindness.

TO WALK MODESTLY [WITH YOUR GOD] – this refers to burying the dead and dowering the bride. Now if, in reference to matters that are not normally done in a secretive fashion,[14] the Torah says, **TO WALK MODESTLY**, how much more so should one act modestly in matters which are normally done quietly.

Isaiah then reduced them to two, as it is written, **THUS SAYS THE LORD: OBSERVE JUSTICE AND ACT WITH RIGHTNESS**[15] (Isaiah 56:1).

[Then] came Amos and reduced them to one, as it is said, **SEEK ME AND LIVE!** (Amos 5:4).

Rav Naḥman bar Isaac objected: Perhaps [Amos] meant **SEEK ME** through all [the commandments] of the Torah!

But Habakkuk came and reduced them to one, as it is said, **THE RIGHTEOUS LIVES BY HIS FAITH** (Habakkuk 2:4).

14. Since they are public acts.
15. The sense here is to balance justice and mercy.

SIXTH TRACTATE
SHAVUOT[1] (OATHS)

*OR WHEN A PERSON UTTERS AN OATH TO BAD OR GOOD PURPOSE
– WHATEVER A MAN MAY UTTER IN AN OATH – AND, THOUGH HE
HAS KNOWN IT, THE FACT HAS ESCAPED HIM, BUT HE LATER
REALIZES HIS GUILT IN ANY OF THESE MATTERS ... HE SHALL
CONFESS THAT WHEREIN HE HAS SINNED, AND HE SHALL BRING
AS HIS PENALTY TO THE LORD ... A FEMALE FROM THE FLOCK ...
AS A SIN-OFFERING.* (Leviticus 5:4–6 JPS)

On vows in general, see introduction to Nedarim.

A person may swear that he will or will not take a certain
action, or that he did or did not act in a certain way. Should
he discover that he has inadvertently broken his oath, or was
mistaken in his assertion about what he had or had not done,
he must confess, and bring an offering to atone for his guilt. An
oath about the past, even if it is a true statement, may be 'vain',
i.e. futile.

CHAPTER THREE

MISHNA:

19b Two [forms of plain] oath [are written in Scripture],[2] making
four oaths [in all]: I swear that I will eat, or I swear that I will

---

1. The noun *shavu'ot* is the plural of both *shavu'a* ('week') and *sh'vu'ah* ('oath');
    Shavuot, in the sense of 'weeks', is the name of a festival.
2. 'To bad purpose' and 'to good purpose' are interpreted as separate categories, viz.
    negative and positive.

not eat; I swear that I ate, or [I swear] that I did not eat.

[If he said,] 'I swear that I will not eat', and he ate [even] the smallest amount, he is liable [to the penalty], according to Rabbi Aqiva.

They said to Rabbi Aqiva, Where do we find that someone who eats a tiny amount is liable?[3] Rabbi Aqiva replied, Where do we find [no lower limit]? With someone who brings a sacrifice on account of speech; this one brings a sacrifice on account of speech.[4]

GEMARA:

When Rav Dimi came, he said in Rabbi Yoḥanan's name, '[I swear that] I shall eat' or 'I shall not eat' is a false oath, forbidden by the verse, YOU SHALL NOT SWEAR FALSELY BY MY NAME (Leviticus 19:12); 'I ate' or 'I did not eat' is a futile oath, forbidden by the verse, YOU SHALL NOT SWEAR IN VAIN BY THE NAME OF THE LORD YOUR GOD (Exodus 20:7); an oath expressed by *qonam* transgresses, HE SHALL NOT BREAK HIS WORD (Numbers 30:3). | 20b

They objected: 'False' and 'futile' are the same. Doesn't this mean that just as a futile oath refers to the past, so does a false oath? No. Each one is what it is; 'the same' means that [God] pronounced as one that which mortals can neither pronounce nor hear. There is [another] case where [two words] were uttered [by God] simultaneously, as Rav Ada bar Ahava said: Women are obliged by the Torah to recite *qiddush*, for Scripture says REMEMBER and OBSERVE,[5] meaning that whoever must observe must remember; since women must observe, they must remember. But what *halakha* could be inferred in our context [from the simultaneous pronouncement of words]? The same [in the citation] means that just as he is liable to flogging for [breaking] a futile oath, he is liable to flogging for [breaking] a false oath.

---

3. Minimum quantities are set for liability in most instances; e.g. for eating forbidden food, it is an olive-size.
4. The sin is breaking his word, not eating per se.
5. These are the alternative expressions in the two versions of the Ten Commandments (Exodus 20:8 and Deuteronomy 5:12); the two versions are said to have been uttered simultaneously by God.

In which direction does the argument go? [You could equally well argue,] Just as he is liable to flogging for [breaking] a false oath, he is liable to flogging for [breaking] a futile oath. Isn't that obvious? You might have reasoned, as Rav Papa proposed to Abbaye, that **HE WILL NOT HOLD INNOCENT** (Exodus 20:7) means not at all, so it has to inform you in accordance with [Abbaye's] reponse.[6]

Alternatively, ['the same' could imply] that just as he must bring sacrifice [to atone for breaking] a false oath, so he must bring sacrifice [to atone for breaking] a futile oath; this would follow the line of Rabbi Aqiva, who holds that a person may be liable for [an oath relating to] the past as well as [for one relating to] the future.

They objected: **A futile oath is where somebody swore contrary to common knowledge;**[7] **a false oath is where he swore contrary to [a contingent] fact.** It could still include an oath about future acts.

When Ravin came he said that Rabbi Yirmiya had told him that Rabbi Abbahu reported that Rabbi Yoḥanan said: [An oath of the form] 'I ate' or 'I did not eat' is false, and derives from **YOU SHALL NOT SWEAR FALSELY BY MY NAME**; 'I shall eat' or 'I shall not eat' transgresses **HE SHALL NOT BREAK HIS WORD**; and what is a futile oath? **A futile oath is where someone swore contrary to common knowledge.**

Chapter Four covers the 'oath of testimony', which functions something like the subpoena in modern legal systems:

IF A PERSON INCURS GUILT – WHEN HE HAS HEARD A PUBLIC IMPRECATION AND – ALTHOUGH ABLE TO TESTIFY AS ONE WHO HAS EITHER SEEN OR LEARNED OF THE MATTER – HE DOES NOT GIVE INFORMATION. (Leviticus 5:1–2 JPS)

---

6. This refers to a complex discussion on the next folio, not translated here.
7. That is, something absurd, for instance that the sun did not rise that morning, rather than something that could have happened, but in fact didn't.

CHAPTER FOUR

MISHNA:

How does the 'oath of testimony' work? If someone said to two [potential witnesses], Come and testify for me! [and they replied], We swear we have no evidence to give on your behalf; alternatively, if they said to him, We have no evidence to give on your behalf, and he said, I adjure you, and they replied, Amen! [In both cases, if they are concealing evidence,] they are guilty.   31b

If he adjured them [even] five times outside the court, and then they entered the court and admitted [that they did have evidence to present], they are exempt [from any penalty]; but if they [still] denied [that they had evidence to present], they are liable to the penalty for each [denial].

If he adjured them five times in the presence of the court and they denied [that they had evidence to present], they are liable only once. Rabbi Simeon said, Why is that? It is because [a witness] cannot retract repeatedly.[8]

If both [witnesses] together denied [on oath that they had evidence to present], both are liable, but if they denied one after the other, only the first is liable.[9] However, if there were two pairs of witnesses, and they successively denied [on oath that they had evidence to present], both are liable, since the evidence could be confirmed by either [pair].

GEMARA:

Shmuel said, If they saw someone running after them and said, Why are you running after us? We swear we have no evidence to give for you! they are exempt [unless and] until they hear from his own mouth [what it is he wants]. What is Shmuel telling us? Surely a Mishna teaches this: **If he sent through his slave, or if the defendant said, I adjure you, that if you have evidence to give on his behalf you will come and give it, they are exempt, unless [and until] they hear from the plaintiff**   32a

8. Once the witness has formally presented evidence by admitting that his denial was false, he cannot repeat the process; therefore only the first oath is valid, and he cannot be held liable for breaking subsequent oaths since these would be invalid.

9. The second, as the single remaining witness, could not testify, since the law requires at least two witnesses.

himself.[10] [Shmuel] needs to tell us that although you might have thought that if [the plaintiff] is running after them it is as if he spoke to them, it is not so.

But surely this also has been stated in [our] Mishna: **How does the 'oath of testimony' work? If someone said to two [potential witnesses], Come and testify for me!** 'If he said', yes, but if he did not [actually] say, no! [No.] 'Said' [in the Mishna] is not to be taken literally, for [if you take it literally,] what about the deposit oath? The Mishna states: **How does the 'deposit oath' work? If he said, Return my deposit which you are holding.** [Here, too,] you would have to say that 'say' is literal, whereas **DEALING DECEITFULLY WITH HIS FELLOW** (Leviticus 5:21) must mean in any way at all. 'Say' is therefore not to be taken literally; here, likewise, 'say' is not to be taken literally.

Where does this lead? If you say that 'say' [in our Mishna] is literal, the Mishna [about the deposit oath] uses the expression in line with this Mishna; but if 'say' is not literal in either context, why use the expression at all? Perhaps it just deals with the normal situation.

A baraita supports Shmuel's view: **If they saw someone running after them and said, 'Why are you following us? We swear we don't know of any evidence for you', they are exempt; but if it was in connection with a deposit, they are liable.**

Chapter Five is dedicated to the 'deposit oath'; someone holds on to a deposit but denies on oath that it is in his possession:

WHEN A PERSON SINS AND COMMITS A TRESPASS AGAINST THE LORD BY DEALING DECEITFULLY WITH HIS FELLOW IN THE MATTER OF A DEPOSIT OR A PLEDGE, OR THROUGH ROBBERY, OF BY DEFRAUDING HIS FELLOW, OR BY FINDING SOMETHING LOST AND LYING ABOUT IT; IF HE SWEARS FALSELY REGARDING ANY ONE OF THE VARIOUS THINGS ... HE SHALL REPAY THE PRINCIPAL AMOUNT AND ADD A FIFTH PART TO IT ... HE SHALL BRING TO THE PRIEST, AS HIS PENALTY TO THE LORD, A RAM WITHOUT BLEMISH. (Leviticus 5:21–25 JPS)

10. Mishna *Shavuot* 35a.

CHAPTER FIVE

MISHNA:

The deposit oath applies to both men and women, relatives   36b
and non-relatives, fit or unfit [to testify], whether or not in
the presence of the court, spontaneous or prompted. Rabbi
Meir says, He is liable only if he has sworn his denial in
court; but the [majority of] Sages say, Whether spontaneous
or prompted, [wherever] he has issued the denial he is liable.
He is liable if he has knowingly sworn an oath, or if he has
unwittingly[11] sworn an oath but was aware he was [wrongfully]
in possession of the deposit. He is not liable if he was merely
unaware [that he was holding the deposit, and therefore had
no intention of uttering a false oath]. What is the penalty
for deliberately [uttering the false oath]? He must bring a
reparation-offering worth at least two silver *selaim*.[12]

GEMARA:

Rav Aḥa bar Huna, Rav Shmuel the son of Rabba bar bar
Ḥana, and Rav Isaac the son of Rav Yehuda were studying [the
tractate] *Shavuot* at Rabba's school. Rav Kahana met them. He
asked them, What happens if someone deliberately swore a   37a
deposit oath, and had been [formally] cautioned [of the seriousness of the offence]? Since [the law of the deposit oath] is
anomalous, as in no other instance does the Torah [accept] an
offering where the offence was deliberate,[13] but here it does, does
it make any difference whether or not he has been cautioned; or
do we say that he only brings a reparation-offering if he has not
been cautioned, but if he has been cautioned, he would receive
lashes and not bring a reparation-offering?

They replied to him, [The answer follows from] a Mishna:
The deposit oath is more serious, since if you utter it deliberately you are liable to flogging, but if unwittingly [just] a

---

11. That is, without realizing it was an offence which would render him liable to a
     reparation offering.
12. Obviously, he must restore the misappropriated article to its rightful owner, but
     that is not a 'penalty'.
13. Rashi points out there are four cases.

reparation-offering worth two silver *sheqels*. Since it prescribes flogging for a deliberate [offence], it follows that he must have been cautioned; it is 'more serious' since a person would find it easier to bring a sacrifice than to submit to flogging.

SEVENTH TRACTATE
EDUYOT (TESTIMONIES –
LEGAL PRECEDENTS)

This tractate, for which there is no Gemara, is a collection of collections of Tannaitic reports in the form of testimonies; most occur elsewhere in appropriate contexts. They include lists of where Rabbi A was more stringent or less stringent than Rabbi B, of where Rabbi X conceded to Rabbi Y, and of what Rabbi C reported to or in the name of Rabbi D. These extracts are chosen for the light they throw on the development of the rabbinic tradition and its mode of operation.

CHAPTER ONE

3. Hillel says, A *hin*[1] of drawn water disqualifies the *miqvé* – a man should use the expression his teacher used; Shammai says, Nine *kabs*. The Sages said, Neither one nor the other. [This remained the situation] until two weavers arrived from the Dung Gate in Jerusalem and testified in the names of Shemaia and Avtalion that three *logs* of drawn water disqualify the *miqvé*, and the Sages confirmed their words.
4. Then why are the words of Shammai and Hillel reported to no [practical] purpose? It is to teach subsequent generations that no one should insist on his opinion [being

1. Most commentators think that the Mishna draws attention here to the expression '*hin*', a biblical measure not normally used by the Sages; Maimonides notes that his teachers told him that Hillel deliberately dropped the 'h' as his Greek-born teachers Shemaia and Avtalion had done.

accepted], for even the great fathers[2] did not insist on their opinions.

5. And why are the words of an individual recorded with those of the majority, seeing that the law goes by the majority? It is in case a later court comes across the individual's words and [mistakenly] relies on them, for no court can annul the decisions of another unless it is greater in learning and number [than the other]; if it is greater is learning but not in number, or in number but not in learning, it cannot annul the decisions of another unless it is greater in both learning and number.

6. Rabbi Judah said, If so, why are the words of an individual recorded with those of the majority to no [practical] purpose? Because if someone says, This is the tradition I have received, they can tell him, That was according to so-and-so[, and was outvoted].

CHAPTER FIVE

7. Aqavia ben Mahalelel testified concerning four matters. They said to him, Aqavia! Retract the four things you have said and we will appoint you Father of the Court of Israel! He replied to them: Better I should be thought a fool all my life than I should be wicked in God's eyes for a moment, and that people should think I changed my opinions to seek office!

8. He held that hair deposited [by a leprous scab] and green-tinted blood were impure, whereas the Sages declared them pure; he permitted [the use by a *Kohen* of] hair that had fallen off a blemished first-born calf and been placed in a window, the calf being subsequently slaughtered, whereas the Sages forbade it; and he held that the bitter waters could not be administered to a convert or a freed female slave, but the Sages held that they could. They said to him: Shemaia

---

2.　Literally, 'fathers of the world', i.e. Hillel and Shammai.

and Avtalion administered the bitter waters to Karkemit, a freed female slave in Jerusalem. He replied, They did that [just] to make an example of her![3] So they excommunicated him, he died under the ban and the court placed stones on his coffin.

Rabbi Judah said, God forbid that Aqavia was placed under a ban! The gates of the Temple courtyard never closed on any son of Israel as wise and God-fearing as Aqavia ben Mahalelel! The man they placed under a ban was Eleazar ben Enoch who ridiculed the washing of the hands, and when he died the court dispatched [an officer] to place a stone on his coffin; this teaches us that if anyone dies under a ban the court places stones on his coffin.

9. As he was dying he said to his son, My son, retract those four things I used to say! Then why did you not retract [them] yourself? He replied, I heard them from a majority who had themselves heard them from a majority; I stood by what I had heard as they had stood by what they heard. But you have heard [rulings on these topics both] from an individual and from a majority; you should relinquish the ruling of the individual and adopt that of the majority.

He asked him, Father, commend me to your colleagues! He refused. Do you find some fault with me? [asked the son.] He replied, No! But it is your [own] deeds that bring you near, and your [own] deeds that drive you away.

CHAPTER EIGHT

7. Rabbi Joshua said, I received [the tradition] from Rabban Yoḥanan ben Zakkai, who heard it from his teacher, and his teacher from his teacher, as a *halakha* received by Moses at Sinai, that Elijah[4] comes not to declare unclean or clean, to drive away or to bring near, but to drive away those who

---

3.   It was an extra-judicial procedure.
4.   Here the harbinger of the Messiah.

have entered by force, and to bring near those who have been driven away by force.[5]

There was a family called the House of Tzerifa in Transjordan that Benzion had forcibly driven away, and another that he had forcibly brought near; those are the kind that Elijah will declare unclean or clean, and will drive away or bring near.

Rabbi Judah says, He will bring near, but not drive [anyone] away. Rabbi Simeon says, He will reconcile those who quarrel.

But the Sages say, He comes neither to bring near nor to drive away, but to bring peace to the world, as it is said, LO, I WILL SEND THE PROHET ELIJAH TO YOU ... HE SHALL RECONCILE PARENTS WITH CHILDREN AND CHILDREN WITH THEIR PARENTS (Malachi 3:23, 24 JPS).

5.　He will decide whether families are recognized as of pure lineage.

EIGHTH TRACTATE
AVODA ZARA (IDOLATRY)

Mishna was compiled for the most part after the disastrous Bar Kokhba Revolt. This was a period of rampant paganization of what was no longer Judaea but had become the Roman province of Syria Palaestina.[1] Towns were refounded as Greek cities with municipal temples; Bet Guvrin became Eleutheropolis, Emmaus became Nicopolis, Lydda Diospolis, Bet Shean Scythopolis, and so on; pagan temples are known to have existed in Aelia (Jerusalem), Sebaste (Shomron, Samaria), Neapolis, Caesarea, Scythopolis, Gadara and Hippos.[2] How were Jews to comport themselves in pagan cities, where public sacrifices were a feature of municipal life? Probably many simply assimilated, whether or not retaining some form of Jewish identity. Others may have taken advantage of the rescript of Severus and Antoninus (Caracalla) allowing Jews to hold municipal office and requiring that they not be obliged to act contrary to their superstitio;[3] *the rabbis themselves were not averse to certain compromises – Gamaliel famously argued that he might bathe in a public bath-place adorned with a statue, since 'We do not say, let us make a bath-place as an adornment for Aphrodite, but let us make a [statue of] Aphrodite to adorn the bath-place.'[4]*

In Sasanian Babylonia, when the Talmud was being produced, the dominant religion was a form of Zoroastrianism, involving fire worship, that Jews regarded as idolatrous.

Many Jews did their best to distance themselves from pagan

1. Belayche, *Iudaea-Palaestina*.
2. Millar, 'Transformations', p. 145.
3. Ulpian, in Justinian, *Digest* 50:2.3.3.
4. Mishna *Avoda Zara* 3:4 (44b). It is uncertain which Gamaliel is meant.

celebrations. *The Mishna offers a glimpse of the social friction this must have generated in towns where pagan festivals were celebrated; the Gemara extends Mishna's teachings to the situation in Babylonia. Christians faced analogous problems, though eventually they adopted many of the local celebrations giving them new significance as Christian saints' days.*

The Sages forbade trade with an idolater for three days before and three days after his festival, in case the trade led him to thank or entreat his idol. Which festivals does this apply to?

CHAPTER ONE

MISHNA:

8a   These are the festivals[5] of the idolaters: Kalends; Saturnalia; *Qartisim*;[6] the birthdays[7] of kings, the day of birth and the day of death. This is the view of Rabbi Meir, but the Sages say, Wherever there is burning at a death, there is idolatry,[8] but where there is no burning, there is no idolatry.

However, the day [an idolater] shaves his beard or his tress of hair,[9] the day he returns from the sea, the day he is released from captivity, or [the day he] makes a feast for his son [are not festivals in the full sense, so it is forbidden to trade] only with that man and only on that day.

5.   The term *eid* is used for an idolatrous festival, in contrast with *ḥag* for a biblical one; it is possibly cognate with Arabic *id*, but in Hebrew bears a pejorative tone, since it is similar to a biblical Hebrew word that means 'distress' or 'calamity' (e.g. Job 21:30).
6.   This is how the Hebrew is commonly read. Lieberman, *Greek*, demonstrated that the word was *kratēsis*, a festival instituted to mark the capture of Alexandria by Augustus on 1 August 30 BCE.
7.   *Genesia.*
8.   That is, if a king is sufficiently important for his possessions to be burnt at his death, his funeral rites are idolatrous.
9.   Upper-class Roman and Greek youths grew their hair long and offered it to the gods on reaching puberty (Jastrow, *Dictionary*). Alternatively, this is a reference to the *Juvenalia* games instituted by Nero in 59 CE to mark the occasion of shaving his beard for the first time.

GEMARA:

The day he shaves his beard. They enquired, Does the   11b
Mishna mean, **The day he shaves his beard *and leaves* his tress
of hair**, or, **The day he shaves his beard *and removes* his tress
of hair**?

There is proof from a baraita that both [are intended, for the
baraita runs]: **The day he shaves his beard and leaves his tress
of hair and the day he shaves his beard and removes his tress
of hair.**

Rav Yehuda said in the name of Shmuel, In Rome they have
another festival. Once every seventy years they bring a fit man,
get him to ride on [the shoulders of] a lame man,[10] dress him
in the clothes of Adam, put the scalp of Rabbi Ishmael on his
head,[11] and drape 200 *zuz* worth of fine gold around his neck
and other [precious stones] on his legs. Then they call out, 'The
brother of our lord was an impostor!'[12] Who sees [the ceremony]
sees it; who does not, does not.[13] They continue: 'What good
did the trickery do to the trickster, or the deceit to the impostor?'
And they conclude: 'Woe to the one when the other triumphs!'[14]

Rav Papa observed, Those wicked people stumbled
with their words. Had they said, Our lord's brother
was an impostor, it would be as they said; but as they
used the words, Our lord was an impostor, it means
that Esau was the impostor.[15]

---

10. This may have been suggested by Roman images of *Judaea capta*. Rabbenu
     Hananel explains that the fit man is Esau, the ancestor of Rome in Jewish legend,
     and the lame man Jacob, the ancestor of Israel (he was injured in his confrontation
     with the angel, Genesis 32:32). The text here is confused; Rashi precedes this with
     an additional phrase that he interprets to mean that Jacob's prophecies concerning
     the end of time were delusory (Tosafot reject this interpretation and apply the
     phrase to Isaac).

11. There is a legend that Rabbi Ishmael was martyred, and his scalp removed and
     used as a charm by kings (*Ḥullin* 123a).

12. Jacob impersonated Esau (Genesis 27:19).

13. If you have missed it, you are not likely to have another chance to see it, since it
     is held only once in seventy years – Rashi.

14. An allusion to Genesis 27:40, where Isaac prophesies that when one brother rises
     the other will fall.

15. In Aramaic this requires only the transposition of two words. Esau is condemned
     as an impostor on the grounds that he allegedly deceived his father into thinking
     he was virtuous.

So why does our Mishna not include this festival? It includes only those [festivals] that take place annually, but not those that do not take place annually.

These are the Roman [festivals]. What about Persian ones? Motradi and Toriski, Moharnaki and Moharin.[16]

These are the Roman and Persian [festivals]. What about Babylonian ones? Moharnaki and Aqniti, Bahanuni and 10 Adar. *A story of the contrasting fates of two rabbis illustrates the ambivalence of Jewish life under Rome (Ḥanina ben Teradion would have been martyred during the Hadrianic persecutions).*

17b   [The Romans] fetched Rabbi Ḥanina ben Teradion and said to him, Why do you study Torah [in defiance of the law]? He replied, As the Lord my God has commanded me (Deuteronomy 4:5). They immediately sentenced him to death by burning, his wife to beheading, and his daughter to a brothel.

18a   He was sentenced to burning because he had uttered the Divine Name as it is written. How could he do that? Doesn't a Mishna state: **These have no share in the World to Come: one who denies that resurrection [of the dead] is [indicated] in the Torah; one who denies that the Torah is from Heaven . . . Abba Saul says, Also anyone who utters the four-lettered Divine Name?**[17] He did it only to learn, as a baraita says, **You shall not learn *to do*** (Deuteronomy 18:9) – but **you may learn to understand and to render thanks.** In that case, why was he punished? He was punished because he uttered the Name in public. **His wife to beheading** – because she didn't stop him; from this we learn that whoever is in a position to prevent a sin [from taking place] but fails to do so is punished. **And his daughter to a brothel** – Rabbi Yohanan said, His daughter was once walking in the presence of some

16. Vowels are inserted in these names and those in the following list for convenience of reading; the Aramaic text has none. The consonantal text itself is certainly corrupt. Three of the Persian festivals have been identified by Taqizadeh, 'Iranian Festivals', pp. 637–9, as Nausard (the New Year), Tirakan and Mihrakan; the final name is thought to be a corruption of the first. See also Kohut, 'Fêtes Persannes'.

17. *Sanhedrin* 90a (see p. 514).

important Romans. They remarked, What elegant steps that girl takes! She straightaway paid attention to her steps. This is [like] what Rabbi Simeon ben Laqish said, What does THE SIN OF MY HEELS SURROUNDS ME (Psalm 49:6) mean? It means that those sins a man tramples on with his heels[18] will crowd around him on the the day of judgement.

When the three of them faced their sentences, they each affirmed God's justice. He said, THE ROCK! HIS DEEDS ARE PERFECT, ETC. (Deuteronomy 32:4); his wife said, A FAITHFUL GOD, NEVER UNJUST, ETC. (Deuteronomy 32:4); his daughter said, GREAT IN COUNSEL AND MIGHTY IN DEED, ETC. (Jeremiah 32:19). Rabbi commented, How great were these three righteous people, that each found a verse affirming God's justice when [their faith in] God's justice [was being put to the test]!

The rabbis taught: When Rabbi Yosé ben Qisma fell ill, Rabbi Ḥanina ben Teradion visited him. Ḥanina, my son, said Rabbi Yosé, Do you not understand that this nation destined by [God] to govern, to demolish His home and burn His Temple, has slain His pious ones and destroyed good people, yet still flourishes! Yet I have heard that you sit and study Torah, gather crowds in public and carry a Torah scroll in your bosom! Ḥanina replied, May Heaven show [me] mercy! [Rabbi Yosé continued,] I talk to you reasonably, and [all you can say is,] 'May Heaven show [me] mercy!' I shall be surprised if they do not burn you and your Torah scroll in fire! Ḥanina [then] asked, Master, what [chance have] I for the World to Come? Have you done anything practical? asked Rabbi Yosé. Money that I had set aside for my Purim celebration got mixed up with money for the poor, so I distributed it all to the poor[, he replied]. In that case, [said Rabbi Yosé,] may my portion be [like] your portion, and my fate [like] your fate![19]

Not long after, Rabbi Yosé ben Qisma died; his funeral was attended by all the great of Rome, and they honoured him with

18. Fails to take seriously.
19. Seeing that you are so generous – Rashi. There is a touch of irony here.

a fine eulogy. On their way back they came across Rabbi Ḥanina
ben Teradion sitting and studying Torah, gathering crowds in
public and clasping a Torah scroll to his bosom. They arrested
him, wrapped him in the Torah scroll, surrounded him with
branches and set them on fire, then brought balls of wool,
soaked them in water and placed them over his heart so that he
should not expire quickly. His daughter said, Is that how I must
see you! He replied, It would be bad enough were I being burnt
alone; but now that the Torah scroll is consigned to the flames
with me, may He who seeks [redress] for the shame of the Torah
seek redress for my shame![20] His disciples asked him, Master,
what do you see? He replied, A scroll burning, and the letters
flying [upwards]. Why do you not open your mouth to let the
flames enter? He replied, Better that He who gave [the soul]
should take it back, and I should not cause my own injury. The
executioner said to him, Master! If I increase the flame and
remove the balls of wool, will you bring me to the World to
Come? Yes, he replied. Swear to me! He swore. At once, he
increased the flame and removed the balls of wool, and [Rabbi
Ḥanina] rapidly expired. Then [the executioner] himself leaped
into the flames. A heavenly voice issued forth and proclaimed,
Rabbi Ḥanina ben Teradion and his executioner are received in
the World to Come!

Rabbi wept [when he heard this story,] and reflected, Some
earn their world in a moment, others only after [labouring]
many years!

*The story goes on to relate how Rabbi Ḥanina's daughter was
rescued from her fate by intervention on the part Rabbi Meir,
husband of her sister Beruria. Nothing is said of her mother's fate.*

Most people are familiar with the Jewish laws on kasher
*food derived from Leviticus 11 and other verses. The 'items of
idolaters' that are forbidden only partly arise from concern with
the observance of biblical food laws; some foods or drinks were*

---

20. He is concerned that if people see the Torah burnt, and himself burnt for teaching
it, it may bring the Torah into contempt.

forbidden because they were directly involved in idolatry, others in order to avoid fraternizing and ultimately intermarriage with idolaters.

CHAPTER TWO

MISHNA:

It is forbidden to eat or drink the following items of idol- 35b
aters, but using them is not prohibited: milk milked by an idolater out of sight of an Israelite; their bread and oil – but Rabbi and his court permitted oil; boiled food and preserves that normally contain wine or vinegar; small salted fish that has been mixed; brine in which no sticklebacks swim; *ḥilleq*; tears of asafoetida; *salqondrit* salt.[21] It is forbidden to eat or drink any of these, but using them is not prohibited.

GEMARA:

What is the problem with **milk**? If they were worried about substitution, permitted milk is white, forbidden milk is green; if they were worried about mixture, let them curdle it, for a teacher said, Permitted milk curdles; forbidden milk does not curdle. If he wants to make it into cheese, that would be all right; but [perhaps] we are dealing here with someone who wants it as food. Then let him take a little of it and see if it curdles. [That won't do, since] even *kasher* milk has some whey in it that doesn't curdle, so it would be impossible to tell. Alternatively, even if he wants to make it into cheese, some [whey] remains in the spaces[, so he could not be sure no non-*kasher* milk was present].

Bread. Rav Kahana said in the name of Rabbi Yoḥanan, Bread was not permitted by [Rabbi's] court. Can we infer from this that there was a court that permitted it? Yes, for when Rav Dimi arrived he said, I once met Rabbi in the country, and an idolater brought him an oven loaf weighing a *seah*; Rabbi said,

21. 'Stickleback' (Jastrow, *Dictionary*) is doubtful; 'asafoetida' is devil's dung; *ḥilleq* is another small fish of uncertain identity; the Gemara suggests later (39b) that *salqondrit* is a kind of salt, popular among high-class Romans, in which small pieces of non-*kasher* fish are mixed.

What good bread this is! Why ever did the Sages forbid it? Why indeed? Surely it was on account of [fraternization leading to] intermarriage! What [Rabbi] meant was, Why did the Sages forbid it even in the country [where fraternization is unlikely]? People [who heard about this incident] thought that Rabbi had permitted bread, but it was not so; Rabbi had not permitted bread.

Rav Yosef – some say, Shmuel bar Yehuda – said, That is not what took place. But Rabbi went to another place and saw that the disciples were short of bread. He asked, Isn't there a baker in the place? People thought he meant even a baker who was an idolater, but he only meant an Israelite baker.

Rabbi Ḥelbo said, Even according to those who permit bread baked by an idolatrous baker, it is only if there is no Israelite baker, but not where there is an Israelite baker. Rabbi Yoḥanan said, Even according to those who permit bread baked by an idolatrous baker, it is only in the country, but not in the town, on account of intermarriage. Aibu used to bite and eat bread in the country, and Rava – some say it was Rav Naḥman bar Isaac – said, Don't talk to Aibu; he eats Aramaean bread.

And oil. Rav says, Daniel issued the decree about oil; but
36a   Shmuel said, It is sprinkled from unclean pots, and that is why it is forbidden. Does everyone eat according to the laws of purity, then? [Shmuel meant,] It is sprinkled from forbidden pots.

Shmuel said to Rav: On my view, that [oil is forbidden] because of sprinkling from forbidden pots, [it makes sense that] when Rabbi Isaac bar Shmuel bar Martha came, he said that Rabbi Simlai had explained in Nisibis that Rabbi Judah and his court had voted to permit oil; this would have been because he held that something that [merely] spoils the taste in permitted. But on your view, that Daniel issued the decree, if Daniel decreed, how could Rabbi Judah ha-Nasi and his court rescind it? Have we not learned that a court **cannot annul the decisions of another unless it is greater in both learning and number?**[22]

---

22. Mishna *Eduyot* 1:5 (see p. 536). Daniel is thought by the rabbis to have presided over the court of the Great Synod.

Are you talking of Simlai of Lydda? asked [Rav]. Lyddans don't take things seriously.

Shall I send to him, then?

Rav was embarrassed;[23] he said, If they didn't explain, should we not do so? It is written, **AND DANIEL RESOLVED NOT TO BE POLLUTED WITH THE KING'S FOOD OR THE WINE OF HIS BANQUETS** (Daniel 1:8).

Scripture speaks of 'banquets' in the plural, one of wine and one of oil. Rav holds, He resolved, and instructed all Israel; Shmuel holds, He resolved, but he did not instruct all Israel.

Did Daniel really issue the decree about oil? Surely Bali said that Abimi Nota'a said in Rav's name, Bread, wine, oil and the daughters of Gentiles were all [prohibited] as part of the Eighteen Measures.[24] You might want to argue that Daniel issued the decree, but it failed to gain acceptance; the disciples of Hillel and Shammai reissued it, and then it was accepted. But in that case, what was Rav testifying? Perhaps Daniel decreed against it in town, and [the Schools] prohibited it also in the country? Then how could Rabbi Judah ha-Nasi and his court rescind something instituted by the disciples of Hillel and Shammai? Have we not learned that a court **cannot annul the decisions of another unless it is greater in both learning and number**? And further, Did not Rabba bar bar Ḥana say in Rabbi Yoḥanan's name, A court may revise any measures taken by another court, but not the Eighteen Measures, for even if Elijah and his court came we wouldn't listen [to the rescinding of the Eighteen Measures]?

Rav Mesharshya said, The reason [the decrees concerning wine and bread took effect] was that they took hold among a majority of Israel; [the prohibition of] oil did not take hold

---

23. The text appears to be corrupt here.
24. Eighteen decrees said to have been passed, centuries after Daniel, on an occasion when the School of Shammai outnumbered the School of Hillel (*Shabbat* 13b; 17b), but there is no agreement as to precisely what they were.

among a majority of Israel. Indeed, Rav Shmuel bar Abba said in Rabbi Yoḥanan's name, Our rabbis sat and enquired, and [ascertained that] the prohibition of oil had not taken hold among a majority of Israel, so our rabbis relied on the words of Rabban Simeon ben Gamaliel and Rabbi Eleazar bar Zadok who used to say, **No decree may be issued to the public that the majority of the public are unable to observe**. Rav Ada bar Ahava said, What verse [shows this]? **You ARE SUFFERING UNDER A CURSE, YET YOU, THE WHOLE NATION, ROB ME** (Malachi 3:9) – if the whole nation backs it, yes; if not, no![25]

36b

Let's examine that statement: Bali said that Abimi Nota'a said in Rav's name, Bread, wine, oil and the daughters of Gentiles were all [prohibited] as part of the Eighteen Measures. What does he mean by 'the daughters'? Rav Naḥman bar Isaac said, They decreed that the daughters should be regarded as menstruant from the cradle. G'neiva said in Rav's name, All the decrees were to do with idolatry, for when Rav Aḥa bar Ada came, he said in Rabbi Isaac's name that they prohibited the bread on account of the oil. Why was oil any worse than bread? [Rather,] they prohibited bread and oil because of wine, wine on account of the daughters, the daughters because of something else, and something else because of something else.

Because of something else? Surely their daughters were prohibited by the Torah, for it is written, **You SHALL NOT INTERMARRY WITH THEM** (Deuteronomy 7:3)! The Torah prohibits marriage with the seven [Canaanite] nations, but not with other Gentiles; they introduced a ban on intermarriage with other Gentiles.

The Gemara establishes (37a) that it was Judah II (Rabbi Judah Nesia, grandson of Judah ha-Nasi) who permitted oil; he had refrained from permitting bread, as he did not wish his court to get a reputation for undue permissiveness.

25. The 'curse' is imposed on the people by the rabbis for infringing the decree; it applies only if the whole nation has accepted the decree.

CHAPTER FOUR

MISHNA:

They asked the elders in Rome, If [God] doesn't want idols   54b
worshipped, why doesn't He destroy them? They replied: If
people worshipped useless things, He would destroy them. But
people worship the sun and the moon and stars and constellations; should He destroy His world because of fools?

Then why doesn't He destroy the useless things and leave the
useful ones? They replied, That would encourage those who
worshipped [the useful things] to believe that they really were
gods, since they had not been destroyed.

GEMARA:

The rabbis taught: **Some philosophers asked the elders in
Rome, If [God] doesn't want idols worshipped, why doesn't
He destroy them? They replied, If people worshipped useless
things He would destroy them. But people worship the sun
and the moon and stars and constellations; should He destroy
His world because of fools? But the world continues on its
course, and the fools who have abused it will face judgement.
Another explanation: If someone stole a *seah* of wheat and
sowed it in the ground, justice [dictates] that it should not
grow. But the world continues on its course, and the fools
who have abused it will face judgement. Another explanation:
If someone slept with another's wife, justice [dictates] that she
should not become pregnant. But the world continues on its
course, and the fools who have abused it will face judgement.**

That is what Resh Laqish [had in mind when he]
said, The Holy One, blessed be He, says, Not only do
they counterfeit my coin, but they force Me to stamp
My seal on it against My will.

A philosopher asked Rabban Gamaliel, It is written in your
Torah, **FOR THE LORD YOUR GOD IS A CONSUMING FIRE, A
ZEALOUS**[26] **GOD** (Deuteronomy 4:24). Why does He direct His

26. 'Zealous' and 'jealous', though etymologically identical, have acquired separate
    meanings in English. The Hebrew covers both, and is translated according to
    context.

zeal toward the worshippers rather than to what is worshipped?
[Rabban Gamaliel] replied, Let me tell you a parable. It is like
a king of flesh and blood who had an only son. The son had a
dog, and named it after his father, and when he uttered an oath
he did so in the name of 'dog-father'. When the king heard
about this, would he be angry with his son or with the dog?
Surely he would be angry with his son.

[The philosopher:] You compare [the idol] to a dog? It is for
real!

[Rabban Gamaliel:] What evidence do you have?

[The philosopher:] Fire once broke out in our city and all the
buildings were consumed apart from the temple.

[Rabban Gamaliel:] Let me give you [another] parable. What
is this like? It is like a king of flesh and blood against whom a
province rebelled. Did he then do battle with the living or with
the dead? Surely with the living.

[The philosopher:] You compared [the idol] with a dog. Now
you compare it with a corpse! If so, why does He not destroy
it?

[Rabban Gamaliel:] If people worshipped only useless things
He would destroy them. But people worship the sun and the
moon, stars and constellations, wells and valleys; should He
destroy His world because of fools? Similarly it says, I WILL
SWEEP EVERYTHING AWAY FROM THE FACE OF THE EARTH –
DECLARES THE LORD. I WILL SWEEP AWAY MAN AND BEAST;
I WILL SWEEP AWAY THE BIRDS OF THE SKY AND THE FISH
OF THE SEA, THE THINGS THAT MAKE THE WICKED
STUMBLE,[27] AND I WILL DESTROY MANKIND FROM THE FACE
OF THE EARTH – DECLARES THE LORD (Zephaniah 1:2 JPS).
Should He destroy things in the world because the wicked
stumble over them? They even worship [other] men – should
He therefore DESTROY MANKIND FROM THE FACE OF THE
EARTH?

General Agrippa asked Rabban Gamaliel, In your Torah is
written, FOR THE LORD YOUR GOD IS A CONSUMING FIRE, A

27. JPS has 'I will make the wicked stumble', but notes that the meaning of the
    Hebrew is uncertain.

JEALOUS GOD. A clever man envies another clever man, a strong man envies a strong man, a rich man envies a rich man. [Rabban Gamaliel] replied, Let me tell you a parable. It is like a man who married a second wife. If the second wife is of higher class than the first she is not jealous;[28] if of lower class, she would be jealous.

Zeno[29] said to Rabbi Aqiva, You and I know in our hearts that there is no substance to idols, yet we see sick people enter [the temples] and come out healed. How does this happen? Rabbi Aqiva replied, Let me tell you a parable. It is like a trustworthy man who lived in a town and everyone in the town entrusted [their valuables] to him without witnesses. A man came to town and deposited something with him before witnesses, but on another occasion forgot, and made a deposit without witnesses. The [trustworthy] man's wife said [to her husband], We can deny it! He replied, Should we undermine our trustworthiness just because this man was foolish? The same is true of suffering. When afflictions are visited on a person, they are made to swear that they will only attack him on such-and-such a day and that they will leave him on such-and-such a day, at such-and-such an hour, by such-and-such a healer and through such-and-such a potion. Once the time has come for them to leave him, if he happens to enter the temple, the afflictions say, By rights we should not now leave him. But then they say, Should we break our oath because of this fool?

This is like Rabbi Yoḥanan's observation: What is the meaning of **BAD BUT RELIABLE DISEASES** (Deuteronomy 28:59)?[30] They are bad when sent, but reliable to leave.

Rava bar Rav Isaac said to Rav Yehuda, In our town there is an idolatrous temple. When rain is needed, [the goddess] appears to them in a dream and says to them, Kill a man for me and I

---

28. The pronouns are indeterminate. Rashi, by whose time Western Jews were strictly monogamous, thinks that the first wife would not spite her husband out of envy for the second. Other explanations are possible.
29. Possible rendering, but cannot be Zeno of Elea or of Cytium.
30. This is a literal translation, to fit the interpretation. JPS has 'malignant and chronic diseases'.

will bring you rain; they killed a man and rain came. [Rav Yehuda] replied, Had I died I would not have told you what Rav said: What is the meaning of **WHICH THE LORD HAS APPORTIONED TO ALL THE PEOPLES** (Deuteronomy 4:19)? He caused them to slip,[31] to remove them from the world. This is like what Resh Laqish said: What is the meaning of, **AT SCOFFERS HE SCOFFS, BUT TO THE LOWLY HE SHOWS GRACE** (Proverbs 3:34 JPS)? If someone seeks impurity, he is given the opportunity [to sin]; if he seeks purity, he is helped.

31. *Ḥalaq* (apportion) and *heḥeliq* (slip) are derived from the same root.

NINTH TRACTATE
AVOT (WISDOM OF THE FATHERS)

The five chapters of this tractate, together with the fuller version known as Avot de Rabbi Nathan, *form a rabbinic counterpart to the Wisdom books of the Bible; the popular title, 'Ethics of the Fathers', is a little misleading.*

But it has another agenda, to demonstrate the authenticity of the rabbinic tradition. Whereas the Bible constantly designates the priests of the tribe of Levi as guardians and teachers of the Torah, Avot *omits them from its chain of tradition, substituting 'elders', who are anachronistically presented as rabbis and Sages who quietly preserved the tradition throughout the biblical period.[1] The 'chain of tradition' becomes two rival chains after Hillel and Shammai: one chain (1:1– 2:4a, presented here) proceeds through the family of the Nasi to Gamaliel III, son of Judah ha-Nasi; the other (2:4b-14) through Yoḥanan ben Zakkai and his disciples.*

CHAPTER ONE

1. **Moses received the Torah at Sinai. He transmitted it to Joshua, Joshua to the elders,[2] the elders to the prophets, and the prophets transmitted it to the men of the Great Synod.**

   They said three things: Be cautious in judgement; raise many disciples; make protective measures for the Torah.

1. On the change from priests to rabbis, see Rivkin, *Hidden Revolution*.
2. 'And Israel served the Lord throughout the days of Joshua and of the elders who [succeeded] Joshua' (Joshua 24:31).

2. Simeon the Just was one of the last Men of the Great Synod. He used to say, The world rests on three things: Torah, Temple service and deeds of kindness.

3. Antigonos of Sokho received [the tradition] from Simeon the Just. He used to say, Do not be like servants who serve their master to receive reward, but be like servants who serve their master without thought of reward; let the fear of Heaven be upon you!

4. Yosé ben Yo'ezer of Tzereda and Yosé ben Yoḥanan of Jerusalem received [the tradition] from him. Yosé ben Yo'ezer said, Let your home be a meeting place for the wise; cover yourself with the dust at their feet; imbibe their words thirstily.

5. Yosé ben Yoḥanan of Jerusalem said, Let your home be open wide; let the poor make up your household; do not talk too much with women. They say [he meant even] with your own wife, how much more so with other men's wives! From this the Sages learned that when a man engages in too much talk with women he brings harm on himself, neglects the study of Torah and ends up in Hell.

6. Joshua ben Peraḥia and Nittai of Arbil received [the tradition] from them. Joshua ben Peraḥia says, Get yourself a master, earn a friend and give everyone the benefit of the doubt.

7. Nittai of Arbil says, Avoid a bad neighbour; do not befriend an evil person; do not despair of punishment.

8. Judah ben Tabbai and Simeon ben Shetaḥ received [the tradition] from them. Judah ben Tabbai says, Don't be a legal counsel;[3] when litigants come before you regard them as guilty; when they leave the court consider them innocent, for they have accepted [the court's] judgement.[4]

9. Simeon ben Shetaḥ says, Examine the witnesses thoroughly, but be careful how you express yourself, so that they do not learn from you to lie.[5]

---

3.   Lawyers who advise on how to present a case in court and are in danger of wresting judgement.

4.   People are of course innocent before the law until proven guilty; Judah simply wants to ensure that both parties to a dispute are questioned thoroughly.

5.   The form of questioning can easily suggest to a witness how to give false answers.

10. Shemaia and Avtalion received [the tradition] from them. Shemaia says, Love work, hate [exercising] authority and don't make yourself known to those in ruling cicles.

11. Avtalion says: Sages! take care how you speak, so that you do not incur the penalty of exile and are exiled to a place where the waters are bad and the disciples who follow you there drink the bad waters and die, profaning the name of Heaven![6]

12. Hillel and Shammai received [the tradition] from them. Hillel says, Be a disciple of Aaron – love peace, pursue peace, love people and bring them to Torah.

13. He used to say: Who pursues fame loses his [good] name; who does not increase his learning decreases it; who does not learn at all forfeits his life; who takes worldly advantage of the crown [of Torah] passes away.

14. He used to say: If I am not for myself, who is for me? If I am for myself, who am I? If not now, when?

15. Shammai says, Let Torah be the focus[7] of your life; say little but do much; receive all men with a cheerful face.

16. Rabban Gamaliel[8] says, Get yourself a teacher and be rid of doubt; do not tithe by guesswork.

17. His son, Simeon, says, I grew up surrounded by Sages, and I found nothing better for myself than silence; not talk, but action is the important thing; too much talk leads to sin.

18. Rabban Simeon[9] the son of Gamaliel says, The world rests on three things: justice, truth and peace; as it is said, RENDER TRUTH AND THE JUDGEMENT OF PEACE IN YOUR GATES (Zechariah 8:16).

6. This is a metaphor for exile to a place where there are pernicious religious influences. Traditional commentators point to Antigonos; since he over-stressed the ideal of service without thought of reward, his disciples left him to follow 'Zadok and Boethius' – possibly Sadducees.
7. Literally, 'the fixed thing'.
8. Gamaliel I – 'the Elder'.
9. Grandson of the Simeon in the preceding paragraph, and son of Gamaliel II, who is not cited here.

CHAPTER TWO

1. Rabbi [Judah ha-Nasi] says, What is the right path for a man to choose? Whatever is honourable to the one who follows it and earns him the respect of others. Take as great care over a small *mitzva* as over a great one, for you do not know the value[10] of each *mitzva*; weigh the loss of neglecting a good deed against the reward for doing it, and the punishment for a sin against the loss of [refraining from] it; reflect on three things and you will refrain from sin: know that above you are an eye that sees and an ear that hears, and that all your deeds are recorded in a book!

2. Rabban Gamaliel,[11] the son of Rabbi Judah ha-Nasi, says, It is good to combine the study of Torah with a worldly occupation,[12] for the two together drive sinful thoughts out of your mind; if [study of] Torah is not combined with work, it becomes an idle pursuit and leads to sin; all who undertake public service[13] should do so for the sake of Heaven, for [then] the merit of their fathers comes to their aid and their good work endures – as for you[, God will say], I grant you great reward as if you yourselves had achieved [these things].

3. Be cautious with government officials, for they only befriend you in their own interest; they act like friends when it suits them, but do not stand up for you when you need them.

4. He used to say: Do His will as if it were your own, then He will do your will as His; negate your will before His, then He will negate that of others before yours.

10. Literally, 'reward'.
11. Gamaliel III, son of Judah ha-Nasi. The inclusion of his sayings is an indication that *Avot*, as we have it, is later than the bulk of the Mishna.
12. This is the meaning of *derekh eretz* here, though it often means 'good manners'.
13. Literally, 'work with the congregation'.

TENTH TRACTATE
HORAYOT (DECISIONS)

Leviticus sets out the atonement procedure for a sin committed unwittingly by the High Priest (4:3–14) or by 'the whole community' (4:13–21), the latter being understood by the Sages to refer to action taken on the basis of faulty rulings issued by the High Court (Sanhedrin, or Bet Din). Deuteronomy 17:8–13 covers the case of a rebellious elder who challenges the High Court's ruling.

The short opening section perfectly illustrates the alternative versions in which a discussion might be transmitted in the academies and preserved by the editors of the Gemara. It addresses the question of what constitutes a 'ruling' rather than a theoretical statement.

CHAPTER ONE

MISHNA:

If the Bet Din issued a ruling contrary to any of the commandments of the Torah and an individual acted on the basis of what they had said, not knowing it was wrong, then whether they acted and he acted with them, or they acted and he acted following them, or whether they did not act but he did, he is exempt [from any penalty], since he relied on them.

If the Bet Din issued a ruling and one member – even a disciple who was capable of ruling – knew it was mistaken, and acted on the basis of what they had said, then whether they acted and he acted with them or they acted and he acted

2a

following them, or whether they did not act but he did, he is liable [to the penalty], since he did not rely on the Bet Din.

The rule is, If he relies on [his own judgement], he is liable; if he relies on [the judgement of] the Bet Din, he is exempt.

GEMARA:

Shmuel said, The Bet Din is not liable unless they say, You are permitted! Rav Dimi of Nehardea said, Unless they say to [specific people], You are permitted to do that! Why? Because otherwise it is not a completed 'ruling'.

Abbaye said, This is clear from the Mishna: **If [the rebellious elder] returned to his town and taught as he had previously taught, he is exempt; but if he instructs people to act, he is liable.**[1]

Rabbi Abba said, We too have found it in a Mishna: **If the court gave her permission to remarry, but she went and committed fornication [and then her husband returned], she must bring sacrifice, for the court only permitted her to marry[, not to commit fornication].**[2]

Ravina said, We too have found it in a Mishna: **If the Bet Din issued a ruling contrary to any of the commandments of the Torah – period!**

Some [give an alternative version of the preceding]:

Shmuel said, The Bet Din is not liable unless they say, You are permitted to do that! Rav Dimi of Nehardea said, Even if they just say, You are permitted!, it is a completed 'ruling'.

Abbaye said, That is not what the Mishna states: **If [the rebellious elder] returned to his town and taught as he had previously taught, he is exempt; but if he instructs people to act, he is liable.**

Rabbi Abba said, But the Mishna says otherwise: **If the court gave her permission to remarry, but she went and committed fornication [and then her husband returned], she must bring sacrifice, for the court only permitted her to marry[, not to commit fornication].**

Ravina said, But the Mishna says otherwise: **If the Bet Din**

1. *Sanhedrin* 86b.
2. *Yevamot* 87b (see p. 323).

issued a ruling contrary to any of the commandments of the
Torah – period!

The concluding Mishnas of this tractate and Order constitute a
clear declaration of the scale of human values as seen by the
Tannaim. Maximum privilege is accorded to Torah learning and
to faithfulness to God's commandments. There is a nuanced
approach to social convention: moral absolutism is firmly
rejected; agonizing choices must be made, and are.

CHAPTER THREE

MISHNA:
A man has priority over a woman in regard to life-saving   13a
and the restoration of lost property. A woman has priority
over a man with regard to clothing and to rescue from captivity,
but if both are at risk of [sexual] abuse, the man has priority
over the woman.
GEMARA:
The rabbis taught: He, his father and his [Torah] teacher
are in captivity; he has priority [for ransom] over his teacher,
and his teacher over his father; the mother has priority over
all of them. The Sage has priority over a king of Israel, for if
a Sage dies he is irreplaceable, but if a king of Israel dies any
Israelite can become king of Israel. The king takes priority
over a High Priest, for it is said, THE KING SAID TO THEM,
TAKE WITH YOU YOUR MASTER'S SERVANTS . . . ZADOK THE
PRIEST (1 Kings 1:33, 34). The High Priest takes priority over
a prophet, for it says, LET ZADOK THE PRIEST AND NATHAN
THE PROPHET ANOINT HIM (1 Kings 1:34) – Zadok is put
before Nathan. Similarly, it says, LISTEN, JOSHUA THE HIGH
PRIEST, YOU AND YOUR FRIENDS . . . [MEN OF WONDERS]
(Zechariah 3:8) – and they were not ordinary people, for they
are called men of wonders, and 'men of wonders' refers to
prophets, as it is said, IF HE GIVES YOU A SIGN OR A WONDER
(Deuteronomy 13:2).
A High Priest anointed with oil takes precedence over one

who [merely] wears high priestly robes; [an acting High Priest] with high priestly robes takes precedence over an anointed High Priest who is suspended owing to a seminal emission; an anointed High Priest who is suspended owing to a seminal emission takes precedence over an anointed High Priest who is suspended owing to a blemish; an anointed High Priest who is suspended owing to a blemish takes precedence over a High Priest anointed for war; a High Priest anointed for war takes precedence over an assistant High Priest; an assistant High Priest takes precedence over an *amarkal* – (What is an *amarkal*? Rav Ḥisda said, One who says (*amar*) everything (*kol*))[3] – an *amarkal* takes precedence over a treasurer; a treasurer takes precedence over the head of the priestly course; the head of the priestly course takes precedence over the head of the father's house; the head of the father's house takes precedence over an ordinary *Kohen*.

The question was asked: With regard to defilement who has precedence, the assistant High Priest or the one anointed for war? Mar Zutra the son of Rav Naḥman settled [this question on the basis of] a baraita: **If the assistant [High Priest] and the one anointed for war were walking along and came across a corpse that required burial, it is preferable for the one anointed for war to defile himself rather than the assistant, since if the High Priest suffers some mishap the assistant must take over from him.** But didn't the baraita [above] state, **A High Priest anointed for war takes precedence over an assistant High Priest?** Ravina said, That was with regard to saving his life.

The following Mishna is a radical statement of the priority of Torah learning over honourable descent, all the more striking in view of the emphasis on pure lineage in Qiddushin *Chapter Four. After discussion of the biblical basis for the order of precedence and its consequences, the tractate concludes with an account of some historical disputes. The story of the plot of Rabbis Meir and Nathan has been worked over in the light of subsequent relations, in Babylonia as well as Palestine, between leaders with conflicting political and academic commitments.*

3.   i.e. an administrator.

MISHNA:

A *Kohen* takes precedence over a Levite, a Levite over an Israelite, an Israelite over a *mamzer*, a *mamzer* over a *natin*, a *natin* over a proselyte, a proselyte over a freed slave. When does this apply? If they are otherwise equal. But if the *mamzer* was a man of learning and the High Priest an ignoramus, the learned *mamzer* takes precedence over the ignorant High Priest.

GEMARA:

The rabbis taught: When the Nasi enters, all the people 13b stand, and they do not sit until he tells them to; when the Father of the Court enters, they make two rows flanking him until he takes his seat; when a [rank-and-file] Sage enters, one rises and one sits[4] until he takes his seat. Children of Sages and disciples of Sages, if they are needed by the people, may step around the people.[5] If someone has to go out for his [bodily] needs, he returns and takes his seat. Children of disciples whose fathers have been appointed as communal leaders may enter and sit facing their fathers, with their backs to the people, if they are capable of understanding the discourse, but if not, they sit in front of their fathers facing the people; Rabbi Eleazar the son of Rabbi Zadok says, Even at feasts they may attach themselves to their fathers.

If someone has to go out for his [bodily] needs, he returns and takes his seat. Rav Papa said, That is only for small needs, but not for big, for he should have tested himself previously; as Rav Yehuda said in Rav's name, A person should [relieve his bowels] early and late so that he doesn't need to go away.[6] Rava[7] said, Nowadays, since people are weak, it applies even for big [needs].

Rabbi Eleazar the son of Rabbi Zadok says, Even at feasts they may attach themselves to their fathers. Rava commented, In their fathers' lifetime, and in their fathers' presence.

---

4. People rise individually as he passes them, then sit.
5. Literally, 'may step over the heads of people'; i.e. no one rises for them, but they may enter even though people are already present.
6. Suitable facilities may have been outside the town.
7. Uncertain reading.

Rabbi Yoḥanan related: This Mishna was formulated in the days of Rabban Simeon ben Gamaliel; Rabban Simeon ben Gamaliel was Nasi, Rabbi Meir was a [leading] Sage, and Rabbi Nathan was Father of the Court. When Rabban Simeon ben Gamaliel was present everyone stood, and when Rabbi Meir or Rabbi Nathan entered everyone stood before them. Rabban Simeon ben Gamaliel said, Should there be no distinction between me and them? So he formulated this Mishna. That day, neither Rabbi Meir nor Rabbi Nathan was present. When they entered the next day, they noticed that people no longer stood before them as they had previously done. They enquired and were told that this had been instituted by Rabban Simeon ben Gamaliel.

Rabbi Meir said to Rabbi Nathan, I am the [leading] Sage and you are Father of the Court; we should do something to protect our positions. What can we do? We will ask him to expound ‘Uqtzin, which he is not familiar with, and as he has not learned it, we will say, **Who can tell the mighty acts of the Lord, proclaim all His praises?** (Psalm 106:2 JPS) – only the one who proclaims *all* His praises[8] is fit to tell the mighty acts – then we will depose him; I will be Father of the Court, and you will be Nasi.

Rabbi Jacob ben Qorshi overheard them. He thought, God forbid, this may lead to deep offence! So he went and sat behind Rabban Simeon ben Gamaliel's room and repeatedly recited [‘Uqtzin]. [Rabban Simeon] thought, What is going on? Perhaps something is afoot in the House of Study. So he put his mind to learning it.

The next day they said, May your honour expound ‘Uqtzin to us? When he had finished he said, Had I not learned it, you would have shamed me! And he gave orders to exclude them from the House of Study. They wrote questions on tablets and threw them in; he answered those he could, and they threw in the replies to those he could not answer.

Rabbi Yosé protested, The Torah is outside and we are in! Rabban Simeon ben Gamaliel said, Then let them come in, but

8.   Who knows every tractate of the Torah, including ‘Uqtzin.

we will penalize them by not allowing any teaching to be repeated in their name; Rabbi Meir's teaching will be given as 'others say', and Rabbi Nathan's as 'some say'.

[Rabbis Nathan and Meir] received [a message] in their dreams: Go, make it up with Rabban Simeon! Rabbi Nathan went, but Rabbi Meir did not; he said, Dreams are of no import. When Rabbi Nathan went, Rabban Simeon ben Gamaliel said to him, Your father's *qamra*[9] may have helped you to become Father of the Court; do you think it will make you Nasi?!

This was Simeon ben Gamaliel II, father of Judah ha-Nasi ('Rabbi'), who in turn had a son named Simeon. The next anecdote explains why, despite Simeon II's decree, Rabbi Meir is frequently cited by name: it is wrong to perpetuate ancient quarrels.

Rabbi taught his son, [the future] Rabban Simeon [III]: **Others say, If it was a substitute it is not offered**. Who are   14a
these 'others' whose waters we drink, but who are not named? asked Simeon. [Rabbi replied,] My son, those are the men who sought to destroy your dignity and the dignity of your father's house. [Simeon:] **THEIR LOVES, THEIR HATES, THEIR JEAL-OUSIES HAVE LONG SINCE PERISHED** (Ecclesiastes 9:6 JPS). [Rabbi:] **THE ENEMY HAS CEASED, BUT THE RUINS ARE FOR-EVER** (Psalm 9:7). [Simeon:] That is if they achieved their purpose; those rabbis did not achieve their purpose. [Rabbi] then taught him again: **Rabbi Meir says, If it was a substitute, it is not offered**.

Rava said, Even Rabbi, who was meek, taught: **They said in the name of Rabbi Meir**; he did not say, **Rabbi Meir said**.

Rabbi Yoḥanan said, Rabban Simeon ben Gamaliel and the rabbis differed; one said, Sinai is preferable, the other said, the uprooter of mountains is preferred.[10]

Rav Yosef was Sinai, Rabba an uprooter of moun-tains. They sent to Palestine: Who takes precedence, Sinai or the uprooter of mountains? Word came back:

9. A belt or sash indicating high position.
10. Sinai is a term for the scholar whose knowledge of tradition is totally reliable; 'uprooter of mountains' is the one who excels in debate.

Sinai is preferred, for as the teacher says, Everyone needs wheat.[11] Even so, Rav Yosef declined to take office. Rabba ruled for twenty-two years, and then Rav Yosef succeeded him. The whole time that Rabba ruled, Rav Yosef wouldn't even allow a bloodletter into his own home.[12]

The tractate concludes with a light-hearted tale about four young students jockeying for position.

Abbaye, Rava, Rabbi Zeira and Rav Matna were sitting together and wanted a leader. Whoever can make a statement that no one can refute shall be leader, they said. All their statements were refuted except Abbaye's. Rabba[13] saw that Abbaye was putting on airs; Naḥmani! he said, Start![14]

They asked, Who takes precedence, Rabbi Zeira or Rabba bar Rav Matna? Rabbi Zeira is sharp and asks hard questions; Rav Matna takes his time but reaches conclusions. They were silent.

---

11. No point in argument unless you have a solid foundation on which to argue.
12. The translation is in accordance with Rashi's first interpretation, that out of respect to Rabba everything had to be done at Rabba's place.
13. The teacher and adoptive father of Abbaye.
14. Rashi's second explanation is that Rabba, addressing him as Naḥmani, was reminding him that he was still a student.

FIFTH ORDER

QODASHIM
(HOLY THINGS)

INTRODUCTION

Rabbi Eleazar said, To act justly is greater than any sacrifice, as it is said, TO DO WHAT IS RIGHT AND JUST IS MORE DESIRED BY THE LORD THAN SACRIFICE (Proverbs 21:3 JPS). And, said Rabbi Eleazar, to act with kindness is greater than to act justly, as it is said, SOW RIGHTEOUSNESS FOR YOURSELVES; REAP THE FRUITS OF KINDNESS (Hosea 10:12) – When a man sows, there is doubt whether he will eat or not; when he reaps, he will certainly eat. (Sukka 49b)

Animal sacrifice was a normal, familiar activity in the ancient world. Aristotle's Athenian Constitution *sets out the responsibilities of the highest officers of the city-state for correct performance of the sacrifices;*[1] *the Roman statesman Cicero (106–43 BCE), drafting his legislation for the ideal state, commences with religious regulations concerning gods, priests and offerings of grain, fruits, milk, offspring and the like.*[2] *The third-century-CE philosopher Porphyry, in a treatise advocating vegetarianism, writes:* 'As it is not necessary, if animals are to be sacrificed, that they are also to be eaten, we shall now show that it is necessary we should not eat them, though it may be sometimes necessary that they should be sacrificed';[3] *while the Emperor Julian (361–3), shocked by Christian opposition to*

---

1. Aristotle, *Athenian Constitution*, Book 8; on Greek sacrifice in general, see Burkert, *Greek Religion*, Part II.
2. Cicero, *De legibus* 2:8.
3. Porphyry, 'Books on Abstinence', p. 71.

traditional religion and sacrifices to the gods, strove to restore temples including that in Jerusalem.[4]

Jewish sacrifice in the late Second Temple period differed from that of most contemporary religions in three radical ways:

It was dedicated to a universal God who could not be represented by any image.

It was limited to one central sanctuary, in Jerusalem.

In common with other systems it articulated personal and collective relationships with the divine (atonement, purification, thanksgiving), but unlike them, it was free of association with any kind of divination; Roman sacrifice, for instance, involved a haruspex whose function was to read the entrails and divine the future.

A sacrifice is essentially a meal that is presented to God, and in most cases shared with Him, i.e. partly or wholly eaten by people (hence 'communion'). It may express atonement, gratitude or simple joy in the Presence of God.

The rabbis called this form of worship avoda ('service' – i.e. the service of God par excellence), and recommended that children should commence their Torah studies with Leviticus – 'Let the pure study the pure.'[5]

The Jerusalem Temple was destroyed by the Romans in 70. Why, then, do the Mishna and Talmud devote so much attention to the Temple procedure? Hopes for restoration remained strong, while the following exchange provides an additional answer:

Rav Naḥman said that Rabba bar Avuha said in the name of Rav, The halakha goes according to what Rabbi Eleazar said in the name of Rabbi Yosé.

Rava [protested], This is a halakha for the Messiah![6]

Abbaye said to him, In that case, none of the tractate Zevaḥim should be taught, seeing that it is [all] halakha for the Messiah! But 'Study, and receive the reward' – here, likewise, study and receive the reward.

4.   e.g. Julian, *Against the Galileans*, pp. 152–5.
5.   *Pesikta d'Rav Kahana* (Mandelbaum) 6:3.
6.   It is pointless, since such a case could only arise in the time of the Messiah.

[Rava retorted:] What I meant was, the halakhic *[decision could be left] for the Messiah! (Zevaḥim 44b–45a)*

Rashi interprets Rava's final words: I expressed surprise that a decision was made. We do indeed need to study the opinions on Temple procedure, for this is Torah, so 'Study, and receive the reward'; but deciding the halakha is relevant only for practice, and the laws are not in practice at this time.

Abbaye and Rava convey an attitude to study of the sacrificial rites which has certainly been common among Jews since that period; it is virtuous ('a mitzva') to meditate on the divinely revealed Torah and its provisions even when it is not possible to put them into practice.

The rabbis regarded the Torah as a seamless, consistent whole, of which the sacrificial laws were an integral part; to neglect the study of any part of it would undermine the logic of the whole, for comparisons could be made and inferences be drawn from one section to another.

There is no precise English vocabulary corresponding to the Hebrew terminology for sacrifices. Within this volume translation of terms used in biblical and Rabbinic Hebrew for sacrifice varies according to context and stylistic requirements:

Hebrew	Range of English equivalents
asham	Reparation- (guilt-, trespass-) offering
ḥatat	Purification-offering, sin-offering
ishshé	Gift,[7] offering by fire, fire-offering
minḥa	Grain offering[8]
olah	Upward-offering, burnt-offering, whole-offering
qorban	Offering (a general word derived from a root meaning 'to approach')
sh'lamim	Well-being, or peace-offering
zevaḥ	Sacrifice (a general word derived from a root meaning 'to slaughter')

7. On the basis of an Ugaritic cognate.
8. Translated in KJV as 'meat', but modern English reserves 'meat' for animal flesh.

FIRST TRACTATE
ZEVAḤIM (SACRIFICES)

The tractate opens with a discussion of intention. The holier an act of service is, the more important it is that the thought that accompanies it is pure and precise.

CHAPTER ONE

MISHNA:

All sacrifices, if offered with an incorrect category in mind, [remain] valid, though they do not fulfil the obligation of their owner.[1] The Passover lamb and the sin-offering are exceptions, the Passover lamb in its proper time [only], and the sin-offering at any time; Rabbi Eliezer says, Also the reparation-offering,[2] for, Rabbi Eliezer argued, The sin-offering comes [to atone] for sin, and the reparation-offering comes [to atone] for sin; just as the sin-offering is invalid if offered with an incorrect category in mind, so the reparation-offering is invalid if offered with an incorrect category in mind.

2a

Yosé ben Ḥoni says, [Offerings] slaughtered [with the thought that they are] Passover lambs or sin-offerings[, but which are not those things], are invalid.

1. The 'owner' of a sacrifice is the person on whose behalf it is offered. For example, if someone has vowed a peace-offering, and the priest offers it thinking that it is some other kind of offering, it is a valid offering per se, but does not fulfil the vow.
2. The repetition here of 'The Passover lamb in its proper time [only], and the sin-offering at any time', found in some copies, is probably a copyist's error.

Simeon the brother of Azaria says, If he slaughtered [an animal] thinking that it was a sacrifice of a higher degree [of holiness], it is valid, but if of a lower degree, it is invalid. How is this? If he slaughtered [sacrifices] of the most holy degree thinking that they were of a lesser degree of holiness, they are invalid, but if he slaughtered [sacrifices] of a minor degree thinking that they were of the highest degree, they are valid.

If someone slaughtered first-born or tithed [animals thinking that they were] peace-offerings, they are valid [offerings]; if he slaughtered peace-offerings [thinking that they were] first-born or tithed [animals], they are invalid.

GEMARA:

Why does the Mishna say, *though* they do not fulfil the obligation of their owner, rather than, *and* they do not fulfil? It is to teach us that though they do not fulfil the obligation of their owner, they retain their sacred status and may not be diverted to any other purpose. [This is in line with] what Rava said, If someone has slaughtered a whole-offering in the thought that it was a different kind of offering, he may not then sprinkle its blood with the intention of making it that kind of offering.

This [position can be justified] by reason or by Scripture.

By reason – Just because one mistake has been made, should he carry on making mistakes?

By Scripture – Scripture says, YOU MUST FULFIL CAREFULLY THAT WHICH ISSUES FROM YOUR LIPS; YOU SHALL ACT ACCORDING TO THE VOW YOU HAVE MADE VOLUNTARILY (Deuteronomy 23:24). VOLUNTARILY? Surely it is a VOW![3] So, if it is as you vowed, then it is a vow; otherwise, it is a voluntary [offering].

But is it permissible to divert a free-will offering [to some other purpose]?

2b

3. A vow creates an obligation, and this must be discharged correctly. If the vow was to bring a sacrifice to the Temple, and the priest or whoever slaughtered the animal did so with the wrong intention, the person who made the vow has failed to fulfil his or her obligation, though the sacrifice may proceed as an anonymous (or additional) voluntary offering.

Ravina said to Rav Papa, You weren't with us last night in the neighbourhood of Bei Ḥarmak[4] when Rava set some excellent statements in opposition and then reconciled them.

What excellent statements? **All sacrifices, if offered with an incorrect category in mind, [remain] valid, though they do not fulfil, etc.** – [They do not fulfil, etc.] because offered with an incorrect category in mind; [this implies that] had they been offered without any explicit category in mind they would fulfil the owner's obligation; that is, the absence of explicit designation is as [good as] the correct designation.

And he set against that: **A *get* that was written without specifying a wife is invalid**,[5] which implies that the absence of right intention invalidates.

He reconciled [the statements like this]: A sacrifice is assumed[, in the absence of evidence to the contrary,] to be designated [as whatever kind of sacrifice it is]; a wife is not assumed[, in the absence of evidence to the contrary,] to be designated for divorce!

And how do we know that sacrifices [offered] without [explicit] designation are all right? If you argue from this Mishna, **All sacrifices, if offered with an incorrect category in mind**, [rather than,] **All sacrifices, if offered without a correct category in mind** – we find the same in regard to a *get*, for the Mishna states: **A *get* that was written without specifying a wife is invalid**, rather than **A *get* that was not written for a specific wife is valid**.

Then perhaps [you can argue] from this Mishna: **How can [an offering] be designated [both] correctly and incorrectly? If he designated it a Passover [lamb] and then designated it a peace-offering.**[6] [This implies] that if he designated it a Passover [lamb] and then [made no designation], it is valid, from which you could infer that without designation is as [good as with the] correct designation. [But] perhaps that [case] is different, since when [continuing the sacrificial procedure,] he does this on the basis of his original designation.

4.   Near Pumbedita (Oppenheimer, *Babylonia*, p. 471).
5.   *Gittin* 24a.
6.   In two separate operations.

Then perhaps [you can argue] from the end [of the same Mishna]: **If he designated it as a peace-offering and then designated it as a Passover [lamb].** The reason [it is invalid] is that he designated it as a peace-offering and then as a Passover lamb, [which implies that] if he made no designation [at first], but only later designated it as a Passover lamb, it would be valid. [But] perhaps that [case] is different [too], since you might have thought that the later designation was [merely] a clarification of the earlier one.[7] Alternatively, since the Mishna taught [what happens] if someone first designated correctly and then incorrectly, it also teaches [what happens] if someone first designated incorrectly and then correctly.[8]

So it must be [inferred] from this [Mishna]: **A sacrifice is designated in six [ways]: for [whichever type of] sacrifice [it is], for the person on behalf of whom it is sacrificed, in the Name [of God], for burning [on the altar], for savour, for pleasantness;[9] sin- and reparation-offerings [are designated in addition] for the sin. Rabbi Yosé said, Even if [the officiating priest] had none of these things in mind, it is valid, for it is a condition imposed by the court.[10]** That is, the court imposed the condition that [the priest] should not actually state what the sacrifice was for, in case he got it wrong [and thereby invalidated it. Now,] if you think that without [explicit] designation the sacrifice is not valid, how could the court impose a condition that would invalidate it? [The conclusion is that the act of making a sacrifice does not require explicit designation.]

Chapter Five summarizes the rules for each kind of offering: its degree of sanctity, the precise location in which it is to be slaughtered, how many times and on which horn of the altar its blood must be sprinkled, which parts are burnt on the altar, which parts are eaten by the Kohanim or others, the time limit

7.   The Passover lamb is, after all, a kind of peace-offering.
8.   That is, it is a question of literary style.
9.   A frequent phrase in Leviticus (e.g. 1:9) is *reah nihoah*, 'a pleasing savour [to the Lord]', here taken as two separate terms.
10. *Zevahim* 46b.

for consumption of the sacrifice, and any special requirements. This is one of very few Mishna tractates for which no dispute is recorded; it is included in the Orthodox daily liturgy as a reminder of the the Temple service.

CHAPTER FIVE

MISHNA:

The upward-offering is of the highest degree of holiness, and is slaughtered on the north [side of the altar]. Its blood must be received in a sanctified receptacle on the north, and two donations, which are four, must be made of its blood [on the altar]. It requires flaying, division into parts and thorough burning as a fire-offering. 53b

GEMARA:

Why does [the Mishna specifically] state that [the upward-offering is] of the highest degree of holiness, [seeing that it has already indicated that it is listing the holiest offerings]? [It is] because Scripture does not refer to it as 'holy of holies'[, as it does with previous items in the list].

Two donations, which are four, must be made of its blood. How is that done? Rav says, He puts and puts again; Shmuel said, He sprinkles it like a Greek *gamma*.[11]

This corresponds to a debate of the Tannaim: **Do you think he should sprinkle [the blood] in one [place] only? It says, [THEY SHALL SPRINKLE THE BLOOD ON THE ALTAR] ROUND ABOUT (Leviticus 1:5). If ROUND ABOUT, perhaps he should draw a line around it? [That is not possible, since] it says, SPRINKLE. So how is it done? Like a *gamma* – two donations that are four. Rabbi Ishmael says, Here we have the expression ROUND ABOUT, and there we have the expression ROUND ABOUT (Leviticus 8:15);**

---

11. How does the *Kohen* manage to get blood on four sides in two acts? According to Rav, he moves from one corner of the altar to the one diagonally opposite, and from each position sprinkles blood on adjacent sides in turn; Shmuel agrees with the positions, but says that from each position the *Kohen* sprinkles only once, covering the angle (the *gamma*) and hence two sides in one motion.

just as there it means four separate donations, so here
also it means four separate donations. Should you
think that just as there it means a donation on each
of the four horns of the altar, so here also it means a
donation on each of the four horns of the altar, [that
cannot be, since] you find that [sprinkling the blood
of] the upward-offering must [commence] ABOVE
THE BASE (Leviticus 4:7), but the south-east horn is
not above the base.

*The altar (see Mishna Middot 3:1) rested on a base 32 cubits
square; above that was the main altar, 30 cubits square and 5
cubits high, surmounted by a fire-grate. The base, however, did
not extend the full length of the southern and eastern sides. The
Gemara, picking up on a theme expounded in* Avot de Rabbi
Nathan *35, relates this anomaly to the geographical location of
the Temple, straddling the ancient boundaries of the tribes of
Judah and Benjamin.*

Why is the south-east horn not above the base? Rabbi Eleazar
said, Because it was not within the territory of THE ONE WHO
SEIZES PREY (i.e. Benjamin – Genesis 49:27). As Rav Shmuel
bar Rav Isaac said, The altar extended one cubit into Judah's
territory.

A baraita[12] states: **Rabbi Levi bar Ḥama said in the name of
Rabbi Ḥama bar Ḥanina, A strip of land extended from the
territory of Judah into that of Benjamin. The righteous Benjamin was constantly distressed through his [unfulfilled] desire
for this, as it is said, HE WORRIES ABOUT IT ALL DAY; [he]
was therefore rewarded by becoming host to the Holy One,
blessed be He, as it is said, HE RESTS BETWEEN HIS SHOUL-
DERS (Deuteronomy 33:12).[13]**

54a

An objection [to the supposition that the base was
incomplete]: **How was the bird purification-sacrifice
performed? [The priest] pinched off its head opposite**

12. This follows the parallel in *Yoma* 12a.
13. Benjamin is described as 'righteous' in the sense that he desired possession of the
holiest spot on earth, that is, the site of the future Temple. The homily depends
on defining the pronouns in the Deuteronomy verse differently from the usual
translations.

the nape of the neck, opened it up and squeezed its blood on the altar wall.[14] If you say there was no base [on the south-east corner], did he do this in mid-air? Rav Naḥman bar Isaac said, Perhaps the arrangement was that the air was Benjamin's territory [hence connected to the altar], and only the ground was Judah's.

What is meant by the statement that there was no base [on the south-east]? Rav said, It was not built; Levi said, [It was built, but as it was in the territory of Judah it was not acceptable for the] blood [of offerings]. That is why Rav paraphrased[15] [Jacob's blessing of Benjamin in Genesis 49:27] as 'in his heritage the altar will be built' and Levi paraphrased it as 'in his heritage a sanctuary will be built' – that is, a place sanctified to receive blood.

However well-defined the law is, human beings inevitably get into situations where laws conflict; the rabbinic mind, with its hatred of legal absolutism, rarely seems happier than when resolving such conflicts. This complex piece illustrates how the rabbis interpreted the Torah as a seamless, consistent whole, whose logic could be transferred from one topic to another.

CHAPTER EIGHT

MISHNA:

If an [animal designated as a] sacrifice has become mixed   70b
with condemned purification-offerings, or with oxen liable to death by stoning, they must all die, even if it is just one in ten thousand.[16]

If it was mixed with an ox with which a sin had been committed, or which had killed a man on the testimony of a   71a

14. Mishna *Zevaḥim* 64b.
15. Literally, 'translated', but neither Amora was concerned with the literal translation. The extant Targum follows Levi's interpretation.
16. Since it is forbidden to make any use of a condemned purification-offering or an ox liable to death by stoning, they cannot be allowed to pasture until they acquire blemishes and then be sold; there is no alternative to allowing them to die, unlike the succeeding cases.

single witness or on the admission of its owner, or had had
sexual intercourse with a man or woman, or had been designated for idolatry or actually worshipped, or had been given
to a harlot as her fee, or was exchanged for a dog, or was
71b cross-bred, damaged or born by Caesarian section – all should
pasture until they become blemished, then be sold, and a new
sacrifice of the same kind purchased equal in value to the best
of them.

If [a sacrificial animal] was mixed with unblemished unconsecrated animals, the unconsecrated animals should be sold[17]
and sacrifices of the same kind purchased with the proceeds.

If consecrated animals became mixed with other consecrated
animals, and if they were designated for the same kind of
sacrifice, each should be offered 'in the name of whoever it
might be'.[18]

If they were not designated for the same kind of sacrifice,
all should pasture until they become blemished and then be
sold, and a new sacrifice of each kind be purchased of equal
value to the best of them; the excess must be paid out of his
own pocket.

If [consecrated animals] had been mixed with first-born or
with tithe, all should pasture until they become blemished and
then be eaten subject to the laws of first-born and tithe animals.

All [kinds of offerings] can become mixed, apart from
purification-offerings with reparation-offerings.[19]

GEMARA:

[Even if it is just one in ten thousand.] Why 'even if'? It
means this: Should a condemned purification-offering or an ox
liable to death by stoning get mixed into other sacrifices, even
if it is just one in ten thousand, they must all die.

Surely the Mishna has stated this once [elsewhere]: **All those
things that are forbidden upon the altar render [others] for-**

17. That is, all the animals are sold; even the one that had been consecrated reverts to
unconsecrated status if it acquires a blemish, though the proceeds may only be
used to purchase a replacement.

18. Only an explicit wrong identification of the owner would invalidate the sacrifice;
it may be offered anonymously.

19. The reparation-offering is a ram, but the purification-offering would be a different
animal, so there could be no mistake.

bidden, even [if they are present only] in the smallest quantity: that which had sexual intercourse with a man or woman, etc.[20]

Rav Ashi said, I repeated this *sh'ma'ta* in front of Rav Shimei, and he said, Both [Mishnas] are necessary. If the point had been made only in the other place, we might have thought that [the one-in-ten-thousand stringency] applied only with regard to [animals to be offered] to the [Most] High, but not in respect of ordinary persons; if it had been made only here, we might have thought that [the one-in-ten-thousand stringency] applied only to things that it was forbidden to make any use of, but not to things that it was permitted to use in some other way. Therefore, both statements are required.

But [our] Mishna does list things that it is permitted to use in some other way! Even so, it doesn't state [in connection with these things] 'even the smallest quantity', whereas the other Mishna does. Then surely the other Mishna should suffice, and ours would not be needed! Ours is still needed, since it offers remedies [in several of the cases].

Another Mishna makes the point with regard to lay matters: **These things are forbidden even in the smallest quantity: wine of [idolatrous] libations; idols, etc.**[21] That is needed too. From that Mishna I might have inferred that it applied only to laymen, but it would be inappropriate to destroy so much sacred property [on account of a mere doubt]; from the Mishna here I might have inferred that [the animals are all condemned] because it would be offensive [to offer something where there is the smallest chance that it might be improper], but in the lay case perhaps things that are banned from use might be rendered negligible if they are mixed with a permitted majority; consequently both Mishnas are required.

Then let things that are banned from use be rendered negligible if they are mixed with a permitted majority! If you want to say that significant items are never rendered negligible, that is all right in the reading of **All that is counted**, but what could

72a

20. *Temura* 6:1 (28a).
21. *Avoda Zara* 5:9 (74a).

you say on the view of those who read, **Whatever is *normally* counted?**

72b

For a Mishna states: **If someone had bundles of fenugreek that had grown as *kil'ayim* with the vine, they must be burnt. If they were mixed with other [permissible bundles of fenugreek], they must all be burnt, according to Rabbi Meir, but the Sages say, They may be ignored if less than 1 part in 201. For Rabbi Meir used to say, Whatever is normally counted pollutes, whereas the Sages said, Only six things pollute (Rabbi Aqiva said, Seven), namely: brittle-shelled walnuts, pomegranates from Badan, sealed barrels, spinach leaves, cabbage stalks and Greek calabash (Rabbi Aqiva adds, Privately baked loaves); they convey the status of *'orla* or of vine-kil'ayim as relevant.**[22]

In connection with that Mishna it was taught: Rabbi Yoḥanan said, The Mishna reads, **Whatever is normally counted**; Resh Laqish said, The Mishna reads, **All that is counted** – it is all right according to Resh Laqish, but what would you say according to Rabbi Yoḥanan?

Rav Papa said, This Tanna[, who holds that significant items are never rendered negligible,] is the Tanna of the pound[23] of figs, who said that whatever is [sold] by number does not become negligible, even if forbidden only by the rabbis, and all the more so if forbidden by the Torah, as a baraita states: **If someone squashed a pound of figs into a fig-cake and doesn't know which fig-cake he squashed it into, or [pressed it] into a jar and doesn't know which jar he pressed it into, or on to a honeycomb and doesn't know which honeycomb he pressed it on, Rabbi Meir says in the name of Rabbi Eliezer that we regard the top [figs] as if detached [from those below], so that the lower ones can be counted to render the top ones negligible;**[24] **[Rabbi Meir says in the name of] Rabbi Joshua,**

73a

22. Mishna '*Orla* 3:6, 7.
23. Hebrew (and Greek) *litra*, Latin *libra*.
24. i.e. less than 1 in 100 (or whatever the relevant quantity).

If there are 100 on top they render negligible [the forbidden one], but if not, all the top ones are forbidden and those underneath are permitted. Rabbi Judah in the name of Rabbi Eliezer says, If there are 100 on top, they render negligible [the forbidden one], but if not, all the top ones are forbidden and those underneath are permitted; [Rabbi Judah says in the name of] Rabbi Joshua, Even if there are 300 on top, they never render negligible. If he squashed them into a fig-cake [and knows which fig-cake they are in] but doesn't know in which position, whether north or south, everyone agrees they can be ignored [against a suitable quantity].

Rav Ashi said, It could even be the opposing rabbis[, who hold that things sold by number can be rendered negligible], for they would agree that living creatures cannot become negligible.

[Reverting to our Mishna:] why not draw out each of the animals in turn and follow the principle that whatever is detached [from a collection] is assumed to have come from the majority[, and is therefore permissible]? [That would not help, since] actively removing one is as if it remained fixed in its place, and whatever is fixed in place is as if it is half-and-half.[25]

In that case, could you push them about, and then assume that whichever animal detached itself [from the crowd] came from the [permitted] majority? Rava said, [No,] in case ten *Kohanim* were to come at once [and each take one of the scattered animals] and offer it up.

Other principles governing mixtures are subjected to criticism and further suggestions are discussed; in later Judaism these rules are developed in relation to the dietary laws.

Three priestly rights are considered in Chapter Twelve: to perform a sacrifice, to a share of the sacrificial meat and to eat it. It is possible to have a right to eat – at someone else's table – without a right to a personal share.

73b

25. There is no majority to render it negligible.

CHAPTER TWELVE

MISHNA:

98b   [A *Kohen* who is] *t'vul yom*, or whose atonement offering is pending, does not take a share of the [meat of] the sacrifice to eat at nightfall.

[A *Kohen* who is] an *onen* may not touch or perform the sacrifice, nor take a share of the [meat of] the sacrifice to eat at nightfall.

[A *Kohen* who has] a [physical] blemish,[26] whether transient or permanent, may share and eat the [meat of] the sacrifice, but may not perform the sacrifice.

Whoever is unfit for service may not take a share of the meat; whoever has no right to a share of the meat has no right to a share of the hides either.

Even if [a *Kohen*] was unclean at the time the blood was sprinkled but clean when the fats [of the offering] were burned, he does not take a share of the meat, for it is said: HE FROM AMONG AARON'S SONS WHO OFFERS THE BLOOD AND THE FAT OF THE OFFERING OF WELL-BEING SHALL GET THE RIGHT THIGH AS HIS PORTION (Leviticus 7:33 JPS).

GEMARA:

99a   How do we know this? Resh Laqish said, Scripture says, THE PRIEST WHO OFFERS IT AS A SIN-OFFERING SHALL EAT OF IT (Leviticus 6:19 JPS) – The [priest] who offers eats; the [priest] who does not offer does not eat.

But what about the rest of the course [of priests]; they did not offer, yet they may [certainly] eat! What we meant was, Those priests who are fit to offer[, even if they did not in fact do so].

Then what about a minor? He is not 'fit to offer', yet he may [certainly] eat! When we said 'eat', we meant 'take a share'. Those who are fit to offer share out [the meat]; those who are not fit to offer do not take a share of [the meat, but may be allowed to eat it].

---

26. Leviticus 21:16–23. *Bekhorot* Chapter Six has the fullest discussion of human and animal blemishes relating to Temple service.

Then what about [a priest] with a [physical] blemish? He is not fit to offer, yet he takes a share! [This is because] Scripture expressly includes him[, as it is written], ALL MALE PRIESTS MAY EAT IT (Leviticus 6:22) – this includes those with a blemish.[27]

But perhaps 'All males' is meant to include *t'vul yom* [rather than blemished priests]? It is more reasonable to include blemished priests [for sharing], since we [already] know that they may eat [the sacrificial meat]. To the contrary, it would be more reasonable to include *t'vul yom*, since he will be able to eat once night falls. [No. *T'vul yom*] is not now in a position to eat[, but a priest with a blemish is].

Rav Yosef said: Now, if you understand 'eat' to mean 'take a share', why does Scripture not say 'take a share'? It must be to teach that those who may eat take a share, while those who may not eat do not take a share.

Resh Laqish asked, What if a blemished priest is unclean? Seeing that the Torah grants him a share notwithstanding the fact that he is unfit [for service], do we say that it makes no difference whether a blemished priest is clean or unclean; or do we say that those who may eat take a share, those who may not eat do not take a share?

Rabba said, Here is a proof: **A High Priest may perform an offering even when he is an** *onen*, **but he neither eats [of the sacrifice] nor takes a share to eat at nightfall.**[28] That proves that [only those who may eat take a share].

Rav Oshaya asked, May a [priest who is] unclean take a share of a public offering[, seeing that in exceptional circumstances public offerings may take place in a state of uncleanness]? Do we argue that the Torah says, THE PRIEST WHO OFFERS IT, and [an unclean priest] might be eligible to perform [a public sacrifice], or do we say that those who may eat take a share, but those who may not eat do not take a share?

27. Leviticus 21:22 expressly states that a priest with a blemish may eat sacrificial meat; Leviticus 6:22 is therefore understood as conferring the right to share – Rashi.
28. Tosefta *Qorbanot* (*Zevaḥim*) 11:2.

Ravina said, Here is a proof: **A High Priest may perform an offering even when he is an *onen*, but he neither eats [of the sacrifice] nor takes a share to eat at nightfall.** That proves that [only those who may eat take a share].

SECOND TRACTATE
MENAḤOT (GRAIN OFFERINGS)

Grain offerings (Leviticus 2) are of wheat or barley flour mixed with oil and frankincense. There are three main categories: the voluntary grain offering, whether plain, baked, griddled or fried (Leviticus 2:1–7), including the grain offering of first-fruit (Leviticus 2:14–18); the purification-offering (Leviticus 5:11–13, brought by those unable to afford an animal or bird sacrifice; the jealousy-offering (Numbers 5:15, 25), lacking oil and frankincense.

The opening Mishna, to do with intent, closely parallels the opening of Zevaḥim. Just as there are four operations, or acts of service (slaughter, collecting the blood, transporting the blood, sprinkling blood on the altar) for an animal sacrifice, so there are four acts of service (taking a handful of flour, placing it in a receptacle, transporting it, casting it on the altar fire) for a grain offering; in both cases the final operation, on the altar, effects atonement. Whereas the slaughter of a beast may be carried out by a layman, a Kohen is required to extract the handful of flour and to perform all other operations on both animal and grain sacrifices.

CHAPTER ONE

MISHNA:

All grain offerings from which the handful of flour was extracted with an incorrect category in mind [remain] valid, even though they do not fulfil the obligation of their owner. 2a

The purification-offering and the jealousy-offering are exceptions.

If [the priest] extracted the handful of flour from a purification-offering or a jealousy-offering with an incorrect category in mind, or if he placed it in a receptacle, transported it or cast it on the altar fire with an incorrect category in mind, or performed one operation with a correct designation and then one with an incorrect designation, or one with an incorrect designation and then one with a correct designation, [the offering] is not valid.

What would be 'with a correct designation and then one with an incorrect designation'? [If one operation was performed on the understanding] that it was a purification-offering and [another on the understanding] that it was a voluntary offering.

[What would be] 'with an incorrect designation and then one with a correct designation'? [If one operation was performed on the understanding] that it was a voluntary offering and [another on the understanding] that it was a purification-offering.

GEMARA:

Why does the Mishna say **even though** rather than simply **and they do not fulfil the obligation of their owner?** It is to emphasize that even though the owner's obligation has not been fulfilled, the offering itself is valid, and should proceed normally. As Rava said, If an upward-offering was slaughtered with the wrong designation, the blood should not be sprinkled with a wrong [but matching] designation[, but with the correct one].

This [position can be justified] by reason or by Scripture. By reason – Just because one mistake has been made, should he carry on making mistakes? By Scripture – Scripture says, You **MUST FULFIL CAREFULLY THAT WHICH ISSUES FROM YOUR LIPS; YOU SHALL ACT ACCORDING TO THE VOW YOU HAVE MADE VOLUNTARILY** (Deuteronomy 23:24). **VOLUNTARILY?** surely it is a **VOW!**[1] So, if it is as you vowed, then it is a vow; otherwise, it is a voluntary [offering].

---

1. A vow creates an obligation, and this must be discharged correctly. If the vow was to bring a sacrifice to the Temple, and the priest or whoever slaughtered the animal did so with the wrong intention, the person who made the vow has failed

But is it permissible to change [the designation of] a voluntary   2b
offering? Perhaps our Mishna conflicts with the opinion of
Rabbi Simeon, for a baraita states: **Rabbi Simeon says, All grain
offerings from which the handful of flour was extracted with
an incorrect category in mind [remain] valid, even though they
do not fulfil the obligation of their owner. Grain offerings are
not like animal sacrifices, for even if [a priest] extracts a handful
of flour from a griddle thinking that it is a frying-pan offering,
the action demonstrates that it is really a griddle; if he extracts
from a dry-grain offering thinking that it is mixed with oil,
the way it is handled demonstrates that it is really dry; but this
does not apply to animal sacrifices, since the act of slaughter is
one and the same, the sprinkling of blood is one and the same,
and the collection [of blood in a bowl] is one and the same.**

Now this is all very well in the view of Rav Ashi, who explains
that one statement is where [the priest] said 'griddle' rather
than 'frying-pan'[2] and the other is where he said 'griddle grain
offering' rather than 'frying-pan grain offering'; [this view is
consistent with our Mishna, since] our Mishna is [analogous to
where he explicitly substitutes] a grain offering [of one kind]
for a grain offering [of another kind]. But what are we to say in
the view of Rabba and Rava?

You might want to follow Rava's distinction between a case
where the priest altered the category of the offering and where
he altered the identity of the owner. However, our Mishna
certainly speaks of altering the category of the offering, for it
continues, **What would be 'with a correct designation and then
one with an incorrect designation'? [If one operation was
performed on the understanding] that it was a purification-
offering and [another on the understanding] that it was a
voluntary offering.** And if you follow Rava and say that one
case was where he extracted the handful [with the thought that

---

to fulfil his or her obligation, though the sacrifice may proceed as an anonymous
(or additional) voluntary offering.

2. This is of no consequence, since he is not designating the offering. Rav Ashi is
commenting on an apparent contradiction between this baraita and another
statement attributed to Rabbi Simeon.

it was] for a grain offering, and the other was where he extracted the handful [with the thought that it was] for an animal sacrifice, our Mishna makes quite clear that it speaks of mistaking one kind of grain offering for another, for it continues, [**What would be**] '**with an incorrect designation and then one with an correct designation**'? [**If one operation was performed on the understanding] that it was a voluntary offering and [another on the understanding] that it was a purification-offering.**

According to Rabba and Rava, then, it is clear that our Mishna conflicts with Rabbi Simeon's view.

THE PRIEST SHALL SCOOP OUT OF IT A HANDFUL OF ITS CHOICE FLOUR AND OIL, AS WELL AS ALL OF ITS FRANKINCENSE; AND THIS TOKEN PORTION HE SHALL TURN INTO SMOKE ON THE ALTAR . . . (Leviticus 2:2 JPS)

If part of the handful the priest must cast on the altar fire is missing, would this invalidate the whole procedure? In general, if part of a mitzva is missing, does this invalidate the rest? The Menora, or Temple Candelabrum, had seven branches (Exodus 25:31–40; Numbers 8:1–4); if a branch was missing, would this render the Menora invalid?

CHAPTER THREE

MISHNA:

28a   The seven branches of the Menora invalidate each other;[3] its seven lights invalidate each other.

The two paragraphs [written] in the *mezuza* invalidate one another; even one [missing] letter invalidates them.

The four paragraphs in the *tefillin* invalidate one another; even one [missing] letter invalidates them.

The four fringes [on the corner of the garment (Numbers 15:37–41)] invalidate one another, since the four [constitute]

3.   If one is missing, the others are invalid.

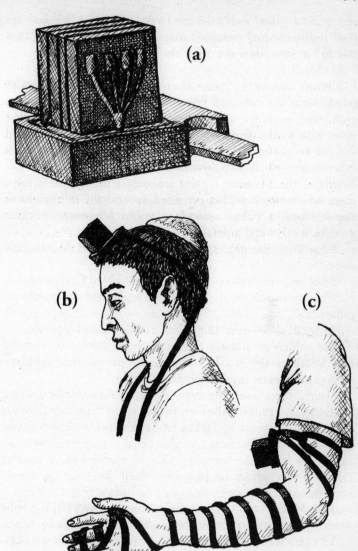

Tefillin (phylacteries)
(a) Four-compartment box for head *tefilla*;
(b) placing of head *tefilla*; (c) placing of arm *tefilla*.

one *mitzva*. [But] Rabbi Ishmael says, The four [fringes] are four [independent] *mitzvot*[, therefore if one is missing that would not invalidate the other three].

GEMARA:

28b Shmuel said in the name of an elder: The Menora was 18 palms high: the base and flowers 3 palms; 2 palms smooth; 1 palm with a goblet, a calyx and a petal; 2 palms smooth; 1 palm with a calyx from which two branches extended upward the full height of the Menora; 1 palm smooth; 1 palm with a calyx from which two branches extended upward the full height of the Menora; 1 palm smooth; 1 palm with a calyx from which two branches extended upward the full height of the Menora; 2 palms smooth; 3 palms left over for three goblets, a calyx and a petal.

What were the goblets like? They resembled Alexandrian cups.

What were the calyxes like? They resembled Cretan apples.

What were the petals like? They resembled the petals on pillars.

[In total] there were 22 goblets, 11 calyxes and 9 petals.

The goblets invalidated one another; the calyxes invalidated one another; the petals invalidated one another; goblets, calyxes and petals invalidated one another.[4]

Clearly, there were 22 goblets, for it is written, AND ON THE LAMPSTAND ITSELF THERE SHALL BE FOUR GOBLETS (Exodus 25:34), and it is written, THREE GOBLETS LIKE ALMOND BLOSSOMS ON EACH BRANCH (Exodus 25:33) – four on [the stem] itself, and 18 on the branches, that is, 22. And there were 11 calyxes – two calyxes on [the stem] itself, one each on the six branches, then CALYX . . . CALYX . . . CALYX (Exodus 25:35) – that is, eleven. But how do we know that there were nine petals? Two on [the stem] itself, and one on each of the six branches, make eight! Rav Salmon says, It is written: IT WAS HAMMERED WORK OF GOLD, HAMMERED FROM BASE TO PETAL (Numbers 8:4 JPS)[, implying there was an extra petal on the base].

Rav said, The height of the Menora was nine palms. Rav

---

4. i.e. if one was missing, the whole Menora would be unacceptable.

Shimi bar Ḥiyya objected to Rav: **The stone in front of the Menora had three steps on which the priest stood to trim the lights.** Rav replied, Is that you, Shimi? What I meant was, From the [lower] edge of the branches upwards.

It is written, **AND THE PETALS, LAMPS AND TONGS WERE OF GOLD [*MIKHLOT ZAHAV*]** (2 Chronicles 4:21). What does *mikhlot zahav* mean? Rav Ammi says, [It means] that it consumed[5] all Solomon's finest gold, for [as] Rav Yehuda said in the name of Rav, Solomon made ten Menoras. He provided a thousand talents of gold for each one, and they refined it a thousand times, reducing it to a single talent.

How can that be so? Is it not written, **ALL KING SOLOMON'S DRINKING CUPS WERE OF GOLD, AND ALL THE UTENSILS OF THE LEBANON FOREST HOUSE[6] WERE OF PURE GOLD: SILVER DID NOT COUNT FOR ANYTHING IN SOLOMON'S DAYS** (1 Kings 10:21 JPS)? We were speaking of fine gold [which he used up completely, though ordinary gold in plenty was left].

Does [gold] reduce that much [when refined]? Was it not taught, **Rabbi Yosé bar Yehuda says, It once happened that the Temple Menora was [found to] exceed that of Moses by the weight of a Kurdish gold denarius; they refined it eighty times in the furnace and reduced it to a talent?** As it had been thoroughly refined in the days of Solomon, further refining had only a small effect.[7]

Rav Shmuel bar Naḥmani said in the name of Rabbi Jonathan: What does **ON THE PURE MENORA** (Leviticus 24:4) mean? [The details of] its manufacture had come down from

5. Deriving *mikhlot* from *kala*, 'finish'.
6. Solomon's palace (1 Kings 7:2).
7. 'Further . . . effect' reads literally, 'Since it stood, it stood.' The meaning is that though refining to pure gold may indeed reduce the bulk a thousandfold, the Temple Menora, since its gold had been refined in the days of Solomon, sustained only a slight reduction, perhaps on account of impurities absorbed over the centuries.

the Pure Place.[8] Then does ON THE PURE TABLE (24:6) [like-wise] mean that [the details of] its manufacture had come down from the Pure Place? Rather, it means it was cleansed from its impurity; similarly, the Menora was cleansed from its impurity.

Now that is according to Resh Laqish, for it was Resh Laqish who said, What is the meaning of ON THE PURE TABLE? [It means] it was cleansed from its impurity. But surely it was a wooden object designed to rest in place, and any wooden object designed to rest in place is not [receptive to] impurity? So what it tells us here is that they raised the table before pilgrims on the festival day and demonstrated the shewbread to them saying, See how God loves you! How did this [show] God's love? As Rabbi Joshua ben Levi said, A great miracle happened; the bread was as fresh when removed as when it had been placed there [a week before], as it is said, TO SET HOT BREAD [AS] ON THE DAY IT WAS TAKEN (1 Samuel 21:7).[9]

Then what about [the Menorah]? Obviously it was cleansed from its impurity – it was a metal object, and metal objects are receptive to impurity. [That is why we said that the details of] its manufacture had come down from the Pure Place.

A baraita stated: **Rabbi Yosé bar Yehuda says, An Ark of fire, a Table of fire and a Menora of fire descended from heaven, and Moses saw [them] and copied them; as it is said, LOOK, AND MAKE THEM IN THE SHAPES THAT ARE BEING SHOWN TO YOU ON THE MOUNTAIN** (Exodus 25:40).

But if so, the same [might be said of the Tabernacle, since it is written,] THEN SET UP THE TABERNACLE ACCORDING TO ITS LAW THAT YOU WERE SHOWN ON THE MOUNTAIN (Exodus 26:30).

[No.] Here, [in the case of the Tabernacle,] the word is LAW; there, [in connection with the Ark, Table and Menora,] it is SHAPE.

Rav Ḥiyya bar Abba said in the name of Rabbi Yoḥanan, [The angel] Gabriel donned an apron and showed Moses how to make the Menora.

8.   From heaven.
9.   The plain meaning is that the bread taken by David and his men was replaced with fresh hot bread.

[Reverting to the previous discussion:]

The two paragraphs of the *mezuza* invalidate one another; even one [missing] letter invalidates them. [Isn't that] obvious? Rav Yehuda said in the name of Rav, It was necessary [to state this] to include the spike of the [letter] *yod*. [Surely that is also] obvious! [Then it must be needed] for the other [ruling] of Rav Yehuda in the name of Rav, for Rav Yehuda said in the name of Rav that any letter not surrounded by [blank] parchment on four sides[10] is void.

[Further discussion on the shapes of the letters follows, then:]

Rav Yehuda said in the name of Rav, When Moses ascended on high [to receive to Torah], he found the Holy One, blessed be He, sitting and tying knots on the letters.[11]

[Moses] said to Him: Lord of the Universe, what are those for?[12]

He replied, After many generations a man will be born called Aqiva ben Joseph; he will infer stacks of laws from each of these marks.

[Moses] said to Him, Lord of the Universe, show him to me! He said, Move back!

[Moses] went and sat in the eighth row [of Aqiva's school], but could not make sense of what they were talking about, and grew faint.[13]

When [the disciples] reached a certain point [in the discussion], they asked [Aqiva], 'Master, on what do you base this?' He replied, 'It is Torah [received by] Moses at Sinai.'

Moses was reassured [that the Torah he received was not forgotten]. He again approached the Holy One, blessed be He, saying:

Lord of the Universe, you have a man like this, yet you give Torah through me!

He said, Silence! Such is My intention!

[Moses] said to Him: Lord of the Universe, you have shown me his learning, [now] show me his reward!

10. That is, any letter touching another.
11. The 'knots' are the decorative *tagin*, or spikes, attached to certain letters.
12. Literally, 'who is stopping you?'
13. Afraid that the original Torah had been forgotten.

He said, Move back!

[Moses] saw that [the Romans] were weighing out [Aqiva's] flesh in the marketplace.[14]

He said, Lord of the Universe! This is his learning, and [is] this his reward?

He said, Silence! Such is My intention!

Chapter Six focuses on the ceremonial reaping of the Omer, a sheaf of barley that was presented in the Temple on the second day of Passover; the new year's harvest was not to be eaten prior to that date:

THE LORD SPOKE TO MOSES, SAYING: SPEAK TO THE ISRAELITE PEOPLE AND SAY TO THEM: WHEN YOU ENTER THE LAND THAT I AM GIVING TO YOU AND YOU REAP ITS HARVEST, YOU SHALL BRING THE FIRST SHEAF OF YOUR HARVEST TO THE PRIEST. HE SHALL ELEVATE THE SHEAF BEFORE THE LORD FOR ACCEPTANCE IN YOUR BEHALF; THE PRIEST SHALL ELEVATE IT ON THE DAY AFTER THE SABBATH . . . UNTIL THAT VERY DAY, UNTIL YOU HAVE BROUGHT THE OFFERING OF YOUR GOD, YOU SHALL EAT NO BREAD OR PARCHED GRAIN OR FRESH EARS; IT IS A LAW FOR ALL TIME . . .

AND FROM THE DAY ON WHICH YOU BRING THE SHEAF OF ELEVATION OFFERING – THE DAY AFTER THE SABBATH – YOU SHALL COUNT OFF SEVEN WEEKS. THEY MUST BE COMPLETE: YOU MUST COUNT UNTIL THE DAY AFTER THE SEVENTH WEEK – FIFTY DAYS; THEN YOU SHALL BRING AN OFFERING OF NEW GRAIN TO THE LORD. (Leviticus 23:9–16 JPS)

The day for elevating, or waving, the sheaf is specified as 'the day after the Sabbath'. Sadducees, not unreasonably, took this to mean Sunday; accordingly, they fixed the Sunday following the first day of Passover as the day of presentation of the sheaf, and celebrated Shavuot (the 'offering of new grain') on the fiftieth day from then, always a Sunday. Pharisees understood

14. The story of the martyrdom of Rabbi Aqiva is told in *Berakhot* 61b and parallels.

'the day after the Sabbath' as the second day of Passover, which could fall on any day of the week; Shavuot would then fall on the same day, seven weeks later. The debate in the following passage is a rabbinic reconstruction, preserving some of the acrimony of the debate. Christians followed Sadducee practice; that is why Easter and Whit (corresponding to Pesach and Shavuot) always fall on Sundays.

The Gemara opens with a citation from Megillat Ta'anit, *a calendar of fasts and feasts still extant in modified form. Two overlapping collections then follow, in which Tannaim attempt to demonstrate that 'sabbath' in 'the day after the sabbath' means the first day of the festival, whichever day of the week that might be.*

CHAPTER SIX

MISHNA:

How did they do it? Officers of the court went out prior to   65a
the festival and bundled the growing [barley] together so that it should be easy to reap. [People from] all the nearby towns assembled there, so that the reaping should take place with maximum excitement. As soon as darkness fell, [the reaper] would say to them, Has the sun set? The [people] would respond, Yes, the sun has set! With this scythe? Yes, with this scythe! Into this box? Yes, into this box! If it was the Sabbath, he would say, Is today the Sabbath? They would respond, Yes, it is the Sabbath! Is today the Sabbath? They would respond, Yes, it is the Sabbath! Shall I reap? Yes, reap! Shall I reap? Yes, reap! Each phrase was said three times. All this was on account of the Boethusians,[15] who denied that reaping the Omer took place on the night following the festival day.

GEMARA:

The rabbis taught: These are the days on which fasting is prohibited; on some of them eulogies are not to be delivered: between the first and the eighth of Nisan, the [matter of

15.   On the identity of the Boethusians, see Herr, 'Who were the Boethusians'. Here it appears to be a code name for Sadducees.

the] daily sacrifice was decided – eulogies are not permitted; between the eighth [of Nisan and] the end of the festival [of Passover,] the date of Shavuot was settled – eulogies are not permitted.

Between the first and the eighth of Nisan, the [matter of the] daily sacrifice was decided: The Sadducees held that a [private] individual might sponsor a daily sacrifice. This is how they interpreted, YOU [singular] SHALL OFFER ONE LAMB IN THE MORNING, AND YOU SHALL OFFER ONE LAMB IN THE EVENING (Numbers 28:4). What reply did [the Pharisees] give? MY OFFERING . . . YOU [plural] SHALL TAKE CARE TO BRING ME AT THE RIGHT TIME (Numbers 28:2) – [meaning,] that all [public] offerings should be paid for out of the Temple treasury.[16]

The First Collection

Between the eighth [of Nisan and] the end of the festival [of Passover], the date of Shavuot was set – eulogies are not permitted: The Boethusians maintained that Shavuot should be on Sunday. Rabban Yoḥanan ben Zakkai joined conversation with them. Fools! he said, What do you base that on?[17] Not one of them could answer him, until an old man stuttered, Moses our Teacher loved the Israelite people: he knew that Shavuot was one day [only], so he fixed it after the Sabbath in order that the Israelites might enjoy themselves for two days. [Yoḥanan ben Zakkai] read him this verse: ELEVEN DAYS' JOURNEY FROM HOREB BY WAY OF MOUNT SEIR (Deuter-onomy 1:2) – if our Teacher Moses loved the Israelites so much, why did he delay them in the desert for forty years? [The Boethusian said,] Rabbi, are you putting me off with that! He said to him, Fool! Is not our perfect Torah superior to your idle chatter? One verse says, YOU SHALL COUNT FIFTY DAYS, and another says, YOU SHALL HAVE SEVEN WHOLE WEEKS (Leviticus 23:16, 15). How does this work out? [SEVEN WHOLE WEEKS] are if [the counting] starts on a Sunday; [FIFTY DAYS] are if it starts mid-week.

65

16. See *Sheqalim* Chapter Three (see pp. 188–9).
17. Why do you interpret 'after the Sabbath' as Sunday, rather than the day following the festival?

Rabbi Eliezer says, That [argument] is superfluous. It says, You shall count [seven weeks] (Deuteronomy 16:9), and that is addressed to the court, on whom the counting depends, since it is they who determine the months [and hence the dates of festivals]; the day after the sabbath therefore cannot mean Sunday, since that could be counted by anyone.

Rabbi Joshua says, The Torah tells us to count days to determine the beginning of the month, and it tells us to count days to celebrate Shavuot; just as the new moon is identified shortly before it appears, so [the day of] Shavuot is identified shortly before it arrives. Now if Shavuot always fell on a Sunday, how could [the day it falls on] be identified [only] shortly before it arrives?

Rabbi Ishmael says, The Torah tells us to bring the Omer on Passover and the Two Loaves on Shavuot; just as [the loaves are brought] on and near the beginning of a festival, so [the Omer is brought] on and near the beginning of a festival.

Rabbi Judah ben Bathyra says, It says Sabbath above and it says Sabbath below; just as in the one case it refers to the beginning of a festival, and in proximity to a festival, so in the other case it refers to the beginning of a festival, and in proximity to a festival.[18]

The Second Collection

The rabbis taught: And you [plural] shall count – each individual must count; from the day after the Sabbath – this means the day following the [first] festival day. Perhaps it means Sunday? Rabbi Yosé bar Judah says, [That cannot be, since] it says, You shall count fifty days; if Shavuot was always on a Sunday, sometimes you would find fifty [days from the beginning of Pesach to Shavuot], sometimes fifty-one, sometimes fifty-two, sometimes fifty-three, sometimes fifty-four, sometimes fifty-five and sometimes fifty-six.

Rabbi Judah ben Bathyra says, This is superfluous. It says, 66a You [singular] shall count; the counting is a matter for the court, and this excludes Sunday, which can be counted by anyone.

18. He refers to Leviticus 23:16 (regarding Shavuot) and 11 (regarding the Omer).

Rabbi Yosé says, THE DAY AFTER THE SABBATH must mean the day after the festival. Is it the day after the festival or is it [always] Sunday? Now, if you say it means the day after the Sabbath [in the middle of] Passover, it says only the day after the Sabbath [without specifying the middle of Passover]. The whole year is full of Sabbaths; how would you find out which one [is meant]? Also, it says Sabbath above and it says Sabbath below; just as in the one case it refers to the beginning of a festival, and in proximity to a festival, so in the other case it refers to the beginning of a festival, and in proximity to a festival.

Rabbi Simeon ben Eleazar says: One verse says, SIX DAYS YOU SHALL EAT UNLEAVENED BREAD (Deuteronomy 16:8), and another one says, SEVEN DAYS YOU SHALL EAT UNLEAVENED BREAD (Exodus 12:15). How can that be? The unleavened bread that you cannot eat for seven days is [unleavened bread made] from the new produce,[19] but you may eat [unleavened bread made] from the new produce for six days. You count FROM THE DAY THAT YOU BRING [the Omer]. Or could it be that you reap, present the Omer, and then start counting whenever you wish? It says, WHEN THE SICKLE IS PUT TO THE STANDING CORN, YOU SHALL COMMENCE COUNTING (Deuteronomy 16:9). Could it be that you reap, count and then present [the Omer] whenever you want? It states, FROM THE DAY THAT YOU BRING. If from the day that you bring, perhaps you can reap, count and present on the day itself? It says, YOU SHALL COUNT SEVEN COMPLETE WEEKS. When are the weeks complete? Only if you start counting at night.[20] Then can you reap, present [the Omer] and start counting at night? It states, FROM THE DAY THAT YOU BRING. How does this work out? The reaping and the counting are at night; the presentation is in the daytime.

Rava said, There are irrefutable objections to all these arguments except those of the last two Tannaim, whether in the first

19. Produce of the current year may not be eaten until the Omer has been brought, that is, from the second day of Pesach onwards.
20. For most religious purposes other than sacrifices Torah regards the night as the commencement of the day.

baraita or the second. Rabban Yoḥanan ben Zakkai's argument falls down since it may be as Abbaye said, It is a *mitzva* to count weeks as well as days.[21] And as for Rabbis Eliezer and Joshua, how do we know that it speaks of the first festival day? Perhaps the final festival day is meant. But there is no objection to [the arguments of] Rabbi Ishmael and Rabbi Judah ben Bathyra. As for Rabbi Yosé bar Rabbi Judah, the fifty [days] do not include the extra six. As for Rabbi Judah ben Bathyra [in the second version], how do we know that it speaks of the first festival day? Perhaps the final festival day is meant. Rabbi Yosé noticed this objection, and that is why he added his explanation.

On that point: Abbaye said, It is a *mitzva* to count weeks as well as days. The scholars at Rav Ashi's school counted days and counted weeks; Ameimar counted days but did not count weeks, saying that [nowadays counting is merely] a remembrance of what took place in the Temple.

As we approach the conclusion of the two major tractates that deal with the Temple service, there are reflections on the Jewish Temple in Egypt and its priesthood. Deuteronomy strictly forbade sacrificial worship anywhere other than in 'the place that God would choose', i.e. Jerusalem. When Judaean independence was restored following Judas Maccabeus' defeat of the Seleucids, Onias IV, a descendant of Simeon the Just, was the presumptive heir to the High Priesthood; however, Alcimus, a strong Hellenizer, was appointed in his place. Onias fled to Egypt and c. 154 BCE, with the permission of Ptolemy VI Philometor, erected a rival temple at Leontopolis.[22] According to Josephus, this temple finally closed under Vespasian, 343 years later.[23]

The story as preserved in the Talmud reveals more of rabbinic attitudes than of history; it leads to unsettling reflections on the pursuit of honour, and on the corruption it brings in its train.

21. Yoḥanan ben Zakkai's argument rested on the fact that the Torah specifies both days and weeks for counting.
22. Josephus, *Antiquities* 12:4, 5; 13:3. On Alcimus, see also 1 Maccabees 7, 9; 2 Maccabees 14. Leontopolis (Tel el-Muqdam) is in the central Nile delta.
23. Josephus, *Wars* 7.10.4.

CHAPTER THIRTEEN

MISHNA:

109a   Priests who served in the House of Onias may not serve in the Holy [Temple] of Jerusalem. It goes without saying that those who have served 'the other thing'[24] may not serve there, since Scripture says, THE PRIESTS OF THE SHRINES, HOW-EVER, DID NOT ASCEND THE ALTAR OF THE LORD IN JERUSA-LEM, BUT THEY ATE UNLEAVENED BREAD ALONG WITH THEIR KINSMEN (2 Kings 23:9 JPS); just like [physically] blemished priests, they had the right to share and eat [the sacred meat], but not to perform offerings.

GEMARA:

109b   Since [the Mishna] says, **It goes without saying that those who have served 'the other thing' may not serve there,** it follows that the House of Onias was not a place of idolatry. A baraita supports the view that the House of Onias was not a place of idolatry, for it teaches: **The year that Simeon the Just died he announced, I will die this year. How do you know? they asked. He replied, Every year on the Day of Atonement a sage robed and wrapped in white meets me and escorts me in and out; this year a sage robed and wrapped in black met me; he escorted me in but not out. After the festival Simeon was sick for seven days, then died. His brother priests ceased blessing with the Holy Name[25] at his expiry. He [had] said, My son Onias shall succeed me. [Onias'] brother, Shimei, who was two and a half years older, was jealous. He said to [Onias], Let me show you how the [divine] service is performed. He dressed him in a tunic and girdle[26] and stood him next to the altar. Then he turned to his brother priests and said, See what this fellow swore to his beloved – 'When I become High Priest I will wear your tunic and girdle'! The other priests wanted to kill [Onias], so he ran away from them and they pursued him to Alexandria in Egypt. He erected an altar there and sacrificed**

24. Idolatry.
25. They felt unworthy to pronounce the four-lettered Name of God.
26. Obscure words, presumably referring to female garments.

to idols. When the Sages got to hear about it they said, If this is what became of [Shimei], who did not pursue [honour], how much more are those who [actively] pursue [honour prone to evil through jealousy]!

This is Rabbi Meir's account, but Rabbi Judah said to him, That is not what happened. Onias declined office since his brother Shimei was two and a half years older, but despite that Onias became jealous of Shimei. He said to [Shimei], Let me show you how the [divine] service is performed. He dressed him in a tunic and girdle and stood him next to the altar. Then he turned to his brother priests and said, See what this fellow swore to his beloved – 'When I become High Priest I will wear your tunic and girdle'! The other priests wanted to kill [Shimei]. He told them the whole story, so then they wanted to kill [Onias]; he ran away and they pursued him. He ran to the king's house, but whoever saw him said, This is the man! So he fled to Alexandria in Egypt. He erected an altar there and sacrificed to Heaven – as it is said, IN THAT DAY, THERE SHALL BE AN ALTAR TO THE LORD INSIDE THE LAND OF EGYPT AND A PILLAR TO THE LORD AT ITS BORDER (Isaiah 19:19 JPS). When the Sages got to hear about it they said, If this is what became of [Onias], who shunned [honour], how much more [do dreadful things happen] to those who pursue [honour]!

It was taught: Rabbi Joshua ben Peraḥia said, At first, if someone had said to me, Go for it!,[27] I would have tied him up and cast him to the lions. Now [that I am held in honour], if anyone says, Give it up!, I would pour a kettle of boiling water over him – Saul fled from honour, yet when he became king he sought to kill David!

Mar Qashisha the son of Rav Ḥisda asked Abbaye, How would Rabbi Meir interpret the verse used by Rabbi Judah in this baraita? After the defeat of Sennacherib Hezekiah went out and saw princes sitting in golden carriages. He made them swear not to serve idols, as it is said: IN THAT DAY, THERE

27. Pursue honour.

SHALL BE SEVERAL TOWNS IN THE LAND OF EGYPT SPEAKING
THE LANGUAGE OF CANAAN AND swearing loyalty to the
Lord of Hosts; one shall be called Town of Heres (Isaiah
19:18 JPS). They went to Alexandria in Egypt, erected an altar
and sacrificed upon it to Heaven, as it is said, IN THAT DAY,
THERE SHALL BE AN ALTAR TO THE LORD INSIDE THE LAND
OF EGYPT.

ONE SHALL BE CALLED TOWN OF HERES. What does that
mean? As Rav Yosef translated, The City of the Sun,[28] which
will be destroyed. It was said, That was one of them. How do
we know that Heres means 'sun'? It is written, WHO SAYS TO
ḤERES, DO NOT SHINE (Job 9:7)!

BRING MY SONS FROM AFAR, AND MY DAUGHTERS FROM
THE END OF THE EARTH (Isaiah 43:6 JPS).

BRING MY SONS FROM AFAR – Rav Huna said, These are
the exiles in Babylonia whose minds are settled, like children
[in the parental home]; AND MY DAUGHTERS FROM THE END
OF THE EARTH – these are the exiles in other lands, whose
minds are unsettled, like daughters.

Rabbi Abba bar Rav Isaac said in the name of Rav Ḥisda
(some say, Rav Yehuda said in the name of Rav): From Tyre to
Carthage they know Israel and their Father in Heaven; from
Tyre to the West and from Carthage to the East they know
neither Israel nor their Father in Heaven.[29]

Rav Shimi bar Ḥiyya objected to [the statement attributed
to] Rav: FOR FROM THE RISING OF THE SUN TO THE SETTING
THEREOF, MY NAME IS GREAT AMONG THE NATIONS; EVERY-
WHERE INCENSE AND OBLATIONS ARE OFFERED IN MY NAME,
WITH PURE GIFTS (Malachi 1:11). He replied, Is it you, Shimi?
It is because everywhere He is known as the God of gods.

*The Sages place Torah rather than Temple at the centre of
Jewish concern, but without derogating from the value of
Temple service.*

---

28. Heliopolis. Rav Yosef read *ḥeres* 'sun', rather than *heres* 'destruction'; many
manuscripts of Isaiah, including the Dead Sea Scrolls, support this reading. (The
Greek Septuagint read *'ir ha-tzedek*, 'town of righteousness'.)
29. Geographically this makes no sense even if 'East' and 'West' are reversed, as has
been suggested; the text must be corrupt.

EVERYWHERE INCENSE AND OBLATIONS ARE OFFERED IN MY NAME. Is that so? Rabbi Shmuel bar Naḥmani said in the name of Rabbi Jonathan, That refers to the scholars who engage in the study of Torah everywhere: [God says,] I regard them as if they offer incense and oblations in My name.

WITH PURE GIFTS. This refers to those who learn Torah in purity; they marry first, and then study Torah.[30]

A SONG OF ASCENTS. NOW BLESS THE LORD, ALL YOU SERVANTS OF THE LORD WHO STAND NIGHTLY IN THE HOUSE OF THE LORD (Psalm 134:1 JPS). Why 'nightly'? Rabbi Yoḥanan said, This refers to scholars who engage in the study of Torah at night; Scripture accounts it as if they were serving [God in the Temple].

AS IS ISRAEL'S ETERNAL DUTY (2 Chronicles 2:3 JPS). Rav Giddel said in the name of Rav, This is the [heavenly] altar on which [the archangel] Michael the Great Prince stands and makes oblation. But Rabbi Yoḥanan said, These are scholars who study the laws of [the Temple] service; Scripture accounts it as if the Temple had been built in their day.

Resh Laqish said, What is the meaning of **THIS IS THE TORAH OF THE UPWARD-OFFERING, THE GRAIN OFFERING, THE PURIFICATION-OFFERING AND THE REPARATION-OFFERING** (Leviticus 7:37)? Whoever studies Torah, it is as if he carried out the upward-offering, the grain offering, the purification-offering and the reparation-offering.

Rava commented, Then it should not say **THIS IS THE TORAH *OF* THE UPWARD-OFFERING, ETC.** but **THIS IS THE TORAH: THE UPWARD-OFFERING, ETC.** What it means is, he who studies the Torah *does not need* the upward-offering, etc.[31]

Rabbi Isaac said, What is the meaning of, **THIS IS THE TORAH OF THE PURIFICATION-OFFERING, THIS IS THE TORAH OF THE REPARATION-OFFERING** (Leviticus 6:17; 7:1)? If you study the law of the purification-offering, it is as if you had brought a purification-offering; if you study the law of the

---

30. To keep their thoughts from straying to illicit sex. See *Qiddushin* 29b–30a (see pp. 407–8).

31. He takes 'This is the Torah for . . .' in the sense of 'This is the Torah in place of . . .'

reparation-offering, it is as if you had brought a reparation-offering.

MISHNA:

Of the upward-offering of cattle it is said, A GIFT OF SWEET SAVOUR and of the upward-offering of birds it is said, A GIFT OF SWEET SAVOUR (Leviticus 1:9, 17). This is to teach you that whether your gift is great or small makes no difference, provided only your heart is directed to Heaven.

THIRD TRACTATE
ḤULLIN
(UNCONSECRATED MEAT)

This tractate, more properly called sheḥitat ḥullin *(slaughter of unconsecrated animals), develops biblical laws about* kasher *food, including:*

- Sheḥita *(slaughter). The Bible does not explicitly lay down a correct method of slaughter for animals, though the rabbis thought it was implied by Deuteronomy 12:21. (Chapters One and Two)*
- *Leviticus 17:15 and 22:8 state that* nevela *(carrion) and* terefa *(that which is 'torn' – injured) are forbidden. On the rabbinic interpretation,* nevela *is any animal that has died other than as a result of correct* sheḥita, *and* terefa *is an animal that has a potentially fatal abnormality or has suffered a lethal injury. (Chapter Three)*
- *The determination of which species may or may not be eaten is based on Leviticus 11 and Deuteronomy 14:3–21. (Chapter Three)*
- *The prohibitions of blood and certain fats derive from Leviticus 7:23–7.*
- *The prohibition of 'the sinew which shrank' – the sciatic nerve – arises from the story of Jacob's struggle with the angel (Genesis 32:33). (Chapter Seven)*
- *The three-times repeated injunction, 'Do not boil a kid in its mother's milk', is interpreted as a prohibition of combining milk and meat. (Chapter Eight)*
- *Leviticus 22:28 forbids the slaughter of an ox, sheep, or goat and its offspring on the same day. (Chapter Five)*
- *Deuteronomy 12:23 is interpreted as a prohibition against eating anything taken from a living animal, other than milk.*

Chapter One is about shehita. *The* shohet's *(slaughterer's) knife must be sharp and smooth. A special knife is reserved for* shehita *and frequently checked for sharpness and possible dents. It is drawn swiftly across the throat, severing the windpipe and oesophagus (the 'signs') and some blood vessels; unconsciousness and death are virtually instantaneous.*

The sugya *below is a collection of rulings by Rav Yehuda bar Ezekiel handed down from his teachers, Rav and Shmuel, interspersed with comments by later Amoraim; it includes the basic 'five laws' of* shehita. *It is followed by a discussion of Rav Huna's principle of presumption.*

CHAPTER ONE

MISHNA:

2a **All may slaughter and what they have slaughtered is** *kasher*, **except a deaf-mute, an idiot or a child, in case they botch the** *shehita*.

GEMARA:

8b Rav Yehuda said in the name of Rav, A butcher[1] needs three knives, one to slaughter with, one to carve the meat and one to cut out the [forbidden] fats.

> Wouldn't it be sufficient to require [just] one to carve the meat, and then to cut out the [forbidden] fats [with it]? [No.] It is a protective rule [in case] he [first] cuts out the fats and then carves the meat.[2] But might he not mix them even now [that he has two knives]? [No.] The requirement for two [separate] knives is a signal [to remind him that he must take care].

Rav Yehuda [also] said in the name of Rav, A butcher must have two water containers, one to rinse the meat and one to rinse the fats.

---

1. It is assumed that the butcher who sells the meat also slaughters.
2. Remains of the forbidden fat might then contaminate the meat.

Wouldn't it be sufficient to require [just] one to rinse the meat, and then to rinse the fats with it? [No.] It is a protective rule [in case] he [first] rinses the fats and then the meat. But might he not mix them even now [that he has two containers]? [No.] If you require him to have two [separate] containers, it is a signal [to remind him that he must take care].

Ameimar said you shouldn't press the loins on to the [rest of the] meat, since the fat oozes out and is absorbed by the meat. [But] if so, even if they are arranged [in the normal way without pressing], fat oozes out and the meat absorbs it! [No, since] a membrane separates them below. If so[, even if the loins are on top there should be no problem, since] there is a membrane on top too! Since the butcher handles [the meat by putting the loins on top, the membrane would] break.

9a

Rav Yehuda [also] said in the name of Rav, A scholar should acquire three [practical skills]: writing, *shehita* and circumcision. Rav Ḥanania ben Shelemia said in the name of Rav, [He should] also [learn to] tie the knot of *tefillin*, [to recite] the wedding blessings and [to tie] the *tzitzit*. [Why did Rav Yehuda not list those too? Because] the others are more common.

Rav Yehuda also said in the name of Shmuel, If a butcher does not know the laws of *shehita*, it is forbidden to eat from [an animal] he has slaughtered, and these are the laws of *shehita*: Pause, Press, Insertion, Misplacement, Ripping.[3]

What is he telling us? [Surely] all these [laws] are taught by the Mishna? He needs [to tell us] that if someone slaughtered correctly two or three times in our presence, [you still cannot rely on him to do it

3.   *Pause*: one fast cut should be made; the least pause invalidates the *shehita*. *Press*: the knife must be drawn across the oesophagus and windpipe, not pressed against them. *Insertion*: the knife must not be inserted between oesophagus and windpipe. *Misplacement*: the cut must be made at the correct location through the oesophagus and windpipe. *Ripping*: oesophagus and windpipe must be cut cleanly, not ripped out.

correctly if he has not learned the laws]; you might
have thought that since he has [slaughtered] correctly
[in the past, you could assume] that what he has done
now [without supervision] is correct too, so [Shmuel]
informs us that since [the slaughterer] has not learned
the laws, he might pause or press without realizing
[that it is wrong].

And Rav Yehuda said in the name of Shmuel, A butcher has
to examine the 'signs' following *shehita*.

Rav Yosef said, That is [implied] in the Mishna:[4] **If
he paused long enough to examine** – surely this means
the length of time needed to examine the 'signs'?
Abbaye said to him, No, for Rabbi Yohanan [clarified]:
[It means] the length of time it would take an expert
[scholar] to [come and] examine. [But if Abbaye was
right,] this would be an indefinite period[, so we must
conclude that Rabbi Yohanan meant the length of]
time for an expert butcher to examine.

What if he didn't examine [them]? **Rabbi Eliezer ben Antigonos said in the name of Rabbi Eleazar ben Yannai, It is
terefa and must not be eaten;** a Tanna says, **It is *nevela*, and
defiles by carrying.**[5]

What is their dispute based on? It is Rav Huna's
[principle], for [Rav Huna] said, So long as an animal
is alive, the presumption is that it is forbidden to eat
[it] until you know how it has been slaughtered; once
it has been [correctly] slaughtered, the presumption is
that it is permitted to eat [it] until you know how it
became *terefa*. [The Tanna] holds that it was presumed
forbidden and is now dead[, and since you do not
know for certain that it was slaughtered correctly, it is
nevela and defiles]; [Rabbi Eleazar] holds there is a
presumption that it was forbidden, but not that it was
defiled.

[Let us consider Rav Huna's principle.] Rav Huna said, So

4. *Hullin* 2:3 (32a).
5. *Nevela* is unclean and defiles; correct *shehita* prevents the animal from becoming
    nevela, even if it is found to be *terefa*.

long as an animal is alive, the presumption is that it is forbidden to eat [it] until you know how it has been slaughtered; once it has been [correctly] slaughtered, the presumption is that it is permitted to eat [it] until you know how it became *terefa*. Why does he not [simply say], Once it has been slaughtered it is permitted?[6] He wants to tell us that even though a contrary presumption may have been introduced[, it is permitted]. This is what Rabbi Abba asked Rav Huna: What if a wolf came and took the intestines?

> Took them? Then they aren't there[, so the question doesn't arise]. So [the question must have been], What if a wolf came and made a hole in the intestines? A hole? Then we can see that [the wolf] made the hole [after the death of the animal, and this would no longer render it *terefa*]. So [the question must have been, What if a wolf] removed the intestines and then returned them with a hole in them? Do we take into account that the wolf may have made the hole where there was already a hole [that would have rendered it *terefa*, but which we can no longer detect], or not?

Rav Huna replied, We do not assume that the wolf made a hole where one was already present.

[Rabbi Abba] objected: **If someone saw a bird peck at a fig, or a mouse nibble melons, we consider that they might have made a hole [where a snake] had already pierced [the fruit and injected venom].**   9b

[Rav Huna] replied, Are you comparing danger [to life] with [religious] prohibition? Danger is different.

Rava asked,[7] Why is it different? Because when there is doubt concerning danger we go to the stricter side [to avoid it]? We go to the stricter side with prohibitions, too.

Abbaye said to him, Then is there no difference between danger and prohibition? If there is doubt about whether something in a public area has been rendered impure, it is regarded as [still] pure; but if there is a doubt as to [whether a snake has

6. i.e. why introduce the legal concept of presumption?
7. Two generations separate Rava and Abbaye from Rav Huna.

drunk from] uncovered water [and injected venom into it], it is forbidden [to drink it]!

Rava responded, [The purity instance] is an [exceptional] *halakha* derived from the case of the suspected adulteress – just as the adulteress [offends] in private [and not in public], so [doubts about] impurity [are treated strictly] in a private [situation but not in a public one].

Rav Shimi objected, **If a weasel held a reptile**[8] **in its mouth and walked across loaves of** *teruma* **and we do not know whether [the reptile] touched them or not, [the loaves remain] pure [despite] the doubt**[9] – but if there is a doubt as to [whether a snake has drunk from] uncovered water [and injected venom into it], it is forbidden [to drink it]!

[The answer:] That also is an [exceptional] *halakha* derived from the case of the suspected adulteress – just as the adulteress can be questioned, so in other cases where questioning is possible [the doubt is resolved in the stricter sense, but you cannot question a weasel, so in this case we take the lenient view].

Rav Ashi said, Here is proof [that danger is more serious than prohibition]: **If someone left a jar uncovered and returned to find it covered, it is impure, for I would say, An unclean person entered and covered it. If he left it covered and returned to find it uncovered, [then] if a weasel might have drunk from it – or a snake, in the view of Rabban Gamaliel – or if dew had fallen into it during the night, it is unfit.**[10] Rabbi Joshua ben Levi said, Why is this? Because creatures uncover things and don't cover them up.[11] [At any rate, we do not assume that it is unclean,[12] whereas] if there is a doubt as to [whether a snake

10a

---

8. Not reptile in a zoological sense, but any of the eight creatures listed in Leviticus 11:29–30; the weasel is not among them.
9. Mishna *Eduyot* 2:7 and *Tohorot* 4:2.
10. That is, unfit for use in connection with the ceremonial of the ashes of the red heifer. This version of Mishna *Parah* 11:1 only partly coincides with the received reading.
11. Some manuscripts insert an alternative reason, but the reading was rejected by the sixteenth-century *halakhist* Solomon Luria.
12. This is one of several interpretations offered by Rashi.

has drunk from] uncovered water [and injected venom into it],
it is forbidden [to drink it]! This proves that danger is more
serious than prohibition.

A Mishna states: **Three liquids are forbidden if left
uncovered – water, wine and milk. How long must they be
left uncovered to become forbidden? Long enough for a reptile
to emerge from nearby and drink.**[13]

> What is 'nearby'? Rav Isaac the son of Rav Yehuda
> said, Long enough for it to emerge from beneath the
> handle of the container and drink. Drink? Wouldn't
> we then see it[, so there would be no doubt]? Rather
> [long enough for it to emerge from beneath the
> handle], drink and return to its hole.

*Leviticus 11 and Deuteronomy 14 list creatures that may or
may not be eaten. Following biblical usage, the rabbis tend to
use the terms 'clean' and 'unclean' rather than* kasher *and* terefa
to indicate the status of the species.

*After reviewing each of the Mishna's categories, the Gemara
clarifies what Leviticus 11 means by swarming and creeping
creatures of air, land or water. The Sages, in common with the
pre-modern world generally, believed in spontaneous generation;*[14] *Rav Huna, for instance, holds that small insects that are
found in liquor made from dates are just part of the liquor, so
it is permitted to drink the liquor containing them unless they
have become detached, in which case they exist independently
as 'swarming creatures'. Terms denoting small creatures are
imprecise; translations such as 'insect' or 'maggot' should not
be taken in a strict zoological sense.*

13. *Terumot* 8:4.
14. The first serious attack on the idea of spontaneous generation was made in 1668
     by Francesco Redi (1626–97), an Italian physician and poet, but few were con-
     vinced before Pasteur's conclusive experiments in 1859.

CHAPTER THREE

MISHNA:

59a The signs of [clean] domestic and wild animals are stated in the Torah.

The signs of [clean] birds are not stated in the Torah, but the Sages said that whatever has an extra toe, a crop and a gizzard that peels easily is clean. Rabbi Eleazar the son of Rabbi Zadok says, Any bird that parts its feet is unclean.

Of locusts, any that has four legs and four wings and leaping legs and whose wings cover most of its body [is clean]. Rabbi Yosé says, It must also be called *ḥagav* [in Hebrew].

[In Leviticus 11:9] *qasqeset* denotes the fixed [scales]; *s'napir* denotes what [the creature] swims with. Any fish that has fins and scales [is clean]. Rabbi Judah says, it must have at least one fin and two scales.

GEMARA:

67a Rav Huna said, Don't filter your date liquor through wood chips at night, because [some small creature] may jump out on to the chips and fall back [into the liquor], and then [when you drink it] you would transgress, [**THESE ARE UNCLEAN FOR YOU OF**] **THINGS THAT SWARM ON THE EARTH** (Leviticus 11:29).

If so, surely the same should apply even when [the liquor] is in a container, since the creatures might adhere to the side of the container and then fall back in? No, since that is their nature. We know this from a baraita: **How do we know that this includes wells, ditches and caves – that you need not refrain from bending down and drinking from them? It says, You MAY EAT WHATEVER IS IN THE WATER** (Leviticus 11:9). Should you not be concerned that the creatures might adhere to the side then fall back in? [No, since] that is their nature; here, likewise, it is their nature.

Rav Ḥisda said to Rav Huna, A baraita supports you: **EVERY SWARMING CREATURE THAT SWARMS ON THE EARTH** (Leviticus 11:42) – **this includes insects that have been filtered out –**

they are forbidden because they have been filtered out, but otherwise they would be permitted.

Shmuel said, If a cucumber generated maggots while still on the growing plant, it is forbidden as a **SWARMING CREATURE THAT SWARMS ON THE EARTH**. Does the following support him? One baraita states: **ON THE EARTH excludes maggots in lentils, caterpillars in peas and worms in dates and figs**; another baraita states: **EVERY SWARMING CREATURE THAT SWARMS ON THE EARTH includes worms infesting the roots of olives and vines.** Don't both of these refer to the fruit, one when it is on the growing plant and the other when it is not on the growing plant? No. Both refer to fruit that is still on the growing plant, but there is no contradiction, since one refers to the fruit and the other to the plant. That is clearly so, since it says: **infesting the *roots* of olives and vines.**

Since the creature is not forbidden until it 'crawls on the ground', the following questions arise:

Rav Yosef asked, If [a creature] left [the host plant] and died [before reaching the ground], what [is its status]? No answer. If [only] part of it [crawled on the ground,] what [is its status]? No answer. If it just went into the air what [is its status]? No answer.

Rav Ashi asked, If [it crawled] on top of a date, what then? Or on top of the pip? Or from one date to another, what then? No answer.

Rav Sheshet the son of Rav Idi said, Flatworms[15] are forbidden because they come from outside. Rav Ashi objected, If they came from outside they would be found in the [host's] excrement.[16]

Others report: Rav Sheshet the son of Rav Idi said, Flatworms are permitted because they are formed [spontaneously] inside [the animal]. Rav Ashi said, That's obvious, since if they came from outside, they would be found in the [host's] excrement.

15. *Ququni*, related to Akkadian *ququnu* (Sokoloff, *Babylonian*), is a general term for parasitic worms; Rashi thinks it refers to worms in liver and lungs, Rabbenu Tam to those in fish.
16. If the animal (or fish) had ingested the flatworms, they would pass through its digestive tract.

67b

The *halakha* is: Flatworms are forbidden since when the animal sleeps they enter through its nostrils.[17]

Parasitic worms found between the flesh and the hide of animals are forbidden, but those in fish are permitted. Ravina said to his mother, Mix them with the fish and I will eat it![18] Rav Mesharshya the son of Rav Aḥa asked Ravina, Why is that different from **YOU SHALL ABOMINATE THEIR CARCASSES** (Leviticus 11:11 JPS) – **to include worms in the flesh**? He replied, An animal is [forbidden until] rendered permissible by *sheḥita*, and as *sheḥita* doesn't affect worms they remain forbidden; fish are permitted simply by gathering them, so their [worms] formed out of something already permitted.[19]

Genesis 32:25–33 tells the story of Jacob wrestling at night with a mysterious opponent, identified by tradition as the guardian angel of Esau. In the course of the conflict Jacob was injured.

THEREFORE ISRAELITES DO NOT EAT THE SINEW OF THE THIGH VEIN[20] TO THIS VERY DAY, FOR HE STRUCK THE SOCKET OF JACOB'S THIGH ON THE SINEW OF THE THIGH VEIN. (Genesis 32:33)

Tradition identifies the 'sinew of the thigh vein' as the sciatic nerve.

As well as generating several halakhic *principles governing food mixtures, the stories of Jacob stimulate some fine* aggada, *including a diversion on Jacob's dream of the ladder (Genesis 28:10–22).*

17. The ruling is probably a Geonic interpolation.
18. They were too disgusting to eat if visible!
19. The 'spontaneously generated' parasites are parts of the animal or fish.
20. This is the probable literal translation. KJV translates as 'the sinew which shrank'; JPS as 'thigh muscle'.

CHAPTER SEVEN

MISHNA:

[The prohibition of] the sinew of the thigh vein applies   90a
both in the Land [of Israel] and outside the Land, whether or
not the Temple is standing, and to unconsecrated as well as
consecrated beasts. It applies to domestic and wild animals, to
the right thigh and the left thigh, but it does not apply to
birds since they lack a socket.[21] It applies to a foetus, but Rabbi
Judah says, It does not apply to a foetus.

In Rabbi Meir's opinion, butchers cannot be trusted [to
remove] the sinew of the thigh vein, but the Sages say, They
can be trusted for that and for [removal of] the forbidden
fats.[22]

GEMARA:

AND JACOB WAS LEFT ALONE (Genesis 32:25). Rabbi Eleazar   91a
said, He went back for some small jars. From this you can infer
that the righteous value their property more than their bodies.
Why so? Because they never put their hand to stolen property.

AND A MAN STRUGGLED WITH HIM UNTIL DAWN (32:25).
Rabbi Isaac said, From this you can infer that a man of learning
should not go out alone at night; Rabbi Abba bar Kahana said,
You can infer that from this verse: HE WILL BE WINNOWING   91b
BARLEY ON THE THRESHING FLOOR TONIGHT (Ruth 3:2
JPS);[23] Rabbi Abbahu said, You can infer it from this verse:
AND ABRAHAM AROSE IN THE MORNING AND SADDLED HIS
DONKEY (Genesis 22:3); [others] said, You can infer it from the
verse, GO AND SEE HOW YOUR BROTHERS ARE AND HOW THE
FLOCKS ARE FARING (Genesis 37:14 JPS); Rav said, From this
verse: AND THE SUN ROSE ON HIM AS HE PASSED PENUEL
(32:32).

---

21. The articulation of the hip joint in birds is similar to that in mammals, but
    perhaps because it is smaller the socket does not appear 'like a spoon', which is
    the literal translation of the term here.
22. Butchers slaughtered their own animals and would have an interest in selling as
    much meat as possible.
23. He would not be returning home alone.

Rabbi Aqiva said, I put this question to Rabban Gamaliel and Rabbi Joshua in the market at Emmaus, where they were looking for a beast to purchase for Rabban Gamaliel's son's [wedding] feast: Scripture says, AND THE SUN ROSE ON HIM. Did the sun rise only for [Jacob]? Surely it rose for the whole world!

Rabbi Isaac said, The sun that had set for him rose for him. It is written, AND JACOB LEFT BEER SHEBA AND WENT TO HARAN; it then states, AND HE HAPPENED UPON A PLACE, FOR THE SUN HAD SET (Genesis 28:10, 11).[24]

When [Jacob] arrived at Haran he reflected: Could I possibly have bypassed the place where my fathers prayed and not have stopped to pray myself? He determined to return; the land shrank[25] and he immediately HAPPENED UPON the place. When he had prayed he wanted to go back [to Haran], but the Holy One, blessed be He, said, This virtuous man has arrived at My lodging; can I let him go without an overnight stay? At once, the sun set.

It is written, AND HE TOOK STONES [plural] FROM THE PLACE [TO PUT AT HIS HEAD], and it is written, AND HE TOOK THE STONE [singular] (Genesis 28:11, 18). Rabbi Isaac said, This teaches that the stones all gathered themselves into one place, each saying, May this virtuous man rest his head on me! It was taught: They all coalesced into one stone.

AND HE DREAMED: BEHOLD, A LADDER STOOD UPON THE EARTH (28:12). It was taught: How wide was the ladder? 8,000 parasangs,[26] for it is written, AND ANGELS OF GOD WERE ASCENDING AND DESCENDING IT. Now, if two angels were ascending and two descending there would be four as they met; it

24. The plain meaning is that Jacob set off for Haran and stopped overnight en route at 'the place' (English translations omit the definite article); Rabbi Isaac reads that Jacob actually arrived in Haran, then regretted that he had not stopped off at the place of prayer. Haran is in Syria; 'the place' (unnamed) is the site of the future Temple in Jerusalem.

25. Or 'jumped'.

26. Since a *parasang* is about $3\frac{1}{2}$ miles this exceeds the circumference of the earth!

is written of an angel, **His body was like Tarsus**[27] (Daniel 10:6), and we have learned that Tarsus was 2,000 parasangs across, so that makes 8,000. It was taught: They ascended to gaze on Jacob's likeness above and descended to gaze on his likeness below. They might have endangered him, but at once, **Behold, the Lord stood above** (Genesis 28:13). Rabbi Simeon said, Had Scripture not stated this it would have been impossible to say it – it was like a man wagging his finger at his son!

The land on which you lie ... What was the big deal?[28] Rabbi Isaac said, This teaches that the Holy One, blessed be He, folded up the whole Land of Israel and placed it beneath our father Jacob, [indicating] that it would be conquered with ease by his descendants.

And he said, Let me go, for morning has come! (32:27). [Jacob] said to him: Are you a thief or a gambler that you are afraid of the morning [light]? I am an angel, he replied, and only now, for the first time since the day I was created, has my turn come to sing the [morning] song [in praise of God]!

This confirms what Rav Ḥananel said in the name of Rav: Each day three courses of ministering angels sing praises; one sings **Holy**, another sings **holy** and a third sings **holy is the Lord of Hosts** (Isaiah 6:3).

As against that: Israel are more loved by the Holy One, blessed be He, than the ministering angels, for Israel recite the Song at all times and the ministering angels only once a day – some say [only] once a week, some say once a month, some say once a year, some

27. Hebrew *Tarshish*, as the name of a location, denotes Tarsus in Asia Minor (Turkey) or perhaps Tartessus in Spain. In Daniel (as in Exodus 28:20, etc.) it more likely refers to a precious stone, perhaps because such items were imported from Tarshish. However, Rashi on Daniel says it is 'the sea of Africa'; Saadia Gaon in his commentary on Daniel suggested it was the depth of the sea.

28. He lay on a mere four cubits – Rashi.

say once every seven years, some say once in
a Jubilee period, some say only once ever.
Also, Israel proclaim the Name after two
words, as it is said, **HEAR, ISRAEL! THE
LORD** . . . (Deuteronomy 6:4), whereas the
ministering angels proclaim it only after
three, as it is said, **HOLY, HOLY, HOLY IS
THE LORD OF HOSTS**.[29] Nor may the ministering angels recite the Song above until Israel
have recited it below, as it is said, **WHEN
THE MORNING STARS SANG TOGETHER**, and
only then, **AND ALL THE DIVINE BEINGS
SHOUTED FOR JOY** (Job 38:7 JPS).

So, one course sings **HOLY**, another sings **HOLY** and
a third sings **HOLY IS THE LORD OF HOSTS**. What
about **BLESSED [BE THE GLORY OF THE LORD IN
HIS PLACE]** (Ezekiel 3:12)? 'Blessed' is sung by the
Ofanim[, not the ministering angels]. Alternatively,
once permission has been granted they continue.

**HE ACTED AS A PRINCE WITH AN ANGEL AND HE PRE-
VAILED; HE WEPT AND IMPLORED HIM** (Hosea 12:5).[30] I would
not know who became prince of whom, but when it says,
FOR YOU ACTED THE PRINCE WITH GOD (Genesis 32:29), it is
[clear that it was] Jacob who became prince over the angel.
[Likewise,] **HE WEPT AND IMPLORED HIM** – who wept [and
implored] whom? When it says, **LET ME GO, FOR MORNING
HAS COME!**, it is [clear that it was] the angel who wept [and
implored] Jacob.

92a

*The phrase 'Do not boil a kid in its mother's milk' occurs three
times in the Torah (Exodus 23:19, 34:26; Deuteronomy 14:21).
It is interpreted later in this chapter (115b) as a threefold prohibition: milk and meat may not be cooked together, and if they
are, the mixture may neither be eaten nor be made use of in any*

---

29. 'The' and 'is the' are not in the Hebrew.
30. Hosea refers directly to the story of Jacob's struggle. *Sarita*, here translated 'acted
    as a prince', is usually translated 'strove'; the same applies to the phrase in Genesis.

other way. The rabbis extended the prohibition to eating or otherwise using a mixture of milk and meat even if uncooked, and later Jewish custom went so far as to insist on separate sets of utensils for foods derived from meat and milk. Although the Torah prohibition applies only to mammals, most Tannaim extended it to birds.

CHAPTER EIGHT

MISHNA:

Fowl may be placed on the table with cheese, though they   104b
may not be eaten together. That is the opinion of the School
of Shammai, but the School of Hillel say, They may neither
be placed on the table [together] nor eaten [together]. Rabbi
Yosé said, That is [a case where] the School of Shammai is
lenient, but the School of Hillel is strict.

What table were they referring to? The table at which you
eat. But you may put one next to the other on the table on
which you prepare food, and you need not worry.

GEMARA:

Surely what Rabbi Yosé says is the same as the first Tanna
[of the Mishna]! You might think that they differed with regard
to eating [cheese and fowl together]; the first Tanna holds that
[the Schools of Shammai and Hillel] differ with regard
to bringing [cheese and fowl on to the table], but not with
regard to [the prohibition of] eating [them together], whereas
Rabi Yosé comments that [with regard to] eating them together,
the School of Shammai is lenient, but the School of Hillel is
strict. But [this cannot be, since] a baraita states: **Rabbi Yosé
says, in six cases the School of Shammai was lenient, but the
School of Hillel was strict; one was that according to the School
of Shammai, cheese and fowl might be placed on the table but
not eaten together, whereas according to the School of Hillel,
they may be neither placed on the table nor eaten together.**

The Mishna, then, simply wants to identify the first Tanna
as Rabbi Yosé, since whoever reports a matter in the name of
the one who [originally] said it brings redemption to the world,

as it is said, **And Esther reported it to the king in Mordecai's name** (Esther 2:22).

Agra the father of Rabbi Abba taught: Fowl and cheese may be eaten without restraint. He taught that and he explained [what he meant]: without rinsing the hands or cleansing the mouth with bread [between one and the other].

Rav Isaac the son of Rav Mesharshya visited Rav Ashi's home. They brought him cheese and he ate it, then they brought him meat and he ate it without rinsing his hands [between]. They asked him, Didn't Agra the father of Rabbi Abba teach: Fowl and cheese may be eaten without restraint – fowl and cheese, not meat and cheese? He replied, That is at night, but in the daytime I could see [that no cheese was left on my hands when I ate the meat].

It was taught: **The School of Shammai say, Clean [the mouth with bread]! The School of Hillel say, Rinse [the hands]!** What do they mean by 'clean' and 'rinse'? Could it be that the School of Shammai meant clean but do not rinse and the School of Hillel meant rinse but do not clean? If so, when Rabbi Zeira remarked, Cleaning is only with bread, he must have been speaking according to the School of Shammai. If the School of Shammai meant clean but do not rinse and the School of Hillel meant [cleaning is necessary, but you must] also rinse, this would be another case where the School of Shammai is lenient but the School of Hillel is strict, and it should be listed among [the cases where] the School of Shammai is lenient but the School of Hillel is strict[, but it is not]. Therefore the meaning must be that the School of Shammai said clean, but rinsing will do and the School of Hillel said rinse, but cleaning will do; there is no dispute between them, but one mentioned one thing and one the other.

Let's look more closely at Rabbi Zeira's remark that cleaning is only with bread. This is only with wheat [bread], but not with rye,[31] and even with wheat only if it is cold, not hot, because if hot it spreads [the cheese in his mouth]; even then only if [the bread is] soft rather than hard.

105a

31. Because it crumbles in the mouth – Rashi.

The *halakha* is: Anything may be used to cleanse
the mouth other than flour, dates or vegetables.[32]

Rav Assi asked Rabbi Yoḥanan, How long must you wait
between meat and cheese? He replied, No time at all. That can't
be right, for didn't Rav Ḥisda say, If you ate meat you mustn't
eat cheese [after it], but if you ate cheese you may eat meat?
[The question must have been,] How long must you wait
between cheese and meat? To this he replied, No time at all.

Let's look more closely at Rav Ḥisda's remark that
if you ate meat you mustn't eat cheese [after it], but if
you ate cheese you may eat meat. Rav Aḥa bar Yosef
asked Rav Ḥisda, What about meat [lodged] between
your teeth? Rav Ḥisda referred him to the verse, THE
MEAT WAS STILL BETWEEN THEIR TEETH (Numbers
11:33).

*Orthodox Jews today refrain from eating milk products after
eating meat or fowl. Customs differ, however, as to whether to
wait one hour, three hours or six, depending on the interpretation of Mar Uqba's remark:*

Mar Uqba said, In this matter I am like vinegar the son of
wine compared with my father, for if my father ate meat one
day he would not eat cheese until the next day, whereas if I eat
meat at one meal I eat cheese at the next.

---

32. The ruling, which conflicts with the previous statement, is probably a Geonic
interpolation.

FOURTH TRACTATE
BEKHOROT (FIRST-BORN)

Bekhorot is about – everything! True, it focuses strongly on laws of the first-born, whether animal or human, but somehow the redactor has managed to relate these laws to almost every halakhic *topic, producing what is commonly known as* Shas qatan, *or 'Talmud in a nutshell'. This makes for a highly compressed style which is difficult to read and calls to be expanded in translation.*

There are three categories of first-born: domestic animals, 'unclean' animals (the ass is specified) and boys:

EVERY FIRST ISSUE OF THE WOMB IS MINE, FROM ALL YOUR LIVESTOCK THAT DROP A MALE AS FIRSTLING, WHETHER CATTLE OR SHEEP. BUT THE FIRSTLING OF AN ASS YOU SHALL REDEEM WITH A SHEEP; IF YOU DO NOT REDEEM IT, YOU MUST BREAK ITS NECK. AND YOU MUST REDEEM EVERY FIRST-BORN AMONG YOUR SONS. (Exodus 34:19–20)

Few in the ancient world would have been surprised had a cow given birth to an ass or a camel; far more drastic transformations are reported by classical writers such as Ovid. Mishna is interested in such marvels for defining the species of the anomalous offspring; is it subject to the laws of the first-born, and what is its status as food? The principle, **That which comes from the clean is clean, and from the unclean unclean,** *may carry social overtones too.*

How do we know that it is permitted to drink milk? At no stage is the law really in doubt, only its derivation from Scripture. The obvious proof, from **A LAND FLOWING WITH MILK**

AND HONEY, is left almost until last; this is an instance of what Louis Jacobs[1] called 'the dramatic construction of the sugya' – *we are kept in suspense awaiting the solution to the problem. Granted milk of 'clean' animals is permitted, how do we know that such permission does not extend to the milk of non-kasher animals?*

CHAPTER ONE

MISHNA:

If a cow gave birth to a kind of ass or an ass to a kind of horse, 5b
[the newborn animal] is exempt from [the laws pertaining to] first-born [asses]; the Torah uses the expression FIRST-BORN ASS twice (Exodus 13:13, 34:20) [to teach] that both the bearer and the born must be asses.

May [such animals] be eaten? If a clean animal gave birth to an animal of unclean species, it is permitted to eat [the newborn], but if an unclean animal gave birth to an animal of clean species, it is forbidden, since that which comes from the clean is clean, and from the unclean unclean.

GEMARA:

May [such animals] be eaten? Why does the Mishna say, 6a
Since that which comes from . . .? It is just a mnemonic, so that you don't get confused and think you ought to go by [appearances] and [decide] it is clean; rather, you must [determine the species] according to the mother.

How do we know this? The rabbis taught: YOU SHALL NOT EAT THE FOLLOWING AMONG THOSE THAT CHEW THE CUD AND[2] HAVE CLOVEN HOOVES (Leviticus 11:4) – There are animals that chew the cud and have cloven hooves, yet you must not eat them. Which are they? Clean [animals] that are the offspring of unclean. Or does it refer to unclean that are the offspring of clean, in which case it means, Do not eat that 6b

1. Jacobs, *Structure and Form*, especially chapter 12 (pp. 95–9).
2. The correct translation in context is 'or'. However, the particle can also mean 'and', and the rabbis play on the ambiguity.

which comes from what chews the cud and has cloven hooves [but does not itself chew the cud and have cloven hooves]? [No. This cannot be correct, since] the text says, THE CAMEL . . . IS UNCLEAN (Leviticus 11:4) – that is, the camel is unclean, but an unclean animal that is the offspring of a clean one is clean, not unclean. Rabbi Simeon says, The word 'camel' is used twice (Leviticus 11:4, Deuteronomy 14:7) [to signify that] both a camel born of a she-camel and a camel born of a cow [are forbidden].

How do the [other rabbis interpret] the repeated use of 'camel'? Once prohibits [eating] the camel itself; twice prohibits its milk [too, but a camel born of a cow is permitted].

On what does Rabbi Simeon base the prohibition of the milk [of a forbidden animal]? He derives it from the particle et^3 that precedes the word 'camel'; the [other] rabbis, however, do not interpret et.

> This is as was taught: Simeon of Emesa interpreted every et in the Torah. When he came to ET THE LORD YOUR GOD YOU SHALL FEAR (Deuteronomy 6:13), he desisted [from this method of interpretation]. His disciples said to him, Master, what is to happen to all those ets you have already interpreted? He replied, Just as I receive a reward for interpreting, so I receive a reward for desisting.[4] Then came Rabbi Aqiva, and taught, ET THE LORD YOUR GOD YOU SHALL FEAR includes the disciples of the Sages.[5]

Rava's son, Rav Aḥa, said to Rav Ashi, So it seems that the rabbis infer [that camel's milk is forbidden] from 'camel' occurring twice, and Rabbi Simeon from et; this [implies that] if not for those interpretations we might have thought that the milk of unclean animals was permitted. Why is this different

3.   This particle indicates the object in a sentence; it is normally untranslated, but sometimes has the force of 'with', and Rabbi Simeon takes this to mean 'in addition to'.

4.   That is, the study of Torah is always virtuous provided it is done in good faith and you are ready to acknowledge your errors.

5.   Respect those learned in Torah as part of your respect for God. Hebrew yir'ah may be translated 'fear', 'awe' or 'respect'. Aquila's translation of the Scriptures consistently translates et by sun, 'with', which results in abominable Greek.

from what was taught: *THE* UNCLEAN (Leviticus 11:29) – [the definite article] is to add juice, gravy and sediments[6] to what is forbidden[, so presumably milk is forbidden too]? [Even so, a verse] is needed [to forbid milk], since without it I might have reasoned: [Permission to drink] milk is an anomaly even in the case of clean animals, seeing that blood becomes turbid and turns into milk, so perhaps the milk of unclean animals is permitted too. [The verse] informs you [that this is not so].

That's all right if you hold that blood becomes turbid and turns into milk, but if you hold 'her limbs are weakened and she doesn't regain full health for twenty-four months',[7] what can you say? [Even in this view a verse] is needed [to forbid milk of unclean animals], since otherwise I might have thought that seeing that nothing else that issues from a living animal is permitted, milk is similar to 'a limb from a living animal', and [since it is permitted even though anything else taken from a living animal is forbidden, it] might be permitted even if from an unclean animal. [The verse] informs you [that this is not so].

But how do we know that the milk of clean animals *is* permitted?

If you say, [It can be inferred] from [the fact that] the Torah forbids milk together with meat that each on its own is permitted, I could [suggest an alternative interpretation, namely:] milk on its own may be used but not drunk, and meat and milk together may not even be used. Even according to Rabbi Simeon who permits the use [though not eating or cooking] of meat and milk together, [the verse] might be [taken to indicate] that cooking meat and milk together incurs the penalty of flogging.

Then perhaps [it can be inferred that milk is permitted] from

6. The words are imprecise; the general idea is that anything exuding from the forbidden meat is forbidden, too. Surely this should include milk!
7. Infants were normally breastfed for 24 months. The question is whether post-partum amenorrhea is due to menstrual blood turning into milk, or simply a consequence of the woman's general weakness; if milk is 'really' blood we would expect it to be forbidden.

[the fact that] the Torah makes clear, in connection with rejected sacrificial animals, YOU MAY SLAUGHTER – but not shear; MEAT – but not milk (Deuteronomy 12:15), which implies that you may drink the milk of unconsecrated animals. [No:] I might still say, [milk of] unconsecrated animals may be used but not drunk, but that of consecrated animals may not even be used.

Then perhaps because it is written, THE GOATS' MILK WILL SUFFICE FOR YOUR FOOD, THE FOOD OF YOUR HOUSEHOLD, AND THE MAINTENANCE OF YOUR MAIDS (Proverbs 27:27 JPS)? Perhaps that is [just] for trade.

Or perhaps because it is written, AND TAKE THESE TEN CHEESES TO THE COMMANDER OF THE THOUSAND (1 Samuel 17:18)? Perhaps that was [just] for trade. [No. Surely] it is not the way of war to trade.[8]

Then you might derive it from here: A LAND FLOWING WITH MILK AND HONEY (Exodus 3:8); Scripture would surely not boast of something unfit.

Or from here: COME, BUY WINE AND MILK, WITHOUT MONEY, WITHOUT PRICE! (Isaiah 55:1).

Next there is some light relief. After discussing the gestation periods of various animals – the snake is (erroneously) said to have been allotted the longest, as a punishment for tempting Eve – it moves on to the extraordinary tale of Rabbi Joshua and the Elders of Athens, a late literary construction combining riddles, folk elements and a memory of Joshua's debating skill in defence of Torah.[9] Medieval and later apologists such as Samuel Edels (Maharsha) have read symbolic, mystical and historical allusions into it. More recently, Peter Schäfer has linked the story of the mule to the virgin birth, and the question about unsavoury salt to Jesus' remarks in Matthew 5:3.[10] Such interpretations are uncertain; the overall purpose of the narrative is to emphasize the superiority of the revealed wisdom of Torah to the 'human' wisdom of the Greeks. The text is poorly preserved and not always intelligible.

8.   Jesse had sent David to his brothers in the army camp with provisions including the cheeses.
9.   Jacobs, *Structure and Form*, pp. 76–80.
10.   Schäfer, *Jesus*, pp. 23–4.

GEMARA:

Caesar asked Rabbi Joshua ben Ḥanania, How long is the   8b
gestation period of a snake? Seven years, he replied. But, [con-
tinued Caesar,] the Sages of Athens coupled them and they gave
birth in three years! Those had already been pregnant for four
years[, responded Rabbi Joshua].

[Caesar:] But they copulated!

[Joshua:] They copulate [when pregnant] as humans do.

[Caesar:] If you're that clever, defeat [the Sages of Athens]
and bring them to me!

[Joshua:] How many of them are there?

[Caesar:] Sixty.

[Joshua:] Then make me a ship with sixty compartments,
each with sixty mattresses.[11]

[Caesar] produced [the ship]. When [Joshua] arrived [in
Athens], he went to a butcher's and found a man flaying carcasses. How much for your head? he enquired. Half a *zuz*,
replied the other. [Joshua] paid him. I didn't mean *my* head,
protested the man when [he realized what had been said], I
meant an animal's head! I'll let you go, said Joshua, if you can
show me the entrance for the Sages of Athens.

[The butcher:] I'm too scared. They kill anyone who shows
the way in!

[Joshua:] Then take a bundle of sticks, and when you pass
there stand it up as if you're taking a breath.

[So Joshua] arrived, and found guards inside and out; if [the
Athenian Sages] saw a foot enter they would kill the outside
guards, and if they saw one going out they would kill the inside
guards. He put his shoe down pointing outwards so they killed
the inside guards, then he put it down pointing inwards so they
killed the outside guards.[12]

So they killed all [the guards] and [Joshua] entered. He found
the young ones above and the elders below. He thought, If I
greet [the younger ones] the others will kill me, since they

11. Rashi says 'thrones', but the word derives from Middle Iranian *bistarak*, 'bedding'
    (Sokoloff, *Babylonian*).

12. The [Athenian] sages themselves killed the guards for failing to prevent the exit
    and entry of unauthorized persons – Rashi.

believe they are more important because they are older and the others are [mere] children. So he greeted the elders.

[The elders:] Who are you?

[Joshua:] I am the Sage of the Jews. I wish to study your wisdom.

[The elders:] Then we must ask you some questions.

[Joshua:] You are welcome! If you outwit me you can do what you like to me. If I outwit you, you must join me for a meal on board my ship.

[The elders:] A man wanted a wife but they wouldn't give her to him. Should he ask for a wife from a better family?

[Joshua] took a peg. He pushed it [in the wall] low down but it wouldn't go, then tried higher up and it went in. This happens [with marriage too, he said;] the superior wife is the one destined for him.

[The elders:] If someone lent money and only got it back by claiming mortgaged property, would he lend again?

[Joshua] went out to a forest and cut a first bundle of wood, but could not carry it. He cut more and added to the bundle until eventually someone came who could carry it.[13]

[The elders:] Tell us a tall story!

[Joshua:] A mule gave birth and they hung a notice round its neck saying his father owed someone 100,000 *zuz*.

[The elders:] But a mule can't give birth!

[Joshua:] That is the tall story!

[The elders:] If salt goes bad, what do they salt it with?

[Joshua:] With the placenta of a mule.

[The elders:] Does a mule have a placenta?

[Joshua:] Does salt go bad?

[The elders:] Build us a house in the air!

[Joshua] uttered a divine Name and suspended himself between the earth and the sky. Pass me up bricks and mortar! he demanded.

[The elders:] Where is the centre of the world?

---

13. The implication is that a lender should not desist on account of one bad debtor, but should persist until he finds someone reliable.

[Joshua:] Here!

[The elders:] How do you know?

[Joshua:] Bring ropes and measure it!

[The elders:] There is a well outside. Bring it into town!

[Joshua:] Make me ropes from bran and I'll bring it in!

[The elders:] We have a broken millstone. Sew it up for us!

[Joshua:] Draw some threads out of it for me and I'll sew it together!

[The elders:] How do you reap a plantation of knives?

[Joshua:] With a donkey's horn!

[The elders:] Does a donkey have a horn?

[Joshua:] Is there a plantation of knives?

They brought him two eggs: Which comes from a white chicken and which from a coloured one?

He brought them two cheeses: Which comes from a dark goat and which from a white one?

[The elders:] If a chick inside an egg dies, which way does its spirit emerge?

[Joshua:] It goes out the way it came in!

[The elders:] Show us something that's worth less than the damage it does.

He brought a mat and spread it out and it wouldn't fit through the door.

[They conceded defeat.] He brought them on board one by one, and when each saw sixty mattresses [in his compartment], he thought the others would join him there.

[Joshua] asked the captain to cast off; meanwhile, he collected soil from their neighbourhood. When he arrived at the place of swallowing waters, he filled a jug with its water. 9a

When they arrived he presented them to Caesar. [Caesar] said, These can't be the ones, they look too miserable! [Joshua] took the soil and threw it down before them. They [brightened up[14]] and spoke overconfidently to the king. [Caesar] said to [Joshua], Do what you like with them! [Joshua] fetched the swallowing waters and placed them in a tub. Fill it up! he said.

14. On smelling the soil of their own land.

They all went and drew water and poured it in but it was swallowed up, so they kept pouring until their shoulders were dislocated and they perished.

If a first-born animal develops a blemish, it loses first-born status and may be slaughtered and eaten by the owner; before the animal is slaughtered an expert is required to confirm that the blemish is serious enough to warrant desacralization. Consideration of what happens if an animal is slaughtered on the advice of an unqualified person leads to the topic of judicial error (see also Sanhedrin *6a (see pp. 498–9)).*

CHAPTER FOUR

MISHNA:

28a   **If someone [first] slaughters a first-born animal and then shows the blemish [to an expert who confirms it], Rabbi Judah says, It is permitted; Rabbi Meir says, If it was slaughtered without [prior] expert approval, it is forbidden.**

If someone who is not an expert views the first-born and it is slaughtered on [the basis of] his declaration, it must be buried, and he must pay for it out of his own pocket.

GEMARA:

Rabba bar bar Ḥana said, All agree without dispute that if [the animal had] a film over the eyes [and the owner slaughtered it before showing it to an expert], it is forbidden, since it is liable to change;[15] the disagreement concerns a bodily defect. Rabbi Meir holds that we uphold the law in the case of bodily defects because of [the likelihood of error with] films over the eye; Rabbi Judah holds that we do not uphold the law in the case of bodily defects because of [the likelihood of error with] films over the eye.

A baraita makes a similar point: **If someone [first] slaughters an animal and then shows the blemish [to an expert], Rabbi Judah says, If it was a film over the eyes it is forbidden, since**

15. It may have been a transient blemish.

it is liable to change, but if it was a bodily defect it is permitted, since it would not have changed; Rabbi Meir says, It is forbidden in both cases, since we forbid on account of that which is liable to change. On account of that which is liable to change? Surely bodily defects are not liable to change! [He means that we forbid that which is not liable to change] on account of that which is liable to change.

Rav Naḥman bar Isaac observed, The Mishna itself is precise on this point, since it states, **It is forbidden, since it was slaughtered without expert approval** – this shows that Rabbi Meir forbade it as a penalty [rather than on strict legal grounds]. 28b

MISHNA:

If he passed judgement and pronounced the guilty innocent and the innocent guilty, the pure impure or the impure pure, what he has done stands and he must compensate out of his own pocket. If he had been authorized by a court [as an expert judge], he is exempt from [paying] compensation.

GEMARA:

Is this anonymous Mishna the view of Rabbi Meir, who upholds the principle of causation?[16] Rabbi Ila said in the name of Rav, This is a case where [the judge] personally involved himself in the transaction [by taking money from the wrong person and giving it to the other]. That is all very well if he declared the innocent guilty: he may have taken money from him and passed it to the other. But what if he declared the guilty innocent? What has he done? If he simply said, You owe nothing, he has not involved himself in the transaction. Ravina answered, [The creditor] may have been holding on to a pledge and [the judge] took it from him.

[If he pronounced] the pure impure or the impure pure. [He may have actively] defiled what was pure by touching it with an [unclean] swarming creature; he may have 'purified' the impure by mixing it with the appellant's pure [food, directly causing him loss].

---

16. i.e. responsibility for indirect damages. Though the judge has not himself handled the money, he has, through his verdict, caused the wrong party to pay. If the 'principle of causation' holds good, it is as if he had personally taken the money from one and given it to the other.

MISHNA:
A cow once had its uterus removed and Rabbi Tarfon fed it to the dogs [on the grounds that hysterectomy was an injury from which it would die, and it would therefore be *terefa* even if correctly slaughtered]. When the case was referred to the Sages in Yavné, they said it was *kasher*; for Theudos the physician of Rome had affirmed that every cow or sow that left Alexandria had its uterus removed, so that it should not give birth.[17] There goes your cow, Tarfon! exclaimed Rabbi Tarfon.[18] Rabbi Aqiva said, Tarfon! You are an expert judge, and expert judges are exempt from compensation.

GEMARA:
Surely he had made an error in a matter stated in the Mishna, and if a judge made an error in a matter stated in the Mishna, the judgement is reversed! Both reasons apply. First, if a judge made an error in a matter stated in the Mishna, the judgement is reversed; also, if the error was in a matter of weighing up opinions, an expert judge is exempt from compensation.

MISHNA:
If [a judge] takes payment to view first-born animals, they may not be slaughtered on his declaration unless he is an expert like Ila at Yavné, who was permitted by the Sages to take four *assarii* for [viewing] a small animal and six for a large one, whether it was blemished or perfect.

GEMARA:
Four *assarii* for [viewing] a small animal and six for a large one. Why? Because one involves much labour and the other does not.

Whether it was blemished or perfect. Now, if it had a blemish he would have given permission [for it to be slaughtered and eaten], but if it was perfect [for what could he claim payment]? It was to avoid suspicion, so that people should not say, [That animal] he declared blemished was really perfect; he

17. This demonstrated that animals did not die as a result of hysterectomy. (The Alexandrians wished to retain a monopoly on their superior breeds of cows and pigs.)
18. He would have to pay compensation to the owner of the cow he had wrongly declared *terefa*.

only declared it blemished to get the payment. If that is so, surely the same would apply if he declared it perfect: people might say, [That animal] he declared perfect was really blemished; he only declared it perfect so he could come back another time and be paid again! The rabbis [therefore] ruled that he should only be paid once, not repeatedly.

MISHNA:

If someone takes payment to judge, his judgements are invalid; [if he takes payment] to testify, his testimony is invalid; to sanctify [the ashes of the red heifer], his water is cave water and his ashes are ashes of the roast.[19] If [the subject of the judgement] was a *Kohen*, and [the judge] had declared him unclean [so that he could not eat] *teruma* [and he consequently had to purchase more expensive food, the judge must] provide him with food, drink and ointment. If [the subject of the judgement] was an old man, he must provide him with a donkey to ride and compensate him for his [loss of] work.

GEMARA:

How do we know this? Rav Yehuda said in the name of Rav, Scripture says, SEE, I HAVE TAUGHT YOU [STATUTES AND JUDGEMENTS AS THE LORD MY GOD COMMANDED ME] (Deuteronomy 4:5) – Just as I [taught] for free, so should you [teach] for free! A baraita makes the same point: AS THE LORD MY GOD COMMANDED ME] – Just as I [learned] for free, so should you [learn] for free! And how do we know that if you are unable to learn for free, you pay to learn? Scripture says, BUY TRUTH! DO NOT SELL IT! (Proverbs 23:23) – you should not say, Just as I had to pay to learn, I take payment for teaching – Scripture says, BUY TRUTH! DO NOT SELL IT!

A first-born son must be redeemed from the Kohen *for five sheqels; he also inherits a double portion. But the definition of first-born differs: for redemption, he is the one who 'opened the mother's womb' (Exodus 13:15); for inheritance, he is 'the first of the father's strength' (Deuteronomy 21:17).*

19.   i.e. not sanctified. See *Berakhot* 28a (see p. 22).

CHAPTER EIGHT

MISHNA:

46a   There is a first-born for inheritance who is not a first-born for the *Kohen*; a first-born for the *Kohen* who is not a first-born for inheritance; a first-born for neither inheritance nor the *Kohen*; and a first-born for both inheritance and the *Kohen*.

Who is a first-born for inheritance but not a first-born for the *Kohen*? One who is born following stillbirths. [That is, even] if the stillborn's head emerged alive, or if a full-term baby's head emerged dead, or if [the mother] had previously aborted something resembling a domestic or wild animal or a bird, according to Rabbi Meir, but in the view of the Sages, only if [she had aborted] something in human form.

If she had aborted a sandal[-shaped object], a placenta, a shaped foetus or detached body parts, any baby born subsequently counts as first-born for inheritance but not for the *Kohen*.

If someone without children married a woman who already had children or a slave woman who was freed or a non-Jewish woman who converted [while pregnant] and gave birth after becoming Jewish, [any son subsequently born to her] is first-born for inheritance but not for the *Kohen*. Rabbi Yosé the Galilean says, He is first-born both for inheritance and for the *Kohen*, since Scripture says, WHO OPENS THE WOMB AMONG THE ISRAELITES (Exodus 13:2) – who opens [his mother's] womb after [she has become] an Israelite.

If a man who already had children married a woman who had not given birth but was already pregnant when converted [if she was not Jewish] or freed [if she was a slave]; or if [an Israelite woman] and a *Kohen*'s wife, or a Levite's wife, or a woman who had previously given birth [both women gave birth, and the babies were mixed up]; similarly, if a woman who had not waited three months after the death of her husband before remarrying, so when she gave birth it was uncertain whether it was a nine-month baby from the first husband or a seven-month baby from the second – [the sons of

all these are] first-born for the *Kohen* but not for inheritance.[20]
There is a widespread belief, endorsed by Hippocrates and still
surviving in many parts of the world, that babies born at seven
and nine months are viable, but 'eight-monthers' are not; the
Gemara rules that the latter are to be treated as stillborn even
if they showed signs of life. If a baby born after eight months
survived, it was held that it was either a delayed seven-month
baby or a premature nine-month one; if a seven- or nine-month
baby died, it was thought likely that it was a premature or
delayed 'eight-monther'. When Shmuel, for instance, speaks of
a stillbirth, he has in mind not necessarily a baby born dead,
but an 'eight-monther' that may appear alive for the moment
but is not really viable.[21]

The passage that follows carries implications for ethical
dilemmas about the end of life as well its beginning. For instance,
if the beginning of life is defined as 'spirit of life' in the nostrils,
i.e. breathing, does the cessation of breathing signify the end of
life, or should other criteria such as pulse or brain activity be
considered?[22]

GEMARA:

Shmuel said, The head of a stillbirth is not sufficient to   46b
exempt [a later birth from the status of first-born]. Why? **ALL**
THAT HAS THE SPIRIT OF LIFE IN ITS NOSTRILS (Genesis 7:22)
– if it has the 'spirit of life' in its nostrils, [it exempts a later
birth from the status of first-born,] otherwise not.

The Mishna spoke of a baby who followed a stillbirth the
head of which had emerged alive or [who followed] a nine-
monther whose head had emerged dead – it speaks of the head
[as what matters, contrary to Shmuel's observation]. When the

20. Several doubtful cases are rather confusingly conflated here. What they all have in
    common is that the baby has 'opened his mother's womb', so should redeem
    himself at some stage (though the *Kohen* is not in a position to demand five *sheqels*
    from the father); he cannot, however, claim a double share of the inheritance, since
    either his father was not Jewish at the time of conception, or his own status is
    doubtful.
21. Reiss and Ash, 'Eighth-month Fetus'; Hippocrates, *De Octímestri Partu*; *Yevamot*
    80a/b.
22. For a modern treatment of this topic drawing on the classical Jewish sources, see
    Sinclair, *Tradition*.

[Mishna] says 'head', it means 'the head and most of the body'. Then why doesn't it say 'and most of the body'? In reality, it should do so; however, since it also has to deal with the case of a nine-monther whose head emerged dead – the point there being that the head was dead, since had it been alive, any son that followed could not have been considered a first-born even for inheritance – it just says 'head' in the first case, too. And what is it telling us? [It is telling us] that once the head has emerged the baby is [regarded as] born.

A Mishna actually states [in connection with animals]: **Once the head emerges, even if it then retracts, it is considered born.**[23] Perhaps that Mishna tells us about beasts but our Mishna speaks of humans; you cannot infer [the law pertaining to] humans from [the law pertaining to] beasts since beasts lack a vestibule,[24] nor that of beasts from that of humans since with humans the face is significant.

But another Mishna speaks of humans: **If it was born normally, then once most of the head has emerged, [it is considered born]. What is meant by 'most of the head'? [It means] when the forehead has emerged.**[25] Shmuel's opinion [that emergence of the head is insufficient to establish birth] must therefore be rejected.

Rabbi Simeon ben Laqish said, The [emergence of the] forehead always exempts [later births from first-born status], except with regard to inheritance. Why [the exception]? Because the Torah uses the expression *yakir*, 'He will recognize'[26] (Deuteronomy 21:17). But Rabbi Yoḥanan said, [The emergence of the] forehead exempts even with regard to inheritance.

What does [Simeon ben Laqish's use of the term] 'always' include? It includes [this case] taught by the rabbis: **A female convert whose baby's forehead**

23. *Ḥullin* 4:1 (68a).
24. The term used normally refers to the vaginal vestibule – in this context, the lower birth canal. Both Rashi and Tosafot think it is used differently here, and that the point is that whereas a calf's head appears completely in the open a baby's head emerges to some extent concealed between the woman's thighs; this reflects the difference in pelvic anatomy.
25. *Nidda* 3:5 (28a).
26. Usual translation: 'He must acknowledge'.

emerged while she was still non-Jewish but who then completed conversion is not subject to the days of purity and impurity nor obliged to offer a birth sacrifice.

They objected [to Simeon ben Laqish's position]: '*Yakir*' means recognizing the face. What is 'recognizing the face'? The facial appearance including the nose. Add the words 'with the nose' [to Simeon ben Laqish's statement].

A proof: **Testimony**[27] **may only be given on the basis of the face including the nose.** Add the words 'as far as the nose' [to Simeon ben Laqish's statement].

A proof: **Testimony may not be given on the basis of the forehead without the face or the face without the forehead; both must be present with the nose.**

Abbaye – some say Rav Kahana – commented, The verse for this is THE RECOGNITION OF THEIR FACES ANSWERS AGAINST THEM[28] (Isaiah 3:9).

[The proof fails, since] the rabbis were particularly strict with regard to testimony [of identification] for women [to remarry].

Were they so strict? Doesn't a baraita say: **It became accepted practice to authorize marriages [on the basis of] one witness reporting another, a woman reporting a woman, or a woman reporting a male or female slave?**[29] They were indeed lenient in the end, but at the beginning [that is, for identification of the husband's corpse] they were strict. Alternatively, 'He will recognize' is one thing; [identification by] facial recognition is another.

47a

---

27. Identification of a corpse.
28. JPS: 'Their partiality in judgement accuses them.'
29. *Yevamot* 87b (see p. 322).

FIFTH TRACTATE
ARAKHIN (VALUATIONS)

For vows in general, see Nedarim *and* Shavuot. *Leviticus 27 sets out a scale of fixed 'valuations' for anyone who vows to donate the value of a person to the Temple:*

SPEAK TO THE ISRAELITES AND SAY TO THEM: IF ANYONE UTTERS A VOW [TO GIVE] THE VALUE OF A LIFE TO THE LORD ... THE VALUATION FOR A MALE OF TWENTY TO SIXTY YEARS OLD SHALL BE FIFTY SHEQELS OF SILVER ... (Leviticus 27:2, 3)

The Gemara implies that lives are to be valued equally irrespective of physical or mental capacity.

CHAPTER ONE

MISHNA:

All – Levites, Israelites, women, slaves – may make value-vows or be the subject of value-vows, may vow or be the subject of a vow.

Persons of indeterminate sex and hermaphrodites may vow, be the subject of a vow or make value-vows, but cannot be the subject of value-vows, for only definite males and females can be the subject of value-vows.

Deaf-mutes, imbeciles and minors can be the subject of vows or value-vows, but they cannot make vows or value-vows since they are not [legally regarded as] of sound mind.

GEMARA:

All . . . may make value-vows. What does 'all' include [that is not specified]? It includes one who is almost an adult, and whose vows are [confirmed] on testing [whether he understands to Whom the vow is made].

Or be the subject of value-vows. ['All' here] includes someone who is ugly or who is covered in boils. You might have thought that since the Torah says, **A VOW [TO GIVE THE] VALUE**, only someone with a purchase value [on the slave market] could be the subject of a value-vow; **VALUE OF A LIFE** teaches us that all lives [are valued equally within their age and gender categories].

The special provisions of Leviticus 25:29–34 with regard to the sale of property in 'walled cities' are developed. Should someone purchase a house in a qualifying city the original owner has the right to 'redeem' it, that is, buy it back, within twelve months. This led to abuse – the purchaser kept out of the owner's way until the time limit elapsed. Hillel's remedy is a precise counterpart of the Roman depositio in aede, *under which a debtor who wants to pay his debt and was unable to do so because the creditor was avoiding him could circumvent the creditor by depositing the sum with the court.*

CHAPTER NINE

MISHNA:

At first, [the purchaser] would hide on the day the twelve months elapsed so that his purchase would become permanent. Hillel the Elder ordained that [the original owner] might place his money in the treasury, break the door [of the house] and enter. [The purchaser] would then collect the money whenever he wished.

GEMARA:

Rava said, It follows from Hillel's edict that if [a man said to his wife,] This is your *get* on condition you give me 200 *zuz*, if she gave it to him with his agreement she is divorced, but if

32a against his will she is not divorced; as Hillel found it necessary
to institute a forced payment it follows that a forced payment
is not normally valid.

Rav Papa – some say Rav Ashi – objected: Perhaps Hillel
only needed to issue his edict for a situation where [the creditor]
was not present, but if he was present it would make no difference whether the payment was [received] voluntarily or against
[the owner's] will.

*Both literary and archaeological evidence point to the listed
towns having been under Jewish occupation in the late Second
Temple period. According to David Adan-Bayewitz, ' "Walled
Cities" ', Iotapata was first settled in the late fourth or third
century BC; numismatic and other evidence points to its having
been settled by Jews in the second century BCE. Gamla's history
extends back to the Chalcolithic Age; it was captured by Alexander Yannai and settled by Jews c. 80 BCE. Adan-Bayewitz
argues that the list, amplified in the Tosefta, predates the Mishna
which has been formed around it.*

MISHNA:

Whatever lies within the wall, other than fields, is considered
a 'house within the walled city'; Rabbi Meir says, Even fields
are included. If a house is built on top of the wall, Rabbi Judah
says it is not considered a house within the walled city; Rabbi
Simeon says it is.

MISHNA:

A city whose roofs wall it in, or which was not surrounded
by a wall in the days of Joshua the son of Nun, is not considered
a 'walled city'. This is what constitutes a walled city: [at least]
three courtyards of two houses [each], surrounded by a wall
in the days of Joshua the son of Nun. Examples are: The old
castra of Sepphoris; the *akra* of Gischala; Old Iotapata; Gamla,
Gadara,[1] Ḥadid, Ono, Jerusalem, and any like those.[2]

GEMARA:

The rabbis taught: **There must be a wall, not just continuous
roofs, around it; this excludes Tiberias, since its 'wall' is the**

1. This seems to be the correct reading; the traditional printed texts have GDUD.
2. *Castra* (Latin, 'camp'); *akra* (Greek, 'high point', 'citadel'). Ono, in the territory
    of Benjamin, is mentioned in the Bible (e.g. Nehemiah 6:2).

lake. **Rabbi Eliezer says, WHICH HAS A WALL** (Leviticus 25:30) – even though it doesn't have one now, so long as it did originally.[3]

It was taught: **Gamla in Galilee, Gadara in Transjordan, Ḥadid, Ono and Jerusalem in Judaea.** What does that tell us? Abbaye said, It means as far as Gamla in Galilee, as far as Gadara   32b in Transjordan, [as far as] Ḥadid, Ono and Jerusalem in Judaea. Rava said, Gamla in Galilee excludes Gamla in any other territory; Gadara in Transjordan excludes Gadara in any other territory; the rest need not have been mentioned since no other towns share those names.

---

3.   Rabbi Eliezer's interpretation depends on the fact that the Hebrew *lo* in 'it has' is spelled like *lo*, 'not'.

SIXTH TRACTATE
TEMURA (SUBSTITUTES)

***ALL TITHES OF THE HERD OR FLOCK – OF ALL THAT PASSES UNDER
THE SHEPHERD'S STAFF, EVERY TENTH ONE – SHALL BE HOLY TO
THE LORD. HE MUST NOT LOOK OUT FOR GOOD AS AGAINST BAD,
OR MAKE SUBSTITUTION FOR IT. IF HE DOES MAKE SUBSTITUTION
FOR IT, THEN IT AND ITS SUBSTITUTE SHALL BE HOLY; IT CANNOT
BE REDEEMED.*** (Leviticus 27:32–3 JPS)

*The rabbis apply the substitution principle to sacred animals
in general.*

*The following Mishna is cited several times in the Talmud; its
underlying theme is the extent to which a particular status can
be transferred. The final example links the Mishna with the
topic of this tractate: can the status of* temura *(substitute) be
transferred from one animal to another?*

CHAPTER ONE

MISHNA:

12a   [Unconsecrated food] that has been contaminated [by an
admixture of *teruma*] contaminates in proportion; leavened
food [that fell into unleavened food on Passover] leavens in
proportion; drawn water invalidates a *miqvé* in proportion;
purification water only becomes purification water when the
ashes are added; a field in which a source of impurity might
be present[1] does not convey [its status of doubtful pollution]

---

1.   *Beit ha-p'ras*, 'a broken field', is a technical term for a field in which a corpse or
     part of a corpse might have been buried.

to another field [with which it is ploughed]; *teruma* does not follow *teruma*;[2] substitute does not make substitute, nor does the offspring [of a sacred animal] make substitute.[3] Rabbi Judah said, Offspring makes substitute; they replied to him, That which is [itself] sacred makes substitute, but its offspring does not.

GEMARA:

[Unconsecrated food] that has been adulterated [by an admixture of *teruma*] adulterates in proportion. Who taught this? Rabbi Ḥiyya bar Abba said in the name of Rabbi Yoḥanan, It is not the view of Rabbi Eliezer, for a Mishna states: If a *seah* of *teruma* fell into less than a hundred [*seahs* of unconsecrated food], contaminating [the mixture], and some of that mixture fell into other [food], Rabbi Eliezer says, [The mixture] contaminates as if it was [all] fully *teruma*, but the Sages say, It contaminates only in proportion [to the quantity of *teruma* it contains].[4]

Substitute does not make substitute, etc. Why [not]? Scripture says, ITS SUBSTITUTE SHALL BE HOLY – its substitute, not its substitute's substitute.

Nor does the offspring [of a sacred animal] make substitute. Scripture says, IT – but not its offspring.

Rabbi Judah said, Offspring makes substitute. Scripture says, SHALL BE – to include the offspring. The Sages say, That is to include an accidental substitution as well as deliberate.

13a

---

2. If someone has separated *teruma* from his crop and then does so again, the second allocation does not acquire the status of *teruma*.
3. That is, if you declare an animal a substitute for another that is itself a substitute for a sacred animal or the offspring of a sacred animal, the declaration is ineffective.
4. Mishna *Terumot* 5:6.

SEVENTH TRACTATE
KERITOT (EXCLUSIONS)

Exodus and Leviticus several times proclaim that a wrongdoer will be 'cut off from his people'. Karet *may originally have meant exclusion from the camp or community of Israel; the rabbis interpret it as a divine punishment, possibly involving premature death, possibly fraught with consequences in the afterlife, but not imposed by any human court.*

Karet *should not be confused with the rabbinic ban or* ḥerem *by which an offender was excluded from normal social intercourse for a period of thirty days, renewable if he failed to comply with the court's demands.*

CHAPTER ONE

MISHNA:

2a

There are thirty-six instances of *karet* in the Torah: A man who has sexual intercourse with his mother, with his father's wife, with his daughter-in-law, with another male or with an animal; a woman who has intercourse with an animal; a man who has intercourse with a woman and her daughter, with a married woman, with his sister, his father's sister, his mother's sister, his wife's sister, his brother's wife, his father's brother's wife(, his mother's brother's wife)[1] or a menstruant; a blasphemer, one who worships an idol, who 'gives his seed to

1. Omitted in some manuscripts.

Molech',[2] a necromancer, a Sabbath desecrator, an unclean person who ate sacred food, one who entered the sanctuary in an unclean state, one who ate forbidden fats, blood, sacrifices that had passed their time of consumption or that had been rendered unfit by incorrect designations, one who slaughters or offers [sacrifices] outside [the Temple]; one who eats *hametz* on Pesach, who eats or who does work on the Day of Atonement, who dispenses oil or incense [for private use according to the formula for the sacred oil or incense], who anoints himself with the [holy] oil and – among positive commandments – one who neglects to observe Passover or circumcision.

In all these cases a deliberate offender is liable to *karet*, an accidental offender brings a sin-offering and one who is in doubt [as to whether he has committed the offence] brings a suspended reparation-offering, with the exception of someone who had defiled the Temple or sacred gifts, since he brings the variable offering (Leviticus 5:1–13). That is Rabbi Meir's view, but the Sages add the blasphemer [to the exceptions], for it says, YOU SHALL HAVE ONE LAW FOR THOSE WHO ACT IN ERROR (Numbers 15:29) – this excludes the blasphemer, since he has not committed an *act*.[3]

GEMARA:

The Sages add the blasphemer. What do they mean by **add the blasphemer?** The Sages heard Rabbi Aqiva[, the author of this Mishna,] list the necromancer but not the wizard (Leviticus 20:27; Deuteronomy 18:11). They asked him, What is the difference [between the two]? Isn't the reason the wizard does not bring sacrifice [if he offended unwittingly] that he [only speaks but] does not commit any act? The blasphemer similarly [only speaks but] does not act[, but is nevertheless listed].

The rabbis taught: **According to Rabbi Aqiva, the [unwitting] blasphemer brings sacrifice, since the term *karet* is applied to him. Moreover, it says, THAT MAN SHALL BEAR HIS GUILT** (Numbers 9:13 JPS). Is it really the case that wherever the term

7a

2. Leviticus 20:2, i.e. to the idol.
3. Speech is not regarded as a physical act.

karet is used the [unwitting wrongdoer] brings sacrifice? *Karet* is used of those who neglect to observe Passover or circumcision, yet they do not bring [an atoning] sacrifice.

This[4] is what [the baraita] meant: According to Rabbi Aqiva the [unwitting] blasphemer brings sacrifice, since [if he was deliberate, the punishment of] *karet* is applied to him as the equivalent of sacrifice. [Rabbi Aqiva] maintains that since [Scripture] has to write *karet*, and it writes it where we would expect sacrifice to be mentioned, he brings sacrifice. With the phrase **Moreover, it says, THAT MAN SHALL BEAR HIS GUILT**, he addresses the Sages, and this is what he tells them: You say that the *m'gadef* [blasphemer] commits no act. But what is meant by *m'gadef*? One **WHO REVILES [M'QALEL] HIS GOD** (Leviticus 24:15). Why, then, does it apply *karet* to him [by using the phrase **THAT MAN SHALL BEAR HIS GUILT**]? They reply, It is [indeed] for the one who reviles God, for it is written of him, **THAT MAN SHALL BEAR HIS GUILT**; [similarly,] it is written of one who fails to observe [even] the Second Passover,[5] **HE SHALL BEAR HIS GUILT** (Numbers 9:13)[, and it also says **THAT PERSON SHALL BE CUT OFF FROM HIS PEOPLE**, so by analogy *karet* applies to the reviler].

The rabbis taught: **HE BLASPHEMES [M'GADEF] AGAINST THE LORD** (Numbers 15:30). Issi ben Yehuda says, It is like the expression 'You have drawn out[6] the pot and diminished [the wood]'; he holds that *m'gadef* means a blasphemer. Rabbi Eleazar ben Azaria says, It is like the expression 'You have drawn out the pot but not diminished [the wood]'; he holds that *m'gadef* means an idolater.[7] Another baraita states: **THE LORD** – Rabbi Eleazar ben Azaria says, Scripture speaks of an idolater; the Sages say, The purpose of the verse is to apply *karet* to the blasphemer.

4. Rashi notes that this text is corrupt and he attempts to emend it.
5. See *Pesaḥim*, pp. 174–6.
6. He relates the root GDF to GRF, 'to draw out' ('r' and 'd' look similar in Hebrew). The *m'gadef* has caused great damage and undermined the foundation of faith.
7. It is a lesser offence, since he has not directly denied God.

EIGHTH TRACTATE
ME'ILA (SACRILEGE)

AND THE LORD SPOKE TO MOSES, SAYING: WHEN A PERSON
COMMITS A TRESPASS AND SINS UNWITTINGLY WITH ANY OF THE
LORD'S SACRED THINGS, HE SHALL BRING AS HIS PENALTY TO THE
LORD A RAM WITHOUT BLEMISH FROM THE FLOCK, ACCORDING
TO ITS VALUE IN SILVER SANCTUARY SHEQELS AS A REPARATION-
OFFERING. HE SHALL MAKE RESTITUTION FOR THAT WHEREIN HE
SINNED WITH REGARD TO THE SACRED THINGS, AND HE SHALL
ADD A FIFTH PART TO IT AND GIVE IT TO THE PRIEST. THE PRIEST
SHALL MAKE EXPIATION ON HIS BEHALF WITH THE RAM OF THE
REPARATION-OFFERING, AND HE SHALL BE FORGIVEN. (Leviticus
5:14–16)

*Trespass, or sacrilege, is misappropriation of designated
offerings or of Temple property. But when does a sacrifice, or
rather its remains, lose its sacred status, so that it is no longer
subject to the laws of sacrilege, and what constitutes misappropriation? How far do the rabbis extend the laws of sacrilege by
forbidding the use of a once sacred item even when it has fulfilled
its purpose and so lost its sacred status?*

CHAPTER ONE

MISHNA:
If he slaughtered a sacrifice of the most holy class on the   2a
south [side of the altar], it [remains] subject to [the laws of]
sacrilege. If he slaughtered it on the south and received its

blood on the north, or slaughtered it on the north and received its blood on the south, or if he slaughtered it in the daytime and sprinkled its blood at night, or slaughtered it at night and received its blood in daytime, or if he slaughtered it [with a designation] for the wrong time or place – [in all of these cases] it [remains] subject to [the laws of] sacrilege.

The principle, said Rabbi Joshua, is that if it had reached the stage at which the priests would be permitted [to eat it], sacrilege no longer applies, but if it had not reached the stage at which the priests would be permitted [to eat it], it remains subject to sacrilege. An example of reaching the stage at which the priests would be permitted [to eat it] would be if [it had been correctly slaughtered and the blood correctly sprinkled], but it had been left [beyond the time allowed for eating it] or had become defiled or left the Temple precinct; an example of not reaching the stage of being permitted to the priests would be if it had been slaughtered for the wrong time or place or if unqualified persons had received or sprinkled its blood.

GEMARA:

The Mishna says, **If he slaughtered a sacrifice of the most holy class on the south [side of the altar], it [remains] subject to [the laws of] sacrilege.** Isn't it obvious that slaughter on the south would not release it from liability to sacrilege? It needs to be stated, for Ulla said in the name of Rabbi Yoḥanan that sacrificial animals that died [of natural causes before being offered] were no longer subject to the Torah law of sacrilege; you might have thought that sacrifices of the holiest class that were slaughtered on the south were as if they had [simply] been strangled[, not slaughtered, and would have lost their sacred status], so [Mishna] informs you that this is not the case – if an animal has died naturally it is in no way fit for the altar, but slaughter on the south side, though wrong for the most holy sacrifices, is proper for less holy sacrifices.

CHAPTER FIVE

MISHNA:

If anyone derives a *peruta* worth of [personal] use from a   18a
holy thing, even if he does not damage it, he is guilty of
sacrilege according to Rabbi Aqiva; the Sages say that if it is
an object liable to damage [by normal use], he is not guilty of
sacrilege unless he actually damages it, but if it is not liable to
damage [by normal use], he is guilty of sacrilege as soon as he
makes use of it. How is this? If [a woman] put a necklace
around her neck or a ring on her finger or if she drank from a
golden cup,[1] she would be guilty of sacrilege as soon as she
had used [the object], but if someone put on a dress or other
garment or used an axe to chop wood, he is not guilty of
sacrilege unless he has actually damaged it.

If someone makes use of a living animal designated as a
sin-offering, he is not guilty of sacrilege unless he has damaged
it, but if it was a carcass, he is guilty of sacrilege as soon as he
has made use of it.[2]

GEMARA:

It was taught: Rabbi Aqiva agrees with the Sages with regard
to an object liable to damage. About what do they disagree?
Rava said, About a middle garment or a very fine linen one.[3]

The rabbis taught: WHEN A PERSON – whether a private
individual, a prince or an anointed priest, COMMITS A TRES-
PASS (Leviticus 5:15) – 'trespass' means changing something, as
it says, IF A MAN'S WIFE HAS GONE ASTRAY AND TRESPASSED
AGAINST HIM (Numbers 5:12), and THEY TRESPASSED
AGAINST THE GOD OF their fathers and went astray after   18b
the Baalim[4] (1 Chronicles 5:25). Could it be that if someone

1. It is understood that these and the objects mentioned later are Temple property.
2. The Gemara explains (19a) that the Mishna means a blemished offering which has
   to be 'redeemed' at its full value; anyone who damages it, reducing its value, causes
   loss to the Temple treasury.
3. A middle garment is not likely to be damaged since it is worn neither in the open
   nor next to the skin; a wearer would take extra care over a very fine linen garment.
4. The Masoretic Hebrew texts and the Septuagint have 'after the gods of the peoples
   of the land'; the Talmud's text is probably a scribal error.

caused damage without benefiting, or benefited without causing damage, or [if the item in question was] land, or if an
agent had not carried out his instructions[,[5] he would be held
accountable]? It states AND SINNED (Leviticus 5:15) – the term
'sinned' is used in connection with sacrilege and also in connection with *teruma* (22:9), just as in the case of *teruma* 'sinned'
implies causing damage, deriving benefit [from the object],
that the one who causes the damage benefits from that which
is damaged, that the damage and the benefit accrue simultaneously, the item is detached from the land, and he bears
liability for an agent who has carried out his instructions, so in
the case of sacrilege 'sinned' implies causing damage, deriving
benefit [from the object], that the one who causes the damage
benefits from that which is damaged, that the damage and the
benefit accrue simultaneously, that the item is detached from
the land, and that he bears liability for an agent who has
carried out his instructions.

5.   Probable meaning in the light of the variant reading in note (b) of *Shita
M'qubetzet*.

NINTH TRACTATE
QINNIM (BIRD PAIRS)

The last three tractates of this Order are not paralleled in the Tosefta and may have been independent baraitot, added at a late stage to the Mishna. Here they are presented in the order in which they appear in printed editions of the Talmud, with pagination; neither Qinnim *nor* Middot *has any Gemara.*

A woman after childbirth brings a lamb as an upward-offering and a pigeon or turtledove as a purification-offering:

IF, HOWEVER, SHE CANNOT AFFORD A LAMB SHE SHALL TAKE TWO TURTLEDOVES OR TWO PIGEONS, ONE FOR AN UPWARD-OFFERING AND ONE FOR A PURIFICATION-OFFERING. (Leviticus 12:8)

A woman who has had an abnormal discharge of blood brings a similar offering of two turtledoves or two pigeons (Leviticus 15:29–30).

Voluntary upward-offerings of turtledoves or pigeons may be made by men as well as women (Leviticus 1:14–17).

These basics are summed up in the opening Mishna; it also defines differences in procedure for upward- and purification-offerings and the difference between a vow and a voluntary offering.

CHAPTER ONE

1. The [blood of the] bird purification-offering [is sprinkled] below [the red line around the altar], and that of the animal

purification-offering above; the [blood of the] bird upward-offering [is sprinkled] above [the red line around the altar], and that of the animal upward-offering below. If [the priest] varied any of them, [the sacrifice] is invalid.

This is the order of bird pairs: for obligatory offerings one [of the pair] is a purification-offering and the other an upward-offering; for vows and voluntary offerings both are upward-offerings.

What is a vow? If someone said, I take it on myself to bring an upward-offering. What is a voluntary offering? If someone said, I declare this [bird] an upward-offering. The only difference between vows and voluntary offerings is that for a vow, if the [birds] died or were stolen he must replace them, but for a voluntary offering, if the [birds] died or were stolen he need not replace them.

22b 2. If a [bird designated for a] purification-offering got mixed up with an upward-offering, or an upward-offering with a purification-offering, even one in 10,000, they must all die.[1]

If a [bird designated for a] purification-offering got mixed up with [a pair of birds designated for] an obligatory offering, only the number of purification-offerings contained in the obligatory offering is valid [and may be offered]. Likewise, if a [bird designated for an] upward-offering got mixed up with [a pair of birds designated for] an obligatory offering, only the number of upward-offerings contained in the obligatory offering is valid, irrespective of whether the obligatory offerings were many and the voluntary offerings few, or the voluntary offerings were many and the obligatory offerings few.

3. Where does this apply? If an obligatory offering was mixed up with a voluntary offering. But if an obligatory offering was mixed up with another obligatory offering – one with one, two with two or three with three – half are valid and half invalid. If there was one from this [set] and two from that, or three from one, or ten from one, or a hundred from

---

6. That is, none of them can be a valid offering, since it is impossible to determine whether the blood should be sprinkled above or below the line.

one, the lower number is valid, whether they belong to one category or two, and whether they are from one woman or two.

4. What does 'one category' mean? Childbirth and childbirth, or discharge and discharge, are one category; childbirth and discharge are two categories. How does this work out? If there were two women each of whom needed to bring a childbirth offering, or two women each of whom needed to bring a discharge offering, that is 'one category'; if one needed to bring a childbirth offering and the other a discharge offering, that would be two categories.

Rabbi Yosé says, If two women purchased their pairs of birds together, or gave the priest money for birds, the priest may offer any of them as a purification-offering for either woman, or as an upward-offering for either woman.

Chapters Two and Three of Qinnim *are* jeux d'esprit *to train the mind of students in combinations and permutations to equip them to pursue a* halakhic *idea to its limits. The principles are tested through highly contrived illustrations, the most bizarre of which is 2:3: there were seven women, one of whom had a pair of birds, the second had two pairs, the third had three and so on to seven, and a bird flew from the first set to the second, from the second to the third, and so on to the seventh (though it was not certain that it was the same bird), and then back again. The questions throughout are (a) how can the priest ensure that he has not confused a purification-offering with an upward-offering, and (b) how can he ensure that he does not sacrifice a bird on behalf of anyone other than its rightful owner? There is an element of fun in the invention of improbable situations – Torah is to be enjoyed!*

TENTH TRACTATE
TAMID (REGULAR TEMPLE PROCEDURE)

This tractate is about daily life in the Temple and may well draw on early material though it is an idealized reconstruction, much of it paralleled in Yoma. *The slaughter and burning of animal sacrifices generates a lot of mess; Chapter Two describes the daily cleaning operation.*

CHAPTER TWO

MISHNA:

28b   When his brother [*Kohanim*] saw him[1] descend [from the altar], they ran quickly to wash their hands and feet in the basin, then took shovels and forks, and went up to the top of the altar. They pushed to one side of the altar any limbs and pieces of fat that had not been completely burnt up, and if there was no room at the side of the altar, they arranged them carefully on the circuit or the ramp.[2] Then they began to heap ashes on top of the pile in the middle of the altar; sometimes there were 300 *kur* of ashes there. They did not remove the ashes on festivals, since they were an embellishment of the

29a   altar. No priest was ever dilatory in removing the ashes [when the time came].

Then they started to fetch wood for the altar fire. Was any

1.   The priest who had formally commenced removal of the ashes.
2.   They were kept in readiness to be burnt after the daily sacrifice – Rashi.

kind of wood acceptable for the altar fire? Yes, all wood other than vine or olive wood was acceptable for the altar fire, but what they customarily used were branches of fig, walnut and persimmon.[3]

GEMARA:

Rava said, [The quantity of ashes stated] is a hyperbole. **They gave the sacrificial animal to drink from a golden cup**[4] – Rava said, That is hyperbole [too].

Rabbi Ammi said, The Torah speaks in hyperbole, the prophets speak in hyperbole and the Sages speak in hyperbole. The Torah speaks in hyperbole: **LARGE CITIES FORTIFIED UP TO HEAVEN** (Deuteronomy 1:28). Did they literally reach heaven? Surely it is a hyperbole. The Sages – what we have said, the pile of ashes and giving the sacrificial animal to drink from a golden cup. The prophets speak in hyperbole, as it is written, **ALL THE PEOPLE THEN MARCHED UP BEHIND HIM, PLAYING ON FLUTES AND MAKING MERRY TILL THE EARTH WAS SPLIT OPEN BY THE UPROAR** (1 Kings 1:40 JPS).

Rabbi Yannai bar Naḥmani said in the name of Shmuel, The Sages exaggerated in three instances, namely the ash pile, the vine and the sanctuary curtain. This excludes Rava's example, for the Mishna states, **They gave the sacrificial animal to drink from a golden cup**, and Rava said, That is an exaggeration – that instance should be rejected, since there is no poverty in the place of wealth.[5] The ash pile is as we have said. The vine is as a baraita states: **A golden vine was spread across poles at the gate of the sanctuary and whoever offered a leaf, a grape or a bunch would bring it and hang it there; Rabbi Eleazar the son of Rabbi Zadok said that 300 priests had to be assigned to move it.** The sanctuary curtain is a Mishna: **Simeon the son of the deputy High Priest said in his father's name, The curtain was a palm thick and woven of 72-fold strands, each thread**

---

3. Literally, 'the oil tree'; persimmon is now commonly called 'Sharon fruit', but the identification is uncertain.
4. This is cited from Chapter Three.
5. The Temple authorities may well have provided a golden cup for the animal to drink from.

being 24-fold. It was 40 cubits long and 20 cubits wide and 82 girls[6] made it. They made two every year and 300 priests were required to immerse each one.[7]

There has been much scholarly speculation as to when and to what extent regular public prayer had taken root outside the Temple before 70. At any rate, the Temple prayers as listed here formed the kernel of the Synagogue service by early rabbinic times; the Ten Commandments were dropped, according to Yerushalmi Berakhot, as a protest against sectarians who held that they constituted the only authentic Torah.[8] See the introductory note to Berakhot.

CHAPTER FIVE

MISHNA:

32b   The officer said to them: Recite a blessing! They recited a blessing. Then they recited the Ten Commandments, the three paragraphs of Shema, the blessing that follows Shema, the blessing over the Divine Service and the priestly blessing. On the Sabbath they also recited a blessing for the departing course of priests.

6.   *Riva* 'a girl' and *ribo* 'ten thousand' are easily confused; an alternative but improbable reading is that it cost 820,000 gold pieces (*Rosh*). Maimonides (*Mishneh Torah: Klei ha-Miqdash* 7:17) omits the phrase.
7.   Mishna *Sheqalim* 8:5.
8.   Reif, *Prayer*, p. 57; Hammer, 'What Did They Bless'.

ELEVENTH TRACTATE
MIDDOT (TEMPLE MEASUREMENTS)

Three successive temples were erected in Jerusalem. The first
was built by Solomon and the second by Ezra and Nehemiah;
the third was Herod's renovation and aggrandizement of the
second. The prophet Ezekiel (Chapters 40–48) 'foresees' the
ritual and dimensions of a future temple, and this is taken by
most rabbis to refer to the temple to be built when the Messiah
comes.

   The Mishna describes Herod's building. Some of the text may
be contemporary, some may be based on personal recollection
transmitted from Sages such as Eliezer ben Jacob; later sages
filled in gaps and adapted material to rabbinic perceptions of
how Temple ritual ought to proceed.

   Josephus left an eyewitness account of Herod's temple which,
though not altogether identical with the Mishna's description,
confirms many of its details.[1] Archaeology supplements the literary accounts, but the main site remains unexcavated as it is
occupied by the Dome of the Rock and the El Aqsa Mosque.
Much of the western wall and part of the southern wall of
Herod's temple enclosure are now exposed to view. A reconstruction of Herod's Temple may be seen in the Israel Museum
in Jerusalem.

---

1.   Josephus, *Antiquities* 15.11.3–7.

CHAPTER TWO

34b   1. The [precinct on the] Temple Mount was 500 cubits by
        500 cubits. Most of [the surrounding space] was at the
        south end, with the east next, the north third, and the least
        on the west; the greatest length corresponded to the greatest
        use.

        2. Whoever entered the Temple Mount turned right, circled
        round and exited on the left,[2] but if someone suffered a
        mishap he circled to the left. [People would ask,] Why are
        you circling to the left? [If he replied, Because] I am a
        mourner, [they would say,] May He Who dwells in this
        house comfort you! If he had been placed under a ban, they
        would say, May He Who dwells in this house put it in their
        hearts to draw you near! That is according to Rabbi Meir,
        but Rabbi Yosé said to him, You make [those who placed
        him under the ban] appear in the wrong; what [people]
        should say is, May He Who dwells in this house put it in
        your heart to listen to your colleagues so that they will draw
        you near!

        3. Within [the wall of the Temple Mount] was a lattice sur-
        round 10 palms high in which 13 breaches that had been
        made by foreign kings had been repaired; they decreed that
        people should bow down at each of the 13. Within that was
        a space 10 cubits wide with 12 steps, each half a cubit high
        and half a cubit wide. All steps [in the Temple compound]
        were half a cubit high and half a cubit wide except those of
        the sanctuary; all doors and gates [in the Temple compound]
        were 10 cubits high and 10 wide except those of the sanctu-
        ary; all the doors had trapdoors in them except that of the
        sanctuary; all the gates had lintels except that of the Tedi
        gate, where two stones were placed one on top of the other;

---

2.   He circulates anti-clockwise, but instead of completing the circuit exits from a
      gate to the left of the one through which he entered. See Ezekiel 46:8–9. Lieberman
      (*Hellenism*, pp. 166–7) remarked that Pythagoreans recommended the same direc-
      tion for entering holy places; however, the source for this is the fourth-century CE
      philosopher Iamblichus (*Life of Pythagoras* 156), far later than the Mishna.

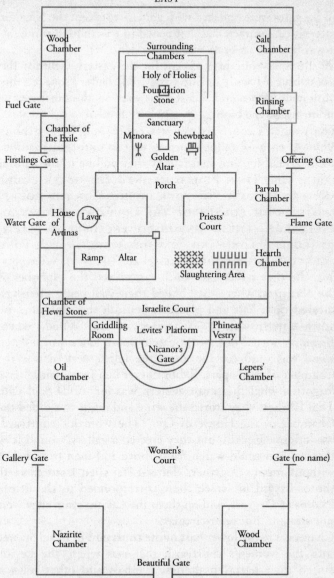

EAST

Wood Chamber
Salt Chamber
Surrounding Chambers
Holy of Holies
Foundation Stone
Fuel Gate
Sanctuary
Rinsing Chamber
Chamber of the Exile
Menora
Shewbread
Firstlings Gate
Golden Altar
Offering Gate
Porch
Parvah Chamber
House of Avtinas
Laver
Priests' Court
Water Gate
Flame Gate
Ramp
Altar
Hearth Chamber
Slaughtering Area
Chamber of Hewn Stone
Israelite Court
Griddling Room
Levites' Platform
Phineas' Vestry
Nicanor's Gate
Oil Chamber
Lepers' Chamber
Gallery Gate
Women's Court
Gate (no name)
Nazirite Chamber
Wood Chamber
Beautiful Gate

Plan of the Jerusalem Temple, derived with modifications from the reconstruction based on Josephus and rabbinic sources in the *Atlas of Israel*, 2nd edn (Jerusalem: Survey of Israel, Ministry of Labour, 1970). Five additional gates (Hulda Gates 1 and 2, Kipponis, Tedi and Susa) controlled entry to the Temple Mount.

all the gates were replaced with gold gates except the Nicanor gate, since a miracle had happened to it – though some say it was because its brass was resplendent.

4. All the walls were high except for the eastern wall, for the priest charged with burning the [red] heifer stood on the Mount of Olives and focused his eyes on the sanctuary as he sprinkled the blood.

5. The women's courtyard was 135 cubits long by 135 cubits wide. At each of its four corners was an unroofed chamber 40 by 40 cubits, and that is how they will be in the future, as it is said: THEN HE LED ME INTO THE OUTER COURT AND LED ME PAST THE FOUR CORNERS OF THE COURT, AND IN EACH CORNER OF THE COURT THERE WAS AN ENCLOSURE. THESE UNROOFED ENCLOSURES, [EACH] 40 [CUBITS] LONG AND 30 WIDE, WERE IN THE FOUR CORNERS OF THE COURT (Ezekiel 46:21–2 JPS). What purpose did they serve? The south-eastern was the Chamber of the Nazirites, where they boiled their well-being offerings, sheared their hair and placed it beneath the cauldron; the north-eastern was the Chamber of the Wood, where *Kohanim* sorted out worm-eaten wood, since worm-eaten wood was unfit for the altar; the north-western was the Chamber of the Lepers. Rabbi Eliezer ben Jacob said, I have forgotten what the south-western was for. Abba Saul said, That is where they stored the wine and oil; it was called the Chamber of the House of Oil. [The women's courtyard] was originally plain, but they erected a gallery around it so that women could watch from above and men from below without mixing together.[3] Fifteen steps led from there to the courtyard of Israel; these corresponded to the fifteen Psalms of Degrees, and on them the Levites sang; they were not straight, but semi-circular.

6. Chambers in the lower part of the courtyard of Israel opened into the women's courtyard; that was where the Levites stored their harps, psalteries, cymbals and other musical instruments. The courtyard of Israel was 135 cubits by 11; it

3. *Sukka* 51b (see p. 222).

was separated from the priests' courtyard by a mosaic.[4] (Rabbi Eliezer ben Jacob says, There was a step one cubit high above which was a stage with three steps, each half a cubit high, so that the priests' courtyard was two and a half cubits higher than the courtyard of Israel.) The whole courtyard [of Israel and the priests] was 187 cubits long and 135 cubits wide and had 13 locations at which to bow – Abba Yosé ben Ḥanan says they corresponded to the 13 gates.[5]

[The 13 gates:] The southern gates at its western end were the Upper Gate, the Fire Gate, the Gate of the First-born and the Water Gate. (It was called the Water Gate because that was the gate through which the jar of water was brought for the *Sukkot* libation. Rabbi Eliezer ben Jacob says, Water streamed through it and will in future stream from beneath the threshold of the House.[6]) Opposite these on the north at its western end were Jeconiah's Gate, the Gate of the Offering, the Women's Gate and the Gate of Song. (Jeconiah's Gate was so called because [King] Jeconiah left that way to go into exile.) On the east was Nicanor's Gate with two small doors, one on the right and one on the left, and on the west were two unnamed gates.

CHAPTER THREE

1. The altar was 32 cubits square.[7] The base rose 1 cubit, then   35b
reduced by 1 cubit, then the circuit rose 5 cubits and reduced
by 1 cubit, leaving [an area of] 28 by 28 cubits [on top].
Each of the corner posts was 1 cubit square, leaving 26 by
26. The priests needed a cubit width all round, so the area
for the fire was 24 cubits square.

---

4. Or 'blocks'.
5. The dimensions of the courtyard are fully explained in Chapter 5 (not translated here); reference was made to the bowing locations in *Sheqalim* 6:1 (see Chapter Six).
6. He has in mind Ezekiel 47:2 and Zachariah 14:8.
7. On the structure of the altar, see *Zevahim* Chapter Five (see p. 574).

Rabbi Yosé said, The base measurement was originally 28 by 28, and as it reduced in this way the area for the fire was 20 cubits square. However, when they returned from exile they added 4 cubits on the north and 4 on the west, like a [Greek] *gamma*, as it is written, NOW THE HEARTH SHALL BE 12 CUBITS LONG AND 12 BROAD, SQUARE (Ezekiel 43:16 JPS). Could that mean that it was only 12 by 12? When it continues, ON ITS FOUR QUARTERS, it indicates that the measurement of 12 is taken from the middle in each direction.

A red line went round it halfway up to distinguish between the blood sprinkled above and that sprinkled below.

The base was continuous along the north and west sides, but projected only one cubit along the south and east.

36a 4. The stones for the ramp and the altar came from the valley of Bet Kerem. They excavated below the virgin soil and brought only whole stones over which no iron had been brandished, for iron would invalidate by touch, and any material would invalidate if it made a dent. If a stone was dented it was rendered invalid, but the others remained valid.

Twice a year, after Pesach and Sukkot, [the stones] are cleaned. The sanctuary [itself] is cleaned annually after Pesach. Rabbi says, [The stones] are cleaned every Sabbath eve with a cloth on account of the blood.

They did not use an iron trowel to lime [the stones] in case it touched them and rendered them invalid. Iron was created to shorten human life, but the altar was created to lengthen human life; it is not right that that which shortens should be brandished over that which lengthens.

SIXTH ORDER

TOHOROT (PURITIES)

INTRODUCTION

Purity, a major concern for the Talmud, was an entirely normal aspect of ancient life, as it still is in much of India and elsewhere. Greeks and Romans were familiar with it in their Temples and even in daily life – Theophrastus (c. 370–287 BCE), for instance, poked fun at 'your Superstitious man such as will not sally forth for the day until he have washed his hands and sprinkled himself at the Nine Springs, and put a bit of bay-leaf from a temple in his mouth'.[1] For the Zoroastrians, among whom the Jews of Babylonia lived, issues of purity affected almost every aspect of life – even at death bodies were exposed rather than buried so as not to contaminate the land.[2] The modern western world has abandoned this concept of purity, though it has retained the vocabulary for matters such as cleanliness and spirituality; subtle changes in the use of words make it difficult to express faithfully what purity meant to our forebears.

Systems of purity have features in common such as the prominence of death and sex as causes of pollution, but there is much that divides them. Whereas the Zoroastrian system links pollution to daevas, or evil spirits, the rabbinic system 'demythologizes' pollution, interpreting it simply as a system of revealed rules giving practical expression to holiness. This sometimes produces counter-intuitive results – a dead snake, though snakes are a cause of death, is not 'unclean', since it is not included in

1. Theophrastus, *Characters* XVI (tr. J. M. Edmonds, Loeb edition (1929), p. 79).
2. On Greek purity, see Parker, *Miasma*; on Zoroastrian, see *Vendidad*, Chapters 5–17, and Boyce, *Zoroastrianism*, pp. 294–330.

the Bible's list of swarming creatures (Leviticus 11:29–30),[3] nor are human urine and faeces sources of uncleanness as they are in most other systems of purity, for the Bible does not specify them as such.

The key words are:

> tahor   *pure, clean*
> tamé   *impure, unclean, polluted, defiled*

These English words have different connotations from the Hebrew they represent; for instance, there could be no confusion in Hebrew between naqi, 'clean' as opposed to 'dirty', and tahor, 'clean (pure)' as opposed to 'unclean (impure)'. The reader will need to set aside modern associations and attitudes and pick up the resonances such words would have had in a society in which degrees of purity and pollution were features of daily life.

Rabbinic literature frequently uses purity and impurity as metaphors; 'sin' and 'the evil instinct' are personified as 'the impure one' (Sukka 52a; see p. 225). Jonathan Klawans has observed that 'the defiling force of sin' continues, in rabbinic literature, to have non-metaphorical as well as metaphorical meaning, but is always clearly distinguished from ritual use.[4]

The System

There are three elements in any purity system: the source of impurity, the recipient (person or object) and the conveyance from source to recipient.

The rabbinic system recognizes twelve sources of impurity.[5] Six emanate from the human body: the male discharge, the female discharge,[6] menstrual blood, childbirth, leprosy, semen.

---

3. Zoroastrian purity law, on the other hand, extends the analogous category of *khrafstra* to aggressive and repulsive creatures in general (Boyce, *Zoroastrianism*, p. 298).
4. Klawans, 'Impurity'.
5. This summary is based on the Elijah of Vilna's succinct and masterly introduction to the Order in his commentary, *Eliyahu Rabba*.
6. The first two are abnormal discharges of semen and blood respectively, as in the tractate *Zavim*.

Three emanate from death: corpse, carrion, reptiles.[7] *Three affect individuals who carry out certain ceremonies: burning the red heifer, burning the sacrificial oxen and goats, and accompanying the scapegoat.*[8]

Ways of conveying pollution vary according to the source, and include touching, lifting, carrying or moving without touching, being under the same roof ('tent'), sitting or lying upon furniture, sexual intercourse.

Food and many objects may become tamé, *but only if they have been 'enabled'. Enablement consists in preparation for human use; a piece of wood, for instance, cannot become* tamé *unless it has been fashioned into some artefact, nor can fruit become* tamé *until it has been harvested and, in addition, been moistened intentionally with one of seven specified liquids.*

The Sages regarded the preceding as mid'Oraita, *law of biblical status, and they instituted additional forms and instances of impurity as safeguards or (in the case of idols) to distance people from other evils. One of the most curious of these is the ruling that sacred scrolls pollute the hands (see the introductory note to* Yadayim 3:4, p. 713).

*Degrees of impurity range from that of a human corpse, deemed to be the 'grandfather' of impurity, through various 'fathers' and then five descending degrees; the third and lower degrees are applicable only in connection with the Temple and priesthood. In general, the holier something is the more it is liable to defilement (*Yadayim 4:6).

Most of the system seems to have been in place by the time of the Schools of Hillel and Shammai early in the first century; their successors at Yavné and Usha elaborate details, classify and add new rulings. A comparison with the Damascus Code and other Dead Sea Scrolls, despite significant divergences, confirms the practice of this form of purity not later than the first century BCE. *How widespread it was is a matter of current debate. Since most Jews frequented the Temple and knew they had to purify themselves before ascending the Holy Mount, it is*

7. That is, the dead bodies of humans, some animals and the eight creatures listed in Leviticus 11:29–30.
8. See tractates *Parah* and *Yoma*.

likely that some form of purity observance was common; they would also strive to keep the teruma *and other offerings pure; moreover, they observed 'idolaters' among whom they lived practising similar rites.*

The Essenes and the ḥaverim *practised a full range of purity rules outside the Temple and made them a criterion of membership. Both were building on popular practice and striving to align it with Bible texts, but whereas Essenes separated themselves from the mass of the people,* ḥaverim *strove to remain within the community, occasionally bending the rules to do so; for instance, they cited 'All the men of Israel gathered to the city as one man,* ḥaverim' *(Judges 20:11) to justify acceptance of the purity standards of* 'amé ha-aretz *in Jerusalem during the festivals.*[9]

9.   Ḥagiga 26a. See also Ḥagiga 22b, and Sanders, *Jewish Law*, especially pp. 242–52.

FIRST TRACTATE
KELIM (ARTEFACTS)

Kelim *can be translated by 'things', 'vessels', 'implements' and a variety of other terms. It can refer to clothes, tools, dishes or to anything that, through human intention, is assigned to human use. The tractate sets out general rules for conveyance of impurity to and by artefacts and proceeds to apply them to a wide selection of household and commercial items, often given Latin or Greek names. Much information about the economic life of third-century Palestine is embedded in the thirty chapters of this tractate.*

Mishnas 1–4 set out degrees of defilement (impurity) in ascending order; Mishnas 6–9 balance this with degrees of holiness.

The terms zav *and* zava *are taken from Leviticus 15, where they refer respectively to a male who has an abnormal seminal discharge and to a female who has an abnormal discharge of blood. Later tractates are devoted to the leper, the* zav *and the* zava.*

CHAPTER ONE

1. The principal sources of defilement are: swarming creatures; semen; a person defiled by contact with a corpse; the leper awaiting purification; purification waters that are insufficient for sprinkling. These defile people and clothes by contact and earthenware vessels by entry.

2. Above those are: carrion; purification waters that are sufficient for sprinkling. These defile people who carry them, to defile [in turn] clothes or unclothed people by contact.

3. Above these: someone who has intercourse with a menstruant, for he defiles a bed beneath him as [others] defile what is on them.

Next come: The discharge of the *zav*, his saliva, semen and urine, and menstrual blood, which defile by contact and carrying.

Next comes riding equipment,[1] for it conveys defilement even if it is beneath a large rock.

Then comes that on which a person lies, for it [conveys defilement] by touch as well as by being carried.

Next comes the *zav* himself, for he generates the defilement of that on which a person lies, whereas that on which a person lies cannot [itself] generate that degree of defilement.

4. Above the *zav* comes the *zava*, for she defiles by sexual contact.

Above the *zava* comes the leper, for he defiles by entrance [into a building].

Above the leper is a barleycorn-size of bone from a corpse, for it causes impurity lasting seven days.

The highest degree [of impurity] is that of a corpse, for it defiles [simply] by being under the same roof, which no other [source of impurity] does.

Mishna 5 lists the prohibitions attaching to various degrees of impurity.

Holiness correlates with purity. The Land is holy since it enables the fulfilment of God's commandments; maximum holiness is attained annually when the High Priest enters the Holy of Holies on the Day of Atonement and brings the people close to God.

6. There are ten degrees of holiness. The Land of Israel is

---

1. Some commentators think this covers all equipment other than the saddle; others restrict it to the reins.

holier than other lands, for the Omer sheaf, the first-fruits and the two loaves [for Shavuot] are brought from its produce, but not from that of other lands.

7. Walled cities [within the Land] are holier, for lepers are excluded from them, and though a corpse may be moved around them, once it has left it may not be returned to them.

8. Within the wall [of Jerusalem] is holier still, for offerings of minor holiness and second tithe may be eaten there.

The Temple Mount is holier still; a *zav*, *zava*, menstruant or newly delivered mother may not enter.

The outer precinct [of the Temple] is holier still; non-Israelites and persons defiled by contact with a corpse may not enter.

The women's courtyard is holier still; a *t'vul yom* may not enter, though he is not liable to a sin-offering [if he inadvertently enters in that state].

The courtyard of Israel is holier still; those who await their atonement offering [to complete their purification] may not enter, and they are liable to a sin-offering [if they inadvertently enter in that state].

The courtyard of the priests is holier still; Israelites may not enter except when they are required to place their hands on the head of the sacrifice, to slaughter it, or for the waving ceremony.

9. Between the portico and the altar is holier still; blemished [priests] or those with untrimmed hair may not enter.

The sanctuary is holier still; none may enter without first washing hands and feet.

The Holy of Holies is holier than any other place; no one may enter but the High Priest on the Day of Atonement as he performs the [divine] service.

Rabbi Yosé said, In five ways the area between the portico and the altar is equal to the sanctuary: no one may enter if blemished, with untrimmed hair, intoxicated or without first washing hands and feet, and they must vacate the area between the portico and the altar when incense is being offered.

Several chapters establish that only objects devised for human use are susceptible to defilement, though not all of them are – for instance, a plain metal object is susceptible to defilement, but a wooden object is only susceptible to defilement if it has a receptacle, that is, if it can hold whatever it is intended for. If an object can no longer fulfil a useful purpose, it is no longer subject to defilement. Measurements (shi'urim), *the topic of this chapter, become important; what size hole would render a container useless and therefore no longer subject to defilement?*

Mishna sets standards for measurements involved in the performance of mitzvot *generally; the Gemara (Yoma 80a) claims that such measurements were received by Moses at Sinai, lost and reintroduced by Jabez and his court in the days of the Judges. Note the use of Archimedes' principle in Mishna 6 and the reference to two official standards for linear measurements in 9.*

CHAPTER SEVENTEEN

1. The measure [of a hole] for [rendering a] household utensil [useless and therefore no longer subject to defilement] is the size of a pomegranate;[2] Rabbi Eliezer says, It depends on the normal use [of that utensil].[3]

    The measure for market-gardeners' boxes is the size of a bunch of greens and for domestic boxes big enough to let straw through; for [the container used by] bath attendants, it is the size through which stubble fuel might drop. Rabbi Joshua says, In all cases [the measure] is the size of a pomegranate.

4. When they referred to pomegranates they meant if three were together [and one fell through the hole]. Rabban Simeon ben Gamaliel said that if it was a basket or a sieve

---

2. If a container has a hole the size of a pomegranate it is deemed useless.
3. Literally, 'whatever it is'.

and he slung it over his shoulder[, and a pomegranate would fall through the hole, that is the size].

As for containers that are not large enough to hold a pomegranate, for instance a quarter- or eighth-*kab* or a small wicker basket, Rabbi Meir holds that the hole would need to be more than half the size [of the container]: Rabbi Simeon says, An olive-size; [that is,] if the container was broken, [the measure] is an olive-size, but if [only] the edge was damaged, then so long as the container can still hold anything [it remains subject to defilement].

5. The pomegranate of which they spoke was neither small nor large, but of average size.

In what connection were Badan pomegranates mentioned?[4] Rabbi Meir says, Because even one of them[, if it was forbidden,] would render any mixture forbidden; Rabbi Yoḥanan ben Nuri said, Because they were the standard for measurement of utensils; Rabbi Aqiva says, It was for both reasons – to measure utensils, and because even one would render any mixture forbidden; Rabbi Yosé said, Badan pomegranates and Geva leeks were specified as certainly requiring tithing wherever they were.

6. The egg of which they spoke was neither large nor small but average.

Rabbi Judah said, You bring the largest and the smallest eggs [you can find], put them into water and divide the [displaced] water.

Rabbi Yosé said, Who can tell me what is the largest and what is the smallest? It is all in the eye of the beholder.

9. The cubit of which they spoke is an average cubit.

There were two [standard] cubits in the Susa Chamber [in the Temple], one in the north-eastern corner and one in the south-eastern corner. The one in the north-eastern corner was half a fingerbreadth longer than that of Moses, and that in the south-eastern corner was half a fingerbreadth

---

4. Badan is said to be a Samaritan town famous for its pomegranates; they cannot have been the standard for measurement since they were not 'average'.

longer still, making it a full fingerbreadth longer than that of Moses.

Why was one long and one short? It was so that craftsmen should take according to the short and return according to the long, avoiding the possibility of trespass.[5]

---

5.   The slight loss occasioned to the craftsmen would save them from accidentally making profane use of Temple property.

SECOND TRACTATE
OHALOT (TENTS)

THIS IS THE LAW. IF SOMEONE DIES IN A TENT, WHOEVER ENTERS THE TENT OR WHOEVER IS IN IT SHALL BE UNCLEAN FOR SEVEN DAYS. (Numbers 19:14)

Ohalot *defines the quantity and state of human and animal body parts that generate impurity, and the dimensions and structure of a 'tent' (roof) that would convey impurity from the source to anyone under its cover.*

Anatomy is by no means as straightforward as it appears from a modern textbook. Do you count the number of bones in a child or those in an adult, in whom some will have fused together? Do you count the coccyx as one or five vertebrae? How many bones form the skull? The answers are to some extent matters of convention.

CHAPTER ONE

6. Human beings do not generate impurity [of the highest degree] until they actually expire. If someone has been severely injured or is in the throes of death, he still either gives rise to or frees from levirate obligation [according to circumstances] and confers or disqualifies from the right to *teruma* [like any living person] until he expires; likewise, domestic and wild animals do not cause impurity [until they expire].

If they have been beheaded they defile [immediately] even

if they are still squirming, as for instance the tail of a lizard squirms [after it has been cut off].

7. [Complete] body parts [convey impurity] irrespective of size; less than an olive-size of a corpse, less than an olive-size of carrion or less than a lentil-size of a swarming creature [conveys impurity if it is a whole body or a complete part].

8. The human body has 248 parts:[1] 30 in the foot (6 in each toe); 10 in the ankle; 2 in the lower leg; 5 in the knee; 1 in the thigh; 3 at the hip girdle;[2] 11 ribs; 30 in the hand (6 in each finger); 2 in the lower arm; 2 at the elbow; 1 in the upper arm; 4 at the shoulder. This makes 101 on each side. Then there are 18 [thoracic and cervical] vertebrae, 9 [parts] in the head, 8 in the neck, 6 in the region of the heart[3] and 5 orifices.[4]

Each [of these parts on its own] defiles by touch, by carrying and by being under the same roof. This is if they are properly covered with flesh, but if they are not properly covered with flesh, they defile by touch and by carrying but not by being under the same roof.

CHAPTER TWO

1. These defile by being under the same roof: a corpse; an olive-size of a corpse; an olive-size of putrid flesh; a ladle full of rotted corpse; a spine, a skull, a complete body part or a part [removed] from a living person if it is properly covered with flesh; a quarter-*kab* of bones if they make up

1. *Ever*, here translated 'part', usually means 'limb', but that would not fit the context. All of the items listed are bones with the possible exception of 'orifices'.
2. Probably Greek *kotulē*, which Galen (*On the Bones*, section 736) describes as the deeper kind of 'hollows that receive the heads'.
3. Literally, 'key of the heart', but it cannot refer to the sternum, which has three sections. Preuss (*Medicine*, Chapter 2, p. 61) thinks it refers to the sternum together with part of the ribs and derives from the breast of the animal that was removed and given to the priest together with these bones.
4. Traditional commentators, following Maimonides, say this refers to the genitals; this is problematic as neither the number nor the absence of bony material would fit the context. Preuss, *Medicine*, suggests sacral vertebrae.

most of the structure or number [of those in the body], or most of the structure or number from the corpse even if they amount to less than a quarter-*kab* – [all these] are unclean. 'Most of the number' is 125.

CHAPTER SEVEN

4. If a woman was experiencing a difficult labour and she was taken from one house to another [and had a stillbirth in the second], the first house is doubtfully unclean, the second certainly unclean. Rabbi Judah said, This is if she had been carried [from one house to the other], but if she walked [on her own] the first house is clean, since once the womb has opened she would not be able to walk; a stillbirth is not regarded as having 'opened the womb' unless its head is as large as a spinner's bobbin.

5. If [she gave birth to two and] the first was dead but the second alive, [the second] is clean. If the first was alive and the second dead, [the first] is unclean; Rabbi Meir says, If they were both in the same sac, [the live one] is unclean; if they were in separate sacs, [the live one] is clean.

The next Mishna has been cited in later rabbinic literature in reference to abortion. Complex though its application may be, the basic principle is simple: the life of the mother takes precedence over that of the unborn child.[5]

6. If a woman was experiencing difficulty in labour, they dismember the foetus inside her and remove it limb by limb, for her life has priority over [that of the unborn] foetus. But if it had mostly emerged they do not touch it, since no life has priority over another.

The New Testament (Luke 10:25–37) tells of a priest who passed by on the other side of the road to avoid a dying man

5.   For later Jewish developments, see D. Feldman, *Marital Relations*, and Jakobovitz, *Medical Ethics*.

who was eventually assisted by a Samaritan.[6] *The basis for the story is that a* Kohen, *even if he is not an acting priest, may not defile himself for the dead other than for his immediate relatives (Leviticus 21:1–4). The rabbis did not uphold this rule in emergencies; in normal circumstances, however, even today, Orthodox* Kohanim *avoid contact with the dead, including being under the same roof as a corpse or walking among graves. A special problem arises when an ancient grave or graveyard has been ploughed over and the area may still contain bones.*

CHAPTER SIXTEEN

1. If someone ploughs over a grave, this creates a *bet ha-p'ras*.[7] How far does it extend? A furlong, or 100 cubits square, sufficient to sow four *seahs;* Rabbi Yosé says, Five. This is if [the land] slopes down, but if it slopes up he should put a quarter-*kab* of vetches on the plough-tail;[8] when he reaches the place where not more than three seeds fall out together, that is the extent of the *bet ha-p'ras*. Rabbi Yosé says, [The law of *bet ha-p'ras* applies only] on a downward slope, not on an upward one.

CHAPTER EIGHTEEN

5. How can a *bet ha-p'ras* be purified? They strip three palms' depth of soil[9] from it or spread three palms of [pure] soil over it; if they stripped half the field and spread [pure soil] on half the field, it is pure.

   Rabbi Simeon says, If they stripped a palm and a half

---

6. Luke implausibly includes a Levite, who would be under no such restriction.
7. This could mean 'place of broken [parts]' or 'place where [body parts] have been spread out'.
8. The Hebrew *borekh*, 'knee', is probably a misreading of Latin *buris*, 'hinder part of a plough'.
9. That is the depth the plough turns over.

from it and spread a palm and a half from elsewhere, it is pure.

If he paves the *bet ha-p'ras* with immovable stones, it is pure.

Rabbi Simeon says, Even if he removes stones from a *bet ha-p'ras*, it is pure.

THIRD TRACTATE
NEGA'IM (PLAGUES)

Leviticus 13 sets out regulations for the priests who are responsible for the diagnosis of leprosy, the quarantine of those with possible symptoms and the isolation of those definitely afflicted. Leviticus 14 outlines the purification process for the recovered leper.

The symptoms listed in Leviticus are not clearly understood, nor is their elaboration by the rabbis; some coincide with symptoms associated with various forms of what is now known as leprosy, or Hansen's disease, but others do not. Like the biblical plague, Hansen's disease exhibits hypopigmented skin lesions (white spots); it is infectious in the early stages. The rabbis understood the biblical term tzara'at *as referring to a special affliction sent by God to punish slanderers; in this tractate they call it simply* nega' *(plague). There is no record of the leprosy laws being implemented in the time of the Mishna or subsequently.*

After first viewing, the victim may be quarantined by the Kohen for a week pending review; on review he may be quarantined for another week, certified as a definite 'leper' or be declared free of the disease and released.

CHAPTER ONE

1. **Appearances of plague are two which are four.**

    The white spot (Leviticus 13:4) is bright as snow; second to that is white like the lime of the sanctuary.

    The swelling (13:10) is like the white of an egg; second to

that is [an appearance] like undyed wool. That is Rabbi Meir's view, but the Sages say that the swelling is like undyed wool, and second to that is like the white of an egg.

2. When the snow[-coloured lesion] is variegated (13:19), it looks like snow mixed with wine; when the lime[-coloured lesion] is variegated, it looks like blood mixed with milk. That is Rabbi Ishmael's view, but Rabbi Aqiva says, The red hue in both of them is like wine mixed with water, but with the snow colour it is bright and with the lime colour paler.

3. These four hues combine to release, to certify and to quarantine.

They may [combine to] quarantine [a sufferer] at the end of a week [after first viewing]; to release him at the end of the second week; to certify anyone in whom a light scar or white hair was found on first viewing, at the end of the first week or the end of the second week or even after being declared free; to certify anyone in whom the lesion spread, at the end of the first week or the end of the second week or even after being declared free; to certify anyone who had been declared free because whiteness had spread all over him (Leviticus 13:12–13); and to declare free anyone over whom whiteness had spread entirely but who had already been certified or quarantined.

These are the appearances of plague on which all [decisions concerning] plague hinge.

The priestly prerogative of diagnosing the plague was downgraded by the rabbis to a mere ceremonial function; the priest is dependent for the diagnosis on an expert 'viewer', that is, a suitably qualified Sage.

CHAPTER THREE

1. All are subject to defilement by the plague except for non-Isaelites and resident aliens.

All may view the plague, but only a *Kohen* may pronounce it impure or pure. [The expert] says to the *Kohen*, 'Say unclean', and he says, Unclean; or he says to the *Kohen*, 'Say clean', and he says, Clean.

Two occurrences should not be viewed simultaneously, whether in one person or two. [The viewer] should first look at one and quarantine, certify or have him declared free, then return to the second.

A victim who is already in quarantine may not be quarantined [on the basis of another occurrence], nor can one who has been certified be certified [on the basis of another occurrence]; the certified may not be quarantined nor the quarantined certified.

At the beginning, [during the week that his status is not determined,] he may be quarantined or certified [on the basis of another occurrence]. After [a period of] quarantine he may be declared free, and after [a period of] being certified he may be released.

2. If [a symptom of] the plague appeared on a bridegroom, he, his house and his clothes are allowed his seven days [of feasting before a formal diagnosis is declared]. Similarly on a festival he is allowed the whole of the festival.[1]

CHAPTER FOURTEEN

1. How is the leper purified? [The priest] brings a new earthenware jar and puts into it a quarter-*log* of 'living water',[2] then he brings two free-flying birds.[3] He slaughters one of them over the earthenware jar and the 'living water', then digs and buries it in front of him. He takes cedar wood and hyssop and scarlet wool, binds them together with the ends of the thread and holds them next to the wingtips, head and tail of the second [bird]. He dips and sprinkles seven times

---

1. Plague is not viewed during a festival even if symptoms have presented.
2. This expression is used several times in Leviticus, and may be translated 'spring water'. See *Miqva'ot* 1:7–8 (see p. 689).
3. Birds that live in the house as well as in the wild.

on the back of the leper's hand – though some say on his forehead. [If purifying a stricken house, (Leviticus 14: 34–53)] he sprinkles on the outside of the lintel.

2. He then releases the living bird. He does not face the sea, the city or the desert, for it is said, HE SHALL SET THE LIVE BIRD FREE IN THE OPEN COUNTRY (14:7 JPS).

He must then shave the leper, passing a razor all over his body.

[The leper then] washes his clothes and bathes. He is now pure to the extent that he no longer defiles by entry, but only as someone who has had contact with a swarming creature. He may enter within the walls [of Jerusalem], but is banned from his [own] house for seven days and forbidden to engage in sexual intercourse.

3. On the seventh day he shaves again as on the first, washes his clothes and bathes. He no longer has the degree of impurity of one who has had contact with a swarming creature, but is like a *t'vul yom* and [if he is a Levite, he] may eat tithe; [if he is a *Kohen*,] when evening comes he may eat *teruma*.

Once he has brought his atonement sacrifice, he may again partake of the sacrifices.

So there are three stages in the purification of a leper, and there are likewise three stages in the purification of a woman following childbirth.

FOURTH TRACTATE
PARAH (THE RED HEIFER)

*The purification ceremony for people defiled by contact with a corpse is described in Numbers 19. A red heifer **IN WHICH THERE IS NO DEFECT AND ON WHICH NO YOKE HAS BEEN LAID** (19:2) is slaughtered, then burnt to ashes with **CEDAR WOOD, HYSSOP AND SCARLET WOOL** (19:6); the ashes are stored in a stone jar which is placed in the Temple. A small quantity of ashes was removed from the jar when required for a purification ceremony and placed in water; this was known as 'purification water'. The whole process from burning the heifer to drawing the water is conducted with maximum attention to purity requirements.*

The dexterous performance described in 3:3 was devised to avoid pollution of the ashes. Like the preceding Mishnas it is not so much an historical record as an attempt by Sages, probably at Usha, to fathom how the rare and delicate procedure could have been carried out avoiding pollution; had it been historical it is unlikely that Rabbi Yosé would have flatly denied that it took place. (The text has been slightly amended by reference to Tosefta 3:2–3, which states that the procedure only took place on the return from Babylon.)

CHAPTER THREE

1. The priest who burnt the heifer was taken from his home seven days in advance and secluded in a chamber called the

House of Stone at the front of the Temple complex, in the north-east.

They sprinkled water of all the available purification-offerings [from earlier times] on him every day. Rabbi Yosé says they sprinkled only on the third and seventh days [of his seclusion]. Rabbi Ḥanina the deputy High Priest says, They sprinkled [purification waters] on the priest who burnt the heifer every day of the seven, but they sprinkled the priest who officiated on the Day of Atonement on the third and seventh days only.

2. There were courtyards in Jerusalem built on rock that had been hollowed out beneath to avoid [pollution from] any burials that might have been in the depths. Pregnant women came to give birth and brought up their children there.[1] They brought oxen with boards on them on which the children sat holding stone vessels.[2] When [the children] arrived at the brook of Shiloah, they dismounted and filled [the vessels from the brook] – but Rabbi Yosé says, They let [the vessels] down on [ropes] to fill them.

3. When they arrived at the Temple Mount, they dismounted, for [the ground] beneath the Temple Mount and courtyards had been hollowed out to avoid [pollution from] deep burials. The jar [containing the ashes] stood ready for the purification waters at the entrance to the courtyard.

They brought a ram and tied a cord between its horns. They tied a brush-ended pole on to the cord, pulled the end of the cord and propelled [the stick] into the jar. Then they hit the ram and it jerked backward[, causing ashes to be catapulted out of the jar on to the oxen. The children] put a visible quantity of ashes into the water, so sanctifying them for use.

Rabbi Yosé said, Don't give the Sadducees an opportunity to ridicule us! [The children] took the ashes directly and placed them in the water.

1.   To the age of eight – Tosefta.
2.   The boards served as a barrier between the children and any unclean thing over which they may have passed.

5. If they could not find [ashes of] seven [previous heifers,] they used six, five, four, three, two or one.

Who made [the earlier ones]? Moses made the first, Ezra the second, and there were five from Ezra onwards, according to Rabbi Meir. The Sages, however, say that there were seven from Ezra onwards. Who made them? Simeon the Just and Yoḥanan the High Priest made two each; Eliehoinai ben ha-Quf, Ḥanamel the Egyptian and Ishmael ben Phoebus made one each.

6. To avoid pollution from deep burials, they made a causeway of stepped arches, each arch next to its neighbour's pier, from the Temple Mount to the Mount of Olives. By way of this the priest who burnt the heifer, together with the heifer itself and whoever was needed to attend to it, walked out to the Mount of Olives.

7. If the heifer was reluctant to move, they did not put a black one with her [to encourage her] in case people would think they were slaughtering the black one, nor could they bring another red one [to accompany her] in case people thought they were slaughtering both. Rabbi Yosé says, That was not the reason; it was because Scripture says, HE SHALL TAKE HER OUT (Numbers 19:3) – her, alone.[3]

Elders of Israel walked ahead to the Mount of Olives, where there was an immersion pool. They defiled the priest who was to burn the heifer – this was [in defiance of] the Sadducees, who insisted that the procedure be done only by a priest on whom the sun had set [following immersion].[4]

8. Then they laid their hands on him and said, Sir! Immerse yourself! He went down, bathed, emerged and dried.

3. Lieberman (*Hellenism*, pp. 159–61) argues that the reason for the causeway was to encourage the goat to go willingly and to prevent its escape; a forced victim, and even more so one that escaped, was popularly regarded in the ancient world as a bad omen.
4. Neusner, *History of . . . Purities*, pp. 242–50, argues that though the procedure of the red heifer was originally carried out in the greatest purity, the standard was downgraded at Usha after the Bar Kokhba revolt, when men began to conceive of purity in the Temple as an ideal that could not be emulated in ceremonies outside the holy precinct. This conflicts with the reference to Sadducees, as they were no longer a threat in Ushan times; also, the *t'vul yom* was rigorously protected from corpse defilement and subjected only to minor defilement by a 'swarming creature'.

Wood had been arranged there [in advance] – cedar, pine, cypress and smooth fig-wood – it was piled up like a tower with windows and faced west.

9. They bound [the heifer] with a cord of bulrushes and set it on the pyre with its head to the south, facing west. The priest stood on the east side, facing west. He slaughtered with his right hand and collected [the blood into a bowl] with his left (Rabbi Judah says, He collected with his right, passed it to his left, then sprinkled with his right). He dipped and sprinkled seven times towards the Holy of Holies [in the Temple], dipping each time before sprinkling. When he had finished sprinkling, he wiped his hand on the carcass of the heifer, descended and kindled the fire with twigs; Rabbi Aqiva says, With palm fronds.

10. When the carcass split open he stood aside from the spot and picked up the cedar, hyssop and scarlet wool. He said [to those standing around], This cedar? This hyssop? This scarlet wool? – each item three times, and they responded 'yes' three times to each.

11. He bound [the cedar and hyssop] with the scarlet wool and threw [the bundle] into the conflagration. When it was burnt they beat it with sticks and sifted it. Rabbi Ishmael says they used stone hammers and sieves [to avoid pollution]. If they found black residue containing ashes, they crushed it, but otherwise they left it; any fragments of bone were crushed.

[The ashes] were then divided into three. One part was placed in the Temple, one left on the Mount of Olives, and one shared out among the courses of priests.

FIFTH TRACTATE
TOHOROT (PURITIES)

ANY PERSON, WHETHER CITIZEN OR STRANGER, WHO EATS WHAT HAS DIED OR WHAT HAS BEEN TORN BY BEASTS SHALL WASH HIS CLOTHES, BATHE IN WATER AND REMAIN UNCLEAN UNTIL EVENING; THEN HE SHALL BE CLEAN. (Leviticus 17:15 JPS)

To avoid superfluity in biblical verses – the general principle of pollution through carrion was expressed in Leviticus 5:2 – the rabbis applied this verse to the anomalous case of the 'carrion of the clean bird' with which this tractate opens.[1] Most of the tractate deals with the resolution of situations of doubt.

CHAPTER ONE

1. Thirteen things were said about the [conditions under which the] carrion of the clean bird [pollutes]: there must be intention [to eat that which is known to be unclean food]; no enabler is required; an egg-size conveys food pollution; an olive-size pollutes when swallowed; one who eats it remains unclean until evening; if someone who ate it entered the Temple [without purification], he is guilty; *teruma* [polluted] by it must be burnt; if anyone ate a limb torn from it while it was alive, he is liable to flogging; if it was correctly slaughtered or 'pinched',[2] it is not carrion (that is Rabbi

1. *Shavuot* 7b.
2. This is a method of slaughter reserved for bird sacrifices, as in Leviticus 1:15.

Meir's view; Rabbi Judah says it is still carrion, but Rabbi Yosé says, Regular slaughter releases it from being carrion, but pinching does not).

CHAPTER FIVE

1. A swarming creature and a frog[3] in a public place; an olive-size from a corpse and an olive-size of carrion; bone from a corpse and bone from carrion; soil from clean land and soil from a *bet ha-p'ras*; soil from the Land [of Israel] and soil from the lands of the nations; two paths, one clean and one unclean, and he does not know which one he trod; he passed under a roof where one of them[4] was present, but does not know which; he moved one but doesn't know which – [in all these cases,] Rabbi Aqiva declares him unclean but the Sages declare him clean.

CHAPTER SIX

4. However many doubts and doubts about doubts you may have [about the presence of pollution] in a private place, it is unclean, but in a public place it is clean.

How is this? Someone enters a cul-de-sac and there is something unclean in one of the courtyards [that leads off it], but he is not sure whether he entered [the courtyard] or not; [or] something unclean is in a house, but he is not sure whether he entered [the house] or not, or even if he had entered whether the unclean thing was there or not, and if it was there whether or not there was enough of it to pollute, and even if there was enough of it whether it was [in fact]

3. Not listed among the 'swarming creatures' in Leviticus 11:29–30, so considered 'clean'.
4. Corpse or carrion – Bertinora, *Commentary*.

unclean or not, and even if it was [definitely] unclean whether he had touched it or not.

Rabbi Eleazar says, If there is a doubt about entry he is clean, but if about pollution he is unclean.

5. If he entered a valley in the rainy season and there was something unclean in a field, and he says, I was in that area but don't know whether I entered that field, Rabbi Eleazar declares him clean but the Sages declare him unclean.

6. Doubts in a private area are unclean unless he is certain that he did not touch [the source of impurity]; doubts in a public area are clean unless he is certain that he did touch [the source of impurity].

What is meant by a 'public area'? The paths of Bet Gilgul[5] and suchlike, though considered private with regard to Sabbath law, are public with respect to pollution; Rabbi Eleazar says, The paths of Bet Gilgul were noted only because they are considered private with regard to both.

Paths that open on to wells, pits, caves and vine presses are private with regard to Sabbath law but public with respect to pollution.

5.   Steep winding paths. Bet Gilgul may be Golgotha.

SIXTH TRACTATE
MIQVA'OT (POOLS)

HE SHALL BATHE IN WATER AND BE CLEAN. (Leviticus 14:8)

BUT A SPRING OR WELL, A GATHERING (MIQVÉ) OF WATER, SHALL BE CLEAN. (Leviticus 11:36)

The principal method of purification is immersion in a miqvé, *literally a 'gathering' of water; this is the origin of Christian 'baptism'.*[1] *Just as there are degrees of pollution there are degrees of purity and efficacy of water. Only 'natural' water can purify; water removed from its source – typically, water stored in jars or tanks – is known as 'drawn water' and is disqualified.*

Rivers in the Land of Israel are not easily accessible, so miqva'ot *were generally hollows in caves or rock into which rainwater had cascaded. Archaeologists have unearthed many of these in Jerusalem, in the towns of Galilee, at Masada and at Qumran, though at desert sites it is not always easy to distinguish between a* miqvé *and a water storage tank.*

CHAPTER ONE

1. There are six degrees of *miqva'ot* one above the other.

   A still pool of rainwater [containing less than 40 *seah* is the lowest degree]. If an unclean person drank [from it] and then a clean person, [the clean person becomes] unclean; if an unclean person drank [from it] and a loaf of *teruma* fell

---

1. Greek *baptizō* is to immerse.

in, even if he rinsed it [in the pool] it is unclean but otherwise it [remains] clean.[2]

6. Above that comes rainwater that forms constant rivulets. If an unclean person drank [from it] and then a clean person, [the clean person remains] clean; if an unclean person drank [from it] and a loaf of *teruma* fell in, even if he rinsed it [in the pool] it [remains] clean.

If he filled an unclean container with it and a clean person drank [from it, the clean person remains] clean; if he filled an unclean container with it and then filled a clean container with it, [the clean container remains] clean; if he filled an unclean container with it and a loaf of *teruma* fell into [the flowing water], even if he rinsed [the loaf in it the loaf remains] clean.

If unclean water fell [into the flowing water] and a clean person drank [from it, the clean person remains] clean; if unclean water fell [into the flowing water] and he filled a clean container with it, [the clean container remains] clean; if unclean water fell in and then a loaf of *teruma* fell into [the flowing water], even if he rinsed [the loaf in it the loaf remains] clean.

This water is suitable for *teruma* and for washing the hands.

7. Above that comes a *miqvé* containing more than 40 *seah*; it is suitable for the immersion of both people and objects.

Next comes a spring with [only] a small flow, to whose waters has been added a larger quantity of drawn water. Like a *miqvé* it purifies when static; like a spring it purifies even when less than 40 *seah* is present.

8. Higher still are salty or hot spring waters, for they purify as they flow.

Highest of all are 'living waters'[3] (Leviticus 15:13); those with discharge are purified by them, they are sprinkled on

2. Water of the lowest degree loses its status if detached from its source; if an unclean person drinks from it he inevitably detaches some, and when detached water falls back in it pollutes the rest, so that the next person who drinks is polluted.
3. Literal translation; JPS has 'fresh water' and KJV 'running water'. See also *Nega'im* 14:1 and p. 679, note 2.

the leper and they may be used as purification water [with the ashes of the red heifer].

CHAPTER TWO

1. If an unclean person entered a pool to immerse himself and there was doubt whether he had actually immersed, or if there was doubt as to whether the *miqvé* contained 40 *seah*, or if there were two *miqva'ot*, one containing 40 *seah* and the other one not, and he bathed in one and doesn't know which, he [remains] unclean [because of the] doubt.

2. If [the quantity of water in] a *miqvé* was measured and found deficient, any purities made on the strength of it, whether in a private or a public area,[4] are retrospectively rendered impure.

That applies only to impurities of high degree, but not to those of low degree. If, for instance, someone ate unclean food or drank unclean liquids, or if his head and most of his body entered drawn water, or if three *logs* or more of drawn water were poured over his head and most of his body, or if he entered a pool to immerse himself and there was doubt whether he had actually immersed, or if there was doubt as to whether the *miqvé* contained 40 *seah*, or if there were two *miqva'ot*, one containing 40 *seah* and the other one not and he bathed in one and doesn't know which – [in all these cases] he is clean [despite] the doubt.

Rabbi Yosé, however, holds that he is unclean, for Rabbi Yosé maintains that whatever is established as unclean remains so until it is known that it is clean; if [on the other hand it is clean] and there is doubt as to whether it has been polluted or has polluted [something else], it remains clean [until proved otherwise].

---

4.   See *Tohorot*, pp. 686–7.

CHAPTER SIX

1. Whatever [body of water] is joined to the *miqvé* is as the *miqvé* itself.

Things may be purified by immersing them in the holes or cracks in a [*miqvé* formed in the rock inside a] cave. [However,] you may not immerse in a pit at the side of the *miqvé* unless it is joined to it by a hole with the diameter of [at least] the opening of a leather bottle;[5] Rabbi Judah explains that that is only if the wall between [the pit and the *miqvé*] can hold firm.

Immersion, whether of people or objects, must be total. This chapter deals with the finer points of what would constitute a ḥatzitza, or obstruction, between the person or object and the water; before entering the miqvé *it is necessary to cleanse the person or object of all such obstructions.*

CHAPTER NINE

1. These are obstructions for persons: wool or linen threads and ribbons on girls' heads. Rabbi Judah says, Wool and hair do not obstruct, since they let the water in.
2. [Also:] matted hair on the chest or beard, or on concealed places in women, secretions next to the eye, crust or bandage on a wound, sap that has dried [on the skin], dried excrement on the skin, dough beneath the nails, crumb-like particles of sweat, *yaven* clay, potters' clay, squashed mud.

What is *yaven* clay? Clay from pits, as it is said, HE LIFTED ME OUT OF THE DESOLATE PIT, THE MIRY [*YAVEN*] CLAY (Psalm 40:3); potters' clay is as it says, but Rabbi Yosé says, Potters' clay is clean[6] so long as it has not been mixed with egg; squashed mud is what gets squashed on to the feet

5. A standard circular measurement also defined as sufficient to turn two fingers.
6. i.e. not an obstruction.

as people walk. These are the kinds of clay in which you cannot immerse nor can you immerse them, but you may immerse in all other kinds of clay so long as they are soft.

You may not immerse with the dust [of a journey] on your feet.

You may not immerse a kettle [containing remains of] burnt coal until you have rubbed off [the coal].

3. These do not obstruct: matted hair on the head, in the armpits or on concealed places in men.[7] Rabbi Eliezer says, There is no difference [in this respect] between men and women; if [an individual] is particular about it, it is an obstruction, if they are not particular, it is not an obstruction.

7.   The assumption is that men are less fussy than women about personal hygiene.

SEVENTH TRACTATE
NIDDA (MENSTRUANT)

Leviticus 15, on purity law, has sections on normal menstruation and on abnormal bleeding – see the introductory note to Zavim. Nidda deals with these matters as well as with the basic prohibition of sexual relations during menstruation (Leviticus 18:19; 20:18); this prohibition has remained operative within rabbinic Judaism.

Sections of the Mishna, including the opening debate between Hillel and Shammai, hark back to Temple times. The opening problem concerns purity law. A woman who suffers menstrual bleeding pollutes teruma *or any other food or drink that should be kept in a state of purity. But how can she be sure precisely when bleeding, hence the possibility of pollution, commenced?*

CHAPTER ONE

MISHNA:
Shammai says, For all women, the time [at which they notice bleeding] suffices; Hillel says, They must revert to the last [self-]examination, even if it was several days previous. The Sages say, Neither one nor the other is correct; a full day reduces the time to the previous examination, and examination reduces the full day.[1]

For any woman whose period is regular, the time [at which she notices bleeding] suffices.

1. That is, she assumes she was unclean only from the shorter of the two times.

SIXTH ORDER TOHOROT (PURITIES)

If a woman examines herself with a piece of material at the time of intercourse, this is as good as [any other] examination; it reduces both the full day and the time to the previous examination.

What is meant by 'the time [at which she notices bleeding] suffices'? If she was handling items to be kept in a state of purity, then moved away and noticed bleeding, she is unclean but the items [remain] clean.

Even though they said she pollutes [retrospectively] for a whole day, she counts [her seven days as menstruant] only from the time she noticed bleeding.

GEMARA:

What is Shammai's reason? He maintains that a woman is presumed to be in her [previously established] state, which was clean. Hillel maintains that we only rely on presumption of the previous state where the body concerned does not change its state for the worse, but since a woman's body is prone to bleeding, we cannot rely on presumption.

Why is this different from [the law governing] *miqvé*? The Mishna states: If [the quantity of water in] a *miqvé* was measured and found deficient, any purities made on the strength of it, whether in a private or a public area, are retrospectively rendered impure.[2] For Shammai the problem arises with regard to retrospection. For Hillel there is a problem with regard to establishing certainty; [Hillel says later[3] that] in the case of *nidda*[, where we declare retrospectively that what she has touched is unclean, we treat it as *doubtfully* unclean,] neither eating it nor burning it, whereas this baraita treats the polluted items as *certainly* unclean.

[A suggested resolution:] The difference is that in [the *miqvé*] case the presumption is that the person was unclean, so we assume that he did not immerse himself [in a valid *miqvé*]. To the contrary – surely we should assume that the *miqvé* was originally in order and that [the volume of water] had not diminished?

2. *Miqva'ot* 2:2 (see p. 690).
3. Baraita on *Nidda* 6a.

[No, since] you see that it is now deficient. Then here also you see that there is blood! She has only just seen it! There also, we have only just seen that [the volume of water] has diminished. [No comparison! In the *miqvé*] case water diminishes gradually; you cannot say that [a woman] saw [blood] gradually. Is that really a problem? Surely it is possible for the onset of bleeding to be gradual! Still, there is a difference: [in the *miqvé*] case you have two contrary indications,[4] here only one. Then how does [our case] differ from [the case of] the barrel? For it was taught: **If someone tested a barrel [of wine] intending to set it aside over a period of time as *teruma* [for the rest of his wine] and subsequently found that it had [turned into] vinegar, he may rely on it [having been wine] for three days [following the test], but after that it would have been doubtful.**[5] Surely this is a problem for Shammai? [No, for] there the presumption is that the produce was not tithed, so we assume that it remained untithed. To the contrary, let us rely on the presumption that the wine was not vinegar and say that it did not become vinegar [until it was found to have turned]! [No comparison!] Wine turns into vinegar only gradually; you cannot say that [a woman] saw [blood] gradually. Is that really a problem? Surely it is possible for the onset of bleeding to be gradual! Still, there is a difference: in the wine case you have two contrary indications, here only one.

Don't the cases of the barrel and the *miqvé* conflict[, seeing that each has two contradictory indications]? Why should one be treated as doubtful and the other as certain? Rabbi Ḥanina of Sura said, The Tanna of the barrel is Rabbi Simeon, and he treats the *miqvé* case as doubtful too, for a baraita states: **If a *miqvé***

4. The fact that the items were certainly unclean, and the fact that the *miqvé* is now deficient.
5. Tosefta *Terumot* 4:8. The problem here is that vinegar may not be given as *teruma* for wine.

was measured and found deficient, any
purities made on the strength of it, whether
in a private or a public area, are retrospectively rendered impure; Rabbi Simeon says,
In a public area they are pure, but in a
private area impure.

THE LORD SPOKE TO MOSES, SAYING: SPEAK TO PEOPLE OF ISRAEL
AND SAY TO THEM: WHEN A WOMAN CONCEIVES AND BEARS A
MALE, SHE SHALL BE UNCLEAN SEVEN DAYS . . . SHE SHALL REMAIN
IN [A STATE OF] PURE BLOOD[6] FOR THIRTY-THREE DAYS. (Leviticus
12:1–2, 4).

The periods of uncleanness and cleanness for a male birth are
7 and 33 days respectively and for a female birth 14 and 66
days (12:5). Since the periods for male and female are different,
it is important to know the gender of the child or the stillborn
foetus. The notion that the foetus does not become a proper
birth until forty days after conception may have something to
do with 'ensoulment'; a practical consequence even today is that
the halakha is lenient (though not unduly permissive) on the
performance of abortions before forty days.[7]
    The allegations of Queen Cleopatra's nasty experiments on
condemned prisoners may be a garbled report of medical experi-
mentation whether in Alexandria or elsewhere; Galen in second-
century Rome used his position as doctor to the gladiators to
do some of his research, but since dissection of human bodies
was strictly forbidden by Roman law, most of his findings were
based on dissections of animals. The rabbis evidently thought
that study of Scripture was a better guide to the human body
than the experimental method!

6. A difficult phrase which is taken to mean that this is not regarded as unclean like
    menstrual bleeding.
7. Aristotle similarly argues that if abortions are needed they should take place 'before
    sense and life (*empsuchē*) have begun in the embryo' (*Politics* 7:1335b20), though
    he does not specify 40 days.

CHAPTER THREE

MISHNA:

If a woman has a miscarriage on the fortieth day [of her
pregnancy], she need not consider that it was a child, but if
on the forty-first day she must sit[8] as if it was a male, a female
or normal menstruation.   30a

Rabbi Ishmael says that if it was the forty-first day, she must
sit as if it was a male or normal menstruation, and if it was
the eighty-first day, she must sit as if it was a male, a female
or normal menstruation, since a male is complete at 41 days
and a female at 81. The Sages, however, say that both are
complete at 41 days.

GEMARA:

Why is a male [birth] mentioned? If for the days of uncleanness[, it is superfluous, since] female [birth, which involves
a still longer period of uncleanness,] is mentioned; if for the
clean days [it is of no avail, since] *nidda* is mentioned[, so there   30b
are no clean days]! It is that if she sees [blood] on day 34 and
then on day 41, she will be unclean until day 48, or[, if the birth
was a female,] if she sees [blood] on day 74 and then on day 81,
she will be unclean until day 88.

Rabbi Ishmael says that if it was the forty-first day, she must
sit as if it was a male or normal menstruation, etc. It was
taught: Rabbi Ishmael says, [Scripture assigns days of]
uncleanness and cleanness for the male and [days of]
uncleanness and cleanness for the female; just as the [days
of] uncleanness and cleanness for the male correspond to the
time of his formation, so the [days of] uncleanness and cleanness for the female correspond to the time of her formation.
They said to him, You cannot infer formation from
uncleanness. They said [further] to Rabbi Ishmael, Queen
Cleopatra of Alexandria[9] had some [slave-girls] who incurred
the death penalty; she experimented on them and found that

8. Observe days of purity and impurity.
9. Seven Cleopatras were queens of Egypt; they were Greek, and their capital was
    Alexandria.

both male and female foetuses were fully formed at 41 days.
Rabbi Ishmael replied, I brought you proof from the Torah,
but you have brought me proof from fools!

What [did he mean by] 'proof from the Torah'? If
**[Scripture assigns days of] uncleanness and cleanness
for the male and [days of] uncleanness and cleanness
for the female,** etc., they had already responded to
him that you cannot infer formation from uncleanness.
[His proof must have been that] the Torah repeats the
word *teled* [she bears] for the female, indicating a
double period of formation.[10]

What [did he mean by] 'proof from fools'? [The
'experiment' was worthless, since] it was possible that
the [slave-girl who gestated a] female had already been
pregnant for 40 days prior to [the one who gestated]
a male. The rabbis assumed that [Cleopatra] had first
made them drink an abortifacient, but Rabbi Ishmael
held that some individuals do not react to the abortifacient.

[An alternative version.] **Rabbi Ishmael said to them, Cleopatra the Greek Queen had some [slave-girls] who incurred
the death penalty. She experimented on them and found that
the male foetus was fully formed at 41 days and the female at
81. They said to him, There is no proof from fools![11]** Why?
Because the one who gestated the female became pregnant 40
days later. Rabbi Ishmael thought that [Cleopatra] had set a
supervisor in charge of them [to ensure they did not become
pregnant], but the rabbis held that there is no [effective] supervisor for sex – the supervisor himself may have got her pregnant.

Perhaps if they had opened up the one with the
female foetus at 41 days, it would have been found
complete? Both had reached the same stage of development[, the male at 41 and the female at 81 days].

The Sages, however, say that both are complete at 41 days.
Isn't that what the first Tanna said? If it was merely to attribute

10. Literally, 'Scripture adds another birth for a female.'
11. This second version is derived from the Tosefta; the explanation, formulated in
Aramaic, is a later comment.

the same statement to an anonymous majority, so that the *halakha* would be decided that way against the individual [Rabbi Ishmael], this is [in any case] obvious. You might have thought that Rabbi Ishmael's position was plausible and has the backing of Scripture, so it makes clear [that even so it is not accepted].

Rabbi Simlai expounded: What is a baby like in its mother's womb? He is like a folded notebook, his hands on his two cheeks, his two elbows on his two knees, his two heels on his two buttocks, his head between his knees, his mouth closed and his navel open; he eats what his mother eats and drinks what his mother drinks, but he does not excrete in case it kills his mother. As soon as he emerges into the fresh air what was closed opens and what was open closes, for otherwise he could not survive. [While still in the womb] a light shines over his head, and he sees from one end of the world to the other, as it is said, WHEN HIS LAMP SHONE OVER MY HEAD, WHEN I WALKED IN THE DARK BY ITS LIGHT (Job 29:3 JPS) – do not be surprised at this, for a man sleeps here and in his dreams sees Spain – and these are the best days of a man's life, as it is said, O THAT I WERE AS IN MONTHS GONE BY, IN THE DAYS WHEN GOD WATCHED OVER ME (Job 29:2 JPS) – the time before birth, when there were months, not years. He is taught the whole Torah, as it is written, HE INSTRUCTED ME AND SAID TO ME, 'LET YOUR MIND HOLD ON TO MY WORDS, KEEP MY COMMANDMENTS AND YOU WILL LIVE' (Proverbs 4:4 JPS), and also, WHEN GOD'S COMPANY GRACED MY TENT (Job 29:5 JPS) – why 'and also'? You might have thought that [the verse in Proverbs] was the prophet speaking [rather than God], so it adds WHEN GOD'S COMPANY GRACED MY TENT.

As soon as he emerges into the fresh air an angel slaps his mouth and causes him to forget the whole Torah,[12] as it is said, SIN CROUCHES AT THE ENTRANCE (Genesis 4:7); [indeed,] he is not allowed out until he swears, as it is said, FOR TO ME SHALL EVERY KNEE BEND AND EVERY TONGUE SWEAR (Isaiah 45:23) – FOR TO ME SHALL EVERY KNEE BEND refers to the

---

12. Plato, for instance in *Meno* 81a–86b and *Republic* X, claims that all knowledge is recollection from previous existence, and is lost at birth.

day of death, as it is said, **ALL WHO DESCEND TO THE EARTH BEND THE KNEE BEFORE HIM** (Psalm 22:30); **EVERY TONGUE SWEAR** is the day of birth, as it is said, **HE WHO HAS CLEAN HANDS AND A PURE HEART, WHO HAS NOT TAKEN A FALSE OATH** (Psalm 24:4) – And what oath is he made to take? 'Be righteous and not wicked. Even if the whole world tells you that you are righteous, see yourself as wicked. Know that the Holy One, blessed be He, is pure and His servants are pure and the soul He has granted you is pure. If you preserve it in purity it will be well, but if not I shall take it from you.'

Galen writes: And what is the semen? Clearly the active principle of the animal, the material principle being the menstrual blood.[13] *The rabbis relate the 'active principle' to God and distribute the material aspects (in ancient physiology this would include the soft matter of the brain) between mother and father.*

31a   Three partners [form] a person: the Holy One, blessed be He, his father and his mother. His father produces the white seed out of which [are formed] bones, sinews, nails, the [soft matter of the] brain in his head and the white of the eye; his mother produces the red seed out of which [are formed] skin, flesh and hair, and the dark part of the eye; the Holy One, blessed be He, puts in him spirit and soul and facial appearance and the seeing of the eye, the hearing of the ear, the speech of the mouth, the movement of the legs, and discernment and understanding. When his time comes to depart from the world, the Holy One, blessed be He, takes His portion and leaves before his mother and father their portion.

The celebration of bar mitzva when a boy reaches the age of 13 is comparatively recent and is not mentioned in the Talmud; bat mitzva for girls of 12 became common only in the late twentieth century. The ages were, however, recognized as stages at which children became responsible for their actions.

13.   Galen, *Natural Faculties*, II:3 (85), p. 134.

CHAPTER FIVE

MISHNA:

[From the age of] eleven years and a day, [a girl's] vows are   45b
tested; from twelve and a day her vows are binding, but they
are tested throughout her twelfth year.[14] [From the age of]
twelve years and a day, [a boy's] vows are tested; from thirteen
and a day his vows are binding, but they are tested throughout
his thirteenth year.

Under that age, even if they say, We know to Whom we
vow, or [We know] to Whom we dedicate [this object], their
vows are not vows and their dedications are invalid.

Over that age, even if they say, We do not know to Whom
we vow, or to Whom we dedicate [this object], their vows are
vows and their dedications are valid.

GEMARA:

The rabbis taught: This is the opinion of Rabbi, but Rabbi
Simeon ben Eleazar said that the words [the Mishna] applied
to a girl applied [also] to a boy, and those applied to a boy
applied to a girl.

Rav Ḥisda enquired: What was Rabbi's reasoning? It is written, **AND THE LORD GOD FORMED THE RIB THAT HE HAD
TAKEN FROM THE MAN INTO A WOMAN** (Genesis 2:22) – this
teaches us that the Holy One, blessed be He, put more understanding in woman than in man.[15]

14. That is, while she is still eleven. For the boy, while still twelve.
15. Hebrew *va-yiven* 'he formed' could also mean 'he understood'; Rav Ḥisda wants
     to explain the earlier maturity of girls.

EIGHTH TRACTATE
MAKHSHIRIN (ENABLERS OF IMPURITY)

IF SUCH A CARCASS FALLS UPON SEED GRAIN THAT IS TO BE SOWN, IT IS CLEAN; BUT IF WATER IS PUT ON THE SEED AND ANY PART OF A CARCASS FALLS UPON IT, IT SHALL BE UNCLEAN FOR YOU. (Leviticus 11:37–8 JPS)

If water falls on seed the seed is receptive to pollution, but otherwise not. The rabbis extrapolated from this that foodstuffs in general could not become unclean unless pollution was enabled through wetting by any of seven specified liquids (Mishna 6:4; see Chapter Six (see p. 704)). From the passive – 'if it be put', rather than 'if it fell' – they inferred that the enabling liquid would have to be put on the foodstuff intentionally, or at least in conformity with human wishes. The opening debate between the Schools is followed, in 1:6 onwards, with detailed discussion by the Sages of Usha.

CHAPTER ONE

1. Any liquid that was at first welcome but later unwelcome or welcome later but unwelcome at first comes under [the heading of] 'if it be put'.

    Unclean liquids pollute whether welcome or not.

2. If someone shakes a tree to dislodge fruit or some unclean thing [and water falls off, the water] does not come under [the heading of] 'if it be put'. If his intention was to shake water [off the tree], the School of Shammai say that [both]

the water that comes out and [the water that remains in the tree] come under [the heading of] 'if it be put'; the School of Hillel say that what comes out is 'if it be put' but what remains is not 'if it be put', since he intended to shake out as much as possible.

6. If someone was blowing lentils to see if they were sound, Rabbi Simeon says, They are not 'if it be put', but the [majority of] Sages say, They are 'if it be put'.

If someone conceals his fruit under water to avoid thieves, it does not come under [the heading of] 'if it be put'[, since he does not really wish it to be wet]. The people of Jerusalem once concealed their figs under water because [they feared] robbers, and the Sages declared them clean.

If someone places his fruit in a stream to float it along with him, it does not come under [the heading of] 'if it be put'.

CHAPTER FOUR

1. If someone bends down to drink, the water that comes up on his mouth or his moustache is 'if it be put', but [that which comes up] in his nose or on his head or beard is not 'if it be put'.

If someone is filling up a jar [from a well], the water on the outside [of the jar] or on the cord holding it and the length of cord needed [to handle it] come under [the heading of] 'if it be put'. How much is needed to handle it? Rabbi Simeon ben Eleazar says, One palm-length. If he filled it from a pipe, [the excess water] is not 'if it be put'.

2. If rain fell on someone, even if he is unclean in the highest degree, the rainwater is not 'if it be put', but if he shakes it off it is 'if it be put'.

If someone stood under a [water-]pipe to cool down or to shower, if he was unclean the water is unclean, and if he was clean it is 'if it be put'.

CHAPTER FIVE

1. If someone bathes in a river and afterwards has to cross another river, the water of the second river [which he enters unwillingly] purifies [any water that remains on him from] the first. If a drunken friend pushed him or pushed an animal into [a second river], the water of the second river purifies [water remaining on him from] the first[, since he entered unwillingly]; however, if his friend pushed him playfully, the water is 'if it be put'.

2. If someone is swimming, what splashes [inadvertently] is not 'if it be put', but if he splashes someone intentionally, it is 'if it be put'.

   If someone blows water bubbles through a hose, neither what comes out nor what remains in the hose is 'if it be put'.

CHAPTER SIX

4. Seven liquids [enable impurity]: dew, water, wine, olive oil, blood, milk and bees' honey.

   Hornets' honey is clean, and may be eaten.

5. Subcategories of water: secretions of the eye, the ear, the nose and the mouth; urine of adults or children.

   Subcategories of blood: blood of *sheḥita*, whether of domestic or wild animals or clean birds; blood extracted for drinking.

   Whey is equivalent to milk.

   Rabbi Simeon says, The dark liquid that exudes from olives after the oil has been extracted is equivalent to olive oil; Rabbi Meir says, [This is so] even if no oil is mixed with it.

   The blood of a swarming creature is unique – like its flesh, it pollutes, but [nevertheless] it does not enable.

NINTH TRACTATE
ZAVIM (DISCHARGES)

If a man has a normal seminal discharge he, and the woman with whom he has had intercourse, must bathe and are unclean until evening (Leviticus 15:16–18). If he suffers an involuntary discharge (spermatorrhoea) without an erection, he enters the category of zav. *One episode means that he must bathe and is unclean until evening; two episodes mean that he pollutes by lying on a bed or sitting on a seat, so he must count seven clean days and then bathe, but is exempt from sacrifice; three episodes (not necessarily three separate days) make him a full* zav, *necessitating a count of seven clean days following which he must bathe and bring a bird sacrifice (15:13–15). Contact or sexual intercourse during any of these periods conveys pollution to varying degrees.*

If a woman has a normal monthly period, she bathes for purification at the end of seven days from the onset (15:19).[1] If she bleeds outside the normal period, she becomes a zava; *if she bleeds one day or two, she 'watches a day for a day' – she bathes and is unclean until evening. If she bleeds for three consecutive days outside the normal period she is a full* zava *and remains so until seven 'clean' days have passed and she has bathed, after which she brings a bird sacrifice (15:28–30). Contact or sexual intercourse during any of these periods conveys pollution to varying degrees.*

The tractate is almost entirely concerned with the male zav *and the ways in which he and the* zava *convey impurity through seat and bed.*

---

1. This was extended by custom, subsequently endorsed by the rabbis, to seven days
    after the cessation of bleeding, to avoid confusion with the *zava*.

CHAPTER ONE

1. If a man has one episode[2] of flux, the School of Shammai say, He is like a woman who watches a day for a day, but the School of Hillel say, He is a *ba'al qeri*.[3]

   If he had one episode, missed a day, and on the third day had two episodes or one episode as long as two, the School of Shammai say, He is a full *zav*, but the School of Hillel say, He defiles through bed and seat and requires immersion in 'living waters', but is exempt from sacrifice.

   Rabbi Eliezer ben Judah says, The School of Shammai agree that such a man is not a full *zav*; the disagreement was about someone who had two episodes or one episode as long as two, missed a day, and on the third day had one – the School of Shammai say, He is a full *zav*, but the School of Hillel say, He defiles through bed and seat and requires immersion in 'living waters', but is exempt from sacrifice.

2. If he is counting seven clean days [following two episodes] and on the third day has a further episode, the School of Shammai say, This cancels out the previous two days[, and he must restart the count of seven]; the School of Hillel say, It cancels out only that day.

   Rabbi Ishmael says, If he has an episode on the second day [of counting], it cancels the previous day. Rabbi Aqiva says, Whether the episode occurred on the second or third day, the School of Shammai say, It cancels the previous days and the School of Hillel say, It cancels only that day. They agree, though, that if it occurred on the fourth day, it cancels that day only.

   All this is only if the episode was *qeri*,[4] but if it was a proper flux, even if it occurred on the seventh day, it cancels the whole previous count.

---

2.   Literally, 'seeing', that is, an involuntary emission of semen.
3.   Literally, 'one who has had an accident', and refers to someone who had a normal seminal emission; the School of Hillel slightly reduce the degree of impurity (*Nidda* 72a–b).
4.   A normal seminal emission.

3. If he had one episode one day and two the next, or two one day and one the next, three in three days or three nights, he is a full *zav*.

A man can only become a zav *if the emission was entirely inadvertent and not attributable to some extrinsic cause such as diet, movement or sexual stimulation.*

CHAPTER TWO

2. Before anyone is confirmed as a full *zav* he is examined in seven ways: food, drink, carrying, jumping, sickness, appearance and thought – whether he thought before seeing or saw before thinking; Rabbi Judah says, Even if he saw animals or birds copulating or saw a woman's brightly coloured clothes.

Rabbi Aqiva said, Whatever he ate, whether good or bad, or whatever he drank [may be regarded as an extrinsic cause]. [The Sages said to him,] If so, no one would ever be a *zav*. He replied, We are not responsible for [ensuring that there are] *zavim*!

Once he is confirmed as a full *zav* no further questions are asked; an accident, a doubt or any seminal emission are unclean, since a likelihood has been established.[5] He is questioned after the first episode and after the second but not after the third. Rabbi Eliezer says, He is questioned after the third, too, since it could render him liable to sacrifice.

Leviticus rules that if a zav *or* zava *lay on a bed or sat on a seat, impurity is conveyed through the bed or seat to anyone who subsequently lies or sits on them. This was generalized by the Sages to include anything on which the* zav *or* zava *exerted pressure, and is known as* tum'at midras, *'pressure impurity'. All sorts of intriguing possibilities arise, of which the following are samples (some of the translations are conjectural).*

5.   Literally, 'the matter has legs'.

CHAPTER THREE

1. If a *zav* and a clean person sat in a boat or on a raft or rode an animal [together], pressure impurity is conveyed even though their garments do not touch one another. If they sat on a plank or a bench, on the platform on which the bed rested or on the beam of a loom if these were not firmly fixed, or if they climbed up a weak tree, on to the weak branch of a sound tree,[6] or up an Egyptian ladder that was not firmly nailed, or on a ramp or a joist or a door that was not mortared in place, they are unclean. Rabbi Judah says, They are clean.

3. If a *zav* and a clean person sat in a large boat – Rabbi Judah says, A large boat is one that cannot be moved by one man – or on a firm plank, bench, bed platform or loom crossbeam, or if they climbed up a strong tree or on to a firm branch or up a Tyrian ladder[7] or a firmly nailed Egyptian ladder, or a ramp, joist or door that was mortared in place even at one end, [the clean one remains] clean.

   If the unclean one struck the clean one, the clean one becomes unclean [by pressure],[8] since if he moved away the unclean one would fall.

Impurity can be conveyed by pressure without touch or by touch alone; it may also be conveyed by moving or carrying. A person polluted in this way may convey the impurity further, though in most cases (the exception being liquids which may convey a higher degree of pollution to hands) the recipient has a lower degree of impurity.

6. Bertinora, *Commentary*, reading *sokha*, 'branch', rather than *sukka*, 'hut'.
7. Apparently ladders made in Tyre were more secure than those made in Egypt.
8. The word translated 'struck' could also mean 'leaned on'. The victim is in any case unclean through touch, but pressure impurity is of a higher degree.

CHAPTER FIVE

1. If someone touches the *zav* or the *zav* touches him, or if he moves the *zav* or the *zav* moves him, he defiles food, drink and rinsable vessels by touch, but not by carrying.

   Rabbi Joshua formulated a rule: Whatever defiles garments by touch defiles food and liquids, conferring on them the first degree [of impurity], while the hands attain second degree; however, it does not defile people or earthenware. Once [the defiled items] have lost contact with the source of impurity, they defile liquids to the first degree, and food and hands to the second degree, but do not defile garments.

2. [Rabbi Joshua] formulated another rule: Whatever is carried on the back of a *zav* is unclean, but what the *zav* is carried on is clean, except for bed, seat and people.

   How is this?[9] If the *zav*'s finger is under a pile of stones and a clean person is on top, he defiles two [degrees] and disqualifies [the third]; when they separate, [the erstwhile clean person] defiles one and disqualifies one.

   If food, liquid, bed, seat or *maddaf*[10] is on top, he defiles two [degrees] and disqualifies [the third]; when they separate, [the erstwhile clean objects] defile one and disqualify one, but bed and seat below defile two and disqualify one, and when they separate, they [still] defile two and disqualify one. However, if food, liquid, bed, seat or *maddaf* is below, they remain clean, since they said that anything which carries or is carried on a bed is clean except for people, and anything which carries or is carried on top of a carcass is clean other than a person who moves it (Rabbi Eliezer said, Only if he carries it). Anything that carries or is carried on top of a corpse is clean unless it is under [the same] roof, and apart from the people who move it.

9. A later comment, perhaps from Usha, rather than the continuation by Rabbi Joshua.
10. Traditional commentaries take this to refer to any object other than a seat or bed, but the precise meaning of *maddaf* is uncertain; see Neusner, *History of . . . Purities*, pp. 63–71.

TENTH TRACTATE
T'VUL YOM (IMMERSED THAT DAY)

HE SHALL BATHE IN WATER AND REMAIN UNCLEAN UNTIL EVENING (Leviticus 15:5 and elsewhere). *This tractate defines the degree of impurity of the* t'vul yom – *one who has bathed that day, but on whom the sun has not yet set. His precise status is said to have divided Pharisees and Sadducees, the former taking a more lenient view and goading the Sadducees by deliberately arranging that the priest who prepared the red heifer should be* t'vul yom.[1] *The opening Mishna places the discussion firmly in the period of the Schools.*

It is assumed that t'vul yom *disqualifies teruma by contact.*

CHAPTER ONE

1. The School of Shammai say, If [a *Kohen*] is gathering pieces of *ḥalla*-dough intending to keep them separate, but they stuck to one another and he is *t'vul yom*, they would be [considered] connected;[2] the School of Hillel say, This is not [considered] a connection.

    Pieces of dough stuck to one another, loaves stuck to one another, buns in an oven lying on top of one another when the dough has not begun to form a crust, bubbles on boiling

---

1. Mishna *Parah* 3:7 (see p. 683).
2. So that if he touched one the uncleanness would be conveyed to all.

water, the first foam on boiling bean gruel, the froth on new wine (Rabbi Judah adds: On boiling rice) – the School of Shammai say, [All these] are connections with respect to *t'vul yom*, but the School of Hillel say, They are not connections.

[The Schools are, however,] in agreement [that all these are connections] for other people who are unclean, whether [they are unclean] to a major or minor degree.

CHAPTER TWO

1. Fluids that emanate from a *t'vul yom*, or any [fluids] that he touches, are clean. But for other people who are unclean, whether [they are unclean] to a major or minor degree, fluids that come out of them are like those they touch; they are of the first degree of impurity except for those that are fathers of impurity.

2. If a pot is full of liquid and a *t'vul yom* touches [the liquid], if the liquid is *teruma*, it is disqualified but the pot remains clean; if the liquid is unconsecrated, it is all clean, whereas someone with unclean hands[3] would render it all unclean. In this respect hands are stricter than *t'vul yom*; but *t'vul yom* is stricter than hands in that in cases of doubt, *t'vul yom* disqualifies *teruma* whereas hands do not.

CHAPTER THREE

2. A woman who is *t'vul yom* may knead dough, cut off a portion for the priest, set it aside and place it in her Egyptian basket or other receptacle [that is not subject to impurity], put it next to the [rest of the] dough and declare that it

3.   Not a *t'vul yom*.

is *ḥalla*, for [*t'vul yom* is only of] the third degree of uncleanness and for unconsecrated food this is regarded as clean.[4]

---

4.   The process ensures that she does not touch the consecrated part – the *ḥalla* – once it has been declared such.

ELEVENTH TRACTATE
YADAYIM (HANDS)

Still today, prior to any meal containing bread, Orthodox Jews formally wash hands by pouring water from a container over each hand in turn, a practice rooted in the purification of the priests prior to divine service.

CHAPTER ONE

1. A quarter-*log* [of water is sufficient] to pour on the hands of one or two [people]; a half-*log* [suffices] for three or four; and a whole *log* for five, ten or a hundred; Rabbi Yosé says, The last one should receive not less than a quarter-*log*.

You may add to the second [rinse] but not to the first.[1]

Among the items that the Sages decided would defile hands were sacred scrolls; this is, paradoxically, a way of confirming that a book is authentic Scripture. The traditional explanation is that the Sages wished to ensure that sacred scrolls were not stored with sacred food such as teruma, *since mice attracted by the food would damage the scrolls; literature they did not approve of might be chewed up by mice! The notion that the holier something is the more it is liable to defilement is articulated in 4:6.*

1. Water is poured twice over each hand and should reach the wrist; for the first rinse this must be done in one action, but as the purpose of the second rinse is only to wash away the first waters which would otherwise pollute, it does not matter if it is not done in one action.

From 3:5 it appears that the canonical status of Song of Songs and Ecclesiastes was still being called into question late in the second century.

CHAPTER THREE

4. Scroll margins, top, bottom, beginning and end, defile the hands. Rabbi Judah says, The margin at the end does not defile unless it is attached to a bar.
5. If a scroll has been erased and 85 letters remain, equivalent to Numbers 10:35–6,[2] it defiles the hands.

A [detached] sheet of parchment containing 85 letters, equivalent to Numbers 10:35–6, defiles the hands.

All sacred Scriptures defile the hands.

The Song of Songs and Ecclesiastes defile the hands. Rabbi Judah says, Song defiles the hands but Ecclesiastes is debated; Rabbi Yosé says, Ecclesiastes defiles the hands but Song is debated. Rabbi Simeon [ben Yoḥai] said, The School of Hillel was stricter than the School of Shammai with regard to Ecclesiastes.

Rabbi Simeon ben Azzai said, I have a tradition through the seventy-two elders that on the day they appointed Rabbi Eleazar ben Azaria president of the assembly,[3] [they decided] that Song and Ecclesiastes defile the hands.

Rabbi Aqiva said, Heaven forbid! No one ever questioned whether Song of Songs defiles the hands. The world was incomplete until the day the Song was revealed to Israel, for all the books are holy, but the Song is the holiest. If they questioned anything, it was Ecclesiastes.

Rabbi Yoḥanan the son of Rabbi Aqiva's father-in-law's son Joshua said, They debated as Ben Azzai reported, and that is how they decided.

2. These two verses are set off in the Torah scroll by a reversed letter *nun* at either end, a Hebrew adaptation of the *antisigma* used by Greek copyists to indicate a displaced section.
3. *Berakhot* 27b–28a (see pp. 18–22).

Having mentioned 'the day they appointed Rabbi Eleazar ben Azaria president of the assembly', the Mishna lists several major decisions allegedly taken 'on that day'.[4] None is historically more significant than that of Rabbi Joshua, who 'at a stroke' dispensed with the Torah's discriminatory legislation against Ammonites, Moabites and by implication other ethnic groups.

That an Ammonite or Moabite might convert to Judaism was accepted by Gamaliel as well as Joshua. Judah had already converted; by 'May I enter the congregation?' he meant 'May I marry a native Israelite woman?'[5]

CHAPTER FOUR

4. On that day Judah the Ammonite proselyte arrived and stood before them in the Assembly. He asked, May I enter the congregation? Rabban Gamaliel said to him, You are forbidden; Rabbi Joshua said, You are permitted.

Rabban Gamaliel said to [Rabbi Joshua], Scripture says, NO AMMONITE OR MOABITE SHALL ENTER THE LORD'S CONGREGATION; NOT EVEN THE TENTH GENERATION (Deuteronomy 23:4).

Rabbi Joshua replied: But are Ammonites and Moabites still in their place? Sennacherib the king of Assyria arose and jumbled the nations, as it is said, I HAVE REMOVED THE BOUNDARIES OF NATIONS AND DESPOILED THEIR TREASURES, AND AS A MIGHTY MAN I HAVE CAST DOWN THEIR INHABITANTS (Isaiah 10:13).

Gamaliel responded, But Scripture says, AFTER THAT, I SHALL RETURN AMMON FROM CAPTIVITY (Jeremiah 49:6), and they have returned!

Joshua: Scripture says, I SHALL RETURN MY PEOPLE

---

4. M. Kahana, 'Mishnaic Controversy', focusing on 4:3 together with *Eduyot* 6:2–3 and *Keritot* 3:7–10, has observed that the lengthy argumentation here 'reflects the transition from the basing of the *halakhot* on ancient traditions to increasing reliance upon logical deduction' (p. vi of the English abstract).

5. Modern biblical scholars understand Deuteronomy 23:4 as banning Ammonites and Moabites from membership of the national council; the notion of conversion is an anachronism.

ISRAEL FROM CAPTIVITY (Amos 9:14), but they have not yet returned!

They permitted [Judah] to 'enter the congregation'.

The Mishna reverts to the question of scrolls that defile the hands.

6. Sadducees say: We criticize you, Pharisees, for you say that sacred scrolls defile the hands, but scrolls of Homer do not defile the hands!

Is that all you have to criticize of the Pharisees? asked Rabban Yoḥanan ben Zaccai. [Pharisees] also say that donkeys' bones are clean, yet the bones of Yoḥanan the High Priest are unclean![6]

[The Sadducees] replied, Uncleanness is in proportion to how much they are loved [by God]; this is so that a man should not fashion the bones of his father and mother into spoons.

[Yoḥanan] replied: Here likewise, sacred scrolls are unclean because they are so greatly loved [by God]; scrolls of Homer are not so loved, therefore they do not defile the hands.

6.   The Zoroastrian *Vendidad* (5:28, 35) states that the most polluting of all corpses is that of a priest, whereas that of a wicked man pollutes 'no more than a frog does whose venom is dried up, and that has been dead more than a year'.

TWELFTH TRACTATE
'UQTZIN (STALKS)

'Oqetz, a stalk or sting, here stands for any inedible attachment of a fruit or vegetable. Are such attachments counted towards the size required for uncleanness, and do they convey pollution to or from the edible part?

CHAPTER ONE

1. Whatever is a handle rather than a protection becomes unclean, makes unclean but is not counted together [with that to which it is attached].[1] Whatever protects but is not a handle becomes unclean, makes unclean and is counted together [with that to which it is attached]. What neither protects nor [functions as] a handle neither becomes unclean nor makes unclean.

4. Shells and peels become unclean, make unclean and are counted together [with that to which they are attached].

   Rabbi Judah says, An onion has three [kinds of] peel. The innermost, whether whole or pierced, is counted together [with the onion]; the middle one is counted if whole but not if pierced; the outermost, whether whole or pierced, is clean.

5. If someone slices [a vegetable] to cook it, even if he has not cut right through, [the slices are] not [regarded as] joined

---

1. It conveys pollution to and from the fruit but is not added to the quantity of fruit to make up the measurement for receptiveness to pollution.

together, but if he intended to pickle or preserve it or to set
it on the table [as it is], it is [regarded as] joined together.
If he had started separating the pieces, only those actually
separated are [regarded as] not joined.

If someone strung together walnuts or onions, they are
[regarded as] joined. As soon as he has started to unstring
walnuts or onions, they cease being [regarded as] joined.

[The shells of] walnuts and almonds are [regarded as]
joined [to the nut] until they are cracked open.

*The final chapter of the Mishna is an appendix of cases not
easily classified; the last of these is a selection of laws relating
to the beehive. The Mishna concludes with a reflection on the
value of peace.*

CHAPTER THREE

10. The beehive – Rabbi Eliezer says: It is [classified as] immov-
    able property, it may be used to underwrite a *prosbul*,[2] it
    cannot become unclean [so long as it remains] in position
    and if anyone removes the honeycomb from it on the Sab-
    bath, he must bring a sin-offering.

    The Sages say, It is not immovable property, it may not
    be used to underwrite a *prosbul*, it may become unclean in
    position, and if anyone removes the honeycomb from it on
    the Sabbath, he is exempt from [the obligation to] bring a
    sin-offering.

11. At what stage does the honeycomb become receptive to
    pollution as a liquid? The School of Shammai say, When
    the bees are smoked out of the hive; the School of Hillel
    say, When [the honeycombs] are crushed.

12. Rabbi Joshua ben Levi says, The Holy One, blessed be He,
    will reward every righteous person with 310 worlds, as it is
    said, I WILL GIVE *YESH*[3] AS AN INHERITANCE TO THOSE

2. Mishna *Shevi'it* 10:3 (see p. 66).
3. *Yesh* means 'substance'; the numerical value of the word is 310.

THAT LOVE ME, AND I WILL FILL THEIR STOREHOUSES (Proverbs 8:21).

Rabbi Simeon ben Ḥalafta said, The Holy One, blessed be He, could find no vehicle of blessing for Israel greater than peace, as it is said, THE LORD GIVES STRENGTH TO HIS PEOPLE; THE LORD BLESSES HIS PEOPLE WITH PEACE (Psalm 29:11).

Timeline

BCE

333 Alexander conquers Judaea, then under Persian rule, and proceeds to conquer Persia (Iran).

c. **300 or 200** Simeon the Just. End of period of 'Men of the Great Synod'.

c. **165** Judas Maccabeus defeats the Seleucids and establishes Judaean independence.

63 Pompey annexes Judaea to Rome.

20 Peace treaty between Rome (Augustus) and Parthia (Phraates IV).

19 Herod commences reconstruction of the Temple.

CE

c. **1 First Generation of Tannaim**: Hillel and Shammai.

6 Augustus established Roman province of Judaea, incorporating Samaria and Idumea.

8 Ovid's *Metamorphoses*.

23 Strabo's *Geography*.

c. **30** Gamaliel I. Jesus's ministry. Aulus Celsus writes *De medicina*.

c. **38–100** Josephus Flavius.

40 Philo leads Alexandrian Jewish delegation to Caligula.

66 First Jewish Revolt against Rome begins in Judaea.

68–9 Death of Nero. Year of the Four Emperors. Vespasian becomes Emperor.

70 Revolt quelled by Titus. Destruction of the Temple.

70s Yoḥanan ben Zakkai sets up school at Yavné. Colosseum built in Rome.

c. **75** Pliny's *Natural History*.

c. **75–110 Second Generation of Tannaim**: Gamaliel II, Joshua ben

Hanania, Eliezer ben Hyrcanus. Gamaliel II defines Jewish prayer forms.

c. 77 Dioscorides begins work on *De materia medica*.

79 Josephus completes *Wars of the Jews*. Eruption of Vesuvius destroys Pompeii.

c. 110–35 **Third Generation of Tannaim**: Aqiva, Tarfon, Ishmael, Eleazar ben Azaria.

113 Trajan commences Parthian wars.

117 Revolt of the Diaspora quelled under Trajan. He dies and is succeeded by Hadrian, who relinquishes eastern conquests.

c. 120 Jewish canon of Scripture finalized. Emergence of Gnosticism. Rebuilding of Pantheon in Rome.

c. 127 Ptolemy's *Geography*.

c. 130 Ptolemy's *Almagest*, setting out geocentric cosmology.

130 Hadrian cleared rubble from Temple site, erected a Temple to Jupiter and renamed Jerusalem Aelia Capitolina, sparking off the Second Revolt.

131 Bar Kokhba Revolt and brief Judaean independence from Rome.

135 Revolt quelled by Hadrian. Jews expelled from Jerusalem.

c. 135–70 Renewal at Usha (Galilee). **Fourth Generation of Tannaim**: Meir, Judah bar Ilai, Simeon ben Gamaliel II, Simeon bar Yohai, Yosé ben Halafta.

c. 150 New Testament canon defined (Christian).

c. 160 Galen of Pergamum commences synthesis of Greek medicine and physiology.

161 Silk-merchant travellers sent by Marcus Aurelius Antoninus reach Han China.

c. 170–220 **Fifth Generation of Tannaim**: Judah ha-Nasi, Nathan ha-Bavli, Symmachus. Completion of Mishna. Huna I, the first recorded Babylonian Exilarch.

195 Septimius Severus establishes Roman province of Mesopotamia, lost to Ardashir I in 226.

212 *Constitutio Antoniniana* ('Edict of Caracalla') confers Roman citizenship on all free men in the Empire.

c. 216–77 Mani Hiyya, founder of Manichaeism.

c. 219 Rav returns to Babylonia and implements Mishna at Sura; Shmuel does likewise at Nehardea. **First Generation of Palestinian Amoraim**: Hanina, Joshua ben Levi.

224 The last Parthian king, Ardavan V, is defeated by Ardashir, who founds the Sasanian dynasty in Iran/Iraq.

241–72 Reign of Shapur I.

250–90 **Second Generation of Amoraim:** *Palestine*: Yoḥanan, Resh Laqish; *Babylonia*: Rav Huna, Rav Yehuda bar Ezekiel.

256 Conquest of Dura (on the Euphrates) by Sasanians.

259 or 263 Sack of Nehardea by Palmyrenes.

260 Shapur defeats and captures the Roman Emperor Valerian. Neoplatonist philosopher Plotinus develops concept of the Great Chain of Being.

290–320 **Third Generation of Amoraim:** *Palestine*: Abbahu, Ammi, Assi; *Babylonia*: Ḥisda, Rabbah bar Huna, Rabba bar Naḥmani, Yosef, Sheshet, Kahana.

297–8 Treaty of Nisibis between Diocletian and Narseh, ceding lands west of the Tigris to Rome.

306–73 Efrem (Syriac Church father).

309–73 Reign of Shapur II.

313 Constantine issues Edict of Milan, granting Christians and others equal authority to observe their preferred religion.

320–50 **Fourth Generation of Amoraim:** *Palestine*: Yonah, Yosé, Jeremiah; *Babylonia*: Abbaye, Rava.

324 Constantine I founds Constantinople as the new Rome.

325 Council of Nicaea (Christians define dogma).

350–75 **Fifth Generation of Amoraim:** *Palestine*: Mani; *Babylonia*: Rav Papa, Rav Zevid, Rav Naḥman bar Isaac.

352 Jewish Revolt against Romans in Palestine brutally crushed by Gallus.

363 Roman Emperor Julian encourages the Jews to rebuild the Temple and offer sacrifices, but is killed in battle. Shapur II concludes peace with Jovian, having regained lost territories.

375–427 **Sixth Generation of Amoraim:** *Babylonia*: Ravina I, Rav Ashi.

395 Rome formally splits into a Western Empire, ruled from Rome, and an Eastern Empire, ruled from Constantinople.

410 Sack of Rome by Alaric the Visigoth.

427–60 **Seventh Generation of Amoraim:** *Babylonia*: Mar bar Rav Ashi (Tavyomi), Geviha of Bei Q'til. Possible editorial activities on Talmud by Stammaim.

438 Publication of *Codex Theodosianus* (Roman Law).

c. 450 'Completion' of Jerusalem Talmud.

c. 450 Compilation of the *Avesta* (Zoroastrian).

451 Council of Chalcedon (Christian).

460–500 **Eighth Generation of Amoraim:** *Babylonia*: Ravina II, Yosé.

c. 484 Mazdak promotes his sect in Iran; its adoption then rejection by

Kavadh II leads to disturbances and possibly persecution of Jews and other minorities.

496 Statutes for School of Nisibis (Christian).

c. **500** Beginning of activity of Sevoraim. *The Book of a Thousand Judgements* (Sasanian Law).

c. **507–11** *Lex Salica* produced under Clovis, King of the Franks.

529–65 *Corpus Juris Civilis* (Roman law code compiled under Justinian I).

532 Peace treaty between Justinian and Khosrow I; renegotiated in 542.

c. **600** 'Completion' of Babylonian Talmud.

614–29 Jerusalem held by Sasanians.

622 Hijrah (flight of Muhammad).

c. **635–6** Arab victories over Sasanians and Byzantines.

642 Sasanian Empire becomes part of Caliphate.

Glossary

Where two forms are given, the first is singular, the second plural; where a third is given, it is an adjective. Alternative spellings are bracketed.

For coins, weights and other measures see Appendix III – Coins, Weights and Measures.

aggada Homily, narrative

'am ha-aretz Common or ignorant person, as opposed to *ḥaver*; see introductory note to *Demai*

Amida 'standing': name of daily prayer

Amora, Amoraim, Amoraic *Strict sense*: lecturer; *broad sense*: sage of the period following the Tannaim

Ashkenazic Relating to Jews of northern and western Europe; see also Sephardic

bar mitzva Boy who has reached age of majority (13)

baraita, baraitot Tannaitic material not incorporated in the Mishna

basilica Palace; large public building

berera Choice; retrospective determination

bet din Court

bet ha-p'ras Field in which a grave has been ploughed

bitter waters Given to a suspected adulteress in Temple times (Numbers 5:23–8)

courses [of priests] Priestly families who took turns to serve in the Temple (1 Chronicles 24ff.)

d'Oraita [Law] instituted by the written Torah

d'rabbanan [Law] instituted by the rabbis

eruv mixture: a group of legal devices for establishing Sabbath boundaries

Essene Ascetic Jewish sect from first century BCE

Exilarch See Resh Galuta

Gaon, Geonim 'Illustrious': title of Head of Academy of Sura or Pumbedita in Islamic times

Gehinnom Hell

get, gittin Bill of divorce

ḥadash Produce of the new season prior to the *omer*

haggada Narration of the Exodus; see also *aggada*

halakha Law; ruling

halakha l'Moshe mi-Sinai Law [received by] Moses at Sinai, but not written in the Torah

ḥalal Man rejected from priestly status

ḥalitza Shoe-loosening ceremony by which a widow is released from the brother of her deceased husband (Deuteronomy 25:5–10)

ḥametz Leaven

ḥanukiya Eight-branched candelabrum used in the celebration of the festival of Ḥanuka. Also called *menora*.

ḥasid, ḥgasidim, ḥasidic 'Pious', 'loving': name given to several ancient and modern sects

havdala Prayer recited at end of Sabbath or festival

ḥaver Member of fellowship group; see introductory note to *Demai*

hefqer Ownerless

ḥerem Ban, excommunication; see introductory note to *Keritot*

karet 'Cut off [from the people]' – a punishment mentioned in Exodus and Leviticus; (see introductory note to *Keritot*)

kasher (*kosher*) All right, especially of food or personal status

kavana Intention; devotion in prayer

kil'ayim Forbidden mixtures of crops

k'lal A collective term; see also *p'rat*

Kohen, Kohanim (*Cohen, Cohanim*) Priest, priests: descendants of Aaron the High Priest.

levir Brother-in-law (Latin)

levirate marriage Marriage to a brother of the deceased husband; see *ḥalitza*)

levitical Pertaining to the tribe of Levi

lulav Palm branch

ma'aser Tithe

Magus, Magi, Magian Zoroastrian priest

Manichaean Strongly dualistic sect, combining Zoroastrian, Jewish and Christian ideas, founded by the third-century prophet Mani

matza Unleavened bread

Mazdean Zoroastrian (from Ahura Mazda, God of Wisdom)

menora see *ḥanukkiya*

Messiah 'Anointed': a Davidic monarch who will preside over a world of peace and spirituality

mezuza Parchment with text of Deuteronomy 6:4–9 and 11:13–21, placed in a receptacle and affixed to doorpost

mid'Oraita See *d'Oraita*

mid'rabbanan See *d'rabbanan*

midrash Interpretation

minyan Number, quorum for prayer

miqvé Immersion pool

mitzva, mitzvot Strict sense: Torah commandment; *broad sense* good deed

mohel Circumciser

muqtzé [mi-da'at] 'Cut off [from the mind]': items it is forbidden to move on a Sabbath or festival

nasi Prince, president

omer Sheaf of barley reaped and offered on second day of Passover

onen Person who has a close relative awaiting burial

Pentateuch The Five Books of Moses (Genesis, Exodus, Leviticus, Numbers, Deuteronomy)

pilgrim festivals Pesach, Shavuot and Sukkot, on which pilgrims would visit Jerusalem

p'rat A specific (as opposed to general) term; see also *k'lal*

qiddush The prayer of blessing for the Sabbath or festival day, recited over a cup of wine

qinyan Formal act of confirmation of a transaction

qonam An expression indicating a vow

Resh Galuta Exilarch: political head of Babylonian Jewish community

Sephardic Relating to Jews whose ancestors lived in the Iberian peninsula; incorrectly applied generally to non-Ashkenazic Jews

shamir Mythical insect said to cut stones

shevarim Sobbing sounds on trumpet or *shofar*

sh'ma'ta Discussion of *halakhic* topic

Shulḥan Arukh Code of law by Joseph Caro (1488–1575)

sudar Garment, possibly a kind of turban, indicating rank

sugya Topic; pericope

sukka Hut, or tabernacle

swarming creatures Forbidden reptiles listed in Leviticus 11:29–30

Syria North and north-east of Palestine, including parts of modern Lebanon and Syria

tahor Pure

talmid ḥakham 'Disciple of the sages': man of learning

tamé Impure

Tanna, Tannaim, Tannaitic *Strict sense*: repeater, *broad sense*: Sage of the period of the Mishna

Targum Aramaic translation of the Bible

tefilla Prayer, especially the *amida*

tefillin Leather boxes strapped on forehead and left arm, containing Exodus 13:1–10 and 11–16; Deuteronomy 6:4–9 and 11:13–21

teqi'a Long note sounded on trumpet or *shofar*

terefa 'Torn' – opposite of *kasher*

teru'a Short, sobbing sounds on trumpet or *shofar*

teruma Priests'-due

teshuva Penitence

Tosafot 'Additions' to Rashi's commentary

t'vul yom Person who has undergone purification and awaits nightfall for it to take effect

tzitzit Fringes on the corners of a garment

usucapio Acquisition by continuous possession (Roman law)

World to Come Life after death. Heaven

yeshiva, *yeshivot* College for study of Torah

yibbum Procedure whereby a man marries his deceased brother's widow

Appendix I
The Jewish Calendar

In the Talmudic period, years were counted according to the Seleucid era for documentary purposes, in accordance with common Near Eastern practice, or from the destruction of the Second Temple. The now general Jewish practice of counting from the supposed date of creation became the norm in the late Middle Ages (see p. 514 n. 36).

The length of years is determined by the seasons; months follow the moon's phases. Since a solar year is approximately 11 days longer than 12 lunar months, it is necessary every so often to compensate for this by intercalating a month, so that some years have 13 months.

The Sages held that, ideally, each month should be proclaimed by the Jerusalem Court, who alone were privileged to fix the calendar. By the end of the Talmudic period, a calculated calendar was in operation, in line with the 19-year cycle calculated by Meton of Athens in the fifth century BCE; 12 of those years had 12 lunar months each, the other 7 had 13.

Here is a list of the months, with those festivals and fast days recognized by the Talmud. Since the dates fluctuate with respect to the civil calendar by almost a month, an arbitrary year (2020–21, corresponding to the Creation Year 5781) has been chosen for comparison.

Date	*Occasion*	*Civil date in 2020–21*
Tishrei		
1–2	New Year	19–20 September
3	Fast of Gedaliah	21 September
10	Day of Atonement	28 September
15	Sukkot, First day	3 October
22	Shemini Atzeret	10 October
Ḥeshvan		
Kislev		
25	First of 8 days of Ḥanuka	11 December

Date	*Occasion*	*Civil date in 2020–21*
Tevet		
10	Fast of 10th Tevet	25 December
Shevat		
15	New Year for Trees	28 January 2021
Adar		
13	Fast of Esther	25 February
14	Purim	26 February
Nisan		
15	Pesach (Passover), First day	28 March
21	Pesach, Final day	3 April
Iyar		
Sivan		
6	Shavuot (Pentecost)	17 May
Tammuz		
17	Fast of 17th Tammuz	27 June
Av		
9	Fast of 9th Ab	18 July
Elul		

The New Moon was marked, but was no longer a festive occasion as it had been in biblical times (cf. 1 Samuel 20:18; 2 Kings 4:23).

In a leap year Purim and its associated occasions are celebrated in Second Adar; 14 Adar I is then Purim Qatan ('minor Purim'). Dates of Purim (see *Megilla* 2a; see p. 262) and some fasts may vary slightly so as not to conflict with the Sabbath.

In the Diaspora, including Babylonia, the following festival days were doubled: first and last days of Pesach, Shavuot, first day of Sukkot, Shemini Atzeret.

Appendix II
Tithes and Sabbatical Years

Numbers (18:8–13, 19–32) and Deuteronomy (14:22–9, 18:1–8, 26:12–15) contain several collections of laws setting out provision for the maintenance of priests (*Kohanim*), Levites and needy persons. Bible scholars see evidence of different, occasionally inconsistent, sources behind this legislation. The Priestly Code of Numbers assigns the tithe to the whole tribe of Levi, including the priests, 'as their share in return for the services that they perform, the services of the Tent of Meeting' (Numbers 18:21 JPS); Deuteronomy views the tithes differently, as a sort of communion, a feast to be eaten in purity in Jerusalem and shared with the Levites, but every third year to be distributed to the local poor.

The Sages did not admit any inconsistency in the Torah; instead, they interpreted the texts in such as way as to create a coherent and consistent system, which they expounded in the Mishna and associated works. The evolution of the system may be seen in the pseudepigraphic Book of Jubilees, the *Temple Scroll* in the Dead Sea Scrolls and other pre-rabbinic writings. David Henshke has demonstrated continuity between the Scrolls and the rabbinic tradition on tithes; the *Temple Scroll* maintains that the tithes were originally (as Leviticus 27:30–31) 'for God', and only subsequently awarded by Him to the Levites (Numbers 18:21–4), and there are traces of this interpretation in the rabbinic tradition, for instance in the debate as to whether the tithes are 'the property of [the One] on high' or 'the property of ordinary [mortals]'.[1]

Tithes were primarily the responsibility of the farmer; others would tithe only if not certain that the farmer had already done so.

Maimonides writes:

Terumot and *Ma'aserot* apply biblically only in the Land of Israel, whether the Temple is standing or not. The prophets ordained that they should be given in the Land of Shinar [Babylonia] too, since it is near the Land of Israel and Israelites travel frequently between the two. The early Sages ordained that [tithes] should be given even in Egypt and in the lands of Ammon and Moab, since they adjoin the Land of Israel.[2]

As understood by the rabbis the offerings comprised:

1. *Teruma* (priests'-due, heave offering). One-sixtieth of the produce was set aside for the priests. This food possessed sacred status, and anyone who was not a *Kohen* or one of his dependants was strictly forbidden to consume it; both the food and those who ate it had to be in a state of purity. (Deuteronomy 18:4)
2. *Ma'aser Rishon* (first tithe). A tenth of the produce was set aside for Levites. This did not have sacred status, but was merely property of the Levites; anyone might eat it subject to the owner's permission. (Numbers 18:21–4)
3. *Terumat Ma'aser* (levitical tithe). The Levite set aside as *teruma* for the *Kohen* one-tenth of his *ma'aser rishon*; this had the same sacred status as the *teruma* set aside by the Israelite. (Numbers 18:25–32)
4. *Ma'aser Sheni* (second tithe). A tenth of the remaining produce was to be taken to Jerusalem, or exchanged for money to be taken to Jerusalem, and consumed there joyfully, sharing it with the poor and needy. (Deuteronomy 14:22–7)
5. *Ma'aser 'Ani* (tithe for the poor). In certain years, in place of the second tithe, a tenth was set aside specifically for the poor. (Deuteronomy 14:28–9 and 26:12)

Offerings varied according to the years of the sabbatical seven-year cycle:

Years 1, 2, 4, 5: *Teruma, Ma'aser Rishon, Terumat Ma'aser, Ma'aser Sheni*.

Years 3, 6: *Teruma, Ma'aser Rishon, Terumat Ma'aser, Ma'aser 'Ani*.

Year 7 (the sabbatical year): No offerings were made, since the land lay fallow and any produce that grew was ownerless (*hefqer*); whoever needed it could help themselves.

In addition to these regular offerings, several gifts related to special situations:

6. *Bikkurim* (first-fruits). Presented at the Temple at the appropriate season. (Deuteronomy 26:1–11)
7. *Ḥalla* (dough). Part of the dough from each batch of bread was set aside by the baker or housewife for the priests. (Numbers 15:17–21)
8. 'The shoulder, the cheeks and the stomach' are set aside by the butcher for the priests. (Deuteronomy 18:3)

9. The first shearings are given to the priests. (Deuteronomy 18:4)
10. First-born animals are offered at the altar, then eaten by the priests. (Numbers 18:15)

The poor benefited from annual gleanings of the harvest (see tractate *Pe'ah*), and from financial and other provisions as appropriate.

Much of this system had become obsolete by the time rabbinic Judaism developed, if indeed it was ever fully operational;[3] the socio-economic structure of Palestine had changed since biblical times, the population of the country had become ethnically and religiously diverse, and the educational functions that were previously the prerogative of the tribe of Levi had been taken over by scribes. Aharon Oppenheimer maintains that the Hasmonean kings, who were themselves *Kohanim*, levied tithes as tax,[4] and the Talmud confirms that tithes in the late Hellenistic period were handed to priests rather than Levites.[5]

Malachi prophesied, 'BRING THE FULL TITHE INTO THE STORE-HOUSE, AND LET THERE BE FOOD IN MY HOUSE, AND THUS PUT ME TO THE TEST – SAID THE LORD OF HOSTS. I WILL SURELY OPEN THE FLOODGATES OF THE SKY FOR YOU AND POUR DOWN BLESSINGS ON YOU' (Malachi 3:10 JPS). By the early first century CE many religious leaders were dismayed at what they regarded as a decline in the spiritual standards of the Temple and a consequent decline in the fortunes of Israel. Some founded groups like those of the Judaean desert who shunned the 'degenerate' Temple, pending its purification under a Messiah figure.[6] Others took the words of Malachi to heart and concluded that the sufferings of Israel were due to neglect of the laws of tithing and of ritual purity; to improve matters they set up fellowship groups devoted to observance of these laws, as well as to Torah observance generally. Many of the Sages of the Mishna were members of such groups (see the introductory note to *Demai*).

NOTES

1. *Qiddushin* 24a. Henshke, 'Exegesis'.
2. Maimonides, *Mishné Torah: Terumot 1:1*.
3. Parts were certainly operational: Nehemiah 10:35–9 attests to the arrangements; archaeologists have unearthed jars with indications that they were reserved for sacred gifts; and there is ample literary evidence from the late Second Temple period. Sources include Apocryphal works (Judith 11:13; Tobit 1:6–7; I Maccabees 3:49–50), Philo (*Special Laws* 1:132–55) and Josephus (*Life* 12:62, 53, 80;

Antiquities 14:10:6; 20:8:8; 20:9:2). A lease signed by Bar Kokhba (*c.* 130) has been discovered in which tenants undertake to pay dues to the landlord after deduction of tithes (Benoît, *Grottes de Murabba'at*, pp. 124–5).

4. Oppenheimer, *'Am ha-aretz*, p. 34. On pp. 41–2 he discusses the question of whether tithes were at this time given only to *Kohanim* or also to Levites.

5. The Talmud (*Yevamot* 86a/b and parallels), elaborating Mishna *Sota* 9:10 and *Ma'aser Sheni* 5:15, attributes the change to Ezra, and its confirmation to Yoḥanan the High Priest (John Hyrcanus, *c.* 175–104 BCE).

6. A similar attitude lies behind the Gospel accounts of Jesus's 'purification' of the Temple (Mark 11 and parallels).

Appendix III
Coins, Weights and Measures

Coins and Weights

The biblical *gera*, *sheqel* and *maneh* are weights of silver or gold (the verb *ShQL* means 'to weigh'), and correspond with the ancient Babylonian *giru*, *sheqel* and *mina*; in the Babylonian sexagesimal system, 60 *giru* = 1 *sheqel* and 60 *sheqel* = 1 *mina*. The Phoenician *sheqel* differed slightly from the Babylonian, and both came in heavy and light varieties. The *sheqel* has been estimated as 8.4 grams.

Specifically Jewish coins were struck only in periods of Jewish independence or revolt;[1] the Talmud assumes that Jews use the general currency.

The three denominations most often mentioned in the Mishna are the Roman *assarius* or *as* (Mishna *issar*), the *denarius* (*dinar* or *zuz*) and the *dupondius* (*pundion*); the silver *ma'a* is probably equivalent to the *sestertius*, originally a small silver coin worth $2\frac{1}{2}$ *assarii*, but by Mishna times a large brass coin worth 4 *assarii*. *Dupondius* and *sestertius* were brass, *denarius* silver, *aureus* gold; the smaller denominations were copper.

Roman coinage was frequently debased, distorting relative values, which also fluctuated with changes in the cost of metals. Major reforms were instituted by Aurelius (270–75) and Diocletian (294–6).

The Bavli sometimes uses Persian terms, for instance *danak* (from Greek *drachma*), equivalent to a *denarius*.[2]

Hebrew / Aramaic name(s)	Latin equivalent(s)	*Perutot*
peruta		1
issar	as, assarius	8
pundion	dupondius	16
(silver) ma'a	sestertius	32
istira, tarp'iq[3] *(tropaikos)*		96
silver dinar, zuz	denarius	192[4]

Hebrew / Aramaic name(s)	Latin equivalent(s)	*Perutot*
silver sheqel		384
silver sela, Torah sheqel		768
gold dinar	aureus	4,800
silver maneh		19,200

Linear Measurement

Unit	Equivalent	Fingerbreadths
fingerbreadth[5]		1
palm	4 × fingerbreadth	4
span	3 × palm	12
cubit	6 × palm	24
ris	$266\frac{2}{3}$ cubit	6,400
mile	2,000 × cubit	48,000
parasang	4 × mile	192,000

Traditional Jewish authorities variously estimate the cubit for religious purposes as 44 or 57.6 cm.[6] Modern estimates of Roman measurements are: *digitus* 18.5 mm; *uncia* (inch, i.e. one-twelfth of a foot) 24.6 mm; *pes* (foot) 296 mm; *cubitus* 44.4 cm; *mille (passuum)* (mile) 1.48 km. Talmudic fingerbreadth and cubit correspond to Roman *uncia* and *cubitus*, but the Talmudic 'mile' is only three-fifths of the Roman.

Land Area

1 *bet kur* (the area required to sow a *kur* of grain) = 30 *bet seah*, or 75,000 square cubits

1 *bet seah* = 24 *bet rovaʿ* (the area required to sow a quarter-*kab* of grain)

Volume

Unit	Equivalent	Egg-sizes
egg-size		1
quarter-*log*	1.5 × egg	1.5
log	6 × egg	6
kab	4 × *log*	24
omer, issaron	43.2 × egg	43.2
seah	144 × egg	144
efah, bat	10 × *issaron*	432
kur, ḥomer	10 × *efah*	4,320

An *issaron* (one-tenth of an *efah*) of flour weighed approximately 1 kilogram; it relates to the daily 'tenth of an ephah' of manna received by the Israelites in the desert (Exodus 16:17, 36).

Olive, fig, date, barleycorn and lentil are used for measurements smaller than an egg-size, but their precise relationships are disputed.

NOTES

1. For details and illustrations, see Banesh, *Middot*, Reifenberg, *Jewish Coins*, and Meshorer, *Jewish Coins*.
2. *Bava Metzi'a* 60b (see Chapter Five).
3. This equivalence is given in *Ketubot* 64a.
4. This is not invariable; *Qiddushin* 2a implies that a *dinar* is 144 *perutot*.
5. Generally identified as the width of the thumb joint (Banesh, *Middot*, pp. 76–92).
6. Banesh, *Middot*, pp. 68–75, summarizes the arguments of Eliyahu Ḥayyim Naeh for the former and Abraham Isaiah Karlitz (*Ḥazon Ish*) for the latter.

Appendix IV
Books of the Bible

In printed Hebrew Bibles the books are arranged in three sections as below, the order differing slightly from that given in *Bava Batra* 12b.

Torah

Genesis
Exodus
Leviticus
Numbers
Deuteronomy

Neviim (Prophets)

Former Prophets

Joshua
Judges
1 and 2 Samuel
1 and 2 Kings

Latter Prophets

Isaiah
Jeremiah
Ezekiel
The Twelve: Hosea, Joel, Amos,
    Obadiah, Jonah, Micah, Nahum,
    Habakkuk, Zephaniah, Haggai,
    Zechariah, Malachi

Ketuvim (Writings, hagiographa)

Psalms
Proverbs
Job
The Five Scrolls: Song (of Songs), Ruth,
   Lamentations, Ecclesiastes, Esther
Daniel
Ezra
Nehemiah
1 and 2 Chronicles

Appendix V

Tractates of the Mishna in Alphabetical Order

Appendix VI
Hebrew Names and Transliteration

The Hebrew Alphabet

The Hebrew alphabet consists of 22 consonants. There is no distinction between upper case and lower case, but five letters take different forms if they occur at the end of a word. The Masoretes who edited the Hebrew text of the Bible in the early Middle Ages devised vowel signs and diacritic points. Some early Mishna and liturgical manuscripts have them, but generally they are omitted from Hebrew texts other than the Bible and prayer books.

The English consonants are only approximate equivalents of the Hebrew. The dagesh is a diacritic dot inserted in vocalized text (i.e. text with vowels) to distinguish between two forms of a consonant.

Consonant	Name	Common transliteration(s)
א	*alef*	(silent letter) ', or omitted
ב	*bet* (without dagesh)	v, b, bh
בּ	*bet* (with dagesh)	b
ג	*gimmel*	g
ד	*dalet*	d
ה	*hé*	h (often omitted at end of word)
ו	*vav*	v, w
ז	*zayin*	z
ח	*ḥet*	ḥ, h, ch
ט	*tet*	t
י	*yod*	y, j
כ, ך	*kaf* (without dagesh)	k, kh, ch
כּ, ךּ	*kaf* (with dagesh)	k, c
ל	*lamed*	l
מ, ם	*mem*	m
נ, ן	*nun*	n
ס	*samekh*	s

ע	'ayin	(a guttural not pronounced in western dialects) ', g, gh, or omitted
פ, ף	pé (without dagesh)	f, ph
פּ	pé (with dagesh)	p
צ, ץ	tsadé	ts, tz, ṣ, ẓ
ק	qof	k, c, q
ר	resh	r
שׁ	shin (right dot)	sh, š
שׂ	sin (left dot)	s
ת	tav (without dagesh)	t, th, s
תּ	tav (with dagesh)	t

The only symbols used in this volume that are not standard English are 'ḥ' (ḥet) and the opening quotation mark for 'ayin, since they are needed to avoid confusion between similar words; however, 'ayin is mostly omitted.

Final 'h' is optional in many words; for instance, 'Mishna' is used instead of the common spelling 'Mishnah'.

In general, vowels are transliterated in accordance with current Israeli pronunciation (hence, kasher rather than kosher). For the most part this is straightforward, but both Hebrew and Aramaic use semi-vowels, and these may be represented in different ways. For instance, the opening 'b' in the word 'baraita' is followed by a semi-vowel, pronounced something like the the first 'a' in 'pajama'; the word may also be spelled 'b'raita' or 'boraita' or 'beraita'.

The Spelling of Hebrew and other Foreign Names

Many Hebrew names have conventional English spellings that do not coincide with the general guidelines for transliteration. Samuel, for instance, is the conventional English rendering of Hebrew Sh'muel; Isaac is the conventional English rendering of Hebrew Yitzḥaq. Here are examples of variation in the spelling of personal names:

        Aqiva, Aqiba, Akiva
        Isaac, Yitzchok
        Jacob, Yaakov, Ya'aqob
        Jerusalem, Yerushalayim
        Johanan, Joḥanan, John, Yoḥanan
        Jose, José, Yosé

Joseph, Yosef
Judah, Yehuda
Salomone, Shlomo, Solomon, Schelomo, Salomon
Samuel, Shmuel, Samwil
Simon, Simeon, Shimon
Yishmael, Ishmael, Ismael, Isma'il

There are additional sources of confusion in rendering the names of people and places:

1. Since there are no vowels, the pronunciation may be unknown.
2. Where a name is of foreign origin, we cannot be sure how Aramaic speakers might have pronounced it. For instance, the name of a well-known second-century Sage is usually pronounced 'Tarfon'; as only the consonants TRFWN appear, the name was probably the Greek 'Tryphon'.
3. Place names cannot always be identified. Even when a place can be identified, a copyist may have muddled the name; most Hebrew copyists write 'Emmaum' rather than 'Emmaus', since they misread the 's' as a final 'm', which looks similar. Sometimes a place has different names in different languages or different periods; e.g. Bet Guvrin became known in Greek as Eleutheropolis.
4. Middle Persian (Pahlavi) names and terms are mostly simplified. For instance, 'Shapur' is used in preference to 'Šābuhr'.

Bibliography

PRIMARY TEXTS

The commonly used text of the Babylonian Talmud is the magnificent edition completed by the Widow and Brothers Romm in Vilnius, Lithuania, in 1886, and frequently reprinted, sometimes with enhancements. The *Mekhon ha-Talmud ha-Yisraeli* (Israel Talmud Foundation) has been engaged since 1971 in producing a definitive modern edition with a full critical apparatus; several volumes have appeared, but the project awaits completion.

Most of the important manuscripts are accessible online through the Hebrew University, Jerusalem, at http://jnul.huji.ac.il/dl/talmud/

English Translations

Several complete English translations of the Babylonia version are in print:

The Soncino Talmud, ed. I. Epstein, 18 vols. (London: Soncino, 1935–48). It is also available on CD and online.

The Artscroll edition: *Bavli. The Gemara: The classic Vilna edition with an annotated interpretive elucidation under the general editorship of Hersh Goldwurm, Schottenstein student edition* (New York: Mesorah Publications, 1996–).

Neusner, J., *The Talmud of Babylonia. An Academic Commentary*, rev. edn (Atlanta: Scholars Press, 1994–6, 1999).

A currently incomplete series is:
The Talmud: With Translation and Commentary by Adin Steinsaltz (New York: Random House: 1989–).

There are in addition numerous single-volume selections and introductions as well as extensive online resources.

Dictionaries and Reference

Every translator is indebted to the prodigious researches of generations of lexicographers, not least those of the Geonic and medieval periods, much of whose work is summed up in the *Arukh* of Rabbi Nathan ben Yehiel of Rome (*c.* 1035–1110).

In modern times, Jacob Levy (1819–92), working in Breslau, East Prussia (now Wrocław, Poland), pioneered Talmudic lexicography, and was quickly followed by the Hungarian scholar Alexander Kohut (1842–94).

Marcus Jastrow's *Dictionary of Talmud Babli, Yerushalmi, Midrashic Literature and Targumim*, 2 vols. (1903) remains deservedly popular.

Michael Sokoloff draws on a further century of research and scholarship in *A Dictionary of Jewish Palestinian Aramaic of the Byzantine Period* (Ramat Gan, Israel: Bar-Ilan University Press, 1990); *A Dictionary of Jewish Babylonian Aramaic of the Talmudic and Geonic Periods* (Baltimore and London: Johns Hopkins University Press, with Ramat Gan, Israel; Bar-Ilan University Press, 2002); and *A Dictionary of Judean Aramaic* (Ramat Gan, Israel: Bar-Ilan University Press, 2003).

Greek and Latin legal terms are covered in Daniel Sperber, *A Dictionary of Greek and Latin Legal Terms in Rabbinic Literature* (Ramat Gan, Israel: Bar-Ilan University Press, 1984).

A new dictionary of the Aramaic language, to be called *The Comprehensive Aramaic Lexicon*, is currently in preparation by an international team of scholars including Sokoloff.

Yitzhak Frank's *The Practical Talmud Dictionary*, 2nd edn (Jerusalem: Ariel, 1994) is helpful for the correct understanding of Talmudic idioms.

For biblical Hebrew, the standard work is still *A Hebrew and English Lexicon of the Old Testament*, ed. Francis Brown, S. R. Driver and Charles A. Briggs (Oxford: Clarendon Press, 1907); my references are to the 1976 reprint. More recent and up-to-date, embodying the latest research is Ludwig Koehler and Walter Baumgartner, *The Hebrew and Aramaic Lexicon of the Old Testament*, 5 vols. (Leiden: E. J. Brill, 1994–2000).

The Cambridge Companion to the Talmud and Rabbinic Literature, ed. C. E. Fonrobert and Martin S. Jaffee (Cambridge: Cambridge University Press, 2007), is another helpful reference work.

SECONDARY WORKS

Comprehensive bibliographies may be found in the specialized works. Books and studies actually cited or used in preparation of this volume are listed here.

Some publishers give the Jewish year of publication, e.g. 5760, which is 3760 years ahead of the commonly used reckoning. As the year runs from September/October rather than January, it overlaps with two civil years, so that 5760 was 1999/2000.

Adan-Bayewitz, David, 'The Tannaitic List of "Walled Cities" and the Archaeological-Historical Evidence from Iotapata and Gamala', *Tarbiz* 66:4 (July–September 1997) pp. 449–70 (Hebrew).

Albeck, Hanokh, *Mavo la-Mishna* (Jerusalem: Mosad Bialik, 1959) (Hebrew).

—, *Mavo ha-Talmud* (Tel Aviv: Dvir, 1969 (Hebrew).

Amit, Aaron, 'The Death of Rabbi Aqiva's Disciples: A Literary History', *Journal of Jewish Studies* 56:2 (Autumn 2005), pp. 265–84.

Artemidorus, *The Interpretation of Dreams (Oneirocriticon)*, tr. and commentary by Robert J. White (Park Ridge, NJ: Noyes Press, 1975).

Aumann, Robert J., and Michael Maschler, 'Game Theoretic Analysis of a Bankruptcy Problem from the Talmud', *Journal of Economic Theory* 36 (1985), pp. 195–213.

Avery-Peck, Alan J., *Mishnah's Division of Agriculture: A History and Theology of Seder Zeraim* (Chico, CA: Scholars Press, 1985).

Avot de Rabbi Nathan: synoptische Edition beider Versionen, ed. Hans-Jürgen Becker and Christoph Berner (Tübingen: Mohr Siebeck, 2006).

Banesh, Chaim P., *Middot v'Shiurei Torah*, 2nd edn (Bnei Braq, Israel: n. p., 5747 (1986/7)) (Hebrew).

Beer, Moshe, 'Notes on Three Edicts against the Jews of Babylonia in the Third Century C.E.', in *Irano-Judaica*, ed. Shaul Shaked (Jerusalem: Ben-Zvi Institute, 1982), pp. 25–37 (Hebrew).

Belayche, Nicole, *Iudaea-Palaestina: The Pagan Cults in Roman Palestine (Second to Fourth Century)* (Tübingen: Mohr Siebeck, 2001).

Benoît, P. et al., *Les Grottes de Murabba'at* (Oxford: Clarendon Press, 1961).

Benson, R. L., and G. Constable (eds), *Renaissance and Renewal* (Cambridge: Harvard University Press, 1982).

Ben Zeev, Miriam Pucci, *Diaspora Judaism in Turmoil: 116/117 CE: Ancient Sources and Modern Insights* (Leuven: Peeters, 2005).

Bokser, Baruch M., *Post Mishnaic Judaism in Transition: Samuel on Berakhot and the Beginnings of Gemara* (Chico, CA: Scholars Press, 1980).

—, 'An Annotated Bibliographical Guide to the Study of the Palestinian Talmud', in *The Study of Ancient Judaism II: The Palestinian and Babylonian Talmuds*, ed. Jacob Neusner (New York: Ktav, 1981), pp. 187–94.

Boyarin, Daniel, *Intertextuality and the Reading of Midrash* (Bloomington and Indianapolis: Indiana University Press, 1990).

Boyce, Mary, *A History of Zoroastrianism: Volume One, The Early Period* (Leiden: E. J. Brill, 1975).

Breuer, Yochanan, 'Rabbi is greater than Rav, Rabban is greater than Rabbi, the simple name is greater than Rabban', *Tarbiz* 66:1 (October–December 1996), pp. 41–60 (Hebrew).

Brock, Sebastian P., *Syriac Perspectives on Late Antiquity* (London: Variorum Reprints, 1984).

—, *The Heirs of the Ancient Aramaic Heritage*, Vol. 2: *The Hidden Pearl: The Syrian Orthodox Church and its Ancient Aramaic Heritage*, ed. Sebastian P. Brock with David G. K. Taylor (Rome: Trans World Film Italia, 2001).

Brody, Robert (Yerahmiel), 'Sources for the Chronology of the Talmudic Period', *Tarbiz* 70:1 (October–December 2000), pp. 75–107 (Hebrew).

Burkert, Walter, *Greek Religion: Archaic and Classical*, tr. John Raffan (Oxford: Basil Blackwell, 1985).

Carmi, T. (ed. and tr.), *The Penguin Book of Hebrew Verse* (New York: Penguin Books, 1981).

Chajes, Z. H., *The Student's Guide Through the Talmud*, tr. Jacob Shachter (London: East and West Library, 1952).

Charles, T. H. (tr.), *Apocrypha and Pseudepigrapha of the Old Testament* (Oxford: Oxford University Press, 1913).

Chepey, Stuart, *Nazirites in Late Second Temple Judaism* (Leiden: E. J. Brill, 2005).

Chernick, Michael (ed.), *Essential Papers on the Talmud* (New York and London: New York University Press, 1994).

Christensen, Arthur, *L'Iran sous les Sassanides* (1936; Copenhagen: Levin & Munksgaard, 1944).

Cohen, Gerson, *The Book of Tradition of Abraham ibn Daud* (London: Routledge & Kegan Paul, 1967).

Cohen, Shaye J. D., 'The Place of the Rabbi in Jewish Society', in *The Galilee in Late Antiquity*, ed. Leo I. Levine (New York: Jewish Theological Society of America, 1992), pp. 157–73.

Cohn, Haim H., *The Trial and Death of Jesus* (London: Weidenfeld and Nicolson, 1972).

Cotton, H. M., and A. Yardeni, *Aramaic, Hebrew and Greek Documentary Texts from Naḥal Ḥever and Other Sites*. Documents from the Judean Desert (*DJD*) XXVII, 1997.

Dahan, Gilbert, Gérard Nahon and Elie Nicolas (eds), *Rashi et la culture juive en France du Nord au moyen âge* (Paris-Louvain: Peeters, 1997).

Dan, Joseph, *The Ancient Jewish Mysticism*, tr. Shmuel Himelstein (Tel Aviv: MOD Books, 1989).

de Lange, Nicholas, *Origen and the Jews* (Cambridge: Cambridge University Press, 1976).

Diamond, Eliezer, *Holy Men and Hunger Artists: Fasting and Asceticism in Rabbinic Culture* (Oxford: Oxford University Press, 2003).

Dunn, J. D. G., *The Parting of the Ways: Between Judaism and Christianity and Their Significance for the Character of Christianity* (London: SCM Press and Trinity International, 1991).

Epstein, Jacob N., *Mavo l'nusaḥ ha-Mishna*, 2nd edn, 2 vols. (Jerusalem: Magnes Press, 1964) (Hebrew).

Erhart, Victoria, 'The Development of Syriac Christian Canon Law in the Sasanian Empire', in *Law, Society, and Authority in Late Antiquity*, ed. Ralph W. Mathisen (Oxford: Oxford University Press, 2001), pp. 115–29.

Eshel, Ben-Zion, *Yishuvei ha-Yehudim b'Bavel bi-T'qufat ha-Talmud* (Jerusalem: Hebrew University, 1979) (Hebrew).

Eshel, Esther, and Amos Kloner, 'An Aramaic Ostracon of an Edomite Marriage Contract from Maresha, Dated 176 B. C. E.' *Israel Exploration Journal* 46 (1996), pp. 1–22.

Feinstein, M., *Igrot Moshe*, Vol. 3: *Even ha-Ezer* I (New York: Balshan Press, 5734 (1974)) (Hebrew).

Feldman, David, *Marital Relations, Birth Control and Abortion in Jewish Law* (New York: Schocken Books, 1974).

Feldman, W. M., *Rabbinical Mathematics and Astronomy* (1931; New York: Hermon Press, n.d.).

Feliks, Yehuda, *Talmud Yerushalmi Masekhet Shevi'it* (Jerusalem: Tzur-Ot, 5740 (1979)) (Hebrew).

—, *Ha-Tsomeaḥ veha-hai ba-Mishnah* (Jerusalem: Makhon l'Heqer ha-Mishna, 5743 (1982)) (Hebrew).

—, *Mishnah Shevi'it* (Jerusalem: Reuben Mass, 5747 (1987)) (Hebrew).

Finkelstein, Menachem, *Conversion: Halakhah and Practice* (Ramat Aviv: Bar-Ilan University, 2006).

Fraenkel, Jonah, *Rashi's Methodology in his Exegesis of the Babylonian Talmud* (Jerusalem: Hebrew University, 1980) (Hebrew).

Frankel, Zacharias, *Mavo la-Yerushalmi* (Breslau (Wrocław): 1870) (Hebrew).

Gafni, Isaiah, 'Ḥibburim Nistoriim k'maqor l'Toldot Yeshivot Bavel', *Tarbiz* 51 (1982), pp. 567–76 (Hebrew).

—, 'L'Ḥeqer ha-Kronologia ha-Talmudit b'Iggeret Rav Sherira Gaon', *Zion* 52 (1987), pp. 1–24 (Hebrew).

—, 'The Institution of Marriage in Rabbinic Times', in *The Jewish Family – Metaphor and Memory*, ed. D. Kraemer (Oxford: Oxford University Press, 1989), pp. 13–30.

—, *Yehudei Bavel bi-T'kufat ha-Talmud* (Jerusalem: Merkaz Zalman Shazar l'Toldot Israel, 5751 (1990)) (Hebrew).

—, 'The Political, Social, and Economic History of Babylonian Jewry, 224–638 CE', in *Cambridge History of Judaism*, Vol. 4, ed. Katz, pp. 792–820.

Galen, *On the Natural Faculties*, ed. A. J. Brock (Loeb edn, 1916).

Geiger, J., 'The Gallus Revolt, and the Projected Rebuilding of the Temple in the Time of Julianus', in *Eretz Israel from the Destruction of the Second Temple to the Muslim Conquest*, ed. Z. Baras, S. Safrai, M. Stern and Y. Tasfrir (Jerusalem: Yad Yitzchak Ben-Zvi, 1982), pp. 202–27 (Hebrew).

Ginzei Talmud Bavli, ed. Abraham Katsah (Jerusalem: Rubin Mass, 1979).

Goodblatt, David M., *Rabbinic Instruction in Sasanian Babylonia* (Leiden: E. J. Brill, 1975).

—, 'Bibliography' (on the Talmud of Babylonia), in *The Study of Ancient Judaism: The Palestinian and Babylonian Talmuds*, ed. J. Neusner (New York: Ktav, 1981).

—, 'The Jews in Babylonia, 66–c. 235 C.E.', in *Cambridge History of Judaism*, Vol. 4, ed. Katz, pp. 83–92.

Goodman, Martin, 'The Roman State and the Jewish Patriarchate', in *The Galilee in Late Antiquity*, ed. Leo I. Levine (New York: Jewish Theological Society of America, 1992).

—, *Mission and Conversion: Proselytizing in the Religious History of the Roman Empire* (Oxford: Clarendon Press, 1994).

—, *Rome and Jerusalem: The Clash of Ancient Civilizations* (London: Penguin Books, 2008).

Goshen-Gottstein, Alon, *The Sinner and the Amnesiac: The Rabbinic Invention of Elisha ben Abuya and Eleazar ben Arach* (Stanford: Stanford University Press, 2000).

Gyselen, Rika, *La Géographie administrative de l'Empire Sassanide:*

Les témoignages sigillographiques (Paris: Groupe pour l'Etude de la Civilisation du Moyen-Orient, 1989).

Habermann, A. M., *Ha-Madpisim bene Soncino* (Vienna: Buchhand-lung David Fränkel, 1933) (Hebrew).

—, *Ha-Madpiss Daniel Bomberg u-Reshimat Sifre Beth Defusso* (Safed, Israel: Museum of Printing, 1978) (Hebrew).

Halivni, David Weiss, *M'qorot uM'sorot (Sources and Traditions)* (Tel Aviv: Devir, 1968).

—, *Midrash, Mishnah and Gemara: The Jewish Predilection for Justi-fied Law* (Cambridge: Harvard University Press, 1986).

—, *Peshat & Derash: Plain and Applied Meaning in Rabbinic Exegesis* (New York and Oxford: Oxford University Press, 1991).

Hammer, R., 'What Did They Bless? A Study of Mishna Tamid 5.1', *Jewish Quarterly Review* 81 (1991), pp. 305–24.

Harries, Jill D., 'Resolving Disputes in Late Antiquity', in *Law, Society, and Authority in Late Antiquity*, ed. Ralph W. Mathisen (Oxford: Oxford University Press, 2001), pp. 68–82.

Harrington, H. K., *The Purity Texts*, Companion to the Qumran Scrolls 5 (London and New York: T. & T. Clark International, 2004).

Harris, Jay, *How Do We Know This?* (New York: SUNY Press, 1994).

Haskin, Charles Homer, *The Renaissance of the Twelfth Century* (Cam-bridge: Harvard University Press, 1927).

Hauptman, Judith, *Development of the Talmudic Sugya: Relationship Between Tannaitic and Amoraic Sources* (Lanham, MD: University Press of America, 1988).

—, *Rereading the Mishnah: A New Approach to Ancient Jewish Texts* (Tübingen: Mohr Siebeck, 2005).

Hecht, N. S., B. S. Jackson, S. M. Passamanek, et al. (eds), *An Introduc-tion to the History and Sources of Jewish Law* (Oxford: Clarendon Press, 1996).

Henshke, David, 'On the History of Exegesis of the Pericopes Covering Tithes: From the Temple Scroll to the Sages', *Tarbiz* 72 (October 2002–March 2003), pp. 85–112 (Hebrew).

Herr, Moshe David, 'Who were the Boethusians?', in *Proceedings of the Seventh World Congress of Jewish Studies: Studies in the Talmud. Halacha and Midrash* (Jerusalem, 1981), pp. 1–20.

Hippocrates, *De Octimestri Partu*, tr. Hermann Grensemann (Berlin: Akademie-Verlag, 1968).

Hoffman, David, *Mar Samuel – Rector der jüdischen Akademie zu Nehardea in Babylonien* (Leipzig: Oskar Leiner, 1873).

Horbury, William, *Jews and Christians in Contact and Controversy* (Edinburgh: T. & T. Clark, 1998).

Ibn Daud, *Sefer Ha-Qabbalah*, see Cohen, Gerson

Jacobs, Louis, *Structure and Form in the Babylonian Talmud* (Cambridge: Cambridge University Press, 1991).

—, *Rabbinic Thought in the Talmud* (London and Portland, OR: Vallentine Mitchell, 2005).

Jacobs, Martin, *Die Institution des jüdischen Patriarchen: Eine quellen- und traditionskritische Studie zur Geschichte der Juden in der Spätantike* (Tübingen: J. C. B. Mohr, 1995).

Jaffee, Martin, *Mishnah's Theology of Tithing: A Study of Tractate Maaserot* (Chico, CA: Scholars Press, 1981).

Jakobovits, I., *Jewish Medical Ethics* (New York: Bloch Publishing Company, 1959). There are later editions.

Jastrow, Marcus, *Dictionary of Talmud Babli, Yerushalmi, Midrashic Literature and Targumim*, 2 vols. (reprinted, New York: Pardes, 1950).

Jellinek, Adolf, *Elischa Ben Abuja gennant Acher* (Leipzig: A. M. Coldotz, 1847).

Josephus, Titus Flavius, *Antiquities of the Jews*, tr. H. St J. Thackeray, Vols. 5–12 (Loeb edn; Harvard: Harvard University Press, 1930–65).

—, *Wars of the Jews*, tr. G. A. Williamson, rev. Mary Smallwood (London: Penguin Classics, 1981).

Julian, *Against the Galileans*, ed. and tr. R. Joseph Hoffman (Amherst, NY: Prometheus Books, 2004).

Kahana, Kalman (ed.), *Seder Tannaim we Amoraim* (Frankfurt-am-Main: Hermon, 1935).

Kahana, Menahem, 'On the Fashioning and Aims of the Mishnaic Controversy', *Tarbiz* 73:1 (October–December 2003), pp. 51–82 (Hebrew).

Kalmin, Richard, *The Redaction of the Babylonian Talmud: Amoraic or Saboraic?* (Cincinnati: Hebrew Union College Press, 1989).

—, *Sages, Stories, Authors and Editors in Rabbinic Babylonia* (Atlanta: Scholars Press, 1994).

Kaplan, Julius, *The Redaction of the Babylonian Talmud* (New York: Bloch Publishing Company, 1933).

Katz, David S., *The Jews in the History of England: 1485–1850*, 2nd edn (Oxford: Clarendon Press, 1996).

Katz, Steven T. (ed.), *The Cambridge History of Judaism, Vol. 4: The Late Roman and Rabbinic Period* (Cambridge: Cambridge University Press, 2006).

—, 'The Rabbinic Response to Christianity', in *Cambridge History of Judaism, Vol. 4*, ed. Katz, pp. 259–98.

Klawans, Jonathan, 'The Impurity of Immorality in Ancient Judaism', *Journal of Jewish Studies* 48 (1997), pp. 1–16.

Kohut, Alexander, 'Les fêtes Persannes et Babyloniennes dans les Tal-muds de Babylon et de Jérusalem', *Revue des Études Juives* 24 (1965), pp. 256–71.

Kovelman, A. B., *Between Alexandria and Jerusalem: The Dynamic of Jewish and Hellenistic Culture* (Leiden: E. J. Brill, 2005).

Kraemer, David, *The Mind of the Talmud: An Intellectual History of the Bavli* (New York and Oxford: Oxford University Press, 1990).

—, *Reading the Rabbis: The Talmud as Literature* (New York: Oxford University Press, 1996).

—, 'The Mishnah', in *Cambridge History of Judaism, Vol. 4*, ed. Katz, pp. 299–315.

Krauss, Samuel, *A Handbook to the History of Christian–Jewish Controversy from the Earliest Times to 1789*, ed. William Horbury, (Tübingen: Mohr, 1996).

Kushelevsky, Rella, 'Hillel as the "Image of a man in the Skylight": A Hermeneutic Perspective', *Revue des Études Juives* 165 (2006), pp. 363–81.

Lamberton, Robert, and John J. Keaney (eds), *Homer's Ancient Readers: The Hermeneutics of Greek Epic's Earliest Exegetes* (Princeton: Princeton University Press, 1992).

Lapin, Hayim, *Early Rabbinic Civil Law and the Social History of Roman Galilee: A Study of Mishna Baba' Meṣi'a'* (Atlanta: Scholars Press, 1995).

Levinas, Emmanuel, *Nine Talmudic Readings*, tr. Annette Aronowicz (Bloomington: Indiana University Press, 1994).

Levine, I. I., 'The Status of the Patriarch in the Third and Fourth Centuries: Sources and Methodology', *Journal of Jewish Studies* 47 (1996), pp. 1–32.

Lewin, B. M., *Iggeret R. Scherira Gaon* (Haifa, 5681 / Berlin: n.p., 1921) (Hebrew).

Lieberman, Saul, *Greek in Jewish Palestine*, 2nd edn (1942; New York: Philipp Feldheim, 1965).

—, *Hellenism in Jewish Palestine* 2nd edn (1950; New York: Jewish Theological Seminary of America, 1962).

Limor, Ora, and Guy G. Stroumsa (eds), *Contra Iudaeos: Ancient and Medieval Polemics between Christians and Jews* (Tübingen: Mohr, 1996)

Linder, Amnon, *The Jews in the Legal Sources of the Early Middle Ages* (Detroit, MI: Wayne State University Press for Israel Academy of Sciences and Humanities, 1997).

Luzzatto, Moshe Chaim, *Mesilas Yesharim: Path of the Upright*, tr. and annotated by Aryeh Kaplan (Jerusalem: Feldheim Publishers, 1977)

Maimonides, Moses, *The Guide of the Perplexed*, tr. S. Pines (Chicago: University of Chicago Press, 1963).

Mandelbaum, Irving, *A History of the Mishnaic Law of Agriculture: Kilayim* (Chico, CA: Scholars Press, 1982).

Mantel, Hugo, *Studies in the History of the Sanhedrin* (Cambridge: Harvard University Press, 1961).

Marx, Tzvi C., *Disability in Jewish Law* (London: Routledge, 2002).

Meshorer, Yaakov, *Ancient Jewish Coins* (Dix Hills, NY: Amphora Books, 1982).

Millar, Fergus, *A Greek Roman Empire: Power and Belief under Theodosius II (408–450)*, (Berkeley: University of California Press, 2006), Chapter III:6, pp. 123-9.

—, 'Transformations of Judaism under Graeco-Roman Rule: Reponses to Seth Schwarz's "Imperialism and Jewish Society"', *Journal of Jewish Studies* 57:1 (Spring 2006), pp. 139-58.

Milson, David, *Art and Architecture of the Synagogue in Late Antique Palestine: In the Shadow of the Church* (Leiden: E. J. Brill, 2007)

Neusner, J., *Fellowship in Judaism: The First Century and Today* (London: Vallentine Mitchell, 1963).

—, *A History of the Jews in Babylonia*, 5 vols. (Leiden: E. J. Brill, 1965–70).

—, *The Rabbinic Traditions about the Pharisees before 70*, 3 vols. (Leiden: E. J. Brill, 1971).

—, *A History of the Mishnaic Law of Purities*, Vol. XXII (Leiden: E. J. Brill, 1977).

—, *Vanquished Nation, Broken Spirit: The Virtues of the Heart in Formative Judaism* (New York: Cambridge University Press, 1987).

—, *The Bavli That Might Have Been: The Tosefta's Theory of Mishnah Commentary Compared with the Bavli's* (Atlanta: Scholars Press, 1991).

—, *The Bavli's One Voice* (Atlanta: Scholars Press, 1991).

—, *Judaism in Society: The Evidence of the Yerushalmi*, 2nd edn (Atlanta: Scholars Press, 1991).

Newman, Louis, *The Sanctity of the Seventh Year: A Study of Mishnah Tractate Shebiit* (Chico, CA: Scholars Press, 1983).

Noam, Vered, 'Divorce in Qumran in Light of Early Halakhah', *Journal of Jewish Studies* 56:2 (Autumn 2005), pp. 206–23.

Novak, David, *The Image of the Non-Jew in Judaism: An Historical and Constructive Study of the Noahide Laws* (New York: Edwin Mellen Press, 1983).

Oppenheimer, Aharon, *The 'Am ha-aretz: A Study in the Social History of the Jewish People in the Hellenistic-Roman Period*, tr. I. H. Levine (Leiden: E. J. Brill, 1977).

—, *Babylonia Judaica in the Talmudic Period* (Wiesbaden: Dr Ludwig Reichert Verlag, 1983).

—, *Between Rome and Babylon: Studies in Jewish Leadership and Society* (Tübingen: Mohr Siebeck, 2005).

Parikhanian, Anahit, *The Book of a Thousand Judgements (A Sasanian Law-Book)*, tr. Nina Garsoïan (Costa Mesa, CA: Mazda Publishers in association with Bibliotheca Persica, 1997).

Parker, Robert, *Miasma: Pollution and Purification in Early Greek Religion* (Oxford: Clarendon Press, 1983).

Philo Judaeus (Philo of Alexandria), *On the Special Laws*, tr. F. H. Colson, Vols. 7–8 (Loeb edn; Harvard: Harvard University Press, 1937–9).

Porphyry of Tyre, 'Four Books on Abstinence from Animal Food', in *Select Works of Porphyry*, tr. Thomas Taylor (1823; reprinted Frome: Prometheus Trust, 1994), pp. 11–138.

Preuss, Julius, *Biblical and Talmudic Medicine* (1961), tr. and ed. Fred Rosner (New York: Sanhedrin Press, 1978).

Ravitsky, Aviezer, 'Prohibited Wars in the Jewish Tradition', in *The Ethics of War and Peace: Religious and Secular Perspectives*, ed. T. Nardin (Princeton: Princeton University Press, 1996), pp. 115–27.

Reed, Anna Yoshiko, and Adam H. Becker, *The Ways that Never Parted: Jews and Christians in Late Antiquity and the Early Middle Ages* (Tübingen: J. C. B. Mohr, 2003).

Reeg, G., *Die Ortsnamen Israels nach der rabbinischen Literatur* (Wiesbaden: Reichert, 1989). This is the documentation volume relating to *Tübinger Atlas des Vorderen Orients* B VI 16.

Reif, Stefan C., *Judaism and Hebrew Prayer: New Perspectives on Jewish Liturgical History* (Cambridge: Cambridge University Press, 1993).

Reifenberg, A., *Ancient Jewish Coins*, 5th edn. (Jerusalem: R. Mass, 1969).

Reiss, Rosemary E., and Avner D. Ash, 'The Eighth-month Fetus: Classical Sources for a Modern Superstition', in *Obstetrics & Gynecology* 71 (1988), pp. 270–73.

Rivkin, Ellis, *A Hidden Revolution: The Pharisees' Search for the Kingdom Within* (Nashville, TN: Abingdon, 1978).

Rosenblatt, Jason P., *Renaissance England's Chief Rabbi: John Selden* (Oxford: Oxford University Press, 2006).

Rouwhorst, G., 'Jewish Liturgical Traditions in Early Syriac Christianity', *Vigiliae Christianae* 51:1 (March 1997), pp. 72–93.

Ruether, R. R., *Faith and Fratricide: The Theological Roots of Anti-Semitism* (New York: Seabury Press, 1974).

Russell, James R., 'Sages and Scribes at the Courts of Ancient Iran', in *The Sage in Israel and the Ancient Near East*, ed. John G. Gammie and Leo J. Perdue (Winona Lake, IN: Eisenbrauns, 1990).

Sanders, E. P., *Jewish Law from Jesus to the Mishnah* (London: SCM Press, 1990).

Sarason, Richard S., *A History of the Mishnaic Law of Agriculture: A Study of Tractate Demai*, Part One (Leiden: E. J. Brill, 1979).

Satlow, Michael L., ' "One who loves his wife like himself": Love in Rabbinic Marriage', *Journal of Jewish Studies* 49 (1998), pp. 67–86.

—, 'Slipping Toward Sacrament', in *Jewish Culture and Society in the Christian Roman Empire*, ed. Richard Kalmin and Seth Schwartz (Leuven: Peeters, 2003), pp. 65–89.

Schäfer, Peter, *Hekhalot Studien* (Tübingen: J. C. B. Mohr, 1998).

—, (ed.), *The Bar Kochba War Reconsidered* (Tübingen: J. C. B. Mohr, 2003).

—, *Jesus in the Talmud* (Princeton: Princeton University Press, 2007).

—, and Klaus Hermann (ed.), *Übersetzung der Hekhalot-Literatur*, 4 vols (Tübingen: J. C. B. Mohr, 1991–5).

Schechter, Solomon, *Aspects of Rabbinic Theology*, with intro. by Louis Finkelstein (1909; New York: Schocken Books, 1961).

Schlüter, Margarete, *Auf welche Weise wurde die Mishna geschrieben?: das Antwortschreiben des Rav Sherira Gaon: mit einem Faksimile der Handschrift Berlin Qu. 685 (Or. 160) und des Erstdruckes Konstantinopel 1566* (Tübingen: Mohr, 1993).

Scholem, Gershom G., *Jewish Gnosticism, Merkabah Mysticism, and Talmudic Tradition* (New York: Jewish Theological Seminary of America, 1960).

Schwartz, J., *Lod (Lydda) Israel: From Its Origins through the Byzantine Period* (Oxford: Oxford University Press, 1991).

Schwartz, Seth, *Imperialism and Jewish Society, 200 B.C.E. to 640 C.E.* (Princeton: Princeton University Press, 2001).

Sendrey, Alfred, *Music in Ancient Israel* (London: Vision Press, 1969).

Shemesh, A., '4Q271.3: A Key to Sectarian Matrimonial Law', *Journal of Jewish Studies* 49 (1998), pp. 244–63.

Shereshevsky, Esra, *Rashi: The Man and His World* (New York: Sepher-Hermon Press, 1982).

Simon, Marcel, *Verus Israel: A Study of the Relations between Christians and Jews in the Roman Empire 135–425*, new edn (Oxford: Littman Library of Jewish Civilization, 1996).

Sinclair, Daniel B., *Tradition and the Biological Revolution: The Appli-*

cation of Jewish Law to the Treatment of the Critically Ill (Edinburgh: Edinburgh University Press, 1989).

Smolenskin, Peretz, *Am Olam*, *Hashachar* 3 (Vienna, 1872), pp. 643–50 (Hebrew).

Sokoloff, Michael, *A Dictionary of Jewish Babylonian Aramaic of the Talmudic and Geonic Periods* (Baltimore and London: Johns Hopkins University Press, with Ramat Gan, Israel: Bar-Ilan University Press, 2002).

Solomon, Norman, 'Extensive and Restrictive Interpretation of Terms in Rabbinic Hermeneutic', in *Jewish Law and Current Legal Problems*, ed. N. Rakover (Jerusalem: Library of Jewish Law 1984). Also *Jewish Law Association Studies*, Vol. I (1985),The Touro Conference Volume.

—, 'Concepts of *ze neheneh* in the Analytic School', in *Jewish Law and Legal Theory*, ed. Martin Golding, International Library of Essays in Law and Legal Theory (Aldershot.: Dartmouth Publishing Company, 1993).

—, 'The Ethics of War in Judaism', in *The Ethics of War in Asian Civilizations*, ed. Torkel Brekke (Oxford: Routledge, 2006), pp. 39–80; and 'The Ethics of War: Judaism', in *The Ethics of War: Shared Problems in Different Traditions*, ed. Richard Sorabji and David Rodin (Aldershot: Ashgate, 2006), pp. 108–37.

Soloveitchik, H., *Ḥiddushei Rabbenu Ḥayyim ha-Levi al ha-Rambam* (Bresc, 1936).

Sperber, Daniel, 'On the Fortunate Adventures of Rav Kahana: A Passage of Saboraic Polemic from Sasanian Persia', in *Irano-Judaica*, ed. Shaul Shaked (Jerusalem: Ben-Zvi Institute, 1982), pp. 83–100.

—, *A Dictionary of Greek and Latin Legal Terms in Rabbinic Literature* (Ramat Gan, Israel: Bar-Ilan University Press, 1984).

—, *Material Culture in Eretz-Yisrael in the Talmudic Period* (Jerusalem: Hebrew University, 1993) (Hebrew).

—, *Magic and Foklore in Rabbinic Literature* (Ramat Gan, Israel: Bar-Ilan University Press, 1994).

—, *The City in Roman Palestine* (Oxford: Oxford University Press, 1998).

Sprengling, Martin, *Third Century Iran, Sapor and Kartir* (Chicago: Oriental Institute, University of Chicago, 1953).

Stern, Sacha, 'The Second Day of Yom Tov in the Talmudic and Geonic Literature', in *Proceedings of the Eleventh World Congress of Jewish Studies*, Vol. CI (Jerusalem: World Union of Jewish Studies, 1994), pp. 49–55.

—, *Calendar and Community: A History of the Jewish Calendar*,

Second Century BCE–Tenth Century CE (Oxford: Oxford University Press, 2001).

Strack, H. L., and G. Stemberger, *Introduction to the Talmud and Midrash* (Edinburgh: T. & T. Clarke, 1991).

Swanson, Robert N., *The Twelfth-Century Renaissance* (Manchester: Manchester University Press, 1999).

Tafazzuli, Ahmad, *Sasanian Society* (New York: Bibliotheca Persica Press, 2000).

Taqizadeh, S. H., 'The Iranian Festivals Adopted by the Christians and Condemned by the Jews', *Bulletin of the School of Oriental and African Studies* 10 (1940–42), pp. 632–53.

Tov, Emanuel, *Textual Criticism of the Hebrew Bible* (Minneapolis, MN: Fortress Press, 1992).

Tübinger Atlas des Vorderen Orients B VI 16 *Israel nach der rabbinischen Literatur* (Wiesbaden: Reichert, 1984). Documentation in Reeg.

van den Broek, Roelof, and Wouter J. Hanegraff (eds), *Gnosis and Hermeticism from Antiquity to Modern Times* (New York: SUNY Press, 1998).

Vendidad. English translation by James Darmesteter, M. N. Dhalla, B. N. Dhabhar, L. Mills, et. al., on www.avesta.org/avesta.html.

Vermes, Geza, *Jesus the Jew* (London: Collins, 1973).

Weinberg, J. (tr.), *The Light of the Eyes by Azariah de' Rossi* (New Haven: Yale University Press, 2001). With an introduction and notes.

Weiss, Zeev, *The Sepphoris Synagogue: Deciphering an Ancient Message through Its Archaeological and Socio-Historical Contexts* (Jerusalem: Israel Exploration Society, 2005).

Wiesehöfer, Josef, *Ancient Persia: From 550 BC to 650 AD* (London: I. B. Tauris, 1996).

Wilken, Robert L., *John Chrysostom and the Jews: Rhetoric and Reality in the Late Fourth Century* (Berkeley: University of California Press, 1983).

Winter, Paul, *On the Trial of Jesus*, 2nd edn (Berlin: Walter de Gruyter, 1974).

Yadin, Y., et al. (eds), *The Documents from the Bar Kokhba Period in the Cave of Letters. Hebrew, Aramaic and Nabatean-Aramaic Papyri* (Jerusalem: Israel Exploration Society, 2002).

Yardeni, Ada, *A Textbook of Aramaic, Hebrew and Greek Documentary Texts from the Judean Desert*, I–II (Oxford: Clarendon Press, 1997).

—, *The Book of Hebrew Script: History, Palaeography, Script Styles, Calligraphy & Design* (New Castle, DE: Oak Knoll Press, 2002).

Yarshater, Ehsan, *The Cambridge History of Iran*, Vol. 3, Parts 1 and 2 (Cambridge: Cambridge University Press, 1983).

Maps

MAP 1: *Palestine of the Mishna*, c. 200 CE

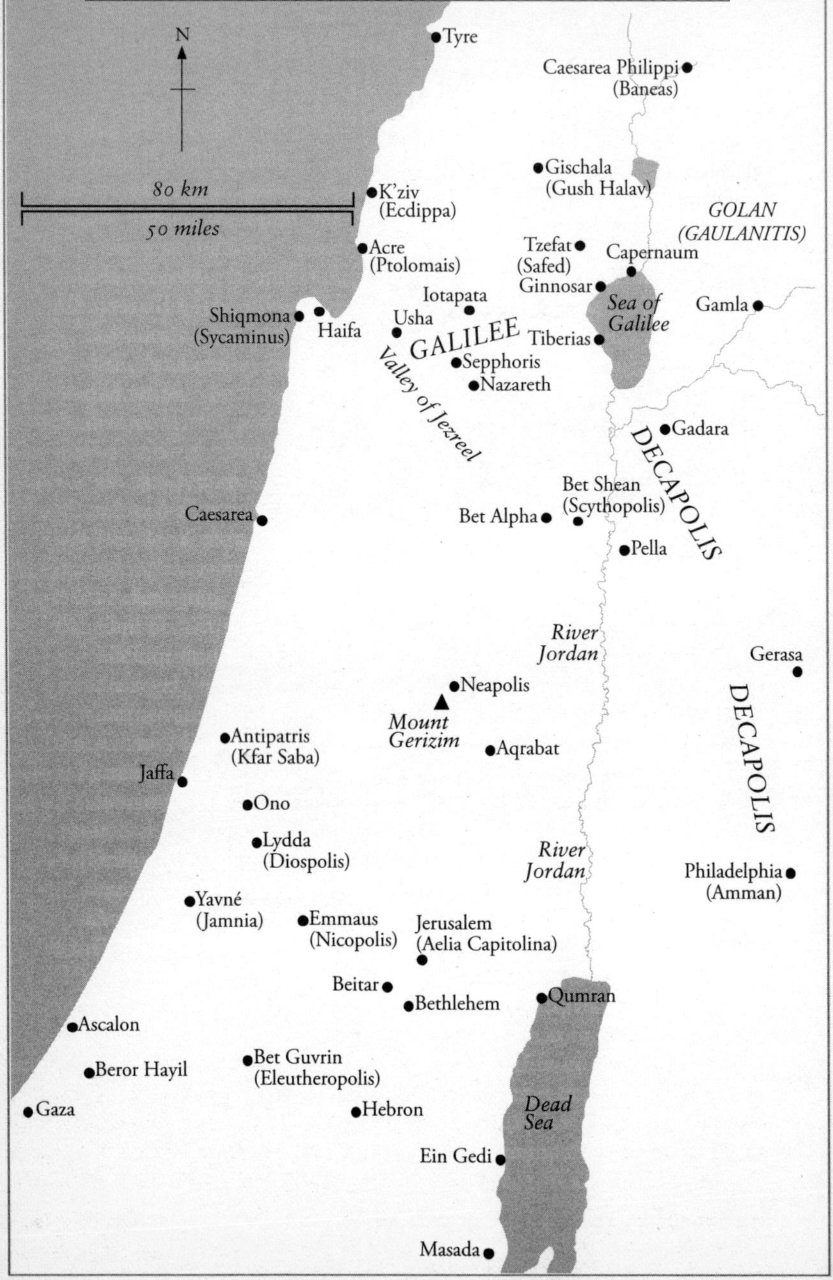

N

80 km
50 miles

Tyre

Caesarea Philippi
(Baneas)

Gischala
(Gush Halav)

GOLAN
(GAULANITIS)

K'ziv
(Ecdippa)

Tzefat
(Safed)

Capernaum

Acre
(Ptolomais)

Ginnosar

Iotapata

Sea of
Galilee

Gamla

Shiqmona
(Sycaminus)

Haifa

Usha

GALILEE

Tiberias

Sepphoris

Nazareth

Valley of Jezreel

Gadara

DECAPOLIS

Caesarea

Bet Alpha

Bet Shean
(Scythopolis)

Pella

River
Jordan

Gerasa

Neapolis

Mount
Gerizim

Aqrabat

DECAPOLIS

Antipatris
(Kfar Saba)

Jaffa

Ono

River
Jordan

Lydda
(Diospolis)

Philadelphia
(Amman)

Yavné
(Jamnia)

Emmaus
(Nicopolis)

Jerusalem
(Aelia Capitolina)

Beitar

Bethlehem

Qumran

Ascalon

Beror Hayil

Bet Guvrin
(Eleutheropolis)

Gaza

Hebron

Dead
Sea

Ein Gedi

Masada

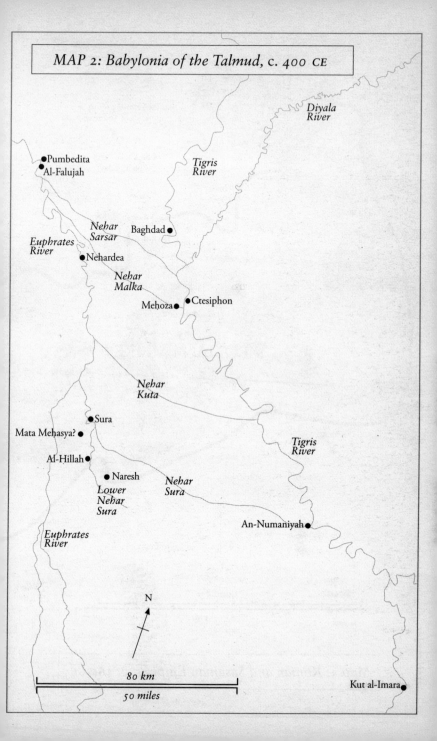

MAP 2: *Babylonia of the Talmud, c. 400 CE*

Diyala River

Tigris River

●Pumbedita
●Al-Falujah

Nehar Sarsar

Baghdad ●

Euphrates River

●Nehardea

Nehar Malka

Mehoza● ●Ctesiphon

Nehar Kuta

Tigris River

●Sura
Mata Mehasya? ●

Al-Hillah ●

●Naresh

Lower Nehar Sura

Nehar Sura

An-Numaniyah ●

Euphrates River

N

80 km

50 miles

Kut al-Imara ●

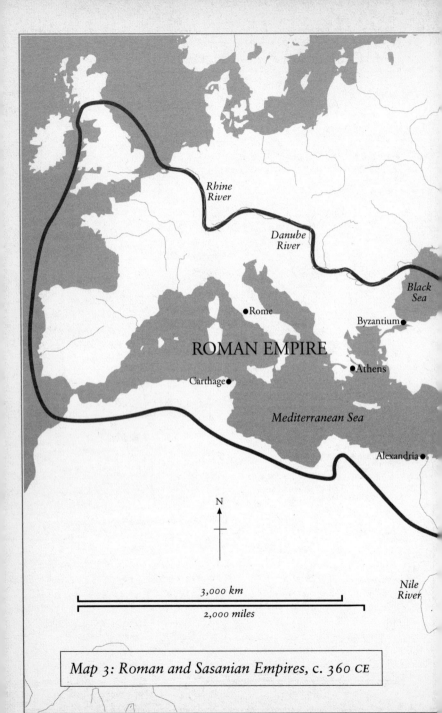

Map 3: *Roman and Sasanian Empires*, c. 360 CE

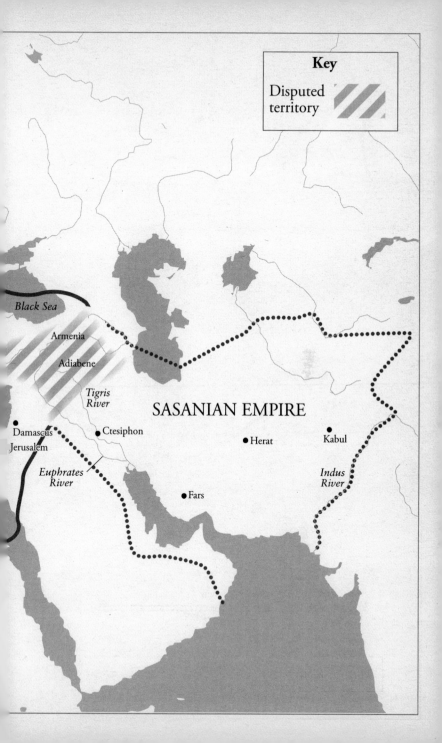

Key

Disputed territory

Black Sea

Armenia

Adiabene

Tigris
River

SASANIAN EMPIRE

Damascus

Jerusalem

●Ctesiphon

●Herat

●Kabul

Euphrates
River

●Fars

Indus
River

Sacred Writings Index

General Index

Page numbers in bold refer to illustrations

Note. In several instances (e.g. Eleazar, Eliezer, Gamaliel, Huna, Judah, Simeon, Yoḥanan, Yosé, Zeiri, Zutra) it is not certain which rabbi of that name is being cited.

Usha, Galilee xxii, xxiii, 55, 60,
  664, 681, 683n, 702, 709n
Ussher, Bishop James 514n
usury *see* interest payments

Valerian, Emperor xxviii
Valmadonna trust 302n
valuations (*arakhin*) *see* vows,
  valuations of
value systems 559–64
  see also morality
verbal abuse *see* insults
Vermes, Geza 249n
Verres 431n
Vespasian (Titus Flavius
  Vespasianus), Emperor 186,
  379, 391, 391n, 394–5, 394n,
  395n
Vilna Gaon lviiin, 134n, 663n
vinegar 64, 77, 149, 150, 545, 695,
  695n
vineyards 28–31, 38, 41–2, 54–5
  definition 55
  planting of 54–6, 87
  tithes on 79
  see also agriculture *and* wine
violence 438–40, 510–13
  see also terrorism *and* war
virgin birth 292n, 624
virginity/virgins 292, 292n,
  328–9, 328n, 332–3, 334, 335,
  498
Vologases I xxvi
volume measurement (capacity)
  476–7, 477n
  see also measurement
vows 300, 325n, 340n, 354–61,
  355n, 356n, 358n, 359n, 452,
  452n, 569, 570, 570n, 584,
  584n, 649, 701
  annulment of 360n
  definition 354, 650

oaths, comparison with 354–5,
  355n
qonam 325, 325n, 727
  on sacrifices 570, 570n, 584n
  valuations of (*arakhin*) 636–7
  by women 358, 359–61, 701

Wahriz (Sasanian general) 459n
walled cities 262, 263, 263n,
  637–9, 668
war 374–6, 375n, 436–40, 560
  types of 374–5
  see also terrorism
war dead 389–90
water
  for drinking 609, 610
  living waters 689–90, 689n
  for purification 681, 682;
    immersion in 683, 688–92
water-drawing ceremony, at
  Sukkot 217, 218, 219–20
wealth 120, 120n, 195–7
weddings *see* marriage
weights 476–7, 735, 737
  see also measurement
Weinberg, J. 222n
Weiss, Z. 24n
white, as colour of purity 255
Whitsunday 593
wickedness *see* sin
widows 335
wills (legal documents) 493
  see also inheritance
wine 28–9, 30n, 148, 149–50,
  149n, 151n, 177–9, 418n, 545,
  547, 548, 577, 578, 609,
  695n, 704
  abstinence from 362, 364, 365
  for anointing 64, 77
  see also food/drink *and*
    vineyards
Winter, P. 498n